AMERICAN EDUCATION

THE COLONIAL EXPERIENCE
1607–1783

AMERICAN EDUCATION

THE COLONIAL EXPERIENCE

1607–1783

Lawrence A. Cremin

HARPER TORCHBOOKS

HARPER & ROW, PUBLISHERS

NEW YORK, EVANSTON, SAN FRANCISCO, LONDON

For Jody and David

CONTENTS

Preface   ix

BOOK I. PLANTATION: 1607–1689

Introduction   3

Part I. Piety, Civility, and Learning

Introduction   27
1. THE PRACTICE OF PIETY   31
2. THE NURTURE OF CIVILITY   58
3. THE ADVANCEMENT OF LEARNING   80

Part II. Institutions

Introduction   109
4. HOUSEHOLD   113
5. CHURCH   138
6. SCHOOL   167
7. COLLEGE   196
8. COMMUNITY   225

BOOK II. PROVINCIALISM: 1689–1783

Introduction   251

Part III. Denominationalism

Introduction   271
9. PIETY RATIONALIZED   273
10. MODES OF ENTHUSIASM   303
11. MISSIONS AND ENCOUNTERS   333

Part IV. Utilitarianism

Introduction   359
12. THE USES OF LEARNING   361
13. THE BUSINESS OF LIVING   387

Part V. Republicanism

Introduction   415
14. CIVILITY LIBERALIZED   419
15. POLITICS AND EDUCATION   444

Part VI. Provincial Education

Introduction   475
16. INSTITUTIONS   479
17. CONFIGURATIONS   517
18. CHARACTERISTICS   544
    EPILOGUE   564

Appendices   571
Bibliographical Essay   577
Index   669

PREFACE

History, Voltaire once quipped, is nothing more than a pack of tricks men play on the dead. He might well have added: on the living too. For, in telling men whence they have come and who they are, history inevitably teaches them the possibilities and limitations of their lives. History can tie men to the service of ancient ideals, or it can free them to define and pursue new ideals, or it can simply demonstrate the futility of all effort to achieve any ideals. It can teach men that they have left Eden or that they are approaching Eden or, indeed, that Eden does not exist and never did. But, whatever history teaches, it helps set the stage on which men act. And that has always been its power in human affairs.

It is doubtless a sense of this extraordinary power that has elicited the widespread dissatisfaction in recent years with traditional versions of the history of American education. Somehow, during a period of intense political conflict touching every phase of educational activity, the time-honored tale of the genesis, rise, and triumph of the public school has seemed flat and inadequate: it has failed to explain sufficiently how Americans have gotten where they are in education, and it has failed to stimulate fruitful debate over where they ought to go. It is coercive rather than liberating history, inspiring ideological commitment rather than informing public policy-making. More than a decade ago, the conference of historians that led eventually to the founding of the Committee on the Role of Education in American History concluded that an imperfect knowledge of educational history had "affected adversely the planning of curricula, the formulation of policy, and the administration of educational agencies in the present crisis of American education."

Consider the typical account of American education, as told in any one of a half-dozen standard texts. The colonists come from Europe bearing a variety of attitudes toward education; in general, backwardness reigns supreme, except in New England, where schools are early erected to confound that old deluder Satan. And these New England schools are destined to be the foundation upon which the American public education system is later erected. At the end of the eighteenth century, it becomes evident that European ways are not working and that the new nation will need a different kind of schooling to nurture and perpetuate its distinctive way of life. There follow diverse efforts to popularize learning, such as Sunday schools, infant schools, and Lancasterian schools, but none of these proves adequate to the needs of the emerging society. And so Horace Mann, Henry Barnard, John Pierce, and others launch a great crusade for public education, in which the forces of progress vie with the forces of reaction for more than a generation. By 1860, the conflict is won, except in the South, that is, where victory must await the regeneration led by northern philanthropists at the end of the nineteenth century. Thereafter, the story is that of the refinement, improvement, and extension of public schooling in response to the conditions of a democratic-industrial civilization. And the moral is always the same: the rise of the public school has been inextricably tied to the progress of the United States; the cause of the one is invariably the cause of the other; hence, it is the duty of both teachers and lay citizens to promote public education, thereby enabling the United States to fulfill its destiny.

Now, no one can deny the central role of public schooling in the American experience during the nineteenth and twentieth centuries: to do so would be patently to distort historical fact. But no one can deny, either, that the traditional chronicle of American education has been narrowly institutional, full of anachronism, and painfully moralistic. True, it has shared those vices with other products of early twentieth-century social-science scholarship, but that has not lessened its unfortunate influence on present-day affairs. Clearly, new approaches are called for if a fuller historical understanding is to be achieved and to make itself felt in policy-making.

Several years ago, in a paper prepared for discussion by a group of American historians, I attempted to formulate some of the questions that might encourage the development of those new approaches.

My queries proceeded along three general lines. First, insisting upon a much broader investigation into the nature and uses of education during different periods of American history, I asked what agencies, formal and informal, have shaped American thought, character, and sensibility over the years and what have been the relationships between these agencies and the society that has sustained them. It seemed to me that to ask these questions would project us beyond the schools to a host of other institutions that educate: families, churches, libraries, museums, publishers, benevolent societies, youth groups, agricultural fairs, radio networks, military organizations, and research institutes. It would permit us to describe such phenomena as the rise of newspapers in the eighteenth century, of social settlements in the nineteenth, and of mass television in the twentieth; and it would provide us a context within which to assess the changing role and influence of schools and colleges, private as well as public. Most important, perhaps, it would enable us to avoid what Herbert Butterfield has called "the abridgment of history," the tendency to oversimplify the past by viewing it strictly in terms of the problems that beset the present.

I found a second source of new questions in certain of the more general developments in recent American historiography: the spirited interest in church history, population history, and the history of science; the use of social-science methods in studying the phenomena of the past; and the addition of a comparative dimension in appraising American achievements. These revisionist thrusts have proved profoundly relevant to the history of education. Whereas an earlier generation was understandably preoccupied with school organization and structure, more recent studies have emphasized the modes and processes of education. Whereas an earlier generation stressed formal legal arrangements and statements of educational aim, more recent works have inquired into actual educational practice. Whereas an earlier generation underscored the separation of education from politics, more recent interpretations have reasserted the complex network of relationships between education and politics. And, whereas an earlier generation concentrated upon the uniqueness of the American educational experience, more recent studies, viewing this experience in comparative perspective, have found it strikingly similar to that of certain European countries.

Finally, I argued that historians of American education must be bolder than they have been in attempting to assess the impact of

American education on the American mind and character. To be sure, there are grave difficulties in such a task: How, after all, does one make demonstrable assertions about the social and intellectual consequences of a new educational institution, or a new curricular trend, or a new tendency in child-rearing? Yet the value of educational history will be considerably diminished if the attempt is not made. However strong and abiding their faith that education makes a difference, Americans are asking more insistently than ever before, What difference?

Shortly after I wrote that paper (it was in the spring of 1964), there occurred one of those unexpected events that often give decisive direction to a person's life and work: W. Stull Holt, then secretary of the American Historical Association, asked whether I would be willing to prepare, in connection with the approaching centenary of the United States Office of Education, a comprehensive history of American education under the joint sponsorship of the Association and the Office. My reply being enthusiastically affirmative, Professor Holt and Francis Keppel, then United States Commissioner of Education, approached the Carnegie Corporation of New York for funds to support the enterprise. The Corporation, under the leadership of John Gardner, responded with a generous grant, which has permitted the research and writing to proceed under the most favorable circumstances. It is a pleasure at this point to state my gratitude to the Association, the Office, and the Corporation for their kindness in furthering the work and at the same time to absolve them of any responsibility for the outcome: characteristically, Messrs. Holt, Keppel, and Gardner arranged for all matters of content to rest wholly and finally in my hands.

At present, I foresee three volumes. This first begins with the transit of civilization from Old World to New, carrying the story through the completion of independence and the efforts of Jefferson's generation to create an education truly "adapted to the genius of the American people." A second volume will deal with the educational endeavors of the young nation, starting with the multifarious schemes of Noah Webster and concluding with the august formulations of William Torrey Harris. And a third volume will consider the more recent experience of metropolitan America, stressing on the one hand the radical changes in the architecture of education wrought by the evolution of the new media of communication and on the other hand the essential changes in the nature of education wrought by the emergence of America as a world metropolis, or exporter of culture. Throughout the work, I shall view education as the deliberate, systematic, and sustained effort to transmit or evoke knowledge, attitudes, values, skills, and sensibilities, a process that is more limited than what the anthropologist would term enculturation or the sociologist socialization, though obviously inclusive of some of the same elements. Education, defined thus, clearly produces outcomes in the lives of individuals, many of them discernible, though other phenomena, varying from politics to commerce to technology to earthquakes, may prove more influential at particular times and in particular instances. There are some who would consider all such phenomena educative, for they invariably shape men and affect their destinies; I myself find such a view so inclusive as to define nothing for the educational historian to study except "history in general," a concept with which I have always had a good deal of difficulty and which should not in any case be mistaken for the history of education.

One or two technical comments about style may be of interest. I have tried to keep footnotes to a minimum, as a rule documenting only quotations, direct assertions involving laws or statistics, specific historical interpretations, and significant historiographical controversies. I have discussed most of the secondary and tertiary literature on which the work rests in the bibliographical essay; hence, those interested in the sources for a particular section should read that essay in conjunction with the text and notes. I have expanded, modernized, and Americanized all spelling and some punctuation in quoted passages; in the case of titles of written works, I have made only those alterations required to follow modern typographical convention. And I have taken dates as they appear in the sources, though I have assumed that the new year began on January 1 instead of March 25 for the period before 1752; thus, March 3, 1716/17, becomes March 3, 1717.

No one engaged in a work of comprehensive scholarship can fail to be aware of the infinite variety of kindnesses that contribute at every point to the progress of his enterprise. Librarians and archivists at a score of research centers in both the United States and Europe were patient beyond measure, not merely with the usual range of bibliographical inquiries, but with every manner of false lead, vague hunch, and wrongheaded hypothesis: in particular, I should like to mention the assistance of Florence Wilkinson, chief reference librarian at Teachers College, whose efforts have always exemplified the attributes of first-rate librarianship. Joanne Hanke Schwarz contributed significantly to my understanding of colonial missions to the Indians; John H. Calam graciously shared with me his insights into the endeavors of the Society for the Propagation of the Gospel in Foreign Parts; Douglas Sloan and Carl F. Kaestle undertook most of the spadework in connection with my studies of New York, Philadelphia, Dedham, and Elizabeth City County; and Miriam Ulltveit-Moe provided valuable assistance in my analyses of Irish literacy. I also profited immensely from Douglas Sloan's pioneering investigations of the pervasive influence of Scottish culture on eighteenth-century American intellectual life. Harold J. Noah, Philip H. Phenix, Robert McClintock, Lambros Comitas, and Martin S. Dworkin endured endless rehearsals of my leading ideas, forcing me again and again to define, sharpen, and clarify; while John H. Fischer and Robert J. Schaefer displayed consistent generosity in creating at Teachers College the circumstances under which I could pursue my study with maximum effectiveness. My assistant, Judy F. Suratt, contributed at so many points and in so many ways, both substantively and editorially, that it is often quite impossible to determine where my work ends and hers begins. Anne Goldstein typed the manuscript with care and intelligence. And Claudia Foster was especially gracious in tendering help on short notice in the final stages of the work. To these and others is owed a good deal of whatever merit the book may possess; responsibility for its failings is most assuredly mine.

The volume began to take form during a period of reflection and writing at the Center for Advanced Study in the Behavioral Sciences in 1964–1965. I delivered the first public statement of my principal theses in the spring of 1966, on the occasion of the Sir John Adams Memorial Lecture at the University of London's Institute of Education. To Ralph W. Tyler, director of the Center during the time of my fellowship, and to H. L. Elvin, director of the Institute, I owe special gratitude.

Finally, there is my incalculable debt to my beloved wife and children, whose devotion and understanding were unfailing, especially on those innumerable occasions when their pleasure and convenience were sacrificed to my continuing education.

L.A.C.

Teachers College, Columbia University
January, 1970

BOOK
I

PLANTATION
1607–1689

INTRODUCTION

For we must consider that we shall be as a city upon a hill, the
eyes of all people are upon us.

JOHN WINTHROP

Sometime in the autumn of 1584—it was probably late in September—the young English preacher Richard Hakluyt obtained an
audience with Elizabeth I in order to present to her the *Discourse
of Western Planting* he had written the previous summer at the
behest of Walter Raleigh. The occasion must have been pleasant
enough, since the queen marked it by bestowing upon Hakluyt the
next canonry or prebend to come vacant in Bristol Cathedral. But
the significance of the visit went far beyond pleasantry. Raleigh,
then at the height of his influence, had persuaded Elizabeth only a
few months earlier to grant him the expired patent of his late half-
brother, Sir Humphrey Gilbert, to search out and colonize such parts
of the New World as were "not actually possessed of any Christian
prince or people." Obtaining the patent was itself something of a
triumph, since others had eagerly sought its privileges. Yet Raleigh
knew better than most that colonizing was a costly enterprise: his
half-brother had spent a fortune on failure. What was desperately
needed, Raleigh had concluded, was access to the royal coffers, and
to obtain that from his parsimonious queen would require a most
persuasive statement of the cause. It was the quest for such a statement that had first led Raleigh to Hakluyt, and he could not have
made a better choice.[1]

---

[1] George Bruner Parks, *Richard Hakluyt and the English Voyages*, edited by James
A. Williamson (2d ed.; New York: Frederick Ungar Publishing Co., 1961), pp. 87-88,
248, 261; and Leonard Woods, "Introduction," in Richard Hakluyt, *A Discourse Con-*

Hakluyt was in his early thirties in 1584 and already a cosmographer of considerable reputation: he had completed his formal education at Oxford in 1577 and had qualified for holy orders sometime thereafter, no doubt in an effort to ensure a continuing source of income. His real education, however, had come from his elder cousin, Richard Hakluyt the lawyer, who had first inspired him to study geography and had then guided his apprenticeship in the field. By the early 1580's, the young scholar had been in touch with most of the leading geographical lights of his time, including Gerhardus Mercator, and had dedicated himself to the systematic collection of treatises, maps, and travelers' reports in all the principal European tongues.

Hakluyt was inevitably caught up in the colonizing plans of Gilbert and his associates—men such as Sir Francis Walsingham, the queen's secretary; Christopher Carleill, Walsingham's stepson; and Sir Philip Sidney, Walsingham's son-in-law. Indeed, Hakluyt's first important collection, *Divers Voyages Touching the Discoverie of America* (1582), had contributed significantly to both the publicizing and the legitimatizing of Gilbert's enterprise. "I marvel not a little (right worshipful)," he wrote in the dedication of that work to Sidney, "that since the first discovery of America (which is now full fourscore and ten years) after so great conquest and plantings of the Spaniards and Portuguese there, that we of England could never have the grace to set fast footing in such fertile and temperate places, as are left as yet unpossessed by them." Having thus gently rebuked his countrymen, Hakluyt offered the earliest public announcement of what was to become his lifelong commitment: the cause of English colonial expansion.[2]

In the spring of 1583, Hakluyt had actually contemplated following Gilbert to America, but he altered his plans and went to Paris the next autumn as chaplain to the English ambassador, Sir Edward

---

cerning [*sic*] *Western Planting,* edited by Charles Deane, in *Collections of the Maine Historical Society,* 2d ser., II (1877), xxxiv. See also the edition of the *Discourse* published as Document 46 of *The Original Writings & Correspondence of the Two Richard Hakluyts,* edited by E. G. R. Taylor, Works Issued by the Hakluyt Society, 2d ser., vols. LXXVI-LXXVII (2 vols.; London: The Society, 1935), II, 211-326. David Beers Quinn, ed., *The Voyages and Colonising Enterprises of Sir Humphrey Gilbert,* Works Issued by the Hakluyt Society, 2d ser., vols. LXXXIII-LXXXIV (2 vols.; London: The Society, 1940), I, 188.

2 *Original Writings of the Two Hakluyts,* I, 175. See David Beers Quinn, *Richard Hakluyt, Editor: A Study Introductory to the Facsimile Edition of Richard Hakluyt's "Divers Voyages"* (1582) (Amsterdam: Theatrum Orbis Terrarum, 1967).

Stafford. There, in addition to his regular duties, he pursued "diligent inquiry of such things as may yield any light into our western discoveries," sending a steady flow of intelligence to Walsingham, Carleill, and Sidney, and asserting his continued readiness to serve in the cause of western planting. Hakluyt's opportunity came soon enough, when Raleigh, probably at Walsingham's suggestion, enlisted his aid in utilizing the new patent. Having obtained leave from his post, Hakluyt returned temporarily to London, where he spent the summer of 1584 privately preparing his manuscript for the queen while publicly "trumpeting" Raleigh's project. He did his work well: the *Discourse* that resulted was unique in its time and remains to this day the quintessential statement of the Elizabethan argument for colonization.[3]

Formally a plea for English settlement of the New World from Newfoundland to Florida, the document is at the same time a treatise on trade, an essay on politics, a sermon on Christian missions, a dissertation on geography, and a disquisition on social policy. Five general theses dominate the discussion: first, Her Majesty has not only the right, deriving from the explorations of Cabot and Gilbert, but the high responsibility, deriving from her role as Defender of the Faith, to establish colonies in the New World; second, if she fails to do so, others will move in her stead; third, colonies will restore the vitality of English trade and make the nation economically self-sufficient; fourth, colonies will alleviate social and political unrest in the commonwealth by drawing off idlers and vagrants; and fifth, colonies will thwart the ambition of Philip II of Spain by striking directly at his lucrative but weakly defended outposts in the West Indies. Protestantism, nationalism, empire, and what came to be known as mercantilism—all the great themes of sixteenth-century expansionism—resound contrapuntally through Hakluyt's effort to enlist Elizabeth in the colonial cause.

So far as its immediate aim is concerned, the *Discourse* must be pronounced a failure. With an all-out naval war against Spain imminent and an army about to enter the Netherlands, it is doubtful whether Elizabeth offered Raleigh much more than encouragement. Raleigh, in turn, tried twice to found colonies at Roanoke: the first expedition, in 1585, failed when the settlers—restive in the face of

<hr />

[3] Richard Hakluyt to Sir Francis Walsingham, January 7, 1584, *Original Writings of the Two Hakluyts*, I, 205; and Sir Philip Sidney to Sir Edward Stafford, July 21, 1584, *The Prose Works of Sir Philip Sidney*, edited by Albert Feuillerat (4 vols.; Cambridge: Cambridge University Press, 1912), III, 145.

depleted numbers, rapidly dwindling supplies, and constant threat from the Indians—went back to England with Sir Francis Drake on his return from military operations against the Spanish in the West Indies; the second venture, in 1587, failed when the colonists disappeared, virtually without trace. In 1589, in an effort at still another beginning, Raleigh assigned many of the privileges under his patent to a company of men, mostly London merchants, among them, interestingly enough, Richard Hakluyt. But England was by then engaged in a dispersed war over several fronts; Raleigh was shortly to fall into disgrace; and no further attempt at permanent settlement would be made during Elizabeth's reign.

The long-range impact of the *Discourse* is more difficult to assess. It gathered together all the arguments for colonization previously advanced and at the same time prefigured most of those that would be put forth over the next generation. Thus, in a unique way, it constituted an ideological link between the unsuccessful ventures of Elizabeth's reign and the more fruitful enterprises of the Stuart era. But the document remained unpublished until 1877; and, though several copies had been made, it is virtually impossible to determine how many people became aware of Hakluyt's program, beyond the queen and Walsingham and Raleigh.

Hakluyt himself remained indefatigable in the cause. In 1589, he published *The Principall Navigations,* a magnificent anthology of exploration, discovery, and adventure, which the historian J. A. Froude later called the prose epic of the modern English nation. In 1598, when a second and enlarged edition of *The Principall Navigations* began to appear, Hakluyt restated England's claims in the New World, venturing the opinion that Raleigh's Roanoke plantation of 1587 had survived; while the following year, in a dedication to Sir Robert Cecil prefacing the second volume of the revised *Principall Navigations,* he recapitulated the arguments for colonizing America, urging Cecil "not to meddle with the state of Ireland, nor that of Guiana, [for] there is under our noses the great and ample country of Virginia." And in 1603 he persuaded the merchants of Bristol to send Martin Pring on a reconnaissance voyage to New England.[4]

4 *The Principall Navigations, Voiages and Discoveries of the English Nation, Made by Sea or over Land, to the Most Remote and Farthest Distant Quarters of the Earth at Any Time Within the Compasse of These 1500 Yeeres* (London: George Bishop and Ralph Newberie, 1589); [J. A. Froude], "England's Forgotten Worthies," *The Westminster Review,* new ser., II (1852), 34; and W. Nelson Francis, "Hakluyt's *Voyages:*

Hakluyt's appearance in 1606, therefore, as one of the leaders in the London company effort to undertake a new plantation in Virginia, was merely one more evidence of his lifelong commitment. The arguments supporting the Virginia venture were familiar: an English colony would spread the gospel to the natives, enhance the power and prestige of the realm, and enrich the nation in general and the sponsors in particular. But this time the conditions surrounding the enterprise were significantly different. Within the British Isles, the union of the English and Scottish crowns and the completion of the conquest of Ireland had finally signaled the domestic consolidation so aggressively sought by the Tudors; externally, Spanish power had waned considerably. Public interest in colonization was running high, thanks in no small measure to Hakluyt; money was increasingly available; organizational forms like the joint-stock company were at hand; and new leaders like Sir Thomas Gates, Sir Thomas Smith, and Sir Ferdinando Gorges had come to the fore. The London company made its initial effort in the winter of 1606-1607, and others followed soon thereafter. Within a generation, English settlements destined to be permanent dotted the eastern shores of North America, from Newfoundland to Barbados; and Hakluyt's dream of empire was on its way to realization.

II

Sometime after Hakluyt had presented the original version of the *Discourse of Western Planting* to the queen, he had occasion to prepare another copy; and with this later draft, probably dating from 1585 or 1586, there appeared an appendix, or twenty-first chapter, setting forth some practical details to be considered by those who would undertake a wilderness plantation. The contents are instructive. There are lists of provisions required to sustain life during the initial phase of settlement, and of the categories of men and materials necessary to increase the value of the colony through husbandry, manufacture, trade, and military and naval operations. In

---

An Epic of Discovery," *The William and Mary Quarterly*, 3d ser., XII (1955), 447-455. Francis notes that "epic" is an erroneous term, since an epic is the creation of an artist, while Hakluyt's *Voyages* is the labor of a scholar. True enough, though, one might add, an artistic labor. For an excellent edition of the work, see the facsimile edited by David Beers Quinn and Raleigh Ashlin Skelton (2 vols.; Cambridge: Cambridge University Press, 1965). *Original Writings of the Two Hakluyts*, II, 423, 456.

addition, there is a fascinating miscellany of advice: one or two preachers should be appointed, "that God may be honored, the people instructed, mutinies the better avoided, and obedience the better used"; a physician, a surgeon, and an apothecary should be recruited, as should a brewer of mead (in light of the reports of abundant honey in the New World); prisons should be borne in mind as excellent sources of manpower, since they are "full of decayed merchants," who, "schooled in the house of adversity, are drawn to a degree higher in excellency, and may be employed to great uses"; known papists should be excluded; and, wherever possible, men of several skills should be chosen, for "the more good gifts that the goers in the voyage have, the more is the voyage benefited."[5]

Taken with the rest of the *Discourse,* the appendix affords considerable insight into the theory of colonization at the time Hakluyt wrote. This theory had several possible sources, including the settlements of the Hanseatic cities in the Baltic and of the Italian cities in the Levant, the ventures of Spain in Central and South America, and the efforts of the English themselves in Ireland. Especially influential were the Venetian *fondachi,* or trading posts, in the Black Sea and the Mediterranean. These were communal enterprises kept under the strictest political control by the metropolis: metropolitan law prevailed; metropolitan authorities appointed the magistrates who administered that law; and metropolitan merchants held a monopoly on trade, the *fondaco* being run as an instrument for metropolitan enrichment. The parallel with the plantations envisioned by Hakluyt is patent. They, too, would be commercial outposts, controlled by adventurers in search of wealth and populated by men hired, pressed into service, or themselves after gain.

Hakluyt's theory doubtless underlay Raleigh's first Roanoke venture: that settlement was thoroughly typical of its time. Interestingly enough, its failure had led Raleigh and his associates to revive Sir Humphrey Gilbert's earlier idea of a colony of households, and a distinguishing mark of the second Roanoke plantation had been the inclusion of women and children. Had the 1587 enterprise proved successful, it could well have heralded a significant change in the theory of colonization; but such insights as might have been gleaned from the experience were lost when the colony disappeared.[6]

5 *Original Writings of the Two Hakluyts,* II, 320-326.
6 David Beers Quinn, ed., *The Roanoke Voyages, 1584-1590,* Works Issued by the Hakluyt Society, 2d ser., vols. CIV-CV (2 vols.; London: The Society, 1955) and *Voyages and Colonising Enterprises of Sir Humphrey Gilbert.*

In any case, there is every indication that at the time the Virginia companies were chartered in 1606 the traditional theory of colonization prevailed. The Jacobean adventurers who banded together to undertake the northern and southern settlements had no more intention of reproducing English villages in the New World than their Elizabethan forebears. They were colonizing for conquest and gain: they conceived of plantation in terms of well-equipped ships, men committed to plunder and production, and capital sufficient to start the profits flowing.

Yet experience played havoc with their plans, and one can trace through the seventeenth century a series of transformations in the nature and character of colonies that simply outmoded much of what Hakluyt had so diligently learned and so passionately taught. One such transformation occurred in Virginia, as what was initially a polyglot band of gentlemen, artisans, and roughnecks slowly and haltingly evolved into an ordered society. Massachusetts represented another departure from the traditional colony, with the successful planting there of Puritan communities drawn together by subscription to an explicit philosophy of the good life, to what the ancients would have referred to as a *paideia*. And still another was New York, where the English early recognized that they had more to gain by tolerating the variegated culture that had grown up under the Dutch than by attempting to suppress it.

In each of these transformations, education in its many modes was deeply involved and profoundly affected. During the first phases of the Virginia settlement, for example, education was in the hands of the ministers, who used it both as an instrument for promoting discipline and order among the colonists and as a device for winning the loyalty of the natives. The arrangement was entirely appropriate for a plantation conceived as a Christian trading post; since there were no families and few children, little else appeared necessary. By 1609, however, despite several "supplies" and the vigorous efforts of Captain John Smith, the colony at Jamestown was on the brink of failure. Two years of frenetic endeavor to locate precious metals to plunder or mine had come to naught, and the realization had begun to dawn that the riches earlier dreamed of were simply not to be had. Commenting on the settlers' lack of success during these first years, Smith himself observed in his *Map of Virginia* (1612) that it had been the Spaniards' good fortune to happen upon well-developed native societies in the New World; all that had been called for was "spoil and pillage of those country people." The English, on the other hand, had found only ignorant primitives and had therefore been forced to "discover the country, subdue the people, bring them to be tractable, civil and industrious, and teach them trades." What was needed, he counseled, was the patience that would enable Virginia ultimately to turn a profit.[7]

In an effort to salvage the venture, the London company resolved to seek a new charter altering its internal organization and "to set and furnish out under the conduct of one able and absolute governor, a large supply of five hundred men, with some number of families, of wife, children and servants, to take fast hold and root in that land." Such a supply had actually left England on June 8, 1609, in nine ships, seven of which had arrived at Jamestown late in August. Though there was still a "starving time" ahead—the colonists had by no means learned to wrest a living from the wilderness—the first step toward the evolution of a community had been taken.[8]

Families continued to come thereafter, as did numerous unaccompanied children to be put out as servants and apprentices. And in 1613-14 Governor Thomas Dale began the distribution of small plots of "clear ground," to be farmed on an individual or familial basis. Slowly, the interest of the settlers shifted from the search for gold to the production of staples—grain, grapes, silk grass, and especially tobacco—and a broadside of 1616 sketched a happy pastorale in which the food problem had been solved and preparations were in progress "to set upon the minerals, whereof there are many sorts." Yet the settlement under Dale was governed far more as a military outpost than as an agricultural society; and education, beyond preaching and catechizing, consisted principally of the colonists going to church twice daily to pray for deliverance from "the delusion of the Devil, the malice of the heathen, the invasions of our enemies, and mutinies and dissensions of our own people."[9]

It was under the treasurership of Sir Edwin Sandys and the gov-

---

7 Captain John Smith, *A Map of Virginia*, in Lyon Gardiner Tyler, ed., *Narratives of Early Virginia, 1606-1625*, Original Narratives of Early American History, edited by J. Franklin Jameson (New York: Charles Scribner's Sons, 1907), p. 178.

8 Alexander Brown, ed., *The Genesis of the United States* (2 vols.; Boston: Houghton, Mifflin and Company, 1890), I, 342.

9 *Ibid.*, II, 776; and William Strachey, *For the Colony in Virginea Britannia: Lawes Divine, Morall and Martiall, &c* (London: Walter Burre, 1612), in Peter Force, ed., *Tracts and Other Papers, Relating Principally to the Origin, Settlement, and Progress of the Colonies in North America, from the Discovery of the Country to the Year 1776* (4 vols.; Washington, D.C.: Peter Force, 1836-1846), vol. III, no. 2, p. 68 and *passim*.

ernorship of Sir George Yeardley that the real transformation of
Virginia into a self-sustaining agricultural community was effected.
The "instructions" Yeardley brought with him from London in
1619 are indicative of the transformation: they set forth the Virginia
Company's intent to lay the foundation for "a flourishing state";
they charged officials to look after the necessary provision of corn
and cattle; they required partitioning of the older holdings in the
colony into four boroughs, to be known as Jamestown, Charles City,
Henrico, and Kecoughtan (later Elizabeth City); they dealt at length
with arrangements regarding the ownership and tenancy of land;
they ordered that a hundred acres of glebe land be reserved in each
of the four boroughs for the maintenance of ministers and ten thousand acres at Henrico for the endowment of a college to train up
the children of the infidels "in true religion, moral virtue and civility
and for other godly uses"; and they sketched a series of elaborate
procedures whereby private plantations, or "hundreds," might be
developed by associated groups of adventurers under the aegis of
the Company. Along with these "instructions," which the colonists
referred to as the "great charter," Yeardley also brought documents
calling for the establishment of a council of state and a general
assembly in the colony.[10]

While much has been made of the assembly as the first representative body in North America, it doubtless derived less from an
interest in democracy than from a desire to make Virginia attractive
to additional English immigrants. In any case, the Company did step
up its efforts to increase the population and put the colony on a
permanent footing by sending three hundred tenants to work its
own land, the governor's land, and the college land; by shipping a
hundred apprentices and servants; and by recruiting, in addition,
a hundred "women, maids young and uncorrupt to make wives to the
inhabitants and by that means to make the men there more settled
and less movable." Scores of others, representing a variety of crafts
and trades, immigrated in subsequent years, in response to a vigorous
campaign on Sandys's part; and, by the early 1620's, the colony had
all the attributes of an ordered community: families, government,
organized property-holding, agricultural production, and an active
religious life.[11]

[10] Susan Myra Kingsbury, ed., *The Records of the Virginia Company of London*
(4 vols.; Washington, D.C.: Government Printing Office, 1906-1935), III, 98-109.

[11] *Ibid.*, I, 255-256, 268-269; and His Majesty's Counseil for Virginia, *A Declaration
of the State of the Colonie and Affaires in Virginia* (London: T. S., 1620), in Force, ed.,
Tracts, vol. III, no. 5, pp. 9-10, 13-17.

It is not without significance that the first sustained attention to the development of formal schooling in Virginia coincided with the transformation wrought under Sandys and Yeardley. The earliest effort was launched by a letter (c. 1617) from James I to the archbishops, soliciting contributions from parishioners throughout the realm to erect in Virginia "some churches and schools for the education of the children of those barbarians." In due course, over two thousand pounds was raised for the college; the Company ordered that land be allotted at Henrico for endowing the university and college; and a number of contributors added individual gifts for the instruction of young Indians in the principles of the Christian religion. Some of these plans would doubtless have come to fruition had it not been for the massacre of March 22, 1622, which cast a pall on the whole idea, in part because several associated with the educational endeavors were thought to have coddled the savages.[12]

Concurrent with these efforts directed toward the Indians, and closely related to them, were the attempts to establish a school at Charles City for the children of the settlers. The key figure there was the Reverend Patrick Copland, chaplain of the *Royal James*, a ship in the East India Company fleet. Returning to England from the Indies in 1621, Copland, "out of an earnest desire to give some furtherance unto the plantation in Virginia," persuaded those aboard the ship to contribute to the work there. Upon hearing of the benefaction, the Virginia Company appointed a committee to discuss with Copland how the money might be spent. The committee "conceived it most fit to resolve for the erecting of a public free school . . . for the education of children and grounding of them in

12 James S. M. Anderson, *The History of the Church of England, in the Colonies and Foreign Dependencies of the British Empire* (3 vols.; London: Francis & John Rivington, 1845-1856), I, 314-316; Kingsbury, ed., *Records of the Virginia Company*, I, 355, 268; III, 102; I, 310-311, 335, 585-589; and Robert Hunt Land, "Henrico and Its College," *William and Mary College Quarterly*, 2d ser., XVIII (1938), 453-498. There is an intriguing passage in Captain John Smith's *Advertisements for the Unexperienced Planters of New-England, or Any Where* (London: John Haviland, 1631), in *Works, 1608-1631*, edited by Edward Arber (2 vols.; Westminster: Archibald Constable and Co., 1895), II, 929, in which Smith, speaking of the charter of 1609, recounts: "At last [they] got a commission in their own names, promising the king custom within seven years, where[as] we were free for one and twenty; appointing the Lord Delaware for governor, with as many great and stately officers, and offices under him, as doth belong to a great kingdom, with good sums for their extraordinary expenses; also privileges for cities; charters for corporations, universities, free schools, and glebe land; putting all those in practice before there was either people, students, or scholars to build or use them, or provision or victual to feed them [that] were then there." Smith seems to have confused the charter of 1609 with the "great charter" of 1618, but his sense of the development of the Company's concern for education is interesting nevertheless.

the principles of religion, civility of life and humane learning." It also recommended that the school—to be named the East India School—"have dependence upon the college in Virginia which should be made capable to receive scholars from the school into such scholarships and fellowships as the said college shall be endowed withal for the advancement of scholars as they arise by degrees and deserts in learning." The quarter court of the Company, which met shortly thereafter, confirmed the committee's report, hence broadening the plan for Henrico College into one that would encompass both Indian and English children.[13]

That same winter of 1621-22, one of the Company's courts took formal notice of a new book by a "painful" schoolmaster, John Brinsley, and appointed a committee, including Copland, to peruse the work with a view to its relevance for the East India School. The action is of special interest, since Brinsley's treatise, *A Consolation for Our Grammar Schooles,* was written explicitly for "all ruder countries and places," including Ireland, Wales, Virginia, and Bermuda, and took the position that education in the colonies was to be "without any difference at all from our courses received here at home."[14]

In the end, none of the educational plans of 1618-1622 was executed, and, though Copland's efforts persisted beyond the great Indian massacre, they came to naught. Nor did anything come of the scheme of Edward Palmer, of London, who had provided in his will of 1624 that in the event he died without heirs his American holdings would be used to found and maintain a university in Virginia, to be known, along with its feeder schools, as Academia Virginiensis et Oxoniensis. But the failure of these endeavors is far less significant than what they indicate about the evolution of English colonial theory. By 1622, it had become apparent that the English experience in the New World would be fundamentally different from that of the Spanish, that its success would be tied to the development of self-sufficient agricultural and trading communities, that self-sufficiency would sooner or later require the planting of families, and that the planting of families would be facilitated by institutions like those of England. Once that stage had been reached,

---

[13] Kingsbury, ed., *Records of the Virginia Company,* I, 532-533, 538-541, 152, 550-551, 558-559; III, 537-540.

[14] *Ibid.,* I, 574; and John Brinsley, *A Consolation for Our Grammar Schooles* (London: Richard Field, 1622).

treatises such as Brinsley's inevitably became relevant; and, after the 1620's, none of the English ventures in the New World could ignore the educational problems they raised and the solutions they proposed.[15]

Some years later, when John Winthrop was weighing the prospects of a Puritan plantation in New England, he observed that the earlier English ventures had been marred by three fundamental errors, which he and his associates would be likely to avoid: they had employed a multitude of rude and undisciplined persons; they had failed to establish proper forms of government; and they had directed their efforts toward carnal rather than religious ends. Winthrop saw no reason for his associates to be deterred, given their commitment to a select company, ordered government, and godly purposes. Properly planned and directed, their undertaking would be not only a profitable commercial enterprise but a service of the greatest consequence to church and commonwealth.[16]

Actually, there had been a number of previous attempts at colonization in the northern part of "Virginia," and at least one had been successful. The earliest English settlement had been at Sagadahoc in 1607, and it had failed for the same reasons that the contemporary venture at Jamestown had almost failed: the settlers had been men of poor character and low ambition, and they had quarreled incessantly, extracting little from the colony of use to themselves or their sponsors. The miracle, as Charles M. Andrews wisely observed, is not that Sagadahoc failed but that Jamestown survived.[17]

Thirteen years after that failure, the Pilgrims founded the Plymouth Colony about six hundred miles north of Jamestown, under a patent obtained from the Virginia Company. A group of Separatists

---

[15] Palmer's will is reproduced in Henry F. Waters, *Genealogical Gleanings in England* (2 vols.; Boston: New-England Historic Genealogical Society, 1901), II, 982-983. Recall Francis Bacon's essay "Of Plantations," probably written sometime around 1620, with its penultimate sentence: "When the plantation grows to strength, then it is time to plant with women as well as with men; that the plantation may spread into generations, and not be ever pierced from without" (*Essays or Counsels, Civil and Moral,* in *The Works of Francis Bacon,* edited by James Spedding, Robert Leslie Ellis, and Douglas Denon Heath [new ed.; 7 vols.; London: Longmans & Co., 1876-1890], VI, 459).

[16] See John Winthrop, "Arguments for the Plantation of New England" (1629), *Winthrop Papers* (5+ vols.; Boston: The Massachusetts Historical Society, 1929-), II, 106-149, especially p. 143. See also the similar observation of John White in *The Planters Plea* (London: William Jones, 1630), in Force, ed., *Tracts,* vol. II, no. 3, pp. 19-22.

[17] Charles M. Andrews, *The Colonial Period of American History* (4 vols.; New Haven: Yale University Press, 1934-1938), I, 93.

who had fled to Holland in 1607 and 1608 to escape Anglican harass-ment, the Pilgrims had realized there that the price of toleration might well be their eventual assimilation into the Dutch population. But even more lamentable, as William Bradford wrote years later in detailing the reasons for their removal to the New World, "and of all sorrows most heavy to be borne, was that many of their chil-dren, by these occasions and the great licentiousness of youth in that country, and the manifold temptations of the place, were drawn away by evil examples into extravagant and dangerous courses, getting the reins off their necks and departing from their parents."[18]

In effect, the Pilgrims came to America as a community seeking to preserve its religious and cultural integrity, and, though they actually ended up only a minority of the population at Plymouth, they set the dominant character and tone of the colony there. As in early Jamestown, their education during the first years of settlement was conducted by family and church rather than through any school or college. They had few men of formal learning among them; they had no ordained ministry; they evidenced little interest in theology or letters; and such literary culture as flourished at Plymouth was maintained largely through the efforts of individual men with sub-stantial libraries, Elder William Brewster, Jr., and Governor Wil-liam Bradford being the leading examples.

The migration that Winthrop eventually led to New England went considerably beyond and, in its very nature, represented yet another transformation in the theory of colonization. Like the Pil-grims, the Puritans who settled Massachusetts came as a community, knit together by ties of family, friendship, and common loyalty. Like the Pilgrims, too, they were attempting to preserve their religious and cultural integrity. But in addition, and more important perhaps, they were seeking to demonstrate to the world at large the nature and practicability of a divinely ordered Christian commonwealth. "We must consider," Winthrop wrote in the oft-quoted peroration to "A Modell of Christian Charity" (1630), "that we shall be as a city upon a hill, the eyes of all people are upon us."[19]

Seeking to execute their special commission from God, the Puritans sought to establish a wilderness Zion, a community of "visible saints" committed to Christian brotherhood and conduct.

[18] William Bradford, *Of Plymouth Plantation, 1620-1647*, edited by Samuel Eliot Morison (New York: Alfred A. Knopf, 1952), p. 25 and *passim*.
[19] John Winthrop, "A Modell of Christian Charity," *Winthrop Papers*, II, 295.

And within such a society education would assume utmost importance, not merely as an instrument for systematically transmitting an intellectual heritage, but as an agency for deliberately pursuing a cultural ideal. Family, church, school, university, the community itself—all would be dedicated to the task of molding men.

Earlier, Winthrop had written of England: "The fountains of learning and religion are so corrupted, as (besides the unsupportable charge of their education) most children, even the best wits and of fairest hopes, are perverted, corrupted and utterly overthrown by the multitude of evil examples and the licentious government of those seminaries." Now, in the new Zion, under the watchful eyes of ministers and magistrates, the reform of education would go hand in hand with the zealous purification of church and commonwealth.[20]

Within the life span of the first generation, which included an extraordinarily high percentage of university-trained men, the Massachusetts Bay Colony enacted legislation requiring families to teach their children to read and understand the principles of religion and the capital laws of the country; it organized its ecclesiastical polity so that each church would have, in addition to a pastor, a teacher, whose special concern was the systematic exegesis of Christian doctrine; it arranged for colonists to settle in towns and then required those towns, when they had grown to fifty householders, to appoint teachers of reading and writing and, when they had grown to a hundred householders, to set up grammar schools; it established a college "to advance learning, and perpetuate it to posterity"; and it welcomed a printing press, in the expectation that it would supply Puritan literature to interested Englishmen on both sides of the Atlantic.[21]

Through this cluster of efforts, Massachusetts had institutionalized a kind of Christian *paideia,* a vision of life itself as deliberate cultural and ethical aspiration. That this *paideia* ultimately deteriorated into what Edmund Morgan has called Puritan tribalism is probably less important than the instruction it afforded both the

20 Winthrop, "Arguments for the Plantation of New England," p. 115.
21 Nathaniel B. Shurtleff, ed., *Records of the Governor and Company of the Massachusetts Bay in New England* (5 vols.; Boston: William White, 1853-1854), II, 6-7, 203; "The Cambridge Synod and Platform, 1646-1648," in Williston Walker, ed., *The Creeds and Platforms of Congregationalism* (New York: Charles Scribner's Sons, 1893), pp. 210-211; *New Englands First Fruits* (London: R.O. and G.D., 1643), in Samuel Eliot Morison, *The Founding of Harvard College* (Cambridge, Mass.: Harvard University Press, 1935), p. 432; and George Parker Winship, *The Cambridge Press, 1638-1692* (Philadelphia: University of Pennsylvania Press, 1945).

New World and the Old in the possibilities of colonization. Education has rarely in history accomplished all that men have hoped to attain through it, but that men have again and again hoped nobly and tried earnestly has been one of the persistent themes of the Western tradition.[22]

England, too, attempted to realize a holy commonwealth in the 1640's and 1650's and witnessed much the same ferment and concern over education as did the Bay Colony during those years. But England tired of Puritanism sooner than Massachusetts, and in 1660 Charles Stuart accepted the judgment of Parliament that the crown had descended to him immediately upon the death of his father "by inherent birthright, and lawful and undoubted succession." The young king returned to England and was everywhere received with acclamation, but he soon learned that acclaim is a poor substitute for coin in the political market place. "I have not so much money in my purse as when I came to you . . . ," he lamented in one of his early addresses to Parliament. "Nor have I been able to give my brothers one shilling since I came into England." This was merely the first of many complaints His Majesty would issue during the next few years over the shortage of cash at court.[23]

That shortage, however, did not prevent him from dispensing honors, offices, and certain grants of land beyond the seas (none of which cost him anything) to the relatives, friends, and supporters who had borne with him during the difficult years of the interregnum. Charles made one such grant in 1664, in the form of a propriety to his brother James, duke of York, which included parts of Maine to the St. Lawrence; Long Island, Martha's Vineyard, and Nantucket; and the entire region from the Connecticut River to the west bank of the Delaware. No doubt he took special pleasure in the last tract, which happened to embrace all of New Netherland. In any case, the duke's charter was granted with unprecedented swiftness between March 8 and 12; on April 2, James appointed his trusted retainer Richard Nicolls deputy governor; and, late in May, an expedition sailed from Portsmouth, whose primary mission was the reduction of the Dutch colony to "an entire obedience and submission" to the king. The fleet reached Boston in late July and then

[22] Edmund S. Morgan, *The Puritan Family: Religion & Domestic Relations in Seventeenth-Century New England* (rev. ed.; New York: Harper & Row, 1966), chap. vii.

[23] *Journals of the House of Commons*, VIII, 16-17; and *His Majesties Gracious Speech to Both Houses of Parliament, on the 29th Day of August 1660* (London: John Bill and Christopher Barker, 1660), p. 7.

proceeded to New Amsterdam, entering the narrows just north of Coney Island the following month. Nicolls issued proclamations offering favorable terms to the Dutch; and, after several days of delay and negotiations, "the place of New Amsterdam, in New Netherland, situated on Manhattan, surrendered to the English, the garrison retiring with all their arms, flying colors and beating drums; and thereby the English, without any contest or claim being before put forth by any person to it, took possession of a fort built and continually garrisoned about forty years at the expense of the West India Company."[24]

The colony that fell to Nicolls had a continuous history extending back to 1624, when the West India Company ship *New Netherland* had deposited groups of colonists, most of them Walloons (French-speaking Belgians), at various points in the newly constituted province of the same name. In 1625, the Company had sent additional families, along with a large supply of livestock, seed, and agricultural implements; and by 1626, following a consolidation of settlers under Peter Minuit, first director-general of the province, the central trading post at New Amsterdam had grown to some two hundred men, women, and children, and was rapidly taking on all the characteristics of a self-sustaining community. "Everyone there who fills no public office is busy about his own affairs," wrote a contemporary observer. "Men work there as in Holland; one trades, upwards, southwards and northwards; another builds houses, the third farms. Each farmer has his farmstead on the land purchased by the Company, which also owns the cows; but the milk remains to the profit of the farmer; he sells it to those of the people who receive their wages for work every week."[25]

Thereafter, the agencies of cultural transmission had appeared in fairly rapid succession. In 1626, Bastiaen Krol and Jan Huygen were already serving as "comforters of the sick," junior church officers who in the absence of a regular minister read Scriptural texts and commentaries each Sunday. In 1628, Domine Jonas J. Michaëlius arrived to undertake the first regular ministry; in 1638, Adam

24 E. B. O'Callaghan, ed., *Documents Relative to the Colonial History of the State of New York* (10 vols. and *General Index;* Albany: Weed, Parsons and Company, 1856-1861), III, 63; II, 415.

25 Nicolaes van Wassenaer, *Historisch Verhael alder ghedenck-weerdichste Geschiedenissen die hier en daer in Europa, etc., voorgevallen syn,* in J. Franklin Jameson, ed., *Narratives of New Netherland, 1609-1664,* Original Narratives, edited by Jameson (New York: Charles Scribner's Sons, 1909), pp. 75-76, 79-80, 82-84.

Roelantsen began the first systematic elementary schooling; and, in 1652, Jan de la Montagne instituted the first formal instruction in the classics.[26]

By 1664, New Amsterdam had become a prosperous Dutch market town of about fifteen hundred inhabitants, which served as the political, commercial, and cultural nucleus of an extensive colonial province with a population of more than five thousand, including not only Dutchmen, as the most numerous single group, but also Englishmen, Walloons, Swedes, Finns, French, Portuguese, and Africans. While New Amsterdam resembled the towns of Holland—at the very least its governmental forms, churches, schools, and architecture were characteristically Dutch—its people were sufficiently heterogeneous for official edicts to be published in three languages and for one contemporary cleric to moralize about the "confusion of tongues" and the "arrogance of Babel."[27]

It was the necessity of bringing this thriving Dutch town and its satellite communities under the control of the proprietor and, through him, within the orbit of England that occasioned yet another transformation in English colonial theory; for the problem was essentially new to the English. They had won military victories in Europe and then imposed limited political solutions on the vanquished; they had prevailed in Ireland, insisting on rather harsh general terms there; and they had from time to time looted their share of colonial ports, temporarily occupying them and carrying off prisoners and plunder. But they had never before captured the distant colonial settlement of another nation with the express intent of incorporating it into their own empire.

The immediate question for Nicolls and the duke was the nature and extent of the control they meant to exercise, though from the outset it was clear that their policies would be moderate and conciliatory. The terms of capitulation, for example, were quite generous —far more so, in fact, than those the Dutch would impose when they recaptured the colony for a brief interval in 1673. The inhabi-

26 *Ibid.*, pp. 83, 120; Dingman Versteeg, *Manhattan in 1628* (New York: Dodd, Mead and Company, 1904); and William Heard Kilpatrick, *The Dutch Schools of New Netherland and Colonial New York* (Washington, D.C.: Government Printing Office, 1912), chaps. iii, vi.

27 O'Callaghan, ed., *New York Colonial Documents*, II, 248. The estimate of the population of the province is based on Stella H. Sutherland's figures in *Historical Statistics of the United States, Colonial Times to 1957* (Washington, D.C.: Government Printing Office, 1960), p. 756. Father Isaac Jogues, "Narrative Reported by Father Buteux, 1645," in Jameson, ed., *Narratives of New Netherland*, p. 253.

tants would remain "free denizens" and enjoy their lands, houses, goods, and ships; the Dutch were assured easy movement to and from the Netherlands and were guaranteed "the liberty of their consciences in divine worship and church discipline"; all civil officials other than the governor were given the option of retaining their posts until the next scheduled election. Two months later, after Nicolls had given assurances that he meant to govern in the spirit of these terms, most of the leading citizens of the town, including Stuyvesant, took an oath of allegiance to the King of England and the Duke of York.[28]

Nicolls' effort over the next four years and, indeed, that of his successors, Colonel Francis Lovelace and Sir Edmund Andros, was to Anglicize as much as possible the administration of the province, leaving substantial latitude in religious and cultural affairs. Even in matters of government, however, Nicolls had to work out policies for the Dutch and Swedish settlements that were quite different from those he was able to develop for the English communities of Long Island and Westchester (the latter were codified in the Duke's Laws of 1665). And, until well into the eighteenth century, there was a persistent problem, at least in New York City, as to whether official records and accounts would be kept in English or Dutch or both.[29]

With respect to religion, Nicolls simply extended the *de facto* toleration that had existed under the Dutch, removing the Reformed church from its position of exclusive political preferment and ensuring that Anglicans would have access to services conducted by the English army chaplain at Fort James. The result was further diversification, and in 1687 Governor Dongan reported in his description of the city: "New York has first a chaplain belonging to the Fort of the Church of England; secondly a Dutch Calvinist, thirdly a French Calvinist, fourthly a Dutch Lutheran—Here be not many of the Church of England; few Roman Catholics; abun-

28 O'Callaghan, ed., *New York Colonial Documents*, II, 250-253; III, 74-77; and Berthold Fernow, ed., *The Records of New Amsterdam, from 1653 to 1674 Anno Domini* (7 vols.; New York: The Knickerbocker Press, 1897), V, 142-145.

29 Albert E. McKinley, "The Transition from Dutch to English Rule in New York," *The American Historical Review*, VI (1900-1901), 693-724; "Lawes Establisht by the Authority of His Majesties Letters Patents, Granted to His Royall Highnes James Duke of Yorke and Albany," *Collections of the New-York Historical Society*, I (1809), 307-428; Fernow, ed., *Records of New Amsterdam*, V, 256; Minutes of the Mayor's Court, November 17, 1674, quoted in I. N. Phelps Stokes, *The Iconography of Manhattan Island, 1498-1909* (6 vols.; New York: Robert H. Dodd, 1915-1928), IV, 303; Mrs. Schuyler Van Rensselaer, *History of the City of New York in the Seventeenth Century* (2 vols.; New York: The Macmillan Company, 1909), II, 174; and Edward T. Corwin, ed., *Ecclesiastical Records, State of New York* (7 vols.; Albany: J. B. Lyon Company, 1901-1916), IV, 2563.

dance of Quaker preachers, men and women especially; Singing Quakers; Ranting Quakers; Sabbatarians; Antisabbatarians; some Anabaptists; some Independents; some Jews; in short of all sorts of opinions there are some, and the most part, of none at all. . . . The most prevailing opinion is that of the Dutch Calvinists."[30]

So it was also in the realm of schooling, where the Dutch institutions were permitted to continue their instruction in Dutch and where, indeed, the Dutch city school of New York was actually granted funds for a time, though that support was withdrawn after the second English conquest in 1674. The Duke's Laws themselves were silent on schooling; neither Nicolls nor Lovelace nor Andros seriously exercised his right to examine and approve teachers; and such English instruction as appeared outside Long Island was modest and intermittent until William Huddleston set up classes as the "Church of England schoolmaster" sometime around the turn of the century.[31]

What prevailed culturally, therefore, in the first three decades of English rule, was a relatively open situation. At the same time as authorities pressed steadily for the extension of English political, legal, and commercial forms, they seemed willing to permit great diversity in the realm of belief, worship, and instruction. The result was a theory of colonization in which a colony became a community with alternate modes of education, formal and informal, each seeking a decisive role in shaping the future. As Duke of York, James doubtless came to the theory as a matter of expediency; his friend William Penn raised it to the level of high principle and made it the basis of a second holy experiment in the New World.

III

The English and Dutch were not the only Europeans to colonize North America during the seventeenth century, as is well known. In fact, they were comparative latecomers to colonization. The Spanish, seeking to protect the northern edge of their trade routes with Central and South America, had established St. Augustine as early

---

[30] O'Callaghan, ed., *New York Colonial Documents*, III, 415.

[31] The quotation is from "An Account of the State of the Church in North America by Mr. George Keith and Others," S.P.G. Journals (S.P.G. mss., United Society for the Propagation of the Gospel, London), Appendix A, p. 178. Huddleston was certainly teaching as early as 1691, when he was listed as "William Huddleston of the said city schoolmaster," in New York City Conveyances (microfilm records, Surrogate's Court, New York City), Liber XVIII, p. 146. And he was early active in the affairs of Trinity Church, which was organized in 1696 and chartered in 1697.

as 1565, destroying in the process the nascent French colony of Fort Caroline and founding the fifst permanent European settlement north of the Gulf of Mexico. The French, following a series of unsuccessful efforts in the sixteenth century, had planted permanent colonies in Acadia (Nova Scotia) and Quebec in 1605 and 1608, seeking during Richelieu's regime to inject into them the same vitality that was already manifest in Virginia and Massachusetts. And the Swedes, anticipating the sort of profitable commerce the Dutch were enjoying with New Netherland, founded New Sweden along the banks of the Delaware in 1638. In addition to these quasi-governmental enterprises, there were also scattered migrations of French Huguenots, Spanish and Portuguese Jews, Scottish Presbyterians, and German sectarians, of whom some came as individuals, some as independent families, and some as groups of families looking forward to sharing a common life under alien but tolerant authorities.

These people came for a variety of reasons, economic, political, religious, and personal; and they brought with them a variety of European traditions. Moreover, this variety of traditions was compounded by the customs of the native Indians and the immigrant Africans, both slave and free. Diversity, therefore, and with it the attendant phenomena of cultural competition, accommodation, and blending, was from the very beginning a fundamental fact of American life. Yet equally striking was the dominance of the English tradition almost from the outset. By 1689, English settlements stretched in a continuous line down the North American coast from Permaquid (in what is now Maine) to the Carolinas (and beyond to the West Indian islands); and of the two-hundred-odd thousand Europeans on the continent the English were by far the majority. Numerically superior to the French, the Dutch, and the Spanish, and technologically superior to the Indians and the Africans, the English were in a unique position to prevail, and indeed they did.

But the decisive influence of their culture was more than a matter of numbers or technology: it was in large measure a matter of education. By the 1620's, the English had moved farther than any other Western power toward conceiving of colonies, not as exploitative bands of transient men, but as permanent, self-sustaining communities; and their concept of colonial communities came gradually to embrace families, churches, missions, print shops, and schools, which would methodically propagate English customs, ideas, language, law, and literature. True, the French, the Dutch, and the Spanish also planted families in North America during the seventeenth century, and even some churches, missions, and schools. But none of these managed to develop education as extensively as the English. As a result, England achieved intellectual as well as political hegemony; and, though that hegemony would be challenged during the intercolonial wars of the eighteenth century, it would not be overthrown.

The processes by which the English succeeded in transplanting their culture to the New World and making it prevail were extraordinarily complex, much more so than Edward Eggleston suggested in his classic study of *The Transit of Civilization from England to America in the Seventeenth Century* (1900). In the first place, English culture was but one version of a more general western European culture: it shared a common heritage with other versions, such as the Dutch, the Spanish, the French, and the Italian, and it remained in continuing contact with them. Thus, the Englishmen who came to America carried Bibles, and the writings of Augustine, and the poetry of Virgil, and the letters of Cicero, all of which Europeans revered in common. Furthermore, they brought as part of their "native" literature treatises by Erasmus, a Dutchman; Vives, a Spaniard; Castiglione, an Italian; and Montaigne, a Frenchman. There was nothing particularly "pure" about the Anglo-Saxon tradition, and a good deal of the cosmopolitanism that marked Renaissance Europe was simply transmitted by the English to the colonies.

Second, English culture was itself changing and in conflict during the seventeenth century, as witness the struggles between Protestant and Catholic, Anglican and Puritan, Royalist and Parliamentarian, scientist and humanist, landlord and tenant, squire and merchant. And these struggles racked the New World as well, though the ferment was, of course, selectively transmitted: neither were all classes of Englishmen represented equally in the migrations to America, nor were all forms of opinion. Some ideas and institutions that were fairly popular at home were barely in evidence in the colonies, and vice versa. There was no simple correspondence of cultures, and, indeed, what correspondence there was tended to diminish with the passage of time.

Third, almost as soon as certain forms were planted in the New World, they began to change in response to unique social and physical conditions. However strong the intent of the English to reproduce English institutions and however characteristic their modes of justification and explanation, there were subtle changes from the beginning, as men were forced to refashion traditional means and invent new ones for coping with a strange environment. Moreover, the very heterogeneity of colonial society made transformation virtually inevitable. English culture may have been dominant, but it was not totalitarian; and alien ways were both tolerated, as in the case of the thriving community of Sephardic Jews in seventeenth-century New York, and incorporated, as witness the permanent influence of Dutch terminology on American English.

Finally, the transmission of culture was a reciprocal process, and from the first years of settlement—in fact, from the earliest voyages of exploration—the New World exerted its influence on Europe. It is not merely that American products, such as white potatoes and maize and persimmons and raspberries and tobacco, were enthusiastically adopted by the English; the very existence of the New World stirred the imagination of the Old, requiring it to rethink many of its time-honored beliefs. From More to Locke, philosophers located their utopias in America; and a steady flow of information concerning the realities of the colonial world—the Indians, the plants and animals, the terrain—worked a transforming influence on English political, religious, and scientific ideas. Indeed, the very traditions that later seventeenth-century English migrants brought with them to America had themselves been modified by American influences.

In all this, education, both formal and informal, played a critical role. On the one hand, education was an important element of the heritage transplanted to the colonies; and, like other aspects of that heritage, it was in ferment, it was transmitted selectively, and it underwent significant changes once established. On the other hand, education was itself part and parcel of the process of cultural transmission. It linked the colonies to the metropolis, affording them access to the accumulated political, moral, and technological wisdom of the West; and it furnished them with the means of modifying, refining, and extending that wisdom in the solution of new and unprecedented problems. Indeed, it is in the relationship between the knowledge the colonists developed for coping with the New World and the agencies they established for transmitting that knowledge, or, alternatively, between the historical processes whereby the colonial character was formed and the institutional processes whereby the colonists sought to form character, that one finds the key to the colonial experience, and the origins of American education.

PART I

PIETY, CIVILITY, AND LEARNING

And the said court, for the better maintenance of the said school, schoolmaster, and usher intended there to be placed, granted one thousand acres of land to the said free school, to be at Charles City, as the most commodious place for health, security, profit, and conveniency: and appointed that with the said £100 8s. 6d., there should be sent over presently an usher, for the instructing of the children there, in the principles of religion, civility of life, and humane learning.

PATRICK COPLAND

INTRODUCTION

"How hard will it be for one brought up among books and learned men to live in a barbarous place where is no learning and less civility," warned Robert Ryece during the summer of 1629, in seeking to dissuade his friend John Winthrop from his projected journey to New England. But there was little that Ryece or any other skeptic could do by that time to dampen Winthrop's enthusiasm. Two weeks after Ryece had written, Winthrop and eleven others entered into an agreement at Cambridge to "embark for the said plantation"; and seven months later, on March 29, 1630, the *Arbella* sailed from Southampton. Winthrop, of course, had no intention of succumbing to the barbarism of the New World. His answer to Ryece lay not only in dreams of a Bible commonwealth but in his carrying from England those works of literature which, through their instruction in piety, civility, and learning, would enable him to maintain the only form of life he thought worth living.[1]

John Winthrop was himself a man of gentle birth, lord of the manor at Groton, a lawyer trained at Gray's Inn. But his effort to overcome the threat of barbarism was to a surprising degree shared by his fellow settlers. North America was colonized during the first phase of Europe's age of print, the initial two-hundred-year period after Gutenberg, when a reading public gradually came into being that for the first time in history was not confined to the clerisy or

[1] Robert Ryece to John Winthrop, August 12, 1629, *Winthrop Papers* (5+ vols.; Boston: The Massachusetts Historical Society, 1929-   ), II, 106; and "The Agreement at Cambridge," *ibid.*, p. 152.

the aristocracy. "Never in any age were books more sought for and better esteemed," wrote a chronicler in 1590; and, at least as far as England was concerned, his observation seems to have been entirely accurate. The work of J. W. Adamson, Louis B. Wright, H. S. Bennett, and others has persuasively documented the fact that reading in the vernacular was an art widely practiced during the Tudor and early Stuart eras, even among the lowest ranks of society. Moreover, it was an art served by an output of printed materials unprecedented in scope and variety. "We live in a printing age," lamented an anonymous commentator in 1591, "wherein there is no man either so vainly, or factiously, or filthily disposed, but there are crept out of all sorts unauthorized authors, to fill and fit his humor." The satirist Thomas Nashe put it more succinctly a year later, ridiculing the fact that "every gross-brained idiot is suffered to come into print." As a result, those who settled America were much less dependent on an oral tradition for the transmission of culture than they might have been even a hundred years earlier. And so along with everything else they forced into the crowded vessels that carried them to the New World—plants, animals, seeds, ploughs, and clothing—the colonists brought books.[2]

Those who came to America, humble and well-born alike, were men of the Renaissance; and, as such, they were heir to all the passions, fashions, and contradictions of that vibrant and expansive era. They accepted witchcraft but were fascinated by the new sciences; they believed in a great and static chain of being but sought at every opportunity to advance themselves; they charged just prices but were really nascent capitalists. They were at the same time credulous and skeptical, mystical and pragmatic. In short, they were medieval men standing on the threshold of modernity. And the books they brought with them embodied their heritage, frequently at its noblest, occasionally at its most base: there were the ancient and the Christian classics, for Renaissance scholarship in England, as everywhere else,

2 Francisco Sansovino, The Quintesence of Wit, translated by R. Hitchcock (London: Edward Allde, 1590), sig. A₂ verso; John William Adamson, "The Illiterate Anglo-Saxon" and Other Essays on Education, Medieval and Modern (Cambridge: Cambridge University Press, 1946), chap. iii; Louis B. Wright, Middle-Class Culture in Elizabethan England (Chapel Hill: University of North Carolina Press, 1935); H. S. Bennett, English Books & Readers, 1475 to 1557 (Cambridge: Cambridge University Press, 1952) and English Books & Readers, 1558 to 1603 (Cambridge: Cambridge University Press, 1965); R. W., Martine Mar-Sixtus (London: Printed for Thomas Woodcock, 1591), sig. A₃ verso; and Thomas Nashe, Pierce Penilesse: His Supplication to the Divell, in The Works of Thomas Nashe, edited by Ronald B. McKerrow and corrected by F. P. Wilson (5 vols.; Oxford: Basil Blackwell, 1958), I, 159.

looked backward to the unexcelled models of the past; there were contemporary works of religion, both contentious and didactic, for Renaissance thought redefined God as well as man, and the proper relationship between the two; there were manuals of law, medicine, politics, surveying, agriculture, and conduct, for the men of the Renaissance were worldly, and those who went to America had to be more worldly than most; there were, less frequently perhaps, the works of poetry, drama, history, and even fiction that for some made the difference between cultivated living and mere existence; and, finally, there were the textbooks that would ensure the continuity of civilization in the New World.

It is largely through these works the colonists carried with them, as well as through the books and pamphlets and sermons and laws they wrote themselves, that we can best know what they understood, believed, valued, and aspired to. There are problems with this assumption, to be sure. In the first place, it tends to disregard (or at best to consider indirectly) the oral tradition, which remained a powerful molding influence throughout the early modern period. Then, too, records of seventeenth-century book ownership are highly fragmentary, and both the range and number of writings available to the colonists doubtless exceeded what can be gleaned from the evidence. And, third, there is the nagging question of whether ownership of written materials actually signifies influence; and here, one can only assume that the cost and difficulty of obtaining books in the wilderness would have militated against idle ostentation.[3]

In any case, there is ample indication of widespread possession of books by the colonists, though small libraries were the rule; and the evidence in letters, diaries, wills, and inventories suggests that these books were both valued and read. And there is every reason to believe that, as the colonies became communities, these books played a fundamental role in articulating the common aspirations of their inhabitants. They were instructive in their own right and profoundly influential in the development of institutions. And, inasmuch as many of them patently set forth standards of character and conduct, they inevitably helped to define education, indicating not only

[3] My argument is that we can neither confine our attention to the writings of the colonists themselves, as Moses Coit Tyler did in *A History of American Literature, 1607-1765* (2 vols.; New York: G. P. Putnam's Sons, 1878), nor assume that writings available in England were uniformly known in the colonies, as Perry Miller did in *The New England Mind: The Seventeenth Century* (Cambridge, Mass.: Harvard University Press, 1939).

the desired outcomes of the process but also the terms in which it would be discussed, the techniques by which it would be carried on, and the agencies through which it would proceed. They were, in effect, the seventeenth-century version of a pedagogical literature, and it is to them we must turn for the ideas of the good life that inspired the colonists and the ideas of education that impelled them.

Chapter 1

THE PRACTICE OF PIETY

To be learned is the lot of only a few; but no one is unable to be
Christian, no one is unable to be pious, and I add this boldly,
no one is unable to be a theologian. For that which is most of
all in accordance with nature descends easily into the minds of
all. But what else is the philosophy of Christ, which he himself
calls a rebirth, than the instauration of a well-founded nature.

DESIDERIUS ERASMUS

No two men of the English Renaissance more consummately symbolized the new education than Desiderius Erasmus and William Tyndale. Yet it is difficult to imagine two more dissimilar personalities.
Erasmus: risen from obscure origins as the illegitimate son of a
Dutch priest, genial, learned, witty, easily the most famous European
scholar of his time, confidant of kings and princes, friend to cardinals
and courtiers, revered and lionized and flattered by his contemporaries; Tyndale: scion of a well-to-do English yeoman, austere, diffi-
dent, self-described as speechless and rude, dull and slow-witted, a
controversialist harried and persecuted in one country after another,
a zealot squalidly betrayed by a false disciple and eventually executed for heresy. As far as we know, the two men never met, though
they shared a large measure of common intellectual commitment and
concern. But, in the end, each in his own way decisively influenced
education in the English-speaking world.

Desiderius Erasmus first came to England in June of 1499, probably at the invitation of William Blount, the youthful Lord Mountjoy, whom he had been tutoring in Paris. Erasmus had been educated
at Deventer and at 's Hertogenbosch by the Brethren of the Common
Life, from whom he had imbibed not only a thorough knowledge

of Latin, including, incidentally, some of the newer critical techniques of Lorenzo Valla, but also the spirit of what the Brethren called the *devotio moderna,* the commitment to a piety stressing imitation of Christ rather than subscription to creed or exploitation of sacramental grace. Then, after a period with the Augustinian canons at Steyn and a tour as Latin secretary to the bishop of Cambrai, he had gone on to the College of Montaigu, at Paris, hoping to obtain a doctorate in theology. The experience there was something less than exhilarating, and by the time of his visit to England—he was probably about thirty—Erasmus had already developed a solid command of the theological tradition and a healthy disdain for theologians.[1]

Thanks to his host, Lord Mountjoy, Erasmus had an opportunity to meet members of the royal family, including the Duke of York (later to become King Henry VIII) and a young barrister-in-training named Thomas More, with whom he shared a lively appreciation of the ridiculous and a thoroughgoing contempt for sham. At Oxford, Erasmus was much taken with John Colet, whose lectures applying the new textual criticism of the Italian humanists to the Epistles of Paul were creating a sensation, and whose circle of friends, including William Grocyn, a specialist in Greek, and Thomas Linacre, a physician, provided unrivaled intellectual stimulation. "I have never yet liked anything so well," Erasmus wrote to his student Robert Fisher. "I have found here a climate as delightful as it is wholesome; and moreover so much humane learning, not of the outworn, commonplace sort, but the profound, accurate, ancient Greek and Latin learning, that I now scarcely miss Italy, but for the sight of it. When I listen to my friend Colet, I seem to hear Plato himself. Who would not marvel at the perfection of encyclopedic learning in Grocyn? What could be keener or nobler or nicer than Linacre's judgment? What has nature ever fashioned gentler or sweeter or happier than the character of Thomas More?" By the time Erasmus returned to Paris early in 1500, he had settled on a vocation as scholar, dedicated to applying the best critical methods of his day to the principal documents of the Christian faith, with a view to purifying the entire Christian tradition.[2]

[1] See Desiderius Erasmus to Thomas Grey, [Autumn, 1497], *The Epistles of Erasmus,* translated and edited by Francis Morgan Nichols (3 vols.; London: Longmans, Green, and Co., 1901-1918), I, 144.

[2] Desiderius Erasmus to Robert Fisher, December 5, 1499, "Selection from the Letters of Erasmus," translated by Barbara Flower, appended to J. Huizinga, *Erasmus of Rotterdam* (London: Phaidon Press, 1952), pp. 199-200.

The fruits of that decision are well known. There was a period of intense preparation, especially in Greek and Greek literature, followed by three decades of indefatigable scholarly production. The result was an outpouring of commentaries and treatises, editions of the Fathers (both Greek and Latin), translations and paraphrases of the New Testament, and compilations of classical and contemporary materials for the use of students. Never long content in one place, Erasmus traveled the length and breadth of Europe, making two additional visits to England; he engaged in voluminous correspondence with most of the intellectual luminaries of his time; and he lived to see his friends and students accede to positions of great power and privilege. But he also lived to know the intense bitterness, hatred, and fratricidal conflict that his own writings doubtless helped bring to pass. "In the death of More I feel as if I had died myself," he wrote in anguish during the summer of 1535 on hearing the word of Sir Thomas' execution. A year later, he himself was dead of dysentery.[3]

Erasmus was no metaphysician: the thrust of his prodigious scholarship was always practical, to free Christendom from the pretentious vacuities of the Scholastics and to substitute for their systems *philosophia Christi*, by which Erasmus understood a simple, rational, undogmatic Christianity. The doctrine is expounded in a number of his works, most clearly, perhaps, in the *Enchiridion militis Christiani* (*Handbook of the Christian Knight*), written in 1501 while Erasmus was under the inspiration of Colet's lectures on Paul, and the *Paraclesis* (*Exhortation*), published in 1516 as the preface to Erasmus' Greek and Latin edition of the New Testament. Together, these treatises proclaim a new piety, not of monks and clerics withdrawn from the world, but of informed laymen living within it according to the precepts of Christ.[4]

The *Enchiridion*, following in the tradition of Thomas a Kempis' *Imitation of Christ*, which Erasmus must have encountered during his years with the Brethren of the Common Life, is essentially a handbook of Christian devotion, which argues primarily that true piety is not assent to creed or performance of sacrament but rather a

---

[3] Desiderius Erasmus to Peter Tomitz, August 31, 1535, in J. A. Froude, *Life and Letters of Erasmus* (New York: Charles Scribner's Sons, 1894), p. 419.
[4] For a modern translation based on Johann Froben's 1519 edition of the *Enchiridion*, see *The Enchiridion of Erasmus*, translated and edited by Raymond Himelick (Bloomington: Indiana University Press, 1963). A modern translation of the *Paraclesis* may be found in *Christian Humanism and the Reformation: Selected Writings of Erasmus*, edited by John C. Olin (New York: Harper & Row, 1965), pp. 92-106.

mode of living that can be learned and practiced by all men. The
principal elements of that mode of living are prayer, which lifts the
spirit heavenward, and knowledge, which informs the spirit with
salutary ideas. And the chief source of knowledge is divine Scripture, itself informed by the interpretations of Paul, the writings of
the Fathers—notably, Origen, Ambrose, Jerome, and Augustine—
and the poetry and philosophy of the ancients. Years later, when
Erasmus prepared a new edition of the *Enchiridion* for the printer
Johann Froben, he added a prefatory epistle to Paul Volz, reaffirming
the work's decidedly pragmatic intent. "Let this little book not
be sharp-witted provided it be pious," he wrote. "Let it not prepare
a person for the mental gymnastics of the Sorbonne but for Christian
peace of soul. . . . Let our aim be not to appear learned but to lead
as many as possible to a Christian life."[5]

The *Paraclesis* is a moving restatement and extension of the arguments of the *Enchiridion,* summoning all Christians to the study of
Scripture as the truest guide to Christ's teaching and calling for the
translation of Scripture into the vernacular, so that it could be known
by the unlettered as well as the learned throughout the world. "I
would that even the lowliest women read the Gospels and the Pauline Epistles," Erasmus wrote in an oft-quoted passage. "And I would
that they were translated into all languages so that they could be
read and understood not only by Scots and Irish but also by Turks
and Saracens. Surely the first step is to understand in one way or
another. It may be that many will ridicule, but some may be taken
captive. Would that, as a result, the farmer sing some portion of
them at the plow, the weaver hum some parts of them to the movement of his shuttle, the traveler lighten the weariness of the journey
with stories of this kind! Let all the conversations of every Christian
be drawn from this source. For in general our daily conversations reveal what we are." Here was a radical doctrine of universal education,
which would soon shatter the unity of Christendom with a force
that even the learned Erasmus could not have imagined as he
wrote.[6]

The *Enchiridion,* issuing as it did from an unknown young cleric

[5] In his well-known letter to Martin Dorp, written at Antwerp in May, 1515, Erasmus noted, "In the *Enchiridion* I simply set down a design for Christian living"
(*Christian Humanism*, p. 59). Desiderius Erasmus to Paul Volz, August 14, 1518, *ibid.,*
pp. 110-112. Volz was abbot of the Benedictine monastery of Hugshofen, in Alsace; he
was much admired by Erasmus, who thought his life exemplary of the principles set
forth in the *Enchiridion.*

[6] Erasmus, *Paraclesis,* in *Christian Humanism,* p. 97.

and containing both explicit and implicit criticisms of contemporary clerical practice, was not an immediate success. The first edition, published at Antwerp in 1503, attracted little attention; there was no demand for a reprint until 1509, nor for a third printing until 1515. With the appearance of the Froben edition of 1518, prefaced by Erasmus' lively defense of the centrality of Scripture and the implied priesthood of believers, interest soared; and thereafter translations and new editions followed one another in rapid succession. Among these was an anonymous English version entitled *A Booke Called in Latyn Enchiridion Militis Christiani, and in Englysshe the Manuell of the Christen Knyght*. First published in 1533, it was probably the translation of William Tyndale, a young priest who had found much to admire in Erasmus and who was already encountering difficulty because of it.

Born in the last decade of the fifteenth century, Tyndale had been educated at Oxford, where he proceeded A.B. in 1512 and A.M. in 1515, and had then gone on to Cambridge to be "further ripened in the knowledge of God's word." At Cambridge, he may well have come to know Hugh Latimer, Thomas Cranmer, Stephen Gardiner, and Thomas Bilney, all of whom were in residence at the time; and he may even have witnessed the burning of Luther's writings in 1521. In any case, though he was both a master of arts and an ordained priest, Tyndale decided against staying at the university or accepting a parish and opted instead to serve as tutor to the children of Sir John Walsh, of Little Sodbury Manor in Gloucestershire. There, in spirited exchanges with local clerics and "other doctors, and great beneficed men," he found himself time and again pointing to Scripture for confirmation of opinions that seemed unorthodox; and, when called upon by Sir John and his wife to defend the practice, it is said that he rendered the *Enchiridion* into English and presented them with the book.[7]

There is no doubt that Tyndale took his Erasmus seriously, and it was during the sojourn at Little Sodbury that he resolved to undertake an English translation of the Bible. If God spared his life, he is said to have proclaimed (echoing Erasmus in the *Paraclesis*), "ere many years he would cause a boy that driveth the plough, to know more of the Scripture than he did." Eager to get on with the work, he traveled to London to see Bishop Cuthbert Tunstall, whose scholarship Erasmus had praised in the annotations to his New

[7] *The Acts and Monuments of John Foxe* (1563), edited by the Rev. Stephen Reed Cattley (8 vols.; London: R. B. Seeley and W. Burnside, 1837-1841), V, 115-116.

Testament, and requested permission and patronage for the venture. Tunstall apparently equivocated, advising him to seek support in the city at large. This proved, as A. G. Dickens has pointed out, the most fateful miscalculation by the English bishops in the matter of Biblical translation. For Tyndale did find assistance, from the wealthy cloth merchant Humphrey Monmouth, who promptly put him in touch with London Lollardry and international Lutheranism. Tyndale began his translation in Monmouth's house, using Erasmus' Greek New Testament in one or more of the early editions (1516, 1519, 1522); and then, in 1524, he went on to complete the work in Germany, where he almost certainly met Luther and used his German edition of 1522. The printing of Tyndale's New Testament was begun at Cologne in 1525 and was completed at Worms, after Tyndale had been forced to flee Cologne by the local magistrates. Despite efforts to prevent its importation, copies were streaming into England by the spring of 1526. Bishop Tunstall and others promptly convinced Henry VIII that the work was subversive, with the result that copies were publicly burned at Paul's Cross in London. Later, in Antwerp, Tunstall commissioned Augustine Packington, a London merchant, to buy up as many additional books as possible, so that they could also be destroyed. But the rapid development of printing had rendered such efforts futile, and Tyndale's translation in its successive editions slowly spread through England. By 1537, Edward Fox, bishop of Hereford, could say to the assembled episcopate: "Make not yourselves the laughing-stock of the world; light is sprung up, and is scattering all the clouds. The lay people know the Scriptures better than many of us."[8]

Tyndale's enterprise had elicited bitter and relentless opposition from a large portion of the intellectual community of western Europe, and the sources and substance of that opposition reveal much about the educational conflicts at the heart of both Renaissance and Reformation. Erasmus' earlier criticism of the Vulgate had itself caused concern among those who believed it unreasonable to suppose "that the universal church has been in error for so many genera-

[8] *Ibid.*, p. 117; and A. G. Dickens, *The English Reformation* (New York: Schocken Books, 1964), p. 70. See the excerpt from Edward Halle's *The Union of the Two Noble and Illustrious Fameles of Lancastre and Yorke* (1548), in Alfred W. Pollard, ed., *Records of the English Bible* (London: Oxford University Press, 1911), pp. 150-153. The passage from Fox is in Richard Watson Dixon, *History of the Church of England from the Abolition of the Roman Jurisdiction* (6 vols.; London: publisher varies, 1878-1902), I, 413-414.

tions in her use of this edition." But Erasmus, with the help of his friend Thomas More, had managed to quiet the controversy by affirming his desire to serve the "common good" and his willingness to retract any opinions that did not stand up in the face of "better doctrine."[9]

Tyndale, on the other hand, was inevitably associated with Lutheranism, and in his case no assurance, however persuasive, would suffice. The same Thomas More who had earlier leaped to the defense of Erasmus was now recruited by Tunstall to "play the Demosthenes" against the Lutheran heretics. Within a year, More obliged with a lengthy and acerbic *Dialogue* (1529), treating "divers matters . . . touching the pestilent sect of Luther and Tyndale." As far as More was concerned, the essential difference between Erasmus and Tyndale was their intent: Erasmus, inspired by John Colet, had prepared a purified version of Scripture to serve the cause of revival and reform within the church; Tyndale, infected by Luther, had made an unauthorized translation, which was replete with heretical errors and which, in the hands of the untutored mob, could only disrupt the church. Tyndale's sin, therefore, lay not in having produced an English version of the New Testament but in having produced an unauthorized version.[10]

"Of all wretches," charged More, "worst shall he walk that, forcing little of the faith of Christ's church, cometh to the Scripture of God to look and try therein whether the church believe aright or not." Tyndale, replying with equal acerbity in *An Answer unto Sir Thomas More's Dialoge* (1531), urged all Christians to judge for themselves whether the pope and his particular interpretations "be the church; whether their authority be above the Scripture; whether all they teach without Scripture be equal with the Scripture; whether they have erred, and not only whether they can." The plea was in its very nature Protestant, a fact that eluded neither the bishops nor the king; and, though the controversy raged for a number of years, growing more bitter with the passage of time, there were few in high places who altered their views. What actually happened was that

[9] Martin Dorp to Desiderius Erasmus, [October, 1514], *Epistles of Erasmus,* II, 169; and Desiderius Erasmus to Martin Dorp, May, 1515, *Christian Humanism,* p. 91.

[10] Cuthbert Tunstall to Thomas More, March 7, 1528, quoted in J. F. Mozley, *William Tyndale* (New York: The Macmillan Company, 1937), p. 213. A facsimile of William Rastell's 1557 edition of More's *Dialogue,* along with a modern version of the same, can be found in *The English Works of Sir Thomas More,* edited by W. E. Campbell (2 vols.; London: Eyre and Spottiswoode, 1931), vol. II.

those in power vacillated to suit their purposes. After initially supporting Tunstall in his efforts to suppress Tyndale's translation,
Henry reversed himself and ordered in 1538 that an English Bible
be placed in every church of the realm (ironically, at about the time
Tyndale suffered execution for heresy). His proclamation was vigorously confirmed by the regency under Edward VI, honored largely
in the breach by Mary, and prudently reconfirmed by Elizabeth.
In this, at least, the Reformation in England was, as Sir Maurice
Powicke once suggested, an affair of state.[11]

Tyndale was far from a democrat, his statement about the
ploughboy notwithstanding; yet there is no denying the popular and
therefore highly radical character of his New Testament. Using the
language of the laity with remarkable artistry, he had actually fashioned an extraordinarily powerful instrument of popular education,
on which nearly all subsequent English versions of the Bible depended in some measure: Miles Coverdale's edition of 1535, the first
complete Bible printed in English; the "Matthew Bible" of 1537
(this included more of Tyndale's work than any other), attributed
to Thomas Matthew but probably prepared by Tyndale's friend
John Rogers; the so-called Great Bible of 1539, published under the
high authority of Thomas Cranmer and Thomas Cromwell; the
Geneva Bible of 1560, produced by the Marian exiles; the Bishops'
Bible of 1568, issued as an official version during Elizabeth's reign;
and, finally, the King James Bible of 1611. Even the Rheims-Douay
Version (New Testament, 1582; Old Testament, 1609-1610), translated by Roman Catholic exiles in France for use by the Catholic
clergy in confuting their opponents, relied to some extent on Tyndale's work. Together, these editions constituted educational instruments of unprecedented influence: by the seventeenth century, the
English had become, in the words of John Richard Green, "the
people of a book, and that book was the Bible."[12]

Preserved Smith once remarked in his biography of Erasmus that
the Renaissance and the Reformation were essentially one, that is,

[11] More, *Dialogue*, in *English Works of Thomas More*, II, 102; and William Tyndale,
An Answer to Sir Thomas More's Dialogue, edited for the Parker Society by
Henry Walter (Cambridge: Cambridge University Press, 1850), p. 9. For the Royal
Injunctions of 1538, see Walter Howard Frere and William McClure Kennedy, eds.,
Visitation Articles and Injunctions of the Period of the Reformation, Alcuin Club Col-
lections, vols. XIV-XVI (3 vols.; London: Longmans, Green & Co., 1910), II, 34-43. Sir
Maurice Powicke, *The Reformation in England* (London: Oxford University Press,
1941), p. 1.
[12] John Richard Green, *A Short History of the English People* (rev. ed.; London:
Macmillan and Co., 1902), p. 460.

two branches of the same movement, and that the sharp encounters over the years between the champions of each had tended to conceal their fundamental similarities. Smith's argument is especially apt for England, where it was the Reformation that gave the Renaissance its peculiar and distinctive character; and it is especially relevant to the work of Erasmus and Tyndale, who complemented each other so uniquely. Both men looked to classical sources as the basis for a revitalization of the civic and intellectual life of their times; both were deeply involved in education, Erasmus substituting the illumination of textual criticism for the obfuscation of Scholastic logic, Tyndale substituting study of the Bible for the authority of the church; and both anticipated much of modernity in the new ideals they proffered and the new freedoms they claimed. Each in his own way asserted a confidence in human reason that was inevitably subversive of the values and styles of medieval Christendom. The militant knight of Erasmus' *Enchiridion,* who was really Everyman, could not but profit from the availability of Tyndale's English Scripture; and the thoughtful reader of the vernacular Bible, also Everyman, could not but profit from the simple prescriptions and caveats of the *Enchiridion.* Both the Renaissance and the Reformation cast Everyman, for the first time in history, in the role of student; and the printing press made that role for the first time feasible. It should be no surprise that some of the sharpest conflicts of the age concerned who would teach Everyman and what and how he would be taught.[13]

II

The *Enchiridion* was read by the American colonists during the seventeenth century, though, like many academics before and since, Erasmus was destined to be known largely through his textbooks— the *Colloquies* (1518), the *Adages* (1500), and the *Paraphrases* (1518-

[13] Preserved Smith, *Erasmus: A Study of His Life, Ideals and Place in History* (New York: Harper & Brothers, 1923), pp. 1-3, 320-324. In arguing his case for the unity of the Renaissance and the Reformation, Smith maintains that "the only important contrast between Renaissance and Reformation is that the first was an aristocratic, the second a popular, movement. The humanist sought to educate the classes; the Reformer to convert the masses" (p. 324). Yet even this distinction fails to stand up fully, as one reads the Erasmus of the *Enchiridion,* the *Paraclesis,* and the letter to Paul Volz dated August 14, 1518 (*Christian Humanism,* pp. 110-112). For the historiographical context, see Wallace K. Ferguson, *The Renaissance in Historical Thought* (Boston: Houghton Mifflin Company, 1948), chap. ix, and Roland H. Bainton, "Interpretations of the Reformation," *The American Historical Review,* LXVI (1960-61), 74-84. For the argument of continuity between Renaissance and Reformation, as it bears on English education, see Fritz Caspari, *Humanism and the Social Order in Tudor England* (Chicago: University of Chicago Press, 1954).

1524). Tyndale, too, was a familiar figure on the colonial scene, though he was encountered far more through the chronicle of his life in Foxe's *Book of Martyrs* than directly through his own writings. Above all, however, the colonists were acquainted with the Bible itself, principally in the Geneva Version but increasingly in the King James Version. The Bible was read and recited, quoted and consulted, early committed to memory and constantly searched for meaning. Deemed universally relevant, it remained throughout the century the single most important cultural influence in the lives of Anglo-Americans. "The Bible, I say, the Bible only, is the religion of Protestants!" the English theologian William Chillingworth proclaimed in 1638; and, while the clergy on both sides of the Atlantic would argue endlessly over details, Chillingworth's assertion did capture the spirit of mid-seventeenth-century Anglo-American Christianity.[14]

Though the Bible had been richly valued for generations, it was not until the seventeenth century that it was widely read and studied. The message of Protestantism was that men could find in Scripture the means to salvation, the keys to good and evil, the rules by which to live, and the standards against which to measure the conduct of prince and pastor. And so men turned to the Bible with reverence and restless curiosity, finding there, not an abstruse exposition of high-flown principles, but an imaginative portrayal of the life of a historic people, contending in their families and communities with day-to-day problems of belief and conduct, freedom and authority, virtue and depravity. Moreover, it was a gripping portrayal, sketched in a highly colorful and powerfully dramatic vernacular; and it depicted a chosen people, acutely conscious of having been selected by God for a special purpose and destiny.

Yet the very attractiveness of Scripture brought with it certain problems: the Bible taught in various modes, not only through the explicit commandments of God to his people, but also through metaphors, allegories, and exemplars; and different men drew different lessons from the text. Hence, there grew up a rich body of oral preaching and devotional literature, both purporting to explicate the true meaning of the word. It has been estimated that over 40 per cent of the books printed in England between 1480 and 1640 were religious in theme, as were some 50 per cent of those printed

[14] William Chillingworth, *The Religion of Protestants, A Safe Way to Salvation*, in *The Works of W. Chillingworth* (12th ed.; London: printed for B. Blake, 1836), p. 465.

by the American press between 1639 and 1689. Bibles, service books, and systematic theological treatises accounted for a good part of this reading matter; but the bulk of it consisted of miscellaneous works of edification, that is, anthologies of prayer, popular sermons, manuals of conduct, exemplary biographies, guides to living and dying —in short, didactic material seeking to specify the nature and character of piety. There were versions for masters and for servants, for nobles and for ploughmen, for each of the four seasons, and for each of the principal callings. No phase of Christian living was without its vade mecum setting forth appropriate thoughts and behavior for every occasion.[15]

"Theology," Helen White observed in her classic analysis of English devotional prose of the early seventeenth century, "lays the ground for and raises the temple of religion, but devotion takes the hand of the believer and leads him into the presence of the God he has been seeking." In an age of theological contentiousness, devotional books tended to avoid doctrinal extremes, concentrating instead on those general values and habits of life that Christians seemed traditionally to share. And hence their delineations of Christian character and the ways of nurturing it managed to achieve broad circulation among men of all persuasions, instructing vast segments of the population in a common heritage of belief and conduct.[16]

In the colonies, devotional works were everywhere read and valued; indeed, except for the Bible and the leading pamphlets and almanacs of the eighteenth century, they and a small number of school texts constituted the best-known general literature in English America. True, the colonists, and especially their ministers, were thoroughly familiar with a wide range of theological writings, from the learned sermons of the most renowned ministers to the more systematic treatises of Calvin, Luther, and Knox. But, for all their usefulness in defining doctrine, these writings were frequently abstruse and almost always technical. By contrast, the devotional literature was insistently popular, addressing itself in a fascinating variety of modes to the day-by-day problems of ordinary men and women.

15 Edith L. Klotz, "A Subject Analysis of English Imprints for Every Tenth Year from 1480 to 1640," *The Huntington Library Quarterly*, I (1937-38), 417-419. The statement regarding colonial imprints is based on analysis of entries in Charles Evans, *American Bibliography* (12 vols. with a 13th edited by Clifford K. Shipton; imprint varies, 1903-1955), vol. I.

16 Helen C. White, *English Devotional Literature [Prose], 1600-1640*, University of Wisconsin Studies in Language and Literature (Madison: University of Wisconsin, 1931), p. 12.

Five such works in particular bear discussion, owing to their immense popularity and influence among colonists of all stations and in every region: John Foxe's *Actes and Monuments* (1563), commonly referred to as the *Book of Martyrs;* Lewis Bayly's *The Practise of Pietie* (c. 1612); Richard Allestree's *The Whole Duty of Man* (1658); Richard Baxter's *The Poor Man's Family Book* (1674); and John Bunyan's *The Pilgrim's Progress* (1678, 1684). Together, these five works went far in defining the Anglo-American *paideia* of the seventeenth century. They were, so to speak, the first statements of educational philosophy in the colonies; and, despite their English origins, they remain the best guides extant to the conventional wisdom about education that prevailed in early America.

John Foxe once remarked that the Lord began the true reformation of his church not with the sword but with the printing press. Certainly, in compiling and publishing his *Actes and Monuments of These Latter and Perillous Dayes, Touching Matters of the Church,* Foxe must have seen himself as an agent of the Lord. Possessed by a vision of human history as an unceasing struggle between the two churches within every church—the true church of grace and election and the material church of nature and reprobation—Foxe dedicated himself to teaching his contemporaries an apocalyptic view of their times, with the English martyrs from Wycliffe to Cranmer as the principal players in the drama.[17]

Beginning the work as an exile "in the far parts of Germany, where few friends, no conference, small information could be had," Foxe in 1554 published in a small Latin octavo of 212 leaves a number of accounts of certain late fourteenth- and fifteenth-century victims of persecution. Five years later, in a Latin folio of over 700 pages, he added the stories of those who had suffered under Henry VIII, Edward VI, and Mary. And then, in 1563, there appeared the great tome, a huge English folio running nearly 1,800 pages and dedicated to Elizabeth I, which included a historical account of the early church and many more reports of the Marian martyrs. A second edition of the *Actes and Monuments,* published, appropriately, in 1570, the year the pope excommunicated Elizabeth, was enlarged by an expanded treatment of ecclesiastical and national history and the addition of still more martyrology. Thereafter, editions issued fairly regularly from the English presses until the appearance of the

---

[17] *Acts and Monuments of John Foxe,* III, 718-722.

ninth and last in 1684. By the end of the seventeenth century, some 10,000 copies had been circulated, probably more than of any other book of similar scope except the Bible.[18]

The first edition of the *Book of Martyrs* was graced by more than fifty woodcuts, many of them representing vivid scenes of torment and torture, and an illuminated title page that did much to convey the general character of the work. At the top of the title page sits the Lord in final judgment, the world at his feet. To his right, kneeling, are sober Protestant patriarchs trumpeting triumphantly in celebration of his majesty; to his left are the tonsured Catholic monks, blowing their trumpets but being dragged downward by Satan into the fires. And below there are the two churches: on the right the church of Christ, in which the faithful hear preaching with Bibles in hand and for which some must suffer martyrdom at the stake on the way to heaven, and on the left the church of Antichrist, in which the faithful hear preaching with rosaries in hand and are turned by the Mass from God to the Devil.

As with the title page, so with the long and loosely constructed text: it is from beginning to end a history of the struggle between light and darkness, with contemporary England as the decisive arena. There is a prosaic review of the early Christian Era, modeled largely on Eusebius' outline of the *Historia ecclesiastica;* there is a detailed chronicle of Yorkist and Tudor political and ecclesiastical history, with emphasis on the triumph of Protestantism; there are intricate reports of theological disputations and inquisitions, with liberal quotations from bulls, decrees, sermons, and letters; and there are the lives of the Protestant heroes—John Wycliffe, William Tyndale, Thomas Bilney, Hugh Latimer, Nicholas Ridley, and Thomas Cranmer; Henry VIII, Edward VI, and especially the "noble and worthy" Elizabeth. It is in these lives, of course, particularly the lives of those who suffered martyrdom, that Foxe's drama becomes most vivid: the martyr's godly efforts to propagate the word; his challenge by the persecutors representing Rome; his disputations with his adversaries during the inevitable trial; and his final agonizing victory at the stake.

The message of all this could not have been lost, even on the least tutored among the faithful. In the first place, Foxe presented a vision of England as the elect nation, singled out to express God's

[18] *Ibid.*, p. 384.

design in the world. In effect, he had transformed the Biblical idea of a chosen people in covenant with God into a nascent modern nationalism, which bound Englishmen together much as the ancient Hebrews had been united. And this vision of English mission must have provided a unique sense of common identity and destiny to colonists in a wilderness across the Atlantic. Second, and equally important, Foxe offered a heroic view of piety, as bearing steadfast witness under extraordinary adversity to the truth of the Protestant faith. It was a view that joined Protestants in their common opposition to Roman Catholicism and, hence, one that could be accepted by Puritan as well as Anglican, by Royalist as well as Parliamentarian. And it was a view that both formed and reinforced the colonists' sense that their enterprise was in the last analysis a fulfillment of England's own special purpose. Finally, Foxe set forth a bold conception of education, at the heart of which stood the martyrs as Christ's intrepid teachers, entrusted with the responsibility for carrying the word to all nations, whatever the hazards or the cost. It doubtless inspired many an American pastor as he ministered to his flock, ever fearful of the lapse into barbarism and ever conscious of his mission as a teacher of the true church of grace and election.

The three most popular handbooks of piety in the colonies—*The Practise of Pietie, The Whole Duty of Man,* and *The Poor Man's Family Book*—were written at different times by quite different sorts of men; yet they were remarkably similar in content and character. Lewis Bayly, a preacher of moderate Puritan propensities, wrote *The Practise of Pietie* while serving as domestic chaplain to King James's son Henry. Henry died in 1612, and Bayly's Puritanism subsequently brought him into disfavor at court, though not seriously enough to prevent his becoming chaplain to the king himself and, eventually, bishop of Bangor, which office he held until his death in 1631. Richard Allestree, who was born a half-century after Bayly, was a scholar of royalist sympathies, who suffered grievously during the interregnum for refusing to submit to the authority of Parliament but who was appointed after the Restoration, first, canon of Christ Church, Oxford, then, Regius Professor of Divinity at the university, and finally, provost of Eton College. In addition to *The Whole Duty of Man,* which he probably began while in the service of Sir Anthony Cope, a royalist gentleman of fortune, Allestree wrote *The Gentleman's Calling* (1660), *The Causes of the Decay of*

Christian Piety (1667), and *The Ladies Calling* (1673), all of which were published anonymously. Richard Baxter, a contemporary of Allestree and one of the best-known English Nonconformists of his day, served first as pastor of Kidderminster, in Worcestershire, then for a time as a chaplain in Cromwell's army, and later, following enactment of the harsh Clarendon Code, with which the Restoration Parliament attempted to suppress dissent, as an itinerant teacher, often hounded by local magistrates and on one occasion actually imprisoned. Baxter wrote voluminously, *The Poor Man's Family Book* being merely one among scores of works. Indeed, that book is best seen as a brief, popularized version of the *Christian Directory* (1673), a monumental *summa* in which Baxter systematically examined Christian ethics (private duties), Christian economics (family duties), Christian ecclesiastics (church duties), and Christian politics (duties to rulers and neighbors), in all their complexity and endless theological ramifications.

A disputatious preacher in the court of James I, a royalist scholar in the entourage of Charles II, and a harried nonconforming lecturer, who complained at the end of his days that he had amounted to little more than a human pen—these three men instructed the colonists in the nature and nurture of piety, teaching them what to believe and how to behave. And they did so in remarkably similar ways, reflecting not only their common roots in a single source—the Bible —but also their common adherence to the method of casuistry and their common employment of the sermonic style made popular by the English Puritan preachers.

Casuistry, or case divinity, was that branch of Christian ethics which dealt with the application of general religious and moral principles to particular human situations. In the scheme of William Perkins, one of the most revered and influential of the early Puritan divines, cases of conscience fell into three categories: questions that "concern man as he is considered apart by himself, without respect unto another"; those that "concern man, as he stands in the first relation, namely to God"; and those that concern him "as he stands in the second relation, to man." The last category included all those cases incident to the life of man as a "member of some society, whether it be a family, the church, or the commonwealth." During the seventeenth century, this triad of self, God, and fellow man became a commonplace, and scholars of every creed found it a useful framework within which to organize their preachments. What Bayly,

Allestree, and Baxter did was to popularize casuistry, defining piety not as something heroic or esoteric but simply as consistently Christian belief and behavior in the day-to-day business of living. As for the sermonic style of the Puritans, it was, as contrasted with the pulpit oratory in vogue among orthodox Anglicans, scrupulously plain. To the Puritan preacher seeking to make his meaning clear to even the most ignorant, simplicity of discourse was paramount. Plainness became the dominant feature of what William Haller aptly dubbed the "democratic rhetoric of the spirit," a rhetoric that was to characterize the devotional literature quite as much as it did the considerable body of Puritan preaching.[19]

Characteristically, Bayly writes in the dedication of his manual that he has endeavored to extract, from the "chaos of endless controversies, the old practice of true piety, which flourished before these controversies were hatched." And that practice of piety consists of (1) knowing the essence of God, (2) knowing one's own self, (3) glorifying God by dedicating one's life to his service, and (4) glorifying God by dying in and for the Lord. The treatise begins with a popular and somewhat attenuated exposition of Calvinist theology, including sections on the nature of God, on the misery and corruption of man without God, on the blessed state of a Christian reconciled to God, and on the character of everlasting life. The language is simple, the rhetoric colorful, the message powerful. From belief, Bayly proceeds to conduct, prescribing in great detail on a vast range of matters—from how to read the Bible to how to perform good works, from how to behave in church to how to govern a family. The advice is practical, concrete, specific, and forthright; and it is interspersed throughout with appropriate prayers, meditations, and citations to Scripture. The goal is always the maintenance of personal, doctrinal, and social stability; and, for a colonial society that saw itself teetering on the brink of barbarism, nothing could have been more apt. Little wonder that many looked upon *The Practise of Pietie* as having an authority equal to that of the Bible itself![20]

The Whole Duty of Man is much like Bayly's handbook, though less Calvinist in tone and orientation. Allestree divides his work into seventeen chapters, directing that one be read each Sunday and the

19 W. Perkins, *The Whole Treatise of the Cases of Conscience* (1608; reprint ed.; London: John Legatt, 1614), p. 275; and William Haller, *The Rise of Puritanism* (New York: Columbia University Press, 1938), p. 130.

20 Lewis Bayly, *The Practise of Pietie* (11th ed.; London: John Hodgetts, 1619), "The Epistle Dedicatorie" and p. 2.

whole traversed three times a year; and it is patent, of course, that like others of its genre the book was meant to be read aloud. Following Perkins, Allestree deals first with man's duty to God, then with man's duty to himself, and finally with man's duty to his neighbor. Under the last, he discusses duties to magistrates, pastors, parents, children, brethren, husbands, wives, friends, and servants. At the end, Allestree adds a series of private devotions, including prayers, excerpts from the Book of Psalms, and a checklist for the reader's use in assessing any "breaches of our duty." As in *The Practise of Pietie,* Allestree's directions are specific and homely, his style simple and epigrammatic. And the emphasis throughout is on order, on the network of mutual obligations and responsibilities that holds a Christian society together. It was an emphasis that must have appealed to Englishmen, who by the 1660's and 1670's would have preferred almost any form of stable Protestant piety to the chaotic dissension of the sects. And, once again, in the New World it inevitably attracted those who saw in that same sort of piety the ultimate defense against barbarism.[21]

The Poor Man's Family Book, a popular compendium of divinity and religion, also follows the Perkins paradigm, teaching men how to become true Christians, how to live as Christians in relation to God, themselves, and others, and how to die as Christians in hope and comfort. The treatise is presented in the form of nine dialogues between Paul, a teacher, and Saul, a learner, along with a lengthy appendix of catechisms, prayers, and hymns. Much the same ground is traversed as in the Bayly and Allestree manuals, though Baxter's theological teachings are by far the most extensive, taking up five of the nine dialogues. Baxter himself justifies the extended doctrinal exegesis, arguing that without a proper understanding and acceptance of Christianity any effort to practice Christian living is destined to failure; but the emphasis on doctrine doubtless cost him readers, his treatise never achieving the popularity in the New World of Bayly's or Allestree's. Nevertheless, *The Poor Man's Family Book* did circulate widely, providing for many a fairly systematic introduction to Christian thought and practice, which went beyond the terse precepts of the catechisms without becoming either abstruse or arcane.[22]

---

[21] [Richard Allestree], *The Whole Duty of Man* (reprint ed.; London: R. Norton, 1676), p. 412.

[22] Richard Baxter, *The Poor Man's Family Book,* in *The Practical Works of the Rev. Richard Baxter* (23 vols.; London: James Duncan, 1850), XIX, 295-297. Baxter also argued, interestingly enough, that a concise style is ineffective in teaching the vulgar to become Christians.

Finally, there was *The Pilgrim's Progress*, which enjoyed a voluminous and continuous readership in the colonies, almost from the time of its publication. The story of Bunyan's authorship is well known. Born in 1628, the son of a Bedfordshire tinker, he spent his youth "without God in the world," tormented by spiritual crises and dreadful visions. He was mustered in a Parliamentary levy during the Civil War, and, though his military life proved uneventful, the aggressive Puritanism of the New Model Army doubtless impressed him profoundly. Following his discharge in the summer of 1647, Bunyan returned to Bedfordshire and tinkering, subsequently marrying a poor woman of fervent piety, who introduced him to two books that helped change his life: Arthur Dent's *The Plaine Mans Path-Way to Heaven* (1601), the devotional dialogue that served as a model for Baxter's *The Poor Man's Family Book,* and Bayly's *The Practise of Pietie.* Under the influence of these and of his wife, Bunyan made an increasingly intense profession of faith, in due course undergoing the classic Puritan conversion. He resolved to live according to the Commandments (what the Puritans called a legal life), entering actively into the affairs of the nascent Bedford congregation, a group of moderate Baptists led by John Gifford, and eventually becoming a lay preacher. Shortly after the Restoration, Bunyan was arrested and charged by the local magistrate with illegal preaching, and spent most of the next twelve years in prison. He probably began *The Pilgrim's Progress* toward the end of his incarceration, publishing the first part in 1678 and a second part, clarifying and reinforcing the message, in 1684.[23]

In effect, Christian s pilgrimage from the City of Destruction to the Celestial City represents a popularization of the martyrdom portrayed by Foxe. The story is woven of common experience by a man of remarkably fertile imagination, who had himself undertaken the pilgrimage, who knew at first hand the Slough of Despond, Doubting Castle, and Vanity Fair, and who was intimately acquainted with the arguments of Faithful, Hopeful, and Mr. Worldly Wiseman. The single, uncomplicated plot, the cast of familiar characters, the popular idiom enlivened by apt metaphors, the homely issues resolved by unequivocal counsel—all combined to make the work consummately engaging to the new, unsophisticated reading public that was slowly coming into being. Bunyan himself insisted

[23] It is interesting to note that Samuel Green produced an American edition of the first part in 1681, just three years after its original publication in England.

in his introductory apology that the book contained "nothing but sound and honest Gospel-strains," and that, of course, was precisely its genius. What the scholarly sermon was to the educated, the tinker's allegory would be to the newly literate. It taught not only that Everyman could live his life as witness to God's teaching but also that the essence of such a life is self-education and self-justification. "This book will make a traveler of thee," Bunyan promised, "If by its counsel thou wilt ruled be":

> It will direct thee to the Holy Land,
> If thou wilt its directions understand:
> Yea, it will make the slothful, active be;
> The blind also, delightful things to see.[24]

III

The devotional books portrayed man as he is and as he might be. In so doing, they did double pedagogical duty, delineating the ideal character to be achieved through education and suggesting the kind of education required for that achievement. The message in all these works was abundantly clear: the ultimate goal of education is the practice of true piety, and that practice proceeds through a succession of steps, viz., conviction of sin, calling to grace, evidence of saving faith, growth of holiness in life, and, finally, glorification. The pilgrimage is inevitably a lonely one, but there is assistance to be gained from responsible families, godly churches, and pious schools.

Thus, for example, Foxe states at the outset that he intends to establish beyond a doubt the continuity between Christ and the Church of England, thereby certifying the accuracy and authority of that church's teaching. Bayly advises those who have been called to the governance of families to rear them in the service and fear of the Lord. And, since the glorification of God is a matter not merely of private devotion but also of public worship, families must attend church services and pay close heed to the minister's sermons, noting the doctrines explained, the sins reproved, and the virtues extolled. Allestree's strictures regarding the parental responsibility to educate

---

[24] John Bunyan, "Grace Abounding to the Chief of Sinners" and "The Pilgrim's Progress," edited by Roger Sharrock (London: Oxford University Press, 1966), pp. 144-145.

children are quite specific: "As soon therefore as children come to the use of reason, they are to be instructed, and that first in those things which concern their eternal well-being, they are by little and little to be taught all those things which God hath commanded them as their duty to perform; as also what glorious rewards he hath provided for them, if they do it, and what grievous and eternal punishment, if they do it not." Baxter, whose pedagogical instructions are especially detailed, points explicitly to the complementary duties of family, school, and church in the education of children: "Parents, schoolmasters, and pastors, have all their several parts to do," he admonishes, "and no one's work goeth on well without the rest." And Bunyan's allegory is, of course, replete with educational suggestions, as witness the crucial role of Evangelist in the first part and of Mr. Greatheart in the second or, indeed, the tenderness with which Dame Mercy catechizes Christiana's children to determine whether they have been properly instructed in the faith.[25]

In addition to the discussions of education in the general devotional works, there were numerous treatises that dealt more systematically with the particular duties of parents, ministers, and schoolmasters. While many of these were Puritan in origin, they were owned and read by Protestants of all persuasions on both sides of the Atlantic. Of those works treating the parental responsibility, the two most widely known in the colonies were *A Godly Forme of Houshold Government*, written in 1598 by Robert Cleaver, a Nonconformist Oxfordshire preacher, and later revised by John Dod, a patriarch of English Puritanism widely revered in New England, and *Of Domesticall Duties* (1622), by William Gouge, the Puritan rector of St. Anne's, Blackfriars. Patriarchalism dominates both treatises: they portray the family as a microcosm of state, church, and school, righteously ruled by a father who serves alternately as prince, pastor, and teacher. And both define a network of mutual responsibilities and obligations that pertain within the family, viewing education as a primary duty parents owe their children and, by extension, their wards, servants, and apprentices.

Dod and Cleaver outline a fourfold duty of parents to their children: to instruct them "in the fear and nurture of the Lord"; to "bring them up in shamefastness, hatred of vice, and love of all

---

25 [Allestree], *Whole Duty of Man*, p. 284; and Baxter, *Poor Man's Family Book*, p. 488.

virtue"; to serve as "examples of all godliness and virtue"; and to "keep them from idleness, the mother of all mischiefs, and bring them up either in learning, or in some good art or occupation." In the explication of this fourfold duty, which constitutes fully a quarter of the manual, there is constant citation of Scripture, the assumption being, of course, that no argument could carry weight without definite Scriptural support. Parents are admonished to instruct their children in the principles of religion, good manners, and civil behavior; to inculcate in them reverence for their elders and superiors; to bring them up in some lawful and gainful calling; to teach them to read and write for both worldly and spiritual ends; to keep them from vice; to chastise and correct them when necessary; to avoid pampering them with too much food, clothing, and affection; and to prepare them to attend church and school with profit. Not unexpectedly, the discussion of the duties of children exhorts them, in turn, not only to obey, serve, fear, love, honor, and revere their parents, but also to follow their good precepts and examples of life and to take correction patiently at their hands.[26]

Gouge's treatise is more formal, but quite similar in scope and character. It postulates three principal duties of parents: to nourish their children, with food and apparel; to nurture them, with discipline; and to instruct them in the ways of God. Like Dod and Cleaver, Gouge draws heavily on Scripture in explicating these duties; and his discourse is relentlessly detailed, though the commonplace allusions to husbandry that mark the Dod and Cleaver manual are not nearly so numerous. The educational counsel is also much the same, with three notable exceptions: first, Gouge devotes far more attention to parental responsibility for the child's health, discoursing at length on proper diet, suitable clothing, and fitting recreation; second, Gouge assigns parents far greater responsibility for training their children in some appropriate calling, advising, interestingly enough, that in choosing a vocation "a child's best ability wherein especially it consisteth, whether in the exercise of mind or of body, is duly to be observed: and also his inclination, to what calling he is most disposed"; and, third, Gouge gives considerably more attention to schoolmasters and tutors, viewing them as surrogate parents charged with instructing children in learning, civility and

[26] John Dod and Robert Clever [sic], *A Godly Forme of Houshold Government* (London: R. Field, 1612), sig. Q.

good manners, and true piety and religion. Like Dod and Cleaver, Gouge also treats the duties of children, exhorting them to obey their parents cheerfully and reverently in all things, to obtain their consent in matters of marriage and calling, and to heed their instructions and emulate their good examples.[27]

Of special significance among the works on familial education, not because of the circulation it achieved, but because it was the first native treatise on child-rearing to issue from the colonies, was Thomas Cobbett's *A Fruitfull and Usefull Discourse Touching the Honour Due from Children to Parents, and the Duty of Parents Towards Their Children* (1656). Cobbett had immigrated to Massachusetts in 1637, with the party led by John Davenport, and was serving as minister of the congregation at Lynn during the winter of 1654-55, when he composed the book. It is, like the manuals of Gouge and of Dod and Cleaver, essentially an application of the Fifth Commandment, albeit somewhat more learned and less popular—probably testimony to the sophistication of the Lynn congregation. Characteristically for the genre, the references to Scripture abound, though they are often supplemented by allusions to the works of the "heathen" ancients. And the advice on education is extensive and detailed: parents are called upon to "observe and pry into the genius . . . and bent and capacity of their children," that they may teach them more effectively; to catechize them often in the principles of religion and to set them "upon actual exercise, and practice" thereof; to teach them to read the Scriptures; to train them up in "some honest, and laudable callings and employments"; to place them under the care of godly ministers; and in every way to serve as fine examples of piety and civility. Children, in turn, are urged to honor their parents through "imitation of what is good in them, and following their gracious counsels." Interestingly, for all of Cobbett's lengthy preachments on the "good and godly education" of children, schools are never mentioned. Since Puritan ministers were not given to forgetfulness, the omission might well have reflected Cobbett's

27 William Gouge, *Of Domesticall Duties* (London: John Haviland, 1622), p. 534. For the classic exposition of the Puritan concept of calling, see William Perkins, *A Treatise of the Vocations* (1603), in *The Works of That Famous and Worthy Minister of Christ in the Universitie of Cambridge, Mr. William Perkins* (rev. ed.; 3 vols.; London: publisher varies, 1612-1613), I, 747-779. Gouge, of course, is speaking of what Perkins would refer to as "specific calling," as opposed to the "general calling" common to all Christians, namely, the calling to Christ.

priorities; on the other hand, it might simply have indicated that Lynn had not yet established a school in 1654.[28]

The colonists also read numerous treatises on ministerial responsibility for the nurture of piety, none more important than *The Arte of Prophecying* (1592) by William Perkins. A fellow of Christ's College, Cambridge, from 1584 to 1594, Perkins was a leading spokesman for the Puritan faction in the university, a teacher and preacher of unrivaled popularity, and an unrelenting enemy of all forms of "Romish" ceremonialism in matters religious. His writings, which ranged from learned disquisitions on predestination to elementary catechisms and conduct books, commanded throughout the seventeenth century a large and heterogeneous audience in England and on the Continent; and in the New World they were studied with that special care and intensity that has always been reserved for the truly inspired and profound.

The Arte of Prophecying, often described as the first modern work on homiletics, is a manual on preaching by one of the most revered of the "godly preachers," as the Puritan clergy were fond of calling themselves. For them, preaching was not simply one more clerical function; it was the essential clerical function. Indeed, by insisting that they were preachers before they were anything else, and preachers with a particular emphasis and style, the Puritans were advancing arguments about the nature of the church, the clergy, and religion which set them apart from both traditional Roman Catholicism and alternative varieties of contemporary Protestantism. The arguments were suggested in the illustrations framing the title page of Foxe's *Book of Martyrs:* preaching rather than ceremonial, they insisted, was the true pedagogy of Christ's church and, ultimately, the only guide to salvation.

Like many of the other great treatises on method, *The Arte of Prophecying* is itself intended to exemplify its prescriptions: it is tightly organized, heavily supported by Scriptural authority, and severely simple in style. Perkins distinguishes two duties of the minister: preaching of the word and prayer unto God; the vehicle for preaching is the sermon, which must be diligently and system-

---

[28] Thomas Cobbet [*sic*], *A Fruitfull and Usefull Discourse Touching the Honour Due from Children to Parents, and the Duty of Parents Towards Their Children* (London: S. G., 1656), pp. 213-243. It is difficult to determine whether or not there was a school at this time, since there are no extant records of the town of Lynn for the period before 1691.

atically prepared and plainly and graciously delivered. Perkins' method of sermon preparation or construction entails reading a passage from Scripture, interpreting it according to true rhetorical principle (in this case, Ramist rather than Aristotelian), gathering from the text several useful points of doctrine, and applying the doctrine "to the life and manners of men." Proper delivery consists in the concealment of "humane wisdom"—the sermon must be free of scholarly ostentation—and the demonstration, in speech or gesture, of divine inspiration.[29]

In all of this, the preacher must bear in mind that most congregations bring together men and women of diverse backgrounds and conditions: some are ignorant and unteachable and must be prepared to receive the word; some are ignorant but teachable and can be catechized; some have knowledge but are unhumbled and have to be stirred to a sense of sin; some are humbled and should be proffered the law and the gospel; some truly believe and also require a particular combination of law and gospel; and some have fallen into error and need to be corrected. The several classes of men, then, require different modes of instruction and receive any given preachment in different ways.[30]

Perkins' method was obviously influential on another handbook of homiletics well known to the colonial clergy, Richard Bernard's *The Faithfull Shepheard* (1607). Bernard had been a student at Christ's College in Perkins' day and had gone on to the vicarage of Worksop, in Nottinghamshire, in 1601. There, he had composed *The Faithfull Shepheard* amidst a series of ideological conflicts with the Separatists. The treatise itself is essentially an elaboration of Perkins', giving somewhat more attention to the personal attributes of the minister (he must be mature, watchful, temperate, modest, hospitable, gentle, righteous, holy, continent, with blameless character, commitment to truth, and considerable aptness to teach), the knowledge required for the proper performance of his duties (grammar, ancient languages, rhetoric, and divinity), and the books he needs to further his studies (works in the liberal arts and sciences, the Bible,

29 William Perkins, *The Arte of Prophecying*, in *Works of William Perkins*, II, 673.
30 As Perry Miller has remarked of their piety, the pedagogy of the godly preachers was essentially Augustinian and assumed, like the *De magistro*, that while the words of the teacher may motivate the learner to search for the interior truth God has planted in his soul, these words must not be confused with the truth itself; ultimately, only God teaches.

dictionaries, concordances and Scriptural commentaries, catechisms, commonplace books, ecclesiastical histories).[31]

Another treatise on ministerial duties which enjoyed considerable vogue in the colonies during the latter half of the seventeenth century was Richard Baxter's *Gildas Salvianus; The Reformed Pastor* (1656). As with all his work, the manual contains abundant evidence of Puritan influence, and, indeed, Baxter may well have been familiar with the homiletic prescriptions of Perkins and Bernard. There has also been speculation concerning Baxter's acquaintance with George Herbert's exceedingly popular *A Priest to the Temple, or, The Country Parson* (1652), which, though Anglican in outlook, bears striking similarities to Baxter's volume. The ultimate source of the treatise, however, was undoubtedly his own experience in the pastorate at Kidderminster. Thus, in addition to the standard instruction on the substance and methods of public preaching, Baxter gives extensive attention to the day-by-day round of pastoral responsibilities: getting to know the members of the congregation, seeing that families are well ordered, instructing the ignorant, advising the perplexed, encouraging the obedient, comforting the sick, admonishing the errant, and receiving the repentant. The ministry Baxter portrays is first and foremost a teaching ministry, but it is also the intensely personal ministry of a pastor with his own doubts and his own profound sense of personal limitation. At least one New Englander, Jonathan Mitchell, explicitly modeled his career after *Gildas Salvianus*. As Cotton Mather later wrote of him: "Herein he visited at fit hours, which he set apart for it, the several families of his flock; not upon trivial designs, but with serious and solemn addresses to their souls upon matter of their everlasting peace; and the *Gildas Salvianus* of Mr. Baxter was herein our Mitchell himself, as well as much read and prized by this faithful pastor, who 'watched for souls, as one that was to give an account.' "[32]

With respect to the schoolmaster's responsibility for nurturing

[31] Richard Bernard, *The Faithfull Shepheard: or, The Shepheards Faithfulnesse* (London: Arnold Hatfield, 1607).

[32] The manual is included in *Practical Works of Richard Baxter*, vol. XIV. One wonders whether the Anglican clergy in the colonies valued Herbert's treatise as much as their brethren in England. The likelihood is that they did, but I have been unable to locate specific evidence of this. Herbert's poetry appeared in a number of colonial libraries, but, as far as we know, *The Country Parson* did not. Cotton Mather, *Magnalia Christi Americana; or, The Ecclesiastical History of New-England* (1702), edited by Thomas Robbins (2 vols.; Hartford: Silas Andrus and Son, 1853-1855), II, 94.

piety, the colonists were steeped in commonplace yea-saying, though they were probably familiar with John Brinsley's *A Consolation for Our Grammar Schooles* (1622), which was especially relevant since it was prepared with the colonies in mind. Brinsley was a Leicestershire preacher and schoolmaster of intense Puritan convictions, once described by a student as "very severe in his life and conversation." He was removed from his posts in 1619 or 1620 for Nonconformity, and thereafter earned his living in London by lecturing, writing, and probably tutoring. The particular circumstances under which *A Consolation for Our Grammar Schooles* came into being are not known; that the Virginia Company was interested in the treatise is clear, but there is no indication as to whether the Company had, in fact, commissioned it. Brinsley himself tended to view the book as a revised version of an earlier work entitled *Ludus Literarius: or, The Grammar Schoole* (1612), though it is actually quite different in character, being much broader in scope and far less detailed in its prescriptions. Yet the very fact that it deals with policy renders its arguments more significant; and, in the matter of the schoolmaster's responsibility for nurturing public piety, its preachments are unequivocal: the two critical duties of the schoolmaster are to promote piety directly by teaching the young to read Scripture, and to promote piety indirectly by educating a select group of ministers, who will in turn instruct a literate laity in the true meaning of the word. The Jesuits in the colonies beyond the seas, Brinsley cautions, have systematically organized their schools "to destroy all the churches of Christ, to extinguish utterly all true learning, to bring in again all their old learning, as (they call it) their palpable delusions, and abominable idolatry." The English nation came close to being "consumed by their furnace," but God intervened and miraculously saved it. It is now up to the schools of the realm "to prepare the way to that glorious appearing, and kingdom, when we with all the children of the light shall shine eternally in the heavens." In the end, Brinsley's schoolmasters are assigned the same awesome responsibility as Foxe's godly preachers: to lead men to the true knowledge of Christ and, ultimately, to salvation.[33]

Interestingly, the propositions Brinsley put forward were reflected

33 *William Lilly's History of His Life and Times* (1715; reprint ed.; London: Reprinted for Charles Baldwyn, 1822), p. 18; and John Brinsley, *A Consolation for Our Grammar Schooles* (London: Richard Field, 1622), pp. 46-48. See also Brinsley's *Ludus Literarius: or, The Grammar Schoole* (London: printed for Thomas Man, 1612).

in works by the colonists themselves, notably in Charles Chauncy's 1655 commencement sermon as president of Harvard, one of the earliest documents to be printed in the colonies. Having immigrated to New England in 1638, Chauncy had been pastor first at Plymouth and later at Scituate, but his unorthodox views, particularly on baptism, had caused growing controversy and eventually rendered his position untenable. Thereupon, he had been offered the leadership of the infant college at Cambridge, and had accepted forthwith, remaining in office until his death in 1672. His 1655 sermon was a resounding defense of learning and a learned ministry, based on a traditional Puritan belief in the essential role of schools and universities in the proper advancement of religion. New England, Chauncy averred, had not only been blessed with agencies for the instruction of its children, it had also been graced with a college for bringing into being a new generation of ministers, pastors, and teachers. "For besides the Lord's former mercies, in sending in to us the old stock of faithful ministers, and thrusting out of his laborers into this vineyard . . . , I say besides those former mercies never to be forgotten, the Lord hath graciously superadded this, in raising up not only means for this end (viz.: schools of learning) but also from thence some of our sons and young men to be prophets and Nazarites." And out of this had come the possibility of continuing the Lord's work in the New World. More than deliverance from any outward enemies, Chauncy insisted, such means were truly the special blessing of God, given to his chosen people that they might walk in his way long after their original teachers had passed from the earth.[34]

[34] Charles Chauncy, *God's Mercy, Shewed to His People in Giving Them a Faithful Ministry and Schooles of Learning for the Continual Supplyes Thereof* (Cambridge, Mass.: Samuel Green, 1655), pp. 28, 6. It is interesting that Chauncy also took the opportunity in his sermon to reply systematically to those English Puritans, notably, William Dell, who rejected the inseparability of religion and learning and pressed for a sweeping reform of the education system that would place schools, colleges, and universities entirely in the hands of the civil government. For the English controversy, see David Johnston Maitland, "Three Puritan Attitudes Toward Learning" (unpublished doctoral thesis, Columbia University, 1959), and Judah Bierman, "Of Learning and Knowledge: An Analysis of the Discussion of Learning in Seventeenth-Century English Essays" (unpublished doctoral thesis, University of California, Los Angeles, 1951).

Chapter 2

THE NURTURE OF CIVILITY

A gentleman is a man of himself, without the addition of either
tailor, milliner, seamster or haberdasher. Actions of goodness he
holds his supreme happiness. . . . Amongst men he hates no less
to be uncivil, than in his fear toward God to be servile. Education
he holds a second nature; which (such innate seeds of goodness are
sown in him) ever improves him, seldom or never depraves him.
Learning he holds not only an additament, but ornament to
gentry. No complement gives more accomplishment.

RICHARD BRATHWAITE

Early in 1515, Erasmus was invited to join the court of Prince Charles
of Burgundy (later to become Emperor Charles V), who was then
sixteen years of age. The invitation came at a particularly propitious
moment in Erasmus' career: his work on the Greek and Latin Testament as well as on the new edition of Jerome was all but completed,
and the prospect of a change must have been attractive. Then, too,
it seemed to offer an opportunity to achieve the sorts of social and
political reform that he and Colet and More had talked endlessly
about, as they had dreamed the optimistic dream of a new Augustan
age. In any case, Erasmus accepted, and in connection with his appointment prepared a treatise entitled *The Education of a Christian
Prince (Institutio principis Christiani)*, which Johann Froben published the following year. It has received too little attention from
students of education, for, beyond its significance as the classic statement of Erasmian political ideas, it was pivotal in the transformation
of the medieval "prince's mirror" into the Renaissance civility book,

a primary vehicle for the systematic exposition of educational theory and practice.[1]

The *Christian Prince* is at once a discourse on politics in the just state and a manual for bringing that state into being. In it, Erasmus deals with a fascinating array of subjects—the arts of peace, the bases of taxation, the encouragement of industry, the enactment of laws, the negotiation of treaties, and the nature of executive, legislative, and judicial duties. His quest, characteristically, is for those reforms that will usher in a golden age of wise and humane government, based on the philosophy of Christ, the most perfect ruler of all time, and the wisdom of the ancients, especially Plato and the later Roman Stoics. And, because he is committed both to monarchy and to the principle that each element in a polity must be properly prepared to take its place in that polity, he sees no task more critical than the education of the future monarch: it is the instrument par excellence for bringing the just state into existence.

"When there is no opportunity to choose the prince," Erasmus points out, speaking of hereditary monarchies, "care should be exercised . . . in choosing the tutor to the future prince. That a prince be born of worthy character we must beseech the gods above; that a prince born of good parts may not go amiss, or that one of mediocre accomplishments may be bettered through education is mainly within our province." The burden of the *Christian Prince* is simply an elaboration of this stricture. Erasmus advises that the entire realm be canvassed for a tutor of fine character, high moral principles, purity of life, and affable manner. He must be one who looks not to personal gain but to the welfare of the state, for his responsibility is nothing less than to ensure that welfare by preparing the young prince to rule, or, in Erasmian terms, by educating him to virtue.[2]

In carrying out his task, the tutor must hew to a middle course between unreasonable severity and unseasoned indulgence: following the ancient dicta of Seneca, he must scold without railing, praise without flattering, control without breaking; and he must enter upon his duties while the mind and character of the prince are still tractable, using every pedagogical device to direct him toward wisdom,

[1] I am using the term "civility book" in at least two senses: the treatise on the formation of elite character (the "governor" or the "gentleman") and the treatise on statecraft, which examines the political role of education in forming the state. Often, a single work went in both directions, in the tradition of Plato's *Republic*.

[2] Desiderius Erasmus, *The Education of a Christian Prince*, translated by Lester K. Born (New York: Columbia University Press, 1936), pp. 140-141.

honor, and virtue. In the matter of formal learning, once the elements of language have been mastered, the prince should study Proverbs, Ecclesiasticus, The Wisdom of Solomon, and the Gospels; then, selected writings of Plutarch, Seneca, Aristotle, Cicero, and— the "most venerable source" of ancient wisdom—Plato; and, finally, the classical historians and the remainder of Scripture. The tutor must bear in mind throughout that literature is inevitably didactic and that it must therefore be presented critically and with discretion. "Whenever the prince picks up a book," Erasmus cautions, "he should do so not with the idea of gaining pleasure but of bettering himself by his reading."[3]

From the rearing of the prince, Erasmus turns to the matter of governance itself, maintaining that the primary goal of the just ruler should be not merely to preserve but to extend the prosperity of the state, and, once again, education comes to the fore, this time as a device for maintaining public docility and order. Properly instructed, the populace will follow the course of right by choice rather than by compulsion, and the need for many laws and punishments will be obviated. Hence, the prince must ensure that children learn the teachings of Christ and of good literature. Indeed, Erasmus really locates the principal hope of the state in education: since it creates the good man—"a sort of divine creature," Erasmus calls him, alluding appropriately to Plato—it is the single most important instrument for shaping the good society.[4]

The *Christian Prince* was written while Erasmus was at the peak of his intellectual influence, and it incorporated all his mature aspirations for a peaceful Christian world ruled by true religion and humane learning. He was proclaiming to the European nobility, in effect, that they would govern well if they governed justly, and that they would govern justly if they followed the teachings of Scripture and the classics. The argument was refreshing in its optimism, departing as it did from the medieval insistence upon war, crime, and injustice as essentially ineradicable evils visited upon sinful men by an inscrutable Providence. And it was radical in its ethics, as is quickly apparent upon comparing it with Niccolò Machiavelli's *The Prince,* a contemporaneous document far more self-consciously descriptive of the realities of Renaissance politics.

[3] *Ibid.,* p. 203.
[4] *Ibid.,* p. 213.

There is no evidence that Erasmus had any knowledge of *The Prince* or, indeed, any intention of answering it. Machiavelli composed the work in 1513, after his forced retirement from Florentine politics, but it was not published until 1532. Gripped by a sense of history as the operation of incomprehensible and uncontrollable forces and despairing of what he perceived as the characteristic humanistic propensity to confuse "how we live" with "how we ought to live," Machiavelli set forth a ruthlessly realistic politics, addressed to the prince who would acquire and hold power; indeed, it is said that his principal model was none other than Cesare Borgia. Erasmus, on the other hand, hoping that man's rational nature could be made to prevail, offered a resolutely moral politics, addressed to the prince who, having acquired or inherited power, would exercise it justly. It is no accident that Erasmus devoted half his treatise to education and ended with a peroration deploring war, while Machiavelli devoted half his treatise to war and omitted the subject of education entirely.[5]

We can only guess what use Charles made of the *Christian Prince,* though it is manifest that his career was something less than testimony to Erasmus' teaching. We do know that the treatise figured centrally in the education of several other prominent sixteenth-century Europeans, among them, Prince Ferdinand of Spain, Prince Eberhard of Württemberg, and the sons of William V, duke of Bavaria. We know, too, that it was uniquely related to More's *Utopia* (1516): the documents were contemporary, and there is every indication that their shared commitment to a humane Christian society was in part the result of sustained and searching conversations over the years. Granted, the *Utopia* was more radical, in its insistence that a truly just society could never be achieved without a drastic equalizing of the human condition, and for that very reason, perhaps, less optimistic. But the two works did bespeak a common commitment to the centrality of education—for the citizenry as well as its officials—in the development of the good society.[6]

Even more important, the *Christian Prince* was profoundly influential on Sir Thomas Elyot's magnum opus, *The Boke Named the Governour* (1531), probably the first major treatise on education

---

[5] Niccolò Machiavelli, *The Prince,* translated by Luigi Ricci and revised by E. R. P. Vincent (London: Oxford University Press, 1935), p. 68.

[6] See St. Thomas More, *Utopia,* in *The Complete Works of St. Thomas More,* edited by Edward Surtz and J. H. Hexter (14 vols.; New Haven: Yale University Press, 1963-), IV, 125-129, 159-161, 181-183, 229.

to appear in the English language. We know little of Elyot's early life. The son of a distinguished jurist, he was admitted to the Middle Temple, one of the Inns of Court, in 1510. While there, he entered upon a career in government, rising from the clerkship of the assize in the West Country to the clerkship of the king's council and also serving intermittently as justice of the peace for Oxfordshire and Wiltshire and as sheriff of Oxfordshire and Berkshire. Elyot was dismissed from the council in 1530, following the fall of Cardinal Wolsey, but was knighted for his service. It was then that he turned to the composition of the *Governour,* which appeared the following year.[7]

The work is divided into two parts, the first (Book One) dealing with the nature of a "public weal" and the proper training of those who would govern it and the second (Books Two and Three) dealing with the manners and virtues ideal governors should possess. "A public weal," Elyot begins, "is a body living, compact or made of sundry estates and degrees of men, which is disposed by the order of equity and governed by the rule and moderation of reason." Within any public weal there ought to be no more than one sovereign governor. "But since one mortal man cannot have knowledge of all things done in a realm or large dominion, and at one time, discuss all controversies, reform all transgressions, and exploit all consultations, concluded as well for outward as inward affairs: it is expedient and also needful that under the capital governor be sundry mean authorities, as it were aiding him in the distribution of justice in sundry parts of a huge multitude: whereby his labors being levigated and made more tolerable, he shall govern with the better advice, and consequently with a more perfect governance." It is to the education of these inferior governors, or magistrates, that Elyot addresses himself in the first and more significant section of his treatise.[8]

Crying out against the "decay of learning among gentlemen" occasioned by the pride, avarice, and negligence of parents and by the lack of competent masters and teachers, Elyot calls for a thoroughgoing reform of education along humanistic lines. The son of

[7] It is possible that he was the Thomas Elyot who received degrees from Oxford in 1519 and 1524, though his most recent biographer thinks this is unlikely. See Pearl Hogrefe, *The Life and Times of Sir Thomas Elyot, Englishman* (Ames: Iowa State University Press, 1967), pp. 48-50.

[8] Thomas Elyot, *The Boke Named the Governour,* edited by Henry Herbert Stephen Croft (2 vols.; London: Kegan Paul, Trench, & Co., 1883), I, 1, 8, 25.

a gentleman should be properly supervised by nurses and other women from his earliest years, taught to speak a clear and polite English and a pure and elegant Latin, and kept generally at activities "wherein is no resemblance or similitude of vice." At the age of seven he should be taken from the company of women and assigned to a tutor, "which should be an ancient and worshipful man, in whom is approved to be much gentleness, mixed with gravity, and, as nigh as can be, such one as the child by imitation following may grow to be excellent. And if he be also learned, he is the more commendable." The primary office of the tutor is the formation of the boy's character: he must understand the child's natural inclinations, extolling and encouraging qualities that are virtuous and reproving those that are not. But he must also be sure that lessons are mixed with some pleasant recreation, such as playing a musical instrument or, if the child is so inclined, painting and sculpture. Once the boy has learned the parts of speech in English, it is time for the father or tutor to locate a master who is "excellently learned both in Greek and Latin, and therewithal is of sober and virtuous disposition, specially chaste of living, and of much affability and patience." The master's task is to introduce the boy to Greek and Latin literature, beginning with *Aesop's Fables* in Greek, proceeding then to the dialogues of Lucian or the comedies of Aristophanes, and moving finally to the great classical poets—Homer, Virgil, Ovid, and Horace, Silius Italicus, Lucan, and Hesiod.[9]

These studies should occupy the boy until he is fourteen, at which time the next stage of education begins, embracing logic (from Cicero or Agricola), rhetoric (in Greek from Hermogenes or in Latin from Quintilian, then from Isocrates, Demosthenes, and Cicero), geography (from Ptolemy), history (from Livy, Xenophon, Quintus Curtius, Caesar, Sallust, and Tacitus), and moral philosophy (from Aristotle, Cicero, Erasmus, Scripture, and, above all, Plato). Nor does Elyot overlook the physical training of the future governor: he insists that studies be interspersed with such varied forms of exercise as wrestling, running, swimming, fencing, riding, hunting, hawking, shooting, and dancing. And throughout there should be constant effort to nurture the cardinal virtues of wisdom, courage, justice, and temperance and the subsidiary virtues of majesty, nobility, affability, placability, mercy, humanity, benevolence, beneficence,

9 *Ibid.*, pp. 113, 98, 35, 36, 50.

liberality, and friendship. "Now all ye readers that desire to have your children to be governors," Elyot concludes, "or in any other authority in the public weal of your country, if ye bring them up and instruct them in such form as in this book is declared, they shall then seem to all men worthy to be in authority, honor, and noblesse, and all that is under their governance shall prosper and come to perfection."[10]

Whence these rather fully developed educational plans? One obvious source was the classical literature that Elyot both cited and recommended. The idea of a public weal, with an ordered hierarchy of men and estates, was a commonplace in Tudor England, though Elyot might well have derived it directly from his study of Plato and Aristotle. The emphasis on caution in the choice of nurses, tutors, and masters, on the need for virtue as well as knowledge, and on the importance of recreation and gymnastic exercises patently followed Plutarch's *The Education or Bringinge Up of Children,* which Elyot himself translated into English. And the recommendation that Greek be taught before Latin, along with a host of other detailed pedagogical proposals, was very likely taken from Quintilian's *Institutes of Oratory.* Other ideas doubtless came from Cicero, Seneca, and Isocrates, all favorites of Sir Thomas.

Elyot's educational scheme also owed a great deal to Erasmus' *Christian Prince,* of which Elyot remarked in the *Governour* that "there was never book written in Latin that, in so little a portion, contained of sentence, eloquence, and virtuous exhortation, a more compendious abundance." There is also evidence that Erasmus' other treatises touching on education, especially the *De copia* (1512), were profoundly influential. Elyot concurred in the Erasmian doctrine that rulers must first be virtuous men and that virtue can only be acquired through the right kind of education. And just as Erasmus took hereditary monarchy as a given and sought to humanize the monarch through education, so Elyot took hereditary nobility as a given and sought to humanize the nobles through education. But in the process, Elyot did much to nationalize Erasmus' cosmopolitan views and make them directly relevant to Tudor England. At a time of political consolidation and a rapid increase in the need for lay administrators and professionals, he addressed his treatise to aspirants entering government service as well as to the traditional aristocracy;

10 *Ibid.,* II, 447.

and, though he instinctively favored the latter, he warned both that only a proper education would qualify them to rule. Furthermore, he defined that education in much more secular terms than Erasmus, making the philosophy of the ancients even more central than the philosophy of Christ.[11]

Yet another influence on Elyot's ideas was More's *Utopia* and, indeed, the whole intellectual life of the More circle. We know that Elyot and More were personally acquainted, drawn together by a common interest "in the pursuit of polite literature," though it should be borne in mind that Elyot was More's junior by some twenty years. In all likelihood, Elyot was a frequent visitor in More's home during the years after 1510, and his wife, Margaret, actually took part in the study of humanistic texts with the children in More's "school." In addition, it is almost certain that the two men met from time to time in the course of their legal and political activities. At any rate, the friendship was sufficiently close for Elyot explicitly to repudiate it in a letter written to Thomas Cromwell following More's execution for treason. At the very least, Elyot imbibed from More a deep commitment to learning and literature and a special taste for Plato and Lucian, among the ancients. Moreover, as John Major has persuasively argued, Elyot's *Governour* bears a unique relationship to More's *Utopia*, standing as a kind of semiofficial reply by a protagonist of Tudor policy, who continued to believe that a strong monarch assisted by a privileged class of rulers could, with proper education, produce a society as just as one that incorporated such radical innovations as social equality, communal wealth, and popular sovereignty.[12]

A final source of Elyot's ideas, though a much more problematical one, is the literature of the Italian Renaissance, especially Machiavelli's *The Prince* and Baldassare Castiglione's *The Book of the Courtier* (1528). True, *The Prince* was not published until 1532; but manuscript copies were available well before that date, and one of them was apparently in the library of Thomas Cromwell, to which Elyot might have had access. There is even stronger evidence that Cromwell owned a copy of *The Courtier*. In any case, even if Elyot did not read *The Prince*, he was at least familiar with its arguments,

11 *Ibid.*, I, 95.
12 Thomas Stapleton, *The Life and Illustrious Martyrdom of Sir Thomas More* (1588), translated by Philip E. Hallett and edited by E. E. Reynolds (New York: Fordham University Press, 1966), p. 40; and John M. Major, *Sir Thomas Elyot and Renaissance Humanism* (Lincoln: University of Nebraska Press, 1964), chap. iii.

and, like Erasmus, he was diametrically opposed to them. As for *The Courtier,* there are obvious similarities between Castiglione's views and Elyot's, only some of which can be attributed to the commonplaces of the age. Both men are partisans of music, painting, and sculpture; both favor physical education, athletics, and dancing; both share regard for antiquity, nobility, and virtue. There are differences, to be sure: Castiglione's emphasis on military pride and prowess is not to be found in *The Governour,* for as Sir Ernest Barker once remarked, "Elyot's governor is a grave magistrate, and the sober background of the public weal is behind his goings and doings: Castiglione's courtier may indeed be a councilor of state, but he is also a man of wit and fashion, of gallantry and the arts." But here, as with Elyot's use of Erasmus, we are simply witnessing the nationalization of an ideal and its adaptation to the conditions of Henrician England.[13]

Elyot's *Governour* set the tone for an immense literature devoted to the education of those who would qualify for positions of leadership in Tudor and Stuart England. The treatise itself went through eight editions in the sixteenth century and was the model for *The Institucion of a Gentleman* (1555), published anonymously, for Sir Humphrey Gilbert's *Queene Elizabethes Achademy* (c. 1572), for Laurence Humphrey's *The Nobles, or, Of Nobilitye* (1563), for James Cleland's *Heropaideia, or, The Institution of a Young Noble Man* (1607), and for Thomas Fuller's *The Holy State, and The Profane State* (1642). It clearly helped pave the way for the immensely popular English version of *The Courtier;* and it patently influenced that most characteristic of Elizabethan treatises on pedagogy, Roger Ascham's *The Scholemaster* (1570), which was "specially purposed for the private bringing-up of youth in gentlemen's and noblemen's houses."[14]

Equally significant, as Fritz Caspari points out in *Humanism and the Social Order in Tudor England,* the conception of the governor was merged with that of the courtier to form the ideal of the Elizabethan gentleman. And that ideal was articulated not only in formal treatises on civility but also in heroic poems such as Sir Philip Sidney's *Arcadia* (1590, 1593) and Edmund Spenser's *The Faerie Queene* (1590, 1596), and in didactic essays such as John Lyly's

---

[13] Sir Ernest Barker, *Traditions of Civility* (Cambridge: Cambridge University Press, 1948), p. 144.

[14] Roger Ascham, *The Schoolmaster,* edited by Lawrence V. Ryan (Ithaca: Cornell University Press, 1967), p. 1.

Euphues (1578, 1580) and Sidney's *The Defence of Poesie* (1595). Furthermore, the ideal was personified in the lives of such Elizabethan luminaries as Sir Walter Raleigh, Lord Burghley, the earl of Essex, and Sidney himself. Indeed, as Caspari clearly demonstrates, one can trace a fairly direct line from the Oxford Reformers, through Elyot, Sidney, and Spenser, to Milton, who praised England as a commonwealth "where under a free, and untutored monarch, the noblest, worthiest, and most prudent men, with full approbation, and suffrage of the people have in their power the supreme, and final determination of highest affairs."[15]

In sum, the humanists prevailed: the gentry took unto themselves the concept of gentility. And in that very process there occurred a momentous shift in English educational thought. For, as Erasmus and Elyot had both realized, the same education that prepared the aristocracy to rule could prepare others to rule; to one convinced of the value of education, it is but a short step from an education that confirms status to an education that confers status. And sixteenth-century England took that step. Whereas Elyot saw education largely as an instrument for humanizing those born to rule, others came to see it as an instrument for qualifying men to rule, whatever the conditions of their birth. A half-century after Elyot, Sir Thomas Smith noted in his widely read *De Republica Anglorum: The Maner of Government or Policie of the Realme of England* (1583): "For whosoever studieth the laws of the realm, who studieth in the universities, who professeth liberal sciences, and to be short, who can live idly and without manual labor, and will bear the port, charge and countenance of a gentleman, he shall be called master, for that is the title which men give to esquires and other gentlemen, and shall be taken for a gentleman." One need not invest the statement with anachronistic democratic meaning to recognize how significant education had become in the formation and re-formation of the English polity.[16]

---

[15] Sidney, of course, thought of the *Arcadia* very much as a heroic poem, despite the fact that it was written in prose rather than verse. Caspari, *Humanism and the Social Order in Tudor England* (Chicago: University of Chicago Press, 1954), pp. 157, 207-208. The passage from Milton is in *Of Reformation Touching Church-Discipline in England* (1641), in *Complete Prose Works of John Milton*, edited by Don M. Wolfe (3 vols.; New Haven: Yale University Press, 1953-1962), I, 599.

[16] Sir Thomas Smith, *De Republica Anglorum*, edited by L. Alston (Cambridge: Cambridge University Press, 1906), pp. 39-40. For a similar observation of a contemporary, see William Harrison, *The Description of England*, edited by Georges Edelen (Ithaca: Cornell University Press, 1968), pp. 113-114; Harrison wrote his *Description* as an introduction to Raphael Holinshed's celebrated *Chronicles of England, Scotlande, and Irelande* (1577, 1587).

II

The American colonists were familiar with the civility literature as well as with those classical works on the conduct of life it drew upon and recommended, though it should be noted that civility was not nearly so popular a concern on either side of the Atlantic as piety. Tutors and schoolmasters in both New England and Virginia taught Cicero and Quintilian as handbooks of style and in the process doubtless conveyed heavy draughts of Roman virtue; and libraries in all the colonies proffered images of man via Plato, Aristotle, Plutarch, Seneca, Homer, Virgil, and Ovid. More's *Utopia* was widely known, as was Machiavelli's *The Prince*, Castiglione's *The Courtier*, and Sidney's *Arcadia*. Curiously, however, the English civility manuals of the sixteenth century were virtually absent. Yet their absence testifies not to a lack of interest in the genre but rather to a demand for another kind of civility book, one very much in the tradition of the *Governour* though tendering somewhat different advice to a somewhat different audience. At least two such works were widely read by the American colonists: Henry Peacham's *The Compleat Gentleman* (1622) and Richard Brathwaite's *The English Gentleman* (1630). Like the manuals of piety, they did double duty pedagogically, defining an ideal character and stating the educational requirements for nurturing that character.[17]

Peacham was born around 1576 at North Mimms, in Hertfordshire, the son of a clergyman. He attended Trinity College, Cambridge, his favorite studies there being history and geography. Sometime before the end of the century, he became master of the free school at Wymondham, in Norfolk, but soon gave up the position in favor of writing. In 1606, he published *The Art of Drawing with the Pen, and Limming in Water Colours,* which appeared subsequently in revised editions as *Graphice* and, alternatively, *The Gentleman's*

[17] Ovid's *Metamorphoses* was early available to the colonists in a lively native translation, prepared by George Sandys during his years in Virginia. Of special interest is Anne Bradstreet's "An Elegie upon That Honourable and Renowned Knight, Sir Philip Sidney," *The Tenth Muse Lately Sprung Up in America* (London: printed for Stephen Bowtell, 1650), in *The Tenth Muse*, edited by Josephine K. Piercy (Gainesville, Fla.: Scholars' Facsimiles and Reprints, 1965), pp. 191-196. I have been unable to find evidence of a single copy of Elyot's *Governour* in a seventeenth-century colonial library. Indeed, given its popularity during the sixteenth century, the book appears much less frequently than one would expect, even in surviving English library lists.

Exercise. In 1613, he agreed to travel on the Continent as private tutor to Hannibal Baskerville and the sons of Thomas Howard, earl of Arundel and Surrey, and passed two years in Holland, France, Italy, and Westphalia. He returned to London in 1615, and it was there that he wrote *The Compleat Gentleman* for William Howard, Lord Arundel's second son.

Peacham's general argument is essentially one with Erasmus' and Elyot's: the foundation of a just society lies in the union of nobility and learning. Nobility, for Peacham as for his forerunners, is inherent and natural; it is part of the great chain of being that establishes the lion as pre-eminent among beasts, the eagle among birds, the whale among fish, the rose among flowers, the diamond among stones, gold and silver among metals. Nobility, then, is given; he who joins it to erudition deserves double honor: "As an engine of the fairest colors he is afar off discerned and winneth to himself both love and admiration, heightening with his skill his image to life, making it precious and lasting to posterity."[18]

Having made the traditional case for a union of lineage and learning, Peacham discusses the educational responsibilities of parents and masters, urging them to begin their efforts early, to accommodate themselves to the differing talents and capacities of their pupils, and to avoid the age-old immoderacies of the teacher—inordinate severity and excessive leniency. Then, after some pointed advice about university life (choose companions prudently, organize time carefully, study Scripture thoroughly), Peacham goes on to the substance of advanced study, taking Latin and Greek for granted and stressing a wide range of subjects not traditionally included in the arts curriculum: English ("while you are intent to foreign authors and languages, forget not to speak and write your own properly and eloquently"); history ("be not a stranger in the history of your own country"); cosmography ("an imitation of the face, by draught and picture, of the whole earth and all the principal and known parts thereof, with the most remarkable things thereunto belonging"); geometry ("a science of such importance that without it we can hardly eat our bread, lie dry in our beds, buy, sell, or use any commerce else whatsoever"); poetry and music ("to sweeten your severer studies"); drawing, limning, and painting ("for your exercise at

18 Henry Peacham, *The Complete Gentleman*, edited by Virgil B. Heltzel (Ithaca: Cornell University Press, 1962), p. 28.

leisure"); heraldry ("it is meet that a noble or gentleman who beareth arms and is well descended be not only able to blazon his own proper coat, derive by pedigree the descent of his family from the original, know such matches and allies as are joined to him in blood, but also of his prince, the nobility, and gentry where he liveth"); and physical exercise ("since the mind from the ability of the body gathereth her strength and vigor"). Finally, there are concluding remarks on friendship, frugality, diet, truthfulness, and the value of travel.[19]

Thus, the substance of Peacham's recommendations. In essence, his complete gentleman—really the Stuart Cavalier—is one more version of the Renaissance union of gentle birth and humane learning. But it is a version much closer to Castiglione's courtier than to Elyot's governor; for, though Peacham explicitly commits his gentleman to public service ("all virtue consisteth in action, and no man is born for himself"), there is, in truth, little in the treatise that would lead the reader to take the commitment seriously. The end of learning—and, indeed, of living—is personal accomplishment, self-realization. Now, whatever the intrinsic merit of such an aim, it was somewhat anachronistic in 1622, increasingly in England, where the traditional court was evolving into an expanding government bureaucracy, and certainly in the colonies, where there was no court and where public service was quickly becoming both the personal and political *raison d'être* of the landed gentry.[20]

Richard Brathwaite was a contemporary of Peacham, the son of a Westmoreland barrister, Oxford and Cambridge trained, and, interestingly enough, also a man of letters. Like Peacham, he had Cavalier propensities; and, indeed, it is said that he served with the royalist forces in the Civil War. But he wrote a very different book on civility. *The English Gentleman* begins with the statement that "virtue the greatest signal and symbol of gentry is rather expressed by goodness of person, than greatness of place." And goodness of person, Brathwaite continues, derives not from descent and title, which only adulterate gentility, but rather from education and piety. Unlike Peacham's treatise, which unites an initial section on nobility of birth with a lengthy discourse on the proper education of nobility, Brathwaite's takes the form of eight discrete essays: on youth, dis-

---

[19] *Ibid.*, pp. 65, 63, 68, 84, 90, 127, 130, 135.
[20] *Ibid.*, p. 12.

position, education, vocation, recreation, acquaintance, moderation, and perfection.[21]

What quickly becomes clear, as one makes his way through the volume, is that Brathwaite's manual of civility is at the same time a manual of piety: his gentleman is actually a Christian man leading a godly life according to Scripture. "He that sigheth not while he is a pilgrim, shall never rejoice when he is a citizen. This is the gentleman, whom I have presumed to recommend to your protection," Brathwaite writes in the dedication. Moreover, his gentleman, nurtured by a proper education, has an obligation to serve the public in some useful calling, an obligation that is especially weighty, since the gentleman's life inevitably serves as an example to others. Indeed, Brathwaite's arguments here, notwithstanding his royalist leanings, fall squarely within the mainstream of Puritan writing, calling to mind William Perkins' classic *A Treatise of the Vocations* some twenty-seven years earlier; and, though Brathwaite discusses at length such characteristic gentlemanly offices as ambassador, military commander, and justice of the peace, he is patently as instructive to aspiring merchants and professionals as he is to landed squires. Finally, in keeping with the genre, Scriptural references abound alongside the classical, making Brathwaite's treatise as distinct from Peacham's in its authorities as in its substance.[22]

In effect, *The Compleat Gentleman* culminated an earlier tradition of civility, while *The English Gentleman* inaugurated a new one. The new ideal was steeped both in Elyot's commitment to public service and in his preoccupation with the secular world, though it was far broader in its definition of gentility and far more religious in its definition of gentlemanly conduct. For colonists at once engaged in the creation of new elites and eager to preserve a Christian social order, Brathwaite's special combination of civility and piety must have proved immensely attractive. True, other contemporary treatises, for example, Richard Allestree's *The Gentleman's Calling* (1660), went in similar directions, but none seemed more suitable to

21 The following comment from the prefatory material in *The English Gentleman* (London: John Haviland, 1630) indicates Brathwaite's own sense of his differences with Peacham: "Now for the title, I am not wholly ignorant, how a subject entitled *The Complete Gentleman*, was heretofore published; which (I can assure you gentlemen) consorts with this rather in title than tenor, name than nature; the proof whereof I refer to the generous and judicious reader." Brathwaite also published *The English Gentlewoman* in 1631, but there is no evidence that it was widely known in the colonies. Brathwaite, *English Gentleman*, "The Epistle Dedicatory."

22 Brathwaite, *English Gentleman*, "Epistle Dedicatory."

the colonial ethos. Indeed, it is more than a little ironic that a man who was not wholly friendly to Puritanism should have articulated so well certain fundamental aspects of the Puritan character.[23]

III

Like manuals of piety, the civility books addressed their educational preachments primarily to families, and this was as true of treatises on statecraft as it was of treatises on gentility. Thus, to take but two examples well known in the colonies, More's *Utopia* made the monogamous, patriarchal family absolutely central in the life of the commonwealth, assigning to it many of the vital regulatory and educational functions of the society. Similarly, Jean Bodin's *The Six Bookes of a Commonweale* (1576), which the colonists read in French and Latin as well as in the popular English edition of 1606 prepared by Richard Knolles, defined the family as "the true seminary and beginning of every commonweal." Within its confines the father had "the right and power to command," as did the prince over his subjects, the magistrate over private men, the master over his scholars, the captain over his soldiers, and the lord over his slaves; and within its confines the foundation of the commonweal would be laid by the father's instruction of his children "in all virtues, but especially in the fear of God." Later, Thomas Hobbes made essentially the same point in the *Leviathan* (1651), which was also known in the colonies, though not so widely in the seventeenth century as the works of More and Bodin. And while Hobbes wanted children taught that fathers had surrendered absolute power over their children when they had established the commonwealth—a matter on which he differed from Bodin—he did grant that they had never relinquished the honor children owed them under the Fifth Commandment for "the benefit of their education."[24]

Within this context of patriarchalism, the traditional genre of the father's advice to a son achieved new popularity as a special form of

23 W. Lee Ustick argues, in "Changing Ideals of Aristocratic Character and Conduct in Seventeenth-Century England," *Modern Philology*, XXX (1932-33), 159, that *The Gentleman's Calling* is "purely a work of piety"; I would contend that its combination of piety and civility is simply different from Brathwaite's, but no less a combination for that reason.

24 Jean Bodin, *The Six Bookes of a Commonweale*, edited by Kenneth Douglas McRae (Cambridge, Mass.: Harvard University Press, 1962), pp. 8, 20, 23; and *Hobbes's Leviathan*, with an essay by W. G. Pogson Smith (Oxford: Clarendon Press, 1909), p. 263.

civility manual, and one of the earliest seventeenth-century examples
to attract wide readership on both sides of the Atlantic was the
Basilikon Doron (Royal Gift) of James I. The book was written in
1599, four years before James acceded to the English throne, and
since it was originally meant solely for his son, Prince Henry, only
seven copies were printed and placed in the hands of trusted royal
assistants. But James subsequently complained that fraudulent copies
were circulating, and he published the treatise in 1603. Sir Walter
Scott once remarked that it was "composed in His Majesty's very best
manner, exhibiting that extraordinary mixture of learning and
pedantry, sense and folly, reason and prejudice, vanity and prudence,
which most deservedly procured James the character of the wisest
fool in Christendom."[25]

The work is brief and is divided into three parts, dealing respectively with a king's duty to God, his responsibility in office, and his
personal behavior. The basic cast of the discussion had become, by
1599, traditional: James doubtless drew on Erasmus and Elyot and in
turn on their sources. The king's duty to God is to love him and to
live according to his law: to do so he must know and follow the
commands and prohibitions of Scripture. Hence, Henry is admonished to study the Bible, to "read it with a sanctified and chaste
heart: admire reverently such obscure places as ye understand not,
blaming only your own capacity: read with delight the plain places,
and study carefully to understand those that are somewhat difficult:
press to be a good textuary; for the Scripture is ever the best interpreter of itself; but press not curiously to seek out farther than is contained therein; for that were over unmannerly a presumption, to
strive to be further upon God's secrets, than he hath will ye be; for
what he thought needful for us to know, that hath he revealed there:
And delight most in reading such parts of the Scripture, as may best
serve for your instruction in your calling; rejecting foolish curiosities
upon genealogies and contentions, which are but vain, and profit not,
as Paul saith." Henry is further cautioned to discern carefully between the commandments of God and the ordinances of men,
between substance and ceremony, between matters touching salvation and the indifferent concerns of the world.[26]

25 Walter Scott, ed., *A Collection of Scarce and Valuable Tracts* (2d ed.; 13 vols.;
London: printed for T. Cadell *et al.*, 1809-1815), III, 260.
26 King James I, *Basilikon Doron*, in *The Political Works of James I*, edited by
Charles Howard McIlwain (Cambridge, Mass.: Harvard University Press, 1918), pp.
14-15.

As for duty in office, James charges that Henry must be a good king who governs justly and equitably, first, by establishing and executing good laws, and second, by teaching his subjects through the example of his own godly life. He must attempt to practice the princely virtues—temperance, justice, clemency, magnanimity, liberality, constancy, humility—making "moderation to be the chief ruler"; but, above all, he must study to know well not only his own calling but every craft. "Delight in reading," James counsels, "and seeking the knowledge of all lawful things." And, "since all arts and sciences are linked every one with other, their greatest principles agreeing in one (which moved the poets to feign the nine muses to be all sisters) study them, that out of their harmony, ye may suck the knowledge of all faculties; and consequently be on the counsel of all crafts, that ye may be able to contain them all in order, as I have already said: For knowledge and learning is a light burthen, the weight whereof will never press your shoulders."[27]

The final book comprises a series of maxims deriving from the proposition that "a king is as one set on a stage, whose smallest actions and gestures, all the people gazingly do behold." Henry is advised to be moderate in his appetites; to speak a plain, honest, natural, comely, clean, and short English; to eschew affectation, pedantry, and uncouthness; to beware of flattery; to avoid violence; to abstain from the idle company of women; and, above all, to bestow love according to the measure of a man's virtue. Thus, "His Majesty's instructions to his dearest son, Henry the prince."[28]

Given its unique authorship, the *Basilikon Doron* was bound to exert a unique influence, particularly in the colonies, where its special blend of sober piety and earnest civility would seem compelling to many who would never be presented at court. Beyond that, the treatise gave impetus to the "advice" genre, and the remainder of the seventeenth century witnessed a steady procession of works by devoted fathers seeking to guide their sons through the labyrinth of life. One such work, which circulated widely in America and which was quite different from the *Basilikon Doron*, was Francis Osborne's *Advice to a Son* (1656). Osborne was born in 1593, the youngest son of a landed Bedfordshire family. He went to London as a youth and there, at court, attracted the attention of the earl of Pembroke, who made him master of the horse in his household.

27 *Ibid.*, pp. 37, 38, 39.
28 *Ibid.*, pp. 43 ff., 3.

Osborne's sympathies lay with the Parliamentary party during the Revolution; and, through the efforts of his brother-in-law, who was a colonel in the Parliamentary army, he was able to obtain a minor office in the city of Oxford around 1650. This gave him an opportunity to oversee the education of his son John, who was then studying at the university and for whom he wrote the *Advice to a Son*.

Osborne's work falls somewhere between the *Basilikon Doron* and the more informal parental instructions written into characteristic wills and letters of the era. The initial section deals with education, and ranges over matters of substance ("the art of music is so unable to refund for the time and cost required to be perfect therein as I cannot think it worth any serious endeavor"), matters of prudence ("a few books well studied and thoroughly digested nourish the understanding more than hundreds but gargled in the mouth as ordinary students use"), and matters of priority ("let not an overpassionate prosecution of learning draw you from making an honest improvement of your estate"). Subsequent sections deal with love and marriage, travel, government, and religion, the section on travel being of special interest in that it criticizes some of the seventeenth-century commonplaces regarding the intrinsic educational value of travel. The emphasis throughout is on a tough-minded pragmatism, one that ended up so much at odds with prevailing pieties that Osborne felt obliged to publish the treatise anonymously.[29]

It is this pragmatism, much of it frankly cynical, that contrasts so sharply with the moralism of the *Basilikon Doron*. Whereas James set out to teach Henry how to live piously and govern justly, Francis Osborne sought to teach John how to get ahead in a troubled world. Marry well, he counseled, for a great estate is the surest palliative for the inconveniences of wedlock; submit quietly to whatever power sits in the saddle of sovereignty; in matters religious, undiscovered hypocrisy is less dangerous than open profaneness; conscience must be kept tender, but not so raw as to occasion imprudence—scores of aphorisms like these are put forward for the use of the young man who would master the art of personal advancement.

"A conceited fellow," Dr. Johnson once said of Osborne in a conversation with James Boswell. "Were a man to write so now, the boys would throw stones at him." Boswell, on the other hand, thought

---

29 [Francis Osborne], *Advice to a Son*, in *Advice to a Son: Precepts of Lord Burghley, Sir Walter Raleigh, and Francis Osborne*, edited by Louis B. Wright (Ithaca: Cornell University Press, 1962), pp. 49, 44, 43.

Advice to a Son lively, original, and full of shrewd observations. In any case, it was certainly one of the more popular books of Restoration England, in its own way capturing the post-Revolutionary disillusionment that characterized the age. For the more enterprising of the colonists the treatise proffered precisely the sort of practical counsel their sons could use to advantage. Not only had civility been made a matter of achievement rather than ascription; the achievement, as Osborne defined it, was thoroughly compatible with worldly success. How apt a doctrine for a family seeking to rise in the relatively fluid social structure of the New World.[30]

For Osborne, as for most others who wrote on the subject, education in civility was first and foremost a family responsibility. But there was assistance for the family, as Osborne noted at the very beginning of *Advice to a Son* in a discussion of the comparative advantages of home and school instruction. Osborne himself thought he had lost a good deal by not having been sent to school, primarily the discipline that derives from the give-and-take of youthful associations. His father, like many of his social class, had chosen to place his sons under the supervision of a tutor at home. For the colonial father without access to a school, there was no such choice: the only supplement to parental education in civility was tutorial education in civility; and even this, of course, was carried on in the familial setting.

One treatise devoted to such tutorial education that was known and read in the New World was Roger Ascham's *The Scholemaster* (1570). Its origins are familiar. Ascham, after a notable career as a Greek scholar at St. John's College, Cambridge, agreed in 1548 to serve as tutor to Princess Elizabeth; and, although he held the position for less than two years, it marked the beginning of a lifelong association with the future queen, culminating in his appointment as her Latin secretary after she acceded to the throne in 1558. The volume itself, as Ascham reports in the preface, grew out of a dinnertime conversation at Windsor Castle in 1563 on the merits of harsh versus gentle pedagogy. Having heard Ascham's view that "young children were sooner allured by love than driven by beating to attain good learning," Sir Richard Sackville, one of Elizabeth's courtiers, asked Ascham to assist him in finding a tutor for his young grandson. The discussion that followed so fascinated Sackville that

30 *Boswell's Life of Johnson* (1791), edited by George Birkbeck Hill and revised by L. F. Powell (6 vols.; Oxford: Clarendon Press, 1934-1950), II, 193-194.

he persuaded Ascham to commit his views to writing. The result, produced over a period of years and not actually published until after Ascham's death, was *The Scholemaster*.[31]

The treatise, long regarded as the quintessential English Renaissance work on pedagogy, is divided into two books, "the first predominantly ethical, the other devoted to method." It is in the first section that Ascham states his wish "that the youth in England, specially gentlemen, and namely nobility, should be by good bringing-up so grounded in judgment of learning, so founded in love of honesty as, when they should be called forth to the execution of great affairs in service of their prince and country, they might be able to use and to order all experiences, were they good, were they bad, and that according to the square, rule, and line of wisdom, learning, and virtue." He clearly recognizes that the opportunity of the schoolmaster—by which he patently means the tutor—is limited at best, commencing only after "wise and good parents" have had charge of the child for some time and lasting only until the youth is ready for the university. Nevertheless, he sees that opportunity as crucial: hence, the need for schoolmasters sage and knowledgeable about their work.[32]

What follows is a commentary replete with specific advice. The schoolmaster is counseled to employ love rather than fear, gentleness rather than beating, encouragement rather than punishment, admonition rather than rebuke, patience rather than irritation. Ascham believes that "learning teacheth more in one year than experience in twenty, and learning teacheth safely"; but he does not want young gentlemen always "poring on a book" to the exclusion of honest pleasures and pastimes. And, though he is aware of the broadening effect of travel, he is unalterably opposed to travel in Italy—indeed, to all things Italian. Regarding the teaching of Latin, he advocates the methods of *translatio linguarum* (double translation, first from a good Latin text into English, then from the English back into Latin) for beginning students and *imitatio* (shaping one's style after certain excellent examples) for more advanced students. Committed thus to *imitatio*, he goes on to an analysis of the great Latin prose models—Varro, Sallust, and Caesar. The text breaks

---

[31] Ascham, *Schoolmaster*, p. 7.
[32] Roger Ascham to Johannes Sturm, [December, 1568], *The Whole Works of Roger Ascham*, edited by J. A. Giles (3 vols. in 4; London: John Russell Smith, 1864-1865), II, 176; and Ascham, *Schoolmaster*, pp. 52, 12.

off abruptly in the middle of the discussion, though, as Lawrence Ryan has suggested, Ascham probably intended that a final section on Cicero would culminate the treatise.[33]

Ascham himself acknowledged his profound intellectual debts to Sir John Cheke, the most celebrated scholar at Cambridge during his tenure there, and to Johannes Sturm, rector of the renowned gymnasium at Strasbourg, with whom he had corresponded for many years. But the reader of *The Scholemaster* will also note Ascham's debts to Plato, Xenophon, Plutarch, Cicero, and Quintilian among the ancients, and to Erasmus and Elyot among his contemporaries. Indeed, if it can be said that Elyot's *Governour* stated the ideal of civility as the union of gentle birth and humane learning, then Ascham's *Scholemaster* proposed the pedagogical means for realizing that ideal. Little wonder, therefore, that Renaissance tutors on both sides of the Atlantic regularly turned to Ascham's treatise for practical guidance in their work.

Ascham's schoolmaster was a tutor, who would rarely be responsible for more than a few children at a time, and these within a family setting. Yet the gap between the tutor's efforts in the home and the master's in the school was one of degree rather than kind during the Renaissance, since most modern techniques of group instruction had not been invented and scholars were still dealt with one by one. Hence, it should be no surprise that John Brinsley, in *A Consolation for Our Grammar Schooles* (1622), cited Ascham's treatise with a respect bordering on reverence, and vigorously urged the adoption of his methods. Equally important, civility stood with piety—or, one might say, civility merged with piety—as one of the central ideals of Brinsley's grammar school, a civility associated both with young Englishmen in the colonies, prepared by learning "to become principal lights; and pillars of their country," and with young Indians in the colonies, lifted by learning from barbarism to civilization. To the extent that Americans shared with metropolitan Englishmen the aspirations Brinsley articulated, the colonial father with access to a school expected that school to supplement whatever familial instruction in civility he himself gave

---

[33] Ascham, *Schoolmaster*, pp. 50, 52, 162 n., xxxii-xxxvii; and Lawrence V. Ryan, *Roger Ascham* (Stanford: Stanford University Press, 1963), pp. 266-270. The proposition about learning and experience is from Erasmus' *De pueris statim ac liberaliter instituendis libellus* (1529), which is printed in William Harrison Woodward, *Desiderius Erasmus Concerning the Aim and Method of Education* (Cambridge: Cambridge University Press, 1904), pp. 191-192.

his children at home. And, indeed, the majority of the colonists did have that expectation: their schools were early cast as agencies of social advancement, however much the rhetoric of educational policy emphasized other, more pious goals.[34]

[34] John Brinsley, *A Consolation for Our Grammar Schooles* (London: Richard Field, 1622), pp. 12, 15. Brinsley also cites his *Ludus Literarius: or, The Grammar Schoole* (1612), which was known in the colonies and in which he recommends the reading of such standard children's books on manners as Francis Seager, *The Schoole of Vertue and Booke of Good Nourture for Chyldren and Youth to Learne Theyr Dutie By* (1557) and William Fiston, *The Schoole of Good Manners* (1609).

Chapter 3

THE ADVANCEMENT OF LEARNING

> For my way of discovering sciences goes far to level men's wits,
> and leaves but little to individual excellence; because it performs
> everything by the surest rules and demonstrations.
>
> FRANCIS BACON

Like all efforts at reform, the humanist program for the reconstitution of learning had both its critical and its constructive sides. On the one hand, there was the mordant attack on the sham and pomposity of the learned—their misplaced emphasis on letter rather than spirit, their incessant quibbling, their gross ignorance, their painful pedantry. On the other hand, there was the heady vision of a new society, in which the benefits of learning would be widely diffused, and the leadership educated to virtue. These two thrusts are symbolized by the two great treatises we have come to associate with the friendship of Erasmus and More, *The Praise of Folly (Moriae encomium)* and the *Utopia.*

Richard Whitford once remarked of the two men, both of whom he knew and loved, that they were "so much alike in genius, character, tastes and studies, that no twin brothers could be found more closely resembling one another." Yet they complemented each other as well, and they influenced each other profoundly: More's ready wit is easily discernible in the *Folly,* the Latin title of which is itself a pun on More's name; and there are sections in the *Utopia,* on the call to counsel, in which More is patently arguing with Erasmus as well as with himself.[1]

[1] Desiderius Erasmus to Richard Whitford, May 1, 1506, *The Epistles of Erasmus,* translated and edited by Francis Morgan Nichols (3 vols.; London: Longmans, Green, and Co., 1901-1918), I, 407. For the pun, see the dedicatory preface to More, in Desiderius

The Praise of Folly was written during Erasmus' third visit to England, in the summer of 1509. King Henry VII had died the previous April, and young Henry VIII had acceded to the throne amidst a chorus of humanist hosannas about a golden age of virtue and learning. "Oh, my Erasmus," young Mountjoy had written in May, "if you could see how all the world here is rejoicing in the possession of so great a prince. . . . When you know what a hero he now shows himself, how wisely he behaves, what a lover he is of justice and goodness, what affection he bears to the learned, I will venture to swear that you will need no wings to make you fly to behold this new and auspicious star." Erasmus, who had received the letter in Rome, hearkened promptly to the call, hoping perhaps for some preferment from the young king, whom he had met a decade earlier. During the wearisome journey from Italy, he found himself contending with the boredom of travel by musing on the varieties of folly in the world. Once in England, he hastened to More's house at Bucklersbury, in London; and there, temporarily without his books and suffering from severe nephritic pains, he proceeded to draft the *Folly,* writing swiftly by day and then reading the manuscript each evening to More and his friends. The treatise was finished in a week but was not published until 1511; it was an immediate success and did more than any other single work to gain for Erasmus an international reputation.[2]

Like all first-rate satire, *The Praise of Folly* can be read at several levels. In its most literal sense, it is a slashing attack on the prevalence of Folly and her attendants—Drunkenness, Ignorance, Self-love, Flattery, Forgetfulness, Laziness, Pleasure, Madness, Wantonness, Intemperance, and Sleep—in every realm of human affairs. In families, among friends, in the churches and schools, in the arts, sciences, and professions, in the highest councils of state, Folly is regnant. Indeed, as she herself declares early in the treatise, "no society, no union in life, could be either pleasant or lasting without me. A people does not for long tolerate its prince, or a master tolerate his servant, a handmaiden her mistress, a teacher his student,

---

Erasmus, *The Praise of Folly*, translated by Hoyt Hopewell Hudson (Princeton: Princeton University Press, 1941), pp. 1-4. For More's differences with Erasmus, see, for example, St. Thomas More, *Utopia*, in *The Complete Works of St. Thomas More*, edited by Edward Surtz and J. H. Hexter (14 vols.; New Haven: Yale University Press, 1963-), IV, 57.

2 William Blount, Lord Mountjoy, to Desiderius Erasmus, May 27, [1509], *Epistles of Erasmus*, I, 457.

a friend his friend, a wife her husband, a landlord his tenant, a partner his partner, or a boarder his fellow boarder, except as they mutually or by turns are mistaken, on occasion flatter, on occasion wisely wink, and otherwise soothe themselves with the sweetness of folly."[3]

As has often been pointed out, the *Folly* stands squarely in the tradition of the "fool" literature, typified by the verses of Sebastian Brant's *The Ship of Fools (Das Narrenschiff,* 1494), which satirized foolishness in no less than 112 different varieties. Erasmus deals in turn with each of the principal callings of his time; and, given his own background and predilections, it is not surprising that some of his sharpest thrusts are reserved for the foibles of philosophers and schoolmen. Have philosophers insisted that they in their wisdom should rule the world? Then consult the historians and learn that "nowhere have princes been so baneful to commonwealths as where the rule has devolved upon some philosophaster or bookish fellow." Have the "logic-choppers" contended that it is knowledge of the sciences that makes man distinctively human? Then recall that the "simple folk of the golden age flourished without any armament of sciences, being guided only by nature and instinct." Has the world honored its teachers? Then mark their lot: they are "hunger-starved and dirty in their schools—I said 'their schools,' but it were better said 'their knowledge factories' or 'their mills' or even 'their shambles' —among herds of boys." Has mankind rewarded its scholars? Then consider the torture they inflict upon themselves: "they add, they alter, they blot something out, they put it back in, they do their work over, they recast it, they show it to friends, they keep it for nine years; yet they never satisfy themselves. At such a price they buy an empty reward, namely, praise—and that the praise of a handful." Do the theologians presume to teach mankind the way to salvation? Then observe the way the "Greeklings, gracklelike," peck at their interpretations of Scripture, with "my Erasmus," Folly adds, at the head of the band. The exposure is brilliant and relentless; as James Kelsey McConica once remarked, it is as if Erasmus hoped that, drenched in the acid of mockery, such presumptions would melt into oblivion.[4]

3 Erasmus, *Praise of Folly*, p. 28.

4 Sebastian Brant, *The Ship of Fools*, translated by Edwin H. Zeydel (New York: Columbia University Press, 1944); Erasmus, *Praise of Folly*, pp. 32, 44, 70, 74, 109; and James Kelsey McConica, *English Humanists and Reformation Politics Under Henry VIII and Edward VI* (Oxford: Clarendon Press, 1965), p. 37.

Yet Erasmus' self-directed barb—and there are several in the treatise—points to a quite different way in which the work can be read, namely, as irony. At the same time that Folly is ridiculing the shallowness, the vanity, and the pretentiousness of much that passes for learning, she is pointing to certain profound truths about its limitations. She mercilessly mocks the scholar who throws away his health and forgoes life's pleasures in favor of pursuing the learned disciplines, only to discover that the Christian religion has no affinity whatsoever for wisdom. After all, Folly points out, those who founded Christianity were bitter foes of literary learning, and those possessed of Christian piety seem the most foolish fools of all, "for they pour out their wealth, they overlook wrongs, allow themselves to be cheated, make no distinction between friends and enemies, shun pleasure, glut themselves with hunger, wakefulness, tears, toils, and reproaches; they disdain life and dearly prefer death; in short, they seem to have grown utterly numb to ordinary sensations, quite as if their souls lived elsewhere and not in their bodies. What is this, forsooth, but to be mad?" Thus, the greatest wisdom with respect to learning may be the recognition of its limitations. Responding some years after the publication of *The Praise of Folly* to Martin Dorp's criticisms of the work, Erasmus argued that his intentions there had been no different from those in the *Enchiridion* and the *Christian Prince*, though what he had done in the *Folly* had been done "under the semblance of a jest." What could be wrong, he asked, quoting Horace, "with saying the truth with a smile"? And the truth, he eloquently insisted, was that knowledge and prayer were complementary: each had its independent function, but neither was sufficient unto itself.[5]

Five years separate the *Folly* from the *Utopia*, five years during which the friendship of Erasmus and More flourished, even as each rode the tide of a successful career, Erasmus in scholarship, More in affairs. The summer of 1516 found them together again in More's home. Several months earlier, Erasmus had accepted the post as counselor to Prince Charles; More on his side was pondering an invitation to serve in the court of Henry VIII. Erasmus doubtless had very much in mind the arguments of the *Christian Prince*, which had just issued from Froben's press in Basel; and More had in hand

[5] Erasmus, *Praise of Folly*, p. 118; and Desiderius Erasmus to Martin Dorp, May, 1515, *Christian Humanism and the Reformation: Selected Writings of Erasmus*, edited by John C. Olin (New York: Harper & Row, 1965), pp. 59-60.

the unfinished draft of the *Utopia,* which he had undertaken during an embassy to Flanders the previous year. It must have been with the same delight that had marked their discussions of the deeds and doings of Folly that the two friends now turned to life on the extraordinary isle of Utopia.

As in Plato's *Republic,* which was patently More's model, men in the *Utopia* are shaped by just laws, sound institutions, and systematic instruction. Properly formed, the Utopians are contemptuous of wealth and possessed of an abiding sense of the proper value of things, derived "partly from their upbringing, being reared in a commonwealth whose institutions are far removed from follies of the kind mentioned, and partly from instruction and reading good books." As in the *Republic,* too, the Utopians draw no sharp line between upbringing and instruction, since education embraces not only systematic learning but also the discipline and training fostered in homes, in churches, and in the day-to-day business of living.[6]

It is the priests of the commonwealth, including, incidentally, older widows and married as well as single men, who are responsible for the education of youth. The most honored citizens of Utopia, they are as concerned with the morals and virtue of children as with their advancement in learning, taking the greatest care "to instill into children's minds, while still tender and pliable, good opinions which are also useful for the preservation of their commonwealth." Every Utopian is instructed in both the art of agriculture and some other craft "to which he is inclined by nature," and all are early introduced to good literature and encouraged to pursue it as a lifetime avocation. For adults, there are public lectures during the hours before daybreak, attended by men and women of every social class. Beyond these opportunities for the citizenry at large, there is provision for a small number of Utopians to be released from manual labor, so that they can devote themselves completely to scholarship; from this group are chosen the ambassadors, the priests, the high officials, and the governor. As with Plato's philosopher-kings, the Utopian scholars combine expertise in affairs with genius in learning: not only have they governed justly and well, they have virtually equaled the ancients in the fields of music, dialectic (classical logic, following Aristotle), arithmetic, geometry, and, indeed, astronomy, which they have managed to separate from astrology. Alas, they have not seemed the equals of contemporary logicians at the picayune

6 More, *Utopia,* p. 159.

business of disputation, for in place of theological hairsplitting they have inquired earnestly into the nature of true happiness, believing that the soul is immortal and by the goodness of God born for happiness.[7]

According to Raphael Hythloday, the discoverer of Utopia, the Utopians were eager to master ancient Greek learning as soon as he had called it to their attention, "for in Latin there was nothing, apart from history and poetry, which seemed likely to gain their great approval." He and his companions taught them the language (using Constantine Lascaris' grammar), which they readily mastered, and then acquainted them with most of Plato's works and several of Aristotle's, as well as with Theophrastus on plants, the dictionaries of Hesychius and Dioscorides, and sundry writings of Plutarch, Lucian, Aristophanes, Homer, Sophocles, Euripides, Thucydides, Herodotus, Herodian, Hippocrates, and Galen. Hythloday also reports that, steeped as they are in learning, the Utopians are especially interested in the study and contemplation of nature (presuming that, like all other artificers, the Author and Maker of nature set forth the visible mechanisms of the world as a spectacle for man, whom alone he has made capable of appreciating it), and they are exceedingly facile in the invention of the arts that promote the advantage and convenience of life. Thereby is learning not only open to all but put to the use of all.[8]

Thus, More's *Utopia,* the greatest educational work of the English Renaissance. Like the *Folly,* it pilloried the arid theologizing of the Scholastics, and like the *Folly,* too, it conveyed a Christian sense of the limitations of learning (the Utopians never discuss philosophy apart from certain fundamental religious principles, in the absence of which they deem reason weak and insufficient). But, beyond that, it imparted an educational message as radical as its economic message. Cicero had argued that to be truly human man must be educated in the studies proper to culture. More projected a society in which all could become human in Ciceronian terms. His concern was for an education that would on the one hand enable every individual to live the virtuous life "according to nature since to this end we were created by God" and on the other hand encourage the practical application of learning to the benefit of the community. Ultimately, he characterized the Utopian not very differently from

[7] *Ibid.,* pp. 229, 127.
[8] *Ibid.,* p. 181.

the way he himself has been characterized, namely, as the "Christian English Cicero," the man of action trained in letters and virtue or, if we may, the Christian knight of the *Enchiridion*.[9]

Over the years, Erasmus and More and the circle of humanists around them issued treatise after treatise setting forth the details of their educational programs. Moreover, they themselves taught in a variety of situations, in the process revealing much about what they hoped to accomplish. Thus, for example, there was More's own household, of which Erasmus once wrote: "You might say that Plato's Academy had come alive again. But I wrong his home in comparing it to Plato's Academy, for in the latter the chief subjects of discussion were arithmetic, geometry, and from time to time ethics, but the former rather deserves the name of a school for the knowledge and practice of the Christian faith. No one of either sex there neglects literature or fruitful reading, although the first and chief care is piety." The students in More's celebrated "school"—his children and grandchildren, and now and then friends of all ages—studied Latin and Greek literature, logic, philosophy, and mathematics; they read Scripture and the classical commentaries on Scripture; they engaged in formal disputations; and they practiced double translation, later to be popularized by Roger Ascham. The quintessential alumna, of course, was More's eldest daughter, Margaret Roper, whose charming correspondence with her father testifies eloquently to the fruitfulness of the enterprise.[10]

There was also the work of John Colet, first at Oxford, where his "singular erudition, eloquence, and integrity" won Erasmus to the cause of humanistic scholarship, and later at St. Paul's School, which Colet refounded around 1509 "specially to increase knowledge and worshiping of God and our Lord Christ Jesus and good Christian life and manners in the children." Significantly, the school, which was supported largely by the private fortune Colet had inherited from his father, was placed under the governance of a lay rather than a clerical body, the Mercers' Company of London. And the statutes Colet wrote for the school in 1518 stipulated that the students, "children of all nations and countries indifferently," would aim at a classical Latin style characteristic of Cicero, Sallust, Virgil,

9 *Ibid.*, p. 163; and Nicholas Harpsfield, *The Life and Death of Sir Thomas Moore, Knight,* edited by Elsie Vaughan Hitchcock, Early English Text Society Publications, no. 186 (London: Oxford University Press, 1932), p. 217.

10 Desiderius Erasmus to John Faber, [December, 1532], *Opus epistolarum Des. Erasmi Roterodami,* edited by P. S. Allen, H. M. Allen, and H. W. Garrod (12 vols.; Oxford: Clarendon Press, 1906-1958), X, 139.

and Terence. In connection with St. Paul's, Colet prepared a cate-chism and accidence under the title *Coleti Æditio,* and Erasmus later published a metrical version of the catechism in Latin entitled *Institutum hominis Christiani (Institution of a Christian Man).* Also, Colet, William Lily, and Erasmus each had a hand in the production of a grammar, which came to be known in various revised editions as *Lily's Grammar,* and Erasmus compiled a textbook of a new kind, the *De copia* (1512), which provided students with a series of techniques, terms, and categories for classifying their knowledge. Erasmus also wrote a treatise on pedagogy for the school, the *De ratione studii (On the Right Method of Instruction),* which appeared initially in 1511 and was included in the first printing of the *De copia* the following year. The treatise obviously pleased Colet, as evidenced by a glowing letter to Erasmus expressing the hope that he might someday lend a hand in teaching the teachers at St. Paul's, when he came "away from those Cambridge people."[11]

Finally, there were the several reform efforts at the two univer-sities, occasionally abortive, always partial, but nonetheless notable. The work of Colet, Linacre, and Grocyn at Oxford in the 1490's has already been mentioned, but this seems to have terminated around 1504, when Colet became dean of St. Paul's. At Cambridge, the chancellorship of John Fisher in 1503 marked the beginning of a concerted effort to lift the educational standards of the clergy, the symbol of which was the appointment of Erasmus to a lectureship in Greek and possibly even to the Lady Margaret professorship of divinity. "I look upon you," the chancellor wrote Erasmus in 1512, "as necessary to the university, and will not suffer you to want, so long as there is anything to spare out of my own poor means." Erasmus himself remained less than three years, but his influence lived on long enough to affect significantly the Royal Injunctions of 1535, which James Bass Mullinger, the historian of the university, has described as "the line that in university history divides the medieval from the modern age."[12]

Meanwhile, at Oxford, Corpus Christi College was organized in

[11] Desiderius Erasmus to John Colet, [1499], *Epistles of Erasmus,* I, 221; "Statutes of St. Paul's School," in J. H. Lupton, *A Life of John Colet,* (2d ed.; London: George Bell and Sons, 1909), pp. 279, 277; and John Colet to Desiderius Erasmus, [October, 1511], *Epistles of Erasmus,* II, 24. In 1529, Erasmus supplemented the *De ratione studii* with a treatise addressed to William, duke of Cleves, entitled *De pueris instituendis (On the Instruction of Children).*

[12] John Fisher to Desiderius Erasmus, [November, 1512], *Epistles of Erasmus,* II, 75; and James Bass Mullinger, *The University of Cambridge* (3 vols.; Cambridge: Cambridge University Press, 1873-1911), I, 631.

1517, embodying in its statutes most of the humanists' ideals. It is said that Richard Fox, one of the founders, had originally intended to establish a college for the young monks of his diocese in an effort to reform the order, but his cofounder, Hugh Oldham, is reputed to have exclaimed: "What my lord, shall we build houses, and provide livelihoods for a company of buzzing monks, whose end and fall we ourselves may live to see? No, no it is more meet a great deal, that we should have care to provide for the increase of learning, and for such as who by their learning shall do good in the church and commonwealth." The first lecturer in Latin (dubbed "humanity") at the new college was Thomas Lupset, a disciple of Colet and Lily; the second was the brilliant Spanish humanist, Juan Luis Vives, who came in 1523 as lecturer in Latin, Greek, and rhetoric at Cardinal College, then housed in Corpus Christi. Vives, thirty-one at the time, had managed to win the admiration and friendship of Erasmus and More and, through More, of Cardinal Wolsey and Queen Catherine, who invited him to tutor her daughter, Princess Mary. A countryman of Catherine, Vives was unfortunately caught up in the politics of the royal divorce and was dismissed from Oxford in 1526 and from England in 1528. But, in the meantime, certain of his texts and treatises had come to be increasingly valued and used, notably, the *De institutione feminae Christianae (On the Education of a Christian Woman,* 1523) commissioned by Catherine, the *De ratione studii puerilis (On the Right Method of Instruction of Youth,* 1523), plans of education prepared for Princess Mary and Charles Blount (the son of Lord Mountjoy), and a little compendium of moral precepts known as the *Introduction to Wisdom* (1524). Often linked with Erasmus and the celebrated Guillaume Budé of Paris in the Renaissance "triumvirate of letters," Vives must also be viewed, with Erasmus and Ascham, as part of a Renaissance "triumvirate of pedagogy." Both groups symbolize the cosmopolitanism of the Renaissance in general, and of the English Renaissance in particular; for the fact is that neither Erasmus nor Vives was ever more than a sojourner in England, yet both profoundly influenced the English conception of learning and the learned man, in their own time and for generations to come.[13]

---

13 *Holinshed's Chronicles of England, Scotland, and Ireland* (1577, 1587), edited by Sir Henry Ellis (6 vols.; London: printed for J. Johnson *et al.*, 1807-1808), III, 617.

II

For all their commitment to learning, the humanists were plagued by a number of ambivalences that were deep in the Western tradition. They were well aware of Stoic admonitions that the disinterested search for truth can easily end up a barren and fruitless enterprise and that grammar, history, and poetry, while useful in their own right, do little to pave the way to virtue. They were thoroughly familiar with the Old Testament dictum that "in much wisdom is much grief," and they comprehended the story of the Temptation and Fall as well as most. And they were doubtless cognizant of the mordant warnings of the Fathers: Jerome's oft-cited dream of being judged by God a Ciceronian rather than a Christian and Augustine's famous characterization of scholarship as "a certain vain and curious longing," which might properly be called "the lust of the eyes."[14]

The humanists were also ambivalent about knowledge of nature. On the one hand, they tended to consider such knowledge of a lower order than ethical wisdom: thus, Erasmus' mockery of the sciences, "which Theuth, that evil genius of the human race, excogitated for the hurt of man, and which are so far from furthering his happiness that they actually hinder it"; and thus, too, his general tendency to characterize naturalists and physicians, along with astrologers, logicians, and theologians, as purveyors of sterile Scholastic learning. On the other hand, the humanists explicitly recognized that the universe is God's creation and that to know the universe is to know God more profoundly: thus, More's suggestion that the Author and Maker of nature "prefers a careful and diligent beholder and admirer of his work to one who like an unreasoning brute beast passes by so great and so wonderful a spectacle stupidly and stolidly."[15]

For those humanists who did commit themselves to the study of nature, the wisdom of the ancients held the same fascination as it did for ethicists and theologians. Much of that wisdom had survived into the medieval period, some of it, notably the works of Aristotle, having been rediscovered in Arabic translations during the twelfth century; but it had all suffered from the characteristic corruptions of erroneous transmission and improper interpretation. Hence, in

<hr/>

[14] Ecclesiastes 1:18; and Augustine, *The Confessions*, translated by J. G. Pilkington, in *Basic Writings of Saint Augustine*, edited by Whitney J. Oates (2 vols.; New York: Random House, 1948), I, 174.

[15] Erasmus, *Praise of Folly*, pp. 43-44; and More, *Utopia*, p. 183.

science as in letters, there was a concerted effort to recover the knowledge of the ancients in its original, unadulterated form. Ptolemy's *Cosmographia (Geography)*, translated into Latin by Jacobus Angelus in 1406, was printed in 1475, while his *Almagest* appeared in a competent *Epitome* by Regiomontanus (Johann Müller) in 1496 and in Greek in 1538. Together, these writings put at the disposal of Renaissance scholars the considerable substance of Alexandrian astronomy and mathematical geography. And, at roughly the same time, the anatomical and physiological treatises of Galen, notably, the *De utilitate partium (On the Use of the Parts)* and the *De facultatibus naturalibus (On the Natural Faculties)*, became available in accurate Latin translations, partly through the efforts of Erasmus' friend Thomas Linacre.

The impact of these works was paradoxical: at the same time that they transmitted the best of classical scholarship, they revealed its fundamental inadequacies; and the physicians, geographers, and astronomers who initially rejoiced over the recovery of ancient learning soon found themselves busily correcting, refining, and extending it. Out of the process came the most important developments in sixteenth-century science: Nicolaus Copernicus wrote *De revolutionibus orbium coelestium (On the Revolutions of the Celestial Spheres,* 1543) to the outline of the *Almagest,* seeking to incorporate the results of his calculations from the new mathematics; Andreas Vesalius undertook *De humani corporis fabrica (On the Structure of the Human Body,* 1543) in an effort to update Galen; and John Dee and Gerhardus Mercator set out to refine Ptolemy's maps, using data brought back by the navigators who were engaged in what J. H. Parry has called "the great reconnaissance."

In all of this, ideas moved easily across political boundaries, facilitated by the use of Latin as the common language of the learned. The Copernican system was fairly well known in England by the 1550's and 1560's, owing largely to the work of Robert Recorde, who referred to it in his *Castle of Knowledge* (1556), published, significantly, in English, and John Dee, who had at least two copies of *De revolutionibus* in his influential library at Mortlake, near London. Later, Thomas Digges, a student of Dee, issued a translation of the critical sections of *De revolutionibus* under the title *A Perfit Description of the Caelestiall Orbes According to the Most Aunciente Doctrine of the Pythagoreans, Latelye Revived by Copernicus and by Geometricall Demonstrations Approved* (1576); and William Gilbert offered his discoveries regarding magnetism as proof of that aspect of Copernican theory which dealt with the earth's rotation. John Dee, in turn, traveled back and forth across the Channel, returning to England in 1547 with some of Mercator's globes, lecturing on mathematics at Paris the following year, and generally making his library an academy of the new sciences. And Vesalius was only the most celebrated of a generation of brilliant anatomists, including Jacques Dubois Sylvius, Charles Estienne, Michael Servetus, Matteo Realdo Colombo, and Gabriel Fallopius, all of whom contributed to the body of knowledge Hieronymus Fabricius imparted to William Harvey at the University of Padua between 1600 and 1602.

Moreover, as scholarship progressed, those who undertook the correction of the humanist documents came also to realize that the ancients, far from comprehending all things, had misunderstood much and failed to note even more. Navigators, using the mariner's compass and sundial, discovered that no combination of Aristotelian syllogisms could explain why they found water where Ptolemy's descriptions and principles indicated there should be land. Anatomists, drawing human organs in a dissecting room, learned that the perfect Galen had portrayed animal as human structures more frequently than perfection should permit. And astronomers, discovering a new star in 1572 and a new comet in 1577 (and this before the Galilean telescope), found themselves sharply criticizing Aristotle on the immutability of the heavens beyond the moon. In fact, John Dee and Thomas Digges hoped to use the appearance of the star and its disappearance a year later to verify the Copernican system. The effort was unsuccessful, but their aspiration symbolized the growing awareness during the late sixteenth century of the need for a new learning based on new methods and using new instruments, a learning that would go beyond what the ancients in all their wisdom had been able to master. "To those men of early times and, as it were, first parents of philosophy, to Aristotle, Theophrastus, Ptolemy, Hippocrates, Galen, be due honor rendered ever," William Gilbert wrote in 1600, "for from them has knowledge descended to those that have come after them: but our age has discovered and brought to light very many things which they too, were they among the living, would cheerfully adopt. Wherefore we have had no hesitation in setting forth in hypotheses that are provable, the things that we have through a long experience discovered."[16]

Here, then, was the context within which Francis Bacon—barris-

16 William Gilbert, *On the Loadstone and Magnetic Bodies*, translated by P. Fleury Mottelay (New York: John Wiley & Sons, 1893), p. li.

ter, essayist, member of Parliament, and learned counsel to the Crown—put forth his program for a complete reformation of learning. A member of Elizabeth's court who had gained the queen's favor through the good offices of the earl of Essex in the 1590's, only to turn against Essex after his abortive coup of 1601, Bacon was justifiably anxious over his future when James I acceded to the throne. He tried every conceivable device to bring himself to the king's attention and actually obtained an audience, but to little avail. All he got was a knighthood—this "almost prostituted title," he called it—and that only after telling his cousin Robert Cecil of his intention to renounce politics in favor of the pen. He never left politics, of course, but one outcome of the decision was the *Advancement of Learning* (1605), which in characteristic Baconian fashion he dedicated to James in the hope of gaining preferment. How James regarded the treatise is not known, though it is clear that Bacon's rise in court did not begin until 1607, when he was named solicitor general. He was made attorney general in 1613, lord keeper in 1617, and lord chancellor in 1621, from which post he was removed for accepting presents from litigants in his court. Meanwhile, he had begun the *Novum organum (New Instrument)*, which he laid aside for a time to compose the *New Atlantis* (an allegory patterned after the *Utopia* of an earlier lord chancellor) and then completed in 1620. Following his fall from grace, he turned full time to his writing, producing a series of works ranging from a *Historie of the Raigne of King Henry VII*, which he presented to Prince Charles in 1622, to revisions of the *Advancement*, issued as the *De augmentis scientiarum* in 1623, and the *Essays,* published in an enlarged edition in 1625. He died in 1626, having been chilled, the story goes, in the process of stuffing a chicken with snow to test experimentally whether freezing preserves flesh.[17]

"I have taken all knowledge to be my province," Bacon wrote at the age of thirty-one to his uncle Lord Burghley, and, indeed, he had, with a verve unrestrained even by that minimal modesty he thought appropriate to civil matters. For he considered the true ends of learning nothing less than the "restitution and reinvesting (in great part) of man to the sovereignty and power . . . which he had in his first state of creation." Men could not be gods, Bacon admitted, but they could still aspire to the dominion over nature that Adam had enjoyed in Paradise. And it was this that Bacon had in mind when

---

[17] Francis Bacon to Robert, Lord Cecil, July 3, 1603, *The Letters and the Life of Francis Bacon,* edited by James Spedding (7 vols.; London: Longman, Green, Longman, and Roberts, 1861-1874), III. 80.

he called his magnum opus, which was to embrace the entire corpus of his writings, *The Great Instauration*.[18]

As is well known, *The Great Instauration* was never completed, but there is every indication that the *Advancement of Learning* constituted an extended prospectus of the larger work. It has two parts: an elaborate defense of learning and a program for its renewal. The effort in the first part is to refute once and for all the ancient charge that learning undermines piety and civility. Quite the contrary, Bacon avers, one need only note the moral virtue of the learned King Solomon or the Fathers (who were "excellently read and studied in all the learning of the heathen"), or the military prowess and civil merit of Alexander the Great or Julius Caesar. Learning, Bacon concludes, has been more than vindicated by her children.[19]

But that in no way implies that all is well with learning, for in Bacon's view it is beset with diseases and distempers. Men study words rather than matter, preoccupying themselves with stylistic niceties instead of substantive realities. They waste their efforts on vain altercations, spinning webs of pseudoscholarship that have little to do with the world. And they wallow in magic and superstition, permitting imagination to dominate reason and the grossest distortions to pass for truth. Worst of all, they pursue knowledge for ignoble ends, seeking victories of wit, curiosity, and greed rather than "the glory of the Creator and the relief of man's estate." What is required, Bacon argues, is a thoroughgoing reform of the purposes, institutions, and organization of learning; and to this end he sets forth his intellectual system, "as it were a small globe of the intellectual world, as truly and faithfully as I could discover; with a note and description of those parts which seem to me not constantly occupied, or not well converted by the labor of man." It is the further development of this system, of course, that he proposes to James, as an "immortal monument" to a unique sovereign, who combines "the power and fortune of a king, the knowledge and illumination of a priest, and the learning and universality of a philosopher."[20]

James did not build the monument, though years later his

---

[18] Francis Bacon to William Cecil, Lord Burghley, [1592], *ibid.*, I, 109; and Francis Bacon, *Valerius Terminus* (1734), in *The Works of Francis Bacon*, edited by James Spedding, Robert Leslie Ellis, and Douglas Denon Heath (New ed.; 7 vols.; London: Longmans & Co., 1876-1890), III, 222.

[19] Francis Bacon, *Advancement of Learning*, in *Works of Francis Bacon*, III, 299.

[20] *Ibid.*, pp. 284, 490, 263.

grandson Charles II took no small pleasure in his role as founder and patron of the Royal Society. But Bacon did spend the rest of his life refining and elaborating the proposal. In the *Novum organum,* he set forth the methods of experimentation and observation, which would derive real knowledge from nature, the hope being that all natural phenomena might eventually be explained by combinations of a few elemental principles that anyone could comprehend. Moreover, in the progression from particular experiments to general axioms that would in turn suggest particular experiments, Bacon saw a mode of intellectual endeavor that would "level men's wits," that would, through the operation of simple and well-defined procedures, or arts, place the amateur scientist in a superior position to both the secretive magician and the bookish scholar. In the process, the "womb of nature" would be delivered of its "many secrets of excellent use, having no affinity or parallelism with anything that is now known, but lying entirely out of the beat of the imagination, which have not yet been found out." Once available, such secrets would doubtless usher in a golden age, during which men would be restored to that original dominion over nature that was theirs by divine ordinance.[21]

In the *New Atlantis* (1627), Bacon portrayed a utopia where that restoration had been achieved, primarily through the efforts of a society of learned men called Solomon's House, or the College of the Six Days' Works, dedicated to "the study of the works and creatures of God." The college was endowed with all the equipment Bacon's imagination could conjure for the pursuit of experimental inquiry: deep caves for the study of minerals; high towers for the study of climate; vast gardens for the study of agriculture; brewhouses, bakehouses, and kitchens for the study of foods; chambers of health for the study of disease and dispensatories for the study of pharmaceuticals; furnaces, perspective houses, soundhouses, perfumehouses, and enginehouses for the study of physical and psychological phenomena; a mathematical house replete with "exquisitely made" mathematical and astronomical instruments; and, last but by no means least, "houses of deceits of the senses" for the study of apparitions, impostures, and illusions.[22]

To conduct the inquiries, there was a company of specialized scholars: men who undertook their own experiments, men who

21 Francis Bacon, *Novum organum,* in *Works of Francis Bacon,* IV, 109, 100.
22 Francis Bacon, *New Atlantis,* in *ibid.,* III, 145-146, 164.

reported on the experiments of others, men who traveled the face of the earth gathering the world's intellectual riches (Bacon's merchants of light), men who organized and classified knowledge, men who searched it for "things of use and practice for man's life," and men who sought to draw from it general axioms and aphorisms about the world (Bacon's interpreters of nature). At the time of the narrator's visit to Bensalem, the men of Solomon's House had already enhanced hearing by means of amplifiers, sharpened vision with telescopes and microscopes, and practiced ornithopterous flight and underwater navigation. Above all, they had realized the Faustian dream—the prolongation of life. Truly, Paradise had been regained in this happiest of human societies.[23]

Throughout the narrative, there was not only a sharp critique of contemporary definitions of learning but an insistent call for the reform of contemporary schools and universities as well as the pedagogy that marked them. And implicit in both the critique and the call was an altered conception of the learned man. For Bacon, the end of the new learning was the "knowledge of causes, and secret motions of things; and the enlarging of the bounds of human empire, to the effecting of all things possible"; the learned man was one who pursued that end for the benefit of mankind, with compassion, humility, and selflessness. Since the new learning was patently central to the progress of civilization, Bacon anticipated that the men who cultivated it would be widely acclaimed, not for gentle birth or scholarly aloofness, but for the intellectual and ethical capacities they displayed in working toward the improvement of man's lot.[24]

Such a view of learning—particularly in its utilitarian aspects—is characteristically modern, though, as has often been pointed out, Bacon's knowledge of contemporary science was at best limited, and of contemporary mathematics virtually nil. But more important, perhaps, such a view is thoroughly characteristic of the English Renaissance. Bacon's humanism is strikingly similar to More's at a number of points: both men envisioned utopias ruled by scholars intent upon honoring God by studying his works; both recognized the potential of man as well as his limitations, and both saw in education a prime instrument for creating and perpetuating the good society. There is little doubt that the Baconians who founded the

[23] *Ibid.*, p. 165.
[24] *Ibid.*, p. 156. For Bacon's pedagogy, see *Advancement of Learning*, pp. 413-417, 439-443, and book II generally, and *Novum organum*, especially book I, pp. 47-115.

Royal Society in 1660 would have felt as much at home on the isle of Utopia as in Solomon's House; and there is no denying that some of the Baconian educational plans of the Commonwealth period resembled nothing so much as the arrangements More had sketched for the Utopians. The point is not to minimize the originality of Bacon's contribution; it is merely to stress that he is quintessentially a product of the English Renaissance and to indicate once again the richness and diversity of that tradition in the sixteenth and seventeenth centuries.

III

The Praise of Folly and the *Utopia* were widely known in the colonies, though it was not until the great Leiden edition of Erasmus' works appeared between 1703 and 1706 that his shorter pedagogical treatises became readily accessible to the intelligentsia. The *Advancement of Learning,* the *Novum organum,* and the *New Atlantis* were also familiar, as were the various editions of Bacon's writings that began to issue during the later seventeenth century. Both ancient and Renaissance science were early in evidence, frequently in original works but more often in learned compendia and popular handbooks. And, later, the founding of the Royal Society accelerated the exchange of information and experiment among interested amateurs on both sides of the Atlantic. In all of this, there was fairly direct transmission of the various views of learning that marked the English Renaissance and, with them, of course, the correlative views of piety and civility.

Two literary genres in particular proved especially congenial to this transmission, namely, the colloquy and the essay. Standing midway in popularity between the scholarly discourse and the more elementary epitome, both genres underwent considerable development during the sixteenth century, largely in response to the spread of printing and the emergence of a new literary audience. And, in the colonies, at least three examples appear to have elicited unusual interest: the *Colloquies* of Erasmus and the *Essays* of Montaigne and of Bacon. Indeed, it is probable that Erasmus and Bacon were better known in America through these works than through anything else they wrote; and that is of special significance, since the colloquy and the essay were so much vehicles for portrayal of the humane life, in all its fullness and with all its foibles.

The *Colloquies* originated as a collection of formulae—elementary language exercises—that Erasmus first developed when he was teaching Latin in an effort to support himself as a theology student during the 1490's. The earliest version consisted of simple idioms, phrases, and dialogues drawn from everyday situations with which one might expect contemporary youngsters to have been familiar. This, together with some materials added during or after Erasmus' first sojourn in England, was published in 1518 as an eighty-page octavo by Johann Froben at Basel, apparently with no authorization from Erasmus and, indeed, to his intense annoyance. That annoyance soon waned, however, as the book caught on: by 1519, Erasmus was contributing prefaces to new editions as well as corrections to the earlier text; and, by 1522, he was adding dialogues addressed not only to callow youngsters but to educated men. The volume was thus transformed from a textbook into a work of belles-lettres, and for two centuries thereafter it did double duty, both in the schools and out.

Pedagogically, the *Colloquies* stood in intimate relation to the *De copia* and the *Adages* (1500). Together, as R. R. Bolgar has incisively pointed out, they set forth the humanist method of imitation at its best: the *De copia* outlined techniques for gathering, classifying, memorizing, and presenting ideas; the *Adages,* an anthology of proverbs and commonplaces taken from classical literature, exemplified the techniques up to the point at which the process of creation began; the *Colloquies* (and, indeed, *The Praise of Folly*) embodied the finished product.[25]

Beyond their pedagogical usefulness, however, both the *Adages* and the *Colloquies* had profound literary merit in their own right. The former constituted a compendium of classical learning; and, however much the selections were meant to illustrate the preachments of the *De copia,* they patently conveyed a good deal of Aristophanes, Cicero, Homer, Lucian, Plato, and Plutarch as well. Similarly, the *Colloquies,* begun in an effort to make "better Latinists and better characters" of schoolboys, ended up as literature, dealing with a wide range of situations and institutions and directed to the forming of men. "Socrates brought philosophy down from heaven to earth," Erasmus wrote in a 1526 edition of the *Colloquies;* "I have brought it even into games, informal conversations, and

[25] R. R. Bolgar, *The Classical Heritage and Its Beneficiaries* (Cambridge: Cambridge University Press, 1954), pp. 297-298.

drinking parties." And indeed he had, for with humor, irony, and suspense he dealt in the various dialogues, not with virtue and vice as abstractions, but with the everyday ethics of courtship, marriage, sports, inns, funerals, horse-trading, churchgoing, and begging. He dealt, too, with education, often implicitly, as in the slashing attack on pedantry in "A Meeting of the Philological Society," though occasionally treating it directly, as in "The Art of Learning," where he argued that there is no easy road to wisdom and that the only sure keys to success are discipline, devotion, industry, and perseverance. In sum, the *Colloquies* teemed with the life of Everyman: they were, as Craig Thompson aptly put it, the literary complement to Brueghel, Holbein, Dürer, Cranach, and Massys. While the reader read impeccable Latin and imbibed appropriate draughts of Christian morality, he also encountered the shock of recognition.[26]

This same sense of recognition was doubtless stirred by Montaigne's *Essays* (1580, 1588, 1595), which the colonists read in both the elegant French of the original and the lambent English of John Florio's 1603 translation. Written over a period of twenty years, these diverse reflections and observations proclaimed an abiding faith in man, rooted in an informed acceptance of all the paradoxes, vicissitudes, and absurdities that mark the human condition. "Our great and glorious masterpiece is to live appropriately," Montaigne declared. "All other things, ruling, hoarding, building, are only little appendages and props, at most."[27]

The story of Michel de Montaigne's retirement from public affairs in 1571 to a life of "freedom, tranquillity, and leisure" is inextricably tied to the development of the essays. Born in 1533 to a prosperous merchant family that had been ennobled in 1477, Montaigne had learned Latin from a tutor, gone on to the Collège de Guyenne in Bordeaux, and then studied law, possibly at Toulouse. Thereafter, he had served as a magistrate, first in a newly created tax court in Périgueux and then in the Parlement of Bordeaux. Finding himself after his father's death both financially independent and unable to advance in the court, he decided to retire, and had painted on the wall of a study adjacent to his library the now famous inscription: "In the year of Christ 1571, at the age of thirty-eight,

---

26 *The Colloquies of Erasmus*, translated by Craig R. Thompson (Chicago: University of Chicago Press, 1965), pp. 3, 360, xxvi.

27 Michel de Montaigne, "Of Experience," *The Complete Essays of Montaigne*, translated by Donald M. Frame (Stanford: Stanford University Press, 1958), p. 851.

on the last day of February, his birthday, Michel de Montaigne, long weary of the servitude of the court and of public employments, while still entire, retired to the bosom of the learned virgins, where in calm and freedom from all cares he will spend what little remains of his life, now more than half run out. If the fates permit, he will complete this abode, this sweet ancestral retreat; and he has consecrated it to his freedom, tranquillity, and leisure."[28]

We do not know precisely what Montaigne intended to do with his new-found freedom; he may have had in mind from the first to write. In any case, he quickly began to formulate his ideas in a series of brief anecdotes, observations, and commentaries, most of them Stoical in character. He had lost his best friend, Étienne de la Boétie, in 1563, his father in 1568, and thereafter, in horrible succession, his brother and five of his six children; and he himself had brushed closely with death. Not surprisingly, his thoughts turned often to fortune, pain, and mortality. Only gradually did the idea of the *essai* as a trial or test of his judgment take form. "Judgment," he wrote around 1578, "is a tool to use on all subjects, and comes in everywhere. Therefore in the tests that I make of it here, I use every sort of occasion. If it is a subject I do not understand at all, even on that I essay my judgment, sounding the ford from a good distance; and then, finding it too deep for my height, I stick to the bank. And this acknowledgment that I cannot cross over is a token of its action, indeed one of those it is most proud of. Sometimes in a vain and nonexistent subject I try to see if it will find the wherewithal to give it body, prop it up, and support it. Sometimes I lead it to a noble and well-worn subject in which it has nothing original to discover, the road being so beaten that it can walk only in others' footsteps. There it plays its part by choosing the way that seems best to it, and of a thousand paths it says that this one or that was the most wisely chosen." The quest throughout is for wisdom, the basic element of which is Socratic self-knowledge tinged with a lively skepticism. Learning is a part of such wisdom, as attested by Montaigne's liberal use of classical quotations in his texts, but by no means the whole, as he makes abundantly clear in his mordant criticism of pedantry.[29]

Returning to public life as mayor of Bordeaux from 1581 to 1585,

---

[28] *Complete Essays of Montaigne*, pp. ix-x.
[29] Michel de Montaigne, "Of Democritus and Heraclitus," *ibid.*, p. 219.

Montaigne continued to develop both his ideas and the genre he had invented. The intellectual shifts that accompanied this development are fascinating: from a brooding concern with the inevitability of death to a confident celebration of the possibilities of life; from an intense preoccupation with the sufferance of pain to a mature acceptance of the entire range of human emotions and sensations; and, most important perhaps, from a haughty disdain for the "brutish stupidity" of the common people to a philanthropic insistence on the unity and similarity of all men. In the process, his humanism became broadly humanitarian; and, like Erasmus, he celebrated the possibility that Everyman might become the *honnête homme* of his later essays.[30]

Throughout, the cultivation of virtue and wisdom remained a central concern; and, indeed, Montaigne's essay "Of the Education of Children" was one of the most appealing to seventeenth-century readers. Like Ascham, Montaigne reiterates the informed commonplaces of the humanists about adapting instruction to the capacities of the pupil; but, unlike Ascham, he is aware that the independence of the pupil is easily compromised by the authority of the teacher. Not surprisingly, he favors a broad association—through travel and the study of history—with men of various stations, countries, and times. "Wonderful brilliance may be gained for human judgment by getting to know men," he remarks. "We are all huddled and concentrated in ourselves, and our vision is reduced to the length of our nose." Judgment: that is ever Montaigne's concern. Once a youngster's judgment has been shaped, learning—in logic, physics, geometry, rhetoric, and the other arts—will inform that judgment and help him use it in the most important art of all, the art of living well. The independent moral being, aware of his limitations, alert to the possibilities for public service, that is Montaigne's ideal of the learned man.[31]

The colonists read in Montaigne's *Essays* the introspections of a man seeking self-knowledge as the key to virtue and happiness. They read in Bacon's *Essays* (1597, 1612, 1625) the observations of a self-styled scientist seeking objective insight into human affairs. Like Montaigne, whose influence is patent, Bacon began his essays while still in his thirties and worked on them throughout the remainder of his life. And, like Montaigne, he returned again and again to

[30] Michel de Montaigne, "That to Philosophize Is to Learn to Die," *ibid.*, p. 58.
[31] Michel de Montaigne, "Of the Education of Children," *ibid.*, p. 116.

particular subjects, reformulating concepts, adding insights, and elaborating examples.

Perhaps the most striking feature of Bacon's early essays is their epigrammatic style, the aphoristic English he saw as an instrument for stimulating debate and popularizing knowledge. The aphorism was Bacon's device for rendering the study of human conduct as objective and scientific as the study of inanimate nature; and, though the later essays are somewhat more prolix and discursive than their predecessors, there is no denying that literary style remained for Bacon a critical element in the new method of science.

Like Erasmus and Montaigne before him, Bacon examined a fascinating variety of human emotions, qualities, and situations: love and envy, beauty and deformity, boldness and cunning, fortune and adversity. In the *Advancement of Learning,* he himself later suggested the theme that seemed to unite many of the topics: in effect, he was dealing with those matters "which are within our own command, and have force and operation upon the mind to affect the will and appetite and to alter manners," or, put another way, those aspects of character which are responsive to intellect and hence to education. On each subject Bacon is the observer: like Machiavelli, whom he cites approvingly, Bacon portrays men as they are, not as they might be. And his assumption throughout is that a sufficient number of propositions regarding human conduct, used inductively as data, will stimulate inquiry, lead on to new data, and in turn yield new propositions.[32]

Education is both a leitmotif of the several essays and a matter of explicit concern. "Of Studies," for example, sets forth some of Bacon's best-known aphorisms, among them, the oft-quoted observation "Histories make men wise; poets witty; the mathematics subtile; natural philosophy deep, moral grave; logic and rhetoric able to contend," and the characteristic assertion "Crafty men contemn studies, simple men admire them, and wise men use them; for they teach not their own use; but that is a wisdom without them, and above them, won by observation." "Of Custom and Education" asserts that habits are best inculcated early in life but then wisely goes on to suggest: "If the force of custom simple and separate be great, the force of custom copulate and conjoined and collegiate is far greater. For there example teacheth, company comforteth, emu-

---

lation quickeneth, glory raiseth: so as in such places the force of custom is in his exaltation." "Of Travel" preaches the educational advantages of experience in a foreign country, enriched by a knowledge of its language, the companionship of informed tutors, and the hospitality of its leading residents. "Of Parents and Children" presents in spare form, and without theological or pietistic trappings, many of the commonplaces of contemporary child-rearing treatises.[33]

While these and other pedagogical propositions by no means constituted a systematic philosophy of education, they did give wide circulation to the Baconian idea that one is educated partly by teachers, studies, and books but mostly by experience, carefully observed and thoughtfully considered. It was an idea that proved especially appealing in America, where Bacon was virtually canonized during the eighteenth century, along with "the incomparable Newton" and "the great Mr. Locke," as one of the true progenitors of the modern world.[34]

IV

In addition to writings on the character of the learned man, the colonists interested themselves in discussions of learning itself. And here they read a varied literature, encompassing almost every phase of Renaissance thought and ranging in format from the systematic treatises studied at Harvard to the popular compendia perused in households.

Harvard's curriculum included all the principal subjects of the arts course at contemporary Cambridge, with the notable exception of music. The traditional trivium—grammar, rhetoric, and logic—stood at the heart of the program, and was supplemented by mathematics and astronomy, the three philosophies (natural, moral, and mental), the ancient languages (Biblical as well as classical), belles-lettres, and divinity. The college library, which began with the four-

---

[33] Francis Bacon, "Of Studies" and "Of Custom and Education," *Essays or Counsels, Civil and Moral*, in *Works of Francis Bacon*, VI, 498, 497, 471-472.

[34] See, for example, Thomas Shepard's letter to his son Thomas, Jr., [1672], advising him on his studies at Harvard: "Let your studies be so ordered as to have variety of studies before you, that when you are weary of one book, you may take pleasure (through this variety) in another: and for this end read some histories often, which (they say) make men wise, as poets make witty" (*Publications of the Colonial Society of Massachusetts*, XIV [1913], 194). Bacon's *Essays* first appeared in a native American edition in 1688, as the third part of Daniel Leeds, *The Temple of Wisdom for the Little World* (Philadelphia: William Bradford, 1688).

hundred-volume bequest of John Harvard and grew to some three thousand titles by the end of the seventeenth century, contained a variety of works in each of these fields, frequently representing diverse philosophical positions. Furthermore, scores of books on a wide range of subjects were privately owned by the students and were passed along from generation to generation.

Amidst all this variety, however, several "favorite authors" are clearly discernible, notably, Petrus Ramus, Johann Heinrich Alsted, and Bartholomaüs Keckermann; together, these favorites tell us much about certain crucial concepts of method and system that decisively influenced Harvard's definition of learning. Although both Aristotelian and Cartesian logic were known and taught at the college before 1700, the logic of Ramus was by far the most popular during the early decades. Ramus, an intensely controversial master at the University of Paris from 1536 until his death in the fierce St. Bartholomew's massacre of 1572, had created a sensation by attempting to develop a logic that would serve more effectively as a tool of learning than the Scholastic versions of Aristotle that had dominated the sixteenth century. Beginning in 1543 with his *Dialecticae institutiones (Education in Dialectic)* and *Aristotelicae animadversiones (Remarks on Aristotle)*, Ramus issued a steady flow of writings which, building on the work of Rodolphus Agricola and Johannes Sturm, claimed for logic the primary responsibility for training in invention (the art of systematic discovery and analysis of subject matter) and arrangement (the art of conducting discourse) and left to rhetoric only training in style and delivery and to grammar only training in etymology and syntax. Beyond this, Ramus formulated three fundamental laws: the law of truth, which insisted that the learned arts consist entirely of universal and necessary propositions; the law of justice, which insisted that a particular proposition can belong to one and only one of the learned arts; and the law of wisdom, which insisted that propositions within any one art must be classified according to the extent and level of their generalization.

Now, a number of observations are relevant here with respect to the significance and thrust of these laws. To begin, Ramism derived from a situation of genuine "pedagogical exigency," that is, from the need to organize the rapidly expanding substance of learning in such a way that it might be taught more economically and effectively. Ramus' laws and definitions offered a logic of communication and, in some small measure at least, a logic of inquiry to take the place of the older Scholastic logic of discourse. (Later, Bacon would insist on orienting logic more fully to inquiry, but, as Paolo Rossi has suggested, there are striking continuities between the Ramist and Baconian logics.) Second, Ramism was intimately related to the development of printing and the consequent emphasis on the visual presentation of material, as the work of Walter J. Ong makes abundantly clear. The problem of spatial arrangement became far more central to pedagogical economy within such a context than it had been when oral discourse was virtually the sole method of education.[35]

Finally, Ramism accelerated the continuing definition of the several arts and of the relationship of one art to another, a philosophical enterprise called *technologia*. Hence the popularity at Harvard of Johann Heinrich Alsted's *Encyclopedia,* which he defined as "the methodical systematization of all things which ought to be learned by men in this life—in short, the totality of knowledge," and of Bartholomäus Keckermann's *Opera omnia* (1614), which embraced "systems" of all the known arts and sciences. Hence, too, the interest there in the work of Alsted's disciple, John Amos Comenius, whose pedagogical writings have often been characterized as Baconian, which is accurate enough if one also understands that both Bacon and Comenius filled their work with Renaissance commonplaces and stood squarely within the broader Ramist tradition.[36]

Such formal treatises as Ramus', Alsted's, and Keckermann's were by no means confined to the Harvard College Library, appearing as they did in the private collections of more than a few ministers and gentlemen in New England and elsewhere. Yet they were in no sense popular books; and, if one wishes insight into more commonly held definitions of learning, he must look to quite different sorts of works, of which Pierre de la Primaudaye's *The French Academie* (1577) is a leading example. Circulating widely in France, England, and the

35 Wilbur Samuel Howell, "Ramus and the Decay of Dialogue," *The Quarterly Journal of Speech,* XLVI (1960), 89; Paolo Rossi, *Francis Bacon: From Magic to Science,* translated by Sacha Rabinovitch (Chicago: University of Chicago Press, 1968), p. 148 and *passim*; and Walter J. Ong, *Ramus, Method, and the Decay of Dialogue* (Cambridge, Mass.: Harvard University Press, 1958), pp. 313-314.

36 *Joan Henrici Alstedii scientiarum omnium encyclopaediae* (2 vols.; Lyons: Jean Antoine Huguetan & Marc Antoine Ravaud, 1649), I, 1. For the science taught by Keckermann and Alsted, see Sister Mary Richard Reif, "Natural Philosophy in Some Early Seventeenth Century Scholastic Textbooks" (unpublished doctoral thesis, St. Louis University, 1962).

colonies, it was not only a piety book and a civility manual but an encyclopedia as well; and, as such, it was relentlessly mined as a reference work by sixteenth- and seventeenth-century authors. Along with the Bible, certain works of conduct, a few anthologies of essays, and a number of school texts, *The French Academie* was popular throughout the colonies among literate but not necessarily learned men; more than any other volume perhaps, it indicates the view of learning held by the average colonist and, by implication, the substance of the liberal education required of those not professionally committed to scholarship.

La Primaudaye himself remains an elusive figure in the annals of Renaissance history. He was born in 1545 to a Protestant family at Anjou, and apparently spent most of his life in the court of Henry III and Henry IV, serving the latter as counselor and as steward of the royal household. *L'Académie Française* was originally published in Paris in 1577; the first English translation was printed in London in 1586. Various additions and augmented versions of the text appeared in English over the next few decades, and, in 1618, the definitive edition appeared, "fully discoursed and finished in four books."[37]

The significance of the work lies less in any fresh thinking it contains than in its utter representativeness: it is, in effect, a complete compendium of Renaissance ideas. Book One treats the "manners and callings of all estates" and is essentially a collection of moral treatises resting heavily on both Scripture and the classics. Books Two and Four deal with man and his relationship to God, utilizing elements of anatomy and physiology, philosophy and theology. Book Three presents "a notable description of the whole world," drawing upon the fields of astronomy, natural history, and natural philosophy.

Book One is cast as a dialogue: the principal characters are four young men of Anjou, whose parents desire to see them, "not great orators, subtle logicians, learned lawyers, or curious mathematicians, but only sufficiently taught in the doctrine of good living, following the traces and steps of virtue, by the knowledge of things past from the first ages until this present that they might refer all to the glory of the Divine Majesty, and to the profit and utility as well of themselves as of their country." The youths are placed under the

[37] Peter de la Primaudaye, *The French Academie, Fully Discoursed*, translated by T. B. C., R. Dolman, and W. P. (London: printed for Thomas Adams, 1618).

tutelage of a "good and notable old man," who directs them to "the moral philosophy of ancient sages and wise men, together with the understanding, and searching out of histories, which are the light of life." After six or seven years of such study, the young men are visited by their fathers and asked what they have learned; the discussions in *The French Academie* are supposed to represent their response. The dialogue form is all but discarded in Books Two and Three and is abandoned entirely in Book Four. What constitutes the real stylistic thread of the work is its rhetoric: following Cicero and Quintilian, La Primaudaye makes expert use of such time-honored devices as amplification, definition, distinction, division, comparison, consequence, and example. That his rhetorical pattern was considered exemplary is attested by the fact that John Brinsley recommended the work in the *Ludus Literarius* as an ideal source for students in search of thematic material.[38]

In substance, *The French Academie* is a fascinating potpourri of sixteenth-century belief: the grand themes of the Renaissance as well as its characteristic contradictions are present in profusion. Augustinian demonology ("the purpose of the devils hath always been to make themselves to be served and honored of men") appears side by side with Ptolemaic astronomy ("the first and universal motion of all the spheric world, is that, which we see is made round about the earth") and Galenic physiology ("and as there are four elements of which our bodies are compounded, so there are four sorts of humors answerable to their natures, being all mingled together with the blood"). The praises of science are loudly sung, with due acknowledgment to Socrates, Plato, and Aristotle; but readers are also warned against the dangers of vain and immoderate curiosity. And, through the thousand pages run the characteristic leitmotifs of sixteenth-century thought: order, the great chain of being, man as a microcosm for whom God created all things, human reason in the service of divine ends. From La Primaudaye the colonist could infer both Renaissance visions of man and the nature of the education they suggested; it is little wonder, therefore, that *The French Academie* remained a New World favorite until well into the eighteenth century.[39]

---

[38] *Ibid.*, p. 2; and John Brinsley, *Ludus Literarius: or, The Grammar Schoole* (London: printed for Thomas Man, 1612), p. 182.

[39] La Primaudaye, *French Academie*, pp. 676, 682, 523.

Part II

INSTITUTIONS

Think not that the commonwealth of learning may languish: and yet our civil and ecclesiastical state be maintained in good plight and condition.

URIAN OAKES

INTRODUCTION

The settlement of America, it has been said, had its origins in the unsettlement of Europe; and that unsettlement holds the key to much that happened on both sides of the Atlantic. The seventeenth century was a period of general crisis throughout the Western world, occasioned, in the interpretation of E. J. Hobsbawm, by "the last phase of the general transition from a feudal to a capitalist economy," or, alternatively, in the interpretation of H. R. Trevor-Roper, by the revulsion from the excesses and inefficiencies of the Renaissance state. Whatever its cause or causes, the crisis was genuine, though it took different forms in different countries. Significantly for the colonies, it culminated in England and the Netherlands in successful political revolutions, which had decisive consequences for the character of the economy and the organization of society.[1]

In England, the crisis derived from a number of highly disruptive changes during the century following 1540. There is every indication that the population of England and Wales grew rapidly, at least until 1620, considerably expanding the labor force and causing a good deal of strain in the traditional class structure, especially since well-to-do families tended to produce more children than the poor. At the same time, prices rose with revolutionary rapidity, somewhere between 400 and 650 per cent between 1500 and 1640. Food costs soared (and with them agricultural profits), and, since wages increased less rapidly, there was cause for persistent discontent. Concurrently, vast tracts of land were put on the market, leading to

[1] E. J. Hobsbawm, "The Crisis of the Seventeenth Century," in Trevor Aston, ed., *Crisis in Europe, 1560-1660* (London: Routledge & Kegan Paul, 1965), p. 5; and H. R. Trevor-Roper, "The General Crisis of the Seventeenth Century," *ibid.*, pp. 93-95.

massive transfers of holdings from institutions to families and from
one family to another. And a considerable expansion of domestic and
foreign trade necessitated greater numbers of craftsmen, merchants,
and entrepreneurs.[2]

One leading social concomitant of all this was an unusual degree
of mobility, both horizontal, that is, from one form of work to another or from one place to another, and vertical, that is, up and
down the social ladder. Geographical movement was constant, especially from the countryside to the city, and more specifically to London, where the younger son of a yeoman or gentleman might obtain
a promising apprenticeship and ultimately establish himself as a
merchant or tradesman. There was also a good deal of movement
across the countryside itself, from village to market town and, indeed, from village to village—a fact of considerable significance,
since, as E. E. Rich has noted, by the early seventeenth century,
Englishmen had become so accustomed to geographical mobility that
migration to the North American colonies may have been for many
a far less disruptive experience than has traditionally been portrayed.[3]

The primary factor in vertical mobility was the buying and selling of land; indeed, land sales reached a peak during the 1610's, by
which time exchanges were occurring at more than twice the rate
of the 1560's. In addition, political preferment, profitable commerce,
favorable marriage, and advanced education were widely sought as
means to higher status. Needless to say, there was downward as well
as upward mobility, particularly among the younger sons of the
gentry, who were frequently forced to seek careers in the professions
as alternatives to the inheritances they failed to receive.

This high degree of mobility, compounded as it was by the social
and religious dislocations of the Reformation, both occasioned and
heightened a widespread sense of instability on the part of individuals and institutions. Among thoughtful men, there were
pervasive feelings of ambivalence, confusion, and restlessness: Renaissance dramatists, for example, were fond of portraying life as a
succession of conflicting situations and inexplicable actions, having
little unity, consistency, or coherence. And, on the institutional side,

2 Lawrence Stone, "Social Mobility in England, 1500-1700," *Past & Present*, no. 33
(April, 1966), pp. 16-55.
3 E. E. Rich, "The Population of Elizabethan England," *The Economic History
Review*, 2d ser., II (1949-50), 264.

time-honored customs embedded in family, church, guild, and village culture seemed suddenly open to question and under attack. Within such a context, Englishmen yearned for definite and authoritative models after which to pattern their lives: hence the persistent demand for conduct guides addressed to men of every social station; hence the quest for disciplines by which to organize family, church, and school; and hence the perception of all institutions as educational, in that they defined, shaped, and rationalized human character.

Yet there is a paradox here, of which Renaissance Englishmen were well aware; for the very institutions that were charged with ensuring social stability were widely perceived as instruments of social advancement and, indeed, were widely used as such. As W. K. Jordan has pointed out, the newly wealthy landowners and merchants who contributed so generously to schools and colleges out of philanthropic and humanitarian motives were not above using those schools and colleges to further their own ideas, to say nothing of the careers of their children. And, as Michael Walzer has made abundantly clear, the patriarchal family projected by William Gouge, the purified church projected by William Perkins, and the "school of the prophets" projected by Sir Walter Mildmay were explicitly charged with developing new forms of character and community, well defined but patently at variance with tradition. Of course, Gouge, Perkins, and Mildmay envisioned a world which would eventually be thoroughly disciplined, that is, once it had been brought into being; but there is no missing the radicalism of that world, when measured against the standard of contemporary England—or, indeed, the instability and turmoil that would inevitably attend its creation.[4]

However much this paradox strained the educational institutions of England, it proved even more unsettling in the colonies. For there, the tensions inherent in change were compounded by the distance from the metropolis, the unfamiliarity of the environment, the newness of the communities, and the ever-present threat of barbarism. However difficult it was for metropolitan Englishmen to define and cultivate piety, civility, and learning, it was even more so for colonial Englishmen. For, though the need may have seemed

4 W. K. Jordan, *Philanthropy in England, 1480-1660* (London: George Allen & Unwin, 1959); and Michael Walzer, *The Revolution of the Saints* (Cambridge, Mass.: Harvard University Press, 1965).

greater to the colonists, given their determination to preserve civilization in the wilderness, the goals themselves were less clear, and their attainment more problematical.

In effect, then, all the uncertainties and instabilities of the Old World were involved in the transit of civilization to the New. They were involved selectively, to be sure, but they were involved nonetheless. The transit of civilization was a transit of institutions in motion and under stress. As these were tried and tested in the colonial situation, some proved viable and took root, some were quickly transformed, some withered and died. As Edward Eggleston himself once remarked, nothing in human history is educed *ex nihilo,* and the institutions of late Renaissance England were the stuff of which colonial society was made: they formed the paradigms with which the colonists began, however imperfect their clarity and however irrelevant their goals.[5]

[5] Edward Eggleston, *The Transit of Civilization from England to America in the Seventeenth Century* (New York: D. Appleton and Company, 1900), p. 231.

Chapter 4

HOUSEHOLD

The original then of state and church being the family, they are
both, in that respect, concerned in it; yea as the family is an
original to states and churches, in their essentials, so also in
their morals, in their manners. As that nursery is better or worse,
and the plants thereof of more or less worth, so are both the
orchards of state and church, (Cantic. 4. 12.) which are thence
stored with trees, better or worse, and their fruits more or less
wholesome; if that school be but well ordered, and the lesser
scholars in it well principled and grounded, (Prov. 4. 4.) those
which afterwards come to be made use of, for more eminent use
and service, in state and church, they will be the more precious
ornaments to them both.

THOMAS COBBETT

In the beginning there was the family. In the Christian West, it was
traditionally monogamous, patriarchal, and, at least until the early
modern era, inclusive of other than blood relatives. It provided food
and clothing, succor and shelter; it conferred social standing, economic possibility, and religious affiliation; and it served from time
to time as church, playground, factory, army, and court. In addition,
it was almost always a school, proffering to the young their earliest
ideas about the nature of the world and how one ought to behave
in it.

Our knowledge of the family in early Renaissance England is at
best fragmentary. We know most, of course, about those selected
segments of society that left written records, particularly the great
noble families that constituted the court, the powerful gentry families that occupied the manor houses of the country shires, and the

rising merchant families that tended to cluster in and around the thriving cities of London, Bristol, and Norwich. An Italian surveying the London scene in the time of Henry VII had only criticism for what seemed to him the utter callousness of such families in the nurture and rearing of their young. "The want of affection in the English is strongly manifested towards their children," he wrote; "for after having kept them at home till they arrive at the age of seven or nine years at the utmost, they put them out, both males and females, to hard service in the houses of other people, binding them generally for another seven or nine years. And these are called apprentices, and during that time they perform all the most menial offices; and few are born who are exempted from this fate, for everyone, however rich he may be, sends away his children into the houses of others, whilst he, in return, receives those of strangers into his own. And on inquiring their reason for this severity, they answered that they did it in order that their children might learn better manners."[1]

For the nobility and gentry, the putting out of children was obviously a holdover from the older chivalric education, which was actually declining during the early Tudor era, though many were prepared to agree with the observation of Sir John Fortescue that the royal household would always be "the supreme academy for the nobles of the realm, and a school of vigor, probity, and manners by which the realm is honored and will flourish." There, the scions of the nobility joined the royal princes under the tutelage of the master of the henchmen, who instructed them in riding, jousting, singing, dancing, religion, manners, and a smattering of languages. The royal household was clearly the model for lesser castles and manor houses, where the master or some trusted retainer might lead boys informally through much the same curriculum, guided perhaps by a manual such as Ramón Lull's *Book of the Ordre of Chyvalry*, printed by William Caxton in 1485 in an effort to rekindle a dying interest in the older ideals of knighthood. For the merchants, the putting out of children was an effort to introduce selected youngsters into the ranks of the gentry and to ensure a livelihood for others. And the fact that sons did not universally follow in their fathers' occupations

---

[1] *A Relation, or Rather a True Account, of the Island of England*, translated by Charlotta Augusta Sneyd, Camden Society Publications, no. 37 (London: John Bowyer Nichols and Son, 1847), pp. 24-25. The term "apprentice" was less generic than here implied, referring only to those bound out specifically to learn a trade or the profession of law.

merely heightened the significance of this particular form of household education.[2]

We know far less about the families of the vast body of early Tudor Englishmen who lived on the land, such insights as we have deriving indirectly from censuses, records of land tenure, and contemporary representations of houses, farms, and villages. The painstaking work of W. G. Hoskins, however, on the social and economic history of Leicestershire, has yielded a wealth of significant information. The typical Leicestershire farm family lived in a one-room cottage built around a hearth and perhaps divided by a partition into a chamber and a hall or kitchen area. Close by were commonly a barn or stable, a variety of hovels or outhouses, and a garden or orchard; together, these constituted the physical household in the village, as opposed to the farm itself, which comprised designated strips in the surrounding fields. Those who pursued crafts and trades in the village—the bakers, coopers, grocers, and chandlers—generally did so while managing a farm, and hence carried on their craftsmanship and commerce within the confines of the household. Familial education involved a process of imitation and explanation, within one's own home or someone else's, and was supplemented by regular instruction tendered by the local parson and by such sporadic instruction as might be proffered by itinerant peddlers, preachers, vagabonds, and minstrels.[3]

[2] *Ibid.*, p. 39; and Sir John Fortescue, *De laudibus legum Anglie* (written 1468-1471), translated and edited by S. B. Chrimes (Cambridge: Cambridge University Press, 1942), p. 111. For examples of later fifteenth-century manuscripts dealing with the substance of household education, see *The Babees' Book: Medieval Manners for the Young: Done into Modern English from Dr. Furnivall's Texts by Edith Rickert* (London: Chatto & Windus, 1923). For allusions to "young gentlemen" undergoing education in an early sixteenth-century household, see *The Regulations and Establishment of the Houshold of Henry Algernon Percy, the Fifth Earl of Northumberland, at His Castles of Wresill and Lekinfield, in Yorkshire* (London: no publisher, 1770). For insights into gentry family life, see *The Paston Letters,* edited by James Gairdner (6 vols.; London: Chatto and Windus, 1904), and *Plumpton Correspondence: A Series of Letters, Chiefly Domestick, Written in the Reigns of Edward IV, Richard III, Henry VII, and Henry VIII,* edited by Thomas Stapleton, Camden Society Publications, no. 4 (London: John Bowyer Nichols and Son, 1839). For insights into merchant family life, see *The Cely Papers: Selections from the Correspondence and Memoranda of the Cely Family, Merchants of the Staple, A.D. 1475-1488,* edited by Henry Elliot Malden, Camden Society Publications, 3d ser., no. 1 (London: Longmans, Green, and Co., 1900). For allusions to the education of well-born women in the later fifteenth century, see *Paston Letters,* II, 237; IV, 213; V, 93; a prime sixteenth-century example, of course, is Anne Boleyn, who was sent by Sir Thomas to Brussels at the age of seven to learn courtesy under the tutelage of Margaret of Savoy.

[3] W. G. Hoskins, *Essays in Leicestershire History* (Liverpool: University Press of Liverpool, 1950), chap. ii; *The Midland Peasant* (London: The Macmillan Co., 1957), chap. v; and *Provincial England* (London: The Macmillan Co., 1963), chap. x.

The actual size and structure of the early Renaissance family are difficult to determine, though it is evident that there was considerable variation from one class to another and from the rural midlands to metropolitan London. There is far more specific information for the later decades of the era and, indeed, for the seventeenth century as a whole, deriving largely from the recent researches of Peter Laslett, E. A. Wrigley, and their colleagues in the Cambridge Group for the Study of Population and Social Structure. Relying primarily on parish records of births, marriages, and deaths, these investigators have come up with fairly precise data on the size and composition of the yeoman, artisan, and laboring families that constituted the greater part of early modern English society. These ranged in size from one or two members to a dozen or more, though they tended to average somewhere between four and five. Moreover, the large majority were nuclear families, that is, they included parents and children and frequently one or more apprentices and servants, but rarely either grandparents or great-grandparents. The following data from the village of Cogenhoe in Northamptonshire for the period between 1616 and 1628 and from the village of Goodnestone-next-Wingham in Kent for 1676 are revealing. While one can scarcely generalize from two villages, we do know that the average size of a household at Stafford in 1622 was 4.02, at Litchfield in 1688, 4.66, at Stoke-on-Trent in 1701, 4.39, and in thirty-three villages of Kent in 1705, 4.47[4]

As can be seen from the figures for Goodnestone-next-Wingham, the families of yeomen tended to be larger than the families of tradesmen, laborers, and the "poor," and those of the gentry tended to be largest of all. This latter fact is borne out by a number of studies indicating that the gentry household commonly included not only husband, wife, and biological children but also grandparents and great-grandparents, wards, household officers, companions (who were sometimes blood relatives), and diverse servants. Members of

4 Peter Laslett and John Harrison, "Clayworth and Cogenhoe," in H. E. Bell and R. L. Ollard, eds., *Historical Essays, 1600-1750, Presented to David Ogg* (New York: Barnes and Noble, 1963), pp. 176, 166; and Peter Laslett, *The World We Have Lost* (London: Methuen and Company, 1965), p. 64. The statistics for gentry households in Goodnestone-next-Wingham have been corrected here on the basis of correspondence with Mr. Laslett and Miss Anne Whiteman, on whose work the table is based. W. G. Hoskins estimates that the average size of a household at Wigston Magna in 1603 was somewhere between 4.25 and 4.75 (*Provincial England*, p. 188). See also Peter Laslett, "Size and Structure of Household in England over Three Centuries," *Population Studies*, XXIII (1969-70), 199-223.

COGENHOE 1616-1628

Date	Total Population	Numbers of Households
1616	187	32
1618	185	33
1620 (May 30)	150	30
1621 (June 29)	154	31
1623	174	34
1624 (Aug. 15)	176	33
1628	180	33

GOODNESTONE–NEXT–WINGHAM 1676

Status of Households	Numbers of Households	Sizes of Households	Numbers of Persons	Numbers of Children	Numbers of Servants	Mean Sizes of Households
Gentry	3	2, 3, 23	28	7	16	9.3
Yeoman	26	2-12	151	64	34	5.8
Tradesman	9	1-8	35	16	2	3.9
Laborer	12	2-6	38	15	0	3.2
Poor	12	1-6	25	11	0	2.1
	62	1-23	277	118	52	4.47

the gentry tended to marry young and to produce more children per marriage, of whom more survived to adulthood. We continue to know less than we might about the families of merchants, lawyers, doctors, clergymen, and administrators, who constituted the semi-independent, occupational hierarchies on the periphery of the formal status system. What information we do have indicates that such families tended to be basically nuclear, though they were frequently a bit larger than average, owing to the presence of one or more relatives or servants.[5]

[5] Peter Laslett, "The Gentry of Kent in 1640," *The Cambridge Historical Journal*, IX (1947), 148-164; W. G. Hoskins, "The Estates of the Caroline Gentry," in W. G. Hoskins and H. P. R. Finberg, *Devonshire Studies* (London: Jonathan Cape, 1952), pp. 334-365; Francis Squire, "The English Country Gentleman in the Early Seventeenth Century" (unpublished doctoral thesis, Yale University, 1935); and Jerome Frank Brown, "Five Somerset Families, 1590-1640" (unpublished doctoral thesis, University of California, Los Angeles, 1966). Since we can assume that in a hierarchical society such as Renaissance England the 4 to 5 per cent of the population that constituted the well-born would tend to defer to the styles and models of its most prestigious segment, the titled peerage, Lawrence Stone's carefully drawn portrait of the aristocracy during

Whatever their size and composition, English families of every rank were inevitably caught up in the social and intellectual turbulence of the Renaissance; and, as their habitual patterns of thought and conduct became more problematical in the face of rapid change, the substance of what they taught their children was altered accordingly. Furthermore, there were changes in the nature of the family itself, which had far-reaching consequences. Chief among these, as Philippe Ariès has persuasively argued, was the invention of the idea of childhood. Whereas in the medieval world the years between birth and adulthood were an ill-defined period during which the infant was being nursed and therefore unable to take his place in society, in the Renaissance that period was increasingly delineated as a separate and desirable stage of the life cycle, with its own requirements and its own activities. Children began to dress in a characteristic mode; they began to appear as subjects in paintings and sculpture; and they began to be identified with a new literature specifically addressed to their needs. Moreover, the family, as the principal nursery and protector of children, took on added significance, with a resultant sharpening of the lines that distinguished it from other social institutions. And, in the course of this demarcation, both the traditional practice of placing children in other families and the informal education that derived from growing up in a village or town gave way to the deliberate domestic nurture preached in the conduct manuals. Among the gentry, the girls, and perhaps the eldest son, were increasingly kept at home for their education, often under a tutor, though the younger sons continued to be sent off as servants in other households (later, younger sons would attend nearby grammar schools or one of the colleges or Inns of Court). And, among yeomen, tradesmen, and professionals, the home became the scene of systematic training of a literary, religious, or technical character.[6]

While this newly significant household education doubtless em-

---

the period between the accession of Elizabeth I and the Revolution is also relevant: more than half the nobles Stone studied were under twenty-two at the time of their first marriage, and more than three-quarters were under twenty-five, as compared with an average marriage age of around twenty-six for the general population. See Lawrence Stone, *The Crisis of the Aristocracy, 1558-1641* (Oxford: Clarendon Press, 1965), chaps. ii, xi.

6 Philippe Ariès, *Centuries of Childhood*, translated by Robert Baldick (New York: Alfred A. Knopf, 1962); and Lawrence Stone, "The Educational Revolution in England, 1560-1640," *Past & Present*, no. 28 (July, 1964), pp. 41-80. For the literature available to "middling people," see Louis B. Wright, *Middle-Class Culture in Elizabethan England* (Chapel Hill: University of North Carolina Press, 1935).

braced the entire range of knowledge, values, and tastes that constituted the "common sense" of the era—we have seen it in one version in *The French Academie*—at least three things about it are notable. First, it remained overwhelmingly oral in character, despite the abundance of printed materials that were issuing from the English and Continental presses (one should bear in mind that the availability of printed matter varied greatly from one social stratum to another and from one region to another). Second, it was, of course, local, and therefore exceedingly variegated in substance, though there were growing areas of commonality deriving from increased communication among families (again, one should bear in mind that there was more communication among the gentry and professionals than among husbandmen and artisans). And third, it became distressingly precarious in mood, at least among yeomen, merchants, certain professionals, and the lesser gentry, who combined the values of social striving with the insecurities of social success and in the process often found themselves searching beyond the household for authoritative guides to familial thought and conduct.

In any case, the role of the family as systematic educator was both emphasized and enlarged by Tudor social policy. On the religious side, the Tudors reaffirmed the traditional responsibility of the Christian family for the elementary spiritual instruction of youth. Thus, the Royal Injunctions of Henry VIII (1536) charged parsons, vicars, and other curates diligently to "admonish the fathers and mothers, masters and governors of youth, being under their care, to teach, or cause to be taught, their children and servants, even from their infancy, their Pater Noster, the Articles of our Faith, and the Ten Commandments, in their mother tongue: and the same so taught, shall cause the said youth oft to repeat and understand." The clergy were instructed in turn to ease the parental burden by discussing the required materials in their regular sermons and by assisting families in obtaining printed texts of the materials for use at home. Similar charges, casting the parent as religious teacher of his family with the vernacular primer as his guide, were repeated in the Injunctions of Edward VI (1547) and Elizabeth I (1559) and were expounded in scores of piety manuals and devotional books. The household was to be a school of religion, with the clergy encouraging and overseeing the instruction.[7]

7 Walter Howard Frere and William McClure Kennedy, eds., *Visitation Articles and Injunctions of the Period of the Reformation*, Alcuin Club Collections, vols. XIV-XVI (3 vols.; London: Longmans, Green & Co., 1910), II, 6-7, 116; and Henry Gee and William John Hardy, eds., *Documents Illustrative of English Church History* (London:

The Royal Injunctions of Henry VIII also required fathers, mothers, masters, and governors to "bestow their children and servants, even from their childhood, either to learning, or to some other honest exercise, occupation or husbandry: exhorting, counseling, and by all the ways and means they may, as well in their said sermons and collations, as other ways persuading the said fathers, mothers, masters, and other governors, being under their cure and charge, diligently to provide and foresee that the said youth be in no manner wise kept or brought up in idleness, lest any time afterward they be driven, for lack of some mystery or occupation to live by, to fall to begging, stealing, or some other unthriftiness; for as much as we may daily see, through sloth and idleness, divers valiant men fall, some to begging and some to theft and murder, which after, brought to calamity and misery, impute a great part thereof to their friends and governors, which suffered them to be brought up so idly in their youth; where if they had been well educated and brought up in some good literature, occupation, or mystery, they should, being rulers of their own family, have profited, as well themselves as divers other persons, to the great commodity and ornament of the commonwealth." This admonition, repeated in somewhat altered form in the Injunctions of Edward VI, represented a patent effort to render household education an instrument of social stability and economic development by linking it to the traditional institution of apprenticeship.[8]

Actually, English apprenticeship had grown up within the guilds over a period of some three hundred years, and by the sixteenth century had acquired a considerable body of customary practices and procedures. But it remained for two highly significant pieces of Elizabethan legislation—the Statute of Artificers of 1563 and the Poor Law of 1601—to regularize these procedures and convert them into a phase of national economic policy. In effect, the Statute of Artificers gave the force of parliamentary law to certain conventions of the trades, using the traditions of the city of London as a model. A preamble stated the need to readjust wage standards and to codify the legislation dealing with employment of servants and apprentices

Macmillan and Co., 1896), p. 420. It is interesting to note that diocesan injunctions by and large repeat the charge to the clergy to teach the laity the elements of Christianity but not the charge to parents and masters, indicating, perhaps, a measure of disenchantment with the promise of formal familial training.

8 Frere and Kennedy, eds., *Visitation Articles and Injunctions*, II, 7-8, 116-117.

(much of this legislation was outdated or at least contradictory, and it varied from place to place and from trade to trade); and then the body of the law went on, in a series of lengthy and detailed regulations, to combine the most pertinent of the customary practices into a general statutory policy. Two sets of provisions stood at the heart of the effort: the first called for compulsory service in husbandry of all persons between the ages of twelve and sixty who were not otherwise employed, thereby establishing the principle of no living without a calling; the second formally established the apprenticeship period as seven years and explicitly defined the responsibilities and prerogatives of master and apprentice during the course of that period.[9]

At the very least, these provisions established a set of common regulations for the realm, clearly designed to guarantee an adequate labor supply to domestic entrepreneurs (the regulations would later be dubbed "mercantilist"). But, in addition, they inaugurated what was destined to become the characteristic Tudor policy of using education, largely within the household, as a device for contending with certain pressing social problems—pauperism, unemployment, alienation from the land. The real genius of the arrangement lay in its mode of recruitment to the trades: as is often the case with education, apprenticeship became at once an instrument of social control and a vehicle for social mobility. Through it, selected individuals were placed in familial situations during a good part of their young adulthood and equipped with the skills that would later enable them to become householders, entrepreneurs, and freemen in their own right.

In yet another way, apprenticeship became a means of relieving poverty; implicit in the Statute of Artificers, the idea lay at the heart of the Poor Law of 1601. That law climaxed a succession of efforts, dating from 1536, to deal with the large group of vagrant persons who had lost their traditional place on the land through the enclosures of the sixteenth century. What the evolving policy sought was to limit their mobility—restrictions on itinerant begging, for example, would complement the commitment to compulsory husbandry—and at the same time set as many of them as possible to

---

[9] For the Statute of Artificers (5 Eliz. I, c. iv, *The Statutes at Large* [9 vols.; London: printed for Mark Basket, 1763-1765], II, 535-543), see R. H. Tawney and Eileen Power, eds., *Tudor Economic Documents* (3 vols.; London: Longmans, Green and Co., 1924), I, 338-350.

work at low-level crafts and trades. The Poor Law of 1601, like the Statute of Artificers, both regularized and nationalized this policy. Each parish was instructed to designate overseers of the poor, who would have the power to levy taxes for the establishment of workhouses, where the impoverished could contribute to the development of England's nascent industries, notably textile manufacturing, and to assign poor children to these workhouses as apprentices (the workhouses would thus supersede their families as the primary agencies of their education).[10]

The twin thrusts of this Elizabethan legislation were characteristic for the age. The Statute of Artificers assumed the primacy of the household as an educative agency and provided that all England be subject to its stabilizing influence, while the Poor Law of 1601 recognized the need for adjuncts to the household—and occasionally surrogates—in the form of workhouses. Simultaneously, the newly self-conscious families of the merchants and gentry began to contribute unprecedented amounts of money to schools and colleges. That they did so was in no way a denial of familial concern for education but rather an affirmation of that concern, which granted that, however responsible the family might feel, it could not perform the task alone in the kind of society that was coming into being, especially if it had ambitions for its children. Hence, what seems a paradox of the late Renaissance is really no paradox at all: it was a time of expanding familial responsibility for education, and it was a time of institution building as well; but the two phenomena were complementary rather than contradictory, and were seen as such by those contemporaries who cared about education and carried it on.[11]

10 For the text of the Poor Law of 1601 (43 Eliz. I, c. ii, *Statutes at Large*, II, 702-705), see Edgar W. Knight, ed., *A Documentary History of Education in the South Before 1860* (5 vols.; Chapel Hill: University of North Carolina Press, 1949-1953), I, 37-45. For the text of the Poor Law of 1597 (39 Eliz. I, c. iii, *Statutes at Large*, II, 684-687), which embodied many of the same provisions, see Tawney and Power, eds., *Tudor Economic Documents*, II, 346-354. For the general policy of the state toward destitute children, see I. Pinchbeck, "The State and the Child in Sixteenth-Century England," *The British Journal of Sociology*, VII (1956), 273-285; VIII (1957), 59-74.

11 I am obviously taking issue here with Ariès (*Centuries of Childhood*, pp. 365-415), arguing against his somewhat simplistic view of "the substitution of the school for apprenticeship" in favor of a conception of school and apprenticeship standing in new and complementary relationships to the natural family. That apprenticeship declined in England certainly had as much to do with the decline of the guilds and the development of a capitalist economy as with the "triumph of domesticity." See O. Jocelyn Dunlop, *English Apprenticeship & Child Labor* (New York: The Macmillan Company, 1912), chap. viii.

II

Dutchmen, Frenchmen, Swedes, Finns, and Walloons notwithstanding, it was predominantly Englishmen who peopled the colonies. But it was not a truly representative cross-section of England that came, and this is important to bear in mind in studying the transplanting of institutions. However active the nobility and elite gentry may have been in sponsoring and financing the colonizing enterprises, few members of these classes actually immigrated, and some who did stayed only temporarily as representatives of the Crown. The lesser gentry, the merchants, and the professionals were somewhat better represented and, indeed, exercised an influence out of proportion to their numbers during the initial decades of settlement. By far the greatest number of migrants were "middling people"— yeomen, husbandmen, artisans, and tradesmen—who acquired their own farms and shops either immediately or after a brief period of indentured servitude. Finally, there were the unskilled laborers, many of whom did not even come voluntarily; virtually all such laborers arrived in some sort of indentured status, though it is important to note that this class never constituted a majority of the indentured servants.

Colonial society, then, was generally representative of contemporary English society, though it had a comparative preponderance of middling people and a comparative paucity of the well-born and the absolutely unskilled. Not unexpectedly, colonial communities comprised a broad range of contemporary familial styles, again with a comparative preponderance of nuclear families characteristic of middling Englishmen and a comparative paucity of both large upper-class households and vagrant unattached laborers. To be sure, the colonists brought with them English ideas of degree, priority, and prestige; and, when they had the wherewithal, many strove to imitate the gentry, in family style as in everything else. Hence, the early acceptance in the colonies of two paradigms, one formed by the accepted norm of the nuclear household, the other formed by the prestigious ideal of the extended household. And hence, too, the coexistence there of nuclear families that spawned additional nuclear families, of extended families that remained extended over several generations, of nuclear families that in a generation or two acquired sufficient land and maintained sufficient stability to become extended, as younger sons and daughters married but remained in the vicinity of the patriarchal household, and of extended families that in a few generations became nuclear, as younger sons and daughters struck out on their own.[12]

Whatever the variation in the size and character of these families, it is clear that their educational responsibilities were both augmented and intensified by the New World situation. The colonists were heir to Renaissance traditions stressing the centrality of the household as the primary agency of human association and education; and they were instructed—indeed harangued—by Puritan tracts and sermons proclaiming the correctness and significance of those traditions. Moreover, at the very time that the need for education seemed most urgent, given the threat of barbarism implicit in the wilderness, they found themselves with far less access than their metropolitan contemporaries to churches, schools, colleges, and other institutions that might share the task. In short, they were Renaissance Englishmen of Puritan loyalties—or at least propensities —who were frightened; and the result was an increased familial responsibility for education, both imposed from without and assumed from within.

The imposition from without came in the form of statutes legally compelling households to do what in England they had long been accustomed to doing. An oft-cited example is the Massachusetts law of 1642 empowering the selectmen of each town "to take account from time to time of all parents and masters, and of their children, concerning their calling and employment of their children, especially of their ability to read and understand the principles of religion and the capital laws of this country," and authorizing them, with the

12 For brief sketches of nuclear middling families, see Edward Spaulding Perzel, "The First Generation of Settlement in Colonial Ipswich, Massachusetts, 1633-1660" (unpublished doctoral thesis, Rutgers University, 1967). For the process by which selected nuclear families evolved into extended households over several generations, see Philip J. Greven, Jr., *Four Generations: Population, Land, and Family in Colonial Andover, Massachusetts* (Ithaca: Cornell University Press, 1970). For portraits of an extended family of Old England that evolved over several generations in New England into nuclear but high-status households, see Robert C. Black III, *The Younger John Winthrop* (New York: Columbia University Press, 1966), Lawrence Shaw Mayo, *The Winthrop Family in America* (Boston: Massachusetts Historical Society, 1948), and Richard S. Dunn, *Puritans and Yankees: The Winthrop Dynasty of New England, 1630-1717* (Princeton: Princeton University Press, 1962). For instances of extended families persisting over several generations, see Louis B. Wright, *The First Gentlemen of Virginia* (San Marino, Calif.: The Huntington Library, 1940).

consent of any court or magistrate, to "put forth apprentices the children of such as they shall [find] not to be able and fit to employ and bring them up." The statute was more than an affirmation of the value of education per se; it came as part of a vigorous legislative effort to increase the political and economic self-sufficiency of the colony. And, significantly, the responsibility for encouraging and overseeing familial education, which had been held by the clergy under the various Royal Injunctions of the Tudor era, was now vested in the selectmen.[13]

Connecticut passed similar legislation in 1650, requiring that children and servants be taught to read English, that they be instructed in the capital laws, that they be catechized weekly, and that they be brought up in husbandry or some trade profitable to themselves and to the commonwealth. New Haven followed suit in 1655, New York in 1665 (the Duke's Laws, after all, were "collected out of the several laws now in force in His Majesty's American colonies and plantations"), and Plymouth in 1671. And, in 1683, an ordinance of the new colony of Pennsylvania provided that all parents and guardians of children "shall cause such to be instructed in reading and writing, so that they may be able to read the Scriptures and to write by the time they attain to twelve years of age; and that then they be taught some useful trade or skill, that the poor may work to live, and the rich, if they become poor, may not want; of which every county court shall take care." Virginia dealt with the matter less directly but no less firmly, by requiring parents and masters to send their children and servants to weekly religious instruction at local churches, by ordering churchwardens to present "such masters and mistresses as shall be delinquents in the catechizing the youth and ignorant persons," and by imposing a substantial fine on parents and masters for failure to comply.[14]

13 Nathaniel B. Shurtleff, ed., *Records of the Governor and Company of the Massachusetts Bay in New England* (5 vols.; Boston: William White, 1853-1854), II, 6-7. It is significant that the 1642 legislation was enacted within months after the laws of the colony had been printed and a catechism prepared under the auspices of the general court.

14 J. Hammond Trumbull, ed. [vols. I-III], *The Public Records of the Colony of Connecticut* (15 vols.; Hartford: publisher varies, 1850-1890), I, 520-521. The Connecticut statute was based on a 1648 version of the Massachusetts law of 1642. See *The Book of the General Lawes and Libertyes Concerning the Inhabitants of the Massachusets, Collected Out of the Records of the General Court for the Several Years Wherein They Were Made and Established* (Cambridge, Mass.: printed according to order of the General Court, 1648), pp. 11-12, and Charles J. Hoadly, ed., *Records of the Colony or Jurisdiction of New Haven, from May, 1653, to the Union* (Hartford: Case, Lockwood

With respect to apprenticeship, there were numerous laws authorizing the putting out of children whose parents were not "able and fit to employ and bring them up," as well as various statutes providing for the public purchase of tools and raw materials for apprentices to use in their work. In addition, there was occasional legislation seeking to force unmarried persons into service within households, or at least into residence within households, and defining minimum standards for the maintenance of households. But the Statute of Artificers itself was never duplicated in the colonies, and the Poor Law of 1601 was explicitly incorporated only in Virginia.[15]

These laws relating to household education are best viewed as essentially normative but only partially descriptive, and we shall never know precisely the extent to which they were actually honored or obeyed. From time to time, one or another of the Massachusetts towns would crack down on parents and masters whose dependents remained ignorant and illiterate, and in 1668 the general court, sensing widespread social discontent, felt obliged to re-enact the law of 1642 and remind the selectmen of their responsibilities under it. On the other hand, there is no evidence that any Virginia parent was ever fined five hundred pounds of tobacco for failing to send his children to religious instruction, as ordered in the law of 1646. Throughout the colonies, the most common relevant judicial actions were those dealing with apprenticeship contracts or with the oversight of orphans or other public dependents.[16]

In any case, there is every indication that the colonial household was even more important as an agency of education than its metro-

---

and Company, 1858), pp. 583-584. "Lawes Establisht by the Authority of His Majesties Letters Patents, Granted to His Royall Highnes James Duke of Yorke and Albany," *Collections of the New-York Historical Society*, I (1809), 307, 334-335; *The Generall Laws and Liberties of New-Plimouth Colony* (Cambridge, Mass.: no publisher, 1672), pp. 26-27; Staughton George, Thomas McCamant, and Benjamin M. Nead, eds., *Charter to William Penn, and Laws of the Province of Pennsylvania, Passed Between the Years 1682 and 1700* (Harrisburg: Lane S. Hart, 1879), p. 142; and William Waller Hening, ed., *The Statutes at Large; Being a Collection of All the Laws of Virginia, from the First Session of the Legislature, in the Year 1619* (13 vols.; imprint varies, 1819-1823), I, 156, 157, 181, 311-312. None of the Virginia requirements appears in the revisal of 1661-62 (*ibid.*, II, 41-162) or in later codes.

15 Shurtleff, ed., *Records of the Governor and Company of Massachusetts*, II, 6-7; Hoadly, ed., *New Haven Colonial Records, from May, 1653, to the Union*, pp. 608-609; and Hening, ed., *Statutes at Large; Being a Collection of All the Laws of Virginia*, I, 336-337; II, 298; IV, 209-210.

16 Shurtleff, ed., *Records of the Governor and Company of Massachusetts*, IV, ii, 395-396. Note the role assigned to the constables in the enforcement of the 1668 statute and the similar role assigned to the newly created tithingmen in 1679 (*ibid.*, V, 240-241).

politan counterpart. As in England, it was the fundamental unit of social organization, serving simultaneously as a center of human association, a producer of food and manufactured articles, and a focus of religious life. Colonial houses were for the most part small and almost always crowded; and, though they provided the family itself with a measure of privacy, they afforded little privacy to the individuals within the family. In their most elemental form, they simply combined sleeping space with living space. The sleeping space comprised one or more bedchambers, in which parents, children, lodgers, servants, and occasional visitors mingled—two, three, or four to a room and often two, three, or four to a bed. The living space was the kitchen, an all-purpose area revolving around a hearth, which might at any time be the scene of eating, working, or playing, cooking, baking, or brewing, knitting, spinning, or weaving, the dipping of candles, the saying of prayers, or the reading of books.

As in England, too, the diurnal business of getting a living was in most households an extension of the activities of the kitchen. On farms, the master of the family and his sons, perhaps with the assistance of a servant or two, worked the fields of rye, wheat, hay, corn, and tobacco, frequently using scythes, hoes, sickles, and shovels that had been fashioned within the home. More often than not, the women managed the several enclosures that constituted the home lot—barnyard, cattleyard, pigpen, garden, and orchard. But there was no sharp division of labor; and, in times of sickness or need, everyone did everything, not only during the busy periods of planting and harvesting, but in the late autumn and early winter, when there was equipment to be repaired, manure to be spread, grain to be threshed, and corn to be husked.

Similarly, shopkeepers and artisans used either part of the home itself or additional houses or sheds on the "homelot" area to pursue their trades. Indeed, farms and shops were often combined, in New England, where a town tradesman might own and cultivate strips of outlying acreage (or have them cultivated by sons, servants, or tenants), as well as in Virginia, where the combination of farm and shop was frequently dictated by the sparseness of settlement. Thus, for example, the extensive and diversified activities at Denbigh, the estate of Captain Samuel Mathews on the north side of the James between Deep Creek and Warwick River: "He hath a fine house, and all things answerable to it, he sows yearly store of hemp and flax, and causes it to be spun; he keeps weavers and has a tanhouse, causes leather to be dressed, has eight shoemakers employed in their trade, has forty Negro servants, brings them up to trades in his house: he yearly sows abundance of wheat, barley, etc. The wheat he selleth at four shillings the bushel; kills store of beavers, and sells them to victual the ships when they come thither; has abundance of kine, a brave dairy, swine great store, and poultry."[17]

Whatever the extent of specialization—and it must have been greater in Captain Mathews' household than in most—the opportunities for varied learning amid such surroundings were legion. One saw and heard and took part as soon as one was able; indeed, given the lack of privacy and the burden of necessity, there was literally no escape from learning. The labor of each child was required as early as possible, and, in the nature of things, the everyday activities of the household provided a continuous general apprenticeship in the diverse arts of living.[18]

But, beyond this, the household was also the scene of a good deal of sustained and systematic instruction. In the first place, there was reading, which was as commonly learned at home as anywhere, both in England and in the colonies. "My younger days were attended with the follies and vanities incident to youth," John Cotton's grandson Josiah (1680-1756) noted in his diary; "howsoever I quickly learned to read, without going to any school I remember." The experience was characteristic in an age when it was assumed that a youngster ready to undertake formal classwork would have a certain rudimentary ability to read in the vernacular. Once again, the evidence is fragmentary, but there is every indication that individual reading, responsive reading, and communal reading were daily activities in many colonial households, and that reading was often taught on an each-one-teach-one basis by parents or other elders, or by siblings or peers. For youngsters growing up in homes in which no one was equipped to teach reading, there was frequently a neigh-

---

17 *A Perfect Description of Virginia* (London: printed for Richard Wodenoth, 1649), in Peter Force, ed., *Tracts and Other Papers, Relating Principally to the Origin, Settlement, and Progress of the Colonies in North America, from the Discovery of the Country to the Year 1776* (4 vols.; Washington, D.C.: Peter Force, 1836-1846), vol. II, no. 8, pp. 14-15.

18 It is interesting to note that, unlike contemporary European representations, colonial portraits of children tended to differentiate them less sharply from adults by dress and stance. But this may be more a reflection of the artists' folk style than of the reality they portrayed. See Mary Black and Jean Lipman, *American Folk Painting* (New York: Clarkson N. Potter, 1966), pp. 1-15, and Madge Garland, *The Changing Face of Childhood* (New York: October House, 1963).

boring household where they might acquire the skill. And, indeed, when an occasional New England goodwife decided to teach reading on a regular basis in her kitchen and charge a modest fee, she thereby became a "dame school"; or, when an occasional Virginia family decided to have a servant (or tutor) undertake the task for its own and perhaps some neighbors' children, the servant became a "petty school." Such enterprises were schools, to be sure, but they were also household activities, and the easy shading of one into the other is a significant educational fact of the seventeenth century.[19]

In the teaching of reading, a family might use a textbook like Edmund Coote's *The English Schoole-Maister* (1596); or a simple hornbook or ABC, which presented the alphabet, a few syllables combining a consonant with a vowel, and a prayer or grace, usually the Lord's Prayer or the Apostles' Creed; or perhaps some combination of hornbook or ABC and primer or catechism, a primer being an elementary book of religious material usually including the Lord's Prayer, the Apostles' Creed, and the Decalogue, a catechism being a series of questions and answers setting forth the fundamentals of religious belief. *The English Schoole-Maister* was the most formal: it was addressed "unto the unskillful, which desire to make use of it for their own private benefit: and unto such men and women of trades (as tailors, weavers, shopkeepers, seamsters, and such other) as have undertaken the charge of teaching others"; and it went systematically from letters, syllables, and words, to sentences, paragraphs, and colloquies. The hornbook, ABC, primer, and catechism, on the other hand, were the most characteristic: they were addressed to the same untutored audience as *The English Schoole-Maister*, but they were explicitly tied to the oral tradition of the liturgy, the characteristic thing about them being that they taught the art of reading using passages with which the learner was probably familiar. This was equally true of the Bible itself, which was fre-

[19] "Extracts from the Diary of Josiah Cotton," *Publications of the Colonial Society of Massachusetts*, XXVI (1927), 278. For references to "dame schools," see, *inter alia*, "The Commonplace Book of Joseph Green (1675-1715)," *ibid.*, XXXIV (1943), 236, and "Autobiography of the Rev. John Barnard" (1766), *Collections of the Massachusetts Historical Society*, 3d ser., V (1836), 178. The phrase "petty schools" is used in *Perfect Description of Virginia*, p. 15. That "dame schools" and "petty schools" were interchangeable terms is suggested by Charles Hoole's observation in *A New Discovery of the Old Art of Teaching School* (London: Andrew Crook, 1660), p. 59: "The petty school is the place where indeed the first principles of all religion and learning ought to be taught, and therefore rather deserveth that more encouragement should be given to the teachers of it, than that it should be left as a work for poor women, or others, whose necessities compel them to undertake it, as a mere shelter from beggary."

quently used as a reading text. Doubtless many a colonial youngster learned to read by mastering the letters and syllables phonetically and then hearing Scriptural passages again and again, with the reader pointing to each word until the relationship between the printed and oral passages became manifest.[20]

Reading was taught for many reasons, not the least so that the Bible might be personally known and interpreted. Yet there was always the inherent Protestant problem of ensuring that the Scriptures would be interpreted and applied properly; and here, too, families were assiduous in their instruction, relying heavily upon the catechetical mode. Initially, of course, English catechisms were used, the most popular of which was probably William Perkins' *The Foundation of Christian Religion, Gathered into Six Principles* (c. 1590). After 1641, however, when the Massachusetts general court "desired that the elders would make a catechism for the instruction of youth in the grounds of religion," there was a steady procession of native catechisms. Hugh Peter and Edward Norris each prepared one for the use of the Salem congregation; James Noyes produced one for Newbury, Ezekiel Rogers for Rowley, John Norton for Ipswich, and Thomas Shepard for Cambridge. John Cotton, characteristically, wrote two catechisms for the members of Boston's First Church, one of which was *Milke for Babes* (c. 1646), later to appear in so many editions of *The New-England Primer*. The Westminster Assembly's Shorter Catechism became available in 1647 and was widely used in the New World, but the proliferation of American catechisms continued unabated. By 1679, Increase Mather felt obliged to observe: "These last ages have abounded in labors of this kind; one speaketh of no less than five hundred catechisms extant: which of these is most eligible, I shall leave unto others to determine. I suppose there is no particular catechism, of which it may be said, it is the best for every family, or for every congregation."[21]

There was also a good deal of systematic study of the more popular devotional works that were acknowledged as authoritative guides to the Christian life. The *Book of Martyrs, The Practise of Pietie, The Whole Duty of Man, The Poor Man's Family Book,* and *The Pilgrim's Progress* have already been discussed. To these must be

[20] Edmund Coote, *The English Schoole-Maister* (London: The Widow Orwin, 1596).
[21] Shurtleff, ed., *Records of the Governor and Company of Massachusetts*, I, 328; and Increase Mather, "Preface," in James Fitch, *First Principles of the Doctrine of Christ* (Boston: John Foster, 1679).

added at least one native product of unrivaled popularity, Michael Wigglesworth's *The Day of Doom* (1662). Cast in contemporary ballad form, 224 stanzas in length, Wigglesworth's poem portrayed Judgment Day in lurid and sulphurous detail: the awesome wrath of God, the fruitless pleas of sinners, and the terrible torments of hell. Many a child learned the ballad early and in its entirety, and remembered it for the rest of his days. And this, of course, is the crucial point about all this material: it was read and reread, often in groups and almost always aloud; much of it was memorized and thus passed into the oral tradition, where it influenced many who could not themselves read; and, ultimately, it provided a world view and system of values that families held in common and that communities could therefore assume as a basis of law and expectation.

For many colonial families, piety simply incorporated civility, and since *The Practise of Pietie, The Whole Duty of Man,* and *The Poor Man's Family Book* dealt in detail with the cardinal virtues and their application in human affairs, there seemed no need to go beyond these manuals in the teaching of conduct. For other families, *The Compleat Gentleman, The English Gentleman,* and *The Gentleman's Calling* served as texts for the nurture of proper deportment and demeanor. Interestingly, one looks in vain for evidence of traditional books of manners, such as Hugh Rhodes's *The Boke of Nurture* (1545), or Francis Seager's *The Schoole of Vertue* (1557), or William Fiston's *The Schoole of Good Manners* (1609), or Richard West's *The School of Vertue* (1619), though the colonists made considerable use of a volume called *The Academy of Complements* (1639), which promised readers "the best expressions of choice complemental language" for every occasion, from a lovers' tryst to a long journey requiring small talk.[22]

Books, of course, were but the visible core of a general household education in values and conduct that was as pointed as it was persistent. The goal was cultivation of piety and civility, and the pedagogy, insofar as it can be gleaned from contemporary biographies and autobiographies, was essentially Hebraic, assuming an overall context of patriarchal surveillance, using the methods of encouragement, emulation, and punishment, and relying heavily on casuistry. "He wanted not the cares of his father to bestow a good education on him," Cotton Mather wrote of his late brother, Nathaniel, "which God blessed for the restraining him from the lewd and wild courses by which too

---

[22] *The Academy of Complements* (London: T. P., 1639), "The Epistle."

many children are betimes resigned up to the possession of the Devil, and for the furnishing him with such accomplishments as give an 'ornament of grace unto the head of youth.' He did live where he might learn, and under the continual prayers and pains of some that looked after him, he became an instance of unusual industry and no common piety; so that when he died, which was October 17th, 1688, he was become in less than twenty years, 'an old man without gray hairs upon him.' " Now, Increase Mather was no ordinary father, and Nathaniel Mather was no ordinary son, but the prayerful and painful education Nathaniel received in his home during the 1670's was exemplary for the age.[23]

Within the context of patriarchal surveillance, fathers, mothers, tutors, and other parent surrogates in the household used a variety of ancient devices for training up the child in the way he should go. At one level, it was assumed, as the Pilgrim preacher John Robinson once put it, that "there is in all children, though not alike, a stubbornness, and stoutness of mind arising from natural pride, which must, in the first place, be broken and beaten down; that so the foundation of their education being laid in humility and tractableness, other virtues may, in their time, be built thereon." In order to beat down "stubbornness and stoutness of mind," parents frequently resorted to castigation and chastisement. At another level, however, they sought to encourage proper behavior by apt example and casuistical reasoning, using shame and fear in place of chastisement and, wherever possible, the promise of salvation in place of all three. Pedagogically as well as politically, the family was truly "an original to states and churches"; indeed, certain essential tactics of the three institutions for the exercise of authority and the enforcement of conformity were virtually interchangeable.[24]

Beyond the nurture of piety and civility, the family undertook the

[23] Cotton Mather, *Magnalia Christi Americana; or, The Ecclesiastical History of New England* (1702), edited by Thomas Robbins (2 vols.; Hartford: Silas Andrus and Son, 1853-1855), II, 157. For Increase Mather's tenderness toward his children, see his diary for the years 1675 and 1676 in *Proceedings of the Massachusetts Historical Society*, 2d ser., XIII (1899-1900), 339-345. The best single summation of Puritan familial pedagogy remains "Some Special Points, Relating to the Education of My Children," which Cotton Mather included in his diary for February, 1706. See *Diary of Cotton Mather* (2 vols.; New York: Frederick Ungar Publishing Co., 1957), I, 534-537, and pp. 487-489 *infra*.

[24] John Robinson, "Of Children and Their Education" (1625), *The Works of John Robinson*, with a memoir and annotations by Robert Ashton (3 vols.; London: John Snow, 1851), I, 246; and Thomas Cobbet [*sic*], *A Fruitfull and Usefull Discourse Touching the Honour Due from Children to Parents, and the Duty of Parents Towards Their Children* (London: S. G., 1656), "The Epistle."

training of children "in some honest lawful calling, labor or employment." In a subsistence economy, this meant at the very least that boys would be instructed by their fathers in the multifarious arts required for the management of household, farm, and shop, while girls would be similarly instructed by their mothers. For those who wished to follow some calling not pursued in their own homes, it meant apprenticeship in another household, where the new mystery or art would be systematically taught by a parent surrogate. For the few who wished to practice one of the more learned professions, a period of formal schooling might be substituted for the apprenticeship, though even here it was assumed that the masters of the school stood *in loco parentis,* and the curriculum either incorporated or was supplemented by an apprenticeship component. The essential pedagogical feature of all such apprenticeship instruction was the combination of direct example and immediate participation. While an occasional household could boast a copy of one or another of the contemporary works on farming, there is no indication that printed manuals played a significant part in training for husbandry or the crafts. Possibly the only assistance beyond the day-by-day demonstration, explanation, and appraisal of parent or master came via an oral tradition that was partly proverbial and partly derived from such popular books as Thomas Tusser's *Five Hundred Pointes of Good Husbandrie* (1557, 1580). Thus, the colonial apprentice to agriculture may have chanted a rhyme such as the following while weeding newly planted shrub cuttings after a spring rain:

> Banks newly quicksetted, some weeding do crave,
>   the kindlier nourishment thereby to have.
> Then after a shower to weeding a snatch,
>   more easily weed with the root to dispatch.

And his sister may have mused over one of the standard commonplaces of contemporary housewifery:

> Good flax and good hemp for to have of her own,
>   in May a good housewife will see it be sown.
> And afterward trim it, to serve at a need,
>   the fimble to spin and the carl for her seed.[25]

[25] *Books of Lawes and Libertyes of Massachusets,* p. 11; and Thomas Tusser, *Five Hundred Pointes of Good Husbandrie,* edited by W. Payne and Sidney J. Herrtage, English Dialect Society Publications, no. 21 (London: Trübner & Co., 1878), p. 113. Both Massachusetts and Virginia made special efforts to encourage the domestic teaching of spinning. See Shurtleff, ed., *Records of the Governor and Company of Massachusetts,* I, 294, and Hening, ed., *Statutes at Large; Being a Collection of All the Laws of Virginia,* I, 336-337.

In the matter of formal apprenticeship, though English custom generally prevailed, a number of departures from contemporary English practice grew directly out of the conditions of colonial life. For one thing, there was a persistent shortage of labor in the colonies, and it is probable that youngsters entered into apprenticeship arrangements earlier than they did in England, that the period during which they served was shorter than the customary seven years, and that traditional entry fees and property restrictions were either relaxed or abandoned entirely. And, for another, the guilds of merchants and craftsmen, which, along with networks of informers, played an important role in enforcing the Statute of Artificers, never became as numerous or as powerful in the colonies. Consequently, access to the trades was comparatively easy in America, and training requirements comparatively lenient—a fact of political as well as economic significance, given the inextricable ties between economic self-sufficiency, the opportunity to start a household, and freemanship.

A final dimension of household education involved the direct transmission of learning itself. Here, the key was almost always the family library, used either for formal instruction by parent or tutor or for systematic self-instruction. Such instruction was certainly given in the household of William Brewster in Plymouth, of Increase Mather in Boston, of Gysberg van Imborch in New Amsterdam, and of John Carter in Lancaster County, Virginia, who provided in his will of 1669 that his son Robert "during his minority have a man or youth servant bought for him that hath been brought up in the Latin school and that he constantly tend upon him not only to teach him his books either in English or Latin according to his capacity (for my will is that he shall learn both Latin and English and to write) but also to preserve him from harm and from doing evil." And, given the utilitarian character of many colonial libraries, with their volumes on law, medicine, husbandry, and military tactics shelved beside the standard works of divinity and belles-lettres, it is not surprising that they were regarded as centers of information and culture, and that borrowing and lending among friends and acquaintances were both frequent and spirited.[26]

[26] Lancaster County Wills and Codicils (ms. records, Circuit Court, Lancaster, Va.), book X, p. 417.

III

The family, then, was the principal unit of social organization in the colonies and the most important agency of popular education; and it assumed an educational significance that went considerably beyond that of its English counterpart. Whereas England had by the 1640's and 1650's placed churches within the reach of virtually every household, schools within the reach of most, and universities within the reach of at least the more ambitious and able, the colonies were only beginning their efforts in those directions. Hence, while metropolitan families could take for granted the ready availability of other institutions to assist in the educational task, colonial families could not. As a result, the colonial household simply took unto itself, by force of circumstance, educational responsibilities that the English family commonly shared with other agencies. And this, of course, was but one manifestation of a more general tendency of institutions to "double up," so to speak, under the wilderness conditions of the initial decades, that is, to assume responsibilities not traditionally carried or carried in some bygone age but subsequently discarded. The phenomenon was nowhere more apparent than in the widespread practice of requiring masters to teach their apprentices reading, writing, and the principles of religion, in addition to the mysteries of a particular trade or trades. In sum, families did more and taught more, in the process nurturing a versatility in the young that was highly significant for the development of colonial society.

Yet, given this generalization, at least two caveats must be entered. First, there were critical educational differences between the dispersed farmsteads of the Chesapeake colonies and the tightly knit agricultural villages of New England. In the former, isolation was a salient feature of existence, and, though the well-to-do managed to get from one place to another rather easily and frequently, the yeomen seem to have had little contact with the outside world. Hence, geography alone would have necessitated a greater educational self-sufficiency on the part of southern households. By contrast, the village communities of the several townships of New England afforded ample opportunity for social intercourse among the members of different families and for joint sponsorship of readily accessible churches and schools. There, it was ideology rather than geography that established the primacy of the household; for the Puritans considered the family the basic unit of church and commonwealth and, ultimately, the nursery of sainthood. True, geographical necessity and ideological propensity often converged both in New England and on the Chesapeake, but it is important to distinguish them if one is to understand the subtle differences in the educational patterns of the two regions.

Second, however much the educational responsibilities of the European colonial family increased under wilderness conditions— and obviously not all families rose equally to the task—it is important to bear in mind at least two ancillary developments: the sharp disruption of family life and education among the native Indians, who withdrew from the tribal context and sought to live according to European ways, and the even sharper disruption of family life and education among those African blacks who were brought forcibly to America as servants or slaves and placed within colonial households. Deprived of their tribal affiliations, the latter played ill-defined roles in the seventeenth century, with some achieving freedom and attempting to live like the European colonists, with others trying to maintain versions of Christian family life within white households, and with still others forced to form matrifocal families unprecedented in Anglo-Saxon or Christian law. We know next to nothing about the education provided in such families: they were often the instruments of white households and white missionaries, and they doubtless transmitted to their young a poignant version of African tribal lore, modified and confused by the effort to adapt it to New World circumstances.[27]

Finally, as the basic unit of social organization, the family was the principal agency through which the colonists worked out responses to the new conditions in which they found themselves, consolidated what they learned, and transmitted that learning to subsequent generations. This is best seen, perhaps, in agriculture, where the production of maize and tobacco was early learned from the Indians and where certain traditional practices associated with the intensive cultivation of valuable but relatively exhausted English soil quickly gave way to quite different practices devised for the extensive cultivation of cheap and relatively virgin American soil. It is seen too in

27 In both instances, of course, the educational problems were exacerbated by race differences and the attitudes attendant upon them. See Alden T. Vaughan, *New England Frontier: Puritans and Indians, 1620-1675* (Boston: Little, Brown and Company, 1965), and Carl N. Degler, "Slavery and the Genesis of American Race Prejudice," *Comparative Studies in Society and History*, II (1959-60), 49-66.

the social and economic arrangements worked out by the New England merchants who, in the face of early Puritan attempts to develop a strictly regulated economy based on agriculture, local fur-trading, and native industry, devised an elaborate commercial network between Boston, London, and the West Indies, which enabled them to challenge and eventually defeat the original restrictive efforts.[28]

The knowledge, skills, and values associated with these innovations were not to be gained from books and manuals or learned in schools and colleges; they were developed, codified into lore, and transmitted orally by families. The enterprise, of course, was far from new for the seventeenth-century English-speaking household, which, given the social and geographical mobility of the Tudor and Stuart eras, had been serving as a mediator of change for several generations. But in the colonies it was crucial. At a time when church, school, college, and press were slowly adapting a fairly explicit and well-defined tradition to colonial needs, the family, for all its commitment to disciplining, civilizing, and spiritualizing children, managed within a single generation to work out and regularize new attitudes and behavior and to transmit these orally to the young. In effect, the colonial family became the critical agency for institutionalizing change—for nurturing the versatility, the flexibility, and the pragmatism so vital to the successful transplantation and modification of metropolitan institutions.

[28] Conversely, the family was also responsible for the stubborn adherence to certain traditional forms, even when they no longer served traditional purposes, as, for example, in the case of the more popular styles of domestic architecture.

Chapter 5

CHURCH

The office of pastor and teacher, appears to be distinct. The pastor's special work is, to attend to exhortation: and therein to administer a word of wisdom: the teacher is to attend to doctrine, and therein to administer a word of knowledge: and either of them to administer the seals of that covenant, unto the dispensation whereof they are alike called: as also to execute the censures, being but a kind of application of the word, the preaching of which, together with the application thereof they are alike charged withal.

THE CAMBRIDGE PLATFORM

Like Judaism, from which it sprang, Christianity has always been an educational system, with Christ as the divine master who commanded his disciples to go forth and teach all nations. And, in the development and maintenance of that system, the ministry, by virtue of its special gifts and obligations, has always played a leading role. "Now you are the body of Christ and individually members of it," Paul told the Corinthians. "And God has appointed in the church first apostles, second prophets, third teachers, then workers of miracles, then healers, helpers, administrators, speakers in various kinds of tongues." Paul's list of ministerial offices is incomplete—elsewhere he mentions evangelists and pastors—and it would seem in any case that he is enumerating functions rather than positions, since in the primitive church a single individual often served in several of the capacities mentioned. But the list does indicate the fundamental continuity between the Judaic and Christian priestly traditions: the ancient Judaic commitment of priests and prophets to teach and interpret the law, as set forth in Leviticus and Deuteronomy, is joined to the newer

Christian commitment of apostles and prophets to proclaim the good news and ultimate meaning of Christ's advent, life, death, and resurrection, as set forth in the Gospels. True, there has long been a controversy over whether the ministry described by Paul was alone entrusted with the keys to the kingdom of heaven, or whether those keys were granted to the entire Christian community. But whatever the outcome of that controversy, there is no denying the essentially educational character of Christianity, as a movement, as a complex of institutions, and as an ideology.[1]

However great the development of ceremonialism during the millennium following the birth of Christ, Christianity retained this essentially educational character; indeed, ceremonialism was itself seen as "a book to the lewd [unlearned] people, that they may read in imagery and painture what clerks read in the book." This was especially so in early Renaissance England, which, for all its outward crudity, was widely perceived as a devout nation by European contemporaries. "Although they all attend Mass every day, and say many paternosters in public," an Italian visitor observed at the close of the fifteenth century, "the women carrying long rosaries in their hands, and any who can read taking the office of Our Lady with them, and with some companion reciting it in church, verse by verse, in a low voice after the manner of churchmen, they always hear Mass on Sunday in their parish church, and give liberal alms, because they may not offer less than a piece of money, of which fourteen are equivalent to a golden ducat; nor do they omit any form incumbent upon good Christians; there are, however, many who have various opinions concerning religion." The observation may, of course, have been partial, in the classic fashion of the traveler's tale, but there is every indication that, next to the family, the parish church was the most visible, accessible, and popular institution of the age. It was not only a place of worship but a center of social life, and that, willy-nilly, made it educative.[2]

Even the ordinary churches were crowded with statuary, paintings, images, and relics, each symbolizing some element of doctrine, some ancient allegory, some eternal verity, some holy mystery. Incorporated as they were into the liturgy, they taught in myriad ways

[1] I Cor. 12:27-28 (R.S.V.); Eph. 4:11-12; I Pet. 2:9; Rev. 1:6; and Matt. 16:18.

[2] *Dives and Pauper* (London: T. Bertheleti, 1534), "The First Commandment," chap. i; and *A Relation, or Rather a True Account, of the Island of England,* translated by Charlotta Augusta Sneyd, Camden Society Publications, no. 37 London: John Bowyer Nichols and Son, 1847), p. 23.

that "the law was given by Moses, but grace and truth came by Jesus Christ." Doubtless most of the laity and many clerics too were ignorant of liturgical Latin, and doubtless many venerated the symbols with no comprehension of doctrine: the age abounded in saint cults, spurious pilgrimages, and specious indulgences. Yet, withal, one must assume some measure of popular understanding of the Gospels, however imperfect, from the regular celebration of the Mass and the seasonal round of holy days, from Christmas to Epiphany to Ash Wednesday to Good Friday to Easter Sunday to Rogation Days to Whitsunday to Trinity Sunday to Corpus Christi to Lammas to Allhallows. And one must assume, too, that some measure of popular conformity to Christian ways resulted from the highly individualized education implicit in the sacrament of penance and from the more general celebration of Christian values in popular pageants, miracle and morality plays, and carols.[3]

Beyond these combinations of liturgy and popular ceremonial, there was the more formal instruction of books of hours, primers, Mass books, and the Scriptures themselves, all of which built on the elemental canonical requirement that children learn by heart the Pater Noster, the Apostles' Creed, and the Decalogue. Thus, John Lydgate, a fifteenth-century monk at Bury, began his *Merita Missae* with the following prayer:

> God of heaven that shaped earth and hell
> Give me grace some word to tell
> To the lewd that cannot read
> But the Pater Noster and the Creed.

The explanations of the Mass that followed were obviously designed to teach, and to be memorized as well as read. So it was also with primers and other vehicles of instruction. We have no precise evidence regarding the extent of literacy, though the abundant circulation of primers, the common practice of posting proclamations, and the spirited interest in the Wycliffite tracts and Bibles indicate that reading was by no means confined to the landed or clerical classes. Yet, in the last analysis, popular Christianity in early Renaissance England was an oral rather than a written religion: it was taught by word of mouth rather than by books or manuscripts and

[3] John 1:17.

was an affair of churches rather than households and of priests rather than parents.[4]

That being the case, the character and education of the clergy were of critical significance. At least in the early Tudor era, the higher clergy were commonly men of affairs, who owed their offices to royal rather than papal patronage. They swore allegiance to Rome but spent their energies in London, serving, in effect, as high officers of the governmental bureaucracy. Clearly, their vocation to the priesthood was often less than compelling, and what education they had tended to be in civil law rather than in theology. Men of ability, they were politicians rather than divines, and they made their contributions to statecraft rather than to religion or education. The inferior clergy were numerous and of dubious qualification. "Every man that offers himself is everywhere admitted without pulling back," lamented John Colet. "Thereof springeth and cometh out the people that are in the church both of unlearned and evil priests." Such jeremiads resounded through the writings of the humanists, who early committed themselves to a radical improvement of clerical education. But one must expect hyperbole from critics, and, despite widespread ignorance and illiteracy among the clergy, their general education was significantly greater than that of any other substantial segment of society, however faint that praise in the context of early Renaissance England.[5]

All this could scarcely have changed overnight, with the proclamation of royal supremacy in 1534, and, indeed, there is evidence that many of the traditional forms, symbols, and ceremonies persisted on the parish level for decades. But there were deeper currents associated with the Protestantizing of England that were destined to alter radically the educational character of the church. To begin, the rendering of the Bible into English and its slow but steady diffusion throughout the realm were of incalculable significance. Prodded by Thomas Cromwell, Henry VIII promulgated ecclesiastical Injunctions requiring that a copy of the English Bible be placed in every

[4] Thomas Frederick Simmons, ed., *The Lay Folk's Mass Book,* Early English Text Society Publications, no. 71 (London: N. Trübner & Co., 1879), p. 148. Lydgate's authorship of the *Merita Missae* has been challenged, but Walter F. Schirmer makes a convincing case for it in his recent biography, *John Lydgate,* translated by Ann E. Keep (Berkeley: University of California Press, 1961), pp. 174, 260-263, 269.

[5] *The Sermon of Doctor Colete, Made to the Convocacion at Paulis* [1511], in J. H. Lupton, *A Life of John Colet* (2d ed.; London: George Bell and Sons, 1909), p. 300.

church and that parishioners be exhorted to "read the same, as that which is the very lively word of God, that every Christian man is bound to embrace, believe and follow if he look to be saved; admonishing them nevertheless to avoid all contention, altercation therein, and to use an honest sobriety in the inquisition of the true sense of the same, and refer the explanation of obscure places to men of higher judgment in Scripture." Though Henry himself later cooled to the idea, the policy proved irreversible, and the consequences irrevocable. Priests and laymen alike were given access to the word, and in studying it they quickly discovered it conflicted with aspects of the oral tradition on the one hand and of the symbolic tradition on the other. Inevitably, the Bible became a judgment on the church itself, an indictment of the worldly prelate and the uninspired priest, a criticism of the selling of indulgences and the exacting of mortuary dues—and this, incidentally, quite apart from Lutheran doctrines of justification by faith alone or Calvinist doctrines of the priesthood of all believers.[6]

But England, of course, could scarcely be insulated from Lutheran or Calvinist doctrines, and, despite Henry's plea, heresy and contentiousness became rife throughout the nation. Pursuing a characteristic Renaissance interest in origins, English theologians followed their Continental teachers in attacking the doctrine of transubstantiation, in assailing the un-Scriptural world of saint cults, pilgrimages, purgatory, and the minor sacraments, and in calling for a purification of the liturgy and a return to the fundamental teachings of the primitive church. These efforts inevitably shifted the function of the priesthood from the exercise of mystical power and the performance of symbolic ceremonial to the systematic proclamation and exegesis of the word.

One indication of the shift is the revival and refinement of preaching. Rooted as it was in the prophesyings of the Scriptures, preaching had been resuscitated in the thirteenth century under the aegis of the mendicant orders; and the itinerant friar calling men to Christ in the language of the people had become a familiar figure on the English countryside. Later, John Wycliffe had taught that "true preaching is better than praying by mouth" and had organized his own company of "poor priests" for the express purpose of pro-

6 Walter Howard Frere and William McClure Kennedy, eds., *Visitation Articles and Injunctions of the Period of the Reformation*, Alcuin Club Collections, vols. XIV-XVI (3 vols.; London: Longmans, Green & Co., 1910), II, 36.

claiming the ultimate authority of the Bible. But Lollardry had been suppressed, and the mendicants had suffered the same decline of fervor and devotion as monasticism generally. With the rise of what John Foxe called spiritual as contrasted with ceremonial religion in the sixteenth century, preaching again came into its own; it was exemplified best in the Henrician and Edwardian years by the ministry of Hugh Latimer and later, in the Elizabethan years, by the Puritans.[7]

Latimer, an early partisan of the translation and dissemination of the Bible, was not only an extraordinary preacher in his own right but an articulate exponent of preaching as the chief instrument whereby God calls men to his kingdom. Widely celebrated by his contemporaries as the "apostle to the English" and martyred during the reign of Mary, he became, through the advocacy of John Foxe, one of the heroic figures of the newly emerging Protestant church. With the accession of Elizabeth I, the "spiritual brotherhood" of Puritans carried Latimer's work forward, rendering preaching a high art and making it the quintessential ministerial office. For men like Richard Cartwright, John Dod, Richard Rogers, and William Perkins, "godly preaching" was expository, edifying, evangelical, and plain: expository inasmuch as it attempted to go beyond the "bare reading" of Scripture to systematic interpretation, edifying inasmuch as it sought to apply doctrine to the everyday affairs of men, evangelical inasmuch as it aimed to turn men from lives of sin to lives of holiness, and plain inasmuch as it addressed itself in ordinary language to the ordinary concerns of ordinary men. In effect, the godly preaching of the spiritual brotherhood was a systematic, self-conscious venture in popular education: the Puritan minister was essentially a teacher, and his church was a "school of Christ."[8]

All this posed thorny problems for the Tudors, whose concern for social stability was ceaseless. It was all well and good for the Crown to follow a hard Erastian line in separating from Rome, in dissolving the chantries, the chapels, and the monasteries, and in appropriating and redistributing much of the vast wealth of the church; but it was quite another matter for English Lutherans to begin to use the

[7] *The English Works of Wyclif Hitherto Unprinted*, edited by F. D. Mathew, Early English Text Society Publications, no. 74 (London: Trübner & Co., 1880), p. 111.

[8] *The Works of Hugh Latimer*, edited for the Parker Society by George Elwes Corrie (2 vols.; Cambridge: Cambridge University Press, 1844-1845), I, 358; and Ivronwy Morgan, *The Godly Preachers of the Elizabethan Church* (London: The Epworth Press, 1965).

rhetoric of individual conscience or for English Calvinists to argue the need for a polity founded on Scripture. How much latitude for inspired preaching? How much conformity to established practice? The Tudor solution, worked out slowly during the reigns of Henry VIII and Edward VI and given final form in the Elizabethan settlement of 1559, was to move a considerable distance toward viewing the church as a "school of Christ" but to insist upon the most stringent regulation of its teachers, its curriculum, and its methods of instruction.

The solution is best seen in two pieces of Elizabethan legislation, the Act of Supremacy and the Act of Uniformity, both of which restored and codified a good deal of pre-Marian policy. The former annexed ecclesiastical jurisdiction to the queen, gave her authority to appoint ecclesiastical commissioners, and prescribed a supremacy oath, setting explicit punishments for refusing it. The latter reinstituted the rites and ceremonies of the Book of Common Prayer as the official liturgy of the Church of England, provided that the clergy follow that liturgy on penalty of removal, and required subjects to attend church services on Sundays and holy days throughout the year. Complementing these laws were the Royal Injunctions of 1559, which specified, *inter alia*, that there be monthly sermons in each parish denouncing superstition (i.e., Romanism), that there be additional quarterly sermons in each parish, that there be regular readings of the authorized homilies and of the Pater Noster, the Creed, and the Decalogue in English, that there be ready access in each church to the Bible and the *Paraphrases* of Erasmus, also in English, and that "every parson, vicar, and curate shall upon every holy day, and every second Sunday in the year, hear and instruct all the youth of the parish for half an hour at the least before evening prayer, in the Ten Commandments, the Articles of the Belief, and in the Lord's Prayer, and diligently examine them, and teach the catechism set forth in the book of public prayer."[9]

The educational thrust of these regulations is perfectly clear: they established a uniform system of instruction through the realm, controlled by the Crown and its appointed ecclesiastical officials, conducted by an orthodox and closely supervised clergy, and embracing an official body of doctrine incorporated in an authorized Bible, an authorized Book of Common Prayer (which included an

[9] Henry Gee and William John Hardy, eds., *Documents Illustrative of English Church History* (London: Macmillan and Co., 1896), pp. 434, 417-467.

authorized catechism, an authorized book of homilies, and an authorized primer), all of which, incidentally, were produced by authorized printers. Such a system was obviously unacceptable to Roman Catholic traditionalists, who saw it as propagating a collection of blatant heresies, and equally repugnant to Puritan radicals, who viewed its preservation of episcopacy and other un-Scriptural practices as odious vestiges of popishness. But it did command sufficient political support to remain in effect until the 1640's, when it was swept away by the reforms of the Long Parliament, only to be restored in its essentials upon the accession of Charles II in 1660.

Absolute uniformity, of course, was never really achieved. For one thing, the English church was subject to that characteristic inertia of all human institutions, which makes them stubbornly resistant to change by fiat—the more so when the change affects historic loyalties and ultimate concerns and when the persons responsible for carrying out the change have life tenure in their positions. For another, the technology of education and politics during the Renaissance permitted only limited standardization and only limited surveillance: the same printing press that made possible the widespread dissemination of authorized Bibles also allowed a spirited circulation of dissenting tracts, which no amount of confiscating or book-burning seemed able entirely to suppress. And, finally, both Elizabeth and James I pursued the policy of uniformity with relative moderation and caution. But the Tudor redefinition of the church did proceed, ever so slowly and haltingly, and with the greatest diversity and variegation.

Consider, for example, the character of the clergy. To shift the priestly function from the exercise of mystical powers to the exegesis of the word was to increase sharply the educational requirements of the ministerial office. Yet, paradoxically, at the very time the shift was taking place, the quality of clerical service was, if anything, in decline. The problem was partly economic, growing out of the widespread impropriation of benefices, leasing of tithes, and "decay" of fees and offerings, partly political, resulting from the general unsettlement of the church during a period of intense religious strife, and partly social, deriving from the tendency of the gentry who controlled so many of the livings to appoint personal favorites, regardless of their qualifications. In any case, during the period preceding Elizabeth's accession in 1558, as many as two thousand of the nine thousand parishes in the realm may have gone unattended, many for years on end; and a considerable portion of the remaining seven thousand were served by pluralists and absentees, many of whose qualifications were at best dubious—the records of ecclesiastical visitations are replete with references to curates ignorant of the Lord's Prayer and the Apostles' Creed and to ministers not only incapable of preaching but unable to read the homilies, and at least one vicar in Nottinghamshire apparently displayed a curious tendency to confuse Jesus with Judas. Indeed, the situation was so acute that the clerical office of reader was created, that is, a layman licensed to conduct the divine service, read the homilies, bury the dead, and teach the catechism.

All this changed decisively between 1558 and 1640, as the shortage of clergymen was gradually alleviated, and their education considerably improved. The statistics presented by Miss D. M. Barratt for the dioceses of Oxford and Worcester are indicative of the change, though it should be recognized that Oxford was somewhat exceptional, owing to the presence of the university.

OXFORD

	1560	1580	1600	1620	1640
Rectors and vicars holding degrees	38%	50%	66%	80%	96%
Parishes vacant for more than 6 months (out of 173)	17	7	7	6	2

WORCESTER

	1560	1580	1600	1620	1640
Rectors and vicars holding degrees	19%	23%	36%	52%	84%
Parishes vacant for more than 6 months (out of 190 in 1560 and 1580; out of 189 from 1600)	12+4?	6	5	5	6

The improvement in the curacy was even more striking: during the 1570's and 1580's, almost all curates were unschooled and itinerant, whereas by the 1640's almost all were university trained and settled. And for clergymen of all ranks who were not so well educated, there were numerous diocesan exercises and examinations designed to encourage and enforce the regular study of Scripture and of suitable sermons.[10]

The possession of a university degree was no guarantee that a clergyman would be licensed to preach or even that he would preach if licensed; but the fact is that both the number of preaching ministers and the number of sermons preached by the average minister increased steadily, so that by 1640 there were very few parishes in which there was no preaching. As might be expected, the Puritans continued to inveigh against inept performance in the pulpit and used their own lectureships to support a vigorous preaching ministry outside the official Anglican fold. But, despite all the bitter debates over how central preaching would actually be in the Church of England, there is no denying that the ministerial office had been dramatically transformed by 1640 and, with it, the nature of the church.

"The country parson desires to be all to his parish, and not only a pastor, but a lawyer also, and a physician," George Herbert wrote in the classic Anglican handbook of the ministry. And so the parson was in the parishes of seventeenth-century England. As in earlier times, he served some two to three hundred of his fellow men as religious leader, moral overseer, civic administrator, legal counselor, medical adviser, and purveyor of news. But, more than ever before, he also served them as educator, preaching sermons on a vast variety of topics (it was a great age of preaching, during which every important question of public policy was hotly debated in the pulpit), catechizing, visiting families, supervising household instruction, frequently teaching English and even Latin in the manse, the church, and neighboring schools, and generally acting as a fount of cultural, political, and technical information. The forms of this education were as varied as the men who proffered it and the parishioners they served; but, given the qualifications of the clergy and the extent of

---

[10] D. M. Barratt, "The Condition of the Parish Clergy Between the Reformation and 1660, with Special Reference to the Dioceses of Oxford, Worcester and Gloucester" (unpublished doctoral thesis, Somerville College, University of Oxford, 1949), pp. 86-89. For the variations in the educational standard of the clergy in different geographical areas, see Lawrence Stone, "The Educational Revolution in England, 1560-1640," *Past & Present*, no. 28 (July, 1964), p. 47. The exercises—or "prophesyings," as they were called—to improve preaching began within the Anglican fold, but they were soon adopted by the Puritans, and have therefore come to be identified with the latter.

their clientele, they doubtless constituted by the end of the Renaissance the largest and most important body of teachers outside the household, and probably the most influential agency of systematic education in the realm.[11]

II

Seventeenth-century America was as much a babel of religion as it was of social class and ethnicity: in addition to English Anglicans, Independents, Puritans, and Quakers, there were French and Spanish Catholics, Swedish Lutherans, Dutch Calvinists, French Huguenots, and Spanish Jews, to say nothing of Indian and African worshipers of ancient tribal gods. Yet, in this realm as in others, English forms and customs came to predominate, providing the context within which other traditions developed, waned, or changed. The thrust that made this domination possible was largely numerical, since English Protestants very quickly outnumbered other groups; but it also derived from an extraordinary missionary zeal, for, beginning with Hakluyt and increasingly in the sermons of impassioned Jacobean preachers, the propagation of the gospel, the conversion of the heathen, and the establishment of God's true church in the western Canaan beyond the seas, were viewed not merely as aspects of English policy but as elements of England's destiny.

Not surprisingly, the initial instruction of James I for the governance of Virginia explicitly provided that Christianity be preached, planted, and practiced by the settlers and propagated among the savages "according to the doctrine, rights and religion now professed and established within our realm of England." In accordance with these instructions, Jamestown was organized as a parish, and, at least according to John Smith, none other than the indefatigable Richard Hakluyt was nominated by the Virginia Company to the rectorship, the nomination being formally confirmed by the archbishop of Canterbury. The appointment was at most honorific, if indeed it was made at all; in the end, it was not Hakluyt but a vicar named Robert Hunt who actually sailed with the initial "supply" and ministered to their needs during the first terrible months of settlement. Hunt remains an ephemeral figure in the early records of Virginia, though Smith later recalled that "we had daily common

---

11 George Herbert, *A Priest to the Temple, or, The Country Parson, His Character and Rule of Holy Life* (reprint ed.; New York: T. Whittaker, 1908), p. 92.

prayer morning and evening, every Sunday two sermons, and every three months the Holy Communion, till our minister died: but our prayers daily, with a homily on Sundays, we continued two or three years after, till more preachers came."[12]

"More preachers" doubtless referred to the Reverend Richard Buck, who landed with Sir Thomas Gates's fleet in the spring of 1610 and remained minister of Jamestown until his death some thirteen or fourteen years later; the Reverend William Mease, who arrived with either Gates or Lord Delaware shortly thereafter and went on to serve for a decade as minister of the newly established parish of Kecoughtan (later Elizabeth City); and the Reverend Alexander Whitaker, who came the following year and acted as minister of both Henrico and Charles City until his death in 1617. Sometime after that, two other ministers appeared briefly on the scene, both of them apparently of Genevan or Presbyterian rather than Anglican ordination; but it was not until 1619, when the Company began to specify arrangements for the creation of new parishes and the appointment of new ministers, that any significant number of additional clergymen arrived.[13]

The year 1619 also witnessed the first session of the newly created general assembly, which, among other things, laid the groundwork for a formal ecclesiastical code by writing into law those customary practices of the Church of England that had gradually come into use in Virginia, and ratified the Company's instructions setting two hundred pounds as the minimum ministerial living in the colony. It ordered all ministers to "read divine service, and exercise their ministerial function according to the ecclesiastical laws and orders of the Church of England"; to catechize every Sunday afternoon "such as are not yet ripe to come to the Communion"; to bring annually to

---

[12] Alexander Brown, ed., The Genesis of the United States (2 vols.; Boston: Houghton, Mifflin and Company, 1890), I, 68; and Captaine John Smith, Advertisements for the Unexperienced Planters of New-England, or Any Where (London: John Haviland, 1631), in Works, 1608-1631, edited by Edward Arber (2 vols.; Westminster: Archibald Constable and Co., 1895), II, 957-958. That Hakluyt was instituted to the rectorship or ever enjoyed the living is disputed by George Bruner Parks in Richard Hakluyt and the English Voyages, edited by James A. Williamson (2d ed.; New York: Frederick Ungar Publishing Co., 1961), pp. 205-206.

[13] The specification began in the "instructions" Governor Yeardley brought with him in 1619, requiring that glebe land be set aside in the new plantations as in the original cities and boroughs (Susan Myra Kingsbury, ed., The Records of the Virginia Company of London [4 vols.; Washington, D.C.: Government Printing Office, 1906-1935], III, 106); it had developed rather fully by the time of the Company's broadside dated May 17, 1620 (ibid., pp. 276-277).

the secretary of estate "a true account of all christenings, burials and marriages"; and, finally, to attempt, in collaboration with the church-wardens, to prevent and punish "scandalous offenses" and "enormous sins" by the usual methods of admonition and excommunication. And it required all parishioners, for their part, to attend church services on Sunday, including both morning and afternoon sermons.[14]

In effect, this legislation confirmed the planting of the Anglican church in America, providing a foundation that lasted well beyond the dissolution of the Virginia Company in 1624. But that foundation had one critical flaw, destined to plague colonial Anglicanism right through the time of the American Revolution: it made no provision for a bishop. The result was that those functions ordinarily performed by an English bishop or his designated surrogates, such as administration of the sacrament of confirmation, ordination of ministers, induction, regulation, and disciplining of clergymen, and licensing of teachers, were either not performed at all in the colonies (confirmation and ordination) or taken over by civil authorities (induction and licensing). It was a result that profoundly affected the fortunes of colonial Anglicanism and, indeed, the ultimate character of the English church in America.

James I unquestionably assumed that his entire western domain would eventually be Christianized "according to the doctrine, rights and religion now professed and established within our realm of England." Yet at the very time the establishment of the Anglican church was being confirmed by the Virginia assembly, a small band of English Nonconformists in Leiden was laying the plans that would culminate the following year in the transplanting of a quite different sort of church to America. Organized as a congregation of Puritan Separatists under the leadership of John Robinson and William Brewster, Jr., they had been harried out of England for their belief that a true church was "a company and fellowship of faithful and holy people" and not the sort of "mixed assemblies" that came together in the ordinary parishes of the Anglican establishment. Acting on this belief, they had separated from the Church of England, preferring to found a "gathered church," composed entirely of faithful Christians linked by a covenant of voluntary association. It was such a church that had moved from Scrooby to Amsterdam in 1607 and

---

[14] "Proceedings of the Virginia Assembly, 1619," in Lyon Gardiner Tyler, ed., *Narratives of Early Virginia, 1606-1625*, Original Narratives of Early American History, edited by J. Franklin Jameson (New York: Charles Scribner's Sons, 1907), pp. 271-273.

1608 and to Leiden in 1609, and that moved from Leiden to New Plymouth in 1620.[15]

The Separatists were never very powerful in Elizabethan or early Stuart England, remaining few in number and humble in circumstance; though it was their Separatism rather than their Puritanism that placed them on the margins of the English Reformation. When they criticized the corrupt membership and un-Scriptural character of the Church of England, they spoke essentially as Puritans, and in so doing they were part of a much larger and more influential movement, which differed with them primarily in its commitment to reforming the church from within, that is, by preaching and persuasion, by the control and occupancy of clerical livings, and by parliamentary action. Like all reform movements, Puritanism was shot through with dissension over doctrine, but virtually all Puritans, at least until the 1640's, shared the ideal of a church as a group of believers "gathered out of the world," led by elected pastors, teachers, ruling elders, and deacons, and practicing Christianity in strict accordance with Scripture. It was Puritans of such belief—in a word, nonseparating Congregationalists—who followed the Separatists to New England in the extensive migration of 1628 to 1643, seeing themselves not merely as propagators of the gospel to the heathen but as exemplars of true Christianity to members of the established Church of England.[16]

In an act of historic significance, the Puritans of Massachusetts Bay founded their first church at Salem in 1629, covenanting with the Lord and with one another "to walk together in all his ways, according as he is pleased to reveal himself unto us in his blessed word of truth," and then ordained the Reverend Samuel Skelton pastor and the Reverend Francis Higginson teacher. The Salem procedure was patently the model for the gathering of churches at Charlestown-Boston and at Watertown the next year (the Dorchester church, also founded in 1630, originated in England) and for New England Congregationalism thereafter. It spread to Connecticut when Thomas

[15] Williston Walker, ed., *The Creeds and Platforms of Congregationalism* (New York: Charles Scribner's Sons, 1893), pp. 33, 51; and *The Works of John Robinson*, with a memoir and annotations by Robert Ashton (3 vols.; London: John Snow, 1851), II, 315, 332.

[16] Albert Peel, ed., *The Seconde Parte of a Register, Being a Calendar of Manuscripts Under That Title Intended for Publication by the Puritans About 1593, and Now in Dr. Williams's Library, London* (2 vols.; Cambridge: Cambridge University Press, 1915), I, 86.

Hooker and Samuel Stone, who had helped form a strong church at Newtown in 1633, moved with a large part of their congregation to Hartford in 1636; and it spread to New Haven when John Davenport and Theophilus Eaton gathered a church there in 1639. And it was brought centrally into the Cambridge Platform of 1648, which was framed by representatives of the four New England colonies (the churches of Massachusetts were by far the best represented) and which outlined what was to become the established form of ecclesiastical polity in Massachusetts throughout the colonial period and in Connecticut until the adoption of the Saybrook Platform in 1708.[17]

Moreover, as with so many reform movements before and since, Nonconformity quickly allied itself with the civil authority to become a new conformity. Church attendance was made mandatory in Massachusetts in March, 1635, and shortly thereafter the question began to be raised whether all who profited from the instruction of the church, rather than simply those who held formal membership in it, ought not to contribute to the support of the ministry. The problem was resolved in 1638, when the general court enacted legislation providing that every "inhabitant who shall not voluntarily contribute, proportionably to his ability, with other freemen of the same town, to all common charges, as well for upholding the ordinances in the churches as otherwise, shall be compelled thereto by assessment and distress to be levied by the constable, or other officer of the town, as in other cases." And, with the organization of the New England Confederation in 1643, the commissioners recommended the Massachusetts policy to the other member colonies. Even Plymouth, which had early determined to keep separate the things of Caesar and the things of Christ, authorized the magistrates in the spring of 1655 to exert pressure on those who had failed to contribute voluntarily to the support of the ministry, "so there may be no just cause of complaints for the future in that behalf."[18]

By 1650, there were twenty-seven Anglican churches in Virginia and fifty-nine Congregational churches in New England: Puritanism

17 Walker, ed., *Creeds and Platforms of Congregationalism*, pp. 116, 100-108.
18 Nathaniel B. Shurtleff, ed., *Records of the Governor and Company of the Massachusetts Bay in New England* (5 vols.; Boston: William White, 1853-1854), I, 240-241; Nathaniel B. Shurtleff and David Pulsifer, eds., *Records of the Colony of New Plymouth in New England* (12 vols.; Boston: William White, 1855-1861), III, 82; J. Hammond Trumbull, ed. [vols. I-III], *The Public Records of the Colony of Connecticut* (15 vols.; Hartford: publisher varies, 1850-1890), I, 111-112; and Charles J. Hoadly, ed., *Records of the Colony or Jurisdiction of New Haven, from May, 1653, to the Union* (Hartford: Case, Lockwood and Company, 1858), p. 588.

as well as Anglicanism had firmly taken root in the New World and had itself become an established religion. Yet it is important to note that both the Puritan and the Anglican establishments in America were early challenged by diversity, both from within and from without. Massachusetts saw fit to banish Roger Williams for his Separatist views in 1635, whereupon he and several others of similar convictions went forth to found the town of Providence on the principle of freedom of conscience. Shortly thereafter, Anne Hutchinson and her adherents were similarly dealt with following the bitter struggle over antinomianism. Virginia felt obliged to adopt strong measures banning Puritan preaching and teaching in the 1640's. And later, both colonies, along with Connecticut, enacted stern legislation against the Quakers, though to little avail.

Outside New England and Virginia, New Netherland sought from the beginning to maintain an establishment of the Dutch Reformed church, but it was an establishment quickly compromised by Dutch traditions of toleration (however poorly they were represented by Peter Stuyvesant) and by the extraordinary heterogeneity of the population. Maryland, initially conceived as a refuge for Roman Catholics, early welcomed Protestants and in 1649 confirmed that welcome with an Act of Toleration. And Pennsylvania was explicitly founded in 1681 as a "holy experiment," based on the doctrines of religious liberty and political freedom.

One response of the established churches to the challenge of diversity was simply an intensification of their efforts to nurture uniformity. Colonial ministers preached, catechized, and taught at least as self-consciously and resolutely as their metropolitan counterparts, perhaps more so, for there were fewer schools to assist them in their task, and they were ever aware of the threat of barbarism lurking in the wilderness. The Puritan ministers of New England were about as remarkable a group of clergymen as gathered anywhere during the seventeenth century, in educational background, in devotion to their calling, and in numerical proportion to their parishioners; indeed, they helped impart a tone and quality to New England intellectual life that early made the Boston-Cambridge region a center for the production rather than the mere consumption of culture. The Anglican ministers of Virginia were less distinguished, perhaps, but no less devoted, and were probably comparable in quality to the clergy of early Caroline England, particularly in some of the more remote parishes. The persistent problem in Virginia, of course, was that of clerical shortage, deriving partly from the absence of a bishop and partly from the delay in establishing a college there. That shortage, coupled with the vast size of the parishes, left many a Virginia household with little or no pastoral care, at least through the 1660's, after which the situation began to improve. Whereas in 1662 there were but ten clergymen to serve some forty-five to forty-eight parishes, by 1680 that number had increased to thirty-five.[19]

From the beginning, both Virginia and New England made preaching a central ministerial responsibility. In Virginia, there is ample evidence that Messrs. Hunt, Buck, and Whitaker, all of whom displayed marked Puritan propensities, sermonized regularly and vigorously in the pulpit, probably at a fairly high level, since all had had university training. Later, after the dissolution of the Company, there was a decline in the amount and quality of preaching, as the colony found it increasingly difficult to attract and hold competent clergymen. Nevertheless, the assembly did reiterate from time to time the requirement that ministers preach on Sundays and, in addition, provided in 1644 that pluralists preach regularly in all their cures. In 1661, it also revived the Elizabethan office of the lay reader, who would conduct divine services and catechize children in parishes "destitute of incumbents." Yet, for all this encouragement of preaching, there remain virtually no records of the sermons themselves, and one can only assume that they ran the contemporary gamut, from fairly learned disquisitions on theology, public affairs, and daily behavior, to the most colorless readings of the homilies.[20]

In New England the effort was to have two ministers for each congregation—a pastor, whose special concern was exhortation and inspiration, and a teacher, whose special concern was doctrinal matters. The two frequently alternated in administering the sacraments of baptism and the Lord's Supper, but in general the pastor was charged with the conduct of church activities, the tendering of moral

[19] R[ichard] G[reen], *Virginia's Cure: or, An Advisive Narrative Concerning Virginia* (London: W. Godbid, 1662), in Peter Force, ed., *Tracts and Other Papers, Relating Principally to the Origin, Settlement, and Progress of the Colonies in North America, from the Discovery of the Country to the Year 1776* (4 vols.; Washington, D.C.: Peter Force, 1836-1846), vol. III, no. 15, p. 4; and "A List of the Parishes in Virginia in 1680," *Colonial Records of Virginia* (Baltimore: Genealogical Publishing Co., 1964), pp. 103-104. There are errors in the transcription of the latter document, which do not involve the numbers of clergymen and parishes and which may be ascertained by consulting the photostatic copies of the original manuscript in the Virginia State Library.

[20] William Waller Hening, ed., *The Statutes at Large; Being a Collection of All the Laws of Virginia, from the First Session of the Legislature, in the Year 1619* (13 vols.; imprint varies, 1819-1823), I, 181, 289-290, 311-312; II, 29-30, 46-47.

advice, and family visitation, while the teacher delivered learned sermons, elucidated points of Scripture, and oversaw the catechizing of youngsters. By 1640, which represented something of a high point for the collegial relationship, approximately twenty of New England's Congregational churches maintained both a pastor and a teacher; with the exodus to England during the Commonwealth period, that number declined, until by 1689 only the First and Second churches of Boston and the churches of Salem, Ipswich, Roxbury, Rowley, Charlestown, and Newbury still had both officers, and, even in those churches, the distinction between the two had largely disappeared.[21]

The typical New England congregation of the seventeenth century ordinarily heard morning and afternoon sermons on the Sabbath and an additional "lecture" during the week, most often on Thursday. Usually an hour or two in length—the hourglass was a standard accoutrement of the New England pulpit—these sermons and lectures, like their English counterparts, ranged widely over matters theological, political, and personal, and sought in a plain and popular style to apply the teachings of Scripture to the conduct of life. Since they were unequivocally put forth and received as instruction, they were commonly précised in writing by members of the congregation and subsequently pondered, both individually and in household groups.

Along with preaching, the catechizing of youth was widely recognized as an important ministerial obligation. In Virginia, Alexander Whitaker referred as early as 1614 to regular catechetical exercises on Sunday afternoons, and the law of 1619 sought to make these standard practice throughout the colony. In 1631, the assembly explicitly required that "upon every Sunday the ministers shall half an hour or more before evening prayer examine, catechize, and instruct the youth and ignorant persons of his parish in the Ten Commandments, the Articles of the Belief and the Lord's Prayer. And shall diligently hear, instruct and teach them the catechism, set forth in the Book of Common Prayer, and all fathers, mothers, masters, and mistresses shall cause their children, servants, and apprentices which have not learned the catechism to come to the church at the time appointed obediently to hear and to be ordered by the minister until

21 Thomas Lechford, *Plain Dealing: or, News from New-England* (1642), edited by J. Hammond Trumbull (Boston: J. K. Wiggin & Wm. Parsons Lunt, 1867), pp. 16-18, 24-25; "The Cambridge Platform, 1648," in Walker, ed., *Creeds and Platforms of Congregationalism*, p. 211; and Vergil V. Phelps, "The Pastor and Teacher in New England," *The Harvard Theological Review*, IV (1911), 388-399.

they have learned the same." Parents who failed to comply were subject to censure by the courts, a penalty that was stiffened in the 1640's in connection with the effort to combat nonconformity in the colony. Later, in the 1660's, the catechizing of youth was made a primary function of the lay reader, both when he served as ministerial surrogate and when he acted as ministerial assistant. The standard text was obviously the catechism from the Book of Common Prayer —interestingly enough, even during the Commonwealth period.[22]

In New England, it was initially assumed that the teaching of the catechism belonged in the home rather than the church, the theory being that a gathered congregation wanted "direct Scripture for ministers catechizing"; and a good deal of early legislation requiring heads of families to catechize their children and servants reflected this assumption. But a combination of clerical diligence and familial laxity seems gradually to have led the church to take over the responsibility, and it became customary for the minister—often the teacher— to spend a significant part of the Sabbath, before and after his sermon, questioning young people on matters of doctrine in general and on the catechism in particular. In Massachusetts, the practice was given civil encouragement in 1669, when the governor and council apparently advised the clergymen of all towns "to catechize and instruct all the people (especially youth) under your charge in the orthodox principles of the Christian religion, and that not only in public, but privately from house to house." Similarly, in Connecticut the legislature ordered in 1680 "that it be recommended to the ministry of this colony to catechize the youth in their respective places that are under twenty years of age, in the Assembly of Divines' Catechism, or some other orthodox catechism, on the Sabbath days."[23]

The process of catechizing was dull and routinized, with repetition being the chief pedagogical technique. Yet, in that process, many a youngster must have found himself, willy-nilly, learning to read, much as he learned to read at home, by matching print to an incessantly reiterated oral liturgy. And, since it was but a short step from catechizing to more general education, many a minister must have

---

[22] Tyler, ed., *Narratives of Early Virginia*, p. 271; and Hening, ed., *Statutes at Large; Being a Collection of All the Laws of Virginia*, I, 181-182, 290, 311-312, 341-342; II, 29, 47.

[23] Lechford, *Plain Dealing*, p. 53; Joseph B. Felt, *Annals of Salem* (2d ed.; 2 vols.; Salem: W. & S. B. Ives, 1845-1849), II, 586-587; and Trumbull, ed., *Public Records of the Colony of Connecticut*, III, 65.

served from time to time as schoolmaster to the children of his congregation, moving from catechism and Scripture to sustained instruction in the arts and ancient languages, in church or manse or even, perhaps, in a separate schoolhouse.

In addition, the minister educated his parishioners informally, advising them in their personal affairs, guiding them in their efforts to "grow in grace," admonishing them for their transgressions, and occasionally threatening them with or even invoking such punishments as excommunication and presentment at court. And, to the extent that he enlisted the churchwardens (Anglican) or elders (Congregational) and the congregation at large in reinforcing this education, it was extraordinarily powerful in confirming his more systematic teaching. The fact is that for most seventeenth-century Americans the church was the most significant community in which they participated outside the family: it served as a forum for the exchange of views, a market place for the transaction of business, and a rostrum for the communication of news. As such, it was inevitably liberating, inasmuch as it afforded individuals direct acquaintance with life styles other than their own. But it was coercive, too, in that it placed a community sanction behind the teaching of the minister. And it is this as much as anything that is meant by the phrase "church discipline," construing discipline in its classic sense, as instruction, as well as in its ecclesiastical sense, as the system whereby the conduct of church members is regulated.[24]

Most colonial ministers limited their educational endeavors to the parish or town; others, who took seriously the injunction to go forth and teach all nations, extended their efforts to the heathen beyond. To do so was to embark upon a long and arduous task, for which few materials and techniques were available. The early literature of colonization had spoken rhapsodically of the opportunity to convert the Indians, forecasting that the savages, thirsting for the gospel, would quickly acknowledge the superiority of an ordered Christian civilization. The actuality, of course, was very different. The earliest settlers of Virginia were initially preoccupied with the problem of survival, though as early as 1612 Alexander Whitaker sent a sermon

---

[24] It is important to note that church discipline extended to the unregenerate as well, following Paul to the Romans 2:14-15. See Wilford Oakland Cross, "The Role and Status of the Unregenerate in the Massachusetts Bay Colony, 1629-1729" (unpublished doctoral thesis, Columbia University, 1957), pp. 76-78 and *passim*.

to England in which he described colorfully the beliefs and institutions of the natives, pointed to their innate sense of piety and civility, and urged support of a vigorous policy of Christianization. Shortly thereafter, Whitaker successfully converted the Indian princess Pocahontas, whose subsequent visit to England marked the beginning of an elaborate plan for missionary activity that included, *inter alia*, the building of the college at Henrico. The scheme went up in smoke, however, with the massacre of 1622, which ended all but scattered missionary efforts in Virginia for the remainder of the century.

For New Englanders, the problem of proselytizing was compounded by the rigorous theology of Congregationalism, according to which conversion involved not merely the sacrament of baptism followed by some sort of minimal acquiescence in Christian belief and behavior but also the experience of saving grace deriving from thorough knowledge of the Scriptures. Until 1663, when John Eliot published an Algonquian edition of the Bible, this meant that a potential convert had either to learn sufficient English to study the Bible and comprehend the subtleties of the faith or to find a clergyman with sufficient command of Algonquian to instruct him in Puritan ways. Moreover, the whole idea of a gathered church assumed that a true Christian would live his life in strict accordance with Scripture; hence, any religious conversion would have to be accompanied by a social conversion to Puritan standards of dress and deportment. Little wonder that by 1640 there were but a handful of Indian converts in all New England.

Thereafter, the situation changed dramatically. In the first place, two extraordinarily gifted ministers, the Reverend Thomas Mayhew, Jr., of Martha's Vineyard, and the Reverend John Eliot of Roxbury, turned their efforts to missionary work, developing the linguistic skills, the preaching techniques, and the organizational devices for using native intermediaries that enabled them to effect conversions in unprecedented numbers. Beginning in 1643 with an Indian named Hiacoomes, "a man of a sad and a sober spirit," Mayhew was able to claim 22 converts by 1650, 199 by 1651, and 283 by 1652. Eliot, conducting his first service at Nonantum (on the Charles River, near Watertown) in 1646, preached with such success that sachems from other villages sought to have him proffer the gospel to their fellow tribesmen; and his visit to Concord persuaded the Indians there to look for an arrangement whereby they could live within the confines of the town, thus ensuring closer adherence to the ways of their new faith.[25]

In the second place, an eight-year effort by agents of the Bay Colony culminated in 1649 in the creation by Parliament of the Society for Propagation of the Gospel in New England, an eleemosynary corporation based in London, composed primarily of prosperous Puritan merchants, and expressly committed to raising funds to support endeavors such as Mayhew's and Eliot's. The Society printed tracts, broadsides, and letters describing successful proselytizing among the Indians in New England (many of them directly from Eliot's pen); it obtained testimonials from the universities of Oxford and Cambridge, from the officials of numerous cities and towns, and from Cromwell himself; and, by 1660, it had collected close to sixteen thousand pounds, from wealthy supporters, from the army, and from parishioners throughout the realm. With the Restoration, the organization was reincorporated as the "Company for Propagacion of the Gospell in New England, and the Parts Adjacent in America," under the leadership of Robert Boyle. And, though its finances between 1660 and 1689 were never wholly satisfactory, it did manage to raise an average of four hundred forty pounds a year during that period.

The Society's interests in New England were represented by the Commissioners of the United Colonies, who were explicitly designated to receive and administer the funds. As one might expect, the coexistence of the Society, the commissioners, and the missionaries themselves created conflicts of interest and perception that dogged the venture from the beginning. Nevertheless, during the quarter-century between 1650, when the commissioners first received confirmation of their responsibilities, and 1675, when King Philip's War radically altered the missionary enterprise, the Society bought clothing, building materials, and tools for the Indians; paid the salaries of ministers, schoolmasters, and civil agents who worked among the Indians; financed the erection of an Indian College at Harvard (which, lamentably, failed to serve its intended purpose for lack of qualified students); provided disbursements for a number of Indian missionaries and teachers; and underwrote the printing of an "Indian Library" in Algonquian, which was translated primarily by Eliot

25 Henry Whitfeld [sic], ed., *The Light Appearing More and More Towards the Perfect Day* (London: T. R. & E. M., 1651), in *Collections of the Massachusetts Historical Society*, 3d ser., IV (1834), 109.

and which included a Bible and a Psalter, Lewis Bayly's *The Practise of Pietie* and Richard Baxter's *A Call to the Unconverted* (1657),
and a grammar, primer, and catechism.

Finally, Eliot pioneered in the development of Indian "praying
towns," committed to the practice of Christian living as well as the
profession of Christian belief. "I find it absolutely necessary to carry
on civility with religion," Eliot wrote in 1649, reflecting the widespread sense that only as the Indians adopted English ways would
they be able truly to embrace Christianity. Having persuaded a number of sachems to his view, he obtained in the summer of 1651 two
thousand acres of land on the banks of the Charles, some eighteen
miles from Boston, and led a group of converts in founding Natick,
the first such praying town. By autumn, they had laid out streets,
assigned house and farm lots, constructed a two-story meetinghouse
(with a room for Eliot on the second floor), readied the land for
spring planting, and even established a civil polity based on Jethro's
instructions to Moses in the Book of Exodus. It would take nine more
years to consummate a church covenant satisfactory to the neighboring ministers, but the pattern was set; and, with the assistance of
funds from the Society, at least thirteen such towns were planted
over the next fourteen years—though only two had bona fide
churches, Natick and Hassawesitt.[26]

On the eve of King Philip's War, there were probably some
twenty-five hundred Christian Indians in New England, representing
roughly 20 per cent of the native population and concentrated mostly
in the praying towns of the Bay Colony and the islands of Martha's
Vineyard and Nantucket, where the Mayhews had proselytized with
such vigor and success. The war itself marked a turning point in the
missionary effort, for, while those Indians who had been converted
were easily among the most loyal to the colonial cause, the hostilities
left them dispersed and under a cloud of suspicion. As a result, the
praying towns declined in number and population, and the colonies
embarked upon a policy of restriction and close supervision. True,
Eliot and a second generation of missionaries persisted, as did the
New England Company; but meanwhile the problem itself was
being transformed, as the Indians increasingly assumed English
ways: they had taught the colonists to plant corn, trap beavers, and
fashion birchbarks, but they had learned from the colonists, too, not

---

[26] Edward Winslow, *The Glorious Progress of the Gospel, Amongst the Indians in
New England* (London: printed for Hannah Allen, 1649), in *ibid.*, p. 88.

merely the ways of piety and civility, but the ways of a dynamic commercial economy and its attendant social arrangements. The education that derived from the contact between the two groups had been mutual but not equal, and it was really the process of acculturation rather than deliberate efforts to nurture piety and civility that ultimately proved decisive.

The same was doubtless true in the case of the African blacks in the colonies, though they lacked even such modest support for their traditional culture as tribal association afforded the Indians. Like the red men, they elicited ambivalent feelings from the clergy, who considered them on the one hand incapable of true Christian profession and practice and on the other hand prime subjects for conversion. Unlike the red men, however, they were generally enslaved, and this posed the question of whether baptism should automatically emancipate them. The Virginia general assembly formally ruled on the question in 1667, declaring that "the conferring of baptism doth not alter the condition of the person as to his bondage or freedom." The assembly appended its hope that, freed of doubt, masters would accelerate the propagation of Christianity by permitting the baptism of slave children, but there is no evidence that the hope was more than partially realized. Some years later, a clergyman named Morgan Godwyn, who had served briefly in Virginia and then for a time in Barbados, issued a strong plea in London for Christianizing the Negroes in both colonies, but it seems at best to have had an indirect impact in stimulating the sort of metropolitan concern that eventuated in the founding of the Society for the Propagation of the Gospel in Foreign Parts in 1701.[27]

In New England, there was no legislative ruling comparable to Virginia's, nor was there any substantial entrance of blacks into the churches. Characteristically, John Eliot argued for the conversion of Negroes, warning slaveholders not to "imagine that the Almighty God made so many thousands of reasonable creatures for nothing but to serve the lusts of Epicures or the gains of mammonists," and, indeed, offered to catechize Negroes if their masters would send them; but there is no evidence whether his views were heeded, or his invitation accepted. In general, the blacks were reached neither by

[27] Hening, ed., *Statutes at Large; Being a Collection of All the Laws of Virginia*, II, 260. In 1682, another act extended the interpretation, barring automatic emancipation by virtue of conversion before immigration to Virginia (*ibid.*, p. 490). See also Morgan Godwyn, *The Negro's and Indians Advocate, Suing for Their Admission into the Church* (London: J. D., 1680).

ordinary ministerial education nor by special missionary education but were left to be influenced by the process of acculturation and the experience of enslavement.[28]

Eliot bears fuller discussion at this point, since he was perhaps the quintessential minister-educator of the seventeenth-century colonies. Every church, of course, had its "apostle to the Indians"— Alexander Whitaker among the Anglicans, Andrew White among the Roman Catholics, John Campanius among the Lutherans, and Johannes Megapolensis among the Dutch Reformed—each of whom ministered to white men and red men alike on the edges of the wilderness. But, more than anyone else, Eliot exemplifies the versatility, the dedication, and the indefatigability that the colonial situation demanded of its clerical teachers.

Born in 1604, the fourth child of a prosperous yeoman family, John Eliot grew up in East Anglia at the time that region was a leading center of Puritan Nonconformity. He attended a local grammar school and then went on as a pensioner at Jesus College, Cambridge, from which he was graduated in 1622. Following this, he returned to his boyhood home at Nazeing, in Essex County, where he served for a while as an usher at Thomas Hooker's school in Little Baddow and thus witnessed Hooker's confrontation with Archbishop Laud in 1629 and 1630 and his ensuing arrest and flight to Holland. Eliot may even have followed Hooker across the Channel and remained with him briefly; in any case, the association was doubtless exceedingly influential in Eliot's subsequent decision to migrate to New England with a group of about sixty people from Nazeing in the summer of 1631.

On debarking in September, Eliot was invited to serve temporarily as pastor in Boston, in place of the Reverend John Wilson, who had returned to England to fetch his wife and children. Thereafter, he took part in the gathering of a new congregation at Roxbury and was ordained teacher of the church there—he was possibly the first New England minister who had not been "bishoped" in England. He held the post for fifty-six years, spending almost half of them as sole minister to the congregation, attending earnestly to matters of doctrine, rendering his pulpit "another Mount Sinai for the flashes of lightning therein displayed against the breaches of law

28 Cotton Mather, *Magnalia Christi Americana; or, The Ecclesiastical History of New-England* (1702), edited by Thomas Robbins (2 vols.; Hartford: Silas Andrus and Son, 1853-1855), I, 581. For the context, see Robert C. Twombly, "Black Puritan: The Negro in Seventeenth-Century Massachusetts," *The William and Mary Quarterly*, 3d ser., XXIV (1967), 224-242.

given upon that burning mountain," zealously tutoring the ruling elders in the knowledge necessary for church membership, vigorously catechizing the young people to preserve them from the "gangrene of ill opinions," and sternly admonishing those who fell prey to Satan's blandishments. In addition, he personally interrogated Mrs. Hutchinson at her heresy trial, pronouncing her views altogether unsatisfactory, collaborated with Thomas Weld and Richard Mather in the preparation of the Bay Psalm Book in 1640, served as an overseer of Harvard College from 1642 until 1685, helped found the Roxbury Latin School in 1645, and played an influential role in the synods that produced the Cambridge Platform of 1648 and the halfway covenant of 1662. This was the man who felt called upon to preach to the Indians in their own language, to catechize their children, to publish books for them, and to look unceasingly after their welfare, right up to the time of his death in 1690. In the end, his apostolate failed, as did his efforts to maintain a uniform piety; but both were merely facets of his larger career as a teacher, a career that in one way or another touched the lives of most seventeenth-century New Englanders, white as well as red and black.[29]

III

Both the Anglican and the Puritan churches were early and firmly transplanted to American soil, under circumstances which, if anything, only intensified their historic commitment to teach. Three thousand miles from the metropolis, they saw themselves incarnating those fundamental values that would ultimately make the colonies true Christian communities. And, steadfastly committed to the struggle against barbarism, they set out to teach those values to all men, becoming, as they were in England, agencies of universal public education supported by the power and resources of the state.

Yet, almost from the beginning, they found themselves struggling not merely against barbarism but against certain stubborn realities of the colonial situation. First, there was the inescapable diversity of colonial religion: of the 260 churches in the colonies in 1689, 71 were Anglican, and 116 Congregational; but, in addition, there were 15 Baptist, 17 Dutch Reformed, 15 Presbyterian, 12 French Reformed, 9 Roman Catholic, and 5 Lutheran, and, beyond these, there were numerous small communities of Quakers, Mennonites,

---

[29] Mather, *Magnalia Christi Americana*, I, 548, 551.

Huguenots, Anabaptists, and Jews, which were lacking either in formal organization or in properly qualified spiritual leaders. All these churches and communities taught quite as vigorously as the established churches, perhaps even more so, since their religious instruction was often merely one aspect of a larger effort to preserve an entire ethnic tradition in the face of English cultural domination.[30]

Such education assumed a variety of forms in the several colonies. It is well illustrated in the work of the Dutch Reformed church in New York, which began as the established church of New Netherland, which enjoyed preferred status along with the Anglican church in New York between 1664 and 1674, and which was then forced to share that status with all the Christian churches in New York under the short-lived Charter of Liberties, enacted by the assembly in 1683. Prior to 1664, the Dutch church developed an elaborate system of ecclesiastical education under the direction of well-educated ministers, lay readers, "comforters of the sick" (who were charged "diligently to instruct the ignorant in the faith, especially out of the word of God"), and precentors (whose duty it was to set the Psalms). Dutch ministers and their lay assistants preached, read from the Scriptures, catechized and instructed the young, and engaged in missionary activities with the Indians in much the same spirit as their theological cousins in New England. And their efforts, along with those of the closely associated Dutch schools, were of crucial significance in preserving the Dutch language and culture long after the Church of England and English culture had become dominant in the province.[31]

The influence of Nonconformist education is also seen in the

---

[30] The statistics are based on Edwin Scott Gaustad, *Historical Atlas of Religion in America* (New York: Harper & Row, 1962), p. 3 and *passim;* Frederick Lewis Weis, *The Colonial Clergy and the Colonial Churches of New England* (Lancaster, Mass.: Society of the Descendants of the Colonial Clergy, 1936), *The Colonial Churches and the Colonial Clergy of the Middle and Southern Colonies, 1607-1776* (Lancaster, Mass.: Society of the Descendants of the Colonial Clergy, 1938), *The Colonial Clergy of Maryland, Delaware and Georgia* (Lancaster, Mass.: Society of the Descendants of the Colonial Clergy, 1950), and *The Colonial Clergy of Virginia, North Carolina and South Carolina* (Boston: Society of the Descendants of the Colonial Clergy, 1955); and Edward Tanjore Corwin, "The Ecclesiastical Condition of New York at the Opening of the Eighteenth Century," *Papers of the American Society of Church History,* 2d ser., III (1912), 81-115.

[31] Edward T. Corwin, ed., *Ecclesiastical Records, State of New York* (7 vols.; Albany: J. B. Lyon Company, 1901-1916), I, 97 and *passim.* For an early statement by a Dutch minister of the inextricable tie between civility and piety in missionary efforts with the Indians, see the Reverend Jonas Michaëlius' letter of 1628 to the Reverend Adrian Smoutius in Amsterdam, *ibid.,* pp. 60-61.

peaceful coexistence of the various congregations of Baptists in Rhode Island and in the spirited competition of Roman Catholics, Puritans, and Anglicans in Maryland. And it is seen best, perhaps, in the rapid expansion of Quakerism during the latter decades of the seventeenth century: despite vicious attempts to suppress the movement in the 1650's and 1660's, by the time George Fox and his companions arrived for a missionary tour in 1672, Quaker meetings, with their characteristic emphasis on mutual instruction and admonition, were thriving in every one of the colonies, from New Hampshire to South Carolina.

Second, there was the inherent localism of all the colonial churches, which manifested itself both in their reluctance to be closely regulated by metropolitan synods, classes, and bishops, and in the vigorous role of the laity in congregational governance and affairs. In the absence of fully developed ecclesiastical organizations and hierarchies, colonial churches simply ventured out on their own, developing principles and procedures that seemed both viable and appropriate: thus the mode of gathering a church and ordaining its ministry that evolved in New England, beginning with the formation of the Salem church in 1629; and thus, too, the rise to prominence of the lay vestries in Virginia and the practice of retaining clergymen on a year-by-year basis by simply neglecting to present them to the governor for permanent induction into office. The result was a subtle shift in the relationship between minister and congregation, which inevitably made ministerial teaching more particular in character and hence less conducive to the advancement of some predefined orthodoxy. And that particularism was only compounded in the latter half of the seventeenth century by the evangelicism forced upon the ministry when, with the passing of the first generation of settlers, religious zeal waned and church membership declined.

Finally, there was the prophetic bent of the American churches: just as Anglicanism in the late Tudor and early Stuart eras had become gradually less liturgical and more prophetic than traditional Roman Catholicism, so colonial Anglicanism and Congregationalism in the seventeenth century became less liturgical and more prophetic than metropolitan Anglicanism. And the resulting emphasis on preaching invariably made for dissonance, as highly learned and incorrigibly rationalistic ministers and their congregations probed the Scriptures for light on every conceivable aspect of human affairs. It was Roger Williams who saw as clearly as any man of his time the inextricable tie between doctrinal dissonance and man's slow progress toward religious truth. And it was Williams, too, who recognized both the injustice and the futility of permitting the state to prohibit that dissonance in favor of some uniform version of the truth. "God requireth not an uniformity of religion to be enacted and enforced in any civil state," Williams proclaimed in 1644; "true civility and Christianity may both flourish in a state or kingdom, notwithstanding the permission of divers and contrary consciences, either of Jew or Gentile."[32]

In the colonial world of divers and contrary consciences, the church taught in many voices. And it was only a matter of time until governments learned that they could do little to suppress the cacophony.

[32] Roger Williams, *The Bloudy Tenent, of Persecution, for Cause of Conscience, Discussed, in a Conference Betweene Truth and Peace*, edited by Samuel L. Caldwell, *Publications of the Narragansett Club*, 1st ser., III (1867), 3-4.

Chapter 6

SCHOOL

Lord, for schools everywhere among us! That our schools may
flourish! That every member of this assembly may go home, and
procure a good school to be encouraged in the town where he
lives! That before we die, we may be so happy as to see a good
school encouraged in every plantation of the country.

JOHN ELIOT

Schools first developed in England during the remarkable religious
and cultural efflorescence that began with the arrival of the "apostle"
Augustine in 597 and culminated in the work of Alcuin at York
during the latter half of the eighth century. And they developed in
response to the novel educational situation that accompanied the
conversion of the English to Christianity. Augustine's mission had
been immensely successful: with the assistance of King Ethelbert
of Kent, he had established himself and his fellow monks at Canterbury; and from there they had ventured forth to spread the gospel,
restoring such ancient churches as they could locate and building such
additional ones as they thought necessary. Yet the very success of
their effort had posed unprecedented educational problems: the new
religion clearly required a native clergy fluent in the Latin language,
steeped in Christian literature, and thoroughly grounded in the
Roman Catholic liturgy; but there were simply no means at hand
for educating such a clergy, and the Romano-British culture that
might have constituted the basis of their education was all but
extinct. To train a clergy, Augustine and his colleagues were forced
to create schools: these they established at their new cathedrals and
patterned after those of the later Roman Empire, in the process

transmitting the structure and substance of the ancient liberal curriculum—grammar, rhetoric, logic, arithmetic, geometry, astronomy,
and music—and introducing the special pedagogical procedures by
which Latin could be effectively taught within an alien culture.

When Alcuin first attended the cathedral school at York in the
730's, England could boast several such institutions at the various
diocesan seats, and the extent to which they had come to incarnate
the classical tradition is clearly revealed in his charming reminiscence
of his revered teacher, Albert, presiding over the studies at York:
"There he moistened thirsty hearts with diverse streams of teaching
and the varied dews of learning, giving to these the art of the science
of grammar, pouring on those the rivers of rhetoric. Some he polished
on the whetstone of law, some he taught to sing together in aeonian
chant, making others play on the flute of Castaly, and run with the
feet of lyric poets over the hills of Parnassus. Others the said master
made to know the harmony of heaven, the labors of sun and moon,
the five belts of the sky, the seven planets, the laws of the fixed
stars, their rising and setting, the movements of the air, the quak-
ing of sea and earth, the nature of men, cattle, birds and beasts,
the divers kinds of numbers and various shapes. He gave certainty
to the solemnity of Easter's return; above all, opening the mysteries
of holy writ and disclosing the abysses of the rude and ancient law.
Whatever youths he saw of conspicuous intelligence, those he joined
to himself, he taught, he fed, he loved; and so the teacher had many
disciples in the sacred volumes, advanced in various arts."[1]

During the next several hundred years, these centers of learning proliferated under various types of sponsorship, but they never
lost their essentially religious character. By the end of the medieval
period, there were, in addition to those schools originally associated
with the several cathedrals, some that had evolved in connection with
certain of the collegiate churches, monasteries, and hospitals, others
that had grown out of chantry foundations, that is, endowments
supporting priests to say masses for the dead, and a few that had
been developed by guilds of one sort or another. These institutions retained their commitment to liberal education, but, given the continuous existence of universities after the twelfth century, they were,
in effect, vestibules to learning, concentrating heavily on Latin gram-

---

[1] Arthur F. Leach, *Educational Charters and Documents, 598 to 1909* (Cambridge:
Cambridge University Press, 1911), pp. 13-15.

mar out of Donatus and Priscian, adding occasional works from selected classical authors, and leavening the whole with appropriate gleanings from the Christian corpus. Many of them were quite small, consisting only of a cleric and a few youngsters; and hence the lines between household, church, and school were frequently fuzzy and sometimes indistinguishable.

Besides these grammar schools, which constituted the principal agencies offering systematic instruction in the arts and languages, there were numerous inferior schools—"petty schools," they came to be called—which introduced youngsters to a more elementary and restricted fare. Some of these were also religious in character, preparing choir and altar boys for the churches and at the same time training them "to say, to sing, and to read." Others were decidedly more secular and served the growing commercial needs of the late medieval economy. Since these latter schools were often sponsored by individual entrepreneurs as well as by guilds and borough authorities, there are fewer records of them than of the ecclesiastical institutions. Yet there is evidence that they existed in substantial numbers, teaching reading (in English) and such writing and arithmetic as were required for conducting commercial transactions and keeping commercial records.[2]

Here, then, were the schools of England on the eve of the Renaissance. They obviously served as leading agencies for recruiting and training the parish clergy. They patently contributed to producing widespread literacy among the laity—once again, consider the success of the Lollards in gaining readers for the Scriptures. And they doubtless liberated countless children from the constrictions of villeinage—witness the 1406 statute providing "that every man or woman, of what estate or condition that he be, shall be free to set their son or daughter to take learning at any manner of school that pleaseth them within the realm." Yet it was these same schools that elicited the relentless criticism of the humanist reformers, and for good reason. They were clerkish and pedantic in character; they had managed to trivialize or lose much that was essential in the very classical wisdom they attempted to convey; and they seemed dominated by narrow conceptions of piety, civility, and learning.

[2] Geoffrey Chaucer, "The Prioress's Tale," *The Canterbury Tales*, in *The Works of Geoffrey Chaucer*, edited by F. N. Robinson (2d ed.; Boston: Houghton Mifflin Company, 1957), p. 161, l. 1690.

Only a thoroughgoing reformation, the humanists insisted, modeled on the refounding of St. Paul's around 1509, could render English schooling sufficient to the needs of a just Christian society.[3]

Such a reformation did occur during the years between 1480 and 1640, and with such vigor and sweep that it might even be described as a revolution. The principal elements in that revolution were the laicizing of sponsorship, the popularizing of access, and the systematizing of the curriculum. The laicizing of sponsorship derived from two phenomena: the dissolution of the monasteries and chantries under Henry VIII and Edward VI and the resultant founding and refounding of grammar schools devoid of the traditional superstructure of ecclesiastical control, and the heavy flow into education of contributions from the merchants and gentry, which crested during the early Stuart era and which, at least in the ten counties surveyed by W. K. Jordan, produced something of a tenfold increase in the number of available grammar schools (and this not counting the numerous private, tuition-supported establishments). Many of these schools sought and received charters from the sovereign; a number were given statutes similar to or actually modeled upon those of St. Paul's. Some were controlled by unincorporated feoffees (trustees to whom endowment was assigned for philanthropic purposes), others by specially incorporated boards of governors, and still others by town corporations, cathedral corporations, or guilds, which also carried additional responsibilities. But the crucial fact was the presence on most such governing bodies of laymen with neither clerical nor teaching responsibilities. The ecclesiastical monopoly over schooling, which had been breached in the late medieval era, was now decisively broken.[4]

This laicizing of sponsorship and control was paralleled by a significant broadening of clientele. The argument of the humanists that the systematic study of letters would produce superior governors as well as superior clerics proved exceedingly persuasive, especially in light of the continuing demands of the Tudor and Stuart bureaucra-

[3] 7 Hen. IV, c. xvii, *The Statutes at Large* (9 vols.; London: printed for Mark Basket, 1763-1765), I, 470.

[4] W. K. Jordan, *Philanthropy in England, 1480-1660* (London: George Allen & Unwin, 1959). In estimating the flow of funds into education, one should note criticisms of Jordan's failure to take sufficient account of the price revolution of the sixteenth century (*The English Historical Review*, LXXV [1960], 686, and *American Sociological Review*, XXV [1960], 296), though his judgment regarding the increase in the number of institutions receiving money is obviously unaffected by these.

cies for lay administrators and professionals. Increasingly, those sons of the gentry and the urban bourgeoisie who aspired to the church, the court, Parliament, or perhaps a local justiceship or the practice of the law streamed into the grammar schools to ready themselves for the universities or Inns of Court. Increasingly, too, the sons of yeomen, husbandmen, and even some laborers attended the petty schools (taught by curates, shopkeepers, and housewives, as well as by career masters), in order to prepare for an apprenticeship, or learn to read the Bible unassisted, or perhaps even enable themselves to claim benefit of clergy upon some confrontation with the law, thereby suffering a substantially milder punishment. Given the paucity of records and the lack of any precise definition of schools or schooling, it is difficult to reach a firm estimate of how many youngsters went to school and for how long. But there is abundant evidence of a considerable broadening in both the size and social composition of the school population during the Tudor and early Stuart eras.[5]

Finally, in keeping with the characteristic Tudor propensity toward uniformity, there was a systematizing of the curriculum, which came about partly through the standardization of textbooks and partly through the licensing of schoolmasters. Textbook standardization was made possible, of course, by the development of printing, which permitted the inexpensive reproduction of written materials on a large scale; surely that lesson could not have been lost on those who took part in the bitter debates over the translation and dissemination of the Bible. What Henry VIII and his counselors did was to convert the possibility into a technique for furthering intellectual uniformity by giving royal sanction to a particular primer (a layman's service book, which brought together selections of Scripture, the liturgy, and prayer, in English or in Latin), a particular catechism (initially, *The Institution of a Christian Man,* produced by Convocation in 1537; under Edward VI, the version included in the Book of Common Prayer), and a particular grammar (the Colet-Lily-Erasmus compilation known as *Lily's Grammar).[6]*

Royal promulgations under Edward VI and Elizabeth I required

[5] Lawrence Stone, "The Educational Revolution in England, 1560-1640," *Past & Present,* no. 28 (July, 1964), pp. 41-80.

[6] The ABC book (an alphabet combined with the Pater Noster, the Ave Maria, the Apostles' Creed, as well as selected short prayers in English or Latin, and, later, the Decalogue) commonly preceded the primer or catechism, but no particular edition was authorized by Edward VI. See *The ABC Both in Latyn & Englyshe,* with an introduction by E. S. Shuckburgh (London: Elliott Stock, 1889).

teachers to use the variant forms of these authorized texts, though, with the growing circulation of the English Bible and the Book of Common Prayer during Elizabeth's reign, the primer was gradually transmuted from a fairly well-defined devotional book with auxiliary instructional intent into a fairly general reading manual with auxiliary devotional intent. And, as is often the case with efforts toward standardization, the materials occasioned a good deal of curricular "leveling upward," however much they may also have constrained a desirable intellectual diversity. Such was certainly the case with *Lily's Grammar*, which, after the study of English grammar had been specifically excluded from the universities in 1570, for all intents and purposes led the general upgrading of grammar-school instruction along the lines suggested by the humanists. One need only compare a curriculum centering on Donatus and Priscian with the one described in Charles Hoole's *A New Discovery of the Old Art of Teaching School* (1660) to realize the scope of the improvement.

The licensing of schoolmasters was a custom that probably gained currency during the early part of the twelfth century, when schools began to grow up independently of churches and monasteries. The vigor with which it was pursued in medieval England varied with the character of the ecclesiastical leadership (licenses were granted by the ordinary of a diocese or his surrogate) and the intensity of doctrinal controversy (not surprisingly, outbreaks of Lollardry occasioned increased surveillance). Curiously, given the heated battles of the 1530's and 1540's, the Royal Injunctions of Henry VIII and Edward VI failed even to mention the licensing of schoolmasters, though one ought not to assume from that failure that the practice therefore ceased. As early as 1553, on the other hand, Queen Mary instructed Bishop Bonner to examine all schoolmasters, preachers, and teachers of children with respect to their orthodoxy and, upon finding them suspect in any way, to remove them summarily. Four years later, Cardinal Pole explicitly restated the directive that schoolmasters be examined and approved by the ordinary, a measure that Elizabeth retained in her Injunctions of 1559. Furthermore, a parliamentary statute of 1562 included "all schoolmasters and public and private teachers of children" among those required to take the oath of supremacy, the object being to prevent them from maintaining or defending the authority of the bishop of Rome. And, beyond this, the regulations governing the several dioceses ordered, in addition, that schoolmasters attend church (Salisbury and Exeter), that they take Communion regularly (Carlisle), and that they be diligent in their work and honest in character (Worcester).[7]

With the excommunication of the queen in 1570 and the incorporation of the licensing principle into the canons of 1571, the vigor with which the various dioceses examined schoolmasters for conformity began to mount. By 1586, Bishop Aylmer of London was inquiring insistently into their sincerity of "religion, life, and conversation," their attendance at church and their partaking of Holy Communion, their use of the authorized catechism, and their private activities, particularly with respect to possible popish teaching or the delivery of lectures preaching "innovations." Whereas in the 1560's and 1570's the practice of licensing had been widely honored in the breach, by the 1590's it had become a potent weapon in the struggle for uniformity.[8]

The principal outcome of the Tudor educational revolution was an unprecedented availability of schooling in early seventeenth-century England, though there was no school system in any latter-day sense. This schooling proceeded at two levels, which were clearly distinguishable, both institutionally and in the literature that emerged after 1580: there were the petty schools, which concentrated on reading but which also offered writing, ciphering, and apparently anything else the students demanded and the instructors felt qualified to teach; and there were the grammar schools, which stressed the reading, writing, and speaking of Latin, also providing instruction in Greek and Hebrew. But, however different the emphases and functions of the two types of school, there was blurring at several points. First, as has already been mentioned, there was considerable blurring between households, churches, and schools all along the line, and both petty-school and grammar-school instruction went on in homes, shops, and chancels, as well as in schoolhouses (not only openly under regularly licensed teachers but also secretly under Puritans and recusants). Then, too, there was the blurring that resulted when petty-

[7] Edward Cardwell, ed., *Documentary Annals of the Reformed Church of England* (2 vols.; Oxford: Oxford University Press, 1839), I, 112; Walter Howard Frere and William McClure Kennedy, eds., *Visitation Articles and Injunctions of the Period of the Reformation*, Alcuin Club Collections, vols. XIV-XVI (3 vols.; Longmans, Green & Co., 1910), II, 425; III, 21, 33, 43, 339, 225; and 5 Eliz. I, c. i, *Statutes at Large*, II, 532.

[8] *A Booke of Certaine Canons* (London: J. Daye, 1571), pp. 25-26; and W. P. M. Kennedy, ed., *Elizabethan Episcopal Administration*, Alcuin Club Collections, vols. XXV-XXVII (3 vols.; A. R. Mowbray & Co., 1924), III, 204-205.

school teachers, particularly the private entrepreneurs, began to extend their offerings to include the ancient languages, grammar, and rhetoric at the same time that grammar-school masters began to establish preparatory classes for "petties," so that the "petties" could obtain the necessary training for the grammar course. This was especially true in the "country schools" that John Brinsley wrote about, which catered to children of all ages and frequently of all classes, teaching the seven-year-olds to read and write English while carrying a few determined youngsters all the way to the university.[9]

The petty schools were expected to render boys—and, as the century progressed, growing numbers of girls—proficient in reading and writing the mother tongue, taking some two or three years to complete the task. The process was the one described by Edmund Coote in *The English Schoole-Maister*: using a hornbook (a small paddle-shaped piece of wood, to which was affixed a layer of horn bearing the letters of the alphabet and a brief prayer or invocation) or an ABC, the youngster learned the alphabet and syllabarium (ba-be-bi-bo-bu, ca-ce-ci-co-cu, etc.) as well as simple words; then, using a catechism or a primer, which set forth well-known liturgical commonplaces, he worked at associating written words with sounds, until he had mastered the art of reading. Along with this core of reading instruction came some writing (perhaps with an independent scrivener), some arithmetic, possibly some singing or music, and occasionally some training in manners from books such as Francis Seager's *The Schoole of Vertue* or Hugh Rhodes's *The Boke of Nurture*.[10]

The grammar schools were expected to give boys a considerable facility in Latin and an elementary knowledge of Greek and Hebrew, this in a period of about seven years, though most students did not complete the entire course. The program of study was commonly divided into eight "forms" (a term probably deriving from the stalls along the walls of the schoolroom, within which students sat on tiers of benches): the lower forms concentrated on Latin gram-

---

[9] John Brinsley, *Ludus Literarius: or, The Grammar Schoole* (London: printed for Thomas Man, 1612), p. 9 and *passim*.

[10] The process is also described in [William Kempe], *The Education of Children in Learning* (London: Thomas Orwin, 1588), sigs. F₁ verso—F₂ verso. For all the emphasis on the authorized catechism, it should be recognized that at least sixty versions were in circulation by the end of the sixteenth century. See Foster Watson, *The English Grammar Schools to 1660: Their Curriculum and Practice* (Cambridge: Cambridge University Press, 1908), pp. 83-84.

mar (out of Lily, though by 1640 there were at least a half-dozen other prominent grammar texts), Latin conversation and composition, and selected Latin writings, notably, *Sententiae pueriles* and Lily's *Carmen de moribus* (both collections of moral maxims to be memorized, parsed, and construed), Cato's *Distichs* and *Aesop's Fables*, Erasmus' *Colloquies*, the comedies of Terence, the *Epistles* and *Metamorphoses* of Ovid, and the Scriptures; the upper forms continued the study of Latin, reading Horace, Virgil, Juvenal, Caesar, Sallust, and Cicero, and initiated the work in Greek grammar (William Camden's *Institutio Graecae grammatices* was the textbook most widely used), Greek literature (Homer, Euripides, Isocrates, Hesiod, and the Greek Testament), and Hebrew grammar. As a rule, mornings were devoted to grammar, afternoons to literature, Fridays to review and the testing of memorization, Saturdays to themes, and Sundays to catechizing and other religious exercises.

Most of the petty schools were taught by a single dame or master; most of the grammar schools were presided over by a master, frequently with the assistance of an usher or two, though it was not uncommon for a single individual to conduct all the instruction in a country grammar school. While we know much less than we should like about the training of early seventeenth-century schoolmasters, Brian Simon's detailed study of Leicestershire between 1625 and 1640 is instructive. Using the records of licensing at the archdeaconry of Leicester—which admittedly do not include several kinds of teachers, among them, Nonconformists who evaded the entire licensing process—Simon found that forty-three of the sixty-two subscribers between December, 1626, and November, 1639, were university graduates and that almost all the nongraduates either had taken their degrees soon after subscription or were designated *literatus* by virtue of having attended the university for a period of time. (Simon also found that subscription by petty-school teachers was not seriously enforced, with the result that there were no subscriptions by women, though contemporary visitation records indicate that women frequently served as schoolmistresses.) Finally, given the canon of 1604, directing that curates in parishes without schools be granted licenses to teach if they were willing and able to do so, it became fairly common for clergymen to undertake schoolteaching; and, in light of the high percentage of university graduates entering curacies by 1640 (virtually 100 per cent in the dioceses Miss Barratt studied), one can reasonably assume there was a rise in the quality of teaching in the grammar schools of the English villages.[11]

It is difficult to know with any certainty the impact of this unprecedented availability of schooling on English life and thought during the seventeenth century. There is every indication that the literacy rate increased—Lawrence Stone has ventured an estimate of 50 per cent for males in Jacobean London, his assumption being that it was lower in the outlying towns and villages—and the increase doubtless contributed to both the religious enthusiasm (deriving from widespread Bible-reading) and the political enthusiasm (deriving from widespread pamphlet-reading) that came to the fore during the Commonwealth period. There is evidence, too, that the grammar schools prepared boys for the universities and Inns of Court in extraordinary numbers, drawing more and more of them from the ranks of the yeomen, artisans, and merchants. And, finally, it is clear that the significance of schooling for the quality of English life was widely recognized—witness the outpouring of educational schemes and proposals during the 1640's and 1650's. True, there was a retreat with the Restoration, as education fell under suspicion as a subverter of authority and as opportunities for schooling were sharply reduced; but the fact is that the century of genius was also a century of unprecedented participation in the political, religious, and intellectual affairs of England. And that participation was a crucial element in the heritage exported to the colonies, where the Restoration was influential but never decisive in determining the course of American social and political development.[12]

I I

At the outset, preaching and catechizing were the forms of education most widely practiced in each of the North American colonies planted during the first half of the seventeenth century. As a rule, schooling came a bit later, as communities achieved greater stability and growing self-confidence. But schooling was rarely far behind, since it was viewed by the colonists as the most important bulwark after religion in their incessant struggle against the satanic barbarism of the

11 Brian Simon, "Leicestershire Schools, 1625-1640," *British Journal of Educational Studies*, III (1954-55), 42-58. For the relevant canon of 1604, see Edward Cardwell, ed., *Synodalia* (2 vols.; Oxford: Oxford University Press, 1842), I, 291.

12 Stone, "Educational Revolution in England," pp. 43, 79-80, and *passim*.

wilderness. "We in this country," wrote Jonathan Mitchell, probably in 1663, "being far removed from the more cultivated parts of the world, had need to use utmost care and diligence to keep up learning and all helps to education among us, lest degeneracy, barbarism, ignorance and irreligion do by degrees break in upon us."[13]

Both the metropolitan sponsors and the colonial planters early manifested an interest in schools. In Virginia, there were the plans for a "public free school" to be located at Charles City, which originated in the subscription of seventy pounds aboard the ship *Royal James* at the behest of the Reverend Patrick Copland and which took form when the Virginia Company granted a thousand acres of land to maintain a teacher and an usher, sent a carpenter and five apprentices to erect the schoolhouse, engaged a Mr. Dike as master, and arranged to secure such books as Dike and his scholars would require. But the East India School, as it was to have been called, never came into being. The funds were mismanaged, and the supplies apparently lost at sea, and in 1624 the Company decided that voluntary contributions like the one collected on the *Royal James* might be better used for a hospital than a school.

There were numerous other metropolitan efforts to establish schools in Virginia, one growing out of an anonymous gift of five hundred fifty pounds, which was designated for educational purposes but which ended up being used to build an ironworks (the profits from which would have gone toward the instruction of Indian children had it not been destroyed in the massacre of 1622), and another embodied in the elaborate plan for Academia Virginiensis et Oxoniensis, written into the will of Edward Palmer in 1624. But none materialized, and indeed there is evidence that by the 1620's— particularly after the massacre—the adventurers in London were simply not assigning a very high priority to schooling, preferring to leave the initiative to the settlers themselves.

Such initiative was in due course exercised, when in 1635 a planter named Benjamin Syms bequeathed two hundred acres of land on the Poquoson, a small tributary of the Chesapeake Bay, and the produce and increase from eight cows for a free school "to educate and teach the children of the adjoining parishes of Elizabeth City and Poquoson," the first produce and increase from the cattle to

---

13 Jonathan Mitchell, "A Modell for the Maintaining of Students & Fellows of Choise Abilities at the Colledge in Cambridge," *Publications of the Colonial Society of Massachusetts,* XXXI (1935), 311.

be used to build a schoolhouse and the subsequent produce and increase to support the education of poor scholars. In March, 1643, the Virginia assembly, hoping to encourage others "in like pious performances," gave legislative sanction to the Syms will by confirming the bequest "according to the true meaning and godly intent" of the testator; and it appears that the school actually came into existence shortly thereafter. Some years later, a surgeon named Thomas Eaton (doubtless inspired by Syms's example) left an even larger bequest, including five hundred acres of land, twenty hogs, twelve cows, two bulls, and two Negro slaves, for similar purposes. And there is every reason to believe that the projected institution was in operation, along with the Syms school, at the time Governor Berkeley thanked God there were no free schools in Virginia.[14]

In New Netherland, too, the metropolitan sponsors early manifested an interest in schooling; in fact, the Dutch West India Company and its colonial representatives played a significant role in founding schools in eleven of the twelve Dutch communities established before the English conquest of 1664. While their efforts are not surprising, given the lively educational tradition of the seventeenth-century Dutch republic (which was at least as well schooled as England, perhaps better), the Company was probably motivated more by a desire to attract additional settlers to the colony than by a concern for culture. In any case, it was the Company that sponsored the establishment of the first town school in New Amsterdam in 1638 and the Company that paid the base salary of the masters, though it was the Classis of Amsterdam rather than the Company that initially oversaw the licensing of schoolmasters. It was the Company, too, acting through the resident director-general and council at New Amsterdam, that encouraged the establishment of similar schools in the outlying villages, albeit the maintenance of these schools gradually passed to the local authorities during the final years of Dutch rule. And it was the Company, acting in concert with the

14 Helen Jones Campbell, "The Syms and Eaton Schools and Their Successor," *William and Mary Quarterly*, 2d ser., XX (1940), 22; and William Waller Hening, ed., *The Statutes at Large; Being a Collection of All the Laws of Virginia, from the First Session of the Legislature, in the Year 1619* (13 vols.; imprint varies, 1819-1823), I, 252. Berkeley made his oft-quoted comment in a 1671 reply to an inquiry from the Commissioners of Trade and Plantations: "But, I thank God, there are no free schools nor printing, and I hope we shall not have these [for a] hundred years; for learning has brought disobedience and heresy, and sects into the world, and printing has divulged them, and libels against the best government. God keep us from both!" See *ibid.*, II, 517.

Classis of Amsterdam and the burgomasters and *schepens* (magistrates), that arranged in 1659 for the establishment of a classical school at New Amsterdam.[15]

Yet all this was not without its tensions between the directors of the Company in Amsterdam and the colonists three thousand miles away, as witness the Grand Remonstrance against Peter Stuyvesant's highhanded rule as chief representative of the Company, which the colonists addressed directly to the States-General in 1649. Pouring out their grievances over the mismanagement that had brought New Netherland "into the ruinous condition in which it is now found to be," the petitioners complained that the "bowl has been going round a long time for the purpose of erecting a common school and it has been built with words, but as yet the first stone is not laid"; and they asserted in their list of demands: "There should be a public school, provided with at least two good masters, so that first of all in so wild a country, where there are many loose people, the youth will be well taught and brought up, not only in reading and writing, but also in the knowledge and fear of the Lord." A reply to the Remonstrance, prepared by Cornelis van Tienhoven, secretary to the governor-general and council, pointed out that the New Amsterdam school was very much in existence, under master Jan Cornelissen, that other teachers offered additional instruction in hired houses, and that "the youth, considering the circumstances of the country, are not in want of schools." After due consideration, the States-General deftly side-stepped the issue by suggesting only that the commonality ought to provide competent schoolmasters; with equal deftness, the Company managed to ignore the suggestion. New Amsterdam did receive municipal powers as a result of the Remonstrance, however, and the eleven years between 1653 and the arrival of the English witnessed a constant tug of war between Stuyvesant and the burgomasters, with Stuyvesant pressing the city to contribute more toward the support of the public school and the city fathers refusing to do so unless they could control it. The outcome was a draw: the Company continued to pay the schoolmaster, the city provided the school-

[15] For a picture of contemporary Dutch schooling, see *Valcooch's Regel der Duytsche Schoolmeesters,* edited by Pieter Antonie de Planque (Groningen: P. Noordhoff, 1926). For specific evidence of the Company's initial interest in schools, see "Particuliere Instructie voor den Ingenieur ende Lantmeter Cryn Fredericxsz alsmede voor den Commes ende Raden om haer daernoer te reguleren," *Documents Relating to New Netherland 1624-1626 in the Henry E. Huntington Library,* translated and edited by A. J. F. van Laer (San Marino, Calif.: The Henry E. Huntington Library, 1924).

house and the master's dwelling, and the burgomasters managed the affairs of the institution, subject, of course, to the "advice" of the director and council.[16]

In New England, the situation was quite different. There, the initiative in the establishment of schools came not from the metropolis but from the plantations themselves. The Plymouth Colony founded no schools during its earliest years, preferring to leave such education as seemed desirable to church and household. But the Bay Colony began rather quickly to experiment with various arrangements for formal instruction. The town of Boston agreed on April 13, 1635, that "our brother Philemon Pormont, shall be entreated to become schoolmaster, for the teaching and nurturing of children with us"; there is evidence that Ipswich maintained a short-lived grammar school in 1636; Charlestown arranged with William Witherell on June 3, 1636, "to keep a school for a twelve-month"; Cambridge, in 1638, set off almost three acres "to the town's use forever for a public school or college"; Dorchester voted on May 20, 1639, to impose an annual rent of twenty pounds on Thomson's Island for the maintenance of a school; that same year, Newbury decided to cede two pieces of land to Anthony Somerby to "encourage" him to keep school, while Salem appointed "young Mr. Norris" as its schoolmaster. Within the first decade of settlement, seven of the twenty-two towns of Massachusetts had taken some public action on behalf of schooling, though they had not all been able to establish viable institutions.[17]

Similarly, the general court of New Haven ordered on February 25, 1642, that a free school be established in the town and instructed the pastor, John Davenport, and the magistrates to consider "what yearly allowance is meet to be given to it out of the common stock of the town." The town of Hartford voted in 1642 that "thirty pounds

16 J. Franklin Jameson, ed., *Narratives of New Netherland, 1609-1664*, Original Narratives of Early American History, edited by J. Franklin Jameson (New York: Charles Scribner's Sons, 1909), pp. 320, 327, 353, 362.

17 *Second Report of the Record Commissioners of the City of Boston: Containing the Boston Records, 1634-1660, and the Book of Possessions* (2d ed.; Boston: Rockwell and Churchill, 1881), p. 5; The Original Records of the Grammar School or as by Some Termed the Free School of Ipswich (ms. records, Town Hall, Ipswich, Mass.); Harry H. Edes, ed., Charlestown Town Records (17 vols.; microfilm records, Boston Public Library), II, 11; *The Records of the Town of Cambridge, Massachusetts, 1603-1703* (Cambridge, Mass.: no publisher, 1901), p. 33; *Fourth Report of the Record Commissioners [of the City of Boston]: Dorchester Town Records* (Boston: Rockwell and Churchill, 1880), p. 39; Newbury Town Records, 1637-1692 (ms. records, Town Hall, Newbury, Mass.), p. 33; and *Essex Institute Historical Collections*, IX (1868), 97.

a year shall be settled upon the school by the town forever." And there is some evidence that Newport, Rhode Island, engaged Robert Lenthal, who had been pastor at Weymouth, Massachusetts, to keep a "public school for the learning of youth" in 1640.[18]

By 1647, Massachusetts had experimented for more than a decade with different sorts of schooling, and at least nine institutions were in operation: Dorchester, Charlestown, Boston, Dedham, and Ipswich maintained town-initiated grammar schools; Salem maintained a town-initiated petty school; Roxbury had a quasi-public grammar school sponsored by a substantial group of householders; Somerby was probably still keeping a private school in Newbury; and Elijah Corlet was conducting a private grammar school in Cambridge. But the majority of the colony's townships had not yet taken action to provide formal schooling—indeed, the impetus to found schools seems to have waned in the 1640's—and the general court therefore felt impelled to provide a modicum of legislative encouragement, as part of its continuing effort to enhance the self-sufficiency of the colony. The result was the school act of November 11, 1647, which would decisively influence the educational history of New England for the remainder of the colonial period:

It being one chief project of that old deluder, Satan, to keep men from the knowledge of the Scriptures, as in former times by keeping them in an unknown tongue, so in these latter times by persuading from the use of tongues, that so at least the true sense and meaning of the original might be clouded by false glosses of saint-seeming deceivers, that learning may not be buried in the grave of our fathers in the church and commonwealth, the Lord assisting our endeavors,—

It is therefore ordered, that every township in this jurisdiction, after the Lord hath increased them to the number of fifty householders, shall then forthwith appoint one within their town to teach all such children as shall resort to him to write and read, whose wages shall be paid either by the parents or masters of such children, or by the inhabitants in general, by way of supply, as the major part of those that order the prudentials of the town shall appoint; provided, those that send their children be not oppressed by paying much more than they can have them taught for in other towns; and it is further ordered, that where any town

[18] Charles J. Hoadly, ed., *Records of the Colony and Plantation of New Haven, from 1638 to 1649* (Hartford: Case, Tiffany and Company, 1857), p. 62; "Hartford Town Votes, Vol. I," *Collections of the Connecticut Historical Society*, VI (1897), 63; and John Callender, *An Historical Discourse on the Civil and Religious Affairs of the Colony of Rhode-Island and Providence Plantations in New-England in America* (Boston: S. Kneeland and T. Green, 1739), pp. 62-63.

shall increase to the number of one hundred families or householders, they shall set up a grammar school, the master thereof being able to instruct youth so far as they may be fitted for the university, provided, that if any town neglect the performance hereof above one year, that every such town shall pay five pounds to the next school till they shall perform this order.

Geraldine Murphy has studied in detail the impact of the law in Massachusetts: during the first decade after its passage, all eight of the hundred-family towns in the colony complied with the grammar-school requirements, whereas only a third of the fifty-family towns complied with the petty-school requirement; thereafter, as new towns reached the stipulated sizes, they tended to disregard both requirements. Meanwhile, Connecticut enacted precisely the same statute in 1650 and virtually the same statute in the legislative revision of 1672, after it had incorporated New Haven. And Plymouth recommended petty schools to its various towns in 1658, mandating grammar schools for towns of fifty or more families in 1677.[19]

By 1650, schooling as an institution had been firmly transplanted to the North American continent, though with varying degrees of enthusiasm. The free school endowed by Benjamin Syms was already in operation in Virginia, and at least one observer reported the existence of "other petty schools" as well. Maryland had a school for the teaching of humanities, conducted by Ralph Crouch, a layman closely associated with the Jesuit mission at Newtown. New Netherland maintained a town school at New Amsterdam, and there may have been schooling in New Sweden, too, given Queen Christina's injunction regarding the maintenance of ministers and schoolmasters. And, in New England, there were at least a dozen schools capable of providing Latin grammar instruction and numerous others offering reading and writing under a master or dame. By that year, too, Massachusetts and Connecticut had enacted pioneering legislation calling for schools in all larger communities, and, although the requirement with

19 Nathaniel B. Shurtleff, ed., Records of the Governor and Company of the Massachusetts Bay in New England (5 vols.; Boston: William White, 1853-1854), II, 203; Geraldine Joanne Murphy, "Massachusetts Bay Colony: The Role of Government in Education" (unpublished doctoral thesis, Radcliffe College, 1960), chap. iii; J. Hammond Trumbull, ed. [vols. I-III], The Public Records of the Colony of Connecticut (15 vols.; Hartford: publisher varies, 1850-1890), I, 554-555; The Book of the General Laws for the People Within the Jurisdiction of Connecticut (Cambridge, Mass.: Samuel Green, 1673), pp. 14, 63; and Nathaniel B. Shurtleff and David Pulsifer, eds., Records of the Colony of New Plymouth in New England (12 vols.; Boston: William White, 1855-1861), XI, 142, 246-247.

respect to petty schools was frequently honored in the breach, the principle remained. Thereafter, the development of schools was about what one would expect from these beginnings: by 1689, Virginia could boast some six schools, Maryland at least one, New York about eleven, and Massachusetts probably around twenty-three.[20]

Nothing is more striking about these institutions than the variety in the modes of their sponsorship and support: virtually every arrangement then current in England was taken as the paradigm for a school somewhere in the colonies. Syms and Eaton bequeathed land and personalty for the purpose of establishing schools, and there is every indication that they intended the property to be administered and used much as it would have been in contemporary England, that is, held and managed in perpetuity by a stipulated board of trustees; Syms's board would consist of "the commander and the rest of the commissioners [later, justices of the peace] of this liberty [county] with the ministers and churchwardens of the said parish where the said school is founded," and Eaton's, of "the commissioners, minister and churchwarden." The school at Newtown, in Maryland, was probably controlled by the Jesuit mission and drew its support from mission funds and tuition, though it did receive at least one bequest from a private citizen.[21]

The schools of New Netherland were initially under the direct regulation of the Dutch West India Company and the Classis of Amsterdam, with the Company paying the salaries of schoolmasters out of general funds. Later, they fell under the mixed control of Company and classis on the one hand and local consistory and court on the other, with support coming from Company contributions, voluntary and enforced subscriptions, and tuition. Under the English, the local consistories and courts continued to employ, oversee, and remove schoolmasters, though it is patent that they competed quite as much as they co-operated in the management of school affairs and the raising of school funds.

New England's experience with various modes of school manage-

---

[20] *A Perfect Description of Virginia* (London: printed for Richard Wodenoth, 1649), in Peter Force, ed., *Tracts and Other Papers, Relating Principally to the Origin, Settlement, and Progress of the Colonies in North America, from the Discovery of the Country to the Year 1776* (4 vols.; Washington, D.C.: Peter Force, 1836-1846), vol. II, no. 8, p. 15; and "Queen Christina's Grant and Privilege for the Establishment of a New Colony in New Sweden," *Pennsylvania Archives*, 2d ser., V (1877), 760.

[21] Campbell, "Syms and Eaton Schools and Their Successor," pp. 22, 24.

ment during this period is especially interesting because of the
number and diversity of the arrangements that were tried. Boston,
for example, employed Philemon Pormont as its master in 1635 but
made no provision for establishing or maintaining a school. The
following year, when Pormont departed in the general exodus of
antinomians, a group of forty-five of the "richer inhabitants," including the selectmen, met to raise a subscription for a grammar
school and named Daniel Maud master. The subscription was insufficient; and, in 1641, the town meeting assigned the rent of
Deer Island for the maintenance of a free school, unless one could
be "otherwise provided for." Rents, however, proved as inadequate
as subscriptions, and the town reluctantly turned to taxation. Charlestown, on the other hand, from the beginning paid its schoolmaster
through the public rate but hoped that assigned rents from lands on
Lovell's Island and the Mystic Weir would eventually support the
school. The inhabitants of Roxbury came together in 1645, agreed
to erect a free school and to allot twenty pounds annually for the
schoolmaster "to be raised out of the messuages and part of the
lands of the several donors," set up a governing board of seven
feoffees with power to "put in or remove the schoolmaster, to see
to the well-ordering of the school and scholars, to receive and pay
the said twenty pounds . . . and to dispose of any other gift or gifts
that hereafter may or shall be given," and stipulated that donors'
children would attend gratis while others would pay a fee. And, at
Hartford and New Haven, a substantial bequest from Edward Hopkins, a former governor of Connecticut, laid the basis for the establishment of two grammar schools "for the education of youth in
good literature." All this, incidentally, above and beyond the numerous arrangements whereby ministers, schoolmasters, and school
dames set up shop independently, attracted such pupils as they could,
and collected tuition from parents.[22]

However diverse the modes of maintenance, there is every reason
to believe that the curriculum was fairly standard, following that
common in contemporary England. Children's textbooks are notori-
ously ephemeral, the more so in a colonial situation, where a single
volume has to serve a large number of readers. We can assume that

---

[22] *Second Report of the Record Commissioners of the City of Boston: Containing
the Boston Records, 1634-1660*, pp. 160, 65; Old School Book (ms. records, Roxbury
Latin School, Roxbury, Mass.); and Charles J. Hoadly, ed., *Records of the Colony or
Jurisdiction of New Haven, from May, 1653, to the Union* (Hartford: Case, Lockwood
and Company, 1858), p. 371.

the study of reading began with the alphabet and syllables, taken perhaps from a hornbook or ABC, and then proceeded directly to a catechism, primer, or Psalter, or even to Edmund Coote's *The English Schoole-Maister*. These were all imported into the colonies in quantity; and there is even evidence that the Cambridge (Mass.) press printed a speller in the 1640's (this may have been Coote's) and a primer and children's Psalter in 1668, but copies of these books have not been located and one can only speculate as to their content. Writing and ciphering were likely taught from a text such as Lewis Hughes's *Plain and Easy Directions to Faire Writing* (before 1650?) or Edward Cocker's *The Tutor to Writing and Arithmetic* (1664), or perhaps from models prepared by the schoolmaster himself. It is also probable that the standard works on piety and civility by Foxe, Bayly, Seager, and Rhodes were read from time to time, though it has not been established that the latter circulated in the colonies.[23]

Like its English counterpart, the grammar-school curriculum emphasized Latin but included an introduction to Greek and occasionally to Hebrew, the level of aspiration being best defined by the Harvard entrance requirements of 1655, which specified an ability to read and understand Cicero, Virgil, or "any such ordinary classical authors," to speak or write Latin in prose and verse, and "to construe and grammatically to resolve ordinary Greek, as in the Greek Testament, Isocrates, and the minor poets." Latin grammar was taught from one of the numerous revisions of Lily, supplemented by texts like John Amos Comenius' *Orbis pictus* (1659), John Brinsley's *Latin Accidence* (1611), and Charles Hoole's *The Common Rudiments of Latin Grammar* (1657); the boys then parsed and construed from the *Sententiae pueriles*, Cato's *Distichs*, *Aesop's Fables*, and the *Colloquies* of Erasmus and Corderius; and from these introductory materials they went on to selected works by Ovid, Cicero, Virgil, Horace, and Juvenal. Greek grammar was usually studied out of Camden, the scholars proceeding from this to Homer, Hesiod, Isocrates, and the Greek Testament. When Hebrew was included, it was most likely taught from the grammars of William Schickard

[23] Robert F. Roden, *The Cambridge Press, 1638-1692* (New York: Dodd, Mead, and Co., 1905), pp. 146, 164. One of the primers imported in large numbers was *The Protestant Tutor*, entered in the Stationers' Registar on June 9, 1683, and published in London by Benjamin Harris. Hughes's textbook, which is known only from a fragment, was "set forth for the benefit of the new-planted vineyards of the Lord Jesus in Virginia, Somers Islands and New England" (Ambrose Heal, *The English Writing-Masters and Their Copy-Books, 1570-1800* [Cambridge: Cambridge University Press, 1931], p. 134).

or John Buxtorf; though, since the language was not required for entrance into Harvard, it was probably not begun in earnest until the freshman year, during which it was vigorously stressed, owing to the Biblical interests of the Puritans and the scholarly interests of Henry Dunster and Charles Chauncy.[24]

As in England, the grammar course ran fairly intensively over seven years and was complemented by appropriate training in piety and civility. As in England, too, youngsters tended to withdraw and return, depending on familial need and circumstance; and, since school was conducted on a year-round basis and instruction organized around particular texts, it was fairly simple for a student to resume study after a period of absence. The rules and regulations of the Hopkins Grammar School at New Haven in 1684 are typical. The purpose of the school is defined as "the institution [education] of hopeful youth in the Latin tongue, and other learned languages so far as to prepare such youths for the college and public service of the country in church, and commonwealth." The master and scholars are enjoined to attend every morning from six to eleven and every afternoon from one to five in summer and from one to four in winter. The master is instructed to begin each day with a short prayer and then to seat his pupils in the schoolroom "according to their degrees of learning." He is also asked to examine them every Monday on the preceding day's sermon and to catechize them every Saturday from one to three in the afternoon. Finally, he is told to preserve appropriate decorum and civility at all times through admonition, correction, and, everything else failing, expulsion. It was a demanding regimen, but one that was very common; and it successfully prepared substantial numbers of students for attendance at Harvard and at the English and Continental universities.[25]

Interestingly enough, the Hopkins regulations explicitly excluded girls, in addition to boys who had not yet learned to read English. Not every school, however, could afford to do so. For all the distinction between reading and writing schools on the one hand and grammar schools on the other in the Massachusetts law of 1647 and the

24 "The Lawes of the Colledge Published Publiquely Before the Students of Harvard Colledge, May 4, 1655," *Publications of the Colonial Society of Massachusetts*, XXXI (1935), 329.

25 *American Journal of Education*, IV (1857), 710. See also "Rules for the Ordering of the Town School of Dorchester in 1645," *ibid.*, XXVII (1877), 106-107, and "Articles of Agreement with Jan Tibout, Employed Schoolmaster for Flatbush, December 18, 1681," in Daniel J. Pratt, *Annals of Public Education in the State of New York, from 1626 to 1746* (Albany: The Argus Company, 1872), pp. 67-68.

Connecticut law of 1650, the fact is that most New England grammar schools—and doubtless those of the other regions too—became "general schools" in the seventeenth century, in the fashion of the country schools at Leicester and for the same reasons, taking "petties" as well as advanced students and instructing each according to his "degree of learning." Thus, the shortage of students (most schools were small, probably enrolling under forty pupils), of masters, and of money proved decisive.

The teachers who conducted the schools of the seventeenth-century colonies were as diverse as the institutions in which they taught, ranging from the literate but relatively untutored housewives who maintained "dame schools" in their kitchens to the cultured university graduates who presided over the better grammar schools. Piety and good character were the stated requirements for teachers everywhere, with piety defined as religious orthodoxy in most of the colonies (Rhode Island and Maryland were notable exceptions). Intellectual qualifications were less commonly specified, though most grammar schools assumed an acquaintance with classical languages and literature.

In Massachusetts, the general court in 1654 commended "to the serious consideration and special care of the overseers of the college, and the selectmen in the several towns, not to admit or suffer any such to be continued in the office or place of teaching, educating, or instructing of youth or child, in the college or schools, that have manifested themselves unsound in the faith, or scandalous in their lives, and not giving due satisfaction according to the rules of Christ." While there is ample evidence that the various town meetings were assiduous in enforcing this prohibition, at least one teacher was certified by a minister rather than the civil authorities. Later, under the short-lived Dominion of New England (1686-1689), Governor Edmund Andros himself assumed the right to approve masters in an effort to extend Anglican influence. In New Netherland, schoolmasters were subject to the approval of the Dutch West India Company, the Classis of Amsterdam, and the local consistory and court, according to a complicated arrangement that converted more than one unsuspecting teacher into a political football. With the English conquest in 1664, the licensing prerogative passed to the governor, where it remained until 1686 (except during the brief period of Dutch reoccupation), when James II ordered that "no schoolmaster be henceforth permitted to come from England and to keep school within our province of New York, without the license of the . . . archbishop of Canterbury." The responsibility passed to the bishop of London in 1689, but the fact is that none of the regulations was stringently enforced, and the Dutch schools continued to operate with impunity well into the eighteenth century. In Virginia, licensing was introduced in 1683, when the governor, Lord Howard of Effingham, was instructed by Charles II that every schoolmaster teaching in the colony had to have a license either from the bishop of London (if he had come from England) or from the governor himself. Prodded by the bishop, the governor issued a general proclamation three years later requiring that all schoolmasters attend the next meeting of the general court at Jamestown, in order to present evidence of their intellectual competence, uprightness and sobriety, and general conformity to the doctrines of the Church of England, on penalty of removal from their posts. Many schoolmasters failed to comply, having been prevented from appearing by the distance and expense; and, after due petition from the House of Burgesses, the governor relented, delegating his licensing powers to one or more appropriate persons in each county.[26]

However stringent the requirements for teaching, the salary remained modest, ranging from ten pounds a year for reading and writing masters in the smaller rural communities, to an average of around twenty-five pounds, to the more generous fifty or sixty pounds received by some of the distinguished grammar-school masters. In addition, there were all sorts of special grants and benefits: gifts of land, houses, and firewood; a share of the tuition fees; exemptions from taxation and military service. Not surprisingly, in view of the persistent shortage of labor in the colonies, these emoluments did not prove sufficiently attractive, and the result was a chronic scarcity of schoolmasters, coupled with transient and part-time service by those who did teach. Transience, of course, was partly a blessing: from 1642 to 1689, about a quarter of Harvard's graduates taught for a period of time, usually before undertaking ministerial training or while awaiting a call from a congregation, and obviously furnished a splendid supply of masters. (It should also be pointed out that only

[26] Shurtleff, ed., *Records of the Governor and Company of Massachusetts*, III, 343-344; "Papers Relative to the Period of Usurpation in New England," *Collections of the Massachusetts Historical Society*, 3d ser., VII (1838), 186; Edward T. Corwin, ed., *Ecclesiastical Records, State of New York* (7 vols.; Albany: J. B. Lyon Company, 1901-1916), II, 916, 991; and H. R. McIlwaine and Wilmer L. Hall, eds., *Executive Journals of the Council of Colonial Virginia* (5 vols.; Richmond: Davis Bottom, 1925-1945), I, 515.

about 3 per cent of the graduates remained in teaching permanently, with much larger numbers going into medicine, business, public service, and especially the ministry, which commanded higher salaries than teaching in the seventeenth century and which, owing to the similarity of motivation and training demanded, consistently drew off the best teachers.) The part-time service of many schoolteachers was simply one more version of the general "doubling up" that occurred in the colonies: not only did teachers serve regularly as readers in Virginia, as *voorlezers* (readers) and *voorsangers* (precentors) in New Netherland, and as ministerial assistants in New England, they also practiced law and medicine, acted as justices of the peace and captains of the militia, and worked as brewers, tailors, innkeepers, and gravediggers.

But there were teachers of distinction in the colonies, who were in every way the equals of their metropolitan counterparts: the Reverend John Bertrand, who kept a school in Rappahannock County, Virginia, in the 1680's and 1690's and taught, among others, the children of William Fitzhugh; Evert Pietersen, who taught first at New Amstel and then at the New Amsterdam school in New Netherland; Elijah Corlet, who kept the "fair grammar school" by the side of the college at Cambridge; Benjamin Tompson, a schoolmaster-physician who taught at Quincy, Boston, Charlestown, and Braintree; and, most notable of all, Ezekiel Cheever.

Cheever's career as a teacher was anything but representative, though it has often been portrayed as such: whereas most of the better colonial schoolmasters were products of Harvard, Cheever had been educated in England; whereas most chose teaching as a temporary occupation, Cheever made a profession of it; whereas most commanded modest salaries, Cheever taught at the Boston Free School for sixty pounds a year; and whereas most enjoyed local reputations at best, Cheever was known throughout New England.

Born in London on January 25, 1615, the son of a spinner, Cheever attended Christ's Hospital and Emmanuel College, Cambridge, and then immigrated to Massachusetts in 1637, as Cotton Mather later put it, "with the rest of those good men, who sought a peaceable secession in an American wilderness, for the pure evangelical, and instituted worship of our Great Redeemer." Removing to New Haven the following year with John Davenport and Theophilus Eaton, he helped found the colony there and, almost from the beginning, ran a school. Though not a wealthy man, he was active in public affairs, participating in the gathering of the church, serving as a deputy to the general court in 1646, and from time to time officiating in the pulpit. In 1649, however, he drew a censure from the congregation for dissenting on certain matters of church discipline, and, for that reason or some other, he left the following year to assume the mastership of the grammar school at Ipswich, Massachusetts. During his tenure there, he became sufficiently renowned to attract scholars from the neighboring towns and, indeed, to elicit from one of the local merchants a generous contribution of a school building and schoolmaster's residence, along with two acres of land. After eleven years at Ipswich, Cheever moved to Charlestown, where he seems to have engaged in a running battle with the town authorities, not only for decent facilities but for his agreed-upon salary of thirty pounds. He eventually persuaded the townspeople to grant him a house plot, but shortly thereafter he accepted an invitation to succeed Benjamin Tompson at the Boston Free School for an annual salary of sixty pounds, in addition to "the possession and use of the schoolhouse." He arrived there in January, 1671, and remained until his death in 1708 at the age of ninety-three.[27]

By all reports, Cheever was an extraordinary teacher. One can glean something of his formal methods from the textbook known as *Cheever's Accidence,* probably compiled in 1709 by his grandson, Ezekiel Lewis, who assisted him during the final decade of his career. One can judge his effectiveness, too, from the attendance at Harvard of large numbers of graduates of the schools over which he presided, whether in upcountry Ipswich or urban Boston. But one senses the power and ability of the man best, perhaps, from Cotton Mather's verse elegy, a section of which is here quoted.

> A learned master of the languages
> Which to rich stores of learning are the keys:
> He taught us first good sense to understand
> And put the golden keys into our hand,
> We but for him had been for learning dumb,
> And had a sort of Turkish mutes become.
> Were grammar quite extinct, yet at his brain
> The candle might have well been lit again.
> If rhetoric had been stripped of all her pride

27 Cotton Mather, *Corderius Americanus: An Essay upon the Good Education of Children* (Boston: John Allen, 1708), "An Historical Introduction"; and *A Report of the Record Commissioners of the City of Boston, Containing the Boston Records from 1660 to 1701* (Boston: Rockwell and Churchill, 1881), p. 57.

She from his wardrobe might have been supplied.
Do but name Cheever, and the echo straight
Upon that name, good Latin, will repeat.
A Christian Terence, master of the file
That arms the curious to reform their style.
Now Rome and Athens from their ashes rise;
See their Platonic year with vast surprise:
And in our school a miracle is wrought;
For the dead languages to life are brought.
   His work he loved: Oh! Had we done the same!
Our playdays still to him ungrateful came.
And yet so well our work adjusted lay,
We came to work, as if we came to play.
   Our lads had been, but for his wondrous cares,
   Boys of my Lady More's unquiet prayers.
   Sure were it not for such informing schools,
   Our Lateran too would soon be filled with owls.
   'Tis Corlet's pains, and Cheever's, we must own,
   That thou, New England, art not Scythia grown.
   That Isles of Silly had o'errun this day
   The continent of our America.
Grammar he taught, which 'twas his work to do:
But he would Hagar have her place to know.
   The Bible is the sacred grammar, where
   The rules of speaking well, contained are.
He taught us Lily, and he Gospel taught;
And us poor children to our Saviour brought.
Master of sentences, he gave us more
Than we in our *Sententiae* had before.
We learned good things in Tully's *Offices;*
But we from him learned better things than these.
With Cato's he to us the higher gave
Lessons of Jesus, that our souls do save.
We construed Ovid's *Metamorphoses,*
But on ourselves charged, not a change to miss.
Young Austin wept, when he saw Dido dead,
Though not a tear for a lost soul he had:
Our master would not let us be so vain,
But us from Virgil did to David train,
Textor's *Epistles* would not clothe our souls;
Paul's too we heard; we went to school at Paul's.[28]

[28] *A Short Introduction to the Latin Tongue, for the Use of the Lower Forms in the Latin School* (Boston: B. Green, 1709); and Mather, *Corderius Americanus,* pp. 28-29.

III

In transplanting schooling during the seventeenth century, the colonists inevitably transplanted something of the revolution in contemporary English education. True, that revolution took on a different flavor in a wilderness three thousand miles from the principal sources of culture, but it remained a revolution nonetheless. The idea that schooling ought to be generally available for the advancement of piety, civility, and learning was accepted throughout the colonies: in New England, that acceptance was manifested by the actual existence of a substantial number of schools; in Virginia and Maryland, where scattered settlement rendered this less feasible, that acceptance was manifested by a continuing concern that more schools be brought into being—e.g., Nathaniel Bacon's insistent questioning of Governor Berkeley as to "what arts, sciences, schools of learning, or manufactories, have been promoted [by those] in authority."[29]

Wherever it took root, schooling was viewed as a device for promoting uniformity, and in that sense the educational revolution was institutionalized in the colonies and put to the purposes of the controlling elements of society; indeed, that institutionalization may well explain why there was no suspicious retreat from schooling in the latter half of the century, comparable to that in Restoration England. Yet, whatever the purposes of those in control, schooling did advance literacy, and it did help immerse a significant number of Americans in the classical tradition. And, like all other institutions of education, schools inevitably liberated at the same time that they socialized, and many a colonial youngster was doubtless freed from the social and intellectual constraints of a particular household, church, or neighborhood by attending a nearby school, which opened doors to new ideas, new occupations, and new life styles.

Granted this, the transplanted revolution encountered a series of novel problems in the colonies. For one thing, there was the initial blurring of lines between institutions, which makes it exceedingly difficult to assess the number and concentration of formally established schools. What the sources clearly indicate is that schooling went on anywhere and everywhere, not only in schoolrooms, but in kitchens, manses, churches, meetinghouses, sheds erected in fields,

29 Mrs. An. Cotton, *An Account of Our Late Troubles in Virginia, Written in 1676 (Richmond Enquirer*, September 12, 1804), in Force, ed., *Tracts*, vol. I, no. 9, p. 6.

and shops erected in towns; that pupils were taught by anyone and everyone, not only by schoolmasters, but by parents, tutors, clergymen, lay readers, precentors, physicians, lawyers, artisans, and shopkeepers; and that most teaching proceeded on an individual basis, so that whatever lines there were in the metropolis between petty schooling and grammar schooling were virtually absent in the colonies: the content and sequence of learning remained fairly well defined, and each student progressed from textbook to textbook at his own pace.

The counterpoint to all this variation, however, was the fact that education became increasingly a matter of "public concernment" in the colonies. The companies, the legislatures, the county and village courts, and the towns were early involved in education, but, as in England, their involvement took quite different forms. Geraldine Murphy provides ample documentation of the diversity in her excellent study of seventeenth-century Massachusetts: the various ways in which the towns initially concerned themselves with schooling; the gradual—and often reluctant—settlement on town-sponsored schooling; the shift from control by the town meeting to control by the selectmen to control by special committees of selectmen; and, finally, the role of the general court in gently guiding these developments. Her study reveals, too, the concomitant variety in sources of support: the initial efforts to raise adequate funds via subscription, rents, tuition, and grants of land, and the gradual—and, again, often reluctant—settlement on town rates, once it became clear that the abundance of land rendered more traditional modes of endowment unsatisfactory. And her study indicates, finally, the multiplicity of meanings of "free school": in Roxbury, the term "free" meant free to the children of subscribers, in Salem free to all poor children, in Ipswich free to a limited number of children, and in Dedham free to all children; as the years passed, the last meaning came to prevail fairly generally throughout the colony.[30]

While these particular lines of development are less clear outside New England, "public concernment" with education was everywhere evident: in the Virginia assembly's abortive effort of 1661 to erect a college and a free school for "the advancement of learning, promoting piety and provision of an able and successive ministry";

[30] Murphy, "Massachusetts Bay Colony: The Role of Government in Education." See also A. F. Leach, *English Schools at the Reformation, 1546-8* (Westminster: Archibald Constable & Co., 1896), part I, pp. 110-114, and Clara P. McMahon, "A Note on the Free School Idea in Colonial Maryland," *Maryland Historical Magazine*, LIV (1959), 149-152.

in the similarly fruitless effort of the Maryland assembly in 1671; and in the general tendency to place the responsibility for certifying and licensing teachers in the hands of lay rather than ecclesiastical officials—the selectmen in New England and the resident governors in New York and Virginia.[31]

Finally, there was the insistent problem of clientele. By the seventeenth century, access to English schools had been substantially increased, and this increase continued in the colonies, where school attendance was a function more often of propinquity than of social status, at least for white children. The accessibility of schooling to Indians and Negroes, on the other hand, was much more problematical. In Virginia, there was an abrupt retreat from neighborliness toward the Indians after the hostilities of 1622. "The way of conquering them is much more easy than of civilizing them by fair means," stated a formal report to the Virginia Company, "for they are a rude, barbarous, and naked people, scattered in small companies, which are helps to victory, but hindrances to civility: Besides that, a conquest may be of many and at once; but civility is in particular, and, slow, the effect of long time, and great industry." In New England, although the Puritans remained as ambivalent about the Indian's educability as they were about his salvation, Indian schooling was vigorously promoted, especially in the years before King Philip's War: there is evidence that, as early as 1650, Indian children were attending the common schools of Massachusetts side by side with whites, and, indeed, the Harvard charter of that year mentioned "the education of the English and Indian youth of this country." In 1653, the Society for Propagation of the Gospel in New England asked the Commissioners of the United Colonies to erect an Indian College at Harvard, and shortly thereafter a program was started in which selected Indian youngsters undertook preparatory studies with Elijah Corlet at the Cambridge Grammar School and with Daniel Weld at Roxbury. Finally, owing largely to the efforts of John Eliot and Daniel Gookin, there were schools for both youngsters and adults in the several praying towns of Massachusetts. No other region did as well as New England, though attempts to school the Indians doubtless accompanied missionary endeavors in all the colonies. As far as the blacks are concerned, it appears that only a handful attended school along with the

[31] Hening, ed., *Statutes at Large; Being a Collection of All the Laws of Virginia*, II, 37, 25; and *Archives of Maryland*, II (1884), 263-264.

whites, and there is no evidence at all of the establishment of any
all-black schools. Apart from the suggestions of John Eliot and
Morgan Godwyn, little was proposed and little was accomplished,
beyond such "schooling" as might have come on the fringes of
household or church instruction for whites.[32]

32 Edward Waterhouse, *A Declaration of the State of the Colony and Affaires in
Virginia* (1622), in Susan Myra Kingsbury, ed., *The Records of the Virginia Company of
London* (4 vols.; Washington, D.C.: Government Printing Office, 1906-1935), III, 557;
and "The Harvard College Charter of 1650," *Publications of the Colonial Society of
Massachusetts*, XXXI (1935), 3.

Chapter 7

COLLEGE

This year, although the estates of these pilgrim people were much wasted, yet seeing the benefit that would accrue to the churches of Christ and civil government, by the Lord's blessing, upon learning, they began to erect a college, the Lord by his provident hand giving his approbation to the work, in sending over a faithful and godly servant of his, the Reverend Mr. John Harvard, who joining with the people of Christ at Charlestown, suddenly after departed this life, and gave near a thousand pounds toward this work; wherefore the government thought it meet to call it Harvard College in remembrance of him.

EDWARD JOHNSON

The origins of English higher education are shrouded in obscurity. One school of historians has located them in the general quickening of theological studies in and around Oxford during the twelfth century, notably the teaching at Beaumont Palace (a favorite of the Plantagenets), the monastery at Abingdon, the priory of St. Frideswide, and a number of the local conventual churches. Another school has associated them more specifically with the recall of English scholars from the University of Paris in 1167, during the long-simmering dispute between Thomas à Becket and Henry II. In any case, there is fairly clear evidence of the gradual emergence of a *studium generale* —a cosmopolitan center of higher learning—at Oxford toward the end of the twelfth century and of the creation of a second *studium* at nearby Cambridge in 1209, after a nasty town-gown encounter at Oxford had sent students and masters in search of more propitious surroundings.[1]

[1] The historiographical controversy is sketched by A. B. Emden in his introduction to the third volume of Hastings Rashdall, *The Universities of Europe in the Middle Ages*, edited by F. M. Powicke and A. B. Emden (rev. ed.; 3 vols.; Oxford: Clarendon Press, 1936), III, xv-xxvi, 5-33, 465-476.

Whatever the particular circumstances of their birth—and it is well to bear in mind Sir John Adams' observation that the medieval universities were not so much founded as they founded themselves —it is clear that the two English institutions, like the University of Paris, were essentially outgrowths of that fascinating convergence of intellectual rebirth and institutional development sometimes referred to as the renaissance of the twelfth century. The story is a familiar one: the era began with only the sketchiest notion of the seven liberal arts, then witnessed the rediscovery of Aristotle, Justinian, Galen, Hippocrates, Euclid, and Ptolemy, and concluded not only with a revivified conception of the arts but also with a new law, a new philosophy, and a new science; here and there, in certain leading centers, particular masters or groups of masters began to attract un-usual numbers of students, to wit, teachers of law at Bologna, or medicine at Salerno, or theology at Paris; the exigencies of medieval life compelled them to form guilds—or universities—to protect and advance their mutual interests (some, like Paris, were guilds of masters, while others, like Bologna, were guilds of students); the guilds became settled and were given privileged status by popes and princes; when a guild began to draw students from a wide radius, its site came to be designated a *studium generale;* as the guilds became institutionalized, they organized themselves into faculties of arts, medicine, law, and theology, with the work in the arts faculty seen as both preparatory to and co-ordinate with that in the others; and, finally, guild and *studium* merged to form the archetype of the modern university.[2]

In this fashion, Oxford—and later Cambridge, which patterned itself closely after Oxford—slowly emerged as a characteristic medie-val university. The earliest extant statutes date from 1253, and the earliest papal authorization from 1254; but, by that time, there were customary curricula for the various degrees, quite similar to those at Paris, though perhaps more flexible. The arts course began with gram-mar out of Priscian and Donatus, logic out of Aristotle and Boethius, and rhetoric out of Aristotle, Cicero, and Boethius, and then went to arithmetic and music out of Boethius, geometry out of Euclid, astron-omy out of Ptolemy, and the three philosophies—natural, moral, and mental—out of Aristotle. After two years of study, the student was expected to take part in disputations and, after four years, in

2 James Hastings, ed., *Encyclopedia of Religion and Ethics* (13 vols.; New York: Charles Scribner's Sons, 1913-1927), V, 172.

lecturing as well. The course in medicine revolved around Galen and Hippocrates, supplemented by the *Liber febrium* (*Book of Fevers*) of Isaac and the *Antidotarium* (*Pharmacopoeia*) of Nicholas; the course in theology, around the Bible and the *Sentences* of Peter the Lombard; and the courses in civil and canon law, around the *Corpus juris civilis* (*Body of Civil Law*) of Justinian, the *Decretum* (a synthesis of church law) of Gratian, and the *Decretals* (*Decrees*) of Gregory IX and his successors.[3]

The programs of study at Oxford were quite typical; indeed, the very similarity of the medieval universities, one to another, permitted the evolution of a cosmopolitan world of learning, in which scholars and ideas passed freely from one center to another. But, in at least two realms, English higher education developed along unique lines: first, with respect to the colleges, and second, with respect to the Inns of Court. The college made its initial appearance at Paris in the twelfth century as a simple device to fill an obvious need: boys were coming to the city from all over Europe at the age of fourteen or fifteen, the university felt no obligation to furnish their housing or maintenance, and so halls or dormitories called *hospitia* grew up, where students could reside while they attended lectures and engaged in disputations. Toward the end of the century, a number of endowed *hospitia,* or *collegia,* were founded to provide lodging and board for poor scholars who were unable to provide these for themselves. There was usually a modicum of supervision in such foundations, by a master or cleric; but, at the beginning at least, the business of instruction remained outside, in the hands of the regent masters and their subordinate bachelors.

In England, groups of scholars frequently hired a hall and shared the cost of living, with one among them, known as the principal, elected to preside over the college. As on the Continent, instruction initially remained external to such establishments; but, with the passage of time, college revenues came to be seen as a prime means for supporting younger masters of arts, who could count on neither benefices nor lecture fees as dependable sources of income. In the process, colleges became teaching as well as residential institutions. One must guard against exaggerating the rapidity of the transformation: at least until the early sixteenth century, the great majority of undergraduates and teachers lived in private lodgings. But the col-

[3] Rashdall, *Universities of Europe in the Middle Ages,* III, 140-168.

leges did equip a small number of able men for positions of power in the church, and there is no denying that it was the colleges rather than the universities proper that attracted the more distinguished patronage of the later medieval period.

Closely related to the evolution of the colleges was the rise of the Inns of Court, whose origin derived from a fundamental difference between the Continental and English legal systems. On the Continent, the introduction of a stable system of law coincided with the development of higher legal studies, and hence the universities became the instruments by which Roman civil law and Christian canon law were diffused throughout the principalities of Europe. In England, on the other hand, the civil courts resisted the introduction of a Roman code and proceeded to create a native common law based on indigenous Anglo-Saxon elements (admiralty law and canon law were exceptions), with the result that there was a sharp disjunction between the legal arts taught at the universities and the legal realities of the courts. Not surprisingly, an apprenticeship system grew up around the great practicing lawyers, not unlike the system of instruction that had grown up around the great practicing clerics; the students required places to live, which in this instance came to be called Inns of Court; and gradually the Inns, like the contemporary colleges, took on teaching as well as residential functions.

Sir John Fortescue described the Inns in his classic treatise on English law, written between 1468 and 1471 for the instruction of Henry VI's ill-fated son, Edward. The laws of England, he noted, were taught in a "public academy, more convenient and suitable for their apprehension than any university"; that academy consisted of some ten lesser schools, called Inns of Chancery, and four greater schools, called Inns of Court; it was situated near the king's courts, in which the laws were daily pleaded and disputed and to which legal students flocked during termtime; and it taught, in addition to law, manners, dancing, singing, "and all games proper for nobles, as those brought up in the king's household are accustomed to practice."[4]

From Fortescue's description as well as from other contemporary documents, it is obvious that the Inns were enjoying something of a golden age during the later fifteenth century, recruiting an elite class of men from noble families, providing them with an essentially

[4] Sir John Fortescue, *De laudibus legum Anglie*, translated and edited by S. B. Chrimes (Cambridge: Cambridge University Press, 1942), pp. 115-121.

practical training in pleading and advocating, and sending them into
the service of the Crown. As W. S. Holdsworth concluded, it was an
arrangement "eminently well suited to the needs of a youthful system
of law, the literature of which was yet of a manageable size." Unfortunately, the same cannot be said of instruction at the two universities. Cambridge, which had remained "provincial" compared to Oxford, was rapidly closing the gap in size and quality during the
fifteenth century; but the fact is that both institutions had suffered
from suspicion and repression in the wake of the Lollard movement.
Absentee chancellors neglected their responsibilities, a narrow Scho-
lasticism suffused the curriculum, and a rapid rise in the number of
graces (dispensations from degree requirements) attested to growing
political domination. Yet, notwithstanding a measure of intellectual
decay, there is every evidence that by the end of the medieval period
the two universities and the Inns had firmly established themselves
within the English institutional structure, and together constituted
an effective system of recruitment and training for scholarship and
the professions.[5]

The very integration of the universities and Inns into the social
fabric inevitably subjected them to the sweeping transformations of
the Tudor and early Stuart eras; and, indeed, the years between 1480
and 1640 witnessed profound changes in English higher education.
In the first place, the universities, like the grammar schools, were
gradually laicized. Having gained their independence from diocesan
authorities by the end of the fifteenth century—Oxford from the
bishop of Lincoln and Cambridge from the bishop of Ely—they
acknowledged direct allegiance to king and pope, though in the conflicts between Oxford and Archbishop Arundel in the early fifteenth
century it had become clear that royal supremacy had begun to prevail. After Henry VIII broke with Rome, the universities were
subject to control by the Crown alone, which manifested its prerogative during the several Tudor reigns, first, by appointing royal
visitorial groups on which prominent laymen were increasingly present, and, second, by appointing a succession of lay chancellors, beginning with Thomas Cromwell at Cambridge in 1535.

Meanwhile, Parliament in 1571 enacted legislation incorporating
the universities and thereby founding their privileges, liberties, and
franchises on civil rather than ecclesiastical authority, a policy that

5 W. S. Holdsworth, *A History of English Law* (12 vols.; London: Methuen & Co.,
1903-1938), VI, 481.

was confirmed when James I granted them representation in Parliament in 1604, choosing to treat them like the ancient boroughs, counties, and cities of the realm rather than like collegiate churches or cathedral chapters. And the same merchant and gentry families that contributed so liberally to grammar schools during the Elizabethan and early Stuart years directed substantial resources to strengthening the older colleges and endowing new ones, such as Emmanuel and Sidney Sussex, in a tide of lay generosity that reached its height during the quarter-century preceding the Revolution.[6]

A second great change of the late sixteenth and early seventeenth centuries was the transformation of the colleges from small, self-contained societies on the margins of the universities into the central units of English higher education. Even before the accession of Elizabeth I, benefactions were pouring into the older colleges and facilitating the establishment of new ones; increasingly willing to accept fee-paying students, these endowed institutions displaced the informal residential halls surrounding the universities, both physically and socially. Then, in 1570, Elizabeth confirmed the shift politically with a new set of statutes for the University of Cambridge, under which most of the authority of the regent masters was transferred to the heads of the colleges, who collectively became the chief governing body of the university. The statutes were obviously an effort by William Cecil, then chancellor of Cambridge, and John Whitgift, then master of Trinity College, to limit religious dissent, as were similar mandates for Oxford, imposed in 1631 by William Laud, then chancellor of the university. Interestingly enough, the transformation of the colleges was accompanied by a decline in the vitality (though not in the drawing power) of the Inns of Court, which were plagued throughout the sixteenth century by an emphasis on form rather than function—by canceled moots and readings, by truncated courses, and by sporadic attendance on the part of students who discovered that the law was more easily learned from books than from lectures or presence at court.[7]

A third change of the late sixteenth and early seventeenth cen-

[6] An Act Concerning the Several Incorporations of the Universities, 13 Eliz. I, c. xxix, The Statutes at Large (9 vols.; London: printed for Mark Basket, 1763-1765), II, 603-605; and James Heywood and Thomas Wright, eds., Cambridge University Transactions During the Puritan Controversies (2 vols.; London: Henry G. Bohn, 1854), II, 207-211.

[7] George Dyer, ed., The Privileges of the University of Cambridge (2 vols.; London: Longman and Co., 1824), I, 181-182; and Strickland Gibson, ed., Statuta antiqua Universitatis Oxoniensis (Oxford: Clarendon Press, 1931), p. 570.

turies was the significant increase in both the size and diversity of the groups attending the universities and Inns of Court. Lawrence Stone has estimated that the number of students annually beginning higher education (including those few who had private instruction or attended foreign institutions) rose from approximately 780 in the 1560's to over 900 in the 1570's and 1580's, then declined at the turn of the century (for reasons that are somewhat obscure, perhaps economic, perhaps ideological), then rose again to a peak of 1,240 in the 1630's, and then dropped precipitously after the Revolution. Of the 1,240, some 430 were probably headed for the church, some 160 for law, and some 30 for medicine, leaving roughly half of those with higher education to enter teaching, politics, business, and other occupations that had not formerly attracted men of learning. Moreover, the students were recruited not only from gentry, merchant, and professional families but also from yeoman, artisan, and even tenant and copyhold families, whose sons worked their way through the universities or Inns as sizars or servitors. Indeed, all but the very poor—and recall that the very poor still constituted the majority of the population—had managed to gain access to higher education.[8]

ENTRANTS TO HIGHER EDUCATION 1560-1699
(decennial averages)

Decade	Universities (estimated numbers)	Inns of Court (50% of total entry)	Private and Abroad (estimated numbers)	Estimated Total (to nearest 10)
1560-1569	c. 654	80	50	c. 780
1570-1579	c. 780	79	50	c. 910
1580-1589	770	103	40	910
1590-1599	652	106	40	800
1600-1609	706	119	40	860
1610-1619	884	140	50	1,070
1620-1629	906	120	50	1,080
1630-1639	1,055	137	50	1,240
1640-1649	557	109	100	770
1650-1659	753	118	80	950
1660-1669	740	118	110*	970
1670-1679	722	124	160*	1,010
1680-1689	558	119	170*	850
1690-1699	499	95	230*	820

* Including entrants to dissenting academies.

8 Lawrence Stone, "The Educational Revolution in England, 1560-1640," *Past & Present*, no. 28 (July, 1964), pp. 54, 41-80; and Joan Simon, "The Social Origins of Cambridge Students, 1603-1640," *ibid.*, no. 26 (November, 1963), pp. 58-67.

Finally, the curriculum, particularly the arts curriculum, changed fundamentally. In the first place, as the colleges and Inns gained prominence, the power of the nonacademic aspects of education was vastly strengthened; the influence of ceremonial, of informal discussion, of day-by-day social intercourse—what Cotton Mather would later refer to as the "collegiate way of living"—grew significantly vis-à-vis that of the formal study of texts. Also strengthened was the role of the tutor, who, with libraries of printed books at his disposal, was able to provide a much more flexible and individualized program of instruction than had previously been possible—one must bear this especially in mind when perusing the prescriptions of college statutes, which often set forth a course of study agreed upon years earlier and then honored increasingly in the breach. And there is evidence that this flexibility permitted a good deal of teaching in the new sciences and mathematics, as well as in modern foreign languages, particularly through what Mark H. Curtis has called the extrastatutory curriculum, and that the universities were therefore much more the nurseries of the new learning than critics such as Francis Bacon, Thomas Hobbes, John Milton, and John Webster allowed.[9]

Considerable insight into what tutorial instruction had become by the early decades of the seventeenth century may be gleaned from the "Directions for a Student in the Universitie," prepared by Richard Holdsworth, who was a fellow at St. John's College, Cambridge, between 1613 and 1620, a Gresham professor from 1629 to 1637, and then master of Emmanuel College between 1637 and 1643. Holdsworth lists the various books to be read and indicates the order in which they should be systematically considered, providing a host of suggestions on the way in which particular works should be approached ("Before you read Ovid's *Metamorphoses* it will be requisite to run over some book of mythology. . . . Also before you read Ovid it will be very good to get two maps one of Old Greece the other of the Roman Empire and spend one afternoon or two in acquainting yourself with them, by the assistance either of your tutor, or some friend") and on the way in which the entire curriculum should be pursued ("A commonplace book ought to be fitted to that profession you follow"; "Many lose a great deal of time in visiting, which must

<hr />

[9] Cotton Mather, *Magnalia Christi Americana; or, The Ecclesiastical History of New-England* 1702), edited by Thomas Robbins (2 vols.; Hartford: Silas Andrus and Son, 1853-1855), II, 10; and Mark H. Curtis, *Oxford and Cambridge in Transition, 1558-1642* (Oxford: Clarendon Press, 1959), pp. 127 ff. and *passim*.

be avoided as much as may be"; "He that will sit tippling in a tavern, and be drunk, shall never find that respect and authority amongst those where he lives, which men of sober carriage do"). And, at one point after another, Holdsworth reveals his patent preference for rhetoric over logic, for belles-lettres over philosophy, and for individual study and conversation over formal lectures on authorized

RICHARD HOLDSWORTH'S OUTLINE OF STUDIES

Morning Study		Afternoon Study
	First Year	
A briefer system and then a more fully developed system of logic	January February March	Richard Holdsworth, "Directions for a Student in the Universitie" Thomas Godwin, *Romanae historiae anthologia* Marcus Junianus Justinus, *Historiarum Philippicarum*
Controversies in logic; another more fully developed system of logic	April May June	Cicero, *Epistles* Desiderius Erasmus, *Colloquies* Terence
Controversies and disputations in logic	July August September	Alexander Ross, *Mystagogus poeticus* Ovid, *Metamorphoses* Greek Testament
A briefer system and then a more fully developed system of ethics	October November December	Terence Cicero, *Epistles* Desiderius Erasmus, *Colloquies* Theognis
	Second Year	
A briefer system and then a more fully developed system of physics	January February March	Latin grammar Lorenzo Valla, *De elegantia linguae Latinae* Greek grammar Franciscus Vigerius, *De praecipuius Graecae dictionis idiotismus*
Controversies in logic, ethics, and physics	April May June	Cicero, *De senectute, De amicitia, Tusculanae quaestiones*, and *De oratore* Aesop's Fables
A briefer system and then a more fully developed system of metaphysics	July August September	Florus Sallust Quintus Curtius

Morning Study		Afternoon Study
Controversies of all kinds	October November December	Virgil, *Eclogues* and *Georgics* Ovid, *Epistles* Horace Martial Hesiod Theocritus

Third Year

Controversies of all kinds for the entire year Julius Caesar Scaliger, *De subtilitate*	January February March	Nicolas Caussin, *De eloquentia*
Aristotle, *Organon*, with commentary by Brierwood	April May June	Cicero, *Orations* Demosthenes, *Orations*
Aristotle, *Physics*	July August September	Famianus Strada, *Prolusiones academi- cae* Robert Turner, *Orationum* Quintilian, *Institutio oratoria*
Aristotle, *Ethics*	October November December	Juvenal Persius Claudian Virgil, *Aeneid* Homer, *Iliad*

Fourth Year

Seneca, *Quaestiones naturales* Lucretius	January February March	Hans Cluver, *Historiarum totius mundi epitome* Suetonius
Aristotle, *De anima* and *De caelo*, with commentary	April May June	Aulus Gellius Macrobius Saturnus Plautus
Aristotle, *Meteorologica*, with commentary	July August September	Cicero, *Orations, De officiis,* and *De finibus*
Marcus Frederik Wendelin, *Christianae theologiae*	October November December	Seneca, *Tragedies* Lucanus Homer, *Iliad* and *Odyssey*

texts, in a sense the epitome of everything the humanists had propounded a century before.[10]

[10] Holdsworth's "Directions" are printed in their entirety in Harris Francis Fletcher,
The Intellectual Development of John Milton (2 vols.; Urbana: University of Illinois
Press, 1956-1961), II, 623-655. For a caution on the use of the "Directions" as a
source, see Christopher Hill, *Intellectual Origins of the English Revolution* (Oxford:
Clarendon Press, 1965), pp. 307-314.

The outcome of these sweeping changes was a shattering of the traditional framework of *imperium-sacerdotium-studium* (state-church-university) and a reconstituting of the mutual relationships between higher education and society, which dramatically affected the commonwealth of England. One must not assume that every tutor was a Holdsworth or that the universities and Inns of Court suddenly became centers of scientific and philosophical inquiry; they remained in large measure institutions where young men of ability could prepare for careers in the church and where young men of wealth and position could acquire a veneer of civility. Yet there is no denying that careers became open to talent on an unprecedented scale, that the quality of political and ecclesiastical leadership was significantly altered, and that the tone of intellectual life was markedly heightened. And, though substantial segments of English higher education remained conservative, learning proved a two-edged sword; and in his history of the Royal Society, Thomas Sprat could with no feeling of ambivalence allude to "those magnificent seats of humane knowledge, and divine; to which the natural philosophy of our nation, cannot be injurious without horrible ingratitude; seeing in them it has been principally cherished, and revived."[11]

I I

Dixon Ryan Fox once suggested that the transit of liberal and professional learning from England to America proceeded through four distinct stages: first, trained men from the metropolis settled in the colonies and practiced their arts; second, the original supply of learned men was renewed when certain of the native-born youth went to the metropolis for advanced education and then returned to America; third, institutions of higher learning sprang up in the colonies, though during their formative years they remained dependent on the metropolis for the education of their teachers; and, finally, the American establishments matured sufficiently to maintain themselves, replace their faculties, and supply the colonies with

11 Thomas Sprat, *The History of the Royal-Society of London, for the Improving of Natural Knowledge* (London: T. R., 1667), p. 328. The principal exceptions to the general advance seem to have been the programs in medicine. See, for example, the Laudian statutes for Oxford, which required the Regius Professor of Medicine "to lecture in Hippocrates or Galen" twice weekly, in G. R. M. Ward, trans., *Oxford University Statutes, Vol. I: Containing the Caroline Code or Laudian Statutes* (London: William Pickering, 1845), p. 25.

educated men. Fox's analysis is useful in tracing the transplantation of higher education to the American colonies, but it requires refinement at a number of points.[12]

Certainly there can be no quarrel with the proposition that the metropolis contributed the original supply of educated men: that is in the nature of colonization. What is especially interesting with respect to the American situation was the extraordinary concentration of educated men in the Great Migration of Puritans to New England. Franklin Bowditch Dexter and Samuel Eliot Morison have identified at least 130 university men among those who immigrated before 1646: 100 had attended Cambridge, and 32 had attended Oxford (obviously, a few had attended both institutions); 87 held the B.A. degree, and 63 held the M.A. Of the 130, 98 served in the ministry in New England, 27 became public officials, 15 taught, 5 entered business, and 3 practiced medicine (again, some practiced more than one profession, and almost all were part-time farmers). True, 43 of the 130 returned to England in the years before the Restoration, but even the remainder constitutes a remarkable number of educated men for a colonial population of around 25,000.[13]

There were far fewer university men in the other colonies, owing to the way in which they were first conceived and settled, but the contrast was not nearly so stark as Dexter and others have portrayed it. By 1646, Virginia had attracted at least twenty-eight university men to the ministry alone; and to those must be added a sprinkling of physicians, such as Walter Russell, Laurence Bohun, and John Potts, and a handful of government officials, such as Thomas West (Lord Delaware) and George Sandys, as well as a succession of public and private men who had attended one or another of the Inns of Court, for example, Gabriel Archer, William Ferrar, Richard Kemp, Roger Wingate, Sir Francis Wyatt, and Edward Digges.[14]

---

[12] Dixon Ryan Fox, *Ideas in Motion* (New York: D. Appleton-Century Company, 1935), pp. 3-36.

[13] Franklin Bowditch Dexter, "The Influence of the English Universities in the Development of New England," *A Selection from the Miscellaneous Historical Papers of Fifty Years* (New Haven: The Tuttle, Morehouse & Taylor Company, 1918), pp. 102-117; and Samuel Eliot Morison, *The Founding of Harvard College* (Cambridge, Mass.: Harvard University Press, 1935), pp. 359-410.

[14] Frederick Lewis Weis, *The Colonial Clergy of Virginia, North Carolina and South Carolina* (Boston: Society of the Descendants of the Colonial Clergy, 1955), pp. 1-57; Wyndham B. Blanton, *Medicine in Virginia in the Seventeenth Century* (Richmond: The William Byrd Press, 1930), pp. 80-84; and J. G. De Roulhac Hamilton, "Southern Members of the Inns of Court," *The North Carolina Historical Review*, X (1933), 278-279.

There is no doubt, either, that colonial families very soon began sending some of their youngsters to the metropolis for advanced study. Among Virginians, John Lee attended Oxford in 1658 and Ralph Wormeley in 1665, Henry Perrott entered Cambridge in 1673 and went on to Gray's Inn the following year, and William Spencer studied at Cambridge in 1684 and proceeded to the Inner Temple a year later. A significant number of New England boys who had been to Harvard chose to cross the Atlantic for additional work in the arts, medicine, law, and theology. James Ward was the first to take advantage of the willingness of the English universities to admit Harvard graduates to advanced standing, by matriculating at Magdalen College, Oxford, in 1648; thereafter, Sampson Eyton, Henry Saltonstall, William Stoughton, and Joshua Ambrose pursued graduate study at Oxford, and John Stone, William Knight, John Haynes, and Leonard Hoar at Cambridge. By 1660, at least a dozen Harvard men had obtained M.A. degrees from the metropolitan universities. In addition, Eyton was admitted to Gray's Inn in 1658, as was Stephen Lake a decade later, while William Wharton attended the Middle Temple in 1681. Samuel Mather and his younger brother, Increase, took M.A. degrees at Trinity College, Dublin, and Nathaniel Brewster acquired a bachelor's degree in theology there. Samuel Bradstreet, Leonard Hoar, and Thomas Oakes studied medicine in England and then returned to the colonies, unlike a number of their fellow medical students, who remained in London to practice.[15]

Thus far, Fox's paradigm explains the Anglo-American experience fairly accurately. But one must bear in mind that the trip to England was uncertain and the expenses high, and those going there for advanced education constituted a trickle at most. By far the greater number of native-born youth aspiring to careers in law or medicine stayed in the colonies and studied independently or with some practitioner, thus occasioning a kind of devolution from the theoretical and systematic education offered by institutions of higher learning to the more practical and informal education associated with apprenticeship. A colonist seeking to equip himself to practice law, for example, could attend one of the Inns of Court or he could attend Harvard, though only a few managed to do either before 1689; but

15 Willard Connely, "Colonial Americans in Oxford and Cambridge," *The American Oxonian*, XXIX (1942), 6-17, 75-77; E. Alfred Jones, *American Members of the Inns of Court* (London: The Saint Catherine Press, 1924); and William L. Sachse, "Harvard Men in England, 1642-1714," *Publications of the Colonial Society of Massachusetts*, XXXV (1951), 119-144.

he could also read law on his own and then seek clients, or he could serve a clerkship in some court (which seems principally to have involved the endless transcribing of documents), or he could serve a clerkship in a private law office, preferably one with a library, mastering the law through some combination of reading, copying, informal association, formal instruction, and practice under supervision. Much the same was true of medicine, though, since there were few if any hospitals in the colonies before 1689, apprenticeships in this field were almost always under an individual. In the realm of divinity, formal study remained a prerequisite to ministerial ordination through the middle of the seventeenth century, owing to the high standards of the Puritan congregations in New England and to the expectations of the English bishops and the Dutch synods. Whereas one could still become a surgeon or a solicitor via apprenticeship in Stuart England, it was difficult to enter the ministry without higher studies; and that difficulty persisted in the colonies—at least until the expansion of the more popular sects after the 1660's, with their emphasis on divine inspiration rather than systematic education as the primary qualification of the clergy.[16]

Concomitant to the devolution of professional training from an aspect of the higher learning to a form of apprenticeship was the tendency, already noted, of colonists to practice more than one profession, a tendency particularly prevalent among educated men who had access to the theoretical and practical manuals of several fields. Thus, in Massachusetts, John Wilson was minister, physician, and schoolmaster at Medfield from 1651 until his death forty years later; Thomas Thacher was a minister-physician, first at Weymouth and later at Boston, and wrote *A Brief Rule to Guide the Common People of New-England How to Order Themselves and Theirs in the Small Pocks, or Measels* (1677), the first known contribution to medical literature in America; Leonard Hoar served as a minister-physician at Boston (where he preached for a while as assistant to Thacher) before accepting the presidency of Harvard in 1672; and John Rogers was a preacher and physician at Ipswich until he became president of Harvard in 1682. In Rhode Island, John Clark, a founder of the

---

[16] There is some evidence that a Giles Firmin delivered a series of lectures based on an "anatomy" (probably a skeleton) in Massachusetts during the 1640's, but Firmin is known to have returned to England in 1654. See Joseph M. Toner, *Contributions to the Annals of Medical Progress and Medical Education in the United States Before and During the War of Independence* (Washington, D.C.: Government Printing Office, 1874), p. 64.

colony who was banished from Boston with Roger Williams, practiced medicine while serving as pastor of the church at Newport. And,
in Virginia, Robert Paulett was a minister-physician at Jamestown
between 1619 and 1622, while Nathaniel Hill combined teaching
and medicine at Henrico after 1686.

If the devolution of professional training represents one needed
refinement of Fox's paradigm, another is required by the extraordinary rapidity with which Harvard College was established and took
root. "After God had carried us safe to New England," the classic account runs, "and we had builded our houses, provided necessaries for
our livelihood, reared convenient places for God's worship, and settled
the civil government: one of the next things we longed for, and
looked after was to advance learning and perpetuate it to posterity."
Accordingly, on October 28, 1636, the general court of Massachusetts "agreed to give four hundred pounds towards a school or college,
whereof two hundred pounds to be paid the next year, and two
hundred pounds when the work is finished, and the next court to
appoint where and what building." Thus, a college was founded by
a legislative body that had been in existence less than eight years for
a colony that had been settled less than ten. As Samuel Eliot Morison
has aptly observed, there has been no comparable achievement in the
history of modern colonization.[17]

The 1636 effort was not the first attempt to found a college in the
English-speaking colonies. The ill-fated plans for the university at
Henrico, in Virginia, have already been discussed: by 1622, over two
thousand pounds in gifts had been collected, a standing committee
of gentlemen had been formed to oversee the project, the large tract
of land which the Virginia Company had contributed was being
cultivated by tenants brought to the colony specifically for that
purpose, a Communion service had been received for the chapel,
the nucleus of a library had been gathered, and the Reverend Patrick
Copland had been appointed rector; but the great Indian massacre
of 1622 and the subsequent dissolution of the Company were blows
from which the project never recovered. There is also evidence that
John Stoughton, a promoter of the Massachusetts Bay Colony who
remained in England, had sometime between 1634 and 1636 con-

17 *New Englands First Fruits* (London: R. O. and G. D., 1643), in Morison, *Found-
ing of Harvard College*, p. 432; and Nathaniel B. Shurtleff, ed., *Records of the
Governor and Company of the Massachusetts Bay in New England* (5 vols.; Boston:
William White, 1853-1854), I, 183.

ceived the idea of "erecting a place where some may be maintained for learning the language and instructing heathen and our own and breeding up as many of the Indians' children as providence shall bring into our hands." It should be noted, however, that both ventures placed heavy, though not exclusive, emphasis on educating the Indians and that both were metropolitan attempts to plant colonial institutions.[18]

The founding of Harvard, on the other hand, represented an indigenous effort to plant an institution that would exercise a beneficent influence not only on the colony but, like Massachusetts itself, on the metropolis as well. The college was patterned after a characteristically English model, which derived from the "prophesyings" that had grown up during the Elizabethan years as instruments for the education of practicing ministers. The Puritans, feeling the increasing pressure toward uniformity after 1570, had used these for their own purposes, converting them initially into "schools of the prophets" conducted in the homes of preachers like Richard Greenham, who sent forth such distinguished disciples as Henry Smith, Robert Browne, and Laurence Chaderton, and later into colleges, of which Emmanuel, founded in 1584 by Sir Walter Mildmay, and Sidney Sussex, founded in 1596 by the countess of Sussex (Sir Philip Sidney's aunt), are leading examples. Mildmay intended Emmanuel to educate preachers "at once learned and zealous, instructed in all that scholars should know, but trained to use their learning in the service of the reformed faith." It is said that Elizabeth once remarked to him, "Sir Walter, I hear you have erected a Puritan foundation." To which Mildmay is reputed to have replied, "No, madam: far be it from me to countenance anything contrary to your established laws; but I have set an acorn, which, when it becomes an oak, God alone knows what will be the fruit thereof." Emmanuel, of course, provided acorns for New England, contributing far more alumni than any of the other Cambridge or Oxford colleges to the ranks of the first settlers, among them, John Harvard.[19]

[18] Morison, *Founding of Harvard College*, p. 415. The only other "collegiate" institution in the English-speaking colonies before the founding of the College of William and Mary in 1693 was the Jesuit college established at Newtown, Maryland, in 1677, though this was probably more like the Latin grammar schools in the colonies and Europe than the English colleges or the Continental universities.

[19] Jonathan Mitchell, "A Modell for the Maintaining of Students & Fellows of Choise Abilities at the Colledge in Cambridge" (c. 1663), *Publications of the Colonial Society of Massachusetts*, XXXI (1935), 309; and Thomas Fuller, *The History of the University of Cambridge* (new ed.; London: printed for Thomas Tegg, 1840), p. 205.

In sum, the higher learning had been a salient feature of the Puritan experience in England, and it remained so in New England. The most educated segment of a commonwealth that may well have been the most educated in the history of the world to that point, had spawned a colony designed to be a city on a hill. The founders of that colony had themselves had widespread experience with advanced studies and considered them a prime requisite for a truly civilized society. They therefore moved quickly to establish an institution of higher learning. Viewed thus, the founding of Harvard remains extraordinary but not surprising: to quote Sir John Adams again, it grew out of the nature of things.

The legislative session following the one that authorized the establishment of Harvard convened two months later in Boston, but it was soon caught up in the antinomian controversy and paid no further heed to education. Hence, the next relevant actions were taken on November 15, 1637, when the college was ordered "to be at Newetowne" (whose name was changed to Cambridge the following May); and on November 20, when responsibility for the college was assigned to a committee—later referred to as the board of overseers —composed of six magistrates and six elders, seven of whom were alumni of Cambridge, one an alumnus of Oxford, and the remaining four fathers or brothers of Cambridge graduates. Before the year was out, Nathaniel Eaton, who had attended Trinity College, Cambridge, and then gone on to study under the distinguished Puritan theologian William Ames at the University of Franeker in the Netherlands, was appointed "professor of the said school" and entrusted with management of the donations to date. It is likely that instruction commenced sometime during the summer of 1638. And, on September 14 of that year, the Reverend John Harvard of Charlestown died of consumption, leaving half his estate (amounting to £779 17s. 2d.) and his entire library to the college. Appropriately appreciative, the general court ordered on March 13, 1639, "that the college agreed upon formerly to be built at Cambridge shall be called Harvard College."[20]

The choice of Eaton proved unfortunate: a former student wrote of him that he was "fitter to have been an officer in the Inquisition,

20 Shurtleff, ed., *Records of the Governor and Company of Massachusetts*, I, 208, 217, 253; and "The Colledge Booke No. 3," *Publications of the Colonial Society of Massachusetts*, XV (1925), 172.

or master of a house of correction, than an instructor of Christian youth"; and, as if that were not enough, his wife served meatless meals, which featured sour bread and dry pudding. Eaton was dismissed on September 9, 1639, and the college was for all intents and purposes closed until the following August 27, when Henry Dunster, an alumnus of Magdalene College, Cambridge, was appointed president. (There is some evidence that John Winthrop, Jr., invited the Moravian educator John Amos Comenius to head the institution when both were in England in 1641, but nothing came of it.) Under Dunster, the history of Harvard began in earnest: by the time he resigned in 1654, the college could boast seventy-four alumni (seventy-two of them still living), a charter granted by the general court in 1650, a fairly respectable library (possibly numbering over a thousand volumes), and three buildings, including a spacious turreted edifice called the "Old College," an auxiliary house known as "Goffe's College," and a president's lodging, which housed a printing press that had become Dunster's responsibility when he married the widow of Jose Glover, a clergyman who had intended to set up a printing establishment in Massachusetts but who had died during the Atlantic crossing.[21]

An excellent picture of Harvard under Dunster is provided in *New Englands First Fruits*, a promotional pamphlet published anonymously in London in 1643 and likely written by Thomas Weld and Hugh Peter. It is clear from the rules set forth there that collegiality was the chief educational principle: every student was to be "plainly instructed" and earnestly pressed to consider that the main end of his life and studies was "to know God and Jesus Christ which is eternal life, Joh. 17. 3. and therefore to lay Christ in the bottom, as the only foundation of all sound knowledge and learning"; everyone was to exercise himself in reading the Scriptures twice a day, so that he "shall be ready to give such an account of his proficiency therein, both in theoretical observations of the language, and logic, and in practical and spiritual truths, as his tutor shall require, according to his ability"; each pupil was to attend diligently all lectures and tutorials, obey strictly the college's rules and regulations, and eschew steadfastly profanity and association with dissolute

---

[21] William Hubbard, *A General History of New England, from the Discovery to MDCLXXX* (2d ed.; Boston: Charles C. Little and James Brown, 1848), p. 247; and "Colledge Booke No. 3," p. 172.

THE TIMES AND ORDER OF STUDIES 1642

	8 A.M.	9 A.M.	10 A.M.	1 P.M.	2 P.M.	3 P.M.	4 P.M.
			First Year				
Monday and Tuesday	Logic; physics				Disputations		
Wednesday	Greek etymology and syntax				Greek grammar, from literature		
Thursday	Hebrew grammar				Hebrew Bible readings		
Friday	Rhetoric	Declamations	Rhetoric		R h e t o r i c		
Saturday	Catechetical divinity	Commonplaces		History; nature of plants			
			Second Year				
Monday and Tuesday		Ethics; politics			Disputations		
Wednesday		Greek prosody and dialects			Greek poetry		
Thursday		"Chaldee" grammar			Practice in Chaldee: Ezra and Daniel		
Friday	Rhetoric	Declamations	Rhetoric		R h e t o r i c		
Saturday	Catechetical divinity	Commonplaces		History; nature of plants			
			Third Year				
Monday and Tuesday			Arithmetic; geometry; astronomy			Disputations	
Wednesday		Theory of Greek [style]			Exercise in Greek style, both in prose and verse		
Thursday			Syriac grammar			Practice in Syriac: New Testament	
Friday	Rhetoric	Declamations	Rhetoric		R h e t o r i c		
Saturday	Catechetical divinity	Commonplaces		History; nature of plants			

company; and no one was to "go abroad to other towns" without the consent of his tutors, his parents, or his guardians. The formal curriculum spanned three years and assumed an understanding of Cicero, along with a fair degree of fluency in Latin and an elementary knowledge of Greek grammar. The themes for disputation were divided into philological theses, organized according to the subjects of the trivium (grammar, rhetoric, and logic), and philosophical theses, organized according to the three philosophies (physics, ethics, and metaphysics).[22]

The program of 1655, set forth by Dunster's successor, Charles Chauncy, was similar: it ratified the additional year Dunster had added to the undergraduate curriculum sometime before the commencement of 1652 as an extension of the first year's studies; it expanded the work in ethics, physics, and metaphysics; it provided additional detail regarding disputations and declamations; and it made explicit the arrangements for the M.A. degree. From the lists of public disputations, the evidence of textbook ownership, and such student notebooks as we have, it is clear that in other respects the curriculum remained much the same throughout the seventeenth century, emphasizing the compendia of Johann Heinrich Alsted, Petrus Ramus, and Bartholomaüs Keckermann, the theology of William Ames, and the logic of Ramus (with considerable attention given to Aristotle as well).[23]

Three academic exercises—the lecture, the declamation, and the disputation—lay at the heart of the education offered at seventeenth-century Harvard; the immediate goal of that education was to enable students to systematize coherently and to contend expertly, abilities highly prized in an oral culture that placed ultimate value on the discovery of philosophical and theological truth. The lecture was the master's way of demonstrating systematic thought at its best: he would commonly cast a proposition as a question, divide and subdivide it into its various elements, dealing with each separately, and then indicate the relationships among the several parts. In a sense, the lecture was an oral textbook—frequently a series of commen-

[22] *New Englands First Fruits*, pp. 434-436, 438-440. Some typical examples of theses are the following: Philological Theses—(1) Greek is the most copious of languages, (2) Rhetoric is different in kind from logic, (3) Universals have no existence outside the mind; Philosophical Theses—(1) Prudence is the most difficult of all the virtues, (2) Form is accidental, (3) Every being is good.

[23] "The Lawes of the Colledge Published Publiquely Before the Students of Harvard Colledge, May 4, 1655," *Publications of the Colonial Society of Massachusetts*, XXXI (1935), 327-339.

taries on some classic treatise—which students often transcribed verbatim and which is exemplified in literary form by a work such as Alsted's *Encyclopedia*. The declamation was also an effort to demonstrate systematic thought at its best, though it was a student rather than a faculty exercise and placed more emphasis on rhetorical grace. Declamations were characterized by an abundance of classical allusions, and it was against the need to parade such learning that most students began early in their careers to gather in commonplace books quotations neatly arranged under such rubrics as war, peace, life, death, virtue, and evil. Finally, the disputation was a highly formalized exchange in which a student argued a position on some question introduced by the moderator, while one or more respondents raised objections to his arguments. As the disputation progressed, the participants sought flaws in each other's logic, as well as errors of fact or substance; and, given the mounting tension and excitement, an apt thrust or a clever pun or just the right axiom from Aristotle could elicit spirited applause from an interested audience. The exercise ordinarily concluded with a "dismissal speech" by the moderator, frequently favorable to one or another of the disputants. At their worst—and they are frequently portrayed at their worst in the reformist literature of the Renaissance—all of these exercises were dull, formalistic, and intellectually barren. At their best, however, they nurtured clarity of expression, grace of style, nimbleness of intellect, and sharpness of wit, all of which were invaluable to men of affairs, to say nothing of teachers in pulpit or classroom. And, in their own way and by the canons of their own time, they were liberating—that is, they provided perspectives of time, place, and the imagination from which to criticize the seventeenth-century present.

In its academic program and in other respects as well, Harvard was similar to the colleges of contemporary Oxford and Cambridge, most notably Emmanuel. It was small in size and collegial in character, embracing at any given time the president and two or three tutors, a steward, cook, butler, and several servants, and from twenty to fifty resident scholars. During Dunster's administration, the median age of entering freshmen was about seventeen; during Chauncy's, it dropped to a little over fifteen, and it remained under sixteen for the rest of the century. While the great majority of the early students were of New England Puritan background, there were enough boys from Virginia, New Netherland, Bermuda, and England to lend a tinge of cosmopolitanism to the college, and, indeed, it was assumed from the beginning that Harvard would be an Anglo-American rather than merely an American institution. As in the English universities, the offspring of magistrates, professionals, and landed families predominated, with a sprinkling of youngsters from artisan and tradesman backgrounds; few sons of husbandmen came, and John Wise of the class of 1673 was probably the first child of an indentured servant to attend. Four years of life in such a community doubtless constituted a powerful education, over and above that provided by the formal curriculum, particularly given the range of recreation, amusements, pranks, brawls, and riots inside and outside the college yard.

Harvard had six presidents between 1640 and 1689—Henry Dunster (1640-1654), Charles Chauncy (1654-1672), Leonard Hoar (1672-1675), Urian Oakes (1675-1681), John Rogers (1682-1684), and Increase Mather (1685-1701)—and forty-three tutors, who served anywhere from a few months to eight years. Dunster and Chauncy were Cambridge men; the remaining presidents were alumni of Harvard, though Hoar held an M.D. from Cambridge and Mather an M.A. from Trinity College, Dublin. That the college was able to produce its own faculty less than a half-century after Massachusetts was settled and less than thirty-five years after its classes first met—and this while maintaining standards sufficiently high to merit an assumption of equivalence on the part of metropolitan institutions—is persuasive testimony to its vitality, and suggests the need for an additional refinement of Fox's paradigm, since Fox implied a significant passage of time before native institutions of higher learning would be capable of maintaining themselves without assistance from the metropolis.

All of Harvard's early presidents were men of ability, though admittedly Chauncy stayed in office well beyond the point at which he should have retired, and Hoar, having come to an early impasse with the students, was quickly forced to resign. Certainly Dunster's administration was the most remarkable: in fourteen years, virtually singlehandedly, he converted an infant institution of uncertain future into a thoroughly acceptable college with every prospect for survival. We know precious little of Dunster's youth in England. He was born in 1609 to a yeoman family in Bury, Lancashire, and attended Magdalene College, Cambridge, taking the M.A. degree in 1634. He returned to Bury shortly after his graduation, as schoolmaster and curate, remaining there until 1640, when he immigrated to Boston with his brother Richard. Three weeks after his arrival, and almost three months to the day before his thirty-first birthday, he was elected president of Harvard.

There is every evidence that Dunster taught the entire curriculum on his own, at least during the early years of his tenure; certainly, the program of 1642 was so arranged that the president could deliver all the lectures himself, instructing the freshmen on Mondays through Thursdays from eight to nine in the morning, the second-year scholars from nine to ten, and the third-year scholars from ten to eleven, meeting with the entire student body on Fridays and Saturdays for work in rhetoric and divinity, and spending afternoons supervising disputations, recitations, and sundry tutorial exercises. Dunster's first assistance in all this came in 1643, when the overseers ordered "that two bachelors shall be chosen for the present help of the president, to read to the junior pupils as the president shall see fit," and appointed John Bulkley and George Downing, both members of the class of 1642, to the newly created positions. Thereafter Dunster had the assistance, in fairly rapid succession, of Samuel Danforth, Samuel Mather, Jonathan Mitchell, Comfort Starr, Samuel Eaton, Urian Oakes, John Collins, and Michael Wigglesworth, all of whom went on to the ministry except Eaton, who served briefly as a magistrate in the New Haven Colony until his untimely death at the age of twenty-five. Wigglesworth left a fascinating diary covering the years of his tutorship, which, though characteristically Puritan in its overweening preoccupation with spiritual self-examination and progress, makes abundantly clear both Dunster's edifying influence on him and his own continuing regard for the piety of his charges.[24]

When Dunster assumed his post, his understanding was that he would teach, and that there would be "no further care or distraction." He could not have been more mistaken. Even though he had the co-operation of a powerful board of overseers, he found himself caught up, during the fourteen years of his presidency, in all

24 "College Book No. 1," ibid., XV (1925), 17; and The Diary of Michael Wigglesworth, 1653-1657, edited by Edmund S. Morgan (New York: Harper & Row, 1965), pp. 7, 9, 11, 26-27, and passim. For lists of Harvard presidents, fellows, and tutors during the seventeenth century, see Albert Matthews' introduction to the Harvard College Records in Publications of the Colonial Society of Massachusetts, XV (1925), clii-clxi.

the concerns of a latter-day university administrator. He had scarcely arrived when he became involved in the completion of the "Old College" building, which had been started under Nathaniel Eaton; he had to regather the dispersed students and recruit new ones; after marrying comfortably in 1641, he found himself unable to collect the salary that had been promised him and forced continually to plead for support from the general court, the New England Confederation, Parliament, and private donors; and, having taken over a college established under legislation of the general court (passed initially in 1637 and re-enacted in 1642), he deemed it advisable during the Commonwealth era to seek a more permanent incorporation and became the prime mover in obtaining a formal charter from the court in 1650. Through it all, he faced the daily necessity of developing the rules, usages, and customs that would shape the character of the college: he borrowed the practice of having commencement theses from the University of Edinburgh, he took the wording of the charter and of the various "rules and precepts" from the ancient statutes of Oxford and Cambridge, he improvised here and invented there, so that by 1654 a unique and autochthonous tradition had been created for the fledgling institution.[25]

Dunster resigned the presidency in 1654, after a series of sharp encounters with the students, the board of overseers, and the General Court, first, over the extension of the undergraduate curriculum from three to four years, then, over the financial management of the institution, and finally—and fatally—over the thorny issue of infant baptism, the propriety and efficacy of which Dunster began to doubt in 1652 and 1653. Many prominent persons in the colony sought to dissuade him from this Baptist heresy, but to no avail. After a public disputation in Boston on February 2 and 3, 1654, in which Dunster argued that infant baptism was un-Scriptural, his position became untenable, and he resigned the following June 10, removing a year later to Scituate, in the Plymouth Colony, where he served as a pastor until his death early in 1659.

III

Harvard College was founded to advance piety, civility, and learning. *New Englands First Fruits* spoke of the longing "to advance learning

---

25 Henry Dunster to the Honored Commissioners for the College *et al.*, December, 1653, in Morison, *Founding of Harvard College*, pp. 448-449.

and perpetuate it to posterity" and the dread of leaving an illiterate ministry to the church, once the initial immigrants had passed from the scene. The charter of 1650 defined the ends of the college as "the advancement of all good literature, arts and sciences" and the education of English and Indian youth "in knowledge: and godliness." The Reverend Jonathan Mitchell, in his "Modell for the Maintaining of Students & Fellows of Choise Abilities at the Colledge in Cambridge," presented to the general court in 1663, insisted not only on the importance of training a learned ministry but also on the necessity of providing masters for the grammar schools, educated gentlemen for the magistracy, and competent practitioners for the several professions. And, in their statement offering assistance to the college in 1669, the residents of Portsmouth, New Hampshire, referred to the need "for the perpetuating of knowledge, both religious and civil, among us, and our posterity after us." In these and other contemporary documents, the three great ends of seventeenth-century Anglo-American education were so intertwined as to be inseparable—except, that is, by an anti-intellectual polemicist like William Dell, and Charles Chauncy gave New England's irrevocable reply to arguments such as his in 1655.[26]

Yet one can grant the explicit purposes of Harvard and still recognize that those who studied there put the education they received to their own uses; and there is no denying the considerable variety of those uses during the period between 1642 and 1689. Whereas just under half the alumni became ministers, the striking fact is that just over half did not, going instead into medicine, public service, business, teaching, or the management of land holdings. And, whatever the spirit in which the classics were taught, there was certainly immense diversity in the manner in which they were learned; indeed the ideas gleaned from them were doubtless discussed, disputed, and eventually acted upon in ways quite at odds with what Harvard's founders had intended. Once again, the similarity to the colleges of contemporary Oxford and Cambridge is patent.[27]

[26] "The Harvard College Charter of 1650," *Publications of the Colonial Society of Massachusetts*, XXXI (1935), 5; Mitchell, "Modell for the Maintaining of Students & Fellows," p. 317; and Shurtleff, ed., *Records of the Governor and Company of Massachusetts*, IV, ii, 433.

[27] Samuel Eliot Morison, *Harvard College in the Seventeenth Century* (2 vols.; Cambridge, Mass.: Harvard University Press, 1936), II, 562.

OCCUPATIONS OF HARVARD ALUMNI OF THE CLASSES 1642-1689

	1642-1658	1659-1677	1678-1689	1642-1689
Clergymen	76	62	42	180
Physicians	12	11	4	27
Public Servants*	13	17	12	42
Teachers**	1	8	4	13
Merchants	3	6	1	10
Planters, Gentlemen	4	5	2	11
Soldiers, Mariners	0	1	4	5
Miscellaneous	2	3	0	5
Died Young***	11	5	11	27
Occupation Unknown****	27	35	6	68
Total	149	153	86	388

* Governors, councilors, judges, deputies (if continuing for a term of years), and permanent officials; local offices not counted.

** Schoolmasters and college tutors who made teaching a career, or who died before doing anything else.

*** Those who died in college or within five years after graduating, without getting a job.

**** Most of these are the nongraduates before 1663, whose careers have never been investigated; some have not even been identified.

The conditions of the colonial environment did, however, occasion certain significant departures from the English pattern. For one thing, Harvard awarded degrees, so far as can be determined, with no explicit authority from the king, or Parliament, or the general court, or any extant *studium* or university: Dunster and the overseers simply went ahead and granted them, thereby virtually declaring independence from Charles I, as Morison appropriately suggests. Then, too, Harvard early innovated in the realm of control. Without evidence to the contrary, one must assume that the founders intended the board of overseers to bring the college into being and then transfer its prerogatives to the master and fellows, much as in the English universities; and, indeed, the charter of 1650, which created a corporation composed of the president, treasurer, and five fellows to govern the college and manage its resources, doubtless envisioned such a transfer. But the charter stipulated that the orders of the corporation would be contingent upon the approval of the overseers, in effect leaving Harvard with two governing boards, one consisting of magistrates and ministers, the other of the college's officers and faculty members. To complicate the arrangement even further, as the seventeenth century progressed a number of tutors were appointed to instruct without being made fellows of the corporation, while a number of influential citizens who had no instructional responsibilities were appointed to the corporation—with the result that the college was governed by two bodies composed primarily of ministers and laymen who did not teach. It was a development quite in keeping with the tendency toward laicization in the English universities, but it was thoroughly indigenous to the colonies.

Harvard also innovated in the realm of support, largely out of necessity. The initial effort to subsidize the institution through endowment, tuition, and the assignment of various fees, like the Boston-Charlestown ferry rent, proved inadequate, and the college shortly began to experiment with schemes such as the fund-raising mission of Hugh Peter, Thomas Weld, and William Hibbins to England in 1641; the "college corn" arrangement proposed by the Commissioners of the United Colonies, whereby "but the fourth part of a bushel of corn, or something equivalent thereunto" would be contributed by every family in New England willing and able to do so; the voluntary collection of the Piscataqua towns of New Hampshire during the 1670's; and direct grants of land and tax revenues from the general court, which agreed to pay the president's salary starting with the accession of Chauncy in 1654. During the period from 1669 to 1682, 52.7 per cent of Harvard's annual income came from the government and government-sponsored subscriptions, while endowment accounted for only 12.1 per cent and tuition for only 9.4 per cent. Once again, the departure from traditional English practice was substantial.[28]

Finally, Harvard sought to innovate in the realm of Indian education, though most of its attempts failed abysmally, largely because of the unspoken assumption that the Indians should aspire to the same social and cultural ends as the whites. Harvard's principal effort was, of course, the Indian College, built around 1654 or 1655 in response to a request from the Commissioners of the United Colonies to erect "one entire room at the college" for the instruction of a half-dozen promising young Indians. Almost as soon as it was completed, however, President Chauncy was complaining that the

[28] Nathaniel B. Shurtleff and David Pulsifer, eds., *Records of the Colony of New Plymouth in New England* (12 vols.; Boston: William White, 1855-1861), IX, 20-21; and Margery Somers Foster, *"Out of Smalle Beginnings . . ."* (Cambridge, Mass.: Harvard University Press, 1962), pp. 148-149.

two-story building was insufficiently used and asking permission to accommodate some white students there, which permission was granted. Unfortunately, Chauncy's complaint became a self-fulfilling prophecy and few Indians ever studied at Harvard. There is evidence that a youngster named John Sassamon attended for a term or two around 1653, before the creation of the Indian College, as a protégé of John Eliot. But it is unlikely that more than four others entered before 1689, of whom only one, known as Caleb Cheeshahteaumuck, completed the work for the B.A.—and he unfortunately died of consumption a year after graduating. Otherwise, the most useful purpose the Indian College served with respect to the red men was to house the press that printed the Indian Bible and the other Algonquian texts prepared by Eliot and his associates.[29]

The presence of Harvard, coupled with both the return of a small number of youngsters to England and the Continent for advanced education and the increasing reliance on apprenticeship to produce physicians, lawyers, and other professionals, created an interesting tension in the colonies between the maintenance of standards commensurate with those of the metropolis and the widening of access to elite positions. The historic regulatory functions of the guilds simply could not be exercised in a land three thousand miles from the seats of power and beset with a chronic labor shortage, and this was as true for the professions as it was for the trades. Hence, there were few serious attempts to restrict entry into the legal and medical professions in the colonies, and these were more often the result of a general animus toward mercenary attorneys and physicians than of a desire to preserve standards—the outstanding exception being Maryland's effort to regulate the practice of law beginning in 1657.[30]

One obvious consequence was a sharp decline in professional standards, which might have been even more precipitous and enduring had not the graduates of Harvard, Oxford, Cambridge, Padua, and Edinburgh been present to exemplify traditional canons of competence. Another outcome, however, was a considerable broadening of access to the professions, extending, to be sure, to many who

29 Shurtleff and Pulsifer, eds., *Records of the Colony of New Plymouth*, X, 107.

30 *Archives of Maryland*, XLI (1922), 10-11. For the short-lived effort to confine the title "counselor-at-law" to barristers certified by the Inns of Court, see William Waller Hening. ed., *The Statutes at Large; Being a Collection of All the Laws of Virginia, from the First Session of the Legislature, in the Year 1619* (13 vols.; imprint varies, 1819-1823), I, 419, 482.

sought little more than a quick and easy shilling, but extending also to those who wanted something better for themselves and for those they served. The resulting situation was egregiously ill-defined, for traditional patterns of professional self-regulation simply failed to take root. But the very lack of definition provided a favorable context for novelty, and when Americans turned to the reconstitution of legal education and medical education in the eighteenth century, they developed these in unique ways: there would be no Inns of Court and no Royal College of Physicians, merely new schools and new faculties of old colleges, open to all who could pay the modest tuition and meet the modest entrance requirements.

Chapter 8

COMMUNITY

> We do settle in the way of townships or villages, each of which
> contains five thousand acres, in square, and at least ten families;
> the regulation of the country being a family to each five hundred
> acres. . . . Many that had right to more land were at first covetous
> to have their whole quantity without regard to this way of settle-
> ment, though by such wilderness vacancies they had ruined the
> country, and then our interest of course. I had in my view society,
> assistance, busy commerce, instruction of youth, government of
> people's manners, conveniency of religious assembling, encourage-
> ment of mechanics, distinct and beaten roads, and it has answered
> in all those respects, I think, to a universal content.
>
> WILLIAM PENN

There is a sense in which all institutions educate, for they subtly
shape the ways men think and act and perceive the world. So, too,
after all, do the laws, which direct the conduct of men along certain
lines defined as just and right and good. And so also do the arts,
which awaken men to visions of human possibility toward which
they themselves may aspire in their efforts at self-perfection. The
ancients, of course, recognized this full well, and their treatises on
education went far beyond a narrow preoccupation with parent
and pedagogue to a broader concern with the formative influence of
civic life in general: of ceremonies, athletics, poetry, music, architecture, government, and philosophy. The men of the Renaissance, re-
covering these insights of a bygone age, made them the basis for a
powerful critique of contemporary institutions, and an insistent
chorus of English humanists from More to Bacon focused attention

on the decisive impact of communities on the character and destiny of men.

The England to which these men addressed their reform programs was a community of rural villages or hamlets, each a cluster of households joined by ties of kinship, marriage, and common experience. These villages varied considerably in size, though the majority remained small, averaging around three hundred people organized into some sixty or seventy families. In most cases, the village proper was at the center of an area of land which the householders had responsibility for cultivating. That land was frequently divided into several sections—one for grazing, two or three for the production of wheat, barley, rye, or legumes, and at least one left fallow—which were rotated from year to year. If the land was held in traditional feudal tenure, the householders farmed it in common, every family receiving the produce of certain designated strips in each of the several fields. If the area had been enclosed, the strips would have been combined to form family farms, owned and tenanted with varying degrees of permanence; but even in such instances much of the work was done in common. Almost all the villages included artisans and craftsmen, who plied their trades in addition to engaging in husbandry. A majority of them also included at least one squire, who lived on a large manor with his substantial household; but at least a fifth did not, and in the absence of a hereditary gentry many of these developed a fascinating array of autochthonous procedures for self-government.

Some 75 to 80 per cent of the population of early Stuart England resided in such villages and hamlets, and, despite the high degree of mobility across the countryside, localism holds the key to what might be called the ecology of English education during the first decades of the seventeenth century. The rhythms and requirements of husbandry set the tone of rural life, the traditional status hierarchy determined its character. And the household, the church, and the village school (if there was one) systematically taught the rightness of that tone and that character, with the household serving as the most important center of day-by-day enactive education and the church as the most important center of iconic and symbolic education. "Take away kings, princes, rulers, magistrates, judges, and such estates of God's order," warned the Homily on Obedience (1547), and "no man shall ride or go by the highway unrobbed; no man shall sleep in his own house or bed unkilled; no man shall keep his wife, children and possessions in quietness; all things shall be common; and there must needs follow all mischief and utter destruction both of souls, bodies, goods, and commonwealths."[1]

True, the church dispensed news as well as homilies, and from time to time royal edicts, parliamentary proclamations, county regulations, and sundry information of more than local significance. True, also, some of the denizens of each village would almost certainly have had first-hand experience in other localities. Moreover, windows on the larger world would occasionally be opened by army musters, manorial courts, county fairs, itinerant preachers and peddlers, and printed matter, especially ballads, broadsides, and chapbooks. And, finally, the children of the wealthier yeomen and gentry might go off to a grammar school or to one of the universities or Inns of Court, or even to the court at London or to the Continent. But most English villagers grew up in a local and predominantly oral culture, within which household and church were the primary agencies of sustained, deliberate instruction—in commonly held opinions, commonly used skills, and a commonly known liturgy incarnating a commonly accepted view of the world.

Alongside the villages stood the towns, varying from those that were not much larger than hamlets to a few, like Norwich, York, and Bristol, that could boast between ten and twenty thousand inhabitants. These towns arose out of a variety of circumstances: most, for example, Bridgewater in Somerset, Cranbrook in Kent, or Stratford-upon-Avon in Warwickshire, emerged as market centers for the territory surrounding them; some, such as Norwich, which developed with the textile industry, or Bristol, which was the second port of the land, served as centers of a particular trade; while others, like Newcastle, York, Salisbury, or Exeter, were cathedral cities and hence centers of ecclesiastical administration.

Households and churches remained pivotal in the social structure of the towns, but other agencies of association quickly appeared, notably assizes, quarter courts, common councils, companies of mer-

[1] "An Exhortation Concerning Good Order and Obedience to Rulers and Magistrates," *The Two Books of Homilies Appointed to Be Read in Churches* (Oxford: Oxford University Press, 1859), pp. 105-106. The terms "enactive knowledge," "iconic knowledge," and "symbolic knowledge" are Jerome Bruner's, the first referring to knowledge that derives directly from acting in context, the second referring to knowledge that derives vicariously from picturing, the third referring to knowledge that derives vicariously from language and other symbolic abstraction. See Bruner's essay "The Perfectibility of Intellect," in Paul H. Oehser, ed., *Knowledge Among Men* (New York: Simon and Schuster, 1966), pp. 15-30.

chants and craftsmen, assemblages of regular and secular clergy, fairs, bridewells, hospitals, and alehouses. Also, with the greater degree of social and economic specialization characteristic of town life, there tended to be more diversity in the nature of households and hence richer opportunities for apprenticeships of various sorts, not only in the crafts and trades, but also in merchandising, medicine, and law. Finally, the higher density of population in the towns made for easier access to advanced education in a grammar school or to private instruction in such subjects as writing or arithmetic. Yet, all this notwithstanding, it is too easy to exaggerate the differences between town and village life. As late as 1688, when Gregory King undertook his memorable survey of the English population, 870,000 individuals were living in cities and market towns other than London, but over half of them resided in communities of less than 1,300. In these smaller towns, as in the rural villages, an oral culture prevailed, and such institutions of deliberate education as existed there devoted themselves largely to transmitting an admixture of folk and formal homilies.[2]

Finally, in a class by itself, there was London, whose rapid growth was one of the salient social phenomena of the English Renaissance. A city of 60,000 in 1500, embracing roughly 2 per cent of the country's population, it had increased to 225,000 by 1600, embracing roughly 5 per cent, and to 550,000 by 1688, embracing roughly 10 per cent. The largest metropolitan center of western Europe, its influence was commensurate with its size: Lewis Mumford has portrayed it as one of the model baroque capitals, incarnating the convergence of royal absolutism, political consolidation, economic dominance, and intellectual vitality that marked the seventeenth century in general and the early Stuart period in particular.[3]

The range of possibilities for formal and informal association in London was dazzling when compared with the relative simplicity of village life: there was the court, with its unrivaled pomp, power, and pageantry; there were the great cathedrals and lesser churches, with their colorful rites and rituals; there were the merchant companies and craft guilds and the Royal Exchange, "where merchants

[2] D. V. Glass, "Two Papers on Gregory King," in D. V. Glass and D. E. C. Eversley, eds., *Population in History* (Chicago: Aldine Publishing Company, 1965), pp. 159-220; and Peter Laslett, *The World We Have Lost* (London: Methuen and Company, 1965), pp. 55-56.

[3] Lewis Mumford, *The City in History* (New York: Harcourt, Brace & World, 1961), chaps. xii-xiii.

most do congregate"; there were the docks and ships and associated agencies of commerce; there were the inns and shops and taverns, wherein a person might encounter men, goods, and ideas from every corner of the civilized world; there were the innumerable amusements, including plays, puppet shows, dancing, fencing, gaming, and bearbaiting; and there were the endless opportunities for learning—at grammar schools, painting schools, calligraphy schools, arithmetic schools, military schools, and the Inns of Court; at sermons at Paul's Cross, public lectures at Gresham College, divinity lectures in the chancel of St. Paul's Church, and anatomy lectures at the Surgeon's Hall; and at the bookshops in St. Paul's Churchyard. Indeed, so abundant were these last opportunities that Sir George Buck referred to London as the "third university of England," at which one could study not only the traditional liberal arts "but also all or the most part of all other arts and sciences proper and fit for ingenious and liberal persons." To this third university came men from all over the realm, to be trained and tried and tested.[4]

Buck, of course, dealt only with formal institutions of learning in his portrayal of the third university, disregarding the unparalleled educational possibilities inherent in the variegated life of the city. The sheer multiplicity of character models available to the apt learner, from the consummately skilled cutpurse to the consummately skilled barrister, and the sheer range of specialized agencies for the conduct of affairs rendered London a school of incomparable richness. Yet its educational influence went even farther. Peter Laslett appropriately describes Stuart England as a "large rural hinterland attached to a vast metropolis through a network of insignificant local centers." The key term is network—or reticulation, as he later puts it—which suggests that the country was a community of hamlets, towns, and shires rather than a mere aggregation of settlements, a community held together by a web of communication. Through that web, London educated the realm, sending forth people, books, and ideas in profusion.[5]

In the first place, London was the political, ecclesiastical, and commercial capital of the commonwealth. Tudor and Stuart policy had cast court and church as the twin centers of the English uni-

---

[4] William Shakespeare, *The Merchant of Venice*, Act I, scene iii, line 50; and Sir George Buck, "The Third Universitie of England" (1615), printed as part of an appendix to John Stow and Edmond Howes, *The Annales, or Generall Chronicle of England* (London: Thoma[s] Adams, 1615), p. 965.

[5] Laslett, *World We Have Lost*, pp. 56-57.

verse, with the monarch symbolizing the union of *imperium* and *sacerdotium*. And numerous contemporary authors had portrayed the court as the exemplary household, over which the king presided as benevolent father and teacher. From such metaphors, it was but a short step to the equation of governance with education: the lords lieutenants and justices of the peace taught and enforced a common law, and the clergy taught and enforced a common liturgy. Moreover, the great London merchants, allied as they were with the Crown, took advantage of the uniformity of laws, expectations, weights, measures, and currency to gain decisive economic dominance over the country. One outcome of all this was the emergence of a vigorous nationalism, which patently ran counter to the localism of the villages and towns. And, indeed, the coexistence of localism and nationalism, together with the dual and often conflicting loyalties demanded by that coexistence, became critically significant to the character of seventeenth-century English education.

London was also the publishing center of the kingdom, owing largely to the incorporation of the Stationers' Company there in 1557. The Stationers' charter, which represented something of a culmination of the effort begun during Henry VII's reign to control printing, gave the master, two wardens, and ninety-four freemen constituting the Company sole printing rights in England (though others might from time to time be granted explicit royal permission to print) and authorized the wardens to search the premises of any printer, binder, or seller of books within the country, to seize and burn any volumes produced "contrary to the form of any statute, act, or proclamation, made or to be made," and to fine and imprison the printers of such confiscated books, dividing the fines between the Company and the Crown. Elizabeth confirmed the charter in 1559 and included the following stipulations in her Royal Injunctions of that year: (1) every new work had to be licensed by the queen herself, by six members of the Privy Council, or by specified persons in the Anglican hierarchy; (2) pamphlets, plays, and ballads had to be licensed by at least three of the ecclesiastical commissioners of the city of London; and (3) the reprinting and circulation of "all other books of matters of religion, or policy, or governance that hath been printed, either on this side the seas or on the other side," had to be supervised by the ecclesiastical commissioners. Twenty-seven years later, a star-chamber decree reaffirmed these orders, adding the requirement that all books, with the exception of those dealing with the law and those produced under the jurisdiction of the queen's printer, be licensed by the archbishop of Canterbury and the bishop of London and leaving responsibility for enforcement jointly in the hands of the Stationers' Company and the ecclesiastical officials. The Stuarts simply built on these regulations, further strengthening the power of the Company, which reached its zenith under Charles I, stringently controlling the number of presses and printing houses, and closely supervising the granting of special patents to the royal printer and other favorites.[6]

The combination of censorship and monopoly was, of course, but another of the Tudor-Stuart instruments for promoting uniformity and avoiding civil dissension; while the regulations themselves were neither strictly obeyed nor wholly disregarded, they did result in a steady flow of politically and theologically orthodox material from London to the provinces. And, given a potential reading public that may have included as many as half the men in the cities and a third of those in the hinterland, that flow was doubtless a leading factor in the gradual homogenizing of the variegated oral culture of Stuart England.[7]

Finally, London was the intellectual center of the nation, with respect to taste and values as well as knowledge and information.

[6] Edward Arber, ed., *A Transcript of the Registers of the Company of Stationers of London, 1554-1640 A.D.* (5 vols.; London and Birmingham: privately printed, 1875-1894), I, xxviii-xxxii, IV, 529-536; Walter Howard Frere and William McClure Kennedy, eds., *Visitation Articles and Injunctions of the Period of the Reformation*, Alcuin Club Collections, vols. XIV-XVI (3 vols.; London: Longmans, Green & Co., 1910), III, 24-25; J. R. Tanner, *Tudor Constitutional Documents, A.D. 1485-1603, with an Historical Commentary* (2d ed.; Cambridge: Cambridge University Press, 1930), pp. 279-284; and Henry R. Plomer, "The King's Printing House Under the Stuarts," *The Library*, new ser., II (1901), 353-375.

[7] The literacy estimates are from Lawrence Stone, "The Educational Revolution in England, 1560-1640," *Past & Present*, no. 28 (July, 1964), 43-44. Sylvia L. Thrupp estimates that 40 per cent of London males could read Latin around 1400 and that at least half could read English (*The Merchant Class of Medieval London* [Ann Arbor: University of Michigan Press, 1948], pp. 157-158). John William Adamson estimates from jury lists of Winchester in 1373 and Norfolk in 1466 that 33 per cent of the males were literate ("*The Illiterate Anglo-Saxon*" *and Other Essays on Education, Medieval and Modern* [Cambridge: Cambridge University Press, 1946], p. 42). Mildred Campbell estimates from the wills, leases, and bonds of some twenty-five hundred to three thousand yeomen in the Tudor and early Stuart eras that the literacy rate was between 60 per cent and 70 per cent (*The English Yeoman Under Elizabeth and the Early Stuarts* [New Haven: Yale University Press, 1942], p. 263). And Godfrey Davies estimates that four-fifths of Cromwell's army signed petitions and hence must have been literate (*The Early Stuarts, 1603-1660* [2d ed.; Oxford: Clarendon Press, 1959], p. 359). All these estimates are based on the assumption that the ability to sign one's name is closely correlated to the ability to read, an assumption open to question (see *infra*, chap. xviii).

One function of the baroque city, Mumford has wisely observed, "was to discredit local goods, which varied in pattern, in color, in stuff, in texture, in decoration, in accordance with local traditions, and give circulation to those in use at the capital." As with material fare, so also with intellectual. The phenomenon is clearly manifest in the impact of the Puritan lecturers of London during the pre-Revolutionary years, in the development of the concept and institution of the newspaper during the Parliamentary era, and in the rapid rise of the coffeehouses after the Restoration, with their extraordinary influence on the genesis of particular modes and schools of thought. It is exemplified best, perhaps, by the efforts of the Royal Society, founded in 1660 and dedicated to promoting "physico-mathematical experimental learning." Meeting initially at Gresham College in London, outside the pale of the two historic universities, and emphasizing "philosophical inquiry" rather than discussions of divinity or politics, the Society sharply challenged the traditional hegemony of Oxford and Cambridge in the world of ideas and, through its correspondence, its *Philosophical Transactions,* and its informal network of communications, profoundly affected English intellectual styles—though not without generating some of the most fundamental, if acerbic, debates of the seventeenth century over the nature, the character, and the ends of education.[8]

Now, the American colonies, too, must be seen as part of the reticulation that was England, as part of the vast rural hinterland attached to London by a series of insignificant local centers. True, the Atlantic posed special problems of communication, though, as E. E. Rich has pointed out, the differences in hazard and difficulty between oceanic and overland travel were not nearly so great as some have assumed. In any case, there was patently a transatlantic community in the seventeenth century, maintained through a network of relationships between London and Boston, London and New York, and London and Virginia, which may well have been closer than the relationships between Boston, New York, and Virginia or, indeed, between Boston and its environs.[9]

[8] Mumford, *City in History,* p. 437; Thomas Birch, *The History of the Royal Society of London for Improving of Natural Knowledge from Its First Rise* (4 vols.; London: printed for A. Millar, 1756-1757), I, 3; and Thomas Sprat, *The History of the Royal-Society of London, for the Improving of Natural Knowledge* (London: T. R., 1667), pp. 52-59. For the debates over education, see Richard Foster Jones, *Ancients and Moderns* (2d ed.; St. Louis: Washington University Press, 1961).

[9] E. E. Rich, "The Population of Elizabethan England," *The Economic History Review,* 2d ser., II (1949-50), 264.

The links in this network, like the links between London and
the metropolitan hinterland, took the form of persons, books, and
ideas. Officials, clergy, and merchants traveled back and forth across
the ocean, their movement varying according to who held power in
London. Thus, there was the procession of governors and administrators to Virginia, sent initially by the Company and then by the
Crown, and there was the burgeoning bureaucracy sent after the
Restoration to all the colonies by the Lords of Trade, the secretary
of state, the admiralty, and the treasury. Conversely, there were the
colonial agents and delegations that made their way eastward, seeking special favors at Whitehall or Westminster or simply representing
the general interests of one or another of the colonies.

Similarly, there were the constant comings and goings of the
clergy. Anglican ministers traveled to and fro between England and
Virginia from the beginning, and, starting with the episcopate of
Henry Compton in 1675, the bishop of London came to play an
increasingly influential role in advancing colonial Anglicanism. Nonconformist preachers moved freely between London and New England, especially during the Parliamentary era. And George Fox's
address in 1659 to "friends in Barbados, Virginia, New England,
and all the islands about" initiated a vigorous Quaker proselytizing
effort beyond the seas, which may have involved as many as a hundred missionaries in the years before 1689.[10]

Finally, there was the transatlantic commercial web, running
largely along well-beaten paths of kinship, friendship, and religious
affiliation, which provided the requisite information, credit, and
capital for goods to flow at a profit. And, once again, the paths led
to London. "The Boston merchants' meeting place in their Town-
house Exchange," Bernard Bailyn has remarked, "was in every way,
except geographically, closer to the 'New England walk' on the London Exchange than to the market places of most inland towns."
Obviously, the paths led also to Amsterdam, the West Indies, and
the West African slaving ports generically known as Guinea. But the
dominance of London was early established, and was decisively confirmed when the city took the lion's share of trade mandated by the
Navigation Acts of 1651 and after.[11]

10 *The Works of George Fox* (8 vols.; Philadelphia: Marcus T. C. Gould, 1831),
VII, 169.
11 Bernard Bailyn, "Communications and Trade: The Atlantic in the Seventeenth
Century," *The Journal of Economic History*, XIII (1953), 383.

London also remained the place from which the colonists imported most of their books. True, at least four presses were operating in the colonies by 1689: one at Cambridge, which dated from 1638, one at Boston, which had been set up in 1674, and those at St. Mary's City and at Philadelphia, which were established in 1685. But these presses never even attempted to produce a complete range of printed materials. Owing partly to costs, partly to the limited availability of type fonts, and partly to censorship, the first colonial printers concentrated on sermons, almanacs, and catechisms, all of which were deemed useful inasmuch as they fulfilled local needs, significant inasmuch as they educated, and economical inasmuch as they could find a ready market. Less ephemeral works of reference, instruction, and entertainment were left to metropolitan publishers to produce and were imported in substantial quantities by both retail booksellers and individual readers. And, since self-instruction from books often took the place of classroom or apprenticeship teaching that was simply not available, London printers had an even greater educational influence in America than they did in the metropolis.

By implication, much the same was true of London's influence in the realm of ideas. Given the very isolation of the colonies, the latest intellectual and aesthetic styles of the capital took on added prestige in America, both because there were few clearly established colonial alternatives and because in many areas sophisticated colonials were forced to turn to the metropolis for like-minded colleagues. The latter phenomenon is clearly illustrated in the career of John Winthrop, Jr., governor of Connecticut, chemist, mineralogist, physician, businessman, and an "original member" of the Royal Society, having been formally elected on May 23, 1663, during one of his sojourns in England. Winthrop returned that year with an unofficial commission as the Society's western correspondent, and there followed a vigorous exchange of letters with Henry Oldenburg (secretary of the Society), Robert Boyle, Sir Robert Moray, Robert Hooke, William Brereton, Isaac Newton, and other luminaries of the new learning, as well as a steady flow of reports to London on the minerals of New England, the aboriginal Indians, the satellites of Jupiter, and the comets visible in North America. Roger Williams was also elected in 1663, but there is no indication that he ever complied with the requirement to come personally to London to sign the membership roll; and it is likely that Thomas Brattle was a fellow too, though his name, curiously, appears nowhere in the Society's records. Further, there is evidence that in 1683 Increase Mather and a number of Boston gentlemen founded an informal philosophical association, clearly conceived on the London model but without the participation of any members of the London group. The Boston association did not survive, however, poignantly testifying to the problems of isolation Winthrop had earlier described in a letter to Theodore Haak, in which he expressed his unhappiness over being at "such a distance, from that fountain whence so many rivulets of excellent things do stream forth for the good of the world."[12]

II

The educational impact of particular communities in seventeenth-century America depended partly on their spatial arrangements, partly on their institutional patterns and cultural characteristics, and partly on their relationships with other communities, both nearby and in Europe. Hence, any assessment of that impact requires a kind of ecological analysis, of both the larger education afforded by various kinds of communal life and the more systematic education afforded by different configurations of formal educational institutions.

Two general types of rural settlement may be discerned in the seventeenth-century colonies: the nucleated agricultural townships of New England and the dispersed farmsteads of the Chesapeake region. In the middle colonies—a residual category, at best, for this and most other analyses—the types were intermingled, though dispersed farmsteads predominated. Granted, New England in due course spawned communities of scattered farms on its frontiers, and the Chesapeake area eventually created hamlets for purposes of trade and communication; but neither of these secondary developments should be permitted to obscure the settlement patterns that prevailed initially.

[12] John Winthrop, Jr., to Theodore Haak, [1668] (Winthrop mss., Massachusetts Historical Society, Boston). For a list of Winthrop's correspondents, see *Philosophical Transactions*, XL (1741), "Dedication." For the writings of a contemporary Virginia minister who corresponded with Robert Boyle, Nehemiah Grew, and other members of the Royal Society, see *The Reverend John Clayton, A Parson with a Scientific Mind: His Scientific Writings and Other Related Papers*, edited by Edmund Berkeley and Dorothy Smith Berkeley (Charlottesville: University Press of Virginia, 1965).

Seventeenth-century New England townships (the word "town" derives from the Old English "tun," meaning rural village; the word "township" refers to both the village and the surrounding land, which was cultivated by the villagers) were grants of land ranging in size from four to ten square miles. Somewhere near the center of each township was the village, which generally included a common, a church, a school, a burying ground, and the home lots of the original settlers. The actual farms of the settlers comprised several parcels of land lying at various distances and in various directions from the village, and were distributed to them by lot. In addition to the home areas and farm acreage, which, significantly, the villagers held in fee simple, there were the common holdings of pasture, meadow, and woodland to which they had access. While no strict equity was practiced in the original apportionment of land—indeed, wealth, family size, and social status were important factors determining the number of parcels assigned a householder—most farms started out small and tended to remain so, though a settler who stayed through the several distributions that normally occurred, sold none of his holdings, and perhaps consolidated those he had via judicious trading, purchasing, and marrying might well have ended up with several hundred acres.[13]

Thus far, one recognizes a contemporary English village without a manor house. But what is important with respect to the ecology of education is that the New England town was much more than a geographical area. It was essentially a body of householders organized for political, social, and religious purposes—an association useful for communal defense, desirable for local government, and utterly indispensable for the creation of an exemplary Christian society. Or, alternatively, it was a gathered political community, just as the church was a gathered religious community. Or, put still another way, it was a commonwealth with a *paideia*. The coexistence of forty or sixty households engaged daily in associated activities held considerable potential for extensive mutual influence; the coexistence of these same households, subscribing to a widely accepted, highly

---

[13] The data on size and arrangement are from Glenn T. Trewartha, "Types of Rural Settlement in Colonial America," *The Geographical Review*, XXXVI (1946), 568-596; Kenneth Alan Lockridge, "Dedham, 1636-1736: The Anatomy of a Puritan Utopia" (unpublished doctoral thesis, Princeton University, 1965), chaps. ii, vi; and Edward Spaulding Perzel, "The First Generation of Settlement in Colonial Ipswich, Massachusetts, 1633-1660" (unpublished doctoral thesis, Rutgers University, 1967), chap. ii.

articulated, and constantly reiterated system of human ideals and aspirations, was in its very nature profoundly educative.

Within such a community, household, church, school, and college both supported and reinforced the informal nurture of daily life. Within such a community, too, responsibilities moved easily from one institution to another, as need and availability interacted: thus, catechizing tended to be transferred from household to church in the 1650's and 1660's, as concern arose that families were ignoring their obligations; and the teaching of reading tended to be transferred from household to school after the 1650's, as schools became more numerous and schoolmasters less insistent that literacy be required for admission. Finally, given the particular character of the New England *paideia,* it was virtually inevitable that the church in such a community would be the chief agency of deliberate, systematic teaching. Households were obviously more numerous, and schools perhaps influenced their students more intensely at any given time; but the churches, operating through households and schools as well as on their own, dominated the educational scene: they called the most vigorous personalities into their service, they reached virtually the entire population (including individuals of every age), and the substance of what they taught was universally deemed to have the utmost significance for this life and for the next.

But the deliberate instruction proffered by these communities, though immensely powerful, was not omnipotent, as the history of New England dramatically illustrates. Indeed, the problem inherent in such education is that it can never fully anticipate the march of events in the outside world. To borrow Vernon L. Parrington's classic categories of "Puritan" and "Yankee," whereas the agencies of formal and informal education in the several towns operated incessantly to nurture Puritans, the opportunities for trade, commerce, and speculation operated incessantly to nurture Yankees, and, indeed, Yankee values early appeared in Puritan nurseries: thus the worldliness that characterized Samuel Sewall's household; thus the utilitarian instruction in writing and arithmetic demanded of town grammar masters; and thus the highly practical use to which a merchant like Robert Keayne put the constant sermonizing on the evils of an "idle, lazy, or dronish life." And this intrusion of Yankee ideals shortly elicited a chorus of jeremiads, which resounded through New England once the first generation had passed. "An overeager desire after the world hath so seized on the spirits of many," Captain Edward Johnson lamented at the end of *The Won-der-Working Providence of Sion's Saviour in New England* (1654), "that the chief end of our coming hither is forgotten; and notwith-standing all the powerful means used, we stand at a stay, as if the Lord had no farther work for his people to do, but every bird to feather his own nest." Or, as Cotton Mather tersely put it a half-century later in writing of Plymouth: "Religion brought forth prosperity, and the daughter destroyed the mother."[14]

CONFIGURATION OF EDUCATIONAL INSTITUTIONS: MASSACHUSETTS[15]

	1650	1689
Population	14,037	48,529
Households	c. 2,339	c. 8,088
Churches	43	88
Schools	11	23
Colleges	1	1
Printing Presses	1	2

The South witnessed a good deal of experimentation, during the first few decades of settlement, with fortified village communities of varying degrees of compactness; but these were random aggregations

14 Vernon L. Parrington, *Main Currents in American Thought* (3 vols.; New York: Harcourt, Brace and Company, 1927-1930), I, 88; "The Apologia of Robert Keayne" (1653), edited by Bernard Bailyn, *Publications of the Colonial Society of Massachusetts*, XLII (1964), 321; *Johnson's Wonder-Working Providence, 1628-1651*, edited by J. Franklin Jameson, Original Narratives of Early American History, edited by J. Frank-lin Jameson (New York: Charles Scribner's Sons, 1910), p. 260; and Cotton Mather, *Magnalia Christi Americana; or, The Ecclesiastical History of New-England* (1702), edited by Thomas Robbins (2 vols.; Hartford: Silas Andrus and Son, 1853-1855), I, 63.

15 I have based the statistics for population on Stella H. Sutherland's estimates in *Historical Statistics of the United States, Colonial Times to 1957* (Washington, D.C.: Government Printing Office, 1960), p. 756; I have derived the number of households by using the simple ratio of 6 persons to a household. Joseph B. Felt indicated a minimum figure of 5.5 in "Population of Massachusetts," *Collections of the American Statistical Association*, vol. I (1845), part II, p. 136; and Evarts B. Greene and Virginia D. Harrington proposed a minimum of 5.7 and a maximum of 6 in *American Population Before the Federal Census of 1790* (New York: Columbia University Press, 1932), p. xxiii. More recently, Richard Le Baron Bowen suggested a figure of 6 white persons per family in 1689 for Bristol, Rhode Island, in *Early Rehoboth: Documented Histori-cal Studies of Families and Events in This Plymouth Colony Township* (3+ vols.; Concord, N.H.: The Rumford Press, 1945-), I, 9-11; Kenneth A. Lockridge gave figures of 6.1 persons per family in 1648 and 6.75 persons per family in 1700 for Dedham, Massachusetts, in "The Population of Dedham, Massachusetts, 1636-1736," *The Economic History Review*, 2d ser., XIX (1966), 326, 343; David Harris Flaherty derived an average figure of 6 persons per family in 1765 for Massachusetts (using the colony-wide census data for that year) in "Privacy in Colonial New England, 1630-1776" (unpublished doctoral thesis, Columbia University, 1967), p. 81.

of individuals rather than extended kinship groups, gathered congregations, or covenanted associations of householders. In its initial
years, Jamestown was for all intents and purposes a quasi-military
society, composed largely of males housed within stockades and
devoted to the production of pitch, tar, and soap ashes for export to
England and, incidentally, to the search for gold. The period from
1611 to around 1619 was one of semicompact settlement, during
which systematic farming was begun, though the settlers remained
servants of the Virginia Company and did not hold land in fee simple.
But after 1619 private enclosures began to be established, so that by
1622, at the time of the great Indian massacre, there were nearly
eighty family farms along the James River, many owned by householders who had been granted tracts of a hundred acres upon the ex-
piration of their terms of service. Thereafter, the Indians were
systematically expelled from the tidewater region, and, with the start
of royal governance in 1624, ownership in fee simple became the rule.

The great turning point in the character of Virginia life, however,
came with the successful cultivation and sale of tobacco, first planted
by John Rolfe in 1612. Following the discovery of this phenomenally
successful cash crop, the population dispersed across the countryside,
hastened by the growing realization that land was a valuable commodity rapidly being exhausted by tobacco-farming and by a rampant
spirit of enterprise, unchecked by any well-articulated theory of the
public interest. In 1622, sixty thousand pounds of tobacco was
exported to England, bringing such great profits that the assembly
found it necessary to require each householder to plant enough food
to feed himself and his dependents. Once the Indians had been successfully harried out of the region, Virginia became a land of small
to middle-sized enclosed farms, spread out along the creeks and
estuaries of the coastal plain, each with its own house and wharf.
Since commerce and trade were carried on largely via waterway,
towns were neither essential nor, indeed, very appealing to the
Virginians.

Under these conditions, households found themselves shouldering
educational responsibilities that in Old and New England were
normally discharged by churches and schools. With parishes running
as large as a hundred square miles and with many of them unstaffed,
churches reached a limited segment of the population at best, and
these people only irregularly. And, with residences scattered across
the countryside, schools became uneconomical, for lack of both

funds and scholars, to say nothing of schoolmasters. Indeed, even the informal education of communal life was missing, as the Reverend Richard Green noted in 1662 when he deplored "the great want of Christian neighborhood, or brotherly admonition, of holy examples of religious persons, of the comfort of theirs, and their ministers' administrations in sickness, and distresses, of the benefit of Christian and civil conference and commerce."[16]

Green, of course, saw towns as the cure for a number of critical social ills facing the colony, but neither his efforts nor any others over the next half-century bore fruit. Yet that should in no way impugn Virginia's interest in education, which was at least as great as that manifested in the outlying regions of the metropolis: the commitment was there, though the resulting configuration of educational institutions was quite different from that of the Bay Colony. Since the community was a less potent educator, the burden of instruction was carried by particular agencies—household, church, school, and college—though, given the circularity that inheres in such situations, the very impotence of the community made it difficult to develop these agencies. Since the colony had no college during the period before 1689, Virginians pursued the higher learning in metropolitan institutions, or at Harvard, or under private tutors, or, occasionally, on their own. Since it had few schools, churches and households assumed functions ordinarily performed by schoolmasters. And, as has already been noted, since parishes were large and overland travel difficult, households often had to bear the total responsibility for education. That they did so with extraordinary effectiveness is indicated at one level by Virginia's high literacy rate throughout the seventeenth century and at another level by the facility with which certain families were able to take on the ways of the gentry, albeit they were not of gentle birth.

The patterns of settlement worked out by those who peopled the middle colonies varied considerably during the seventeenth century. There were the great proprietary grants to men such as Carteret and Penn, who looked upon their holdings as sources of income and sold them to individuals and groups in tracts of various sizes. There were the characteristic Puritan village communities of Long Island

---

16 R[ichard] G[reen], *Virginia's Cure: or, An Advisive Narrative Concerning Virginia* (London: W. Godbid, 1662), in Peter Force, ed., *Tracts and Other Papers, Relating Principally to the Origin, Settlement, and Progress of the Colonies in North America, from the Discovery of the Country to the Year 1776* (4 vols.; Washington, D.C.: Peter Force, 1836-1846), vol. III, no. 15, pp. 5-6.

CONFIGURATION OF EDUCATIONAL INSTITUTIONS: VIRGINIA[17]

	1650	1689
Population	18,731	52,101
Households	c. 3,122	c. 7,232+
Churches	27	52
Schools	1+	8
Colleges	0	0
Printing Presses	0	0

and East Jersey, so similar to New England townships in spatial arrangements and social composition. And there were the settlements of Dutch, Swedes, Germans, French, and Finns, who tended to maintain forms of community organization typical of their metropolises. In general, the proprietary colonies developed dispersed farmsteads, like those of Virginia during its commonwealth period; and, indeed, William Penn observed in 1685 that many early Pennsylvanians, covetous as they were of land, seemed unimpressed by the obvious cultural advantages of villages. The Puritan townships of Long Island and, to an extent, the smaller ethnic settlements of Swedish Reformed, Finnish Lutherans, and French Calvinists, were inclined to be fairly compact and therefore to resemble the frontier communities of New England in the ecology of their education, retaining social and intellectual cohesiveness without the messianism of the first-generation Puritans.[18]

By far the largest of the non-English settlements was the Dutch colony of New Netherland. Like Virginia, it was in its initial years little more than a collection of fortified trading posts dealing primarily in furs with the Indians. But the metropolitan authorities were also interested in establishing communities, and they formulated plans for land distribution whereby vast estates would be granted to patroons charged with finding settlers to develop them, while smaller holdings would be assigned directly to bona fide farmers. Early settlement on patroon manors was relatively compact, though once

17 The statistics for population are based on *Historical Statistics of the United States, Colonial Times to 1957,* p. 756; the estimate of the number of households in 1650 was derived by dividing the population by 6, the number in 1689 by dividing the white population by 6 and indicating with a plus sign the presence of an additional but unknown number of free black households.

18 It is interesting to note that, as early as 1673, Governor George Calvert of Maryland had complained in a letter to Lord Baltimore that "the remoteness of the habitation of one person from another, will be a great obstacle to a school" (*The Calvert Papers* [3 vols.; Baltimore: J. Murphy & Co., 1889-1890], I, 286).

the Indian menace had declined tenants began to move out onto more isolated farms. Similarly, the yeomen receiving direct grants scattered across the countryside; and, despite persistent efforts of the Dutch West India Company to group them in villages, "as the English are wont to do," they remained dispersed throughout the seventeenth century.[19]

By 1664, with a population just over five thousand, New Netherland included a dozen Dutch villages, among them New Amsterdam, a handful of Puritan townships on Long Island, and a scattering of small Swedish and Finnish settlements along the Delaware. The ecology of education in these communities was not unlike that in contemporary New England. Residences were sufficiently concentrated to provide social, economic, and intellectual intercourse beyond the confines of a single home; and household, school, and church were mutually supportive in the education they bestowed. In many instances, the *voorlezer* and schoolmaster were actually the same person, and indeed Carel de Beauvois of Breyckelen served not only as *voorlezer*-schoolmaster during the 1660's but also as *voorsanger*, sexton, and court messenger. The Dutch villages differed from the New England towns in having less clearly defined powers of self-government and a less clearly articulated *paideia*, though New Netherland could boast a fairly rich culture, which drew freely on the flourishing intellectual life of the contemporary Dutch republic.[20]

If the nucleated village communities of New England and the dispersed agricultural settlements of Virginia provide two characteristic educational patterns of the seventeenth-century colonies, the several market towns in evidence by 1689—notably, Boston, New York, and Philadelphia—afford yet another. Having begun as villages, they had come increasingly to resemble such metropolitan commercial centers as Bristol or Southampton rather than the larger agricultural settlements. Like their English counterparts, they early displayed that diversity of people and institutions which itself enlarged the range of educational opportunities available to their inhabitants. Households, churches, shops, markets, businesses, taverns, courts, and prisons were more numerous and more varied than in the

19 E. B. O'Callaghan, ed., *Documents Relative to the Colonial History of the State of New York* (10 vols. and *General Index*; Albany: Weed, Parsons and Company, 1856-1861), I, 153.

20 For Carel de Beauvois's contract, see Daniel J. Pratt, *Annals of Public Education in the State of New York, from 1626 to 1746* (Albany: The Argus Company, 1872), p. 31.

CONFIGURATION OF EDUCATIONAL INSTITUTIONS:
NEW NETHERLAND–NEW YORK[21]

	1650	1689
Population	4,116	13,501
Households	c. 686	c. 2,250–
Churches	8	34
Schools	7	11
Colleges	0	0
Printing Presses	0	1

towns, as were the schools and classes offering instruction in every conceivable art, from fencing to embroidery. The resulting configuration of educational institutions was far more complex, and its influence on individuals far more diverse: some received their education largely from a household, a church, a school, and a neighborhood subscribing to a common religious view; the education of others furnished a patchwork of conflicting values and ideas, inevitably confusing in their impact but at the same time potentially liberating.

Like their English counterparts, too, colonial market towns became leading communications centers, through which ideas, values, and styles from abroad (particularly from London) were filtered and transmitted to the colonial hinterland, and central gathering points for those colonial products sent to the metropolis in return. Boston and Newport served these functions for New England, New York and Philadelphia for the middle colonies. The market town of the South was for all intents and purposes London (with the assistance of Bristol), which catered to the planters' preference for dealing directly with the metropolis.

III

The North American colonies were settled in the main by one of the most literate societies of the West during a peak period in its cultural development. Not surprisingly, institutions of formal education were early established in those colonies, and played a critical

[21] The statistics for population are based on *Historical Statistics of the United States, Colonial Times to 1957*, p. 756; the estimate of the number of households in 1650 was derived by dividing the population by 6, the number in 1689 by dividing the total population by 6 and indicating the presence of a substantial but unknown number of slaves (the black population in 1689 was 1,623), who did not have their own households, with a minus sign.

role in the transmission of European civilization to the New World. By 1689, there was clear evidence of a vigorous Anglo-American culture there, which afforded the colonists access to most, if not all, of the accumulated wisdom of the West, particularly as represented by the knowledge, values, and aspirations of contemporary Englishmen. Books were present in large numbers, and ranged over the standard categories of scholarship, belles-lettres, and popular literature; and literacy remained as widespread as it was in the metropolis, often more so, owing to the initial selectivity of the colonial migration and to the failure of the Restoration to dampen educational enthusiasm in the colonies. Moreover, the colonists had the intellectual techniques for criticizing, refining, recategorizing, and correcting the body of learning they had inherited: they were well versed in the traditional logic of both Ramus and Aristotle and were increasingly aware in the 1680's of the newer methods of Descartes, and, furthermore, their one native institution of higher learning tended to welcome heterodoxy in this respect; they were acquainted, too, with the new sciences, as witness the prompt adoption of Charles Morton's "Compendium physicae" at Harvard after his arrival in New England in 1686; and they possessed several thriving presses, which were already producing autochthonous materials like almanacs and codifications of the law, as well as New World versions of such traditional materials as catechisms and Psalters.

Now, this was all well and good, and doubtless crucial in avoiding the lapse into barbarism so universally feared and declaimed upon. But the question must be raised as to the relationship between the agencies of education and the general quality of life in the colonies. One gets the sense that colonial life was generally quite similar to that of the outlying regions of England, such as Devon, or York, or Lancashire. In everything from court procedure to domestic architecture, recreation to the decorative arts, textile manufacturing to town planning, the initial styles were comparable to those of the metropolis; and, indeed, they remained so in the 1670's and 1680's, after the first generation had passed, owing largely to education.

But the colonists were learning from experience as well as from schools and churches, and one must also question the extent to which the institutions of education articulated and codified the insights gained from that experience and passed them along to subsequent generations. Here, the record is mixed, as one would expect. The

COMMUNITY

household was the most flexible, transmitting new ideas about methods and materials in the realm of agriculture and the crafts well before these were incorporated into books or even almanacs. The churches, the schools, and the colleges, on the other hand, and the press as long as censorship prevailed, were less adaptable, precisely because they taught more systematically and were more concerned with symbolic and codified learning. The very institutions that possessed the formal techniques for criticizing common sense were also the institutions that proffered learned theological treatises on witchcraft, learned medical treatises on bloodletting, learned pharmacological treatises on the doctrine of signatures, and learned scientific treatises on the souls of the aboriginal Indians—all of which conveyed error authoritatively and, if anything, made their readers even less receptive to truth than the average untutored individual. But the colonists were no worse off in this respect than their metropolitan cousins; indeed, their incessant confrontations with novelty and exigency (to say nothing of those aboriginal Indians) may have made them somewhat more sensitive to the limitations of scholarship. "They have few scholars," the Reverend John Clayton wrote of the Virginians in 1684, "so that everyone studies to be half physician, half lawyer and with a natural acuteness [that] would amuse thee. For want of books they read men the more." And something of the same spirit may have occasioned Cotton Mather's observation five years later that the youth of New England seemed "very sharp, and early ripe in their capacities."[22]

On the whole, then, the American colonies enjoyed striking success in transplanting the institutions of education and in granting their inhabitants access to the cultural tradition of the West, though each faced problems of reconciling and adapting that tradition to the demands of the New World experience. Yet, from the beginning, the several colonies seemed intent upon stressing certain differences among themselves, which they often associated with differences in education. Even before the Puritans left England, they emphasized the distinction between their godly purposes and the Virginians' quest for gain, and the rhetoric contrasting plantations of religion

---

22 John Clayton to [Dr. Edward Williamson], April 24, 1684, *Reverend John Clayton*, p. 4; and Cotton Mather, *The Way to Prosperity: A Sermon Preached to the Honourable Convention of the Governour, Council, and Representatives of the Massachuset-Colony in New-England on May 23, 1689* (Boston: R. Pierce, 1690), p. 34.

with plantations of trade persisted throughout the seventeenth century. The Virginians, in turn, saw no special godliness in dissent and celebrated the superiority of their own Anglican piety. The residents of Maryland, Pennsylvania, and New York were less given to self-congratulation, though it is patent from Jasper Danckaerts' journal entries dealing with his visit to New England in 1680 that he found little to praise in either the churches or Harvard College.[23]

That there were qualitative differences among the several colonies, resulting from religious, ethnic, and social diversity, is doubtless true. That New England played something of a special role as producer of culture during the seventeenth century, owing to the early presence there of a college, a press, and a high concentration of intellectuals who had created the college and press and then served as their clientele and audience, is also doubtless true. On the other hand, it is the educational similarities among the colonies that come to the fore when they are compared not with one another but with the outlying regions of the metropolises and with that profoundly different seventeenth-century English plantation, Ireland.

Throughout the seventeenth century, plans for the colonization of Ireland and America were consistently interwoven in the minds of English expansionists, and, after 1606, they had become increasingly competitive with respect to funds and personnel. Whereas Elizabeth had attempted to settle the problem of Irish land tenure by having the chief of each region surrender his holdings to the Crown and then having them regranted to him in return for his allegiance, the so-called flight of the earls in 1607 had paved the way for the Stuart policy of widespread confiscation and plantation. That policy had brought roughly 45 per cent of Ireland into Protestant hands by the time of the 1641 uprising, and the Cromwellian settlement had quickly raised that proportion to 90 per cent; moreover, there had been a sustained effort to populate the country with English and Scots gentlemen and yeomen, who would hold the Irish in check and guarantee the eventual Anglicization of the territory. By 1672, William Petty estimated that the total population of Ireland was

---

[23] *Winthrop Papers* (5+ vols.; Boston: The Massachusetts Historical Society, 1929-   ), II, 143; John White, *The Planters Plea* (London: William Jones, 1630), in Force, ed., *Tracts*, vol. II, no. 3, pp. 19-22, 33, 37; and *Journal of Jasper Danckaerts, 1679-1680*, edited by Bartlett Burleigh James and J. Franklin Jameson, Original Narratives, edited by Jameson (New York: Charles Scribner's Sons, 1913), pp. 252 ff.

1,100,000, including 800,000 Irish Catholics and 300,000 English, Scottish, and Welsh Protestants.[24]

Now, although the size and density of the native population were far greater in Ireland than in English-speaking America, the two colonial enterprises had certain fascinating similarities. In both cases, a minority of English had seized land held under a loose kinship system by an indigenous population, and in both cases the English became committed not merely to economic exploitation of the newly acquired territory but to its eventual Anglicization. But the venture in North America was destined to be far more successful than that in Ireland, for a variety of reasons. First, there was Whitehall's quite different treatment of the two regions, owing, no doubt, to the unequal widths of the Irish Sea and the Atlantic Ocean. Second, there was the vastly different nature of the two native populations: however much English observers tended to analogize between the Irish and the Indians in the 1620's and 1630's, the Irish were much more similar to the English socially and politically, far more advanced technologically (by Western standards), and patently Caucasian (thereby affording greater possibility for assimilation, according to English criteria). Third, there were the differences in the character and motivations of the respective groups of colonists: Ireland simply never had anything comparable in organization, intellectual attainment, or missionary zeal to the Great Migration of the 1630's. And, finally, there was the fact that Ireland did not have the sort of involuntary immigration from Africa that in America provided the foundation of the slave system.

Given a decisive technological superiority and a less unfavorable numerical disadvantage, the English settlers of North America were

[24] Sir William Petty, *The Political Anatomy of Ireland*, in *The Economic Writings of Sir William Petty*, edited by Charles Henry Hull (2 vols.; New York: Augustus M. Kelley, 1963), I, 121-231. Petty's figure was almost certainly low, as was his figure of 1,300,000 as the population in 1687 in "A Treatise of Ireland, 1687," *ibid.*, II, 610. The more recent figure of K. H. Connell for the latter year is 2,167,000, and assumes that Petty calculated correctly the number of persons per household but that he grossly underestimated (by two-thirds) the number of households. Since the greatest deficiencies in Petty's 1687 estimate appear to have derived from his failure, in using hearth tax figures, to make sufficient allowance for householders who either evaded the tax or had no hearth, and since that class of householders would more likely be Irish Catholic than English, Scottish, or Welsh Protestant, the chances are that the proportion as well as the number of Irish Catholics would be higher in any revised estimate. See K. H. Connell, *The Population of Ireland, 1750-1845* (Oxford: Clarendon Press, 1950), pp. 4, 22, 25, 259-260.

able to defeat the Indians in a series of bitter battles and push them inland. Given a less decisive technological superiority and a more unfavorable numerical disadvantage, the English settlers of Ireland were never really able to overthrow the Irish completely, and, of course, there was no area comparable to the trans-Allegheny region into which they could be pushed. The resultant garrison mentality did not conduce to a maximum educational effort on the part of either group. The conquered Irish were cut off from schooling and left in the hands of a poorly trained and overly parochial native clergy. Possessed of an oral culture rich in music and poetry, their economy and social organization remained medieval and relatively unproductive, calling to mind Thomas Babington Macaulay's observation that the Irish had always been distinguished by the qualities that make men interesting rather than prosperous. And the conquering English, land rich but labor poor, did not attract an intellectual class or a learned clergy or even a sufficient supply of schoolmasters, except to Dublin, the second-largest city in the British Isles at the end of the seventeenth century and the home of a flourishing Anglo-Irish culture revolving around Trinity College, a philosophical society, a medical school, a thriving theatre, an energetic press, and a host of taverns, coffeehouses, and bookshops. But the intellectual and economic liveliness of Dublin and such smaller towns as Cork, Limerick, Kilkenny, and Galway could not compensate for the overwhelming inertia of a peasantry caught up in the superstitions, rhythms, habits, and chronic scarcities of a medieval pastoral existence. Even in Ulster, with its concentration of Scottish Presbyterians, the dominant Protestant society maintained a relatively restricted cultural life, while the "mere Irish" inclined toward apathy. It is this combination of constraint and inertia that Petty described so compellingly in his pioneering treatise on *The Political Anatomy of Ireland* (1672) and that, when compared with the social and intellectual vitality of the average New World English community, renders less significant the time-honored controversies over which American colony was the best educated and therefore the most cultured.[25]

[25] Lord Macaulay, *The History of England from the Accession of James the Second*, edited by Charles Harding Firth (6 vols.; London: Macmillan and Co., 1913-1915), I, 56.

BOOK
II

PROVINCIALISM
1689-1783

◦❧◦

INTRODUCTION

He is an American, who, leaving behind him all his ancient prejudices and manners, receives new ones from the new mode of life he has embraced, the new government he obeys, and the new rank he holds. He becomes an American by being received in the broad lap of our great alma mater.

J. HECTOR ST. JOHN DE CRÈVECOEUR

The Glorious Revolution, as George Macaulay Trevelyan pointed out years ago, was not nearly so glorious as it was sensible, and far less a revolution than a series of compromises and accommodations that saved England from a second civil war. Politically, the events of 1688-1689 culminated a decade of maneuvering between James Stuart, younger brother of Charles II and a professed Roman Catholic, and William of Orange, husband of James's daughter Mary and a Reformed Protestant by birth and education. Yet that culmination scarcely represented any radical break with the past. True, the convention that invited William and Mary to the throne did issue a ringing Declaration of Rights asserting its grievances against James II and setting forth the "ancient rights and liberties" of Parliament, and in the process obviously established certain limitations on the royal prerogative—much to William's dismay, one might add. But the fact is that the so-called Revolutionary settlement was essentially conservative in its initial phase and in some respects quite reactionary, and only later ushered in a period of personal freedom under Whig hegemony.[1]

In the realm of religion, the settlement, as embodied in the Toleration Act of May 24, 1689, marked the end of the effort by

---

[1] George Macaulay Trevelyan, *The English Revolution, 1688-1689* (London: Thornton Butterworth, 1938).

the state to coerce the entire populace into doctrinal uniformity. Yet here, too, the initial break with tradition was limited at best: Nonconformists remained excluded from public office and the universities; the Prayer Book continued unaltered; and Roman Catholics were left legally outside the pale, though in fact they came to enjoy most of the prerogatives of Protestant Dissenters. The real advance of 1689 lay in the ending of active religious persecution; and once again it was only later that this initial reform ushered in a period of more genuine religious toleration.

Whatever the realities, the widespread belief in both England and America was that there had indeed been a glorious revolution, and that the realm had been narrowly saved from absolutism, Catholicism, and James. Politically, the most immediate manifestation of the revolution in the colonies was the rapid collapse of James's hastily contrived Dominion of New England. The rebellion began in Boston in April, 1689, quickly spread to New York and Maryland, and even affected Virginia, where the House of Burgesses actually harried the governor, Lord Howard of Effingham, out of the colony. The longer-range political impact is best seen, perhaps, in the new charter Increase Mather won for Massachusetts in 1691: that instrument retained the institution of the royal governor, but it also mandated a representative assembly to be chosen by the freeholders of the several towns on the basis of property (but not religious) qualifications; and it explicitly granted the governor and assembly full power "to make, ordain and establish all manner of wholesome and reasonable orders, laws, statutes and ordinances, directions and instructions either with penalties or without (so as the same shall be not repugnant or contrary to the laws of this our realm of England) as they shall judge to be for the good and welfare of our said province or territory." Religiously, the impact of the Toleration Act was twofold: it confirmed the pluralism that was already manifest in the colonies, providing a legal precedent for claimants of the right to dissent; and it released metropolitan Anglicans from their consuming preoccupation with the threat of James's Catholicism, thereby enabling them to intensify dramatically their missionary efforts in the New World.[2]

All this obviously affected colonial education, chiefly through the

2 Francis Newton Thorpe, ed., *Federal and State Constitutions, Colonial Charters, and Other Organic Laws* (7 vols.; Washington, D.C.: Government Printing Office, 1909), III, 1882.

freeing of Dissenters to preach and teach according to their own lights, though also at such points as the licensing of schoolmasters and the chartering of colleges. Yet, on the whole, the Glorious Revolution touched education somewhat tangentially and ultimately quite diffusely. It was rather the intellectual upheavals surrounding the Glorious Revolution and inextricably associated with it—the upheavals symbolized by Newton's *Principia mathematica* (1687) and Locke's *Letters Concerning Toleration* (1689, 1690, 1692), *An Essay Concerning Human Understanding* (1690), and *Two Treatises of Government* (1690)—that exerted the more direct and profound influence, working their way into every aspect of purpose, process, and program, and eventually marking a watershed between an overwhelmingly derivative colonial culture of the seventeenth century and an increasingly creative provincial culture of the eighteenth.

The tie between the political and intellectual revolutions of the 1680's has been much discussed by historians, and in recent years has been a matter of spirited scholarly controversy. The two principal figures on the intellectual side, Isaac Newton and John Locke, were essentially contemporary and curiously similar in a number of important respects. Locke was born in 1632 near Bristol, the son of an attorney of moderate means and excellent connections; Newton was born on Christmas Day, 1642, the son of a small landholder in Lincolnshire who had died the previous October. Locke attended Christ Church, Oxford; Newton, Trinity College, Cambridge. Both turned away as students from the regnant peripatetic philosophy of the universities, Locke through the lectures of Seth Ward on astronomy and of John Wallis on geometry as well as through his reading of Descartes, Newton through his studies with Isaac Barrow, the mathematician who first occupied the Lucasian chair at Cambridge. Both men gave early evidence of concern with the themes that would dominate their mature work, Locke during the first years of his senior studentship at Christ Church, after 1658, when he ventured his initial—and surprisingly Hobbesian—speculations on civil government and religious toleration, Newton during those two remarkable years of the plague, 1665 and 1666, when he worked avidly at the mathematical calculations and optical experiments that foreshadowed the *Principia* and the *Opticks*. Both men managed to retain their university connections without taking holy orders, though Locke was eventually forced out of Christ Church and practiced medicine privately. Both men were elected to the Royal Society,

Newton serving as its president from 1703 until his death in 1727. Neither man ever married. Newton sat as a Whig in the Convention Parliament that invited William and Mary to the throne; Locke returned to England with Mary on the *Isabella* in February, 1689. In due course, both men were appointed to government posts by William, Locke to commissionerships of appeals and of trade, and Newton to the wardenship and then the mastership of the mint.

The two men met for the first time at Lord Pembroke's salon after Locke's return to London in 1689, and there ensued a spirited exchange of ideas on philosophy, science, politics, and religion. The friendship was briefly marred by Newton's delusion in 1693 that Locke was somehow trying to embroil him with women, but Locke displayed characteristic patience, and several weeks later an apology by Newton repaired whatever slight damage might have been done. Thereafter, all was tranquil until Locke's death in 1704. It is said that Locke sought assurances from the Dutch mathematician Christian Huygens as to the accuracy of Newton's computations before studying the more general propositions of the *Principia,* and, indeed, there is extant a manuscript of Newton's demonstration that the inverse-square law of gravitation holds in an elliptical orbit that may well have been prepared especially for Locke. In any case, Locke found the general propositions impressive and paid tribute to their author in his prefatory reference in the *Essay* to the "incomparable Mr. Newton." There is evidence, too, that Newton considered and commented upon a number of Locke's writings as they took form in the 1690's, especially those that dealt with the substance and politics of religion.[3]

That the two men actually did know one another, however, was of no great significance for their work, most of which had been completed before the start of their friendship. But it does symbolize the intertwining of the two major seventeenth-century traditions they articulated and synthesized, the new empirical science as represented by Newton and the new empirical politics as represented by Locke. Both men, in Newton's oft-quoted phrase, stood on the shoulders of giants. Newton himself brought together, *inter alia*, Galileo's persuasive demonstration of the distinction between the real and apparent

---

[3] Isaac Newton to John Locke, [March, 1690], in H. W. Turnbull, ed., *The Correspondence of Isaac Newton* (4+ vols.; Cambridge: Cambridge University Press, 1959-), III, 71-77; and John Locke, *An Essay Concerning Human Understanding,* edited by Alexander Campbell Fraser (2 vols.; Oxford: Clarendon Press, 1894), I, 14.

motion of celestial bodies; Tycho's and Kepler's mathematical hypotheses concerning the elliptical character of planetary orbits; Descartes's analytical geometry and Huygens' application of that geometry to theoretical physics; and Bacon's irrepressible faith in man's ability to know nature. His synthesis changed radically the way men conceived the cosmos, from a mysterious realm which an unknowable God ruled at will according to his infinite wisdom to an ordered universe set in motion by an infinitely wise God who permitted men to know his handiwork.[4]

Locke, applying the methods of the new natural philosophy to the problems of mental and moral philosophy, brought together the classical commitment to mixed government as it had come down through Thomas Aquinas, Machiavelli, More, and Sir Thomas Smith; the methods of historical and comparative observation exemplified by Sir Edward Coke, Algernon Sidney, and James Harrington; the inductive political analyses of Thomas Hobbes and Sir William Temple; and the same Baconian faith in man's ability to know nature coupled with Bacon's characteristic insistence upon locating human affairs within the sphere of nature. His synthesis, which, like Newton's, combined elements of empiricism and rationalism, conceived of man and society as knowable phenomena within a knowable universe and of politics and education as processes best ordered by the light of reason informed by experience and experiment. It was but a short step to such characteristic Enlightenment doctrines as government by the consent of the governed, education for the business of living, and the possibility of progress in the world. And, indeed, such doctrines were readily at hand at the time of the Glorious Revolution, to justify its Whig proponents, to impose larger meaning on the political events which constituted it, and thereby to affect its subsequent course.

Newton and Locke were not merely extraordinarily original synthesizers who gathered up the innovative ideas of an era and gave them systematic and coherent exposition; they served also, in a manner of speaking, as intellectual prisms through which these innovative ideas, once gathered, were diffused to a larger public at various levels and in various forms. As part of that broad dissemination from London, Newtonian and Lockean ideas quickly reached the Amer-

[4] For the possible irony in Newton's assertion "If I have seen further it is by standing on the shoulders of giants," see Frank E. Manuel, *A Portrait of Isaac Newton* (Cambridge, Mass.: Harvard University Press, 1968), pp. 144-145.

ican colonies. Thomas Brattle of Massachusetts had actually participated in the development of Newton's work by sending a series of
comet observations to the Greenwich Observatory in England, from
which they were communicated to Newton. And it is probable that
certain concepts of the *Principia* were known to colonial intellectuals
such as Cotton Mather as early as the 1690's, though the earliest
extant copy of the work for which the evidence is undisputed is the
copy James Logan obtained for his personal library in April, 1708.
Locke's works arrived even sooner; in fact, as early as 1700 a substantial parcel of books reached Pennsylvania on consignment to the
proprietor from the London booksellers Awnsham and John Churchill, including several copies each of *An Essay Concerning Human
Understanding, Some Thoughts Concerning Education* (1693), *Two
Treatises of Government, Letters Concerning Toleration,* and *The
Reasonableness of Christianity* (1695). Beyond the works themselves,
there is clear evidence of the widespread dissemination of Newtonian
and Lockean ideas via popularizations, such as Henry Pemberton's *A
View of Sir Isaac Newton's Philosophy* (1728) or Isaac Watts's *The
Improvement of the Mind* (1741, 1751), via popularizations of the
popularizations in almanacs, newspapers, sermons, and pamphlets of
one sort or another, and, last but not least, via reformulations and
restatements in native form by colonists who found in them keys to
understanding the new world of America as it was and as it might
conceivably become.[5]

II

The colonies that took Newton and Locke to heart were still in 1689
a series of separate plantations stretching along the Atlantic coast
from Penobscot to Charleston: for all their 200,000 settlers, they
were scattered, sparsely populated and separated by considerable
stretches of wilderness, often hemmed in by hostile Indians, and
patently in better communication with the metropolis than with one
another. Three-quarters of a century later, at the time of the crisis
surrounding the Stamp Act, the colonial population had increased
ninefold, to 1,800,000, the coastal colonies had been joined and the

[5] Frederick E. Brasch, "James Logan, A Colonial Mathematical Scholar, and the
First Copy of Newton's *Principia* to Arrive in the Colony," *Proceedings of the Amer-
ican Philosophical Society,* LXXXVI (1943), 3-12; and Edwin Wolf, 2nd, "A Parcel of
Books for the Province in 1700," *The Pennsylvania Magazine of History and Biography,*
LXXXIX (1965), 428-446.

hinterland up to the Appalachian ridge had been settled, the French and their Indian cohorts had been defeated in a series of intermittent wars, thereby making possible the eventual expansion to the Mississippi, and a flourishing network of intercolonial communication was already contributing significantly to the development of a vigorous provincial culture and an emergent provincial community.

The rapid expansion of population after 1689 was primarily the result of an unusually rapid rate of natural increase, clearly related to conditions of relative social stability and economic prosperity; hence, the majority of the colonists in the eighteenth century, as in the seventeenth, remained of English background. But one of the chief developments of the eighteenth century was also the radical shift in the character of colonial immigration, which brought large numbers of Scots, Scotch-Irish, French, Germans, and Africans, particularly to the middle and southern colonies. The reasons for the shift are complex and often elusive: the Africans, of course, both those who came directly from the West African slaving ports and those who came indirectly via Latin America or the West Indies, were brought involuntarily and under unspeakable conditions; the Germans were fleeing a land that had served as a political and religious battleground at least since the Thirty Years' War; the Scots from Ireland were discontented with a land system that seemed to victimize them with high rents and short leases, and when the spate of thirty-year arrangements made in the wake of the Glorious Revolution began to expire in 1718, large numbers of them chose to move yet again to America; the Scots from Scotland were escaping poverty and depression deriving from successive crop failures and cattle blights; and the French Huguenots were harried out of Europe by the intolerance associated with the revocation of the Edict of Nantes in 1685. To all except the Africans, America meant cheap land (it was frequently free to squatters), the opportunities implicit in a chronic labor shortage, and religious toleration. In the course of a few decades, these immigrants filled the interstices of the older settlements, pushed westward across the Alleghenies as far as Pittsburgh and then south into the Virginia Piedmont and the Carolina back country, and swelled the populations of Philadelphia, New York, and a dozen smaller inland market towns. In their wake, they brought a rich cultural diversity that inevitably exerted profound and permanent influence on the character of American life.

The immediate impact of the new diversity varied considerably from colony to colony. It was weakest in New England, which remained suspicious of cultural differences throughout the eighteenth century and hence inhospitable to the new immigrants. It was substantial in Maryland, Virginia, and the Carolinas, which, beyond peopling their western regions, firmly established slavery as an economic and social system. It was ironically significant in Georgia, which was organized as a refuge for debtors at precisely the time England was beginning seriously to discourage emigration and was therefore early dependent on alternative sources of population. And it was decisive in the development of the middle colonies, notably the Jerseys, Delaware, and, above all, Pennsylvania. Indeed, the first century of Pennsylvania history epitomizes the diversification of the American population during the provincial era and with it the transformation of the colonial community.

From the beginning, William Penn conceived of his vast holdings in the New World as a haven for the persecuted, and he actively recruited the oppressed of England and the Continent through a vigorous promotional literature, personal visits, and promises of land. Along with the original English Quakers who settled the colony in the years after 1682, there were substantial numbers of Welsh and German Protestants, who organized their own communities in order to preserve their native languages and customs; and there was a small but vocal cadre of Anglicans, who settled in Philadelphia and from the outset formed a political faction in opposition to the Quaker majority. The Welsh were for the most part Quakers. The Germans of the initial period were mainly Mennonites, Dunkers, Amish, and Schwenkfelders; later, after the announcement of a new emigration policy by Queen Anne in 1702, they were joined by a much larger stream of Lutherans and Reformed recruited by the British government in the Palatinate, as well as by an incredible variety of Labadists, New Born, New Mooners, Separatists, Zion's Brueder, Ronsdorfer, Inspired, Gichtelians, Depellians, and Mountain Men. These later German migrants tended to push out from the initial settlements around Philadelphia to an arc of rich farmland that stretched from Easton on the Delaware River southwest to the Susquehanna and across into the Cumberland Valley. After 1702 there were also large numbers of Scotch-Irish immigrants to the colony, the earliest arrivals settling with the Germans in Bucks and Lancaster counties, their successors, toughened by a century of conflict in Ireland, pressing out to the westward region along the Susquehanna and its tributaries and there forming something of another arc on the edges of the German settlements. In 1766 Franklin estimated the population of the colony at around 160,000 whites, a third of whom were Quakers, another third Germans, and the remainder inclusive not only of English Anglicans and Scots and Scotch-Irish Presbyterians but also of Moravian Brethren, French Huguenots, and scattered handfuls of Swiss, Celtic Irish, Dutch Reformed, and Swedish Lutherans. In addition, there was a black population that probably numbered over 5,000, of whom at least several hundred may have been freemen.[6]

In one sense, the social situation in eighteenth-century Pennsylvania was not unlike the one that had confronted the English along the Hudson with the creation of New York in 1664: it was a polyglot society under English hegemony that had yet to become a community. But there were fundamental differences between the two colonies that had important bearing on education. In the first place, the English were conquerors in New York but founders in Pennsylvania, and as founders they held the reins of government tightly unto themselves, not really beginning to share political power until shortly before the Revolution. Second, the English in New York were content to Anglicize the administration of the province while at the same time permitting considerable diversity among religious and cultural institutions; the English in Pennsylvania embarked upon a deliberate policy of cultural Anglicization. And third, New York in 1664 was far more isolated from its sister plantations than was either New York or Pennsylvania in the eighteenth century, when intercolonial communication had so vastly expanded.

Of the several groups that actually settled Pennsylvania in the colonial period, it was the Germans who most consistently educed the fears of the English Quakers and Anglicans. The first German migrants of the seventeenth century had been middle-class Pietists, not unlike the Quakers in outlook and character; the Germans who followed them, however, were of peasant origin and strikingly different in language, religion, values, and manner. Arriving in con-

---

6 Franklin's estimates were included in his "Examination" before the House of Commons (1776), *The Writings of Benjamin Franklin*, edited by Albert Henry Smyth (10 vols.; New York: The Macmillan Company, 1905-1907), IV, 415-416. George Bancroft estimated the number of blacks in 1751 as 11,000, but that estimate is almost certainly high, given the figure of 10,274 at the time of the first census. See Evarts B. Greene and Virginia D. Harrington, *American Population Before the Federal Census of 1790* (New York: Columbia University Press, 1932), p. 116. More recent estimates by Stella H. Sutherland place the Pennsylvania population for 1766 at over 200,000, including at least 5,000 blacks; see *Historical Statistics of the United States, Colonial Times to 1957* (Washington, D.C.: Government Printing Office, 1960), p. 756.

siderable numbers after the 1720's, they soon tried the patience of
the founders, changing an earlier spirit of hospitality into a sullen
mood of grudging toleration and suspicious concern. "At this rate,"
James Logan wrote John Penn in 1727 concerning the German
immigration, "you will soon have a German colony here, and perhaps
such a one as Britain once received from Saxony in the fifth century."
And, indeed, that same year the Pennsylvania assembly passed a law
requiring an oath of allegiance to the Crown by all male German immigrants over the age of sixteen. Two years later, Logan again voiced
his dismay over the "vast crowds" of Palatines that seemed to be in-
undating the province, while the provincial assembly sought to slow
the German influx by levying a tax of twenty shillings upon each
"foreigner" brought in as a servant—a measure, incidentally, which
proved entirely ineffective as a deterrent.[7]

In the 1740's, Benjamin Franklin joined the chorus of concern,
having failed to attract the German community to his plan to raise an
extralegal militia against the French, and his letters and pamphlets
soon crackled with criticism. The Germans "underlived" the English
and were therefore able to "underwork" and "undersell" them; the
German clergy had insufficient control over their parishioners, who
"seem to think themselves not free, till they can feel their liberty in
abusing and insulting their teachers"; the Germans were politically
unreliable and would almost certainly side with the French against
the English in the wars that were racking the frontier; and, worst of
all, the Germans threatened to drive the English out of their own
province or at the least to overwhelm them culturally. "This will
in a few years become a German colony," Franklin wrote his friend
James Parker in 1751. "Instead of their learning our language, we
must learn theirs, or live as in a foreign country. Already the English
begin to quit particular neighborhoods surrounded by Dutch, being
made uneasy by the disagreeableness of dissonant manners; and in
time, numbers will probably quit the province for the same reason."[8]

[7] James Logan to John Penn, September 23, 1727 (Logan mss., Historical Society of
Pennsylvania, Philadelphia); *Minutes of the Provincial Council of Pennsylvania, from
the Organization to the Termination of the Proprietary Government* (10 vols.; imprint
varies, 1852), III, 283, 359-360; and James Logan to James Steel, November 18, 1729
(Penn mss. [official correspondence], Historical Society of Pennsylvania, Philadelphia).
[8] Benjamin Franklin to James Parker, March 20, 1751, *The Papers of Benjamin
Franklin*, edited by Leonard W. Labaree and Whitfield J. Bell, Jr. (13+ vols.; New
Haven: Yale University Press, 1959-), IV, 120-121; Benjamin Franklin to Peter
Collinson, May 9, 1753, *ibid.*, pp. 484-485; "Observations Concerning the Increase of
Mankind," *ibid.*, p. 234; and Whitfield J. Bell, Jr., "Benjamin Franklin and the German
Charity Schools," *Proceedings of the American Philosophical Society*, XCIX (1955),
381-387.

So persuasive and alarming was Franklin's fear that the English would ultimately be Germanized rather than the Germans Anglicized that his friend Peter Collinson, a member of Parliament, was moved to recommend measures that would prohibit the publication of official documents in German, suppress all German printing houses in the province, prevent the importation of German books, restrict the immigration of German nationals, require the establishment of English schools, introduce an English literacy requirement for the suffrage, and encourage the intermarriage of English and German residents. Similar measures were introduced in the provincial assembly, but neither Parliament nor the assembly took action.[9]

Franklin's concern did, however, play a significant role in the development of the so-called charity schools in the province and in their early and rapid conversion into agencies of deliberate Anglicization. The schools originated in the appeal by the Reverend Michael Schlatter, who came to Pennsylvania in 1746 under the direction of the Synod of Amsterdam, for assistance from the synod in providing "faithful teachers and pastors" for the "destitute" German children of the province. A considerable sum of money was raised in Holland, and, in addition, Schlatter's appeal attracted the attention of the Reverend David Thomson, pastor of the English Reformed Church in Amsterdam, who carried the cause to the General Assembly of the Church of Scotland and who was a leading figure in the establishment in London of an elite philanthropic organization called the Society for the Propagation of Christian Knowledge Among the Germans in Pennsylvania. Once the appeal reached London, however, political as well as religious and educational considerations intruded, as witness a letter to the Society in December, 1753, from William Smith, who was about to associate himself with the Philadelphia academy and had traveled to England to take Anglican orders before doing so. Waxing enthusiastic over the Society's proposed undertaking, Smith commented: "By a common education of English and German youth at the same schools, acquaintances and connections will be formed, and deeply impressed upon them in their cheerful and open moments. The English language and a conformity of manners will be acquired, and they may be taught to feel the meaning and exult in the enjoyment of liberty, a home and social endearments. And

---

9 Peter Collinson to Benjamin Franklin, August 12, 1753, *Papers of Benjamin Franklin*, V, 21. See also Franklin's reply [1753], *ibid.*, 158-160. *Votes and Proceedings of the House of Representatives of the Province of Pennsylvania* (4 vols.; Philadelphia: printer varies, 1752-1754), IV, 283.

when once these sacred names are understood and felt at the heart;—when once a few intermarriages are made between the chief families of the different nations in each country, which will naturally follow from school acquaintances, and the acquisition of a common language, no arts of our enemies will be able to divide them in their affection; and all the narrow distinctions of extraction, etc., will be forgot—forever forgot—in higher interests."[10]

That the Society hearkened to hopes such as Smith's is evident from his appointment to the board of trustees empowered to oversee its work in the province, along with James Hamilton, the provincial governor; William Allen, the provincial chief justice; Richard Peters, the provincial secretary; Conrad Weiser, the provincial agent for dealing with the Indians and, incidentally, the only German on the board; and, not surprisingly, Franklin. Schlatter was engaged to direct the undertaking, and early in 1755 the first schools were organized and set in operation. Later, in October of that year, the Pennsylvania trustees also purchased a "Dutch" press as part of their educational effort from none other than Franklin, who contributed twenty-five pounds toward the cost. Yet from the beginning the venture was destined to failure. Christopher Saur, the leading German publicist of the province, excoriated the plans even before the schools were opened, condemning the movement in general and Schlatter in particular for portraying such a false and imprudent picture of German culture and loyalties. His criticism was devastatingly effective: the movement found little support among the German community; at its peak, in 1759, it never served more than 600-750 children, some two-thirds of them German; and thereafter it failed gradually, expiring in 1764. In the long run, its most important impact on the Germans was probably in stimulating them to redouble their efforts to perpetuate their own language and culture.[11]

[10] H. Harbaugh, *The Life of Rev. Michael Schlatter; with a Full Account of His Travels and Labors Among the Germans* (Philadelphia: Lindsay & Blakiston, 1857), p. 213; William Smith to Society, December 13, 1753, in Horace Wemyss Smith, *Life and Correspondence of the Rev. William Smith* (2 vols.; Philadelphia: S. A. George & Co., 1879-1880), I, 30-31. See also *ibid.*, pp. 34-38, for Smith's specific proposals.

[11] Samuel Chandler to James Hamilton, William Allen, Richard Peters, Benjamin Franklin, Conrad Weiser, William Smith, March 15, 1754, in Smith, *Life and Correspondence of William Smith*, I, 40-42; William Smith, *A Brief History of the Rise and Progress of the Charitable Scheme, Carrying on by a Society of Noblemen and Gentlemen in London, for the Relief and Instruction of Poor Germans* (Philadelphia: B. Franklin and D. Hall, 1755); William Smith to the Rev. Messrs. Reiger and Stoy, September 30, 1754, in Smith, *Life and Correspondence of William Smith*, I, 81-84; Christopher Saur, *Pensylvanische Berichte, oder Sammlung*, September 1, 1754, pp.

Nevertheless, the Germans were Anglicized and ultimately reconciled to the Pennsylvania of Franklin and Smith, and the phenomena involved in that reconciliation tell us much about the broader education implicit in provincial life. Many of these phenomena were internal to Pennsylvania and operative during Franklin's lifetime. During the 1750's, for example, the traditional pacifism of the Germans had been shaken by Indian attacks on their settlements in the Blue Mountain region, and, despite Saur's unrelenting opposition to a militia, they found themselves increasingly in common cause with the British and hence with Franklin and Smith. With Saur's death in 1758 and the subsequent banishment of his son from the province for criticizing the authorities, an important source of separatist propaganda was removed, and, though the Germans remained apart ecclesiastically, they began to adopt English speech and culture. When the vast majority of the German community sided with Franklin in a tough stand favoring American independence, the reconciliation was complete; indeed, it was Smith who had to leave the province because of his opposition to a break. In effect, though the Germans retained separate schools and churches and later even organized Franklin College at Lancaster in 1787 to train their own religious and civic leaders, the broader education implicit in politics was to prove decisive.

But there were also educational factors beyond the borders of Pennsylvania that were centrally involved in the reconciliation. The fact is that intercolonial communication increased vastly during the eighteenth century, and obviously with profound impact on the several individual provinces. It was the rejection by the Pennsylvania assembly of the Albany Plan of Union (first proposed by Franklin) that initially made the Germans vulnerable to Indian depredation and later mobilized them to make common cause with Franklin. It was the growth of intercolonial as well as transatlantic trade that made Philadelphia a cosmopolitan American city as well as a local provincial port. It was the growth of an intercolonial post and through it an intercolonial audience that gave the productions of Franklin's press regional and even national rather than local signi-

2-3; Henry Melchior Mühlenberg to Benjamin Franklin, August 3, 1754, *Papers of Benjamin Franklin*, V, 418-421; Christopher Saur to [a Friend], September 6, 1755, in Smith, *Life and Correspondence of William Smith*, I, 94-96; and Samuel Edwin Weber, *The Charity School Movement in Colonial Pennsylvania* (Philadelphia: George F. Lasher, [1905]), pp. 47, 55-56.

ficance. It was the development of an intercolonial science that
made Philadelphians such as Franklin and David Rittenhouse and
Benjamin Rush intellectuals of North American rather than local
repute. It was the growth of intercolonial political co-operation that
caused Franklin to be appointed agent for Georgia in 1768, for New
Jersey in 1769, and for Massachusetts in 1770, as well as for Pennsylvania. It was the interdenominational—or one might more literally
say denominational—character of the Great Awakening that made
it possible for the German Lutherans and German Reformed to see
themselves as not wholly unlike the several varieties of English Protestants. And it was the combination of all these factors and several
others that enabled the Germans to conceive of themselves as reconciled less to a historic English community than to an emergent
American community. The great Mr. Locke and the incomparable
Mr. Newton contributed mightily to the conceptualization and
developing awareness of that emergent community, but what came
forth as its ultimate articulation was as characteristically indigenous
and as different from the original formulations of 1687-1690 as were
the Germans who served under Washington from their fathers and
grandfathers who had fled the Palatinate a half-century before.

III

Pioneers, Edward Eggleston observed in *The Transit of Civilization*,
"have no time to invent; necessity rarely brings forth anything better
than imitation and adaptation." In the extent to which provincial
America remained a pioneer society, imitation remained a fundamental method of survival, in education as elsewhere. The Germans,
the Scotch-Irish, the French, and even, in a special way, the Africans
who came as slaves, brought with them time-honored ideas and institutions; and though they transplanted those ideas and institutions
within a civilization already decisively English in character and tradition, they transplanted them with no less vigor or resolve or intent
toward permanence than their seventeenth-century predecessors.[12]

But imitation and adaptation are far more subtle and complicated
processes than Eggleston doubtless meant to suggest, and one need
not posit either mystical theories of cultural autogenesis or rationalistic theories of a "rejection of Europe" to account for the genuine

[12] Edward Eggleston, *The Transit of Civilization from England to America in the
Seventeenth Century* (New York: D. Appleton and Company, 1900), pp. 231-232.

novelty that became a leading phenomenon of eighteenth-century America. As Constance Rourke pointed out years ago in a brilliant critique of Eggleston's theses, the "seeds of influence" may fall but not germinate, they may germinate but yield very different fruit amidst altered circumstances, or they may combine into hybrid forms that are essentially new and historically unprecedented. One need only consider Franklin's proposals for the Academy of Philadelphia to see the several processes at work. Franklin admitted quite forthrightly that he had borrowed liberally from John Milton, John Locke, Obadiah Walker, Charles Rollin, George Turnbull, and David Fordyce (whose work Franklin mistakenly attributed to Francis Hutcheson); yet the educational program he put forth was strikingly original and characteristically American in its overall structure and content. Franklin's model was clearly drawn from the dissenting academies of contemporary England, notably, Philip Doddridge's at Northampton; yet what emerged in Philadelphia was quite different from any extant English institution, including Doddridge's, and, as a matter of fact, sufficiently different from what Franklin himself had had in mind to elicit bitter criticism from him in later years. Moreover, quite apart from the prototypes in Northampton and Philadelphia, every manner of school sprang up under the name of academy in late eighteenth-century America, the various institutions differing as much among themselves as they did from either the English or the Philadelphian model.[13]

The processes of imitation and adaptation described here were repeated countless times and at every conceivable point in the education system. The Moravians of Bethlehem, Pennsylvania, for example, successfully transplanted the Moravian choir system, whereby the community was rigidly stratified according to age, sex, and marital status, and under which traditional family life was obviously drastically altered. Yet within thirty years of the founding of Bethlehem, in 1741, the system had begun to come apart, families had coalesced along more traditional lines, and the choirs were degenerating into boardinghouses for lodgers who paid rent. Or, to take a set of quite different examples, one can find instance after instance of a particular sect or denomination founding a school to perpetuate and advance its particular way of life in the New World, only to find that an inevitable broadening of the school's clientele

[13] Constance Rourke, *The Roots of American Culture and Other Essays*, edited by Van Wyck Brooks (New York: Harcourt, Brace and Company, 1942), pp. 49 ff.

for economic reasons inexorably broadened the school's purposes. The phenomenon was as characteristic of Anglican efforts in New York as it was of French Ursuline efforts in Louisiana, German Pietist efforts in Pennsylvania, or Irish and Scots Presbyterian efforts in New Jersey.

Meanwhile, contemporary with these eighteenth-century transplantations and adaptations, there was the continuing transformation of institutions that had been set down in earlier decades: consider the novel use Jonathan Edwards made of the church as an educative agency, or the way in which Franklin employed the almanac as an instrument of public enlightenment, or the responsibilities Thomas Jefferson assigned to the lower schools in his Bill for the More General Diffusion of Knowledge (1779). Given such radical changes in the concept and character of traditional educational agencies, and given the fact that they inevitably entered into new relationships with one another and with the communities that sustained them, the emergence of characteristically American modes of education in the provincial era is not difficult to explain.

Beyond this, it is important to bear in mind that educational institutions always confront novelty in at least two quite different forms: on the one hand, they themselves undergo change and adaptation, the tempo and intensity of which vary according to circumstance; on the other hand, they are required by the very nature of their task to come to terms with change and adaptation in the ways they transmit knowledge, values, tastes, and skills to the oncoming generation. They may choose self-consciously to resist change, defining it as pernicious and teaching the knowledge and values of a traditional way of life; they may choose to ignore change, thereby unavoidably taking a stand in relation to it; or they may, willy-nilly, ally themselves with change and seek to nurture the values that encourage it. Again, Franklin's career is instructive, for one need only contrast the education he received during a year at the Boston Latin School with his own proposals for the Academy of Philadelphia some thirty-five years later to recognize the problem every educational institution had to confront in eighteenth-century America: namely, how and how much to make life as it was and would be, rather than life as it had been, the central fact of the curriculum. Moreover, this was as true of families as it was of churches, schools, and colleges—recall that Josiah Franklin pulled Ben out of the Latin school and placed him first in George Brownell's school to learn writing and arithmetic and then in apprenticeships with his cousin Samuel and his brother James.

Finally, for all the novelty that provincial education manifested and taught, it remained in the last analysis provincial, and this was as stubborn and significant a fact of life as its own autochthonous development. The dialogue with the metropolis continued, and, much as in the seventeenth century, the colonists tended to take their cultural and educational cues from London—and increasingly from Edinburgh and Paris as well. Yet, as with everything else, the nature and character of the dialogue changed: it became far more a mutual exchange than a one-way flow westward, and it was increasingly charged with a kind of tension between the values of cosmopolitan sophistication and the virtues of native simplicity. In 1689, the question in the minds of most Europeans was whether North America was yet sufficiently civilized for habitation. A century later, the question was rather what Europe could learn from America: a new education in a new land had wrought new men who seemed to hold the future in their hands. "The epoch," an Italian churchman wrote a friend in Paris, "has become one of the total fall of Europe, and of transmigration into America. Everything here turns into rottenness: religion, law, arts, sciences; and everything hastens to renew itself in America. This is no jest, nor is it an idea growing out of quarrels among the English: I have been saying it, announcing it, preaching it for twenty years: and I have always seen my prophecies fulfilled. Therefore, do not buy your house in the Chaussée d'Antin; buy it in Philadelphia. My misfortune is that there are no abbeys in America."[14]

[14] L'Abbé Ferdinando Galiani to Madame D'Épinay, May 18, 1776, *Lettres de L'Abbé Galiani à Madame D'Épinay, Voltaire, Diderot, Grimm, Le Baron D'Holbach, Morellet, Suart, D'Alembert, Marmontel, La Vicomtesse De Belsunce, Etc.*, edited by Eugène Asse (2 vols.; Paris: Bibliothèque-Charpentier, 1903), II, 225-226.

Part III

DENOMINATIONALISM

I think I never parted from a place with more regret; for America in my opinion is an excellent school to learn Christ in.

GEORGE WHITEFIELD

INTRODUCTION

George Whitefield's star was obviously rising when he first embarked for the colonies in the winter of 1737-38. A maverick deacon of the Anglican church and sometime counselor to the Methodist students of Oxford, he had already begun with John and Charles Wesley the work among the disinherited poor of England and Wales that would culminate in the emergence of Methodism as a major religious force on both sides of the Atlantic. Persuaded that the spirit of God had taken possession of his soul, Whitefield was preaching to immense audiences in church after church, soliciting men for Christ and funds for the charity-school children of London and the benighted denizens of Newgate. "It was wonderful to see how the people hung upon the rails of the organ loft, climbed upon the leads of the church, and made the church itself hot with their breath, that the steam would fall from the pillars like drops of rain," he wrote in his journal for 1737. "Sometimes, almost as many would go away, for want of room, as came in; and it was with great difficulty that I got into the desk, to read prayers or preach."[1]

Whitefield had been called to Georgia by the Wesleys the previous year to assist in the conversion of the heathen there and the founding of an orphanage for the unusually large number of children in the colony lacking one or both parents. He arrived at Savannah on May 7, 1738, bearing an appointment from the trustees authorizing him to serve as a deacon of the church in that town and at nearby Frederica. Embarking upon his duties with characteristic zeal, he preached, baptized, and catechized, ministered to clusters of outlying

[1] *Whitefield's Journals,* edited by William Wale (London: Henry J. Drane, 1905), p. 77.

families, established at least three schools, and visited with the Salzburgers at Ebenezer to study their orphanage there. Having resolved with the Wesleys on the absolute necessity of a larger orphan house for the colony, he decided to return to England to obtain a grant of land from the trustees and a subscription of funds from the public. Setting sail from Savannah on August 28, he was touched by the many expressions of affection tendered by the members of his flock. "My heart was full, and I took the first opportunity of venting it by prayers and tears," he noted in his journal. "I think I never parted from a place with more regret; for America in my opinion is an excellent school to learn Christ in, and I have great hopes some good will come out of Savannah because the longer I continued there, the larger the congregation grew."[2]

Whitefield was destined to return to America again and again over the next twenty-five years as one of the most charismatic teachers in that school of Christ, and the school itself was destined to develop an extraordinarily powerful program of education marked by diversity, originality, and considerable contradiction. In the vast open spaces of the New World, refugees from every corner of Europe were seeking the opportunity to start life anew, setting down new roots and establishing new sects with special versions of the truth which they diligently nurtured in the young. Yet, in the very process of rooting, the young, the truths, and the sects themselves seemed to change. At the same time, men in Boston, New Haven, New York, and Philadelphia were imbibing the heady new philosophies of the Old World, of Locke and Newton and their disciples and detractors, and finding their views on everything that mattered challenged, shaken, and transformed. And, once they came to terms with these new philosophies and appropriately modified their conceptions of the true, the good, and the beautiful, they too tried to communicate their insights to others, so that everyone might do what was needed to be saved. Amidst the resulting cacophony of conflicting voices proffering conflicting instruction, new pieties emerged and, with them, new outlooks and life styles. Provincial America was indeed an excellent school to learn Christ in, though its faculty, its students, and its curriculum were in constant flux as it defined and redefined the meaning of Christ for man.

2 *Ibid.*, p. 159.

Chapter 9

PIETY RATIONALIZED

> Christianity is principally an institution of life and manners;
> designed to teach us how to be good men, and to show us the
> necessity of becoming so.
>
> JONATHAN MAYHEW

There is a curious paradox in Locke's religious writing with respect
to the problem of schism in the Christian community. Locke conceived of churches as free and voluntary societies of individuals joined
together for the public worship of God according to their own lights,
and, as such, committed by their very nature to techniques of persuasion rather than coercion. Magistrates, in turn, had the high
responsibility to tolerate all such efforts, save those that threatened
direct harm to individuals or to the state itself. The assumption, of
course, was that for the foreseeable future, while fallibility remained
an inescapable fact of the human condition, men would differ in their
perceptions of the truth, and Christianity would remain fragmented
and rent by controversy.[1]

Yet, like many of his contemporaries, Locke despaired of the
dissension and schism that surrounded him, believing that, if somehow an essential Christianity demanding a minimum of subscription
could be defined, it would quickly attract a maximum of subscribers.
This interest in placing Christianity on a new and sounder basis was
clearly the enterprise of *An Essay Concerning Human Understanding* (1690). In an "Epistle to the Reader" at the beginning of that

---

[1] John Locke, *A Letter Concerning Toleration* (1689), translated by William Popple
and edited by Patrick Romanell (Indianapolis, Ind.: Bobbs-Merrill Company, 1950),
pp. 17-25 and *passim*.

work, Locke located the origins of his inquiry in an informal discussion some twenty years before. "Five or six friends meeting at my chamber, and discoursing on a subject very remote from this, found themselves quickly at a stand, by the difficulties that rose on every side. After we had awhile puzzled ourselves, without coming any nearer to a resolution of those doubts which perplexed us, it came into my thoughts that we took a wrong course; and that before we set ourselves upon inquiries of that nature, it was necessary to examine our own abilities, and see what objects our understandings were, or were not, fitted to deal with." One of the friends, James Tyrrell, later noted in his copy of the *Essay* that the subject of the discussion had been "the principles of morality and revealed religion." Even in the absence of such particular evidence, it is clear that Locke's examination of "the grounds and degrees of belief, opinion, and assent" was in essence an inquiry into how, in general, there could be genuine knowledge about religion, and what, in particular, could reasonably be believed about the Christian faith.[2]

By the end of his *Essay* Locke had made a great deal more progress in clearing away rubble than in erecting a dependable scheme for answering his questions. Recall the progress of his argument. In his critical discussion of the relation of faith and reason, he attempts to distinguish among propositions that are "according to, above, and contrary to reason." Those according to reason are "such propositions whose truth we can discover by examining and tracing those ideas we have from sensation and reflection; and by natural deduction find to be true or probable." Those above reason are "such propositions whose truth or probability we cannot by reason derive from those principles." And those contrary to reason are "such propositions as are inconsistent with or irreconcilable to our clear and distinct ideas." The existence of one God Locke takes as according to reason; the existence of many gods, as contrary to reason; and the resurrection of Christ, as above reason. Now, since "the existence of a God, reason clearly makes known to us," those propositions that come from God "in some extraordinary way of communication"—Locke refers to the discovery of such truths as "revelation"—can at the same time be above reason and yet governed by it. Seen thus, Locke concludes, faith and reason are not contrary, as popular usage would have it; rather, faith is "nothing but a firm assent of the mind: which, if it

[2] John Locke, *An Essay Concerning Human Understanding*, edited by Alexander Campbell Fraser (2 vols.; Oxford: Clarendon Press, 1894), I, 9, 26.

be regulated, as is our duty, cannot be afforded to anything but upon good reason; and so cannot be opposite to it."[3]

There is an ambivalence here, of course, that dogged both disciples and critics of Locke for generations. On the one hand, Locke accepted God as revelation, and the Bible as the word of God, placing himself squarely in the classic Protestant position. "The Holy Scripture is to me, and always will be, the constant guide of my assent," he wrote to Bishop Edward Stillingfleet in 1697; "and I shall always hearken to it, as containing infallible truth, relating to things of the highest concernment. And I wish I could say, there are no mysteries in it: I acknowledge there are to me, and I fear always will be. But where I want the evidence of things, there yet is ground enough for me to believe, because God has said it: and I shall presently condemn and quit any opinion of mine, as soon as I am shown that it is contrary to any revelation in the Holy Scripture." This was the Locke of simple common-sense piety. On the other hand, there was the Locke who concluded the principal discussion of religion in the *Essay* with the flat assertion, "Reason must be our last judge and guide in everything"—the skeptical Locke of the new "way of ideas," the Locke, indeed, whom the Deists cited against the latitudinarian Locke whom they thought all too ready to live uncritically with the mysteries of traditional Christianity.[4]

Locke himself went on in his less well-known work *The Reasonableness of Christianity* (1695) to amplify the rather gentle and generally rational piety suggested in the *Essay*. There, his enterprise was an "attentive and unbiased search" of Scripture for an understanding of the Christian religion. And there, he concluded that the primary obligations of the Christian are to believe in Christ and to live in accordance with his morality as the revelation of God. Moreover, like Erasmus before him, Locke argued that there was no contradiction between that morality and the morality taught by the ancients, though the ancients had grasped merely a portion of the

3 *Ibid.*, II, 412-413, 325, 416, 413.

4 John Locke, "A Letter to the Right Reverend Edward, Lord Bishop of Worcester, Concerning Some Passages Relating to Mr. Locke's Essay of Human Understanding, January 7, 1697," *The Works of John Locke* (10th ed.; 10 vols.; London: T. Davison, 1801), IV, 96; Locke, *Essay*, II, 438. See also "A Letter to the Reverend Mr. Richard King, August 25, 1703," *Works of John Locke*, X, 306. For Locke's own definition of his "way of ideas," see "A Letter to the Right Reverend Edward, Lord Bishop of Worcester. . . , January 7, 1697," *Works of John Locke*, IV, 61-62; and, more generally, John W. Yolton, *John Locke and the Way of Ideas* (London: Oxford University Press, 1956).

truth. "He that shall collect all the moral rules of the philosophers," Locke observed, "and compare them with those contained in the New Testament, will find them to come short of the morality delivered by our Saviour, and taught by his apostles; a college made up, for the most part, of ignorant, but inspired fishermen." Finally, like Erasmus in the *Enchiridion* and like the Averroists before Erasmus, Locke contended that, while reason must eventually confirm the truths of revelation, most men have neither the aptitude nor the patience for reason and hence must rely on revelation for their moral and religious truths. "The greatest part cannot know," Locke declared, "and therefore they must believe. And I ask, whether one coming from heaven in the power of God, in full and clear evidence and demonstration of miracles, giving plain and direct rules of morality and obedience, be not likelier to enlighten the bulk of mankind, and set them right in their duties, and bring them to do them, than by reasoning with them from general notions and principles of human reason?"[5]

In effect, what Locke really produced in *The Reasonableness of Christianity* was an intellectual's devotional book. It made no attempt to provide advice for every occasion or prayer for every event, and different men doubtless drew differing instruction from its arguments, as they did from the *Essay*. Yet its fundamental Arminianism, holding that, however stern the law of works, the law of faith afforded all believers access to immortality "as if they were righteous," and its essential latitudinarianism, holding that the one requisite element of faith was belief in the mission and message of Jesus as told in the New Testament, won spirited acceptance for its doctrines in many quarters of the Anglo-American community.[6]

For those who desired more explicit guidance on how precisely to nurture the sort of piety outlined in *The Reasonableness of Christianity*, there was Locke's other treatise, essentially contemporary with the *Essay*, entitled *Some Thoughts Concerning Education* (1693). Fashioned during the period of his Dutch exile, when Locke was devoting himself primarily to the composition of the *Essay*, the *Thoughts* took form in a series of letters to Edward Clarke on the upbringing and education of Clarke's children. Owing to their origin, the *Thoughts* are loosely organized and tend to be repetitive, and

---

[5] John Locke, *The Reasonableness of Christianity* (1695), edited by I. T. Ramsey (Stanford: Stanford University Press, 1958), pp. 24, 30-31, 61-66; *Essay*, II, 443-444.
[6] Locke, *Reasonableness of Christianity*, p. 30.

Locke seems not to have perceived them as systematically related to the problems and doctrines of the *Essay*. Yet, like *The Reasonableness of Christianity*, they are inextricably tied to the *Essay* and stand squarely on its doctrines of epistemology and human nature.[7]

Some Thoughts Concerning Education has often been alluded to as a civility manual in the tradition of *The Governour*, and indeed it is explicitly put forth as a treatise on the education of gentlemen. But it is also a devotional manual in the tradition of *The Practise of Pietie*, though its rational and benevolent conception of virtue (by which Locke meant belief in Christ and conduct according to his teaching) is a world apart from Bayly's strident Calvinism. "That which every gentleman (that takes any care of his education) desires for his son," Locke asserts, "besides the estate he leaves him, is contained (I suppose) in these four things, virtue, wisdom, breeding, and learning. . . . I place virtue as the first and most necessary of those endowments, that belong to a man or a gentleman; as absolutely requisite to make him valued and beloved by others, acceptable or tolerable to himself. Without that I think, he will be happy neither in this, nor the other world."[8]

The place where virtue is to be nurtured is the household; there are few references to churches and schools in the *Thoughts*, and most of those are barbed. And the methods by which virtue is to be nurtured are those especially adapted to childhood as a particular stage of life with its own appropriate concerns. In keeping with the spirit that would later mark *The Reasonableness of Christianity*, Locke speaks of "a true notion of God" as the single most certain foundation of virtue. Parents are advised to begin early with the Lord's Prayer, the Creeds, and the Decalogue, then to teach reading following the "ordinary road of the hornbook, primer, Psalter, Testament, and Bible," and then to ensure that the Bible itself is systematically studied as the foundation of all morality. Even more intriguing, perhaps, is the emphasis throughout on teaching virtue by practice rather than rule, in the earlier years by the deliberate use of praise and shame as techniques of reinforcement (Locke preached only the rarest use of corporal punishment), in the later years by the

[7] M. G. Mason has documented the extent to which parts of the *Thoughts* were composed as early as 1684, as evidenced by an unpublished manuscript on education now in the Bodleian Library, in "How John Locke Wrote 'Some Thoughts Concerning Education,' 1693," *Paedagogica Historica*, I (1961), 244-290.

[8] *The Educational Writings of John Locke*, edited by James L. Axtell (Cambridge: Cambridge University Press, 1968), pp. 240-241.

systematic encouragement of self-conscious efforts at self-control. "These are my present thoughts concerning learning and accomplishments," Locke concludes. "The great business of all is virtue and wisdom.... Teach him to get a mastery over his inclinations, and submit his appetite to reason. This being obtained, and by constant practice settled into habit, the hardest part of the task is over."[9]

II

"A Christian I am sure I am," Locke wrote in his *Second Vindication of the Reasonableness of Christianity* (1697); and, when it came to a choice of church with which to associate himself, he chose the Anglican, into which he had been baptized. Yet his ideas in the realm of piety and education exerted their influence without regard to sect or denomination, and, indeed, came to be associated far more with the mercantile and dissenting communities in England and the colonies than with the dominant elements of the gentry and the established church. Certainly this was true of Locke's most significant popularizers known to the colonists, Isaac Watts, Philip Doddridge, and James Burgh. Watts was an Independent, Doddridge and Burgh were Presbyterians. And even the briefest perusal of their writings reveals major disagreements with Locke, notably in matters of theology and church discipline. Yet what they shared with their mentor and with one another was a generous sense of tolerance for such disagreements, along with a benevolent conception of piety on the one hand and a general penchant for educational reform on the other.[10]

Watts was easily the most influential of the three, both in his own time and after. Born in 1674 to a Nonconformist family that had suffered persecution for its beliefs, educated at Thomas Rowe's academy at Newington Green and there introduced to the works of Descartes and Locke and more generally to the world of free philosophic inquiry, Watts was a sometime tutor to the son of Sir John Hartopp, a well-to-do London Dissenter, and pastor to one of London's most exclusive Independent congregations, the Mark Lane Meeting. But he suffered ill health during much of his life, and spent most of his last four decades in semiretirement at one or another

9 *Ibid.*, pp. 241, 260, 153-159, 313-314.
10 *A Second Vindication of the Reasonableness of Christianity* (1697), in *Works of John Locke*, VII, 359.

of the homes of his friend Sir Thomas Abney. Yet his writing during that time and his extensive network of personal and professional associations made him immensely influential in ecclesiastical and educational circles. As a member of the Congregational Fund Board and the Coward Trust, he was called upon repeatedly to appraise candidates for tutorships in English academies, to recommend curricula, and to propose courses and textbooks. And as friend and counselor to many colonial leaders he maintained a spirited involvement in colonial affairs: he carried on a vigorous correspondence with Cotton Mather that extended over a decade and even weathered Mather's utter dismay with Watts's tract *The Arian Invited to the Orthodox Faith* (1724); he served as literary agent for Benjamin Colman and Elisha Williams; he contributed to the libraries of Harvard and Yale and played a part in founding and filling the Hollis professorship of mathematics at Harvard; he solicited funds for missionary work among the Indians; and he took an active part in the controversy over revivalism in New England during the 1740's.

Above all, Watts influenced education through his writings, notably his hymns, his devotional works for children, his textbooks on logic and pedagogy, and his essays on educational policy. In the field of hymnody, Watts made radical innovations that decisively influenced the liturgy of English Protestantism: he Christianized and nationalized the Psalms of David, recasting them to appeal to the "level of vulgar capacities," as he put it, and, reaching beyond the Psalms to the New Testament, he combined substance, diction, imagery, meter, and melody in such a way as to create what was essentially a new popular liturgical form.[11]

Watts's devotional works for children, especially his *Divine Songs* (1715) and his *Catechisms* (1730), were also innovations, though in substance rather than form, emphasizing as they did a more benevolent piety and beneficent pedagogy than their precursors. The *Divine Songs* was almost certainly modeled upon John Bunyan's *A Book for Boys and Girls* (1686), which circulated for more than a century under the title *Divine Emblems*. But one need only compare their gentle piety with the acerbic theology of *The Day of Doom* to recognize their quantum leap toward benevolence. Consider the following example:

---

[11] Isaac Watts, *Hymns and Spiritual Songs, 1707-1748*, edited by Selma L. Bishop (London: Faith Press, 1962), p. liv.

The praises of my tongue
I offer to the Lord,
That I was taught and learned so young
To read his holy word.

That I am brought to know
The danger I was in;
By nature, and by practice too,
A wretched slave to sin.

That I am led to see
I can do nothing well;
And whither shall a sinner flee,
To save himself from hell?

Dear Lord, this book of thine
Informs me where to go,
For grace to pardon all my sin,
And make me holy too.

Or another:

What blest examples do I find
Writ in the word of truth,
Of children that began to mind
Religion in their youth!

Jesus, who reigns above the sky,
And keeps the world in awe,
Was once a child as young as I,
And kept his Father's law.

Or yet another:

Let love through all your actions run,
And all your words be mild;
Live like the Blessed Virgin's Son,
That sweet and lovely child.

The counsel toward the pious life is not different from Wigglesworth's; but the substance of the counsel and the definition of the pious life are a world apart. And the same is true in comparing Watts's *Catechisms* with John Cotton's *Spiritual Milk for American Babes*. Again, the intent is not different: Watts, like Cotton before him, wants children brought up "in the nurture and admonition

of the Lord." But the Lord of Watts's *Catechisms* is a more beneficent deity, and the processes of nurture and admonition are gentle
by comparison.[12]

Watts's textbooks, especially the *Logick* (1725) and *The Improvement of the Mind* (1741, 1751), and his essays on educational policy,
notably *A Discourse upon the Education of Children and Youth*
(1753), which circulated in America as an appendix to several of
the popular editions of *The Improvement of the Mind,* played a
critical role in the dissemination of Lockean views of the purpose
and character of education. The *Logick* set forth a characteristically
empirical view of the nature and uses of knowledge, while *The Improvement of the Mind,* which Watts saw as a supplement to the
Logick, was for all intents and purposes a utilitarian treatise on
pedagogy suitable for self-education as well as formal teaching.
Similarly, the *Discourse* spoke in its own terms of concepts not unlike
virtue, wisdom, and learning, and, beyond that, included working-
class as well as middle-class children within its purview, so that
Watts's strictures on the need to attend to the moral, intellectual,
physical, and vocational training of all children, each according to
his aptitude and station in life, patently broadened contemporary
conceptions of educational purpose and opportunity.[13]

Like Watts, Doddridge was born to a dissenting family, his
paternal grandfather, John Doddridge, having been an ejected English rector, and his maternal grandfather, John Bauman, an exiled
Lutheran preacher. Like Watts, too, he attended a dissenting academy, entering the school kept at Kibworth, Leicestershire, by John
Jennings in 1719, shortly after he had reached the age of seventeen.
Jennings himself was an Independent, but there was an eclectic
flavor about the school, and several of the students, including Doddridge, were assisted by scholarships from the Presbyterian Fund.
More importantly, Jennings, like Watts's tutor, Thomas Rowe, was
committed to "the greatest freedom of inquiry," and his four-year

[12] Isaac Watts, *Divine and Moral Songs, Attempted in Easy Language for the Use
of Children* (London: John Van Voorst, 1848), pp. 20-21, 33-34, 39. Watts himself
insisted to the reader "that you will find here nothing that savors of a party: the
children of high and low degree, of the Church of England or Dissenters, baptized in
infancy or not, may all join together in these songs." See also *Dr. Watts' Plain and
Easy Catechisms for Children; To Which Are Added Forms of Prayer, Adapted to the
Smallest Capacities* (Cambridge, Mass.: William Hilliard, 1806), p. 3.

[13] Those sections of the *Discourse* that deal with the education of the poor call to
mind Locke's 1697 memorandum on working schools, printed in H. R. Fox Bourne,
The Life of John Locke (2 vols.; New York: Harper & Brothers, 1876), II, 377-391,
rather than *Some Thoughts Concerning Education.*

course included not only such standard readings as the Scriptures in Hebrew, Greek, French, and English, and the traditional Latin and Greek classics, but also selections from *The Spectator* and *The Tatler,* Grotius' *De jure belli ac pacis* (*Concerning the Law of War and Peace*) (1625), Bacon's *Essays* (1597, 1612, 1625), Tillotson's *Sermons* (1695-1704) and Locke's *An Essay Concerning Human Understanding* and its supplement, *Of the Conduct of the Understanding* (1706). Apparently Doddridge throve under Jennings' strict regimen: at least one account of his reading at Kibworth during a typical six-month period indicated that he had carefully perused sixty books, abridging some, excerpting from others in his commonplace book, and inserting particularly attractive passages in his interleaved copy of the Scriptures.[14]

Having completed his formal work with Jennings, Doddridge entered the ministry, accepting a pulpit at Kibworth in 1723 and then moving to the neighboring town of Market Harborough in 1725. Meanwhile, Jennings died suddenly and prematurely of smallpox in 1723, leaving abundant evidence that Doddridge was his personal choice to continue his work. Doddridge himself apparently felt the responsibilities of discipleship, for he developed on his own a lengthy treatise on education for the ministry that was essentially an elaboration of Jennings' ideas. Interestingly, through the offices of a mutual friend, this treatise came into the hands of Isaac Watts, then at the peak of his powers and influence. Watts found himself intrigued by the ideas of the younger man and took steps to make his acquaintance; Doddridge in turn was immensely flattered, having long revered Watts from afar for his "valuable and successful services for the advancement of practical Christianity." The outcome was a lifelong association as master and disciple, as well as an initiative on Watts's part that led to the establishment of a new academy at Market Harborough in July, 1729, with Doddridge as tutor. When Doddridge accepted a call to the Castle Hill Independent Church of Northampton a few months later, he took the academy with him, and launched there a distinguished and influential career as teacher and pastor that was to last until his death in 1751.[15]

14 Philip Doddridge to Samuel Clark, September, 1722, *The Correspondence and Diary of Philip Doddridge,* edited by John Doddridge Humphreys (5 vols.; London: Henry Colburn and Richard Bentley, 1829-1831), I, 155; and Job Orton, "Memoirs of the Life, Character and Writings of the Late Rev. P. Doddridge, D.D., of Northampton," *The Works of the Rev. P. Doddridge,* (10 vols.; Leeds: Edward Baines, 1802-1805), I, 22.

15 Philip Doddridge to Isaac Watts, April 5, 1731, *Correspondence and Diary of Philip Doddridge,* III, 74.

In England, Doddridge came to be widely known as a proponent of "moderate orthodoxy," who had accepted the "way of ideas" set forth in Locke's *Essay* and who had come far—indeed, much farther than his mentor Watts—toward accepting the benevolent and undogmatic theory of *The Reasonableness of Christianity*. "Mr. Locke and many others with him," Doddridge wrote in his divinity lectures, "maintain, that the only fundamental of Christianity is, that Christ is the Messiah: but here a question arises concerning the extent of these words: perhaps it may be sufficient to answer it by saying, that whenever there appeared to be such a persuasion of the dignity of Christ's person and the extent of his power, as should encourage men to commit their souls to his care, and to subject them to his government, those who professed such a persuasion were admitted to baptism by the apostles, and ought to be owned as Christians." Doddridge was well reputed too for his work at the Northampton academy, where the program employed English as the vehicle of instruction, where students were encouraged to interest themselves in a wide variety of subjects, including history, geography, modern languages, and the natural sciences, as well as the more traditional fields of logic, rhetoric, philosophy, mathematics, and divinity, and, most importantly perhaps, where the most difficult and controversial philosophical and theological questions were debated and discussed in a spirit of mutual respect and inquiry. And Doddridge was also connected in the public mind with the world of missionary enterprise, having interested himself in the work of Count Nikolaus Ludwig von Zinzendorf and George Whitefield, and having introduced to the English public an abridged edition of David Brainerd's diary and journal.[16]

In the colonies, Doddridge was known primarily as the author of a number of popular works on practical theology, particularly *The Rise and Progress of Religion in the Soul* (1745), an immensely compassionate devotional work owing much to the influence of Watts and Richard Baxter, that urged men to take their Christianity into the world in the form of service to the common good. And he was widely regarded, too, for several books on Christian nurture, especially the *Sermons on the Religious Education of Children* (1732), addressed mainly to parents, and *The Principles of the Christian Religion* (1743), directed primarily to the young.

The *Sermons on the Religious Education of Children* were origi-

16 "Lectures on Divinity," *Works of the Rev. P. Doddridge*, V, 226; Orton, "Memoirs of the Late Rev. P. Doddridge," pp. 59-79.

nally delivered to the congregation of Northampton in 1732, and first appeared in a colonial edition in 1763. There are four of them in all, each squarely in the format and rhetorical tradition of the Puritan manuals of piety. But the substance and flavor of Doddridge's precepts are quite different from those of John Dod and Robert Cleaver, and of William Gouge. Piety is defined, traditionally enough, as the "way which God has in his word marked out for us; the way which all the children of God have trodden in every succeeding age; the way, the only way, in which we and ours can find rest to our souls." But, when Doddridge goes on to explicate these generalities, his phrases convey a characteristically latitudinarian flavor: "obedience to parents," "benevolence to all," "diligence," "integrity," "self-denial," and "humility"—all summed up best, perhaps, by the Lockean concept of virtue. Indeed, much of Doddridge's advice on the mechanics of familial education is in the spirit of *Some Thoughts Concerning Education,* though there is no explicit recommendation of shame as a pedagogical technique: parents are urged to teach their children plainly, seriously, tenderly, and patiently; temptations must be kept out of reach; the rod must occasionally be used, but moderately and always as a last resort; and the whole enterprise must go forward prayerfully, with God's assistance.[17]

The Principles of the Christian Religion, penned in 1743 and first published in the colonies in 1754, consists of twenty-four lessons of "plain and easy verse" designed, like Watts's *Divine Songs,* to suit the fancy of the young. There is no shrinking from the stark possibilities of damnation: the terrors of God's wrath are dramatically portrayed, with fierce fires, terrifying devils, and souls in infinite despair. But these possibilities are followed by the good news of salvation through Christ and the blessings available to every child who chooses repentance and belief. And there is a warmth and tenderness about Doddridge's teaching, even on death and sin and judgment, that once again stands in sharp contrast to the earlier preachments of Wigglesworth and his contemporaries:

> Awake, my soul, without delay;
> That if God summons thee this day,
> Thou cheerful at his call mayest rise,
> And spring to life beyond the skies.[18]

---

[17] *Sermons on the Religious Education of Children,* in *Works of the Rev. P. Doddridge,* II, 14, 40-58.
[18] *The Principles of the Christian Religion,* in *ibid.,* IV, 241.

In the end, Doddridge made his peace with the rationalized piety of *The Reasonableness of Christianity,* though not without considerable explanation and amplification of his own. His mentor Watts ultimately turned away from it, persuaded that Locke's treatise had "darkened the glory of the gospel, and debased Christianity." James Burgh, on the other hand, was an unreserved admirer of Locke, and recommended *The Reasonableness of Christianity* as one of the three or four best books extant on the nature, character, and evidences of true religion. Born the son of a minister at Madderty, Perthshire, in 1714, Burgh was educated for a time at St. Andrews University with a view to following in his father's footsteps. But illness forced a change in plans, and he became instead a teacher, establishing his own academy at Stoke Newington in 1747. It was in connection with the launching of that enterprise that he wrote his *Thoughts on Education,* which was republished in the colonies two years later; and it was at the peak of his powers as a teacher, in 1754, that he issued *The Dignity of Human Nature,* which was widely read by the colonial intelligentsia as one of the richest and most representative of the dissenting treatises on education.[19]

Burgh's *Thoughts,* essentially an extension of Locke's *Thoughts,* is concerned with the "virtuous and religious education of the youth." And in Burgh's view that education consists of two elements, the "accomplishing a person in such parts of knowledge as may be useful for qualifying him to pass decently and comfortably through the present life," and the "right directing him how to prepare himself for the everlasting duration after this life is at an end." The chief studies in Burgh's scheme, beyond the usual classical languages and literature, are the grammar, orthography, and writing of the mother tongue, French, drawing, music, mathematics, astronomy, anatomy, history, and biography. The chief methods are those that appeal to young people "as rational creatures, . . . teaching them to exert their reason, and to judge rightly of men and things." And the chief values are those of liberty and piety, piety being defined essentially as it is in the treatises of Locke, Grotius, and Samuel Clarke.[20]

Toward the end of the *Thoughts on Education,* Burgh suggests that nothing is so valuable in fixing the direction of true morality

[19] *The Works of the Rev. Isaac Watts* (9 vols.; Leeds: Edward Baines, 1812-1813), IX, 271; James Burgh, *Thoughts on Education* (Edinburgh: no publisher, 1747), p. 39.
[20] Burgh, *Thoughts,* pp. 3, 7, 21, 39.

for the young as a letter from a parent or teacher setting forth the chief maxims of prudence and virtue, summing up briefly the central doctrines and precepts of Christianity, and adding such directions, encouragements, and warnings as will keep the student on the path of righteousness. And for parents who have not the leisure or ability, Burgh has assurances that there are any number of judicious persons, both lay and clerical, who stand ready to assist with the task. Apparently Burgh took his own advice, for *The Dignity of Human Nature,* which appeared seven years later, is really such a letter, though it runs over two hundred thousand words and deals as fully and profoundly as any document of its time with the ends and means of education in an enlightened age.

The treatise is presented in four sections, discussing prudence, knowledge, virtue, and revealed religion. The first section is really a compendium of wisdom for getting on in the ordinary business of life, setting forth maxims on every conceivable activity, from the management of a business to the rearing of a family. The character is Baconian, the formulations, utilitarian. The second section is essentially a discourse on the curriculum, explicitly rooted in the methods of Locke's *Essay* and organized in such a way as to be equally useful to teachers and students. The third and fourth sections are treatises on moral philosophy and divinity, setting forth Burgh's Lockean doctrines and their implications for belief and conduct. The temper of the discussion is reasoned, sensible, and uncontentious; the outlook, always optimistic: Burgh anticipates the day when all human beings will live lives of dignity in this world and achieve salvation in the next. And the thrust is, above all, practical: piety and civility ultimately merge, and virtue comes to describe the network of mutual rights and obligations that mark a nation of free moral agents, men who use their God-given reason to discover the universal scheme and to govern their lives according to the dictates of their place in it.[21]

III

"Seldom any new book of consequence finds the way from beyond-sea, to these parts of America," Cotton Mather noted in his diary for 1706, "but I bestow the perusal upon it." And indeed he did

21 See also [James Burgh], *Youth's Friendly Monitor: Being a Set of Directions, Prudential, Moral, Religious, and Scientific* (London: printed for M. Cooper, 1756).

bestow the perusal upon an extraordinary range of contemporary literature, not merely in theology, but also in politics, medicine, and natural philosophy. He was patently familiar with the doctrines of Newton and Locke, though occasionally it is difficult to determine whether he had come by his knowledge of a particular point directly or through some intervening source, as, for example, when he excerpted in his "Quotidiana" substantial passages from a book entitled *Faith and Reason Compared,* which he explicitly characterized as "a book against the modern rationalists, and particularly Locke." At the very least he probably knew Locke's *Essay* and *The Reasonableness of Christianity* firsthand and was doubtless familiar with the writings of such commentators on Locke as Isaac Watts and William Whiston. And, whether or not he had studied the *Principia* himself, he felt sufficient confidence in his acquaintance with the new experimental philosophy to urge young candidates for the ministry to obtain "as thorough an insight as you can get into the principles of our perpetual dictator, the incomparable Sir Isaac Newton."[22]

Certainly the most erudite man in the New England of his time, Cotton Mather may also have been the most typical: one encounters in the vast corpus of his work all the ardent faiths, gnawing uncertainties, uneasy reconciliations, and glaring contradictions of the latter-day Puritan mind. Born in 1663, the eldest son of Increase Mather, then minister at Dorchester and later teacher of the Second Church in Boston and president of Harvard College, he was the scion of two of New England's most distinguished families, the Mathers and the Cottons. Indeed, much of his life can be explained in terms of the inherent competition between an able son and an illustrious father. He was educated at home and at the Boston Latin School under Ezekiel Cheever and was then sent off to Harvard at the age of twelve, the youngest student ever admitted to that time.

[22] *Diary of Cotton Mather* (2 vols.; New York: Frederick Ungar Publishing Co., 1957), I, 548; "Quotidiana" (4 vols.; Mather mss., American Antiquarian Society, Worcester, Mass.), II [1720-1722], 135-138; *Utilia. Real and Vital Religion Served, in the Various and Glorious Intentions of It* (Boston: T. Fleet & T. Crump, 1716), p. 261 (in which Mather paraphrases Locke on truths that conform to reason and truths that go beyond it); *Manuductio ad Ministerium: Directions for a Candidate of the Ministry* (Boston: printed for Thomas Hancock, 1726), p. 50. The volume cited in "Quotidiana" is obviously *Faith and Reason Compared; Shewing That Divine Faith and Natural Reason Proceed from Two Different and Distinct Principles in Man. Against the Notions and Errors of the Modern Rationalists. Written Originally in Latin by a Person of Quality in Answer to Certain Theses, Drawn from Mr. Lock's Principles Concerning Faith and Reason* (London: B. Cowse, 1713).

A stammer kept him from aspiring to the ministry, so he settled initially on medicine as his life's work; but in 1680 he began to assist his father at the Second Church and performed so admirably that he was ordained there in 1685 and served the congregation for the remainder of his life.

Young Mather involved himself in Massachusetts politics during the 1680's and was a leading figure in the opposition to Sir Edmund Andros, the royal governor. He also played a central role in the Salem witchcraft trials of 1692, though he did urge rather more stringent tests of guilt than were employed by the court and less severe penalties as well. But he was never able to realize his lifelong ambition to succeed his father in the presidency of Harvard, losing out to John Leverett in 1707 and to Benjamin Wadsworth in 1725. Bitterly disappointed in the political arena, he turned increasingly to scholarship and good works, producing over three hundred books and pamphlets during the years after 1700, taking seriously his election to the Royal Society, and laboring indefatigably in such causes as the assistance of itinerant ministers and the advancement of Indian missions. He died in 1728, eulogized by friend and foe alike for his universal learning, exalted piety, extensive charity, and zealous endeavors in the service of Christ.

In the realm of education, Mather displayed an astonishing versatility and range of concern, symbolizing better than anyone else of his time both the continuities and the transformations in provincial educational thought. Aware of the breadth and diversity of education, he dealt in detail with the roles and responsibilities of parents, masters, ministers, teachers, and neighborhood associations in such treatises as *A Family Well-Ordered* (1699), *Cares About the Nurseries* (1702), *Corderius Americanus* (1708), and *Bonifacius* (1710). Aware too of the didactic possibilities of literature, he explicitly set out in the *Magnalia Christi Americana* (1702) to teach New England the true significance of its heritage, much as John Foxe had done for Reformation England in the *Actes and Monuments*. Persuaded as to the centrality of the clergy in the work of education and of education in the mission of the clergy, he discussed the training of ministers in the *Manuductio ad Ministerium* (1726), elaborating a complete curriculum of reading, study, devotions, and good works. Convinced that the study of nature provided insight into God's infinite wisdom, he construed the new science as an essential aspect of learning and both explicated and exemplified its systematic study in *The Christian Philosopher* (1721). And, possessed of a characteristic Puritan need for self-scrutiny, he used his diaries as instruments to clarify, *inter alia,* his educational commitments, dealing at length with the day-by-day business of familial training, as he thought it ought to be and as he himself carried it on in his household. His works circulated briskly on both sides of the Atlantic, making him perhaps the best-known American of his era among intellectuals in England and on the Continent.

For Mather, piety remained the chief end of education and the decisive element in determining its content and character. "All the learning that many have," he wrote in 1690, "serves only as a bag of gold about a drowning man; it sinks them the deeper into the scalding floods of the lake that burns with fiery brimstone: But the knowledge of the Lord Jesus Christ is a saving thing." In matters of doctrine, Mather's piety was essentially conservative: observing "how powerfully the devices of Satan are operating, to bring on apostasies and innovations upon our churches," he sought to reassert the old Congregationalism in the face of growing factionalization and secularization in New England life. In other respects, however, his piety partook of many of the more liberal tendencies in Enlightenment religious thought. Thus, he openly embraced the growing spirit of toleration, at least as far as most of the Protestant sects were concerned. And his views on toleration were closely tied to the idea that piety had to be revitalized and rendered "practical," so that it might become an engine of benevolence and social regeneration. Adopting an increasingly humanistic view of the function of religion, he appealed to all men to do good works, assuming that benevolence might well be a nonsectarian enterprise. Thus, he counseled candidates for the ministry in the *Manuductio:*

> For Communion in these churches, and admission to all the privileges and advantages of the evangelical church-state, I would have you insist upon it, that no terms be imposed, but such necessary things, as heaven will require of all, who shall ascend into the hill of the Lord, and stand in his holy place. Be sure to stand by that golden rule, Receive ye one another, as Christ has received us unto the glory of God; that is to say, those of whom it is our duty to judge, that our Saviour will receive them to his glory in the heavenly world, we ought now to receive unto all the enjoyments of our Christian fellowship. And let the table of the Lord have no rails about it, that shall hinder a godly Independent, and Presbyterian, and Episcopalian, and Antipedobaptist, and Lutheran, from

sitting down together there. Corinthian brass would not be so bright a composition, as the people of God in such a coalition, feasting together on his holy mountain.[23]

In all this, Mather believed himself eminently "reasonable," though his definition of reason constantly shifted, meaning at one point knowledge through experience, at another, innate ideas, and at yet another, obedience to an ultimate moral law. More importantly, perhaps, he used reason to verify his Calvinism but never to criticize it, believing with Locke that there are many doctrines in the Christian religion that are above reason but none contradictory to it. "There is a thought which I have often had in my mind," he wrote in his diary for 1711; "but I would now lay upon my mind, a charge to have it yet oftener there; that the light of reason, is the work of God; the law of reason is the law of God; the voice of reason is the voice of God; we never have to do with reason, but at the same time we have to do with God; our submission to the rules of reason is an obedience to God."[24]

Mather's pietism suffuses his discussions of education. The chief purpose of education is to prepare children for conversion, and the way to accomplish this is through an understanding of the Bible. "Our knowledge of the Holy Scriptures," he observed in *Corderius Americanus,* "is that by which we come to know the rules of religion, and be religiously wise unto salvation. The rules of our holy religion are all of them delivered in those oracles of God, which we call the Holy Scriptures. If ever we come unto salvation, it must be by conversing with the Holy Scriptures." Hence, all parents, masters, ministers, and tutors must "begin betimes in teaching of children, the early knowledge of the Holy Scriptures, that so they may be wise unto salvation." Children must be made familiar with the historical portion of the Bible, so they may draw appropriate religious lessons from the narratives. They must acquire doctrinal knowledge, too, with the aid of a proper catechism. And they must learn the commandments of the Scriptures, that they may properly govern their conduct. "We must know and hear our duty," he counsels; "and we must be doers of the word, and not hearers only. Else we are not wise unto salvation." Piety for Mather is practical as well as intel-

---

[23] Cotton Mather, *Addresses to Old Men, and Young Men, and Little Children* (Boston: R. Pierce, 1690), p. 11; *Diary of Cotton Mather,* I, 363-364; and Mather, *Manuductio,* pp. 126-127.

[24] Mather, *Utilia,* p. 261; and *Diary of Cotton Mather,* II, 144.

lectual; it involves the performance of good works as well as the knowledge of correct doctrine.[25]

This pragmatic thrust of Mather's piety was scarcely new: it stood in a direct line with the practical divinity of William Perkins and his contemporaries. What was new, though, was the communal character it assumed in Mather's thought, an aspect he developed most fully in his tract *Bonifacius,* subtitled *An Essay upon the Good.* The context for *Bonifacius,* of course, was the general spirit of benevolence that pervaded the English-speaking world after 1700 and, more specifically, the work of the societies for the reformation of manners that sprang up in England during the 1680's and 1690's. Growing out of a Puritan effort to resurrect the more stringent morality of pre-Restoration society, these associations conducted a relatively abortive campaign against debauchery and profanity, using legal as well as educational weapons. Mather knew of these societies and his acquaintance with them was doubtless responsible for his own attempts to initiate similar enterprises in the colonies. Now, communalism too was scarcely new in late seventeenth-century America; it had been a feature of Congregationalism from the beginning. What was new was Mather's explicit linking of communalism and piety in his definition of the good life and his formulation of novel disciplinary, hence educational, mechanisms for encouraging men to lead the good life in collaboration with their neighbors.

Written during a period of declining religiosity, *Bonifacius* is at the same time a call for popular piety and a primer on how to achieve it: Mather attempts in the volume to teach magistrates, ministers, physicians, lawyers, schoolmasters, and "wealthy gentle-

[25] Cotton Mather, *Corderius Americanus: An Essay upon the Good Education of Children* (Boston: John Allen, 1708), pp. 5, 7, 6-7. Robert Middlekauff has commented in an unpublished paper on an "apparent paradox" of Puritanism, that a system so repressive should have liberated so much social, psychological, and political energy. And he locates his explanation in the connection within Puritan thought between the psychology of religious experience and the psychology of learning, a connection he finds central in Mather's assumption that the educative process is really an analogue of the conversion process. "God initiated conversion; he drew men to himself by infusing their souls with grace; without him, men were helpless. In education, too, the process was initiated from outside the mind of the child. Something had to be put in before he could act, even if his reason were conceived of as a storehouse of unborn ideas. The release of ideas could be triggered only from without; but once release was given, once the trigger was pressed, the child could do much, indeed, he had to do much for himself, just as the soul that craved salvation had to do much once it received so little as a seed of grace." The characterization is especially apt and, incidentally, one more evidence of the Augustinian character of New England Puritanism.

men" how they may do good, providing detailed instructions on the responsibilities of each group to relatives, neighbors, and servants, in short, to the community. His first admonition to parents, and the one he explicates most fully, is to educate, to nurture children in piety, civility, and learning:

> Parents, Oh! how much ought you to be continually devising, and even travailing, for the good of your children. Often devise: how to make them wise children; how to carry on a desirable education for them; an education that shall render them desirable; how to render them lovely, and polite creatures, and serviceable in their generation. Often devise, how to enrich their minds with valuable knowledge; how to instill generous, and gracious, and heavenly principles into their minds; how to restrain and rescue them from the paths of the Destroyer, and fortify them against their special temptations. There is a world of good, that you have to do for them.

Once individual households have been properly instructed, they must organize into societies of associated families, committed to gathering regularly "in the exercises of religion." The function of these societies is not merely to insure doctrinal orthodoxy, though that is certainly one of their prime responsibilities, but also to assume a major role in the formation and shaping of character. "It should be like a law of the Medes and Persians to the whole society—," Mather counsels, "that they will upon all just occasions, lovingly give, and as lovingly take, mutual admonitions of anything that they may see amiss in each other." Beyond this, Mather sees the associated families as institutionalizing benevolence by insisting that their members perform good works, or, to use an older phrase, that they practice piety. In sum, they must self-consciously assume many of the social and educational roles that church congregations had traditionally carried informally, all, needless to say, under the watchful eyes of the clergy.[26]

Much more might be written about the inseparability of piety and education in Mather's thought; suffice it to say that in the vast corpus of his work, written over an eventful lifetime spanning more than a half-century, there were different emphases at different times, depending on Mather's particular concerns and the circumstances in which he found himself. His piety was sufficiently rational for the historian Herbert Morais to consider him the first American deist,

[26] Cotton Mather, *Bonifacius: An Essay upon the Good,* edited by David Levin (Cambridge, Mass.: Harvard University Press, 1966), pp. 42, 64, 65.

largely on the basis of *Reasonable Religion* (1700). Like Locke, however, Mather was not a deist: both men wrestled with the problems of reason and revelation, but resolved them in a fashion that Conrad Wright has aptly termed "supernatural rationalism." Mather's rationalism did lead on, however, to at least two threads in American Puritanism that dominate the eighteenth century. One was the more radical rationalism of Jonathan Mayhew and Charles Chauncy, with its conception of a benevolent deity who rules the world in his infinite goodness as well as wisdom, its assertion that all men are capable of salvation, and its view of education as a central concern of a free Christian community in which each individual has an "indispensable duty" to exercise private judgment and to act on the basis of that judgment. "Christianity is principally an institution of life and manners; designed to teach us how to be good men, and to show us the necessity of becoming so," Mayhew sermonized in 1748. And the test of that institution in this world is not the prevalence of belief in certain notions and doctrines but the ultimate effect of belief on individual conduct.[27]

The other thread, of course, was the brilliantly rationalized orthodoxy of Jonathan Edwards, with its conception of an awesome deity ruling the world with absolute self-sufficiency and independence, its assertion of moral necessity and total depravity, and its insistence upon an education concerning itself not merely with understanding and conduct but also with the affections, or, in Edwards' words, the "more vigorous and sensible exercises of the inclinations and will of the soul." "If it be so," Edwards argued in 1746, "that true religion lies much in the affections, hence we may infer, that such means are to be desired, as have much of a tendency to move the affections. Such books, and such a way of preaching the word, and administration of ordinances, and such a way of worshiping God in prayer, and singing praises, is much to be desired, as has a tendency deeply to affect the hearts of those who attend these means." He devoted his life to the development and explication of such means, and to the purposes they might serve in the hands of inspired teachers and preachers.[28]

27 Herbert M. Morais, *Deism in Eighteenth Century America* (New York: Columbia University Press, 1934), p. 8; Conrad Wright, *The Beginnings of Unitarianism in America* (Boston: Starr King Press, 1955), pp. 3-4; Jonathan Mayhew, *Seven Sermons* (London: John Noon, 1750), pp. 42-66, 145, 156.
28 *A Treatise Concerning Religious Affections*, edited by John E. Smith (New Haven: Yale University Press, 1959), pp. 96, 121.

IV

The world of Cotton Mather was self-consciously cosmopolitan: he reached constantly and resolutely for the latest ideas from England and the Continent so that he could quote, refine, and rebut them in his "many treatises, on a copious variety of subjects." Less than a hundred miles away, at the infant college at Saybrook, Connecticut, Mather's younger contemporary Samuel Johnson found himself in a world of studied provincialism, dominated by Latin, Greek, and Hebrew exercises and "the scholastic cobwebs of a few little English and Dutch systems." Having been educated first by his grandfather and then by a succession of grammar masters in his native town of Guilford, Johnson had entered the college at the age of fourteen, in 1710. He completed the bachelor's degree four years later, having heard of a new philosophy of Descartes, Boyle, Locke, and Newton but having been warned against it as a subversive force that would "soon bring in a new divinity and corrupt the pure religion of the country."[29]

The year 1714 was a crucial one at Saybrook, since it marked the arrival from England of some seven hundred volumes that Connecticut's agent Jeremiah Dummer had gathered for the library. Rarely has such a collection of up-to-date metropolitan literature burst upon a colonial institution of higher learning with more instantaneous and pronounced effect. As Johnson himself later reminisced about his own awakening, "He had then all at once the vast pleasure of reading the works of our best English poets, philosophers and divines, Shakespeare and Milton etc., Locke and Norris etc., Boyle and Newton etc., Patrick and Whitby, Barrow, Tillotson, South, Sharp, Scott and Sherlock etc. All this was like a flood of day to his low state of mind."[30]

The story of Johnson's intellectual odyssey thereafter has become a familiar chapter in American history. He and his classmate Daniel Browne, retained as tutors after the college moved to New Haven in 1717, "introduced the study of Mr. Locke and Sir Isaac Newton as fast as they could," together with mathematics and the Copernican system of astronomy; and Johnson himself labored earnestly over

[29] *Diary of Cotton Mather*, I, 547; Samuel Johnson, "Memoirs of the Life of the Rev. Dr. Johnson," in Herbert Schneider and Carol Schneider, eds., *Samuel Johnson, President of King's College: His Career and Writings* (4 vols.; New York: Columbia University Press, 1929), I, 6.

[30] Schneider and Schneider, eds., *Samuel Johnson*, I, 7.

"Euclid, algebra, and the conic sections, so as to read Sir Isaac with understanding." They also discussed endlessly the various works on theology in the Dummer collection and found themselves drifting slowly toward the conviction that the Church of England most nearly approached the "purity and perfection" of the primitive church. After 1720, when Johnson resigned from full-time service at the college to accept a pulpit in West Haven, gnawing doubts about the validity of Presbyterian ordination compounded their discontent with the Connecticut establishment.[31]

By 1722 rumors of heresy were sufficiently rampant at the college —now dubbed Yale in honor of a generous benefactor—for the trustees to launch a full-scale investigation. The inquiry confirmed their worst fears: not only Johnson and Browne, but the rector himself, Timothy Cutler, were guilty of "Arminianism and prelatical corruptions." Cutler was duly "excused" from the rectorship on October 17, and a month later the three men were off to England to seek ordination in the Anglican church. Browne subsequently died of smallpox. Cutler was appointed minister of the newly formed Christ Church in Boston, which became during his incumbency the militant center of New England Anglicanism. And Johnson acceded to the pulpit of the Anglican church at Stratford, Connecticut. There, he immersed himself in the literature of the deist controversy, deploring the "progress of infidelity and apostasy in this age of mighty pretense and reasoning from the well meaning but too conceited Mr. Locke, down to Tindal, and thence to Bolingbroke, etc. etc." A reading of George Berkeley's *A Treatise Concerning the Principles of Human Knowledge* (1710) in 1728 and a visit with the English philosopher the following year, when he came to America with a view to founding a college in Rhode Island, confirmed his sense of the dangers of reason unrestrained by faith, and he became a convert to Berkeley's idealistic critique of Newton and Locke. For the rest of his life, which he spent mostly at Stratford, the principal interruption being his service as president of King's College from 1754 to 1763, Johnson sought to develop and extend that idealism, working it in the end into an antiscientific defense of orthodoxy that proved a blind alley with respect to further American influence.[32]

[31] *Ibid.*, pp. 8-9.

[32] Franklin Bowditch Dexter, ed., *Documentary History of Yale University Under the Original Charter of the Collegiate School of Connecticut, 1701-1745* (New Haven: Yale University Press, 1916), pp. 232-233; and Johnson, "memoirs," p. 23. A fourth Connecticut "heretic," James Wetmore, traveled to England alone but was ordained there with the others.

Johnson's principal work, the achievement of a lifetime of study and reflection, was his *Elementa Philosophica (The Elements of Philosophy)*. Begun as a logic he prepared for his own use in connection with the education of his sons, whom he tutored along with several other boys, the work grew by accretion and was published in full by Franklin and Hall in 1752, the first textbook in philosophy to appear in English-speaking America. The overall system of thought within which the work is located Johnson calls *cyclopaedia,* or learning, by which he means "the knowledge of everything useful to our well-being and true happiness in this life, or our supreme happiness in the life to come." *Cyclopaedia* embraces grammar, rhetoric, oratory, history, poetry, mathematics, mechanics, geology, astronomy, natural history, metaphysics, and moral philosophy. *Elementa Philosophica,* which is intended to introduce mature students of sixteen or seventeen to the last two subjects, is divided into two parts: *Noetica,* or matters relating to the mind or understanding, and *Ethica,* or matters relating to moral behavior.[33]

The treatise is admittedly indebted to Berkeley and actually includes various excerpts and borrowings from his writings. But it also sets forth many of Johnson's own definitions and propositions that are much more generally representative of the benevolent rationalism of the age, and this is certainly true of the sections on education. The final chapter of the *Noetica,* for example, is a discourse on "the progress of the mind, from its first notices, towards its utmost perfection," which treats of such topics as the nature of ideas, the pedagogical function of praise, blame, shame, and guilt, the character of moral training, and the substance and order of the curriculum. "Hence also it appears," Johnson asserts, "that we ought to think little children to be persons of much more importance than we usually apprehend them to be; and how indulgent we should be to their inquisitive curiosity as being strangers; with how much candor, patience and care, we ought to bear with them and instruct them; with how much decency, honor and integrity, we ought to treat them; and how careful it concerns us to be, not to say or do anything to them, or before them, that savors of falsehood or deceit, or that is in any kind indecent or vicious."[34]

The *Ethica,* in turn, sets forth what is fundamentally a benevo-

33 *Elementa Philosophica* (1752), in Schneider and Schneider, eds., *Samuel Johnson,* II, 361.
34 *Ibid.,* pp. 422, 424.

lent Arminian piety characterizing Jesus as first and foremost a teacher come from God and clothed with divine authority, and the church as "the school of Christ, wherein immortal spirits clothed with flesh, are to be trained and bred up as candidates for eternal glory." And, on the basis of that piety, it prescribes conduct within the classic casuist categories of duties to God, duties to others, and duties to ourselves.[35]

The essentially rational and humane pedagogy of *Elementa Philosophica* is also reflected in a number of Johnson's other works, notably his "Sermon upon the Reasonableness of Religion and Obedience," preached in 1716, his *Short Catechism for Young Children* (1765), and an unpublished rhapsody entitled "Raphael; or, The Genius of English America," in which, even though his overwhelming concern is to warn his countrymen against "spiritual pride and conceitedness and affectation of singularity or novelty," his preachments favor a reasonable though unindulgent familial education and an intellectually solid though religiously sound school education—all, incidentally, very much with a Lockean flavor. Indeed, what is most noteworthy about "Raphael," which was probably written around 1763, is its call for an education that will nurture a noble and generous patriotism toward the colonies, a call that was appropriately symbolic of the new self-consciousness of English America, though seemingly innocent of the growing ambivalence of that self-consciousness toward the mother country.[36]

V

For Samuel Johnson, the philosophy of George Berkeley provided a way out of the glaring difficulties he saw in Locke's rationalism, particularly its encouragement of "high soaring and conceited speculations in matters of religion." For John Witherspoon, Berkeley's idealism was "a wild and ridiculous attempt to unsettle the principles of common sense by metaphysical reasoning, which can hardly produce anything but contempt in the generality of persons who hear it, and which I verily believe, never produced conviction even on the persons who pretend to espouse it." Yet Witherspoon was as distressed as Johnson about the tide of unorthodox religious think-

[35] *Ibid.*, p. 514.
[36] Samuel Johnson, "Raphael; or, The Genius of English America," in Schneider and Schneider, eds., *Samuel Johnson*, II, 590.

ing and as determined as Johnson to stem it through his teaching.[37]

Born in Scotland in 1723, Witherspoon came to maturity during the period of intellectual ferment aptly referred to as the Scottish Enlightenment. Like Johnson, he early encountered Locke and then George Berkeley and Thomas Reid in their efforts to contend with the unresolved problems in Locke. He studied *An Essay Concerning Human Understanding* under John Stevenson, one of the first professors to teach the Lockean system at the University of Edinburgh, and produced while not yet twenty a master's thesis in the field of epistemology that drew eclectically on the classics, Locke, and Berkeley to prove that mind is eternal, divine in its qualities, and destined for immortal bliss "on condition that in this life it pursues correctly the path assigned to it by God."[38]

Having been graduated from the university with a divinity degree in 1743, he was licensed to teach by the Haddington Presbytery and was subsequently ordained to the ministry, serving first at Beith in Ayrshire and then at the thriving town of Paisley, a few miles to the north. An avid participant in the theological disputes of his time, he came via his study of Reid and the common-sense philosophy to the intellectual leadership of that dissenting minority within the National Presbyterian church who called themselves the Popular Party. Strongly committed to the essential Calvinism of the Westminster Confession, they tended to support the rights of congregations (in the covenant tradition) as against the rights of individual patrons in the appointment of pastors, to insist upon the centrality of the pastoral role in the ministry, and to uphold the most rigorous standards of personal and professional conduct for members of the clergy. Above all, they lamented the drift toward a more liberal benevolent piety and proclaimed the need for a return to the traditional orthodoxy of Scottish Presbyterianism.

Through Reid, too, Witherspoon was led to abandon his earlier adherence to Berkeleyan idealism, the thrust of which seemed to him inexorably skeptical, in favor of a common-sense philosophy of realism that asserted the validity of both mind and matter and the reality of both sense experience and the object sensed. Insisting that the essential acts of the mind are "judgments of nature—judg-

[37] *Ibid.*; and *The Works of the Rev. John Witherspoon* (3 vols.; Philadelphia: William W. Woodward, 1800), III, 279.

[38] John Witherspoon, "Philosophical Disputation: Concerning the Immortality of the Mind," in George Eugene Rich, "John Witherspoon: His Scottish Intellectual Background" (unpublished doctoral thesis, Syracuse University, 1964), p. 166.

ments not got by comparing ideas, and perceiving agreements and disagreements, but immediately inspired by our constitution," Reid followed Francis Hutcheson in positing a moral sense, or conscience, which provides every human being with original conceptions of right, wrong, merit, and demerit by which to guide his conduct. Witherspoon seized upon this epistemology as the basis for a new synthesis of empirical philosophy and Calvinist piety, which he put forth as a rational alternative to the increasingly influential theological liberalism of his time.[39]

It was this mature Witherspoon, a powerful protagonist of orthodoxy familiar with all the major currents of the Scottish Enlightenment, whom the trustees of the fledgling College of New Jersey brought to America in 1768. The college itself had taken shape during the great revivals of the 1730's and 1740's that had split the Presbyterian church into New Light and Old Light factions and set each to founding academies for the training of its own ministers. Established in 1746 by the New Light Synod of New York, the college had existed first in the home of Jonathan Dickinson in Elizabethtown, New Jersey, then in the parsonage of Aaron Burr, Sr., in Newark, and then at Nassau Hall in Princeton, under Burr, Jonathan Edwards, Samuel Davies, and Samuel Finley. At the time of Finley's death in 1766, the college had become a center of controversy as the Old Lights, jealous of its growing influence, had schemed to place it on a "better foundation." Determined not to be finessed, the New Light trustees had promptly elected Witherspoon to the presidency. The story of Witherspoon's refusal, indecision, and eventual acceptance under the gentle but insistent prodding of Benjamin Rush has been recounted in detail by Lyman H. Butterfield in his charming volume *John Witherspoon Comes to America*. Suffice it to say that Witherspoon arrived at Princeton to take up the post in August, 1768, and remained until his death a quarter-century later, reshaping the college and with it substantial segments of American education, taking an active part in the reorganization of the American Presbyterian church, and playing a unique role in

[39] *The Works of Thomas Reid*, edited by Sir William Hamilton (8th ed.; 2 vols.; Edinburgh: James Thin, 1895), I, 110; II, 589-590; John Witherspoon, "Remarks on an Essay on Human Liberty," *Scots Magazine*, XV (1753), 165-170; and *Works of the Rev. John Witherspoon*, III, 281. The essentially Newtonian posture of the Scottish realists, in seeking through observation and induction certain empirical touchstones for human conduct, is explicated in Gladys Bryson, *Man and Society: The Scottish Inquiry of the Eighteenth Century* (Princeton: Princeton University Press, 1945), pp. 19-20.

the founding of the Republic. As Moses Coit Tyler later remarked in a now-classic appraisal, "He seems to have come at the right moment, to the right spot, in the right way."[40]

For all his ability as a controversialist, Witherspoon at Princeton was first and foremost a teacher, and hence it is his lectures on moral philosophy, which as president he delivered regularly to the senior class, that afford the fullest insight into his thought in America. Upon his arrival at Princeton, he found Berkeleyan idealism in the ascendancy among tutors and students, and, not surprisingly, he took it upon himself to substitute the realism of Reid and the Scottish common-sense school. The lectures reflect this in their heavy reliance on Reid and Francis Hutcheson and in their sharp attack on immaterialism, which, according to Witherspoon, "takes away the distinction between truth and falsehood." They are firmly committed to reason, asserting that "the whole Scripture is perfectly agreeable to sound philosophy"; but they argue that reason itself is based on certain first principles or dictates of common sense that can be grasped intuitively, that both intimate and enforce duty, and that are previous to reason. It is these first principles, abstracted into a faculty called the moral sense, that Witherspoon explicates, giving attention not only to the traditional concerns of practical divinity, i.e., duties to God, self, and others, but also in unusual measure to politics, economics, and jurisprudence. At the end, a brief bibliography suggests both the usual literature of the deist controversy and of Scottish common-sense realism, and also a substantial literature of politics, including Grotius, Pufendorf, Hobbes, Harrington, Locke, Sidney, and Montesquieu.[41]

Witherspoon's views on education are scattered through his sermons, his lectures on divinity, his treatise on eloquence, the announcements of the college during his administration, and an intriguing series of "letters on education" published initially in *The Pennsylvania Magazine* and *The American Museum* and later in book form. At the college, he sought on every possible occasion "to unite together piety and literature—to show their relation to, and their influence one upon another—and to guard against anything that may tend to separate them, and set them in opposition one to

[40] L. H. Butterfield, *John Witherspoon Comes to America* (Princeton: Princeton University Press, 1953); and Moses Coit Tyler, *The Literary History of the American Revolution, 1763-1783* (2 vols.; New York: G. P. Putnam's Sons, 1897), II, 321.

[41] *Works of the Rev. John Witherspoon*, III, 279, 271, 373-375.

another." He persistently advocated a broadened curriculum, extending the substance of his own teaching beyond the traditional classical and philosophical studies to include systematic work in the English and French languages, in history, and in oratory and eloquence. He brought new vigor to the grammar school that operated in the basement of Nassau Hall, and even gave attention to the problems of educating those not destined for college. And, in his letters on education, he set forth a characteristically Lockean pedagogy, urging concern for the health of the young and for the adaptation of teaching to their differing temperaments, and stressing the diversity of techniques available to parents in establishing as early as possible their moral authority over their children.[42]

Most important, perhaps, Witherspoon redirected the effort of the college toward the nurture of pious men suited to positions of service in the commonwealth as well as the church. And in this, of course, he was extraordinarily successful, his graduates including a president of the new nation (James Madison), a vice-president (Aaron Burr), ten cabinet officers, sixty members of the Congress, and three justices of the Supreme Court. Witherspoon himself might well have argued that his teaching of these men, while significant, was not decisive, for he displayed a lively sense of the limitations of education. Yet there is no denying the extent of Princeton's influence under his charismatic presidency: it helped create the leadership of the new Republic in philosophy as well as politics, and it profoundly shaped the character of nineteenth-century American education.[43]

VI

Johnson and Witherspoon were not so widely read in America as Locke, Watts, and Doddridge. Yet the conservatism they put forth in the face of growing religious skepticism was strongly supported by a popular devotional literature that continued to circulate in the colonies and to proffer a conventional wisdom about education for piety. *The Practise of Pietie, The Whole Duty of Man, The Poor Man's Family Book,* and *The Pilgrim's Progress* were widely read by a broad spectrum of Americans, as were later volumes such as

---

[42] *The Works of the Rev. John Witherspoon* (2d ed., rev.; 4 vols.; Philadelphia: William W. Woodward, 1802), IV, 10.

[43] John Maclean, *History of the College of New Jersey, from Its Origin in 1746 to the Commencement of 1854* (2 vols.; Philadelphia: J. B. Lippincott & Co., 1877), I, 357-364.

Daniel Defoe's *The Family Instructor* (1715; first colonial edition, 1740), Robert Dodsley's *The Oeconomy of Human Life* (1750; first colonial edition, 1765), and Samuel Richardson's *Pamela* (1740; first colonial edition, 1744), which in essence presented a traditional piety in novel form. Like the precursors on which they were modeled, these later works tended to proffer the nonsectarian orthodoxy characteristic of the devotional genre; and, inasmuch as they were increasingly written by free lances in search of large audiences, their nonsectarian traditionalism was a deliberate attempt at popularity. For all the doctrinal refinements and subtleties of Mather, Johnson, and Witherspoon, conventional piety retained a central place in eighteenth-century educational thought.[44]

On the other hand, there were radical transmutations of piety in the writings of deists like Benjamin Franklin and Thomas Jefferson, which sounded new themes of direct relevance to colonial education. In Franklin, a new version of popular piety appeared in the utilitarianism of Poor Richard, who proclaimed that virtue and trade were a child's best portion. And, in Jefferson, a new ideal of secular piety appeared in the sturdy republican yeoman acting according to the dictates of conscience as informed by a free press. Both men rationalized piety in the extreme, the result being that, although they remained nominally Christians, Christian piety in its traditional form no longer remained the chief end of education. Together, they pointed the way for other institutions than the church to play the decisive role in the education of the people.

44 For the debate over the authorship of *The Oeconomy of Human Life*, see Henry Tedder's biography of Dodsley in the *Dictionary of National Biography*, which attributes the work to the earl of Chesterfield, and Ralph Straus's *Robert Dodsley* (London: John Lane, 1910), pp. 169-181, which argues persuasively in favor of Dodsley's authorship. For the values incorporated into Richardson's novels, and for a general analysis of the early novel as conduct manual, see Herbert Schöffler, *Protestantismus und Literatur* (Leipzig: Bernhard Tauchnitz, 1922), pp. 163 ff.

Chapter 10

MODES OF ENTHUSIASM

> If it be so, that true religion lies much in the affections, hence we may infer, that such means are to be desired, as have much of a tendency to move the affections. Such books, and such a way of preaching the word, and administration of ordinances, and such a way of worshiping God in prayer, and singing praises, is much to be desired, as has a tendency deeply to affect the hearts of those who attend these means.
>
> JONATHAN EDWARDS

In Locke's view there were three possible grounds on which to base assent to religion: reason, or inferential thought; faith, which reaches beyond reason to revelation but never contradicts reason; and enthusiasm, which lays reason aside and blindly accepts revelation without it. "Whereby in effect," Locke argued, "it [enthusiasm] takes away both reason and revelation, and substitutes in the room of them the ungrounded fancies of a man's own brain, and assumes them for a foundation both of opinion and conduct."[1]

In the fourth edition of the *Essay,* published in 1700, Locke actually added a chapter on enthusiasm in which he lashed out against the conceits and vanities of the enthusiast, who fatuously argued that what he believed was revelation because he so firmly believed it and that he firmly believed it because it was revelation. Throughout history, Locke mused, there had been men possessed of a sense of special and immediate familiarity with God, and from that presumptuous sense had stemmed some of the darkest thoughts and acts of humankind.

[1] John Locke, *An Essay Concerning Human Understanding,* edited by Alexander Campbell Fraser (2 vols.; Oxford: Clarendon Press, 1894), II, 430.

There was no mistaking the most immediate targets of Locke's animus, the left-wing sects of the Reformation that had flourished so freely in England and Holland during the period of the Commonwealth. Under conditions of relative religious toleration, Baptists, Familists, Ranters, Seekers, Quakers, Fifth Monarchists, and other millenarians of infinite variety had argued vociferously and incessantly over matters of doctrine, each claiming the illumination of some inward light affording special insight into divine truth. Essentially religious in inspiration, the sects were inevitably political in effect, purveying as they did radical doctrines of equality, democracy, and individuality that in their very nature seemed subversive of social order. And in education they tended toward simplicity of doctrine, a contempt for learned theologizing that frequently deteriorated into outright anti-intellectualism, and a radical separation of church and state that would leave schools and universities under the direct control of the civil magistrate. Locke had encountered the sects in his years at Oxford and had been repelled by their "passions" and "fancies" and "enthusiasms." Years later, having modified his earlier fear that toleration invariably meant anarchy, he had not yet gotten over his revulsion.

Meanwhile, on the Continent, a related pietism swept the Lutheran, Moravian, and Reformed churches, growing initially out of the teaching of Gysbertus Voetius, a seventeenth-century theologian at Utrecht, and Philipp Jakob Spener, a pastor at Frankfurt am Main in the 1670's, and then spreading via the efforts of August Hermann Francke, a professor at the newly founded University of Halle (1694), and of Francke's student Count Zinzendorf, who literally recreated Moravianism in the eighteenth century. Stressing Christianity as an experience of God within and as a way of life rather than a fixed creed with historic rituals, pietism infused new spirit not only into the traditional churches but also into a host of smaller sects, such as the Mennonites, the Dunkers, the Schwenkfelders, and the Inspirationists.

Now, sectarianism, of course, had appeared in English America as early as the 1630's, when antinomianism had rent the unity of the Bay Colony, leading to the banishment of Anne Hutchinson and her followers. Later, Quaker missionaries had appeared in several of the colonies, eliciting at first sharp persecution and then reluctant toleration. But it was in the last two decades of the seventeenth century that members of the sects had begun to arrive in appreciable numbers, settling largely but by no means exclusively in the middle colonies, notably, Pennsylvania. There, under conditions of toleration that excelled even Rhode Island's, they formed communities, organized churches and schools, and in general developed educational arrangements according to their special visions of the pious man and the good society.

For the Quakers themselves, there was a curious paradox in Pennsylvania, in that they were the proprietary party and yet brought with them self-consciously sectarian concepts of education. As a steady flow of epistles from the London meeting exhorted, Quakers were a "peculiar" people, and their children were to be trained as such, that is, taught to "outstrip and exceed the world in virtue, in purity, in chastity, in godliness, and in modesty, civility, and in righteousness, and in love." And that meant, first, an indoctrination in the history and beliefs of the Society of Friends, and, second, a protection from the corrupting influences of the world, or, as it has frequently been put, a "guarded education." These commitments were clearly reflected in the writings of William Penn, whose letters abound with allusions to family prayer, regular attendance at meetings, and systematic parental instruction and oversight as prime devices by which children may be led to that inward communion with God and outward activity in his causes that are the unmistakable marks of true piety. Moreover, in honoring these commitments, Penn, who as a member of the Royal Society was doubtless familiar with the work of Sir William Petty, John Dury, Samuel Hartlib, and other proponents of Baconian methods in education, proposed a pedagogy remarkably similar to Locke's in its outward manifestations. "The first thing obvious to children, is what is sensible," Penn wrote in *Some Fruits of Solitude* (1693), an "enchiridion" composed toward the end of his life, "and that we make no part of their rudiments. . . . We press their memory too soon, and puzzle, strain and load them with words and rules; to know grammar and rhetoric, and a strange tongue or two, that it is ten to one may never be useful to them; leaving their natural genius to mechanical and physical, or natural knowledge uncultivated and neglected; which would be of exceeding use and pleasure to them through the whole course of their life." Not surprisingly, Penn displayed a familiar Quaker contempt for the inordinate pursuit of learning, particularly as a qualification for the ministry, and he was savage in his attacks on the universities; but there is no denying his deep concern for the education of all children in "useful knowledge, such as is consistent with truth and godliness."[2]

For all his characteristic Quakerism, however, Penn was also the proprietor and governor of a province and as such committed to education as a fundamental instrument of public order and enlightenment. "There is scarcely any one thing," he wrote in 1679, "that so much needs the wisdom of the nation in the contrivance of a new law, as the 'education of our youth,' whether we consider the piety or prudence of our manners, the good life, or just policy of the government." The principle was enacted into law in the early frames of government in Pennsylvania, but it was not realized in practice for decades; and the reasons are profoundly instructive. The early Quaker leaders were committed on the one hand to education for piety and on the other hand to toleration; and in the very nature of the dual commitment the civil polity was limited to the broad encouragement rather than the direct sponsorship of education. For the first time in earnest—Rhode Island had never faced the problem squarely—Americans had to contend with the dilemmas of public education in a pluralistic society.[3]

For some, such as Thomas Budd, a convert to Quakerism and a member of the provincial assembly, Pennsylvania's natural resources and strategic location for purposes of trade afforded a unique potential for a thriving plantation, and a comprehensive scheme of education could play a central role in the development of that potential. In a pamphlet entitled *Good Order Established in Pennsilvania & New-Jersey in America* (1685), Budd set forth proposals calling for seven years of schooling for all children in "all the most useful arts and sciences that they in their youthful capacities may be capable to understand," including not only reading and writing in English and Latin and arithmetic and bookkeeping but also some trade or mystery such as joinery, weaving, or shoemaking for the boys and spin-

2 *Epistles from the Yearly Meeting of Friends, Held in London, to the Quarterly and Monthly Meetings in Great Britain, Ireland, and Elsewhere, from 1681 to 1817 Inclusive* (London: W. E. S. Graves, 1818), pp. 96, 21; *Extracts from the Minutes and Advices of the Yearly Meeting of Friends Held in London* (2d ed.; London: W. Phillips, 1802), pp. 121-129; "Some Fruits of Solitude," in *The Select Works of William Penn* (3d ed.; 5 vols.; London: James Phillips, 1782), V, 120; *A Letter from William Penn, to His Wife and Children* (Penrith: Anthony Soulby, 1797), p. 6.

3 "An Address to Protestants of All Persuasions," *Select Works of William Penn*, IV, 51-52; Staughton George, Thomas McCamant, and Benjamin M. Nead, eds., *Charter to William Penn, and Laws of the Province of Pennsylvania, Passed Between the Years 1682 and 1700* (Harrisburg: Lane S. Hart, 1879), p. 142.

ning, knitting, or sewing for the girls. Schools would be provided "in all towns and cities," to be supported, first, by the rents from lands set aside as endowment (one thousand acres would be assigned to each school), and, second, by the work of the students, who would produce cloth, the boys (with their fathers) cultivating flax and hemp and the girls (with their mothers) spinning and weaving it. And interestingly enough these "public schools"—they were so called only to contrast them with "private" familial education—would cater to poor as well as rich, to Indians as well as colonists, and, at least so far as can be determined, to children of all religious persuasions.[4]

Nothing resembling Budd's plan was adopted; indeed, aside from the employment of Enoch Flower in 1683 and the establishment of the Friends' Public School—later the William Penn Charter School —in 1689, the provincial authorities did little to realize the educational aspirations of the founder, leaving to the Yearly Meeting of Philadelphia and the various monthly meetings of the province the actual responsibility for establishing and maintaining schools. The meetings assumed their responsibilities with the utmost seriousness, generally using voluntary subscriptions and tuition rates to support their teachers and often using the meetinghouses themselves as schools until separate buildings could be erected. By mid-eighteenth century, there were some fifty particular meetings in Pennsylvania, organized under seventeen monthly meetings; and of these a goodly majority—possibly as many as forty—were conducting schools.[5]

Given the clear Quaker position on human equality, there was one realm in which the outward thrust of Quaker education stood in sharp contrast to any notion of "guardedness," and that was with respect to the schooling of Negroes and Indians. George Fox himself had written explicitly and forthrightly of the Quaker responsibility to teach "Indians and Negroes, and all others" how Christ had died for all men. And Penn, though he acquiesced in slavery in the province and assumed a generally paternalistic attitude toward black men and red men alike, had often reiterated the Christian obligation

---

[4] Thomas Budd, *Good Order Established in Pennsilvania & New-Jersey in America* [1685], in *Gowans' Bibliotheca Americana* (New York: William Gowans, 1845), pp. 339-343. Note Budd's interesting reference to Andrew Yarranton's *England's Improvement by Sea and Land* (London: R. Everingham, 1677), which advanced a plea for workhouse schools where children might early be turned into producers of wealth for themselves, their families, and their country.

[5] Thomas Woody, *Early Quaker Education in Pennslyvania* (New York: Teachers College, Columbia University, 1920), pp. 270-271 and *passim*.

to proffer the gospel to all human beings. During the eighteenth century, Quaker teachers such as John Woolman and Anthony Benezet went far beyond Penn, arguing the unmitigated evil of slavery, describing the calamitous conditions among the enslaved Negroes in the colonies, and calling for their manumission and education. Given the traditional Quaker opposition to slavery and the character of the Pennsylvania economy, there was never a large black population in the province, the number reaching around three thousand in 1750. So far as can be determined, many were tutored in the homes of their masters, while a few actually attended schools with whites, though descriptions of the conditions under which they attended are lacking. And in Philadelphia, where the concentration of blacks made possible the establishment of separate schools, one was actually started in 1758, under the auspices of Thomas Bray's Associates, an English philanthropic society, and another in 1770, largely through the efforts of Benezet, who presided over it during the last two years of his life.[6]

Penn's policy of toleration, his own active recruitment of settlers on the Continent, and the common tendencies toward quietism that the Quakers shared with the Mennonites, the Amish, the Dunkers, and the Schwenkfelders, led to the immigration of large numbers of these and other Anabaptists to Pennsylvania. Like the Quakers, these sectarians brought with them concepts of a guarded education that envisioned closely allied efforts of home, meetinghouse, and school, and amid the benevolent cultural conditions of Pennsylvania the educational activities of these sects throve in the eighteenth century. Like the Quakers, too, they eschewed a learned ministry in favor of inspired brethren who knew their Scripture well. Yet they did spawn schools wherever they settled, and they managed to produce from within their ranks the teachers to oversee them. Among the most able of these teachers were Francis Daniel Pastorius, a cultivated Frankfurt lawyer who migrated to Pennsylvania in 1683 and presided over the founding of Germantown, and Christopher Dock, who came to the colony around 1714 and shortly thereafter opened a school on the Skippack Creek in Montgomery County, beginning a teaching career that, with minor interruptions, lasted until his death in 1771.

Pastorius taught at the Friends' Public School from 1698 to 1700,

6 "Memoir of the Life of George Fox," *The Friends' Library*, I (1837), 79. See also George Fox's sensitive understanding of the plight of the slave family denied the privilege of monogamous marriage in *Gospel Family-Order, Being a Short Discourse Concerning the Ordering of Families, Both of Whites, Blacks and Indians* (1671), pp. 17-18.

and then served from 1702 until shortly before his passing in 1720 as master of the newly founded subscription school at Germantown. He was himself superbly educated in the classics and virtually encyclopedic in his interests, but there is evidence that, like Penn, he had moved by 1700 toward a much more utilitarian view of the proper education of children. Dock's schools were well known among the Germans of the Schuylkill Valley, and from the descriptions of a posthumous treatise called *Schulordnung* (*School Management*), which his friend Christopher Saur prevailed upon him to write, it is clear that a gentle benevolence suffused his classroom ("how I treat the children with love that they both love and fear me"), that a modified monitorial system, by which older students (called *Wächter*, or guards) helped in the instruction of the younger, was in operation, and that religious music played as central a role in the curriculum as it did in the larger life of the sects themselves. Most important, perhaps, Dock managed to deal with children of various religious persuasions without ignoring Christian doctrine on the one hand or exciting sectarian controversy on the other. Given the heterogeneous population of eighteenth-century Pennsylvania, his experience was doubtless representative, in that schools started by one or another of the sects or denominations more often than not found themselves catering to a diverse clientele. As such, the *Schulordnung* stands as one of the earliest systematic discussions of what was to be the characteristic American problem of common schooling in a pluralistic society, though it is interesting to note that while Dock's schools were religiously diverse they were ethnically homogeneous, in a community where Germans were a minority group.[7]

In light of these developments, it may be that the traditional harsh judgment of the Quaker educational effort in eighteenth-century Pennsylvania is far from wholly justified. True, the opposition of George Fox and others to the heathen authors in general and to the education provided by the Anglican leadership in particular did become in some Quaker quarters a general opposition to all learning; and true, too, the Quakers in Pennsylvania, unlike their Puritan predecessors in New England, failed to realize their own early aspirations to widespread civil support for education. Yet there was considerable schooling in Pennsylvania and the Quakers contributed more than their share of effort and money.

Rufus Jones, the Quaker historian of the colonial Quakers, has

[7] Martin G. Brumbaugh, *The Life and Works of Christopher Dock* (Philadelphia: J. B. Lippincott Company, 1908), pp. 124, 121, 56.

called them to task for their failure to establish institutions "adapted to the right education of Quaker youth, as Harvard and Yale were to the education of the Puritan youth," arguing that had they done so they would have won that commanding place in American civilization of which their early history gave promise. Yet he himself praises the colonial Quakers for the quality of life produced among the rank and file of their membership and for the quality of character manifested in the outstanding examples of their leadership, not realizing that it was Quaker education in the largest sense that helped produce such men. Moreover, Jones fails to recognize that what the Quakers permitted to come forth by way of educational diversity in Pennsylvania may have been quite as worthy in its own right as what their Puritan cousins mandated in New England— perhaps more so in view of the long-range destiny of the North American continent. And who can deny in any case the Quaker mark on much that did come forth? George Fox urged in his auto- biography the establishment of schools to teach children whatever things were "civil and useful in the creation"; a century later, Ben- jamin Franklin proposed an academy to teach young people what- ever was "most useful and most ornamental." Franklin was no Quaker, but his academy did come into being in a Quaker city that under Quaker leadership had become a thriving hub of the empire. And that is no small tribute to a people as viciously persecuted as any in history, who, when they themselves gained power, treated others only as they themselves had wanted to be dealt with.[8]

II

Mysticism and evangelicism, as Ronald Knox pointed out in his classic analysis of *Enthusiasm*, are related and occasionally similar phenomena but actually quite different in their inspiration, the former bypassing the theology of grace and concentrating on the God within, the latter acutely conscious of man's fallen state and ever concerned with redemption. And, just as the mysticism of the sectarians had its origins in Europe and found fertile soil in the open spaces of America, so too did the more evangelical pietism that

[8] Rufus M. Jones, *The Quakers in the American Colonies* (London: Macmillan and Co., 1911), pp. xxvii, xxix, xxxi; *The Journal of George Fox*, edited by Norman Penney (2 vols.; Cambridge: Cambridge University Press, 1911), II, 119; *The Papers of Benjamin Franklin*, edited by Leonard W. Labaree and Whitfield J. Bell, Jr. (13+ vols.; New Haven: Yale University Press, 1959-   ), III, 404.

emanated from Utrecht, Lingen, Frankfurt, and Halle transplant itself to the New World and flourish amidst traditional churches seeking to redefine their role in the wilderness.[9]

The chief agents in the transplantation are well known. One of the earliest was the Dutch pastor Theodorus Jacobus Frelinghuysen, who accepted the call of a number of Dutch Reformed churches in New Jersey's Raritan Valley in 1720 and almost immediately became a source of theological and ecclesiastical controversy. Trained at the University of Lingen and deeply affected by the pietism of the Dutch Voetians, Frelinghuysen launched upon his duties with unprecedented earnestness, stressing inner religion over outward conformity, demanding that his parishioners "lay aside all pride, haughtiness, and ideas of inherent worthiness, and humble themselves deeply before the Lord," and insisting that only penitent, believing, upright, and converted persons be invited to the Lord's table. Charges of heresy burst upon him but Frelinghuysen managed to contend with them, and meanwhile his congregations flourished and his influence spread, not only within the circles of the Dutch Reformed but also among powerful Presbyterian protagonists such as Gilbert Tennent, who apparently took Frelinghuysen as a model for his preaching.[10]

Tennent, of course, had been well prepared for Frelinghuysen's influence by twenty years of systematic education under his father, William Tennent, first in Ireland and later in various manses in the American colonies. The elder Tennent, a former priest of the Church of Ireland, had migrated to America sometime between 1716 and 1718 as a result of his disenchantment with episcopacy and Arminianism and had affiliated with the Presbyterian Synod of Philadelphia. In a succession of posts in New York and Pennsylvania, he had preached with evangelical zeal the doctrine that only the truly converted can properly partake of the Lord's Supper. Equally important, perhaps, he had created a Log College—so called in derision —for the training of like-minded clergymen, among them his sons. From the Log College, as well as from dozens of other academies maintained by Scottish and Scotch-Irish immigrants and their disciples, a vehement evangelicism suffused the Presbyterian church,

9 Ronald A. Knox, *Enthusiasm* (Oxford: Clarendon Press, 1950), p. 581.
10 Theodorus Jacobus Frelinghuysen, *Sermons*, translated by William Demarest (New York: Board of Publication of the Reformed Protestant Dutch Church, 1856), pp. 34, 51 ff.

splitting it into Old Side and New Side factions and drastically transforming its character and doctrine.

Paralleling the work of Frelinghuysen among the Dutch Reformed and of the Tennents among the Presbyterians were the efforts of Michael Schlatter among the German Reformed and of Henry Melchior Mühlenberg among the Lutherans. Both men had imbibed the heady pietism of the Continental awakenings, and indeed Mühlenberg had been intimately associated with the Franckes at Halle and had actually been persuaded to accept the call to America in part by the enthusiasm of August Hermann Francke's son, Gotthilf. Once in America, both men, like Frelinghuysen and the Tennents, traveled extensively among the dispersed congregations of their respective churches, awakening zeal in place of lethargy, preaching the centrality of the conversion experience, encouraging the establishment of schools and churches, and arranging for a dependable supply of well-trained ministers.

Finally, there were the culminating efforts of George Whitefield, whose seven itinerations through America between 1738 and 1770 took him to every quarter of the seaboard colonies, from Portsmouth, New Hampshire, to Savannah, Georgia, and brought him into contact with virtually every sect and denomination. An Anglican priest by ordination, a Methodist by affiliation, and a Calvinist by orientation, Whitefield was quintessentially undenominational in outlook, preaching the doctrine of the new birth, or conversion, to huge audiences of every conceivable composition under every conceivable sponsorship. As William Howland Kenney III has suggested, he was in many ways the first authentic American hero, eliciting the most extravagant praise from the most unlikely quarters. One ecstatic listener who signed himself "Juventus" spoke for an unprecedented number of Americans when he wrote in the *The New-York Weekly Journal* in 1739:

> Whitefield! that great, that pleasing name
>   Has all my soul possessed:
> For sure some seraph from above
>   Inspires his godlike breast.
>
> He comes commissioned from on high
>   The gospel to proclaim;
> And through the wide extended world
>   To spread the Saviour's name.

See! See! He comes, the heavenly sounds
   Flow from his charming tongue;
Rebellious men are seized with fear
   With deep conviction stung.

Listening we stand with vast surprise,
   While rapture chains our powers,
Charmed with the music of his voice,
   Know not the passing hours.

Blasphemers hear the dreadful sound
   Inspired with trembling awe;
While he declares their crimson guilt,
   And loud proclaims the law.

While, Whitefield, to thy sacred strain
   Surprised we listen still.
Immortal heights we seem to reach,
   Celestial transports feel.

Approach ye mortals here below
   And flock around the song:
With pleasure hear the Saviour's name
   Sound from a mortal tongue.[11]

The essential effect of men such as Frelinghuysen, the Tennents, Schlatter, Mühlenberg, and Whitefield was to articulate, strengthen, and confirm a developing autochthonous evangelicism that was already in evidence at the beginning of the eighteenth century as one response of the colonial churches to the predicament in which they found themselves. If New England may be taken as an example, several problems had converged to create a genuinely precarious situation for Congregationalism some two or three generations after its emergence as the "New England way." In the first place, there were the difficulties implicit in recruiting new members for gathered churches: the children and grandchildren of the original settlers were simply not demonstrating the appropriate evidences of election in sufficient numbers to keep the congregations alive, and the problem was only exacerbated by the spread of religious alternatives, especially Anglicanism after the 1690's.

[11] *The New-York Weekly Journal*, no. 311, November 26, 1739. The verses were reprinted in *The American Weekly Mercury*, no. 1040, December 6, 1739.

The halfway covenant, developed between 1657 and 1662, under which the children of covenanters could become birthright members of the parents' congregations (though they were denied the Lord's Supper until they themselves had received indication of grace), represented one effort to deal with the situation; but it in no way stemmed a widespread sense of religious decline, at least on the part of the clergy. Toward the end of the seventeenth century, a number of New England churches held "harvests," or designated periods during which halfway covenanters might own the covenant in full, the assumption being that participation in Communion would not in itself guarantee salvation but would at least assist the participant toward the ultimate experience of grace. From there, it was but a short step for some ministers—Solomon Stoddard of Northampton was the leading example—to extend the opportunity to families that had not previously owned the covenant at all. The emphasis during these "harvests" on the sort of preaching that would call forth the experience of conversion in as many of the unregenerate as possible had already made revivalism a somewhat familiar part of the religious scene by the time the pietism of Voetius, Spener, Francke, Frelinghuysen, and the Tennents began to be known among the intellectuals.

Compounding these ecclesiastical problems was the closely related theological problem of what actually constituted evidence of true regeneration in the first place. From the beginning, the New England clergy had insisted that good works were merely the adornments of the elect and not the instruments of their election, that only the personal experience of grace from heaven itself could be the mark of true salvation. Yet, if precise and widely shared definitions of the nature of that personal experience were difficult to obtain during the early days of the "city upon a hill," they were well-nigh impossible to achieve among the "mixed multitudes" of the eighteenth century, distracted as they were by religious alternatives on the one hand and by earthquakes, epidemics, wars, and incessant population movement on the other.

It was amidst this context of uncertainty, aggravated by a widespread sense of moral and spiritual decline, by a general tendency toward formalism on the part of now well-established churches, and by the simple drabness and loneliness of life on the frontier, that the awakenings of the 1730's and 1740's came to pass. The chief figure, of course, was Jonathan Edwards, who played a central role in the revivals themselves and whose theologizing in connection with the revivals remains pre-eminent in the sphere of eighteenth-century American thought. Born in 1703 and educated at Yale during the era of Samuel Johnson's tutorship, Edwards was one of the first to taste the delights of the Dummer library, notably the writings of Newton, Locke, and the Cambridge Platonist Ralph Cudworth. It was during the Yale period, too, that he underwent his conversion, "a sweet burning in my heart," as he described it, and began his intellectual odyssey toward a vigorous subjective idealism that would demonstrate the "gross mistake" of "those who think material things the most substantial beings, and spirits more like a shadow." Possessed of a "sense of the glorious majesty and grace of God," which seemed to him flatly to deny a modish deism on the one hand and a fashionable Anglicanism on the other, Edwards dedicated his life to comprehending, teaching, and acquiescing in God's unqualified sovereignty, excellency, and infinitude.[12]

Graduation from Yale in 1720 was followed by two years of theological study in New Haven, a brief ministry in New York, a tutorship at Yale, and then a call to the pulpit at Northampton, where he served first as colleague to his grandfather Solomon Stoddard, and then, upon Stoddard's death in 1729, as pastor. It was in Northampton over the next two decades that "the spirit of God began extraordinarily to set in, and wonderfully to work" among Edwards' parishioners. A pervasive concern over matters religious gripped the townspeople, especially the young; theological discussion was ubiquitous; and conversions multiplied. By the summer of 1735 the town "seemed to be full of the presence of God."[13]

Other towns in Massachusetts and Connecticut and "some parts of the Jerseys" were similarly gripped; and as word spread of the Northampton revivals Edwards himself became much in demand as a preacher. Meanwhile, his sermons began to be published and read and with them his more elaborate dissertations, particularly *A Treatise Concerning Religious Affections* (1746), in which he developed his characteristic argument that "a great part of true religion lies in the affections" and that the true Christian possesses a "new spiritual sense" generated by the Holy Spirit that manifests itself in gracious affections, or, in effect, tendencies toward sainthood.[14]

12 *The Works of President Edwards*, edited by Sereno E. Dwight (10 vols.; New York: S. Converse, 1829-1830), I, 61, 708.

13 *A Faithful Narrative of the Surprizing Work of God* (1737), in *ibid.*, IV, 21, 23.

14 Jonathan Edwards, *A Treatise Concerning Religious Affections*, edited by John E. Smith (New Haven: Yale University Press, 1959), pp. 96, 271.

For all his identification with enthusiasm, it is clear that by 1742, when Edwards began work on the *Treatise*, he was already trying to steer a middle course between unreserved partisans of evangelicism such as George Whitefield and unreserved critics such as Charles Chauncy. In many ways he succeeded, going farther than any contemporary toward establishing the intellectual respectability of "religion of the heart." Yet, by the time he began his efforts to moderate, the awakenings had become national in scope, undenominational in character, and quite independent of the intellectual formulations of any particular individual—even Whitefield. New Light factions were appearing in all the traditional churches, and, indeed, within many a particular congregation or parish; and inspired clergymen, both tutored and untutored, were coming forth to lead them. Clearly, evangelicism had answered a fundamental need of a significant segment of the colonial population, and, though it would wax and wane from decade to decade and assume vastly differing forms at different times and places during the eighteenth century, it would remain an established feature of American life.

The awakenings have been portrayed as religious, social, and political movements, but never as the large-scale educational movements they obviously were. In their very essence, they transformed the churches as teaching institutions. In the first place, they radically attacked the dominant legalism that seemed in every region to render traditional preaching tediously formalistic. Benjamin Franklin described this legalism in his *Autobiography* in a passage sharply criticizing the sermons of Jedediah Andrews, minister of the Presbyterian church in Philadelphia: "His discourses were chiefly either polemic arguments, or explications of the peculiar doctrines of our sect, and were all to me very dry, uninteresting, and unedifying, since not a single moral principle was inculcated or enforced, their aim seeming to be rather to make us good Presbyterians than good citizens." Of course, Andrews' aim was clear: preaching to a mixed congregation of "divers nations of different sentiments" amidst keen denominational rivalry, he saw his task as one of holding his congregation together by teaching a piety emphasizing correct doctrine and good behavior from a Presbyterian point of view. For many members of his congregation, however, that piety proved acutely unsatisfactory as an answer to the gnawing question "What shall I do to be saved?" The outcome, in Philadelphia and in the colonies at large, was the painful "religious dilemma" of the 1730's and 1740's, the crisis that afforded the opportunity for the revivalists.[15]

In place of the traditional sermons of men like Andrews, the Frelinghuysens and Tennents and Edwardses and Whitefields adopted a radically new preaching style that awesomely portrayed the terrors of hell, insistently held the mirror to the vile hearts of the unconverted, and ruthlessly exposed the false assumptions that commonly led sinners to think themselves saved. The emphasis was always, of course, on stimulating that new birth that would mean another victory for Christ. A contemporary description of Gilbert Tennent in the pulpit conveys the character and power of such preaching at the peak of the Great Awakening: "He seemed to have no regard to please the eyes of his hearers with agreeable gesture, nor their ears with delivery, nor their fancy with language; but to aim directly at their hearts and consciences, to lay open their ruinous delusions, show them their numerous, secret, hypocritical shifts in religion, and drive them out of every deceitful refuge wherein they made themselves easy, with the form of godliness without the power." The responses to Tennent's preaching are legendary. Members of a congregation would weep, sob, and cry out in terror, falling to their knees and calling for salvation. And his younger brothers John and William literally sank into comas—with William actually pronounced dead by a physician and prepared for burial—before reviving to report the indescribable beauty of the conversion experience.[16]

The chief differences between the Old Light and New Light factions in the various traditional churches turned in the last analysis on the validity of such conversion experiences. For the Old Lights, the terror of the experience was little more than a delusion: correct doctrine and good works were the essence of piety and the marks of grace. For the New Lights, correct doctrine and good works could themselves be delusions unless an individual had been truly regenerated and given evidence of saving grace. For the Old Lights, education and nurture were crucial to piety; for the New Lights, these were secondary to the transformation wrought by conversion

---

[15] *The Autobiography of Benjamin Franklin,* edited by Leonard W. Labaree, Ralph L. Ketcham, Helen C. Boatfield, and Helene H. Finerman (New Haven: Yale University Press, 1964), p. 147; Jedediah Andrews to Benjamin Colman, April 7, 1729 (Colman mss., Massachusetts Historical Society, Boston).

[16] Thomas Prince, Jr., *The Christian History, Containing Accounts of the Revival and Propagation of Religion in Great-Britain and America &c. for the Years 1744-5,* Vol. II (Boston: S. Kneeland and T. Green, 1745), p. 385.

—indeed, in the case of the more radical New Lights, irrelevant and even deleterious to piety. Thus the charge of the Old Lights that their enthusiastic opponents "disparaged humane reason and rational preaching"; and thus, too, the efforts of some of the New Light clergy, notably Jonathan Edwards, to distinguish between their own theology and the theology of those they deemed truly misguided enthusiasts.[17]

Inseparable from the Old Light–New Light controversy were questions of who would teach and who would be taught within the church. The first issue was boldly raised by Gilbert Tennent in his famous Nottingham, New Jersey, sermon of 1740 on *The Danger of an Unconverted Ministry*. In Tennent's view, only God's call could properly bring a man to the ministry, and this quite apart from the action of any church judicatory. Beyond that, God's call would obviously be addressed only to those who had themselves undergone regeneration. "Natural men have no call of God to the ministerial work . . . ," Tennent insisted; "our Lord will not make men ministers, until they follow him." The effect of such a view on Presbyterianism in 1740 was to tear the church asunder: ministers were branded unconverted and forced either to mount a successful defense of their regeneracy or resign; congregations were divided into hostile camps, with factions frequently seceding in order to gain the freedom to call their own ministers. And, through it all, the cacophony of charges and countercharges mounted, with the question of who had the keys to the kingdom inevitably becoming, as it always had been, the question of who had the right to educate.[18]

Obversely, there was the question of who would be admitted to the church to be educated; and here, at the very least, there was ambivalence among the New Lights. On the one hand, they deeply believed that only the converted should enjoy the privilege and blessing of the Lord's Supper and that only gathered congregations could constitute a true church. They were opposed in this respect to the easy Arminianism they associated with eighteenth-century Anglicanism, and they mounted in their opposition what might be described as a second dissenter revolution that would purify the existing churches and originate new ones free of corruption. On the

17 *The Sentiments and Resolution of an Association of Ministers Convened at Weymouth, Jan. 15, 1744/5 Concerning the Reverend Mr. George Whitefield* (Boston: T. Fleet, 1745), p. 5.

18 Gilbert Tennent, *The Danger of an Unconverted Ministry* (Philadelphia: Benjamin Franklin, 1740), pp. 7-8.

other hand, the New Lights in the very nature of their enterprise reached out to new communicants, seeking to educate them to Christ. The ambivalence is patent in the preaching of Frelinghuysen and Tennent, who argued at the same time that man is totally helpless before God and that he needs to "choose" Christ and "undertake" regeneration. Tennent even went so far as to conclude one sermon with a reading list designed to guide the penitent toward conversion. While arguing theoretically that God in his infinite wisdom grants grace, the revivalists taught men actively to seek grace through their own efforts, and, indeed, to recognize it when bestowed.[19]

This tendency was especially apparent in the New Light posture toward young people, who in the very nature of things constituted a prime source of unconverted souls. Resident ministers like Stoddard and Edwards addressed special preaching to them and even developed new definitions of early piety to satisfy New Light canons—thus the portrait of Phebe Bartlet, in Edwards' *A Faithful Narrative of the Surprizing Work of God* (1737), who shortly after her fourth birthday began to manifest all the classic signs of repentance, retiring frequently for secret prayer, displaying an overwhelming interest in matters religious, reciting the catechism incessantly, listening enrapt to Edwards' preaching, and generally having "very much of the fear of God before her eyes, and an extraordinary dread of sin against him." The great itinerants also addressed themselves directly to the young, with Whitefield on one occasion in Boston advising children to choose Christ and go to heaven alone if their parents refused to join them.[20]

Inherent in these efforts were the thorny problems the New

---

[19] Frelinghuysen, *Sermons*, pp. 117-118, 121-122, 291-294; and Gilbert Tennent, *Solemn Warning to the Secure World, from the God of Terrible Majesty* (Boston: S. Kneeland and T. Green, 1735), p. 191.

[20] Edwards, *Faithful Narrative*, in *Works*, IV, 67. Edwards' companion delineations of adult piety were his sketches of Sarah Pierrepont (his wife) and David Brainerd; see *Works*, I, 114-115, 171-190; X, 31-32. Some contemporaries took a dim view of youthful conversion, arguing that the religious enthusiasm of children derived from their ignorance and was ultimately a "delusion"; see, for example, John Smith to James Pemberton, July 20, 1741 (Pemberton mss., Historical Society of Pennsylvania, Philadelphia), commenting critically on a letter in *The American Weekly Mercury* for July 9-16, 1741, which praised the work of the New Light clergy among young children. William Howland Kenney III develops statistical support for the preponderance of the young and the female in New Light congregations in "George Whitefield and Colonial Revivalism: The Social Sources of Charismatic Authority, 1737-1770" (unpublished doctoral thesis, University of Pennsylvania, 1966), pp. 149-153. See also Cedrick B. Cowing, "Sex and Preaching in the Great Awakening," *American Quarterly*, XX (1968), 624-644.

Lights faced of relating conversion and nurture, of defining the human effort that would follow God's action in bestowing grace. On the one hand, there were matters of doctrine to be clarified and communicated. Thus, for example, Gilbert Tennent in 1744 published a volume of twenty-three sermons on the essentials of Scripture for the newly converted. "The knowledge of divine truths in their due series and connection, much confirms our belief of them, and thereby inflames our love, and influences our practice," he wrote in the introduction. And elsewhere in his preaching he dealt again and again with the principles and practices of the believing Christian. In this respect, the New Lights taught a piety following conversion that was not unlike what the Old Lights taught preceding conversion.[21]

On the other hand, there was the whole arsenal of institutions the New Lights developed as adjuncts to the church for the war on Satan: the private associations of families, the societies of young covenant-owners, and the neighborhood meetings for prayer and self-examination modeled in part after the pietistic societies of August Hermann Francke and in part after the societies for the reformation of manners that grew up in late seventeenth-century England. Such organizational efforts vastly strengthened the educational thrust of the churches, which not only revivified their own internal teaching under the influence of the awakenings but also extended anew the penetration of that teaching into households, communities, and colleges. True, the radical piety of the New Light churches often clashed with familial and political authority—recall Whitefield's invitation to the young. True, too, some of the more radical enthusiasts were quite ready to substitute inspiration for any traditional concept of nurture. But in the end the force of the awakenings was to enhance the educative influence of the churches and through them to strengthen the role of Christian teaching and works in the everyday life of the colonists.

Finally, for all the contrast between conversion and nurture, at least one additional point remains clear: people not nurtured in religion care not what they must do to be saved. In this respect the awakenings ultimately testify to the success rather than the failure of religious education in the previous generation. Especially was this

---

[21] Gilbert Tennent, *Twenty-Three Sermons upon the Chief End of Man* (Philadelphia: William Bradford, 1744), "The Preface."

so in New England, where, as Lawrence Gene Lavengood has demonstrated, the quality of intellectual debate over the awakenings was surely superior. "I am an old light new snuffed," the Reverend Solomon Reed of Framingham, Massachusetts, exclaimed in the course of a debate with members of a rival congregation, pointing to the renewal that revivalism gave traditional as well as novel piety. In the last analysis, it was less that the revivalists downgraded religious education than that they changed its pedagogy. As in earlier dissenter revolutions, prophecy replaced edification as the central technique of churches once again awakened to their mission in the world.[22]

III

The religious crisis of the 1720's and 1730's was only partly one of precept and purpose; it was also in many ways a crisis of leadership. A century after settlement, it was abundantly clear that the metropolis was neither able nor prepared to supply the colonies with ministers in the numbers needed, while the colonies on their side seemed ill-equipped to undertake the task. The result, in every region and among all denominations, was a growing disparity between the number of congregations in need of pastors and the supply of available clergymen. In New England, where Harvard's efforts had been supplemented by the founding of Yale in 1701 for the "upholding and propagating of the Christian Protestant religion by a succession of learned and orthodox men," and where the two institutions together managed to graduate some 850 ministers between 1701 and 1740, shortages persisted, particularly in the outlying settlements. And, in the South, the establishment of the College of William and Mary in 1693 as, *inter alia*, "a seminary of ministers of the gospel" did little to alleviate the chronic undersupply of Anglican clergymen, given the paucity of graduates and the continuing absence of a colonial bishop. Yet the situation was most acute, perhaps, in the middle colonies, where the Presbytery of Philadelphia seemed constantly to be reaching east to the British Isles and north to New England for ministers but never quite able to obtain them in sufficient numbers, where at least half the Anglican rectorships went for

22 J. H. Temple, *History of Framingham, Massachusetts* (Framingham: The Town of Framingham, 1887), p. 214.

years without incumbents, and where a handful of Reformed and Lutheran ministers desperately attempted to serve thousands of communicants.[23]

It was into this crisis of leadership that Gilbert Tennent hurled his warnings on *The Danger of an Unconverted Ministry* and advanced his proposals to remedy the situation. "The most likely method to stock the church with a faithful ministry, in the present situation of things," he advised, "the public academies being so much corrupted and abused generally, is, to encourage private schools, or seminaries of learning, which are under the care of skillful and experienced Christians; in which those only should be admitted, who upon strict examination, have in the judgment of a reasonable charity, the plain evidences of experimental religion. Pious and experienced youths, who have a good natural capacity, and great desires after the ministerial work, from good motives, might be sought for, and found up and down in the country, and put to private schools of the prophets; especially in such places, where the public ones are not."[24]

What Tennent was urging, of course, was more institutions of the sort his father, William Tennent, had conducted over the years for the training of a New Light clergy. The evidence on the conduct and curriculum of Tennent's school is fragmentary. It was apparently begun sometime after he took up permanent residence at Neshaminy, Pennsylvania, in 1727, and was patently founded on the educational program he had been conducting for his sons in the years before—recall that Gilbert, the eldest of the four, had been licensed to preach by the Presbytery of Philadelphia in 1725. But the first clear indication of the school's significance came in 1739, after George Whitefield visited Tennent at Neshaminy and described the institution in glowing terms. "It happens very providentially," Whitefield wrote in his *Journal*, "that Mr. Tennent and his brethren are appointed to be a presbytery by the synod, so that they intend breeding up gracious youths, and sending them out from time to time into

23 Franklin Bowditch Dexter, ed., *Documentary History of Yale University Under the Original Charter of the Collegiate School of Connecticut, 1701-1745* (New Haven: Yale University Press, 1916), p. 20; Bailey B. Burritt, *Professional Distribution of College and University Graduates* (Washington, D.C.: Government Printing Office, 1912), pp. 79, 83; and Henry Hartwell, James Blair, and Edward Chilton, *The Present State of Virginia, and the College,* edited by Hunter Dickinson Farish (Charlottesville: University Press of Virginia, 1964), p. 72.

24 Tennent, *Danger of an Unconverted Ministry*, p. 16.

our Lord's vineyard. The place wherein the young men study now is, in contempt, called the college. It is a log house, about twenty feet long, and nearly as many broad; and, to me, it seemed to resemble the schools of the old prophets. That their habitations were mean, and that they sought not great things for themselves, is plain from that passage of Scripture, wherein we are told, that at the feast of the sons of the prophets, one of them put on the pot, whilst the others went to fetch some herbs out of the field. From this despised place seven or eight worthy ministers of Jesus have lately been sent forth; more are almost ready to be sent; and a foundation is now laying for the instruction of many others."[25]

Beyond Whitefield's description, what can be said about the Log College must be inferred from the prior training of its master and the subsequent performance of its alumni. Tennent is known to have attended the University of Edinburgh in the early 1690's on the eve of the Scottish Enlightenment; and, though the university had not yet entered upon the succession of reforms that would later grow out of the Parliamentary Visitation Commission of 1690, it had already begun to quicken intellectually under the general influence of students returning from the Continental universities, notably, Leiden, after the thaw of 1689, and under the particular influence of professors such as David Gregory, the mathematician, and Robert Sibbald, the physician. There is evidence that Tennent did obtain a thorough classical training, and, for all the derision directed against the Log College, it is probable that Tennent's instruction in divinity was demanding and systematic, if not, perhaps, wholly traditional. As for the alumni, they were as dedicated a lot as issued from any institution during the 1730's and 1740's: most of the twenty-one who have been fairly clearly identified became leading New Light preachers; at least three, Samuel Blair, Samuel Finley, and William Robinson, went on to organize schools of their own; and one, Dr. John Redman, became a physician.[26]

The model for Tennent's Log College and for the host of

25 *Whitefield's Journals*, edited by William Wale (London: Henry J. Drane, [1905]), p. 351.

26 Thomas C. Pears, Jr., and Guy S. Klett, "Documentary History of William Tennent, and the Log College," *Journal of the Department of History (Presbyterian Historical Society)*, XXVIII (1950), 199-200; and A. Alexander, *Bibliographical Sketches of the Founder, and Principal Alumni of the Log College* (Princeton, N.J.: J. T. Robinson, 1845).

similar institutions founded over the next half-century by Congregationalists, Dutch Reformed, Baptists, and Methodists as well as by
Presbyterians, was patently derived from the dissenting academies of
contemporary England and Ireland. Established as one major
response to the odious requirements of the Act of Uniformity (1662)
and the Five Mile Act (1665), the academies had provided an outlet
for the considerable talents of numerous ejected ministers and at
the same time had served as a source of renewed leadership for the
Nonconformist churches. Obviously receptive to influences from the
Reformed universities of France, Holland, and Scotland, many of
the academies—though by no means all—had become centers of
intellectual and educational innovation, introducing English as the
language of instruction, the sciences and politics as suitable curricular
content, and liberty of inquiry as a fundamental academic principle.
In form and character, they were almost infinitely variegated. Some,
such as Richard Frankland's at Rathmell or Francis Hutcheson's at
Dublin, were conducted as individual enterprises; others, such as
David Jardine's at Abergavenny, were established under denominational auspices, in that particular instance, by the Congregational
Fund Board. A few, like Abergavenny, were open only to theological
students; most, on the other hand, trained men for other professions
as well. Certain of the tutors, such as David Jennings of Wellclose
Square, were explicitly committed to orthodoxy; others, including
Joseph Priestley of Warrington, who later immigrated to America,
were well known for their liberalism. Perhaps the one generalization
that can be made is that the academies were in their very nature
alternatives to established patterns of higher education; and, while
Oxford and Cambridge were by no means as somnolent in the eighteenth century as some historians have portrayed them, it was the
academies that tended to break the fairly traditional molds of the
higher learning.

In England, however, the dissenting character of the academies
inevitably limited their ultimate role and influence; in America, particularly in New Jersey, Pennsylvania, and Delaware, where there were
no colleges representing "standing orders" of religious and civil
government, there was relative freedom after 1689 for academies to
expand in number, scope, and power. And the result was an unprecedented multiplication of institutions that significantly enlarged
opportunity for schooling in the colonies and in the process substantially altered the content and character of education. Douglas

Milton Sloan has authenticated at least fifty-two academies maintained by Presbyterian clergymen alone between 1727, when Tennent settled at Neshaminy, and 1783, when the Presbyterians founded four new institutions (two colleges and two academies), and there were doubtless more; certainly no other denomination even approached that figure, though the total number of academies maintained by ministers of all faiths may well have exceeded a hundred. By 1783, the academy as an institution was rapidly diversifying in format and emphasis, and the practice of legislative chartering was becoming widespread, creating an essentially new situation for which any statistics would carry radically new significance.[27]

One of the most interesting aspects of the Presbyterian academies was their strong tie with the Scottish universities, either directly, as alumni of Edinburgh or Glasgow came to the New World and established schools, or indirectly, as students of these alumni went on from academies in Ulster or America to found additional institutions of their own. Tennent, of course, was a case in point; so was Francis Alison, another alumnus of Edinburgh, who conducted an academy in his home at New London, Pennsylvania, from 1742 until 1752, when he moved to the Academy of Philadelphia; so too were Samuel Blair, who went on from the Log College to found an academy at Fagg's Manor in Pennsylvania, and Samuel Finley, who established an academy at Nottingham, Maryland, after his studies with Tennent. All four were expert classicists and all four had a hand in training some of the most distinguished Presbyterian clergymen of the eighteenth century. And Alison at least is known to have taught English grammar and composition (using *The Spectator* and *The Guardian* as models), belles-lettres, and natural and moral philosophy, along with the usual Latin and Greek, clearly reflecting the instruction he himself had had from John Stevenson at Edinburgh and from Francis Hutcheson, with whom he is thought to have studied either at the Dublin academy or during a period of residence at Glasgow.

Like their English and Irish counterparts, the American academies were almost infinitely variegated. Some, like Alison's at New London, were formally sponsored by a presbytery or synod; others,

27 Douglas Milton Sloan, "The Scottish Enlightenment and the American College Ideal: Early Princeton Traditions" (unpublished doctoral thesis, Columbia University, 1969), pp. 500-504.

like Joseph Bellamy's at Bethlehem, Connecticut, were conducted unofficially and privately by a single individual. Some, like Alison's, were probably as excellent and advanced in scholarship as any contemporary New World college; others were more elementary in character, serving essentially as preparatory institutions on the grammar-school level. In the unsystematized world of provincial education, there was need and opportunity for every venture.

Yet, given the shortage of certified ministers and the absence of powerful and long-established universities, it was virtually certain that some of the more advanced academies would themselves evolve into degree-granting institutions and that other degree-granting institutions would be founded *de novo;* and such indeed was the case. Thus, for example, the College of New Jersey may be said to have evolved from the work of Tennent's Log College, though in actuality there was no direct connection between the two institutions, and as a matter of fact plans for the college had to await the passing of the elder Tennent so that fear of possible competition would be eliminated. The seven men who "first concocted the plan and foundation of the college" included four New Light ministers of the recently founded Synod of New York and three influential laymen active in New York provincial affairs. The purpose, of course, was to insure a supply of clergymen for the new synod who could combine the zeal indicative of divine grace with solid academic learning. But the problem, since the founders did not wish to rely either on extant private academies or on a substantial scholarship program at Yale (which seemed to them to grow more rigidly traditional by the day), was to gain a broad enough constituency to make a regularly chartered college financially feasible and politically possible. They accomplished their goal, obtaining an initial charter in 1746 and a permanent charter two years later, but in the very process transformed the character of the projected institution by opening admission to adherents of all denominations, by dedicating it to the education of men aiming to be useful in other learned professions as well as in the ministry, and by moderating the New Light emphasis of its theological curriculum. The college opened in May, 1747, at Elizabethtown, New Jersey, under the tutelage of Jonathan Dickinson, who had maintained an academy there for years; and, though it was not to have its own expansive quarters at Nassau Hall for almost a decade, its very existence forced a corresponding transformation of the Presbyterian academies, both New Side and Old Side, which became in increasing measure preparatory institutions for the college that was now available.[28]

In a manner somewhat similar to the College of New Jersey, the College of Rhode Island emerged from the work of the Hopewell (New Jersey) Academy, founded in 1756 by the Philadelphia Association of Baptist Churches "for the promotion of learning amongst us." Under the leadership of the Reverend Isaac Eaton, the Baptist pastor at Hopewell, the academy was so successful in supplying preachers, lawyers, and physicians that the Philadelphia Association felt "encouraged to extend their designs of promoting literature in the society by erecting on some suitable part of this continent a college or university, which should be principally under the direction and government of the Baptists." In due course, Rhode Island was chosen as the colony "wherein education might be promoted, and superior learning obtained, free of any sectarian religious tests," and a twenty-four-year-old graduate of Hopewell who had gone on to complete his education at the College of New Jersey, James Manning, was named to lead the work. After more than a year of negotiations, a charter was obtained, once again, as with the College of New Jersey, considerably extending the purview and constituency of the project by broadening the curriculum, by excluding all sectarian opinion from the "public and classical instruction," by granting equal privileges to all Protestant denominations, and by specifying an interdenominational board of trustees that would include Quakers, Congregationalists, and Anglicans as well as Baptists. Shortly after obtaining legislative approval of the charter, Manning accepted a pulpit at Warren, Rhode Island, and organized a Latin school in that community; in 1765, when the first board of trustees elected Manning president, he simply added the few undergraduates to that institution, maintaining the College of Rhode Island in the parsonage, much as Dickinson and Burr had maintained the College of New Jersey. Only later, in 1770, did the college move to Providence and

---

[28] Jonathan Dickinson to unknown correspondent, March 3, 1747 (unpublished ms., Manuscript Division, Princeton University Library); and *An Account of the College of New-Jersey* (Woodbridge, N.J.: James Parker, 1764), pp. 6-10, 28, and *passim.*

to quarters of its own, modeled, not surprisingly, on Nassau Hall at Princeton.[29]

Somewhat the same dynamics were involved in the transformation of the Reverend Eleazar Wheelock's academy at Lebanon, Connecticut, into Dartmouth College, chartered in 1769 by the province of New Hampshire. Wheelock was a New Light Congregationalist minister, who found himself early caught up in the enthusiasm emanating from Northampton, and who later came more directly under the spell of Whitefield during the great itinerant's 1740 tour of New England. Wheelock's particular vocation turned out to be Christianizing the Indians, which he undertook to accomplish by tutoring selected Indian youths in his parsonage along with a small number of white youngsters aspiring to careers as missionaries. The venture was expensive and Wheelock became involved in large-scale fund-raising efforts in the British Isles; indeed, a pair of his agents, one an Indian alumnus of his academy named Samson Occom and the other a Connecticut minister named Nathaniel Whitaker, gathered over twelve thousand pounds in Great Britain between 1766 and 1768, possibly more than was raised by any other colonial school or college in the years preceding the Revolution. As with other institutions, the raising of the funds and the subsequent obtaining of a charter from the province of New Hampshire required a constant broadening of the enterprise, and, once again, the college that emerged at Hanover was far different in character and spirit from the academy that had existed at Lebanon.

One collegiate institution that grew *de novo* out of the awakenings was Queen's College, founded by a New Light faction of the Dutch Reformed church in New Jersey in 1766. The moving spirit in that enterprise was the Reverend Theodore Frelinghuysen, son of Theodorus Jacobus Frelinghuysen, who feared that the willingness of the Dutch pastors of New York City to unite with the Anglicans in the establishment of King's College in 1754 would ultimately threaten the very existence and identity of the Dutch Reformed church in America. In response, the younger Frelinghuysen called a

[29] *Minutes of the Philadelphia Baptist Association, from A.D. 1707, to A.D. 1807,* edited by A. D. Gillette (Philadelphia: American Baptist Publication Society), p. 74; David Howell, Memorandum of April 12, 1774 (David Howell mss., Brown University); Isaac Backus, *A Church History of New-England. Vol. II. Extending from 1690, to 1784* (Providence: John Carter, 1784), p. 235; "The Charter of 1764," in Walter C. Bronson, *The History of Brown University, 1764-1914* (Providence: published by the University, 1914), pp. 500-507.

conference of like-minded ministers and elders in 1755, which resolved after due deliberation "to plant a university or seminary for
young men destined for study in the learned languages and in the
liberal arts and who are to be instructed in the philosophical sciences;
also that it may be a school of the prophets in which young Levites
and Nazarites of God may be prepared to enter upon the sacred
ministerial office in the church of God." The usual long-drawn
negotiations—in this case on both sides of the Atlantic—were involved; a characteristic broadening of the purposes of the projected
institution occurred as funds and a charter were sought; and, when
the institution finally opened in New Brunswick in 1771, its purpose
was described as "the education of youth in the learned languages,
liberal and useful arts and sciences, and especially in divinity;
preparing them for the ministry, and other good offices."[30]

One effort at college founding that failed during the 1760's is of
special interest in view of its unimpeachable New Light sponsorship, namely, the attempt of George Whitefield to convert the
Bethesda Orphan Asylum in Georgia into a fully chartered degree-
granting institution. The asylum had originated in Charles Wesley's
desire to create an institution modeled along the lines of the orphan
house described in August Hermann Francke's *Pietas Hallensis*
(1705); but ill-health had forced Wesley to abandon the project and
Whitefield had taken it on in his stead, resolving "to prosecute it
with all my might." Money was collected, a grant of land was obtained
from the Georgia trustees, and in 1740 the venture was launched,
growing rapidly to a point where the "family" regularly numbered
between fifty and seventy-five. It was this institution that Whitefield
sought to have chartered as a college between 1764 and 1767. But,
as fate would have it, he applied to the metropolitan Privy Council
rather than to the provincial assembly for the charter, and there
Thomas Secker, archbishop of Canterbury, a member of the council
and no lover of Whitefield's enthusiasm, was relentless in his insistence that any charter specify the daily use of the Anglican liturgy

30 "Our Salutation in the Lord to All Who May Read This Letter," in E. T.
Corwin, J. H. Dubbs, and J. T. Hamilton, *A History of the Reformed Church, Dutch,
the Reformed Church, German, and the Moravian Church in the United States* (New
York: The Christian Literature Co., 1895), p. 151. The statement of purpose is taken
from the second charter, granted by the governor of New Jersey in the name of the
king on March 20, 1770; the charter is given in its entirety in Elsie W. Clews, *Educational Legislation and Administration of the Colonial Governments* (New York: no
publisher, 1899), pp. 336-347.

at the college. Whitefield, who had steadfastly maintained that the institution would be undenominational in character, found himself unable to accept, and therefore withdrew the application. A subsequent plan to have Bethesda chartered as an academy by act of the Georgia legislature failed in 1770, when Whitefield died before the legislation could be enacted, and no further attempt was made to convert the orphanage into an institution of higher learning.[31]

IV

The experience of these newly launched academies and colleges, as purpose, clientele, and constituency broadened, was as characteristic of Old Light as of New Light institutions and, indeed, generally characteristic of provincial religious life. However circumscribed and guarded the intent of the founders, the institutions themselves became less sectarian as time progressed. Thus Yale, established principally to give Connecticut its own fount of learning but certainly partly as a reaction against the perceived theological liberalism of Harvard, was initially placed under the control of a board of Congregational ministers, who promptly required that all students be instructed in a system of divinity prescribed by them and no other. And as late as 1754 President Thomas Clap defined the college as a religious society "of a superior nature to all others. For whereas parishes, are societies, for training up the common people; colleges, are societies of ministers, for training up persons for the work of the ministry."[32]

Yet the purposes of Yale, like Harvard's before it, were always broader than those of a divinity school, and, whereas well over half of its alumni entered the ministry during the early years, that percentage had fallen to a third by the later 1760's. Moreover, the same President Clap observed in 1766 that "persons of all denominations of Protestants are allowed the advantage of an education here, and no inquiry has been made, at their admission or afterwards, about

31 *The Works of the Reverend George Whitefield* (6 vols.; London: printed for Edward and Charles Dilly and Messrs. Kincaid and Bell, 1771-1772), III, 463, 446-447, 497.

32 Dexter, *Documentary History of Yale University*, p. 32; Thomas Clap, *The Religious Constitution of Colleges, Especially of Yale-College in New-Haven in the Colony of Connecticut* (New-London: T. Green, 1754). For a sharp reply to Clap, asserting that it was nothing less than popery to argue that colleges were religious societies, see Benjamin Gale, *The Present State of the Colony of Connecticut Considered* ([New-London: T. Green], 1755).

their particular sentiments in religion." At Harvard, where no religious tests for students had ever been countenanced, a climate of theological liberalism prevailed under President Holyoke, within which the faculty could denounce Whitefield as an enthusiast whose passionate preaching had deluded his hearers with "dangerous errors" and "blasphemy," within which the Hollis Professor of Divinity, Edward Wigglesworth, could invite his classes critically to examine competing theological systems, and within which students whose parents desired it could attend Anglican rather than Congregational services.[33]

For all intents and purposes, the academies and colleges of America, like its churches, had become denominational; in fact, inasmuch as they trained a growing proportion of the clergy, they not only reflected but accelerated and even led the movement toward denominationalism. However much the rivalry of New Light versus Old Light, dissent versus orthodoxy, and sect versus church had given rise to particular institutions, and however much the continuing evolution of sectarian into denominational institutions had inevitably occasioned the establishment of new sectarian institutions, the very character of provincial society—its heterogeneity, its openness, its lack of custom and tradition—accelerated the development of a general Christian education. As Sidney Mead once put it, zealous sectarianism tended to be swallowed up in a larger whole; and in the academies and colleges, even more, perhaps, than in the churches, Americans found common ground, common opportunity, and common cause.[34]

Moreover, in providing that common ground, based as it was on classical as well as Scriptural models of man, the academies and colleges resolutely humanized religious life in general and religious enthusiasm in particular. However much the New Lights, going well beyond the Old Lights in this respect, conceived of those institutions as religious societies par excellence and used them to advance the cause of evangelicism, the edges of that evangelicism were inevitably smoothed and the core inevitably leavened, as diverse groups of young men found their theology broadened by philosophy

[33] Thomas Clap, *The Annals or History of Yale-College* (New Haven: John Hotchkiss and B. Mecom, 1766), p. 83; *The Testimony of the President, Professors, Tutors and Hebrew Instructor of Harvard College in Cambridge, Against the Reverend Mr. George Whitefield, and His Conduct* (Boston: T. Fleet, 1744), p. 13.
[34] Sidney E. Mead, *The Lively Experiment* (New York: Harper & Row, 1963), p. 77.

and their world views broadened by one another. In effect, the very academies and colleges that were established to perpetuate the awakenings ended up taming them and moving American Protestantism toward a common Christianity within which the various churches were seen as "but several branches (more or less pure in minuter points) of one visible kingdom of the Messiah."[35]

[35] Gilbert Tennent, *The Divine Government over All Considered* (Philadelphia: William Bradford, 1752), p. 45.

Chapter 11

MISSIONS AND ENCOUNTERS

Go, British worthies, go diffuse your day,
Let England evangelic light display;
Go, plant your Saviour, where you plant your queen,
Let both be with united scepters seen.

ELKANAH SETTLE

One key to the character of eighteenth-century religion was the trans-atlantic network of communities that made possible a continuing cultural and clerical interchange between the European metropolis and the American colonies. Organized along national as well as de-nominational lines, this network included Anglo-American Quakers, Netherlands-American Dutch Reformed, Franco-American Hugue-nots (especially after the revocation of the Edict of Nantes in 1685), German-American Lutherans, and Spanish-American Catholics. All served variously as sources for the supply of clergymen to vacant colonial pulpits, as devices for the recruitment of able colonials to the metropolis for training and placement, as instruments for the regula-tion of colonial ecclesiastical affairs, and as vehicles for the exchange of religious and cultural ideas. Most important, perhaps, all were agencies of missionary endeavor, organizations for the political, re-ligious, and cultural education not merely of first- and second-generation Europeans in the colonies but also of recently arrived African blacks and long-established indigenous Indians.

Among the many communities, few were as ardent or expansive during the provincial era as the Anglicans, who managed to extend their enterprise in less than a century from scarcely more than thirty clergymen in Virginia and Maryland in 1671 and less than forty in the colonies as a whole to a vast array of ministers, missionaries, and teachers laboring from the northern reaches of New England all the way to southernmost Georgia. The story of this massive effort begins with the accession of Henry Compton to the bishopric of London in 1675. No sooner had he entered upon his duties than he took steps to establish his authority over the churches of the various plantations beyond the seas, assuming in the process that he was merely carrying forward prerogatives assigned in the initial charters of Virginia. Whatever the nature and intent of that original assignment, Compton did manage to have it reaffirmed, initially gaining the right to certify clergy for appointment to colonial parishes and then slowly building up precedents for the exercise of ecclesiastical jurisdiction.

A critical element in the latter effort was Compton's decision to appoint ecclesiastical commissaries to represent him in the colonies, officers who brought with them to the New World all of the traditional power to reinforce diocesan authority except the right to collate ministers to benefices, to grant licenses for marriage, and to probate wills. These commissaries went energetically about their duties, reaffirming the force of English ecclesiastical law to clergy and laity alike, serving as judges, visitors, and administrators, and generally representing the London ecclesiastical hierarchy in the dominant circles of colonial society. Most interestingly, perhaps, they found themselves acting more and more as cultural emissaries, proclaiming traditional English values in an alien world that paid scant attention to formal commissions from Fulham and even less to the traditional privileges of ecclesiastical office.[1]

There is evidence that ecclesiastical commissaries may have been appointed by Compton as early as 1686, during the reign of James II, but it was only after the bishop had been removed by James and subsequently restored by William III that commissarial government came into its own. On December 15, 1689, Compton appointed James Blair his commissary to Virginia, marking the beginning of a major commissarial role in the mainland colonies. Blair was a Scot who had attended Marischal College and the University of Edinburgh and then settled as a Scottish Episcopal minister at Cranston, near Edinburgh, only to find himself standing firm against the requirement of the Test Act of 1681 and hence ejected from his charge and cut off

[1] It should be borne in mind that the commissaries, beyond the ordinary powers excepted in their commissions, did not traditionally have the right to ordain ministers or confirm communicants in England or in the colonies.

from further employment in his native land. He had then moved on to London, where, through the good offices of his former professor of divinity Laurence Charteris, he had met a number of eminent clergymen, among them Compton, who appointed him a missionary to Virginia. He had settled in the colony in 1685 as rector of the frontier parish of Varina, in Henrico County, spending the next four years in the usual round of clerical duties and in addition marrying favorably and thereby gaining entry into the influential families that clustered around Jamestown. By the time of his appointment in 1689, he had managed to combine the education, the experience, and the social contacts on both sides of the Atlantic that augured excellently for the new role in which he found himself.[2]

Blair's commission gave him sweeping though ill-defined powers, and he lost no time in setting himself an ambitious program. On July 23, 1690, he convened the clergy in Jamestown for what at least one historian has called potentially the most momentous ecclesiastical meeting held in Virginia during the colonial period. There are neither minutes of the proceedings nor records of who attended, but there is evidence that at least two actions were taken, one, the establishment of a system of ecclesiastical courts to enforce the ecclesiastical laws against both lay and clerical offenders, the other, a resolution appealing for assistance in the establishment of a college. The first plan soon foundered on the contempt of the House of Burgesses; the second went forward to establish Blair's permanent place in the history of American education.[3]

The proposal that the clergy endorsed "for the better encouragement of learning by the founding [of] a college in this country" envisioned an institution embracing a grammar school, a philosophy school, and a divinity school—the first to be taught by a master and usher; the second, by two professors competent in logic, natural philosophy, and mathematics; and the third, by a professor of oriental languages and a clergyman, who would also serve as president. The proposal was apparently submitted to the lieutenant governor and council at about the same time and won endorsement from both, with the result that a committee was appointed to raise a subscrip-

[2] The Bishop of London's Commission to Mr. Blair, December 15, 1689 (ms. archives, Public Record Office, London), CO 5, no. 1305, no. 28.

[3] "Papers Relating to the Founding of the College," *The William and Mary College Quarterly*, VII (1898), 158-159; and George Maclaren Brydon, *Virginia's Mother Church and the Political Conditions Under Which It Grew* (2 vols.; imprint varies, 1947-1957), I, 280-283.

tion and obtain legislative approval from the assembly. That approval was given at the spring session the following year in actions petitioning the king and queen for a charter and appointing Blair the assembly's agent for the project.[4]

Blair went to London that summer, where he enlisted the support of several leading churchmen, some of whom he had come to know during his earlier residence in that city; and particularly through the good offices of Archbishop Tillotson he obtained audiences with Queen Mary and King William. His petition was well received, and the cause referred to the offices of the treasury and of plantations for legal and administrative clearance, an enterprise that consumed eight months, since the assignment of certain colonial revenues was involved and since in any case some feared lest a college detract the planters from their labors "and make them grow too knowing, to be obedient and submissive." However that may be, a charter was issued on February 8, 1693, authorizing the establishment of "the College of William and Mary in Virginia," with Blair as the first president and Compton as the first chancellor.[5]

For all Blair's apparent success, however, the institution was actually some time in getting under way. In the first place, Blair demanded a salary of one hundred fifty pounds a year as president, a sum that consumed most of the college's income, leaving little for the other officers contemplated in the charter. Then, too, Sir Edmund Andros replaced Francis Nicholson in the Virginia government in 1693 and proved nowhere near as friendly to the nascent college as his predecessor. Moreover, when Nicholson returned as governor in

[4] "Papers Relating to the Founding of the College," pp. 158-164.

[5] "Commissary Blair to Governor Nicholson, December 3, 1691," in William Stevens Perry, ed., Historical Collections Relating to the American Colonial Church (4 vols.; Hartford, Conn.: Church Press Company, 1870-1878), I, 38; [Gilbert Burnet], Bishop Burnet's History of His Own Time (3d ed.; 4 vols.; London: T. Davies, 1766), III, 165; and Henry Hartwell, James Blair, and Edward Chilton, The Present State of Virginia, and the College, edited by Hunter Dickinson Farish (Charlottesville: University Press of Virginia, 1964), p. 78. It was during the period 1692-1693, when Blair was awaiting the assignment of revenues and the granting of the charter, that Sir Edward Seymour, on being urged by Blair to speed the considerations because there were souls to be saved in Virginia as well as in England, is supposed to have replied, "Souls, damn your souls. Make tobacco!" Apart from Benjamin Franklin's report of this bit of William and Mary lore in a letter to Mason Weems and Edward Gant, July 18, 1784 (The Writings of Benjamin Franklin, edited by Albert A. Smyth [10 vols.; New York: The Macmillan Co., 1907], IX, 240), there seems to be no evidence for the event or the remark. See Samuel Roop Mohler, "Commissary James Blair, Churchman, Educator and Politician of Colonial Virginia" (unpublished doctoral thesis, University of Chicago, 1940), pp. 171-173.

1698 he and Blair promptly began to quarrel over political matters. And, as if these difficulties were not sufficient, a fire destroyed the institution's building, which had been erected in the 1690's from plans drawn by Sir Christopher Wren. The result was that instruction initially went forward only at the grammar-school level, under the Reverend Mungo Inglis, and it was not until 1717, when Hugh Jones became professor of mathematics, that any instructor in the philosophy school seems to have been in office more than a few months. Even Jones's service was intermittent—as late as 1724 he described the institution as "a college without a chapel, without a scholarship, and without a statute"—and it was only after the assembly appropriated additional revenues in 1726 that the college was able to recruit additional faculty and get seriously under way. Thereafter the development of the college began in earnest, and with the accession of professors like William Small in 1758 and the arrival of substantial numbers of students—there must have been over a hundred by the time Small arrived, including those who resided in town and those who attended an Indian school that had been built with a legacy from Robert Boyle—the college came into its own.[6]

One of the most interesting aspects of the College of William and Mary during this formative period was the pronounced Scottish flavor of its customs and regulations. Blair patently had Scottish models in mind when he decreed in the statutes of 1727 that two years would be required for the bachelor's degree and four for the master's. Likewise, he clearly defined the duties of the two professors in the divinity school along Scottish rather than English lines, including the requirement of lectures and the prohibition of fee-taking. And finally, as in Edinburgh, the students were left free to live away from the college if they chose, since it was intended that "the youth, with as little charge as they can, should learn the learned languages and other arts and sciences."[7]

In truth, few students seem actually to have taken the bachelor's degree during the eighteenth century, the practice having been to spend a year at William and Mary either preceding or following study with a private tutor or in England. But that fact should not

[6] Hugh Jones, *The Present State of Virginia,* edited by Richard L. Morton (Chapel Hill: University of North Carolina Press, 1956), p. 108.
[7] "The Statutes [1727]," *The William and Mary College Quarterly,* XXII (1914), 293.

obscure the influence of the college at a time when the substance of the training given was far more significant than the award of any certificatory degree. As Herbert Baxter Adams pointed out years ago, the unique quality of that substance derived as much from the college's location at Williamsburg as from anything in the formal curriculum. "The gathering together of the best people of Virginia," Adams observed, "and the forming of student associations with all that was best in the history and politics of that colony and of mother England were of untold influence in molding the intellect, in testing the character, and in cultivating the manners of the rising generation. Whatever schoolmen may say, there is no school like the world of human society, like contact with men."[8]

At precisely the time Blair was attempting to organize the recently chartered College of William and Mary in 1695, his friend Nicholson, who had gone on to the governorship of Maryland, wrote to Bishop Compton requesting the appointment of a commissary there to oversee the staffing and maintenance of some twenty-five parishes newly created by an assembly zealous for the development of Anglicanism in that province. Compton's choice for the post, once he had decided to grant Nicholson's request, was an able young priest from Sheldon, in Warwickshire, named Thomas Bray, whose recently published *Catechetical Lectures* had impressed the bishop as a work of solid learning and commendable orthodoxy. Bray was laboring on a second volume of the *Lectures* at the time of the invitation but resolved to lay it aside and accept the opportunity, concluding "that there might be a greater field for doing good in the plantations." His resolution was happily a firm one, since it was not until 1700, after several years of incessant wrangling over the legalities attending the establishment of the church in Maryland, that Bray finally sailed for America to take up his duties.[9]

During the intervening period, however, the young commissary-designate developed plans for the organization of his work that would dramatically and permanently affect education in the New World. The key to these plans lay in Bray's realization that only the poorer clergy would respond to the missionary call from a distant colony of uncertain stability, and that, if they were to perform at a competent

---

[8] Herbert B. Adams, *The College of William and Mary: A Contribution to the History of Higher Education, with Suggestions for Its National Promotion* (Washington, D.C.: Government Printing Office, 1887), p. 26.

[9] [Samuel Smith], *Publick Spirit Illustrated in the Life and Designs of the Reverend Thomas Bray* (London: printed for J. Brotherton, 1746), p. 10.

level, they would need to be instructed along with the laity under their cure. Bray's instrument for this continuing instruction was the parochial library, a select body of theological, humanistic, and scientific works that would incorporate in an eminently practical way all that the colonial parson and his parishioners needed to know.

Bray first set forth his plans in his *Proposals for the Incouragement and Promoting of Religion and Learning in the Foreign Plantations* (1696), the appearance of which launched a personal subscription campaign with the solid support of the Anglican hierarchy. More comprehensive versions of the plan, along with advice on the administration of the libraries, appeared in *An Essay Towards Promoting All Necessary and Useful Knowledge, Both Divine and Human, in All the Parts of His Majesty's Dominions, Both at Home and Abroad* (1697), in *Bibliotheca Parochialis* (1697), and in *Bibliotheca Catechetica; or, The Country Curate's Library* (1699), all of which, incidentally, addressed themselves to the rural regions of the metropolis as well as to the outlying regions of the colonies. And in 1699 Bray and a group of friends formed themselves into the Society for Promoting Christian Knowledge (S.P.C.K.) to advance the work. Not unexpectedly, in an age of societies for moral and religious reformation, the Society's conception of its purposes soon broadened beyond the support of libraries to include free catechetical schools for poor planters' children, missionary activities for the reduction of the Quakers "to the Christian faith" as well as the conversion of the Indians, and charity schools for the youthful poor of the motherland. Funds flowed in almost immediately and the Society was able to lift from Bray's shoulders some of the burdens he had personally assumed in gathering almost twenty-five hundred pounds for the support of the work.[10]

Bray arrived in Maryland to a succession of disappointments. The Quakers on both sides of the Atlantic had been active in obtaining an order of council disallowing the Maryland Church Act; Nicholson had gone to Virginia to take up the governorship there, leaving a careerist named Nathaniel Blakiston in his place; and, last but scarcely least, there were no funds for his support. Bray remained for

[10] Edmund McClure, ed., *A Chapter in English Church History: Being the Minutes of the Society for Promoting Christian Knowledge for the Years 1698-1704* (London: Society for Promoting Christian Knowledge, 1888), pp. 21-22; and "Dr. Bray's Accounts, 1695-1699" (ms. records of Dr. Bray's Associates, United Society for the Propagation of the Gospel, London [Library of Congress photostats]).

three months, lobbying in the legislature, touring the province to gain firsthand knowledge of the religious situation, and gathering the clergy in Annapolis to urge the advisability of regular catechizing, the advantages of frequent preaching, the usefulness of organizing the vestries into religious societies for the reformation of manners, and the desirability of converting the Quakers in neighboring Pennsylvania. He returned to England in the spring of 1700 determined to negotiate a satisfactory church act between the provincial assembly and the Board of Trade, and, indeed, the Act for the Establishment of Religious Worship According to the Church of England, and for the Maintenance of Ministers (1702), is testimony to the success of his effort. But he had gotten caught up in numerous causes and projects in the meantime, and he eventually persuaded Compton to appoint another commissary.[11]

Apart from the future he secured for Anglicanism in eighteenth-century Maryland, Bray's principal contribution during the period of his commissaryship was embodied in the libraries he left on the North American mainland. The first, numbering 1,095 volumes, was founded at Annapolis in 1696—the earliest lending library formally established as such in the English-speaking colonies. During the next three years, before Bray ever set foot in the New World, over thirty others were established in Boston, New York, Philadelphia, Charleston, and the parishes of provincial Maryland. The design of these collections was based on an elaborate scheme that embraced metaphysics, ethics, and economics; politics, law, and history; physiology, medicine, and mathematics; trade and commerce; and grammar, rhetoric, poetry, and logic. Detailed instructions were also given for housing, shelving, and circulating the collections. The books themselves ranged from the Bible, the Book of Common Prayer, and *The Whole Duty of Man* (which was apparently Bray's most frequent recommendation) to such mundane items as Franciscus Arcaeus' *A Most Excellent and Compendious Method of Curing Woundes in the Head and in Other Partes of the Body with Other Precepts of the Same Art* (translated by John Read, 1588) and Gervase Markham's *A Way to Get Wealth, Containing Six Principall Vocations or Callings, in Which Everie Good Husband or House-wife May Lawfully Imploy Themselves* (1631). What is abundantly clear is that Bray had the laity as much in mind as the clergy in his selection of books and

[11] "An Act for the Establishment of Religious Worship in This Province According to the Church of England, and for the Maintenance of Ministers," *Archives of Maryland*, XXIV (1904), 265-273.

that, however top-heavy the libraries may have been with theological and devotional writings, they were also sufficiently diverse and utilitarian to be powerful agencies for popular education in the communities that possessed them. In earlier years as a youth, Bray had gone to school at the library of a local clergyman in the Shropshire hamlet where he grew up; now, through his efforts, that same opportunity had been afforded to thousands of his countrymen in the colonies beyond the seas.[12]

II

At least one of the numerous causes and projects that preoccupied Bray after his return to London in the summer of 1700 was the development of a new organization that would more effectively muster the considerable resources needed to channel large numbers of competent missionaries into the colonies. Bray doubtless initiated conversations on the matter with leading churchmen and with his associates in the S.P.C.K. shortly after he reached England, for the matter was brought before the lower house of Convocation on March 13, 1701, and that body appointed a committee of twelve "to inquire into ways and means for promoting Christian religion in our foreign plantations" in collaboration with the bishop of London. Neither Bray nor his friend Compton seemed very patient with this procedure, however, for less than a month later, in early April, Bray addressed a petition directly to the king for the creation of a new society dedicated to the propagation of the gospel in the provinces of America. William appeared favorably disposed; a charter was drafted and considered by the membership of the S.P.C.K. at its May 5 meeting; and a subscription was launched to finance the arrangements for the incorporation. On June 16, 1701, a charter was issued to Dr. Bray and a group of distinguished associates, creating the Society for the Propagation of the Gospel in Foreign Parts, with the archbishop of Canterbury, Thomas Tenison, as president.[13]

Setting forth in appropriately grave phrases the mean state of the church in many of His Majesty's plantations, colonies, and factories

---

[12] Thomas Bray, "Bibliothecae Americanae Quadripartitae" (Bray mss., Sion College Library, London [Library of Congress photostats]); and *A Brief Account of the Life of the Reverend Mr. John Rawlet*, in *Missionalia* (London: W. Roberts, 1727-1728).

[13] The relevant minute from the lower house of Convocation and the charter are reprinted in C. F. Pascoe, *Two Hundred Years of the S.P.G.* (London: The Society, 1901), pp. 4, 932-935.

beyond the seas and the consequent vulnerability of these plantations to atheism, infidelity, and the "popish superstition and idolatry" purveyed by "divers Romish priests and Jesuits," the documents
commissioned the new Society to recruit and maintain an orthodox
clergy that would minister to the needs of the colonists and undertake the conversion of the heathen. And it brought into being an
organization that would be quasi-public in character, distinct from
the state yet responsible for reporting to certain of its designated
officials and equally distinct from the church yet embracing a majority of the episcopal bench among its membership. In a sense, both
the purpose and the structure were unprecedented, combining as
they did imperial evangelism with philanthropic benevolence and the
power of a royal charter with the force of private initiative.

The granting of the charter launched one of the most ambitious
educational efforts of the eighteenth century, the more impressive
because of its transatlantic span. John Calam has described it in
colorful detail in "Parsons and Pedagogues: The S.P.G. Adventure
in American Education." Between the latter months of 1701,
when the first letters of inquiry went forth to colonial officials seeking
information on existent needs and opportunities, to the years during
and following the Revolution, when the Society's enterprises were
either dissolved or transformed, the Society established at least 169
missionary stations, extending from North Stratford in New Hampshire to St. George's in Georgia, and as far west as Johnstown, New
York, Cumberland County, Pennsylvania, and Rowen County, South
Carolina. In addition, more than eighty schoolmasters and some
eighteen catechists labored for periods of time varying from a few
weeks to a quarter-century, teaching charity-school children to "read,
write, and cast accounts," leading prayers in the absence of the
clergy, and itinerating in the cause of Anglicanism. Beyond these
efforts, the Society distributed literally thousands of Bibles, prayer
books, anniversary sermons, devotional works, and school texts, not
only in English, but also in French, German, Dutch, and the various
Indian dialects. Through pulpit, classroom, library, and tract, S.P.G.
missionaries spread the religious and cultural doctrines of Anglicanism among a polyglot people of uncertain and conflicting loyalties.[14]

14 Mr. Huddleston to secretary, February 23, 1712, S.P.G. Letter Books
(S.P.G. mss., United Society for the Propagation of the Gospel, London), Series
A, VII, 146. Calam presents maps of the stations and lists of the missionaries,
schoolmasters, and catechists (usually men in deacons' orders serving in somewhat the same capacity as readers) in the appendices of his monograph "Parsons
and Pedagogues: The S.P.G. Adventure in American Education" (unpublished doctoral
thesis, Columbia University, 1969), pp. 356 ff.

As might be expected, the men who served as the Society's missionaries were themselves a mixed company, varying from romantic idealists to disillusioned adventurers, and including French refugees, displaced Scottish Episcopalians, and converted Irish Dissenters. Of sixty-four men commissioned by the Society between 1701 and 1725, only a third were of English nativity, the rest having come principally from Scotland, Ireland, Wales, and the colonies themselves. The Society at least had the good judgment to try to match the missionaries with their clientele, so that men of English birth tended to be assigned to the Carolinas or New England, while men of Scottish, Irish, or Welsh birth were more often placed in the middle colonies among groups of their countrymen. As for the Society's schoolmasters, few were actually recruited in England, the tendency being to employ men who were already resident in the colonies.[15]

Very soon after its founding, the Society issued detailed instructions to guide the efforts of its missionaries and schoolmasters, which reveal much about its priorities and its expectations. The missionary clergy were enjoined to preach often concerning the fundamental principles of Christianity and the duties of a sober, righteous, and godly life that derive from them; to instruct the people in the nature and uses of the sacraments; to take special care to catechize the young and the ignorant; to teach the heathen, beginning with the principles of natural religion and proceeding to revelation as contained in Holy Scripture; to distribute the Society's literature among their parishioners; and to encourage the establishment of schools and the employment as schoolmistresses of the widows of clergymen who had died in service as missionaries.[16]

Teachers in turn were enjoined to instruct and dispose children to believe and live as Christians, to teach them to read that they might study the Holy Scriptures and other pious and useful books, to catechize them thoroughly, to "teach them to write a plain and legible hand, in order to the fitting them for useful employments, with as much arithmetic as shall be necessary to the same purpose, to lead them in morning and evening prayer, to oblige them to attend church services, to exercise special care concerning their manners, to en-

[15] John Kendall Nelson, "Anglican Missions in America, 1701-1725: A Study of the Society for the Propagation of the Gospel in Foreign Parts" (unpublished doctoral thesis, Northwestern University, 1962), pp. 31-32.

[16] S.P.G. Minutes, May 18, 1705, Journals, I, 194. The instructions to missionaries are printed in *A Collection of Papers, Printed by Order of the Society for the Propagation of the Gospel in Foreign Parts* (London: Joseph Downing, 1706), pp. 22-32.

courage them to be industrious, and at all times to set them appropriate examples of virtue and piety."[17]

Beyond the ordinary human difficulties in observing such instructions to the letter, there were the special problems presented by the colonial situation. In the first place, there were the harsh realities of the colonial environment, for which most of the missionaries were simply unprepared by training or temperament. Living conditions were rude; travel was difficult; the climate was debilitating; and poverty, hunger, discomfort, and disease seemed ubiquitous. Then, as if physical hindrances were not sufficient, there was the ever-present hostility of the Dissenters. For churchmen accustomed to membership in an establishment, the animus of the New England Congregationalist or the Pennsylvania Quaker must have been at the least dispiriting. And, finally, there was the conspicuous absence of a bishop, so crucial to Anglican protocol and discipline, and the consequent confusion of authority and responsibility as between resident governors and commissaries and the distant officials of the Society. Not a few of the Society's enterprises collapsed in the New World simply for want of a mediator to referee conflicts.

Despite these obstacles, there were noteworthy examples of success in every region. In South Carolina, for example, the Society was intimately involved in the initial establishment of Anglicanism in what was for all intents and purposes a wilderness. The settlements were scattered; the Indians were hostile; malaria, dysentery, and smallpox were frequently epidemic; inflation was rampant; and the government in Charleston was incessantly uncooperative. Beyond this, the settlers themselves were unrelentingly suspicious in matters of religion. "Never was a people so wretchedly crippled concerning the use of the sacraments," Commissary Gideon Johnston observed, "and between the church and conventicles, as they are generally here, for they have gotten such strange notions and whims in their heads about these things, and have fallen into such a comprehensive and latitudinarian way, that it is the hardest thing in the world to persuade them out of it." Yet a succession of over fifty missionaries, including Johnston, Alexander Garden, Francis Le Jau, and Thomas Hassel, were able to plant the church sufficiently firmly for the

17 S.P.G. Minutes, May 17, 1706, June 21, 1706, July 19, 1706, Journals, I, 237-238, 244, 246; and "Instructions for Schoolmasters Employed by the Society," *A Collection of Papers*, pp. 33 ff.

Society to withdraw during the 1760's, leaving a well-financed network of local parishes to minister to the settlers.[18]

In Connecticut, to choose a quite different example, the Society from the beginning worked under a cloud of official hostility, and, indeed, the defection of Timothy Cutler, Daniel Browne, Samuel Johnson, and James Wetmore in the notorious Yale episode of 1722 only made the task more difficult. Yet it was precisely the publicity given the Yale affair that made Anglicanism a matter of general interest throughout the colony, and it was only after 1722 that the Church of England gained more than a precarious foothold in the colony. Thenceforth, under the aggressive leadership of S.P.G. missionaries such as George Pigot, Richard Mansfield, Samuel Andrews, Richard Samuel Clarke, and Samuel Johnson, the church made significant gains. And, though all of the S.P.G. churches were closed during the Revolution, Anglicanism lived on to emerge in a transformed American version after the termination of hostilities.

In New York, to choose yet another example, the Society played a significant role in the spirited competition between English and Dutch religious and cultural institutions and in the eventual triumph of English forms. In no other colony did the Society mount an effort of such prodigious scope and diversity. S.P.G. funds supplied a German Church of England minister to the Palatinates along the Hudson and a French priest in Anglican orders, who actually lured an entire Huguenot congregation into the Anglican fold, using S.P.G. financing as bait. The Society also made New York the headquarters for its early forays into Congregationalist New England and the scene of its most intensive efforts at charity schooling. At least one and sometimes as many as three schoolmasters were partly or wholly supported in each of the parishes staffed by an S.P.G. missionary, with enrollments averaging around forty pupils; and, in the case of the Society's charity school in New York City, a distinguished succession of masters, including William Huddleston, Thomas Noxon, and Joseph Hildreth, attracted classes that ran as high as eighty-five or ninety. And the chartering of King's College in 1754 represented perhaps the single most important institutional formation to which the Society contributed in North America.

Doubtless there were significant differences between what the S.P.G. missionaries and schoolmasters intended to teach in all this

[18] Commissary Johnston to secretary, July 5, 1710, S.P.G. Letter Books, Series A, V, 446.

effort and what was actually communicated. But the intentions, at least, were clear and went far beyond the alphabet, the catechism, the Prayer Book, and the Scriptures. Books such as Richard Allestree's *The Whole Duty of Man*, Archbishop William Wake's *The Principles of the Christian Religion* (1699), and William Stanley's *The Faith and Practice of a Church of England-Man* (1688) formed the staples of the S.P.G. curriculum, preaching as they did a piety and civility emphasizing respect for monarchy, belief in episcopacy, unerring obedience to minister and magistrate, and quiet acceptance of place and station. Not surprisingly, it was the apiary that appeared again and again as the prize metaphor, with royalty regnant, with each individual accepting of his order and his work, and with the hive an organic unity representing the general good.

Beyond these staples, which were as widely read in the metropolis as in the colonies, there were the special preachments of the S.P.G. anniversary sermons, delivered annually at St. Mary-le-Bow in London by some of the leading lights of the Church of England. Together with the theological commonplaces of High-Church Anglicanism, these conveyed a sense of the pre-eminence of England vis-à-vis the rival imperial efforts of Roman Catholic Spain and France, a view of the colonies as mines of wealth for the metropolis, a conception of the denizens of the colonies as ignorant, immoral, and unlettered malcontents, and an assertion of the obligation of the colonists to proffer filial reverence to the mother country. All these doctrines and images persisted through the century, though with the sharpening crisis of the 1760's there appeared a tendency on the part of the Society's policy-makers to stress familial imagery and particularly the ties that bound the colonists to their motherland.

As has been suggested, the reception accorded the Society's efforts was anything but uniformly friendly. Even in instances where S.P.G. missionaries were formally requested by the colonists themselves they were held at arm's length once they arrived. Colonial governors desirous of retaining their prerogative to institute clergymen to benefices and to collect certain traditional ecclesiastical revenues and colonial legislatures reluctant to appropriate substantial sums for an established church were none too eager for the political machinations on the part of the clergy that they had come to accept as traditional in England. And, in instances where S.P.G. missionaries represented the aggressive thrust of mili-

tant Anglicanism into confirmed Dissenter territory, there was outright opposition. In Connecticut the Society was accused of sending
"foreigners" into the colony to take the rightful pulpits of native
sons, while in Massachusetts Jonathan Mayhew's *Observations on
the Charter and Conduct of the S.P.G.* (1763) denounced the Society
as a political instrument rather than a humanitarian agency. In
Mayhew's view, the Society's charter had made its principal purpose
the conversion of the heathen to Christ, but the Society's program
had been nothing less than the planting of an Anglican bishop in
the colonies and the return of the colonies to conformity. "Is it not
enough, that they persecuted us out of the Old World?" he asked.
"Will they pursue us into the New to convert us here?—compassing
sea and land to make us proselytes, while they neglect the heathen
and heathenish plantations!" Sentiments like Mayhew's became
dominant during the Revolution, after which most of the Society's
missionaries were suppressed or forced to retire to Canada or the
West Indies, or to return home. The Society ended its work in the
independent colonies in 1783, to go on to other crusades in other
parts of the world.[19]

III

Whatever the validity of Mayhew's charge that the S.P.G. had set
altar against altar in New England while at the same time neglecting the conversion of the heathen, there is no denying that the
Society from the beginning had pursued a twofold aim. In the very
first of the prestigious anniversary sermons, the Reverend Richard
Willis, dean of Lincoln, had stated the goals thus: "The design is
in the first place to settle the state of religion as well as may be
among our own people there, which by all accounts we have, very
much wants their pious care; and then to proceed in the best
methods they can toward the conversion of the natives." Later, in

[19] Jonathan Mayhew, *Observations on the Charter and Conduct of the Society
for the Propagation of the Gospel in Foreign Parts* (Boston: Richard and Samuel
Draper, Edes and Gill, and Thomas and John Fleet, 1763), p. 156. For another
sharp critique of the Society as an instrument to convert Dissenters to Anglicanism
rather than heathen to Christianity, see William Douglass, *A Summary, Historical
and Political, of the First Planting, Progressive Improvements, and Present State
of the British Settlements in North America* (2 vols.; London: R. Baldwin, 1755),
I, 232; II, 126-140.

1710, with the visit to England of a troupe of Indian chieftains, it looked for a time as if the Society might come to concentrate exclusively on the second goal; but that prospect, as embodied in a pair of resolutions adopted on April 28 of that year, proved temporary, and the subsequent activities of the S.P.G. continued to reflect a dual purpose. However that may be, the Society was early and enthusiastically in the business of ministering to the indigenous Indians and the immigrant blacks and remained so throughout the period of its presence in the North American colonies.[20]

The visions of Indian and Negro education that shone through the anniversary sermons over the years are indicative of the hopes and expectations of the Society and the preconceptions on which they were founded. The Indian was portrayed as a noble savage whose plight combined great dignity with infinite pathos. Of tractable, sweet, and gentle disposition, he was quite "capable of receiving the impressions of the Christian religion, and easily inclined to embrace it." Had he not been barbarously used, continuously tricked, and ruthlessly destroyed by the Spanish and the French, he would gladly have embraced Christianity. Even so, he remained receptive to the propagation of the gospel when treated decently, approached gently, and addressed in his own tongue. The Negro, in turn, was seen as in the very nature of his situation even more tractable, since slaves were scarcely in a position to refuse what their masters demanded. Yet, in the case of the Negro, the masters themselves posed a formidable obstacle, fearing as they did that conversion would inevitably imply manumission, or, if not manumission, at least certain obligations with respect to charity, humanity, and subsequent sale. Bishop Fleetwood of St. Asaph undertook to down such fears in his anniversary sermon of 1711, arguing that the conversion of a slave to Christianity affected neither his salability nor his civil status and implied no more by way of humanity than that minimal compassion Christ demanded of his followers toward all men, including Jews, savages, and infidels. "And all that can consider seriously these things," Fleetwood concluded, "will certainly consent, nay, and be glad, that slaves, though Christians, might be bought and sold, and used like slaves, rather than still be bought

---

[20] Richard Willis, *A Sermon Preached Before the Society for the Propagation of the Gospel in Foreign Parts, at Their First Yearly Meeting on Friday February the 20th. 1701/2. at St. Mary-le-Bow* (London: printed for Matt. Wotton, 1702), p. 17; S.P.G. Minutes, April 28, 1710, Journals, I, 479.

and sold, and used like slaves, and not permitted to be Christians."[21]

The Society's first mission to the Indians began a little more than a year after the signing of the charter, in the appointment of Samuel Thomas to "Christianize" the Yamasee tribe in South Carolina. Thomas arrived at Charleston on Christmas Day, 1702, with ten pounds' worth of "stuffs for the use of the wild Indians." But the situation was inhospitable to his efforts, what with the Yamasees having just returned from an unsuccessful war against the Spanish to the south; and Thomas decided instead to accept Governor Johnson's invitation to serve as personal chaplain and rector of the nearby parish of St. James. The Society never did appoint another missionary to the Yamasees, though its representatives in South Carolina visited them from time to time and reported their experiences back to London.[22]

The Society's next missions to the Indians were undertaken in New York, where the maintenance of good relations with the Iroquois had long been a matter of concern to the Board of Trade. In 1703 Thoroughgood Moore was appointed to work among the Mohawks, who were deemed the Iroquois nation most friendly to the English. He duly made his way to Albany, where he presented his credentials to the Indians and asked permission to live among them and instruct them in the principles of Christianity. The Mohawk response was evasion, and less than a year after his arrival Moore left Albany for a rectorship in Burlington, New Jersey. Later, in speculating on the failure of his mission, Moore blamed the continued mistreatment of the Indians at the hands of land speculators, the disreputable behavior of the military garrison at Albany, and the persistent misrepresentation of English motives by Dutch merchants eager to maintain their trade with the Iroquois. The missionary, he implied, could scarcely carry on his work in the face of this larger and more powerful education.[23]

Some years later, after a visit to London by four Mohawk chiefs,

[21] John Williams, *A Sermon Preached Before the Society for the Propagation of the Gospel in Foreign Parts. At the Parish-Church of St. Lawrence Jewry, February 15, [1705]/1706* (London: Joseph Downing, 1706), pp. 26-27; and William Fleetwood, *A Sermon Preached Before the Society for the Propagation of the Gospel in Foreign Parts, at the Parish Church of St. Mary-le-Bow, on Friday, the 16th of February, 1710/11* (2d ed.; London: Joseph Downing, 1725), p. 36.

[22] Samuel Thomas to Thomas Bray, January 20, 1703, S.P.G. Letter Books, Series A, I, no. 86; S.P.G. Minutes, June 26, 1702, Journals, I, 76.

[23] S.P.G. Minutes, September 17, 1703, Journals, I, 117; Thoroughgood Moore to secretary, November 13, 1705, S.P.G. Letter Books, Series A, II, no. 122.

the Society mounted a more ambitious effort. In 1712, William Andrews was appointed to take up residence among the Mohawks, at the unprecedented annual salary of one hundred fifty pounds plus an additional allowance of sixty pounds for an interpreter. Andrews promptly set about catechizing according to the rules of the Society and also saw to the establishment of a school, which at least in its initial period attracted as many as forty students and which became the occasion for the production and printing of hornbooks, primers, and catechisms in the Indian language. But interest in the work soon flagged and Andrews' reports to London began to talk less of the civil and generous Mohawks and more of the filthy and brutish Mohawks. He left his post in 1719 for a parish in Virginia, having taught many but converted few.[24]

Undaunted, the Society instructed its missionaries in Albany during the 1720's and 1730's to include the Christianizing of the Indians among their duties and later in the century mounted yet another effort among the Mohawks, organizing a school under the tutelage of one Colin McLeland in 1769 and commissioning a clergyman solely to minister to the Mohawks the following year. Yet, like their precursors, these ventures produced little by way of permanent results, overwhelmed as they were by the much more powerful education of tribal folkways on the one hand and white exploitation on the other. They were apparently supported from London until 1782, when they vanished along with most of the rest of the Society's program in North America.[25]

The situation with respect to the blacks was both similar and dissimilar in significant ways. The blacks were generally first-, second-, or third-generation involuntary immigrants, torn from their tribal contexts and frequently from their familial roots as well and set down amidst a dominant white society in a servile or at best ill-defined status. Like the Indians, they must have perceived an immense gap between what the missionary said about the brotherhood of man and what the slaveowner did (and in the case of missionaries who were slaveowners their skepticism must have been overwhelming). Unlike the Indians, they were integrated into white society willy-nilly and lacked even the choice—such as it was

24 S.P.G. Minutes, March 20, 1712, Journals, II, 178; William Andrews to secretary, March 9, 1713, S.P.G. Letter Books, Series A, VIII, 147; and April 17, 1718, ibid., XIII, 323.

25 William Johnson to secretary, December 10, 1769, S.P.G. Letter Books, Series B, II, 291; and E. B. O'Callaghan, ed., The Documentary History of the State of New York (4 vols.; Albany: publisher varies, 1850-1851), IV, 261.

—of moving westward. And, unlike the Indians, they were possessed of a culture infinitely more difficult to observe and preserve in its authentic form, Africa being some five thousand miles away.

Yet the S.P.G. was nothing if not intrepid, and, having assured colonial slavemasters that baptism implied no manumission, its missionaries went forth to teach the Negroes. In 1704 the Society appointed a conforming French Protestant named Elias Neau its catechist to the Negro population of New York City, thereby launching an enterprise that would continue until Neau's death in 1722. Neau was apparently indefatigable about his work, regularly meeting his Negro catechumens at five o'clock on Wednesday, Friday, and Sunday evenings and spending the remainder of his time going from house to house, instructing, catechizing, and exhorting all who would listen, comforting the sick, and praying for the dead. Swelled by the attendance of whites and Indians as well as blacks, the enrollment of his school, which met in the house where he lodged, frequently passed a hundred. The enterprise even survived a Negro uprising in 1712, when Neau's school "was charged as the cause of the mischief, the place of conspiracy and that instruction [that] had made them cunning and insolent." After "the strictest inquiry and severest trial" failed to indicate the complicity of any of the blacks Neau had taught and baptized, the school was permitted to continue despite vocal opposition. On Neau's death in 1722, his work was taken up for two years by William Huddleston, who presided over the S.P.G. charity school in the city; thereafter, it was continued in turn by James Wetmore, Richard Charlton, and Samuel Auchmuty, all of whom served concurrently as assistant rectors of the Trinity Church.[26]

Another venture of a quite different sort was undertaken by Commissary Alexander Garden in Charleston, South Carolina. He developed a plan whereby Negro children from various parts of the colony would be taught to read so that they might in turn instruct their fellows. A school for that purpose was established by subscription in 1743, and the Society was persuaded by Garden to purchase two young blacks named Harry and Andrew to be trained to serve as its schoolmasters. The records of the venture are fragmentary, though there is evidence that as many as sixty pupils on

---

26 Elias Neau to secretary, July 24, 1707, S.P.G. Letter Books, Series A, III, no. 128; and memorandum of the Reverend John Sharpe, March 11, 1713, "Bibliotheca Lambethana" (unpublished mss., Lambeth Palace Library, London), vol. DCCCXLI, no. 18, p. 18.

the average may have been in attendance during the twenty years
of the school's existence. It was closed in 1764 for reasons that are
not entirely clear. Yet another effort went forward in the 1750's,
when an Italian convert from Judaism named Joseph Ottolenghe
was sent by the Society to Georgia to work as a catechist to the
Negroes of that colony. Ottolenghe spent at least three evenings a
week between 1751 and 1753 instructing adult slaves in "such principles of our holy religion, as suits best with their condition and
capacity," with such effectiveness that he was encouraged to turn
some of his attention to the catechizing of white children. But he
was apparently devoting an increasing portion of his time to politics, for he subsequently went on to a series of public offices in the
colony and the Society eventually cut him off from his allowance.[27]

However interesting these particular enterprises may have been,
they were limited in scope and local in influence. By far the larger
impact of the Society in respect to black education derived from
the instructions given all S.P.G. missionaries and schoolmasters to
teach the heathen and infidels. Doubtless some honored such instructions in the breach, but many followed them in the best of
spirit, continually teaching small numbers of free and unfree blacks
and eventually baptizing many of them. A typical example was the
Reverend Francis Le Jau, the Society's missionary in Goose Creek,
South Carolina, between 1706 and 1717. When Le Jau first arrived,
he found several Negroes already attending church regularly, while
the Indians appeared "very quiet, sweet humored and patient, content with little which are great dispositions to be true Christians."
His efforts with the latter came to naught, ultimately collapsing in
the great Yamasee uprising of 1715. But his efforts with the Negroes
were patient and persistent. Describing his methods in a 1710 report
concerning some fifty Negro and Indian slaves who were invited to
remain for a time after the regular Sunday service, he wrote:

[27] Alexander Garden to secretary, May 6, 1740, S.P.G. Letter Books, Series
B, VII, 235-238; April 9, 1742, ibid., X, no. 138; September 24, 1742, ibid., X,
no. 139; and Robert Smith to secretary, July 25, 1759, ibid., V, no. 252. Although
the colony passed legislation in 1740 prohibiting the teaching of slaves, the efforts
of the Charleston school do not appear to have been confined to free Negroes. See
John F. Grimke, ed., The Public Laws of the State of South Carolina from Its
First Establishment as a British Province Down to the Year, 1790, Inclusive (Philadelphia: R. Aitken & Son, 1790), p. 174; Joseph Ottolenghe to secretary, September 9, 1751, S.P.G. Letter Books, Series B, XIX, no. 149; and Joseph Ottolenghi
[sic] to Benjamin Martin, September 11, 1753, in The Colonial Records of the
State of Georgia, XXVI (1916), 437.

We begin and end our particular assembly with the collect *Prevent Us O Lord* and I teach them the Creed, the Lord's Prayer, and the Commandments; I explain some portion of the catechism, I give them an entire liberty to ask questions, I endeavor to proportion my answers and all my instructions to their want and capacity: I must acknowledge that the hand of God does visibly appear on this particular occasion, I had often attempted and proposed a time, a method and means easy, as I thought, for the instruction of those poor souls, but all in vain, till this last was put in my mind by special mercy, the most pious among their masters stay also and hear; others not so zealous would find fault, if possible, their murmurings sometimes reach my ears, but I am not discouraged.

Le Jau took care to assure the secretary, incidentally, that any slave who requested baptism was required to declare that he had not asked for that sacrament out of any design to free himself from his duty and obedience to his master.[28]

In addition to the efforts of its missionaries, the Society lobbied vigorously for parliamentary action forcing owners of slaves to provide them with religious instruction. When this effort seemed to fail, the Society obtained from the bishop of London a "Letter to the Masters and Mistresses in the English Plantations Abroad, Exhorting Them to Encourage and Promote the Instruction of Their Negroes in the Christian Faith," as well as a similar letter to the Society's missionaries soliciting their assistance in the effort. Some twelve thousand copies of these letters were circulated in the colonies to stimulate such interest and activity as they could.[29]

The S.P.G. was the largest but by no means the sole British missionary agency to the heathen. The Society in Scotland for Propagating Christian Knowledge supported a number of missions to the Indians, notably the work of Azariah Horton on Long Island, the work of David Brainerd among the Delawares and the Susquehannas (made famous on both sides of the Atlantic by the publicizing of Jonathan Edwards), and the work of Eleazar Wheelock at Dartmouth College. Similarly, an organization known as Thomas Bray's Associates, founded initially by the good doctor with a bequest from King William's secretary, Abel Tassin, Sieur D'Allone,

---

28 Francis Le Jau to secretary, December 2, 1706, S.P.G. Letter Books, Series A, III, no. 68; October 20, 1709, *ibid.*, V, no. 49; and June 13, 1710, *ibid.*, no. 120.
29 S.P.G. Minutes, March 17, 1727, Journals, V, 119; June 16, 1727, Journals, V, 125; and *Two Letters of the Lord Bishop of London* (London: Joseph Downing, 1729).

established a school for Negroes in Philadelphia in 1758 and then, with the advice of Benjamin Franklin, similar schools in New York, Newport, and Williamsburg two years later. There is evidence, too, of support from the Society in London for Promoting Knowledge Among the Poor, for the work of Samuel Davies in the catechizing of Negroes in Hanover County, Virginia, during the 1750's; while numerous gifts of money and energy from John and Charles Wesley and George Whitefield advanced any number of charities in the various colonies involving missions to the heathen.

All these efforts failed, once again, because the formal education of the missionary was controverted by the informal education of day-by-day existence. True, many Indians and blacks became Christians; some became literate; a few were permitted to pursue decent careers as free tradesmen; and a handful even left marks on the intellectual life of their time—the Indian clergyman Samson Occom and the black scientist Benjamin Banneker come immediately to mind. But the vast majority of the Indians were formed by tribal values for a way of life that was at best marginal to the social mainstream, and at worst crumbling; while the vast majority of the blacks were decisively formed by the slave system and the attitudes toward race that supported it. However well such men and women may have repeated the Christian litany, neither their hearts, nor their minds, nor their bodies were in it.

IV

The S.P.G. failed to Christianize the heathen, but it doubtless helped to Anglicize the colonists. And in this its effort not only coincided with but strengthened the larger education that derived from affairs, confirming as it did the political direction that was ultimately decided in the colonial wars. Yet even here success was qualified at best, for, in less than two decades following 1763, the separation of the colonies from England was debated, fought over, and consummated. What remained at that point was a bond of language, law, and custom that would endure for years to come, despite the severest political strains. It would be difficult to assess the extent to which the Society's schools, tracts, and missions contributed to this bond; but that they strengthened it is undeniable. Curiously, ironically, and perhaps even tragically, then, it was in the broader cultural realm rather than the religious and political realms where it so desperately sought to serve that the S.P.G. achieved its greatest success.

The Society's own sense of this irony was at best imperfect. On the one hand, for all its militant High-Church Anglicanism, it seemed more than willing from time to time to make common cause with other denominations. Thus, the Society placed major library collections at Congregational Yale and Harvard as well as at Anglican King's. And it voted funds on several occasions to Swedish Lutheran pastors in New Jersey and Pennsylvania, who had, in addition to their regular responsibilities, ministered to leaderless Anglican congregations. Similarly, it seemed quite ready to cross ethnic lines in the effort to gain converts: witness its willingness to support French- and German-speaking missionaries to the Huguenot and Palatine communities of New York and Pennsylvania.

Yet, when it came to the Roman Catholic missionaries of France and Spain and particularly to the Jesuits, the Society was unbending: the papists were the enemy, the Antichrist who deserved defeat at all costs. In this, the Society was well aware that the Spanish to the south and the French to the north and west had for years been propagating both Christian and imperial gospels, with immense effectiveness. The Roman Catholic clergy, celibate and subject to authority, seemed infinitely more mobile, adaptable, and successful than their Anglican counterparts, and the Spanish and French laity, though by no means free of commonplace eighteenth-century attitudes toward race, seemed somewhat more ready to intermarry with the Indians and to accept them on a basis of rude equality.

Except for sporadic encounters with the Spanish in northern Florida during the late seventeenth and early eighteenth centuries, the English had little contact with them. Spain's principal missionary effort on the North American continent after 1700 was west of the Mississippi, and it was there, among the Indians of Texas, New Mexico, and California, that the Jesuits, the Franciscans, and, after the expulsion of the Jesuits in 1767, the Dominicans established their mission posts, teaching the gospel, settling the nomadic tribes in pueblos complete with farms, workshops, and occasional mines, and tying the pueblos to presidios with their cohorts of troops and civil agents. The French on the other hand were in direct political, economic, and cultural competition with the English, in Canada, in northern New England, in upper New York, and in the Great Lakes region. Under the leadership of the Jesuits, the Récollets, and the Sulpicians, they courted the Algonquians and the Iroquois in these several regions, erecting chapels, forts, and trading posts, and relentlessly seeking converts, furs, and military assistance.

Now, all this effort very obviously went forward in the context of national and international politics, and the missionaries themselves were scarcely unaware of it. The Spanish knew full well that they were occupying Alta California in order to hinder possible Russian thrusts there. The French moved into Louisiana at least in part to check the expansion of the English in Maryland, Virginia, and the Carolinas. And the English sent missionaries to the Iroquois in upper New York in the full knowledge that they were promoting an alliance against the French. Naturally, such efforts were often accelerated for political or military reasons. Thus, in 1756, with the quickening of the Seven Years' War, the S.P.G. gave new instructions to its missionaries in the colonies, urging them to redouble their efforts with the Indians, "which good work is not only pious and charitable in the more important views of religion, but highly beneficial likewise in a civil view, as promoting the security and interest of the American colonies: an advantage of which our enemies are by no means insensible or negligent." And two years later the archbishop of Canterbury wrote to Samuel Johnson, then president of King's College, urging the placement of additional missionaries on the frontier; "for missionaries there might counteract the artifices of the French papists; and do considerable services, religious and political at once, amongst the neighboring Indians; both which points the Society hath been heavily charged, on occasion of the present war, with having neglected."[30]

To point to these political realities is less to denigrate the instruction of the missionaries than to view it and its impact in context. The Indian was no fool, and the competition for his loyalty was not lost upon him. His response, not surprisingly, was often cynical, and he was known to drive a hard bargain for his ultimate choice of doctrine. The moral is not merely that the missionary frequently produced educational effects he did not intend, but that often, when he achieved his intended effect, it was of questionable worth. But that did not seem to deter the missionary then, and it has not seemed to deter the many generations of missionaries since, who have carried on their work in plantations beyond the seas.

[30] S.P.G. Minutes, March 11, 1757, Journals, XIII, 126; and E. B. O'Callaghan, ed., *Documents Relative to the Colonial History of the State of New York* (10 vols. and *General Index;* Albany: Weed, Parsons and Company, 1856-1861), VII, 347.

Part IV

UTILITARIANISM

A great stock of learning, without knowing how to make it useful in the conduct of life, is of little significancy.

WILLIAM SMITH

INTRODUCTION

No quality so marked the character of provincial America as its expansiveness, in material as well as in spatial terms. Fed by a high natural birth rate and a continuing flow of migrants from Europe and Africa, colonial agriculture, industry, and commerce flourished with an unprecedented vitality; and, for those disposed to read the future in the developing traits of the new society, that vitality held the key to much that was distinctive. "We are all animated with the spirit of an industry which is unfettered and unrestrained, because each person works for himself," observed the *émigré* farmer Crèvecoeur in an idyll addressed to an audience of faintly envious Frenchmen. From the involuntary idleness, servile dependence, and useless labor of Europe, the eighteenth-century American had passed on to a new form of honest toil, founded upon the most fundamental of natural principles, self-interest. That honest toil, Crèvecoeur asserted, had transformed a continent, bringing forth new men endowed with an ample subsistence and marked by a proud and stubborn independence of mind and character.[1]

The fruits of that honest toil were everywhere apparent: in the incessant conversion of forest into arable land; in the rising exports of tobacco, rice, and indigo produced as cash crops; in the developing extractive and manufacturing industries such as fishing, lumbering, fur-trading, shipbuilding, ironmaking, and textile manufacturing; in the thriving internal commerce between New England and the West Indies and among the various continental colonies (much of it involved in the not so honest slave trade); and in the burgeon-

[1] J. Hector St. John de Crèvecoeur, *Letters from an American Farmer* (1782), edited by Warren Barton Blake (New York: E. P. Dutton & Co., 1957), pp. 36-39.

ing towns and cities of the mainland with their diversified shops
and services and their varied cultural fare. And, given the operation
of the principle of self-interest, the outcome of that honest toil
was a constant reshuffling of wealth and status, as fortunes were
garnered and consolidated, and social alliances contracted and
cemented.

Inevitably, education entered in, having long served both social
and utilitarian ends in the English tradition. For the ambitious
entrepreneur, there were the preachments of Daniel Defoe and
Benjamin Franklin, who celebrated trade as a most noble and instructive way of life and who counseled the aspiring young tradesman to seek at least the knowledge requisite to his business. For
the ambitious farmer, there were the practical advices of Jared
Eliot's *Essays upon Field-Husbandry in New-England* (1748-1760),
to say nothing of the more traditional social wisdom of Henry
Peacham and Richard Brathwaite, stressing learning as one component of gentility. And for all enterprising Americans there were
the characteristic Baconian adages about knowledge in general
serving to increase men's power over nature and thereby "multiply
the conveniences or pleasures of life."[2]

Not everyone, of course, partook of the new expansiveness. It best
suited those who were already participants in the cheap land and
wage system, though it was patently relevant to those who labored
under indenture. But it simply did not apply to the enslaved—or
even the free—Indian or Afro-American. For the slave, the expansiveness of the economy was a daily fact of life, in whose burden
he participated but in whose fruits he did not share. What rhetoric
there was about his education dealt largely with those creedal
necessities associated with baptism or those technical skills associated with a farm or household economy. And, for the free Indian,
black, or mulatto, access to occupations was sufficiently restricted by
social covenant and convention to make any substantial education a
luxury. Once again, particular blacks and Indians transcended all
obstacles and made their way into the world of affairs and intellect.
But the stark fact of provincial America is that color was generally
a bar to economic advancement and hence a basis for educational
deprivation, setting in motion a circle of failure and despair that was
destined to persist for generations.

[2] *The Papers of Benjamin Franklin*, edited by Leonard W. Labaree and Whitfield J. Bell, Jr. (13+ vols.; New Haven: Yale University Press, 1959-   ), II, 282.

Chapter 12

THE USES OF LEARNING

Most of the learning in use is of no great use.

BENJAMIN FRANKLIN

"I have lately got a little leisure to think of some additions to my book, against the next edition," John Locke wrote to his friend William Molyneux on April 10, 1697, "and within these few days have fallen upon a subject that I know not how far it will lead me. I have written several pages on it, but the matter, the further I go, opens the more upon me, and I cannot yet get any sight of the end of it. The title of the chapter will be *Of the Conduct of the Understanding,* which, if I pursue, as far as I imagine it will reach, and as it deserves, will, I conclude, make the largest chapter in my *Essay.*" The *Conduct* did not appear in the next edition of the *Essay,* nor in any other for that matter; it was eventually published in a posthumous collection of essays and letters, in the unfinished form in which Locke had left it. But it would indeed have made the largest chapter of the *Essay,* and one of the most significant. For it drew from the body of that work many of Locke's most profound insights into the nature and character of education, and organized them into a systematic presentation that remains essential to a proper understanding of Locke's overall philosophy.[1]

Recall for a moment the central arguments of *Some Thoughts Concerning Education,* which Locke had composed a decade earlier. The four great ends of education are set forth there as virtue, wis-

---

[1] John Locke to William Molyneux, April 10, 1697, in *Some Familiar Letters Between Mr. Locke, and Several of His Friends* (London: printed for A. and J. Churchill, 1708), p. 194.

dom, breeding, and learning, with virtue conceived as the good life based on belief in Christ, wisdom as the able management of one's business affairs, breeding as the ability to think well of oneself and others, and learning as the possession of an ample stock of useful knowledge. Recall, too, that of the four learning explicitly comes last, as of little value unless joined to a properly formed character, and patently receives the fullest discussion, given Locke's grave doubts about traditional conceptions and his earnest desire to put forward a more defensible view.

There is a marked utilitarian flavor about the formulations of the *Thoughts,* nowhere more pronounced, perhaps, than in Locke's lengthy treatment of the curriculum. The child is to begin by learning to read and write as painlessly as possible in his native tongue, using the traditional progression from hornbook to primer to Psalter to Bible. Once this is under way, he should be introduced conversationally (rather than grammatically) to the study of Latin and at least one modern language, possibly French. Then, in place of the usual preoccupation with ancient languages and abstruse philosophy, Locke recommends some introduction to arithmetic, geometry, astronomy, geography, chronology, anatomy, aspects of history, and "all other parts of knowledge of things, that fall under the senses, and require little more than memory." Later, he suggests certain more abstract studies such as ethics, law, logic, rhetoric, and natural philosophy. And, to ensure that there are accomplishments other than those to be had from studies and books, Locke also counsels early instruction in dancing, music, fencing, horsemanship, and some such manual art as gardening, joinery, metalwork, or bookkeeping. Finally, he briefly commends the advantages of travel for the facilitation of language learning and the advancement of prudence and wisdom that derive from "seeing men, and conversing with people of tempers, customs, and ways of living, different from one another, and especially from those of his parish and neighborhood." Thus Locke's advice to those who would "dare venture to consult their own reason, in the education of their children, rather than wholly to rely upon old custom."[2]

In addition to these substantive proposals, Locke's treatise is replete with the best of the Renaissance commonplaces about pedagogy, many of them obviously gleaned from Montaigne and Bacon.

[2]*The Educational Writings of John Locke,* edited by James L. Axtell (Cambridge: Cambridge University Press, 1968), pp. 270, 321, 325.

There are the characteristic caveats against overreliance on authority, excessive rote learning, preoccupation with words, and all other forms of pedantry. And there are the characteristic prescriptions concerning the adaptation of teaching to temperament, the substitution of encouragement for punishment, and, more generally, the apt pursuit of method. In history, Locke counsels, the order of time should govern; in philosophy, the order of nature, that is, the progression from that which is already known to that which lies next and is coherent to it. The supreme model, of course, is the reasoning of "the incomparable Mr. Newton" in his admirable work, the *Principia*.[3]

The *Thoughts* clearly pertains to a tutorial relationship in which an aspiring young gentleman is systematically introduced to a variety of studies by an able and informed teacher of good character. But Locke is quite explicit about his belief that any gentleman who would penetrate more deeply into one or another of these studies must do so on his own, "for nobody ever went far in knowledge, or became eminent in any of the sciences by the discipline and constraint of a master." And it is here that *Of the Conduct of the Understanding* becomes complementary to the *Thoughts,* as a kind of manual of general method for the young man who would venture even farther into the world of learning.[4]

Locke's problem in the *Conduct* is the training of the understanding so that it will more effectively guide behavior. With appropriate allusions to Bacon he lashes out against the traditional logic taught in the universities and explains his presumption in proposing a superior one on the simple grounds of necessity. In characteristic Baconian fashion, too, he divides his discussion between hindrances to the understanding, such as prejudice, passion, haste, and partiality, and aids to the understanding, such as objectivity, observation, analysis, and perseverance. Also in a Baconian vein, he is as sharp with those who attribute all knowledge to the moderns as he is with those who assume it resides wholly with the ancients. "Some will not admit an opinion not authorized by men of old, who were then all giants in knowledge . . . ," he laments. "Others, with a like extravagancy, contemn all that the ancients have left us and, being taken with the modern inventions and discoveries, lay by all that went before, as if whatever is called old

3 *Ibid.*, p. 306.
4 *Ibid.*, p. 198.

must have the decay of time upon it and truth too were liable to mold and rottenness."[5]

As in the *Thoughts,* Locke assumes in the *Conduct* that men are variously endowed by nature but largely shaped by education. Hence, he is at pains to point to the need for the proper training and exercise of the powers and faculties given at birth. In the absence of training and exercise, powers atrophy and there is no reviving them. As in the *Thoughts,* too, the approach is thoroughly empirical. Assuming the central role of experience, Locke cautions insistently against any substitute for personal observation. "Knowing is seeing," he asserts, "and, if it be so, it is madness to persuade ourselves that we do so by another man's eyes, let him use never so many words to tell us that what he asserts is very visible." And, assuming the value of reflection, he advises that relentless probing beyond masses of simple facts that yields true principles on which to base new knowledge or wise action. "Particular matters of fact are the undoubted foundations on which our civil and natural knowledge is built," he observes; "the benefit the understanding makes of them is to draw from them conclusions which may be as standing rules of knowledge and consequently of practice."[6]

Finally, the whole temper of the *Conduct* is thoroughly utilitarian. Locke's enterprise, here as in the *Thoughts,* is to reconceive the pursuit of learning, not as the special vocation of the cleric or scholar but rather as the general obligation of the gentleman of affairs. Hence his insistence that the value of truths be measured "by their usefulness and tendency." Hence his countless allusions to the workaday world by way of example. And hence, too, his frequent and savage cuts at scholastics, logic tricksters, and overly bookish men full of contention and bereft of judgment. The ultimate business of learning is not mastery of a particular science, or, indeed, of all the sciences, but rather the development of the capacities that enable a man "to attain any part of knowledge he shall apply himself to or stand in need of in the future course of his life." For Locke as for Bacon, learning is of the world and for the world: it enables the learner to know more of life so that ultimately he can live more richly.[7]

[5] *John Locke's* "Of the Conduct of the Understanding," edited by Francis W. Garforth, Classics in Education, no. 31 (New York: Teachers College Press, 1966), p. 79.

[6] *Ibid.,* pp. 86, 64.

[7] *Ibid.,* pp. 87, 63.

II

Locke's views both symbolized and strengthened a developing utilitarianism about learning that was coming to prevail in the Anglo-
American world at the time of his death in 1704. The colonists
were thoroughly familiar with the *Essay* and the *Thoughts,* which
circulated briskly in all regions and were commonly referred to
in letters and periodicals; and the *Conduct* was available in one or
another of the editions of the *Collected Works,* first published in
1714. Yet, in the realm of learning as in the realm of piety, Locke
was even better known through a burgeoning popular literature
that reflected—or at least coincided with—some of his most characteristic views; and, indeed, toward the end of the century, that
literature was increasingly wont to attribute commonplaces to him,
whether or not they were his. A flood of pamphlets, periodicals,
almanacs, children's books, and manuals of advice deliberately undertook to instruct the public in the precepts of "Lord Bacon, the
incomparable Mr. Newton, and the great Mr. Locke," as the litany
went; and, while the Lockean views that came through such popularizations were almost as often imputed as they were properly inferred, there is no denying that such popularizations did give
enormous circulation to certain aspects of Locke's corpus.

Consider, for example, the characteristic utilitarianism proffered
by the popular English serials, *The Tatler, The Spectator,* and *The
Guardian.* Representing the full flowering of the periodical essay
that was so much a part of the Augustan age in English letters, the
three journals contributed significantly to a developing hagiography
that stood Bacon, Boyle, Newton, and Locke alongside Homer,
Plato, Aristotle, and Cicero as among the greatest men of all time.
"I find you frequently mention him," Penance Cruel interjected in
relating to Mr. Spectator a story about Mr. Locke's contempt for
gaming. And indeed Mr. Spectator had.[8]

Richard Steele, a young Dubliner who had entered upon a
career of letters after a period of study at Oxford and a short-lived
venture with the military, launched *The Tatler* in 1709, in the form
of a single unfolded sheet containing two columns of print on both
sides and published three times a week at a penny a copy. "What

---

[8] *The Spectator,* edited by Gregory Smith (rev. ed.; 4 vols.; London: J. M. Dent
& Sons Ltd, 1945), no. 532, Nov. 10, 1712, IV, 181.

mankind does is grist for us," the motto proclaimed, followed by the promise of a mixed fare of poetry, learning, foreign and domestic news, accounts of gallantry, pleasure, and entertainment, and whatever else the editor chose to offer on any other subject. The promise was more than fulfilled, as subsequent issues presented to a growing audience not only the wit of Steele and the political urbanity of his old friend Joseph Addison but contributions also from Jonathan Swift, John Hughes, Eustace Budgell, and William Congreve. In 1711 the thrice-weekly *Tatler* gave way to the daily *Spectator,* with its single theme dominating each issue and with its occasional disquisitions from Hughes, Budgell, and Alexander Pope. For over five hundred numbers, the journal commented brilliantly and bitingly on the Britain of Queen Anne, its foremost men and women, its treasured customs and sentiments, and its favorite fads and foibles, with a familiarity and directness that made its columns the common fare of coffeehouse and drawing-room conversation throughout the English-speaking world. Finally, *The Guardian* came into being in 1713, some three months after the discontinuance of *The Spectator,* and lasted through 175 issues, until October 1, 1713.[9]

From the beginning, the purpose of the Addison-Steele effort was explicitly moral and self-consciously didactic. The very first issue of *The Tatler* spoke of "instructing" those politic persons "who are so public-spirited as to neglect their own affairs to look into the transactions of state." The third issue told of the paper's interest in the reformation of manners and the suppression of profanity. And the final issue sketched the general purpose of the whole effort as the recommendation of "truth, innocence, honor, and virtue, as the chief ornaments of life." Similarly, through its cast of fictional characters, *The Spectator* sought satirically as well as directly to convey useful knowledge and creditable standards of taste at the same time that it mocked absurdity, pretentiousness, and affectation; while *The Guardian* proclaimed as its prime purpose the protection of the modest and industrious, the celebration of the wise and valiant, the encouragement of the good and pious, the confrontation of the impudent and idle, the contemning of the vain and cowardly, and the disappointment of the wicked and profane.[10]

9 *The Tatler,* edited by George A. Aitken (4 vols.; New York: Hadley & Mathews, 1899), no. 1, April 12, 1709, I, 11. .

10 *Ibid.,* no. 1, April 12, 1709, I, 11; no. 271, December 30, 1710, to January 2, 1711, IV, 375; *The Spectator,* no. 10, March 12, 1711, I, 31-34; no. 434, July 18, 1712, III, 343-345; *The Guardian* (7th ed.; 2 vols.; printed for J. and R. Tonson, 1740), no. 1, March 12, 1713, I, 11.

With respect to education, the journals were unequivocally committed to a heightened role for learning in the life of affairs and relentlessly critical of pedantry in all its forms. Addison remarked at one point, much in the spirit of Erasmus, that he was ambitious to have it said of him that he had brought philosophy out of closets, libraries, schools, and colleges, to dwell instead at clubs, assemblies, tea tables, and coffeehouses; and, time and again thereafter, he and Steele came back to the value of useful knowledge in promoting individual success and thereby the public good. Not surprisingly, this view was often accompanied by an advocacy of business as an appropriate career for the gentleman and by allusions to learning as a road to gentility.[11]

As for the agencies of education, the journals were full of Lockean exhortations about proper parental training and Lockean criticisms of the tyranny of schooling. More intriguing, perhaps, there were frequent remarks concerning the educational value of good conversation in coffeehouses—at one point Addison referred to them as the "British schools of politics"—and occasional comments too about the educational role of the Royal Society, though the latter were tempered by criticism of those virtuosi who had displayed the new pedantry of the scientific dilettante. On the whole, such pedagogical precepts as the journals ventured were quite specific, and the aspiring middle-class family that sought to follow them doubtless found, upon gathering the several papers together, that it had in hand a delightfully urbane guide to activity, virtue, and sensibility in this world and to the anticipated fruits of the next. Little wonder that the papers were avidly read in the colonies by enterprising young men who were seeking to live by their wits.[12]

Lockean views on learning were also disseminated in the colonies by the works of James Burgh and Isaac Watts. Burgh included a major section on knowledge in *The Dignity of Human Nature* (1754), which presented a detailed plan of studies for children from the age of six to maturity and a comprehensive series of booklists with which the ambitious might instruct themselves in every significant field. "The present," Burgh counseled his readers, "is by no means an age of indulging ignorance. A person, who thinks to have any credit among mankind, or to make any figure in conversation, must

11 *The Spectator*, no. 10, March 12, 1711, I, 31-32; *The Tatler*, no. 246, October 31, 1710, IV, 246; *The Spectator*, no. 105, June 30, 1711, I, 321-323; *The Guardian*, no. 94, June 29, 1713, II, 50-54; no. 111, July 18, 1713, II, 109-112.
12 *The Spectator*, no. 305, February 19, 1712, II, 417; *The Guardian*, no. 1, March 12, 1713, I, 9-13.

absolutely resolve to take some pains to improve himself. We find more true knowledge at present in shops and countinghouses, than could have been found an age or two ago in universities. For the bulk of the knowledge of those times consisted in subtle distinctions, laborious disquisitions, and endless disputes about words. The universal diffusion of knowledge, which we observe at present among all ranks of people, took its rise from the publishing [of] those admirable essays, the *Spectator, Tatler,* and *Guardian,* in which learned subjects were, by the elegant and ingenious authors, cleared from the scholastic rubbish of Latin and logic, represented in a familiar style, and treated in a manner which people of plain common sense might comprehend."[13]

Arguing that the chief differences among men had always inhered in different degrees of knowledge, Burgh went on to assert the moral obligation of all men to enlarge their understanding and ennoble their minds. And the key to achieving that end, he insisted, would be schooling conducted by teachers of unexceptionable character, good breeding, and knowledge of the world, teachers totally disengaged from other pursuits and wholly committed to the instruction of youth under their care "in all the branches of useful and ornamental knowledge, suitable to their ages, capacities, and prospects, and especially in the knowledge of what will make them useful in this life, and secure the happiness of the next." Having departed in this instance alone from Locke, that is, in his devotion to schooling, Burgh then proceeded to propose a thoroughly Lockean education, based on Locke as authority and rooted in Locke as substance. Indeed, only Milton, Addison, and Steele were tendered equal respect as pedagogues, and only Newton as thinker—the Newtonian philosophy being referred to as "the summit and pinnacle of knowledge, the utmost reach of human capacity."[14]

Not surprisingly, the chief books Burgh recommended for "putting young persons in the way of reasoning justly" were Locke's *Essay* and Isaac Watts's *Logick.* From the latter, the reader would have gleaned a fairly down-to-earth presentation of the subject, drawn essentially from the writings of Aristotle and the French philosopher Jean Le Clerc, and from Locke's *Essay.* Watts's textbook was widely used in the colonial colleges and academies as an explicitly Lockean

---

[13] James Burgh, *The Dignity of Human Nature* (new ed.; London: printed for C. Dilly, 1795), p. 121.
[14] *Ibid.,* pp. 141-142, 145, 179.

introduction to the systematic study of logic, and it doubtless led many a reader to the *Essay* itself. Yet even its influence as a disseminator of Lockean ideas was vastly exceeded by another of Watts's works, *The Improvement of the Mind*, which had first been published in 1741 as an extension of the *Logick* expressly intended to bring reason into the domain of everyday affairs.[15]

Watts's biographer once remarked that, while the *Logick* was meant to make reason comprehensible, the *Improvement* was meant to make it usable. And, indeed, Watts is at pains throughout the volume to deal with the multifarious commonplace occasions that demand the exercise of judgment and understanding on the part of the average man and woman. Defining logic as instruction in "the right use of reason in the acquirement and communication of all useful knowledge," he sets forth a series of maxims which, if followed, promise significant improvements in understanding among the "common and busy ranks of mankind." Five prime means are suggested for improving the mind: observation, reading, lectures, conversation, and systematic study. For each Watts sets forth principles for obtaining maximum advancement. In connection with observation, for example, he cautions against hastily erected generalizations drawn from a small number of data. In connection with books, he argues that the central task is not merely to know the opinions of the author but also to subject them to criticism and appraisal. In connection with lectures, by which Watts means to embrace the whole realm of oral instruction, he admonishes against "pert young disciples" who fancy themselves wiser than their teachers. In connection with conversation, he urges the avoidance of "everything that tends to provoke passion, or raise a fire in the blood." And, in connection with study, by which he also means to imply meditation, he urges a sensible pace that would prevent too much of any one subject from being presented all at once or too many different subjects at the same time. Beyond these strictures, there are special chapters dealing with the fixing of attention, the improvement of memory, and the nature of the several sciences and their particular uses to the several professions.[16]

A second part of *The Improvement of the Mind*, written by Watts

15 *Ibid.*, p. 155.

16 Arthur Paul Davis, *Isaac Watts* (privately printed, 1943), p. 89; Isaac Watts, *The Improvement of the Mind: or, A Supplement to the Art of Logic. In Two Parts. To Which Is Added a Discourse on the Education of Children and Youth* (Exeter, N.H.: J. Lamson and T. Odiorne, 1793), part I, pp. 3, 57, 78.

during the last years of his life but published only posthumously in 1751, presented rules and principles for the communication of useful knowledge to others. "If the treasures of the mind should be hoarded up and concealed," Watts argues, "they would profit none besides the possessor, and even his advantage by the possession would be poor and narrow, in comparison of what the same treasures would yield, both to himself and to the world, by a free communication and diffusion of them." Believing thus, Watts goes on to deal with preaching and teaching, styles of instruction (a style fit for instruction should be "plain, perspicuous, and easy"), modes of prejudice and ways of overcoming it, types of sermon ("wisdom [is] better than learning in the pulpit"), and principles for the writing of books addressed to the general public.[17]

In all of this, there is no denying that Watts was writing essentially on pedagogy; and, indeed, *The Improvement of the Mind* may well have been the single most popular tract on the subject to circulate in eighteenth-century America, standing in relation to the *Logick* much as Locke's *Of the Conduct of the Understanding* stood in relation to the *Essay*. That this pedagogical essence was well perceived at the time is indicated by the inclusion in some editions of the work of Watts's *Discourse on the Education of Children and Youth*, which also appeared posthumously, in 1753. Arguing that children ought to be instructed in "those things that are necessary and useful for them in their rank and station, and that with regard to this world and the world to come," Watts proposed that six considerations be uppermost in mind: proper training in religion; systematic cultivation of the understanding, the memory, the judgment, the faculty of reason, and the conscience; fundamental training in reading, spelling, and writing; systematic instruction in the conduct of human life and the art of self-government; the teaching of some proper trade, business, or profession; and, finally, an introduction to the ornaments of life, namely, history, poetry, painting, and the like. Parents are cautioned concerning their crucial role in the proper management of such education; and the "middle way" is put forth as the guide in matters of liberty and authority, freedom and restraint. The cast is Lockean, the spirit utilitarian, the character moderate— all, once again, qualities that seemed exceedingly attractive to an audience of enterprising colonials intent upon equipping their chil-

[17] *Ibid.*, part II, pp. 1, 8, 36.

dren with the best education possible for seizing upon the opportunities of the new society they were helping to build.[18]

III

"About this time," Benjamin Franklin reminisced in a memorable
passage of the *Autobiography*, "I met with an odd volume of *The
Spectator*. It was the third. I had never before seen any of them. I
bought it, read it over and over, and was much delighted with it. I
thought the writing excellent, and wished if possible to imitate it.
With that view, I took some of the papers, and making short hints
of the sentiment in each sentence, laid them by a few days, and then
without looking at the book, tried to complete the papers again, by
expressing each hinted sentiment at length and as fully as it had
been expressed before, in any suitable words, that should come to
hand." Franklin was probably around fourteen or fifteen years of
age at the time and serving as an apprentice to his brother James,
who was publisher of *The New-England Courant*. The immediate
outcome of his effort is well known: on April 2, 1722, the so-called
Silence Dogood letters began to appear anonymously in the *Courant*,
commenting satirically from time to time on politics, religion, manners, education, and, during James Franklin's brief incarceration for
overly forthright criticism of the authorities, freedom of the press.
But there was a larger outcome of this and countless other such
efforts that holds the key to understanding Franklin in particular and eighteenth-century American education in general: that outcome was Franklin himself, the earliest symbol of the self-made
American, self-made in that he was self-educated.[19]

The story of Franklin's life is familiar, in large part from his own
masterful telling of it. He was born in Boston in 1706, the youngest
son of a tradesman's family of old English Protestant stock. All his
brothers were put out as apprentices; but Ben, seeming more inclined
to books than the others, was regarded by his father as the "tithe of
his sons to the service of the church." He was duly started on his
studies at the age of eight, first at the Latin school and then in the
classes of George Brownell, who specialized in the teaching of writ-

18 *Ibid.*, p. 60.
19 *The Autobiography of Benjamin Franklin*, edited by Leonard W. Labaree,
Ralph L. Ketcham, Helen C. Boatfield, and Helene H. Fineman (New Haven: Yale
University Press, 1964), pp. 61-62. Only a century and a half later was it definitely
established that the letters had flowed from Ben Franklin's pen.

ing and arithmetic. After two years, however, his father took him out in favor of an apprenticeship, first in the elder Franklin's own candlemaking establishment, then in the cutler's shop of Ben's cousin Samuel, and then in his brother James's print shop. He learned the printing trade well, but broke his indenture in 1723 and began an odyssey that would take him to Philadelphia for a time, then to London, where he worked as a printer for almost two years, and then back to Philadelphia, where he eventually organized his own printing business with Hugh Meredith in 1728. Together they purchased *The Pennsylvania Gazette* from Samuel Keimer and had begun to make a success of it when Meredith's propensity for drink and gaming forced Franklin to dissolve the partnership and strike out on his own. By 1730, at the age of twenty-four, he was the sole owner of the establishment and of the *Gazette,* and launched upon the series of publishing ventures that were destined to make his name a household word, first in the colonies and later in Europe as well.

As Franklin's shop prospered he found time to contribute to various public enterprises, beginning with his clerkship to the Pennsylvania assembly in 1736. By 1748, he was able to retire from business and give his entire energies to public affairs and private pursuits, serving as deputy postmaster general to the colonies, as Penn's delegate to the Albany Congress, as colonial agent in London for Georgia, New Jersey, and Massachusetts, as delegate to the Continental Congress, as diplomatic representative of the new Republic in London and Paris, and as member of the Constitutional Convention, and carrying on a voluminous correspondence with many of the leading scientists and philosophers of Europe and America. He died in 1790, much honored by his countrymen and universally acclaimed as one of the most civilized men of his era.

Franklin's education holds the key to his profound influence on his own and subsequent generations. As reported in the *Autobiography,* which was explicitly written with a didactic purpose in mind, his entire life was a succession of projects, experiments, and observations, or, as Bernard Bailyn once put it, a series of problems in education. Franklin recalled four works as having had an early and lasting impression on his outlook: John Bunyan's *The Pilgrim's Progress,* Cotton Mather's *Bonifacius, The Spectator*, and Daniel Defoe's *An Essay upon Projects* (1697) (which set forth Defoe's varied schemes for social and economic uplift and which Franklin quoted approvingly in one of the Dogood letters). His penchant for reading persisted throughout his life, the fare ranging from Thomas Tryon's *The Way to Health, Long Life and Happiness* (1683), with its vegetarian bias, to John Locke's *Essay*, with its empirical bias. He recalled, too, a youthful effort to achieve "moral perfection" by cataloguing thirteen key virtues (from temperance to humility) and arranging to give a week's strict attention to each in the effort to improve his character, assuming it would take thirteen weeks to go through the cycle and that four cycles might be accomplished in a year. And he recalled such enterprises as the launching of *Poor Richard's Almanack*, the invention of the Pennsylvania fireplace, the founding of the Philadelphia academy, and the carrying out of the experiments with electricity. The common thread in these and countless other projects in Franklin's life was self-instruction, the ability to learn from an experience that in its very nature was unprecedented and hence unprepared for: that experience was the rise to political and intellectual prominence of a candlemaker's son who had never gone to school more than two years and who had learned everything else he knew on his own.[20]

Self-education also holds the key to several other domains of Franklin's activity. The junto, for example, founded in 1727 as a "club for mutual improvement," was clearly a joint venture in self-education on the part of Franklin and his friends. Modeled in part on the neighborhood associations recommended by Mather in *Bonifacius* and possibly influenced too by John Locke's plan for a mutual improvement society in England, the junto served for forty years as an intellectual adjunct to Franklin's own educative activities. Similarly, like Mather before him, Franklin used his voluminous correspondence as an enterprise in self-education on an astonishing variety of topics—on slavery with Anthony Benezet, on orthography with Noah Webster, on electricity with Peter Collinson, on human character with his sister Jane Mecom, on the English language with David Hume, on constitutionalism with the Duc de la Rochefoucauld d'Enville, and on printing and publishing with William Strahan. Obviously, Franklin's efforts toward the establishment of the Library Company of Philadelphia in 1731 represented simply an extension

---

[20] *Ibid.*, pp. 43-44. Franklin doubtless saw the *Autobiography* as a conduct manual, much in the genre of Francis Osborne's *Advice to a Son* (1656) and William Penn's *Fruits of a Father's Love* (1726).

of the junto's opportunities for mutual education; while his *Proposal for Promoting Useful Knowledge Among the British Plantations in America* (1743), which led to the founding of the American Philosophical Society, was aimed at the creation of a more formal and prestigious junto.[21]

As in his own experience, so in his advice to others: Franklin saw in self-education the key to the successful conduct of life and he based his major educational efforts on the principle. The quintessential example, of course, was the annual *Poor Richard's Almanack*, which Franklin first issued in December, 1732, and which he continued thereafter for twenty-five years. "I endeavored to make it both entertaining and useful," he later reminisced, "and it accordingly came to be in such demand that I reaped considerable profit from it, vending annually near ten thousand. And observing that it was generally read, scarce any neighborhood in the province being without it, I considered it as a proper vehicle for conveying instruction among the common people, who bought scarce any other books. I therefore filled all the little spaces that occurred between the remarkable days in the calendar, with proverbial sentences, chiefly such as inculcated industry and frugality, as the means of procuring wealth and thereby securing virtue, it being more difficult for a man in want to act always honestly, as (to use here one of those proverbs) it is hard for an empty sack to stand upright."[22]

The "proverbial sentences" that Franklin alluded to were in effect a popular latter-day *Adagia* for the instruction of the eighteenth-century American. They were taken largely from anthologies such as Thomas Fuller's *Introductio ad Prudentiam* (*Introduction to Prudence*) (1726-1727), *Introductio ad Sapientiam* (*Introduction to Wisdom*) (1731), and *Gnomologia: Adages and Proverbs; Wise Sayings and Witty Sentences, Ancient and Modern* (1732); James Howell's *Lexicon Tetraglotton, An English-French-Italian-Spanish Dictionary* (1660); François de la Rochefoucauld's *Réflexions ou Sentences et Maximes Morales* (*Moral Maxims and Reflections*) (1665); and Samuel Richardson's "Moral and Instructive Sentiments," published as

21 *Autobiography of Benjamin Franklin*, p. 116; and Benjamin Franklin, *A Proposal for Promoting Useful Knowledge Among the British Plantations in America* (1743), in *The Papers of Benjamin Franklin*, edited by Leonard W. Labaree and Whitfield J. Bell, Jr. (13+ vols.; New Haven: Yale University Press, 1959-   ), II, 378-383.

22 *Autobiography of Benjamin Franklin*, pp. 163-164.

an appendix to the 1750-1751 edition of *Clarissa*. And they were re-phrased in Franklin's terse and homely language in such a way as quickly to become proverbial in the English-speaking colonies. They taught the virtues of industry, frugality, and prudence in the conduct of life, the possibilities of power and station to be derived from the pursuit of one's calling, and the principles of utility and self-help in the quest for education. "The doors of wisdom are never shut," Poor Richard counseled, warning also that "most of the learning in use is of no great use" and that "experience keeps a dear school, yet fools will learn in no other."[23]

It was virtually inevitable that one who espoused such sentiments would early come into conflict with the dominant ideals of con-temporary schooling, and Franklin early did. One of the Silence Dogood letters of 1722 reported Mrs. Dogood's dream of a temple whose entrance was guarded by two porters named Riches and Pov-erty, who permitted only those who had gained the favor of Riches to enter. Inside, on a stately and magnificent throne, sat Learning, surrounded by volumes in all languages; to her right sat English, smiling pleasantly and attired handsomely, while to her left sat Latin, Greek, and Hebrew, essentially reserved in character, their faces veiled. All who entered the temple tried to ascend to the throne, but most gave up and contented themselves with sitting at the foot in the company of Madam Idleness and her maid, Ignorance. On awakening, Mrs. Dogood was given to recognize that she had been dreaming about Harvard College.[24]

Some years later, after he had established himself in Philadelphia, Franklin drew up his *Proposals Relating to the Education of Youth in Pennsylvania*, a document apparently begun in 1743 but not actually published until 1749. Concerned in the first place "to pro-cure the means of a good English education," he sketched a plan for a school that would be largely residential in character and under the tutelage of a man of good understanding, learned in languages and the sciences, and especially versed in English. In the matter of the curriculum, Franklin suggested that it would be well if the students could be taught "everything that is useful, and everything that is ornamental: but art is long, and their time is short. It is therefore proposed that they learn those things that are likely to be most

23 *Papers of Benjamin Franklin*, V, 473; III, 347; II, 373; I, 281-282.
24 *Ibid.*, I, 14-18.

useful and most ornamental, regard being had to the several professions for which they are intended."[25]

From this now-classic statement of principle, Franklin went on to detail the specific subjects that would be included. All should be taught "to write a fair hand" and "something of drawing"; arithmetic, accounts, geometry, and astronomy; English grammar out of Tillotson, Addison, Pope, Sidney, Trenchard, and Gordon; the writing of essays and letters; rhetoric, history, geography, and ethics; natural history and gardening; and the history of commerce and principles of mechanics. Instruction should include visits to neighboring farms, opportunities for natural observations, experiments with scientific apparatus, and physical exercise. And the whole should be suffused with a quest for benignity of mind, which Franklin saw as the foundation of good breeding, and a spirit of service, which he regarded as "the great aim and end of all learning."[26]

Franklin later elaborated the *Proposals* in the *Idea of the English School,* published in 1751. There he sketched a curriculum extending over six years (or, in any case, over six classes), which would include most of the essential studies mentioned in the *Proposals,* and specifically cited Johnson's *Noetica* as the textbook for the work in logic and Johnson's *Ethices Elementa* as the textbook for the work in ethics (both of which, incidentally, Franklin intended shortly to publish). Insisting throughout that the purpose of the program was not to turn out scholars, poets, or scientists but rather to produce able men of affairs, Franklin concluded, "Thus instructed, youth will come out of this school fitted for learning any business, calling or profession, except such wherein languages are required," and qualified "to pass through and execute the several offices of civil life, with advantage and reputation to themselves and country."[27]

Now, however fresh these ideas might have seemed to contemporaries and however characteristically American they may seem in retrospect, they were less than wholly original. Franklin himself acknowledged at the beginning of the *Proposals* that many of his thoughts were derived from Milton's tractate *Of Education* (1644), Locke's *Some Thoughts Concerning Education,* David Fordyce's *Dialogues Concerning Education* (1745) (recall that Franklin attrib-

25 *The Writings of Benjamin Franklin,* edited by Albert Henry Smyth (10 vols.; New York: The Macmillan Company, 1904-1907), X, 10; and *Papers of Benjamin Franklin,* III, 404.
26 *Papers of Benjamin Franklin,* III, 404, 419.
27 *Ibid.,* IV, 108.

uted it to Francis Hutcheson), Obadiah Walker's *Of Education, Especially of Young Gentlemen* (1673), Charles Rollin's *De la Manière d'Enseigner et d'Étudier les Belles-Lettres* (*The Method of Teaching and Studying the Belles-Lettres,* 1726-1728), and George Turnbull's *Observations upon Liberal Education in All Its Branches* (1742). Of the six, Locke's work was by far the most influential, though beyond Franklin's specific citations it is difficult to determine precisely which ideas he took from the *Essay,* as contrasted with the *Thoughts,* and which ideas he drew from an increasingly Lockean common sense, as contrasted with one or another of Locke's works. From Milton, Franklin drew support for his proposals regarding civic education, an apt use, given the colonists' tendency by 1749 to link Milton with Sidney, Harrington, and Locke as an archetypical republican. From Rollin, who as principal of the Collège de Beauvais was the only practicing schoolman quoted in the *Proposals,* Franklin drew support for his ideas on the teaching of history and the sciences. From Turnbull, an Anglican clergyman; Fordyce, an Aberdeen professor; and Walker, a private tutor, Franklin seemed to have taken what were at best routine ideas. In addition to these sources specifically cited in the *Proposals,* there were doubtless more general influences on Franklin's educational views that came via his acquaintance with men such as George Whitefield and his personal knowledge of the various schools that went under the name "academy" in and around eighteenth-century London.

But, beyond these external sources, there was Franklin's own appraisal of the colonial experience and the sort of schooling that would produce men qualified "to pass through and execute the several offices of civil life, with advantage and reputation to themselves and country." However much Franklin may have borrowed the parts of his educational plan or at least sought authority for the parts, the schemes in their entirety are as original and autochthonous as the rephrased commonplaces of Poor Richard. The schemes have from time to time been labeled narrowly vocational, crassly materialistic, and even vaguely anti-intellectual; but they are actually none of these. If anything, they are anti-academicist, seeking to bring education into the world and place it in the service of particular men as well as mankind in general. Sir Humphry Davy once wrote of Franklin's contribution to science that he "in no case exhibited that false dignity, by which philosophy is kept aloof from common applications, and he . . . sought rather to make her a useful inmate and servant in the common habitations of man, than to preserve her merely as an object of admiration in temples and palaces." As with science, so with learning in general: Franklin sought to make her a useful inmate and servant in the common habitations of man.[28]

I V

By the 1750's and 1760's, Philadelphia had become a center of educational debate and innovation, not merely because of Franklin's various plans and activities, but because of a continuing influx of men and ideas from all over the Anglo-European world. Carl and Jessica Bridenbaugh have pictured the ferment largely as a struggle between those committed to a more traditional elitist-classical education and those pressing for a more novel democratic-vocational education, and certainly that conflict was central. But the fact is that Philadelphia also became something of a testing ground for a much broader range of educational theories and proposals, drawing not only from Milton, Locke, and Watts in England but from Rousseau, Rollin, and Fénelon on the Continent and from William Robertson, Lord Kames, William Cullen, and Adam Smith in Scotland. Indeed, as Douglas Milton Sloan has ably demonstrated, the impact of the Scottish Enlightenment on colonial educational thought was absolutely pervasive, going far beyond John Witherspoon and the College of New Jersey to touch every conceivable realm of curricular substance and method; and that pervasive impact was abundantly evident in Philadelphia, most notably in the writings of two leading educators, William Smith and John Morgan.[29]

Smith was born in Aberdeen in 1727, the son of a landholder of some means, and educated at King's College of the University of Aberdeen. He seems to have gone afterward to London, where there is some evidence of his having worked for a time as a clerk for the S.P.G. Then, in 1751, he immigrated to New York in the capacity of tutor to the children of Colonel Josiah Martin of Long Island. It was in the course of that service that he prepared a pamphlet entitled *A General Idea of the College of Mirania* (1753), which was quickly to call him to the attention of influential citizens of New York and Philadelphia, among them Benjamin Franklin. "I received . . . your

<hr>

28 *The Collected Works of Sir Humphry Davy*, edited by John Davy (9 vols.; London: Smith, Elder and Co., 1839-1840), VIII, 264-265.

29 Carl Bridenbaugh and Jessica Bridenbaugh, *Rebels and Gentlemen* (2d ed.; New York: Oxford University Press, 1962), chap. ii.

new piece on education," Franklin wrote to Smith on April 19, 1753, "which I shall carefully peruse; and give you my sentiments of it as you desire, per next post. . . . If it suits your conveniency to visit Philadelphia, before you return to Europe, I shall be extremely glad to see and converse with you here, as well as to correspond with you after your settlement in England. For an acquaintance and communication with men of learning, virtue and public spirit, is one of my greatest enjoyments."[30]

The origins of *Mirania* are shrouded. The probability is that Governor James De Lancey and others interested in the college projected for the province of New York had invited Smith to prepare it. The ideas of *Mirania*, however, are quite clear and explicit, the utopian form providing an excellent vehicle for proposals on which Smith had doubtless been ruminating at least since his own collegiate experience at Aberdeen. Mirania, the reader is told, is a province of the New World first settled by the English early in the seventeenth century. By the 1740's, the Miranians have become a "mighty and flourishing people, in possession of an extensive country, capable of producing all the necessaries, and many of the superfluities of life." Well aware of this, they have concluded that the only way to secure these advantages on any permanent basis is "to contrive and execute a proper scheme for forming a succession of sober, virtuous, industrious citizens, and checking the course of growing luxury." And what they see as decisively important in that scheme is "to accustom youth early to distinguish the true from the false, by directing their studies to such things as come more immediately home to their business and bosoms."[31]

Having reached these conclusions, the Miranians have proceeded to build a seminary appropriate to the needs of their province. With regard to learning, they have divided the people into two groups, one headed for the learned professions (divinity, law, medicine, and agriculture) and public office, the other headed for the mechanic professions, the trades, and all other occupations. The two groups are given their first three years of schooling in common, the effort being to dissolve prejudices and to encourage "indissoluble connections and

[30] Benjamin Franklin to William Smith, April 19, 1753, in *Papers of Benjamin Franklin*, IV, 467-470.
[31] [William Smith], *A General Idea of the College of Mirania* (New York: J. Parker and W. Weyman, 1753), pp. 9, 12-13. See also Smith's earlier essay *Some Thoughts on Education: With Reasons for Erecting a College in This Province, and Fixing the Same at the City of New York* (New York: J. Parker, 1752).

friendships." Then they enter upon two quite different curricula. Those destined for the trades proceed to a six-year mechanic's school, the program of which quite closely resembles that of the English school recently projected for the city of Philadelphia. Those destined for the professions proceed to a Latin school with a five-year program (four given over almost wholly to Latin with some minor studies in English and writing, and a fifth divided between Latin and Greek) and then to an undergraduate curriculum spanning four years —the first under a professor of mathematics, who teaches algebra, geometry, astronomy, chronology, and navigation along with such logic, metaphysics, and practical surveying as time and weather permit; the second under a professor of philosophy, who teaches ethics (out of Plato, Cicero, Locke, and Hutcheson), physics, natural history, and mechanical and experimental philosophy; the third under a professor of rhetoric and poetry, who teaches the precepts of oratory and the canons of taste and criticism (out of Cicero, Quintilian, Demosthenes, and Aristotle); and the fourth under the direction of the principal himself, who teaches agriculture and history, the former conceived as embracing hygiene, chemistry, and anatomy, and the latter conceived as a series of lessons in ethics and politics. The Miranians are explicit about their intention not to form poets, orators, and scientists in the final two years but rather men rational about the business of life. "A great stock of learning, without knowing how to make it useful in the conduct of life, is of little significancy," the narrator, Evander, points out. The ultimate object of the college is to make of youth masters of writing, speaking, acting, and living—in short, men sufficient to the responsibilities of virtuous and patriotic citizenship in Mirania.[32]

Smith's *Mirania* is easily the most characteristic and comprehensive formulation of the altered conceptions of piety, civility, and learning that underlay the development of education in eighteenth-century America. Yet it was Samuel Johnson, not Smith, who won the presidency of King's College when it was finally established. And it was in Philadelphia, in connection with Franklin's academy, rather than in New York, that Smith had the chance to realize his vision. Embarking on his duties there in 1754, he played a central role, together with Francis Alison, in developing the academy into the College of Philadelphia, and then accepted the post of provost in the new institution. The curriculum worked out for the college, which was first published in *The Pennsylvania Gazette* on August 12, 1756, represented a skillful detailing of Smith's earlier proposal, one that rested solidly on Scripture and the classics but was then enriched with a wide range of modern works such as Bacon's *Essays* (1597, 1612, 1625), Hutcheson's *A System of Moral Philosophy* (1755), Watts's *Logick* (1725, 1741, 1751) and *Brief Scheme of Ontology* (1733), Locke's *Essay* and *Two Treatises of Government* (1690), Newton's *Principia*, Pufendorf's *De jure naturae et gentium* (*On the Law of Nature and Nations*) (1672) and Sidney's *Discourses Concerning Government* (1698). To those who thought the three-year sequence overly demanding in its scope and intensity, Smith pleaded for the fair trial he thought was clearly due, given "the particular circumstances of these colonies, where very few youth can be detained for a long period at infant unendowed colleges, where they must wholly maintain themselves at a considerable expense, and where the genius seems not only to be sooner ripe, but where there is also a more immediate demand, and a more easy settlement to be obtained, in all the ways of genteel employment, for young men of parts, than there is in European countries."[33]

Smith's curriculum was patently rooted in King's College, Aberdeen, where he himself had been trained only a decade before, though it was also derived from some of the more recent reforms at Marischal College, Aberdeen, in 1753, where, following the general principles of Scottish realism, the curriculum progressed from particular and concrete studies to general and abstract studies and particular professors were made responsible for the conduct of particular phases of the course. It was also indebted to Franklin's *Proposals*, which Smith explicitly mentioned and had obviously read. Finally, as Theodore Hornberger pointed out some years ago, it was quite obviously drawn in part from Robert Dodsley's popular compendium of knowledge entitled *The Preceptor* (1748), to which the English Samuel Johnson had contributed a major preface on the scope and content of education.[34]

Yet, as in the case of Franklin, the existence of these sources must not overshadow the originality and uniqueness of Smith's proposals. Their recognition of the diversity of the middle colonies and the

[33] *The Pennsylvania Gazette*, no. 1442, August 12, 1756. See also "Account of the College and Academy of Philadelphia," *The American Magazine and Monthly Chronicle for the British Colonies*, I (1757-58), 630-640.

[34] Theodore Hornberger, "A Note on the Probable Source of Provost Smith's Famous Curriculum for the College of Philadelphia," *The Pennsylvania Magazine of History and Biography*, LVIII (1934), 370-377.

WILLIAM SMITH'S PROPOSED CURRICULUM FOR THE COLLEGE OF PHILADELPHIA 1756*

LECTURE I	LECTURE II		LECTURE III	PRIVATE HOURS
		FIRST YEAR		
Latin and English exercises	Arithmetic Decimal arithmetic Algebra	First Term	Homer, *Iliad* Juvenal	*The Spectator, The Rambler,* and monthly magazines for the improvement of style and knowledge of life
	Fractions and extracting roots Simple and quadratic equations Euclid, *Elements,* demonstrated by Edmund Stone (Books I-VI)	Second Term	Pindar Cicero Livy	Isaac Barrow, *Geometrical Lectures* Ignace Gaston Pardies, *Short, but Yet Plain Elements of Geometry and Plain Trigonometry* Colin Maclaurin, *A Treatise of Algebra* John Ward, *The Young Mathematician's Guide* John Keill, *The Elements of Plain and Spherical Trigonometry*
Logic with metaphysics William Duncan, *The Elements of Logick,* Jean Le Clerc, *Logica,* or Jean Pierre de Crousaz, *A New Treatise of the Art of Thinking*	Euclid, *Elements,* demonstrated by Edmund Stone (Books I-VI) Logarithmical arithmetic Henry Wilson, *Trigonometry Improved* Henry Sherwin, ed., *Mathematical Tables*	Third Term	Thucydides or Euripides Dionysius Periegetes, *Geography,* translated by E. Wells	Isaac Watts, *Logick, Philosophical Essays on Various Subjects,* and *Brief Scheme of Ontology* John Locke, *An Essay Concerning Human Understanding* Francis Hutcheson, *Metaphysicae synopsis* Bernardus Varenius, *A Compleat System of General Geography,* corrected by Peter Shaw William King, *An Essay on the Origin of Evil,* with notes by E. Law
Occasional disputation		Throughout	Occasional declamation	
		SECOND YEAR		
Logic, etc., reviewed Surveying and dialing Navigation	Plane and spherical trigonometry	First Term	"Rhetoric," in Robert Dodsley, *The Preceptor* Longinus	Gerhard Johannes Vossius, *Elementa rhetorica* René Le Bossu, *Traité du Poème Épique* Dominique Bouhours, *The Art of Criticism* John Dryden, *Select Essays on the Belles Lettres* Joseph Spence, *An Essay on Pope's Odyssey* Joseph Trapp, *Lectures on Poetry* Dionysius of Halicarnassus, *De structura orationis liber*
Conic sections Fluxions	Euclid, *Elements,* demonstrated by Edmund Stone (Books XI-XII) Architecture with fortification	Second Term	Horace, *Art of Poetry* Aristotle, *Art of Poetry* Quintilian	Demetrius Phalereus, *De elocutione, sive dictione rhetorica* Famianus Strada, *Prolusiones academicae oratoriae, historicae, poeticae, etc.* Archibald Patoun, *A Complete Treatise of Practical Navigation* David Gregory, *A Treatise of Practical Geometry* Charles Bisset, *The Theory and Construction of Practical Fortification* Thomas Simpson, *Elements of Plane Geometry*
David Fordyce, *The Elements of Moral Philosophy* (Fordyce well understood will be an excellent introduction to the larger ethic writers.)	John Rowning, *A Compendious System of Natural Philosophy* ("The Properties of Bodies," "The Mechanic Powers," "Hydrostatics," and "Pneumatics")	Third Term	Cicero, *Pro Milone* Demosthenes, *Pro Ctesiphon* (During the application of the rules to these famous orations, imitations of them are to be attempted on the	Colin Maclaurin, *A Treatise on Fluxions* William Emerson, *The Doctrine of Fluxions* Andrea Palladio, *Architecture,* translated by Isaac Ware Richard Helsham, *A Course of Lectures in Natural Philosophy* Willem Jakob Gravesande, *Mathematical Elements of Natural Philosophy* Roger Cotes, *Hydrostatical and Pneumatical Lectures* Desaguliers, J. T.

Exercises	Subjects and prescribed texts	Period	Recommended reading
Occasional declamation (models of perfect eloquence.)	John Rowning, *A Compendious System of Natural Philosophy* ("Light," "Colours," and "Optics") (Anonymous Jesuit) John Keill, *An Introduction to the True Astronomy* (Rowning's System may be supplemented by the larger works recommended for private study.)	Throughout	Pieter van Musschenbroek, *Elementa physicae* John Keill, *An Introduction to Natural Philosophy* Benjamin Martin, *Philosophia Britannica* Isaac Newton, *The Mathematical Principles of Natural Philosophy* Colin Maclaurin, *An Account of Sir Isaac Newton's Philosophical Discoveries* Jacques Rohault, *Natural Philosophy*, with notes by S. Clarke
		THIRD YEAR	
Occasional disputation	Francis Hutcheson, *A Short Introduction to Moral Philosophy* Jean Jacques Burlamaqui, *The Principles of Natural Law* Introduction to civil history Epictetus, *Enchiridion* Cicero, *De officiis* and *Tusculanae quaestiones* Xenophon, *Memorabilia* Denys Petau, *Rationarium temporum*	First Term	Samuel von Pufendorf, *Law of Nature and Nations*, with notes by Jean Barbeyrac Richard Cumberland, *A Treatise of the Laws of Nature* John Selden, *Of the Judicature in Parliaments* Montesquieu, *Spirit of the Laws* Algernon Sidney, *Discourses Concerning Government* James Harrington Seneca Francis Hutcheson, *A System of Moral Philosophy* John Locke, *Two Treatises of Government*
	Introduction to laws and government Introduction to trade and commerce Natural history of vegetables Natural history of animals Plato, *Laws* Hugo Grotius, *De jure belli ac pacis*	Second Term	Richard Hooker, *Of the Lawes of Ecclesiastical Politie* Joseph Justus Scaliger, *Opus novum de emendatione temporum* Robert Dodsley, *The Preceptor* Jean Le Clerc, *Compendium historiae universalis*
Review of the whole Examination for degree of B.A.	Composition and declamation on moral and physical subjects Philosophy acts held Hermann Boerhaave, *A New Method of Chemistry*, with notes by Peter Shaw Natural history of fossils Natural history of agriculture	Third Term	David Gregory, *The Elements of Astronomy* John Fortescue, *A Learned Commendation of the Politique Lawes of Englande* Nathaniel Bacon, *An Historical and Political Discourse of the Laws & Government of England* Francis Bacon, *Works* John Locke, *Several Papers Relating to Money, Interest and Trade* Charles Davenant, *Discourse on the Publick Revenues, and on the Trade of England* Joshua Gee, *The Trade and Navigation of Great-Britain Considered* John Ray, *The Wisdom of God Manifested in the Works of Creation* William Derham, *Physico-Theology* N. A. Pluche, *Spectacle de la Nature* Guillaume Rondelet, *Libri de piscibus marinis* Bernard Nieuwentijt, *The Religious Philosopher* Holy Bible
Study of the French language at leisure hours, if desired		DURING ALL THREE YEARS	Holy Bible to be read daily

* It is perhaps significant that while Smith specified particular classics to be used as texts, he suggested that alternative works might be substituted for these whenever necessary.

responsibility of education in the face of that diversity was profound, anticipating by a century the arguments for common schooling that would later be advanced by Horace Mann and his contemporaries. And the course of study itself was as comprehensive and thorough as any proposed in the pre-Revolutionary period. Smith himself proved less able as a teacher and academic leader than the Aratus of his utopia, who presided over the college of Mirania with consummate wisdom, goodness, and piety. A contemporary described Smith as a "haughty, self-opinionated, half-learned character"; and he seems to have spent a good part of his later life in political and legal controversy. But then, one might well inquire how many men with the versatility of a Thomas More the world has come to know in the centuries since the appearance of More's utopia.[35]

John Morgan was a student of William Smith and a member of the first graduating class of the College of Philadelphia. Indeed, his academic career provides dramatic testimony to the pervasiveness of Scottish influence on eighteenth-century American education. Morgan was sent at the age of ten or eleven to Samuel Finley's academy at Nottingham, Maryland, where he studied English and then went on to the classics, mathematics, and some work in natural philosophy. Thereafter, in 1750, at the age of fifteen, he entered upon an apprenticeship to Dr. John Redman, who had studied medicine in London and Edinburgh and who held a doctorate from the University of Leiden. Significantly, both Finley and Redman had studied with William Tennent at the Log College during the heyday of that institution.

While pursuing his work with Redman, Morgan enrolled in the new baccalaureate program of the College of Philadelphia and from 1754 to 1756 undertook a course of studies more or less like the one Smith published in *The Pennsylvania Gazette*. Having satisfactorily completed his work with Redman and Smith in the spring of the latter year, he accepted appointment as a regimental surgeon with the Pennsylvania militia, a commission he held for four years. Then, with a degree, an apprenticeship, and a varied medical experience, he set out for additional study in Europe, determined to establish himself as one of Philadelphia's leading physicians. Armed with letters of introduction to Thomas Penn and Benjamin Franklin, he went first to London, where he studied anatomy with Dr. William Hunter

[35] *The Literary Diary of Ezra Stiles*, edited by Franklin Bowditch Dexter (3 vols.; New York: Charles Scribner's Sons, 1901), III, 350.

and walked the wards of St. Thomas Hospital under the tutelage of
the attending surgeons there. Then, following in the footsteps of
his friend and fellow Philadelphian, William Shippen, Jr., he went
on in 1761 to the University of Edinburgh medical school, where he
studied chemistry with William Cullen and physiology with Robert
Whytt, read anatomy from the lecture notes of Alexander Munro,
made rounds in the Royal Infirmary under David Clerk and Colin
Drummond, and took active part in the weekly sessions of the medical
society, the oldest and most prestigious of the student societies at the
university. He completed his studies there in two years, taking the
M.D. degree in the summer of 1763 with a thesis on the formation of
pus that contravened a number of traditional theories on the basis
of experimental evidence.[36]

It was at Edinburgh, in innumerable conversations with his fellow students from America, that Morgan formed his idea for establishing a first-rate institution of medical education in America.
Shippen had actually returned to Philadelphia in 1762 and introduced a course on anatomy there, with a view to developing an independent medical school in the city. Morgan, after managing to gain
election to the Royal Society, the Royal College of Physicians of
London, and the Royal College of Physicians of Edinburgh, returned
to Philadelphia in 1765 with a plan for establishing medical studies
under the aegis of the College of Philadelphia, and was promptly
elected professor of the theory and practice of medicine there at a
meeting of the trustees on May 3. Four weeks later, at the end-of-May
commencement exercises, Morgan delivered his *Discourse upon the
Institution of Medical Schools in America*, an occasion his biographer
has aptly called "the hour of his greatest triumph."[37]

Morgan's *Discourse* intertwined two essential themes: a diagnosis
of the medical problem of the colonies and a proposal for its cure.
First, he lamented the deplorable state of medical practice, contending that the chief causes were inadequate training and insufficient
specialization. Under the apprenticeship system, he argued, practitioners were trained by other practitioners, themselves inadequately

36 Significantly, the medical faculty at Edinburgh had been profoundly influenced
by the teaching of Hermann Boerhaave, the Dutch physician, botanist, and chemist,
who had introduced the methods of clinical instruction at the University of Leiden;
hence, Morgan encountered at Edinburgh the best of both Continental and British
medicine. See J. D. Comrie, "Boerhaave and the Early Medical School at Edinburgh,"
Nederlandsch Tijdschrift voor Geneeskunde, LXXXII (1938), 4828-4835.

37 Whitfield J. Bell, Jr., *John Morgan: Continental Doctor* (Philadelphia: University of Pennsylvania Press, 1965), p. 118.

prepared, and were thereby subjected to the worst kind of instruction, which transmitted error as well as truth and offered few canons for separating the one from the other. Once trained as apprentices, practitioners were forced, owing to tradition and economic circumstance, to function not only as physicians but also as surgeons and pharmacists, doing all interchangeably and none well.

Morgan's solution to the problem was twofold: first, the separation of physic (which is "conversant about the cure of inward diseases, and such complaints as require the use of medicines") from surgery (which "principally regards external disorders, and those inward maladies which need the manual assistance of a dexterous operator to relieve them") and pharmacy; and, second, the development of a scientifically founded professional education for the preparation of physicians that would rest on a firm base of liberal education in the arts, sciences, and languages and include systematic training in anatomy, materia medica, botany, chemistry, the theory of physic (physiology and pathology), and the practice of medicine—in that order, since it was necessary to proceed from the more obvious facts of anatomy to the more abstract truths of medical theory if a genuine logic was to inhere in the curriculum.[38]

Morgan's *Discourse* has properly been celebrated as the charter of medical education in the colonies; and, though Morgan's ideas on the complete separation of physic, surgery, and pharmacy proved initially unfeasible, even for himself in Philadelphia, his ideas on medical education proved immensely influential, not only in Philadelphia but also in New York. Yet the significance of the *Discourse* goes far beyond medicine; for, in an era when neither the universities nor the professions were as sharply compartmentalized as they would later become, Morgan really provided a plan whereby the formal teaching of science within the university might go rapidly forward, on something of a Scottish model. The fact is that science was not nearly so wholly an amateur activity in eighteenth-century America as has traditionally been assumed; it was as vigorously and professionally pursued under the aegis of the medical faculties in Philadelphia and New York as it was under the William Smalls and the John Winthrops. And that this was so is of the utmost significance for understanding the aims of scientific inquiry in pre-Revolutionary America, as well as its extent and character.

[38] John Morgan, *A Discourse upon the Institution of Medical Schools in America* (Philadelphia: William Bradford, 1765), p. 5.

Chapter 13

THE BUSINESS OF LIVING

> If mankind would spend their time in the pursuit of true philosophy, and in the study of things of solid use and benefit, that they consume in cobweb learning to catch flies, they would be more judicious and knowing at twenty years of age, than usually they are at seventy.
>
> JAMES FRANKLIN

"Diligence is the mother of good luck," Poor Richard counseled, and, indeed, nothing so characterized Benjamin Franklin's life as diligence in the pursuit of his varied interests. About this he was quintessentially the eighteenth-century American. In a society where the cake of custom had been broken by a fundamentally new experience, where cheap land, flourishing commerce, and a persistent scarcity of labor had placed a premium on human ingenuity and enterprise, and where the right of each man to the fruits of his labor had been proclaimed as something of a Lockean gospel, diligence became, after inheritance, the leading way to wealth, status, and power, and hence truly the parent of fortune.[1]

That diligence, which so marked the character of Franklin and his contemporaries, pertained in education as elsewhere. Since the Renaissance at least, Englishmen had used the devices of education to advance their worldly estates, not merely in the arts and professions but in the trades and business as well. Now, in a new world marked by boundless opportunity, education seemed more than ever a key to advancement. As Franklin tried to teach in the *Autobiography*,

---

[1] *The Papers of Benjamin Franklin*, edited by Leonard W. Labaree and Whitfield J. Bell, Jr. (13+ vols.; New Haven: Yale University Press, 1959-), II, 138.

however, it was no narrow view of education that fired the imagination of the colonists but rather a vision as open as their land and its possibilities. "The doors of wisdom are never shut," Poor Richard taught, recognizing that life itself could be a continuing education for those enterprising men and women who would make it so. In the very business of living, the greatest profits accrued to those who learned most diligently.[2]

One Renaissance institution to which the colonists turned in growing numbers in their pursuit of education was didactic literature. By 1762 each of the thirteen colonies could boast at least one press, and the country as a whole around forty, with the result that there was a vast upsurge in the number of newspapers, almanacs, magazines, textbooks, manuals, sermons, legal codes, and pamphlets of every sort and variety available to the literate public. Charles Evans' *American Bibliography* lists over eighteen thousand titles that issued from the native presses between 1689 and 1783, and there is good reason to believe that there were actually four or five times that number, including broadsides, individual issues of newspapers, posters, legal and commercial forms, and other ephemera. Much of this material, including some with the largest circulation, was explicitly and self-consciously didactic in character and was so perceived by an expanding audience eager to partake of its instruction.

The printers themselves were a fascinating if sometimes puzzling and elusive group, involved as they were in entrepreneurial activity, public affairs, and cultural leadership; and one must bear in mind that Franklin was merely the best known among a diverse fraternity. There was his partner David Hall, for example, a native of Edinburgh and a journeyman in William Strahan's shop in London before Franklin called him to Philadelphia in 1743. An able craftsman and a prudent editor, Hall entered into a partnership with Franklin in 1748 and carried the major responsibility for the firm until 1766, when Franklin sold Hall his interest in the enterprise. Thereafter, Hall invited his journeyman William Sellers into partnership and continued the firm until his death in 1772. Also in Pennsylvania, there was Andrew Bradford, who had been trained in his father's shop in New York and who had then set up his own business in Philadelphia, where his father had earlier maintained a press; and

2 *Ibid.*, V, 473.

there was Christopher Saur, who was reportedly skilled in two dozen trades beyond the printer's and whose shop at Germantown was for years a cultural center of the German community there.

In New England, which continued to dominate colonial printing until well into the 1760's, there were men such as Bartholomew Green, who served nearly four decades as printer to the governor and council of Massachusetts; Thomas Fleet, whose more than two hundred fifty publications during the period between 1713 and 1758 reflected a phenomenal catholicity of interest, ranging from ecclesiastical controversy to Indian warfare; and James Franklin, who began his business in Boston and then moved it to Newport, Rhode Island, after a period of harassment by the Massachusetts authorities. In New York there were William Bradford, who came from Philadelphia in 1693 as printer to the government and continued in that capacity for over fifty years, and John Peter Zenger, who learned the trade in Bradford's shop and whose acquittal from charges of criminal libel brought by the governor and council of the province was perceived as a major victory for freedom of the press in the colonies. And in the South there was William Parks, whose dual responsibilities as public printer of Maryland and Virginia afforded him opportunity for extraordinary influence on the life and culture of both colonies.

One could easily argue that the entire output of these men educated the public, in that larger sense in which literature inevitably shapes the character and outlook of men. But in particular their almanacs, newspapers, and magazines, on the one hand, and their primers, manuals, and textbooks, on the other, were deliberately designed to teach and readily available to those desirous of learning. The almanac, for example, evolved into a major instrument of public education during the eighteenth century, and Franklin's sense that it could serve as "a proper vehicle for conveying instruction among the common people" was widely shared by both printers and their audiences. The first native almanacs of the seventeenth century had issued very quickly from the native presses and had looked, not surprisingly, much like their contemporary English counterparts. William Pierce's *An Almanack for the Year of Our Lord 1639* was the second publication of the Cambridge press and the first book printed in British North America, preceding even the Bay Psalm Book. John Foster's *An Almanack of Coelestial Motions for the Year of the Christian Aera, 1675* was the first item to appear from the first Boston press, while

Samuel Atkins' *Kalendarium Pennsilvaniense* (1685) was the first to appear from William Bradford's press and the first book printed in the middle colonies. These and other seventeenth-century issues, most of which were prepared at Harvard and printed in New England, contained the usual calendars and accompanying astronomical data, weather predictions, chronological tables of "memorable things," schedules of forthcoming events, occasional excursions into satire and practical advice, and, as the century progressed, brief scientific essays increasingly expounding the Copernican view. The evidence is that they circulated widely among the literate public, though it is important to bear in mind that they were prepared by the best-educated segment of the community.

As the number of presses increased after 1689, the number of almanacs rose proportionately: virtually every press published one, and almost always in large printings, so that a relatively popular issue, such as the Ames almanacs, could circulate on the average of sixty thousand annually between 1725 and 1764. Moreover, as circulation rose there was a corresponding popularization of content that both reflected and stimulated an increasingly diverse audience. The business of authorship tended to pass out of the hands of the academic intelligentsia, and, while some of the more popular series continued to emanate from men such as Theophilus Grew, who was the first professor of mathematics at the College of Philadelphia, a growing number were prepared by men who had educated themselves or whose formal education had been minimal. Roger Sherman, whose almanacs appeared in New England and New York from 1750 to 1761, was a self-taught shoemaker, who later went on to a notable political career as a member of the First Continental Congress. Nathaniel Ames and Nathaniel Whittemore were physicians who, so far as can be determined, learned their craft via the usual route of apprenticeship. And James Franklin, Benjamin Franklin, and Isaiah Thomas were self-educated printers.

These men brought new talents and sensibilities to their work and new perspectives concerning what the public needed and wanted by way of education. And in their enterprising hands the range and content of the almanacs broadened significantly to include the best of English poetry and prose, an infinite variety of essays on topics from anatomy to zoology, a wealth of vigorous political polemic, and every manner of practical advice, from remedies for minor diseases to hints on successful farming, from counsel on the management of household accounts to general advice on the conduct of life. "If mankind would spend their time in the pursuit of true philosophy, and in the study of things of solid use and benefit, that they consume in cobweb learning to catch flies," Poor Job lamented in James Franklin's almanac for 1755, "they would be more judicious and knowing at twenty years of age, than usually they are at seventy." And there was no missing Job's faith that his almanac presented just such a curriculum of "solid use and benefit."[3]

As with the almanac, so with newspapers and magazines: native issues began to appear in considerable numbers during the eighteenth century, and with explicitly didactic ends. The first American newspaper was issued by the Boston printer Benjamin Harris, under the title *Publick Occurrences, Both Forreign and Domestick,* on September 25, 1690. Four days later, however, the governor and council of Massachusetts declared their "high resentment and disallowance of said pamphlet" and ordered it suppressed. With that, Harris' venture collapsed, and it was not until 1704 that the next effort was made, in the form of John Campbell's *Boston News-Letter,* which first appeared on April 24 of that year and lasted until 1723 (at which time it was taken over by Bartholomew Green, Campbell's printer). Thenceforth, there was a continuing though erratic growth in the number and circulation of newspapers, right up to the onset of the Revolution, when there were thirty-seven in all.[4]

The first magazine published in British North America was Samuel Keimer's reprint of *The Independent Whig* of London, which he issued weekly for twenty numbers in 1724. The earliest native journals, interestingly enough, appeared within three days of one another in 1741, when Andrew Bradford published *The American Magazine, or, A Monthly View of the Political State of the British Colonies* on February 13 and Benjamin Franklin published *The General Magazine, and Historical Chronicle, for all the British Plantations in America* on February 16. Neither lasted more than six months, and it was not until the Boston printers Gamaliel Rogers and Daniel Fowle issued *The Boston Weekly Magazine,* later *The American Magazine and Historical Chronicle,* in September, 1743, that a magazine of any significant duration appeared—and even this

---

[3] *Poor Job. 1755, An Almanack* (Newport, R.I.: James Franklin, [1754]).

[4] *By the Governour & Councel,* Boston, September 29, 1690. For a checklist of colonial newspapers published between 1690 and 1783, see Clarence S. Brigham, *History and Bibliography of American Newspapers, 1690-1820* (2 vols.; Worcester, Mass.: American Antiquarian Society, 1947).

was discontinued in December, 1746. There followed a varied succession of serials, mostly from Philadelphia, Boston, and New York, all more or less transient. By 1783, there had been twenty-two in all, not counting *The Independent Whig*, though only one, *The Boston Magazine*, was actually appearing that year.[5]

It would be foolish to assert that all or even the major part of this periodical literature was explicitly designed to instruct anybody in anything. Issuing principally from the seaport towns, which were economic and political as well as cultural centers, the newspapers provided commercial intelligence from farmers in the hinterland and merchants on the waterfront, legislative and legal intelligence from the councils and the courts, and literary and scientific intelligence from local colleges, theatres, and societies; while the magazines presented a varied fare of fact and fiction that the Boston printer Benjamin Mecom once summed up as:

> Old-fashioned writings, and select essays,
> Queer notions, useful hints, extracts from plays,
> Relations wonderful, and psalm, and song,
> Goodsense, wit, humor, morals, all dingdong;
> Poems, and speeches, politics and news,
> What some will like, and other some refuse;
> Births, deaths, and dreams, and apparitions too;
> With something suited to each different *gou[t]*,
> To humor him, and her, and me, and you.[6]

Yet, granted the character of this miscellany, the printers and editors of these early serials also saw themselves as teachers and took ever so seriously their responsibility to communicate useful information to an increasingly literate public. Thus, Samuel Keimer pledged in 1728 that *The Universal Instructor in All Arts and Sciences; and the Pennsylvania Gazette* would contain "the theory of all arts, both liberal and mechanical, and the several sciences both humane and divine"; while Christopher Saur introduced *Der Hoch-Deutsch Pensylvanische Geschicht-Schreiber* with a promise of "timely remarks and questions for serious people to ponder, and perhaps even some honest answers." And three decades later, after the periodical press

---

[5] For a checklist of colonial magazines published between 1741 and 1783, see Lyon N. Richardson, *A History of Early American Magazines, 1741-1789* (New York: Thomas Nelson and Sons, 1931), pp. 363-369.

[6] *The New-England Magazine*, August, 1758, p. 1.

had begun to carry the debate over independence to the general public, John Holt of *The New-York Journal* boldly proclaimed the triumph of the newspaper as popular educator:

> 'Tis truth (with deference to the college)
> Newspapers are the spring of knowledge,
> The general source throughout the nation,
> Of every modern conversation.
> What would this mighty people do,
> If there, alas! were nothing new?[7]

An American could buy Ames's *Almanack* in 1750 for one shilling sixpence, while a common subscription rate for newspapers and magazines in that year was twelve shillings annually, with extra charges for post. Even granting the variations and fluctuations in colonial currencies, it is clear that such materials were by no means cheap, given a wage of two shillings a day for ordinary labor. Yet it was common for several readers to peruse each item, particularly in those more populated places readily accessible to the post, and, by mid-century, isolation was probably a greater hindrance than cost to obtaining the benefits of periodical literature. So also, however, was illiteracy, and many a colonial doubtless invested the sixpence or shilling it took to purchase a primer in order to gain access to what increasingly appeared as the joys and advantages of print.[8]

There is no determining how many Americans actually learned to read on their own or informally with the help of friends and relatives. Given the extraordinary circulation of primers, both local

[7] *Advertisement* [for *The Pennsylvania Gazette, or, The Universal Instructor,* October 1, 1728]; *Der Hoch-Deutsch Pensylvanische Geschicht-Schreiber,* August 20, 1739; *The New-York Journal,* no. 1424, April 19, 1770, p. 12. In their didacticism, American editors were merely imitating the high art of Addison, Steele, and their successors, one that embraced elements of style going beyond mere literary grace to include modes of argument not unlike secular preaching. The urbane writer addressing a newly literate audience in essay form was in many respects the eighteenth-century bearer of the word, and, in the manner of his progenitors, his ultimate goal was to convey truth, heighten sensibility, and improve conduct.

[8] Prices of Ames's almanacs may be gleaned from Sam Briggs, *The Essays, Humor, and Poems of Nathaniel Ames* (Cleveland, Ohio: Short & Forman, 1890), p. 20 and *passim.* For prices of newspapers and magazines, see Frank Luther Mott, *American Journalism* (rev. ed.; New York: The Macmillan Company, 1950), p. 59, and *A History of American Magazines* (5 vols.; Cambridge, Mass.: Harvard University Press, 1930-1968), I, 33-34. For prices of primers, see Charles F. Heartman, *American Primers, Indian Primers, Royal Primers, and Thirty-Seven Other Types of Non-New-England Primers, Issued Prior to 1830* (Highland Park, N.J.: printed for Harry B. Weiss, 1935), p. 109 and *passim.*

and imported, the number must certainly have been appreciable. By far the most common of these texts was *The New-England Primer*, the earliest known edition of which issued from the press of Benjamin Harris in Boston in 1690, though there may well have been London editions dating from the 1680's. Thoroughly characteristic of its genre, *The New-England Primer* introduced one important innovation that rendered it easily the most popular reading instructor of the eighteenth-century colonies, namely, it combined into a single volume the substance of the traditional hornbook (the alphabet and the syllabarium) with the substance of the traditional primer (the Lord's Prayer, the Creed, and the Decalogue) and an authorized catechism.

"He who ne'er learns his ABC, forever will a blockhead be," warned one edition. "But he who to his book's inclined, will soon a golden treasure find." The content of the primer was essentially religious, as its words ("godliness," "holiness," "benevolence," "fidelity"), couplets ("In Adam's fall, we sinned all"), and texts ("Holiness becomes God's house forever") made abundantly clear. But the key that opened the path to salvation also opened the door to opportunity, and the coincidence could not have been lost on ambitious youngsters. Once the art of reading had been mastered, there was no end to the useful knowledge that might be gleaned from manuals of every sort and variety. As in the seventeenth century, every field of learning and every vocation had its vade mecum, designed to convey the essentials as fully and systematically as possible; and, while most of these were intended and used as textbooks in connection with apprenticeship and schoolroom instruction, some were doubtless studied without the assistance of a master. Especially interesting in this connection were the manuals explicitly advertised as self-instructors, which were widely imported and reprinted in the colonies. One such volume was John Hill's *The Young Secretary's Guide: or, A Speedy Help to Learning*, which was sold in Boston as early as 1694 and later reprinted by Thomas Fleet. Another was William Burkitt's *The Poor Man's Help, and Young Man's Guide*, which was first reprinted by Bartholomew Green in 1731. And by far the most popular was Mrs. Slack's *The Instructor: or, Young Man's Best Companion*, which Franklin and Hall reprinted as *The American Instructor* in 1748 and which was subsequently reissued by a number of colonial publishers.[9]

[9] *The New-England Primer* (Boston: E. Draper, c. 1785).

In effect, *The American Instructor* was an encyclopedia for the aspiring young tradesman, filled with useful information that he might need in the course of a varied and successful career. Instruction in English came first, the use of the mother tongue being acknowledged universally as "a necessary and principal qualification in business"; then, advice on "a good, fair, free, and commendable hand"; and then, an extensive compendium of useful knowledge, including familiar form letters for use in social and commercial intercourse, some elements of arithmetic and bookkeeping (along with models of bills of lading, invoices, and receipts), certain geographical observations concerning the British Isles and the North American colonies, some principles of measurement for carpentry, joinery, and bricklaying, a series of handy legal forms (deeds, wills, bonds, and indentures), and, finally, some helpful hints on gardening and preserving, the movements of heavenly bodies, the value of currencies, and the treatment of disease. One can imagine ambitious youngsters systematically mastering the various sections and then applying for positions, using clichés from the form letters of Daniel Diligent, George Generous, and Titus Tradewell. More likely, the volume and others of its genre served families in much the fashion of *The French Academie* (1577), furnishing a useful—and, incidentally, secular—potpourri of the world's knowledge explicitly designed for townspeople eager to participate in the expanding commerce of the Anglo-American world.[10]

II

Newspaper and magazine subscriptions remained rather expensive throughout the eighteenth century, while the cost of certain almanacs tended to decline, as circulation and print runs mounted: for example, Ames's *Almanack,* which sold for one shilling sixpence in 1750, had decreased in price to six coppers by 1763. What rough evidence there is on the cost of books in that same period indicates that this was about equivalent to the cost of hardcover books in the twentieth century. Yet the reading public that was coming into being

[10] [Mrs. Slack], *The American Instructor: or, Young Man's Best Companion* (9th ed.; Philadelphia: B. Franklin and D. Hall, 1748), "The Preface" and *passim.* For those who desired an advanced course with an equally secular bent, there was Robert Dodsley's popular anthology of compendia *The Preceptor* (2 vols.; London: printed for R. Dodsley, 1748), with its authoritative articles and extensive bibliographies.

in the eighteenth century was in no way comparable to the audience for present-day publishing. In the first place, it was a newer audience, in that many families—or at least their younger members—were finding literacy to be a novel need and a novel opportunity. In the second place, it was an audience of more limited taste, in that neither its own interests nor the publishing industry that would eventually serve those interests had yet undergone that sweeping diversification that would mark the nineteenth and twentieth centuries. And, finally, it was an audience not yet in the habit of buying books, in part because the distribution of books, especially in the colonies, was so undeveloped as a technology.[11]

In the face of these limitations, the library assumed critical importance, not only for those who lacked the means to purchase books but also for those who had neither access to nor taste for the book market. As in the seventeenth century, there were hundreds of small personal libraries numbering anywhere from five to a dozen books and almost always including a Bible, a catechism, a selection of devotional works, and an almanac or two. And as in the seventeenth century, too, there were increasing numbers of larger personal libraries noted for their size and diversity. Cotton Mather referred again and again in his diaries to his "well-furnished library," which, numbering around four thousand volumes and embracing topics going far beyond theology, was probably the largest and best of its time in the colonies—John Dunton referred to it as "the glory of New England, if not of all America." James Logan's collection included over two thousand volumes in 1749, the year he drew a will bequeathing it to the people of Pennsylvania. And the collection assembled by William Byrd II in the new brick mansion he built at Westover was shelved in twenty-three black-walnut cases holding over three thousand books and pamphlets. All the evidence indicates that these and other sizable personal libraries held the best products of contemporary British-American publishing in all fields and that they were continually consulted by friends, neighbors, and even strangers with a taste for literature (one of Benjamin Franklin's most charming anecdotes recounts the way in which he deliberately cultivated the friendship of a political adversary—probably Isaac

11 Briggs, *Essays, Humor, and Poems of Nathaniel Ames*, pp. 20, 133; and Lawrence C. Wroth, "Book Production and Distribution from the Beginning to the American Revolution," in Hellmut Lehmann-Haupt *et al.*, *The Book in America* (2d ed.; New York: R. R. Bowker Company, 1951), p. 42.

Norris—by borrowing a certain "scarce and curious book" from his personal collection for a few days).[12]

Institutional libraries also increased dramatically in number and breadth during the eighteenth century as a result of philanthropic efforts on both sides of the Atlantic. The Harvard collection, which began with the 400 volumes (representing some 329 titles) bequeathed by John Harvard in 1638, had grown to approximately 3,500 volumes (representing 2,961 titles) by the time the catalogue of 1723 was compiled, and extended over the following fields:

DISTRIBUTION OF BOOKS IN THE HARVARD COLLEGE LIBRARY 1723

Subject	Number of Titles	Percentage of Titles
Theology	1726	58
Literature	277	9
Science	232	8
Philosophy	219	7
History	202	7
Law	57	2
Geography	49	2
Government	49	2
Biography	23	1
Arts	9 ⎫	
Commerce	2 ⎬	4
Other	116 ⎭	

The Harvard collection was almost entirely destroyed by the fire of January 26, 1764, with the exception of some 400 books on loan to faculty and students; yet, when Ezra Stiles visited the library at the 1766 commencement, he estimated a total of 4,350 volumes, largely purchased in the intervening two years through an outpouring of gifts from donors as varied as the legislature of New Hampshire, the Society for the Propagation of the Gospel in Foreign Parts, and Thomas Hollis of Lincoln's Inn, the nephew of the founder of the Hollis professorships. By 1783, the collection had more than doubled in size and number of titles.[13]

[12] Diary of Cotton Mather (2 vols.; New York: Frederick Ungar Publishing Co., 1957), I, 36; John Dunton's Letters from New England, Publications of the Prince Society, vol. IV (Boston: T. R. Marvin & Son, 1867), p. 75; and The Autobiography of Benjamin Franklin, edited by Leonard W. Labaree, Ralph L. Ketcham, Helen C. Boatfield, and Helene H. Fineman (New Haven: Yale University Press, 1964), p. 171.

[13] Catalogus librorum bibliothecae Collegij Harvardini quad est Cantabrigiae in Nova Anglia (Boston: B. Green, 1723); Joe Walker Kraus, "Book Collections of Five Colonial College Libraries; A Subject Analysis" (unpublished doctoral thesis, University of Illinois, 1960), p. 114; and Franklin Bowditch Dexter, ed., Extracts from the Itineraries and Other Miscellanies of Ezra Stiles 1755-1794 (New Haven: Yale University Press, 1916), p. 206.

The libraries of the other colonial colleges were smaller but no less significant for their particular regions. One collection at the College of William and Mary was destroyed by fire in 1705 and another pilfered by troops quartered at the college in 1781; nevertheless it was sufficiently large and diverse in 1779 to require classification and cataloguing, which would put it almost certainly at two or three thousand volumes. The significance of the library at Yale, particularly after the arrival of the first Dummer collection in 1714, has already been noted. That library was further enlarged by a gift from Bishop Berkeley in 1733 and had grown to some twenty-five hundred volumes by 1783, representing almost two thousand titles. The collection at the College of New Jersey numbered around two thousand at the beginning of the Revolution, but much of it was destroyed during the hostilities which swept Princeton during the winter of 1776-77. The libraries of the other colleges founded after 1750 were less impressive, not the least of the reasons in the case of King's College and the College of Philadelphia being the ready availability of nearby collections.

Town and parish libraries also multiplied during the eighteenth century, the former dating from the establishment of the earliest public collections at Boston, Concord, and New Haven during the 1650's and 1660's, the latter deriving largely though not wholly from the efforts of the Reverend Thomas Bray and the S.P.G. In addition, beginning in 1762, a number of circulating libraries were started by ambitious booksellers such as William Rind of Annapolis, George Wood of Charleston, Garrat Noel of New York, and John Mein of Boston, all of whom in the very nature of their enterprise catered to the interest of local audiences in more popular works of "polite literature, arts, and sciences."[14]

Perhaps the most interesting innovation in the library field, however, was the subscription library, a form which was initially imported from England but which proved peculiarly appropriate to the American environment. The first such library in the colonies was established at Philadelphia in 1731 through the efforts of Benjamin Franklin. As the story is recounted in the *Autobiography,* several members of the junto agreed to contribute books to a common collection that would be held for the use of the members in the meeting room the club maintained at the house of Robert Grace.

14 John Mein, *A Catalogue of Mein's Circulating Library* (Boston: [Mein and Fleeming], 1765), title page.

Seeing the advantages of this arrangement, Franklin "proposed to render the benefit from books more common by commencing a public subscription library." The plan he drew up provided for an association of subscribers, each of whom would contribute forty shillings for the initial purchase of books and ten shillings per annum for the subsequent enlargement of the collection. The instrument of association, which was drawn in 1731, carried fifty signatures, indicating that the Library Company started with an initial capital of one hundred pounds and a projected annual income of twenty-five pounds. The first selection of books was made by Franklin and Thomas Godfrey, a member of the junto, in consultation with James Logan, and included such varied titles as Homer's *Iliad* and *Odyssey*, Plutarch's *Lives*, Richard Bradley's *A Complete Body of Husbandry* (1727), Algernon Sidney's *Discourses Concerning Government* (1698), and *The Tatler*, *The Spectator*, and *The Guardian*. It was patently a practical library, filled with the atlases, histories, and handbooks that would attract enterprising young men; and, significantly, there was not a theological title in the initial collection.[15]

Characteristically, Franklin claimed in the *Autobiography* that the Philadelphia enterprise had served as the "mother of all the North American subscription libraries" that were subsequently established throughout the colonies. "These libraries," he reflected in the early 1770's, "have improved the general conversation of the Americans, made the common tradesmen and farmers as intelligent as most gentlemen from other countries, and perhaps have contributed in some degree to the stand so generally made throughout the colonies in defense of their privileges." Clearly, Franklin's venture had been influential in the development of the Union Library Company, the Association Library, and the Amicable Company, which were subsequently founded in Philadelphia, as well as in the establishment of similar libraries at Germantown, Lancaster, Trenton, New York, Charleston, and elsewhere. But clearly, too, such institutions as the Philogrammatical Library, established in 1739 at Lebanon, Connecticut, by the Reverend Solomon Williams and an association of

---

[15] *Autobiography of Benjamin Franklin*, p. 142; *Papers of Benjamin Franklin*, I, 209-210; "A Book of Minutes, Containing an Account of the Proceedings of the Directors of the Library of Philadelphia Beginning November 8, 1731" (ms. records, Library Company of Philadelphia), p. 8. Interestingly enough, the collection soon expanded to include scientific apparatus, fossils, and other curiosa, transforming the institution into something of a museum and laboratory as well as a library.

neighbors, or the Redwood Library, established in 1747 at Newport, Rhode Island, by Abraham Redwood, had managed to get under way quite independently of the Philadelphia model. Be that as it may, the idea of a subscribers' association maintaining a library for mutual benefit and general improvement provided a propitious instrument of education in eighteenth-century America, and dozens of them appeared in the years following the Revolution.[16]

III

In addition to self-instruction from books, the enterprising young provincial in search of useful knowledge could get more systematic instruction from teachers; and, if he was fortunate enough to reside in one of the larger towns, it was increasingly likely that he could obtain that instruction without obligating himself to a long period of apprenticeship. In Boston, New York, Philadelphia, and Charleston, as in contemporary London, a thriving market for skilled labor combined with a sufficiently large concentration of potential clients to encourage the emergence of the private entrepreneurial teacher, more or less versed in some art or skill and willing to teach it to all comers for a fee. Apprenticeship continued as a formal institution, to be sure; but apprenticeship meant a long and costly education for an ambitious young man, and, particularly in those arts which seemed to rest on some intellectual base that could be systematically studied, such as surveying or navigation or bookkeeping, schooling for a fee became a more economical arrangement for youths seeking to obtain maximum competence in a minimum period of time.

Boston had at least eight private schoolmasters prior to 1689, several of whom taught writing and at least one of whom was given liberty "to teach children to write and to keep accounts." Thereafter, any number of teachers advertised instruction in a fascinating variety of subjects, notably those associated with such common vocations as surveying, navigation, and commerce as well as with such polite arts as dancing, needlework, and fencing; and, while the advertisement did not in every case guarantee the existence of a school, there is no denying the diversity of private instruction available to the eighteenth-century Bostonian. This same richness of opportunity also prevailed in New York, Philadelphia, and Charleston, and

[16] *Autobiography of Benjamin Franklin*, pp. 130-131.

doubtless to a lesser degree in some of the secondary market towns such as New Haven, Albany, and Norfolk.[17]

Many of the advertisements for private instruction announced that students could be accommodated during the morning, afternoon, or evening hours, according to their convenience. Others, however, specified solely the evening hours, implying that either the master or the students or both would be otherwise occupied during the daytime. In some instances, masters of regular day schools undertook evening classes to supplement their income. In others, men who worked during regular business hours as scriveners, accountants, translators, surveyors, or merchants taught certain aspects of their own or other trades during the evening hours. Obversely, the possibility of evening instruction allowed some students to hold jobs at the same time that they continued their education and permitted others to serve simultaneously as apprentices and students. Indeed, the possibilities inherent in this last arrangement must have proved as attractive to masters who were enjoined by indentures to teach their charges to read and write as it was to apprentices who wished to supplement the practical instruction they received from their masters with the systematic theoretical instruction their masters may have been incapable of imparting.

Whatever the competence and steadfastness of particular private teachers in the eighteenth-century colonies, their efforts were inevitably transient to a degree. George Brownell, who taught Franklin and who may well have been the most versatile private schoolmaster in the colonies, offered a curriculum that ranged from arithmetic to embroidery and taught at one time or another in Boston, New York, and Philadelphia for a period that extended over almost a quarter-century. Andrew Lamb taught bookkeeping and navigation in Philadelphia for some twenty years, as did John Hutchins in New York. Yet, when these teachers and scores of others like them were no longer able to offer instruction, their "schools" simply vanished.

[17] *A Report of the Record Commissioners of the City of Boston, Containing the Boston Records from 1660 to 1701* (Boston: Rockwell and Churchill, 1881), p. 36. Years ago, Robert Francis Seybolt reported in *Source Studies in American Colonial Education* (Urbana: University of Illinois, 1925) that he had found some 200 teachers at work at one time or another in the private teaching of bookkeeping, navigation, and surveying between 1709 and 1775 in the colonies, excluding New Hampshire and North Carolina. More recently, Carl and Jessica Bridenbaugh reported in *Rebels and Gentlemen* (2d ed.; New York: Oxford University Press, 1962) evidence of over 125 private teachers of all subjects between 1740 and 1776 in Philadelphia alone. My own figure for the same period in Philadelphia is very close to that of the Bridenbaughs, namely, 136.

Some recognition of the ephemeral character of such instruction may well have been in Franklin's mind when he first drafted plans for an academy at Philadelphia in 1743. By that time, the city had been witness to some modest debate over education, deriving not merely from the usual religious and ethnic differences over curricular content but also from fundamental philosophic differences over educational purpose. Franklin, clearly recalling his own experience at the hands of George Brownell and doubtless aware of the innovations inaugurated by private schoolmasters in the colonies and in England (it was Whitefield who introduced him to Doddridge's work at Northampton), must certainly have envisioned an institution that would incorporate on a permanent basis many of the more practical studies available only as particular individuals chose to offer them.[18]

Nothing came of the 1743 proposal, which lay dormant until Franklin published his *Proposals Relating to the Education of Youth in Pennsylvania* in 1749 and undertook, with the support of a group of friends, to raise a sufficient subscription to open and support an academy. Some fifty or more prominent citizens pledged support and appointed Franklin and Tench Francis, attorney general of the province, to draft a set of Constitutions of the Public Academy in the City of Philadelphia. Twenty-four of the larger subscribers agreed to serve as trustees, meeting on November 13, 1749, to sign the Constitutions and to elect Franklin their president. Their first major decisions were to purchase the so-called new building on Fourth Street, which had been erected in 1740 and 1741 as a chapel for George Whitefield to preach in and for subsequent use as a charity school, to employ David Martin as the first rector, and to arrange for the commencement of classes on January 7, 1751. A charter was obtained two years later, designating the corporation "The Trustees of the Academy and Charitable School in the Province of Pennsylvania" (the charitable school still symbolizing the early hope associated with the new building); and in 1755, under the leadership of William Smith, a new charter was obtained redesignating the corporation "The Trustees of the College, Academy, and Charitable School of Philadelphia in the Province of Pennsylvania."[19]

[18] See, for example, the vehement attack of a writer in *The American Weekly Mercury*, no. 784, December 31–January 7, 1734-35, and no. 785, January 7-14, 1735, on the grammar masters for ignoring the needs of "trade, commerce, and the business of the world" in favor of a time-honored preoccupation with "the Roman language."

[19] *Papers of Benjamin Franklin*, III, 422-428, 435-436.

The Constitutions of the Public Academy provided for two schools, a Latin school and an English school, the master of the former to be "styled, the rector of the academy." The Constitutions also required the trustees to employ an English master and to endeavor with all convenient speed "to engage persons, capable of teaching the French, Spanish and German languages, writing, arithmetic, algebra, the several branches of the mathematics, natural and mechanic philosophy, and drawing." Rector Martin served as master of the Latin school until his death in 1751, after which Francis Alison took charge of the work. David James Dove was appointed master of the English school in 1750, while Theophilus Grew was employed "to teach writing, arithmetic, merchants accounts, algebra, astronomy, navigation, and all other branches of the mathematics." Dove soon found himself in disagreement with the trustees on matters of hours and attendance, with the result that he was replaced in 1753 by Ebenezer Kinnersley. In effect, it was Alison, Kinnersley, and Grew who shaped the institution during its formative phase.[20]

Years later, shortly before he died, Franklin pronounced the academy a failure as measured against his initial vision. From the outset, he charged, the trustees had been persistently partial to the Latinists, thereby eroding the quality and attractiveness of the English school. There is in mankind "an unaccountable prejudice in favor of ancient customs and habitudes," Franklin lamented, "which inclines to a continuance of them after the circumstances, which formerly made them useful, cease to exist." That prejudice, he concluded, had operated to wreck the experiment.[21]

Now, it has been commonly observed that, at the very time Franklin penned these sentiments, ideas such as his on the value of a more practical English education were being realized by other men at other places, notably at the two Phillips academies, at Andover, Massachusetts, and at Exeter, New Hampshire. Surely, if one studies the constitutions of these academies, the aim of "instructing youth, not only in English and Latin grammar, writing, arithmetic, and those sciences, wherein they are commonly taught; but more especially to learn them the great end and real business of living," shines

[20] *Ibid.*, pp. 424, 425; Trustees of the College, Academy, and Charitable School of Philadelphia, Minutes (unpublished mss., University of Pennsylvania, Philadelphia), December 17, 1750.

[21] "Observations Relative to the Intentions of the Original Founders of the Academy in Philadelphia," in *The Writings of Benjamin Franklin*, edited by Albert Henry Smyth (10 vols.; New York: The Macmillan Company, 1904-1907), X, 30.

through. And so too does the desirability of more practical activities, such as agriculture and gardening. Yet, if one turns from the constitutions to the actual instruction proffered by Eliphalet Pearson in the first school and William Woodbridge in the other, he must conclude that the systematic study of English and the useful arts and sciences received even scantier attention than it did at the Philadelphia academy. The prejudice in favor of ancient customs and habitudes was as vigorous in these institutions as at Franklin's; indeed, some of the better Presbyterian academies of the middle colonies may well have given more attention to English and the sciences than any of the oft-cited New England academies of the eighteenth century.[22]

The more advanced segment of Franklin's venture, namely, the College of Philadelphia, provided quite another story. There, under the vigorous leadership of William Smith as provost and Francis Alison as vice-provost—recall that both were products of Scottish higher education—the college offered first-class instruction in the classics, complemented by a wide range of systematic work in rhetoric and philosophy, mathematics and the sciences, and history and politics. And, while there is no certainty that the curriculum announced by Smith in 1756 was followed to the letter, there is evidence that it was more or less authentic. Moreover, with the creation of the medical department in 1765, additional resources in the basic and applied sciences became available; and, given the small enrollment of the philosophy and medical schools combined, one must assume that there were no hard lines separating their students, their faculty, or their instruction. By the 1760's and 1770's, the College of Philadelphia differed substantially in character and emphasis from its sister institutions, the central reason lying not so much in its nonsectarian origins as in the vision of its leadership and the urban context in which that vision was realized.

In this respect, the unique relationships and similarities between the colleges of Philadelphia and New York are especially significant. Talk of a college in the latter city had begun as early as 1704, when Governor Lewis Morris of New Jersey had written the secretary of the S.P.G. concerning the prospects of obtaining certain lands for such an institution. Yet nothing had really materialized until 1746, when the general assembly of New York authorized a public lottery

---

[22] *The Constitution of the Phillips Academy in Andover* (Andover, Mass.: Flagg and Gould, 1828), p. 3.

"for the advancement of learning and towards the founding of a college" in the colony. By 1751, almost thirty-five hundred pounds had been collected, and the assembly created a board of trustees, two-thirds of whom turned out to be communicants of the Church of England. A vituperative controversy ensued over the religious and political complexion of the intended college, the opponents charging that it would be nothing more than a narrow establishment seminary. Nevertheless, the assembly in due course authorized the trustees to engage a suitable faculty, and in 1754 a royal charter was granted by George II.[23]

The crisscrossing of personalities between the colleges of Philadelphia and New York during the early 1750's is manifest at many points, nowhere more forcefully than in the correspondence of Benjamin Franklin, Samuel Johnson, and William Smith. It is clear that Franklin eagerly sought Johnson as rector of the academy and indeed offered him the position in 1751. It is clear, too, that Smith published *Mirania* in the spring of 1753 in an effort to seize upon the opportunity then developing in New York. When the New York trustees finally settled on Johnson in the autumn of 1753, Johnson launched a concerted effort to recruit Smith as his colleague. But Smith decided instead to accept the post at Franklin's academy that subsequently became the provostship of the College of Philadelphia.[24]

The traditional tendency to contrast the nonsectarian origins of the Philadelphia institution—it later fell under Anglican control—with the Anglican auspices of the New York institution has too often obscured the important similarities in the two colleges. Like Smith,

23 Lewis Morris to secretary, [Summer, 1704]. S.P.G. Letter Books (S.P.G. mss., United Society for the Propagation of the Gospel, London), Series A, I, no. 171; Abraham Lott, Jr., ed., *Journal of the Votes and Proceedings of the General Assembly of the Colony of New-York. Began on the 8th Day of November, 1743; and Ended the 23d of December, 1765* (New York: Hugh Gaine, 1766), II, 128-129; and *The Colonial Laws of New York* (5 vols.; Albany: James B. Lyon, 1894), III, 607-616, 842-844. The charter is given in its entirety in Elsie W. Clews, *Educational Legislation and Administration of the Colonial Governments* (New York: no publisher, 1899), pp. 256-271.

24 See, for example, the Franklin-Johnson correspondence in *Papers of Benjamin Franklin*, IV, 37-42, 71-72, 74-76, 146-147, 222-223, 260-262, 324-325; and William Smith to Samuel Johnson, [May, 1753], in Herbert Schneider and Carol Schneider, eds., *Samuel Johnson, President of King's College: His Career and Writings* (4 vols.; New York: Columbia University Press, 1929), I, 167-169. Incidentally, the two colleges also undertook a joint fund-raising mission to the British Isles in 1762-1764, under the direction of Smith and Sir James Jay; see Letters Patent, in *ibid.*, IV, 231-236.

Johnson was an Anglican clergyman committed to working out new patterns of education for the new society that was coming into being —his "Raphael" is the best indication of that commitment. And, like the College of Philadelphia, King's College was located in a major seaport city and drew its students largely from the surrounding community. As a result, despite Johnson's idealist propensities, one notes a pronounced scientific and mathematical element in the first curriculum, not unlike that of Philadelphia. The announcement of the opening of the college that appeared in *The New-York Gazette* for June 3, 1754, spoke of the usual admissions requirements (Latin as far as Cicero's *Orations* and Virgil's *Aeneid,* Greek as far as the Gospel of John, and mathematics as far as the arithmetic of division and reduction), promised a religious orientation "in the best manner expressive of our common Christianity," and then proposed "to instruct and perfect the youth in the learned languages, and in the arts of reasoning exactly, of writing correctly, and speaking eloquently; and in the arts of numbering and measuring, of surveying and navigation, of geography and history, of husbandry, commerce and government, and in the knowledge of all nature in the heavens above us, and in the air, water and earth around us, and the various kinds of meteors, stones, mines, and minerals, plants and animals, and of everything useful for the comfort, the convenience and elegance of life, in the chief manufactures relating to any of these things: and, finally, to lead them from the study of nature to knowledge of themselves, and of the God of nature, and their duty to him, themselves, and one another, and everything that can contribute to their true happiness, both here and hereafter." For assistance with the classical instruction, Johnson turned first to his son William Samuel Johnson and then, in 1755, to Leonard Cutting, an alumnus of Cambridge University; for the work in mathematics and natural philosophy, Johnson called Daniel Treadwell, a graduate of Harvard, and then, upon Treadwell's death in 1760, Robert Harpur, who had been educated at Glasgow.[25]

Following the lead of Philadelphia, King's College inaugurated a medical department in 1767, which made available instruction in anatomy under Samuel Clossy, a graduate of Trinity College, Dublin; in surgery under John Jones, who had studied with William Hunter in London and Jean Louis Petit in Paris; in physiology and pathology under the Scotsman Peter Middleton, who had been

25 *The New-York Gazette,* no. 592, June 3, 1754.

trained at the University of St. Andrews; in chemistry under James Smith, a graduate of Leiden; in midwifery under John V. B. Tennent, also a Leiden alumnus; and in the theory and practice of medicine under Samuel Bard, a fellow student of Morgan in London and at Edinburgh. True, the school at King's College initially lacked the splendid opportunity made possible by the presence in Philadelphia of the Pennsylvania Hospital; and, even after Bard, Middleton, and Jones had led in organizing the Society of the Hospital in the City of New-York in America and in collecting sufficient funds for the establishment of that institution, fire and military upheaval prevented the development of a genuine hospital in New York until 1791. Yet pre-Revolutionary King's, like its counterpart in Philadelphia, was always small, and the availability of the instruction associated with the medical department left its mark on the entire institution. One need not exaggerate the overall impact of King's to argue that, with the College of Philadelphia, it marked something of a new departure in American higher education, in the degree to which the useful sciences found a significant place in the curriculum and an aura of urbanity surrounded the enterprise as a whole.

IV

Franklin's junto, based as it was on various Anglo-American models for voluntary association in the cause of mutual enlightenment, provided yet another pattern by which eighteenth-century colonials pursued their education. The story of its formation and career is one of the most charming in the *Autobiography*. In the autumn of 1727, Franklin recounts, "I . . . formed most of my ingenious acquaintance into a club for mutual improvement, which we called the junto. We met on Friday evenings. The rules I drew up required that every member in his turn produce one or more queries on any point of morals, politics or natural philosophy, to be discussed by the company, and once in three months produce and read an essay of his own writing on any subject he pleased. Our debates were to be under the direction of a president, and to be conducted in the sincere spirit of inquiry after truth, without fondness for dispute, or desire for victory; and to prevent warmth all expressions of positiveness in opinion, or of direct contradiction, were after some time made contraband and prohibited under small pecuniary penalties."[26]

[26] *Autobiography of Benjamin Franklin*, pp. 116-117.

The first members, in addition to Franklin, included a copier of deeds, a self-taught mathematician, a surveyor, a shoemaker, a joiner, a merchant's clerk, two fellow employees of Franklin at Samuel Keimer's printing shop, an Oxford scholar who had come to the colonies as a bond servant, and a young gentleman of means. This variegated group, Franklin once observed, provided "the best school of philosophy, morals and politics that then existed in the province." The conversation ranged widely over every realm of human concern; topics were announced a week in advance in order that members might read and reflect by way of preparation; and rules were drawn up and enforced to preserve a minimal civility. The club had its ups and downs, apparently thriving during the 1730's and 1740's, then languishing in the 1750's, then reviving in the 1760's under a new name, the American Society Held at Philadelphia for Promoting and Propagating Useful Knowledge, and finally merging with the American Philosophical Society. But it doubtless rewarded most of its members over the years with amusement, information, and instruction, to say nothing of the benefits that redounded to the commonwealth in significant laws, useful institutions, and valuable social reforms.[27]

The point has often been made that the American Philosophical Society really arose as a kind of intercolonial junto. Once again, Franklin played an influential role as proposer and organizer, though in this instance it was John Bartram, a local farmer and self-taught botanist, who seems to have originated the idea. An indefatigable correspondent on matters scientific with naturalists on both sides of the Atlantic, Bartram as early as 1739 had discussed with Cadwallader Colden of New York the idea of a scientific academy where "ingenious and curious men" might exchange knowledge of "natural secrets, arts and sciences." Colden may even have given Bartram the idea, since he himself had suggested the establishment of a similar organization to Dr. William Douglass of Boston a decade before. In any case, Franklin probably had the help of Bartram in drafting his 1743 proposal for a society of "virtuosi or ingenious men residing in the several colonies, to be called the American Philosophical Society; who are to maintain a constant correspondence." The Society would have its headquarters at Philadelphia, where at least seven members would always be in residence. These members would meet

27 *Ibid.*, p. 118.

once a month to receive, read, consider, and disseminate communications and queries from nonresident members. Possible subjects for correspondence would include:

All new-discovered plants, herbs, trees, roots, and etc. their virtues, uses, and etc. Methods of propagating them, and making such as are useful, but particular to some plantations, more general [thus Bartram's principal concerns]. Improvements of vegetable juices, as ciders, wines, and etc. New methods of curing or preventing diseases. All new-discovered fossils in different countries, as mines, minerals, quarries, and etc. New and useful improvements in any branch of mathematics. New discoveries in chemistry, such as improvements in distillation, brewing, assaying of ores, and etc. New mechanical inventions for saving labor; as mills, carriages, and etc. and for raising and conveying of water, draining of meadows, and etc. All new arts, trades, manufactures, and etc. that may be proposed or thought of. Surveys, maps and charts of particular parts of the seacoasts, or inland countries; course and junction of rivers and great roads, situation of lakes and mountains, nature of the soil and productions, and etc. New methods of improving the breed of useful animals, introducing other sorts from foreign countries. New improvements in planting, gardening, clearing land, and etc. And all philosophical experiments that let light into the nature of things, tend to increase the power of man over matter, and multiply the conveniences or pleasures of life.

Correspondence would be maintained with the Royal Society of London and the Dublin Society. And abstracts, reports, and transactions would be circulated regularly to the membership.[28]

Under the leadership of Bartram, Franklin, and Thomas Bond, the physician, and with the support of Cadwallader Colden in New York, the Society was duly organized, probably early in 1744. An initial enthusiasm both in Philadelphia and abroad soon gave way to apathy and wrangling, however, and within a year the Society was moribund. And indeed it was not until the organization was revived virtually *de novo* by Thomas Bond late in 1767 and united a year later with what had become the rival American Society Held at Philadelphia for Promoting and Propagating Useful Knowledge that it began truly to serve the ambitious aims projected by Franklin. Thereafter, during the period before the Revolution, the Society was able to mount a number of significant scientific and utilitarian projects, including a major series of observations on the transit of

[28] *Papers of Benjamin Franklin*, II, 378-383; and Cadwallader Colden to [William Douglass, c. 1728], *The Letters and Papers of Cadwallader Colden*, vol. I, in *Collections of the New-York Historical Society for the Year 1917*, L (1918), 272.

Venus in 1769, supported in substantial measure by the Pennsylvania assembly, and a characteristically utilitarian survey that same year of possible canal routes from the Delaware River to the Chesapeake Bay, supported by the merchants of Philadelphia. It was also able to publish a volume of *Transactions* in 1771, which became the principal means by which its work was known abroad.

In effect, the activities of the junto on the one hand and the American Philosophical Society on the other symbolize in their local and intercolonial character what came to be a critically important dimension of provincial education, namely, mutual education. Locally and regionally, formally and informally, systematically and haphazardly, face-to-face and through correspondence, Americans instructed one another, in taverns and coffeehouses, in Masonic lodges and militia musters, and in tradesmen's associations and chambers of commerce, as well as in formal institutions and societies organized to advance and communicate one sort of knowledge or another. William Livingston, William Smith, Jr., and John Morin Scott organized a Society for the Promotion of Useful Knowledge in 1748 in New York in an effort to combat the view in some quarters that the city was a cultural wasteland; and it was in connection with the Society that they projected *The Independent Reflector* for "correcting the taste and improving the minds of our fellow citizens." A Virginia Society for the Promotion of Useful Knowledge appeared in Williamsburg in 1773, with John Clayton, the well-known amateur naturalist, as president. An American Academy of Arts and Sciences was chartered by the Massachusetts general court in 1780, with such distinguished men as John Adams, James Bowdoin, and John Hancock among the founding members. And a New Jersey Society for the Promotion of Agriculture, Commerce, and Art was started in 1781, the forerunner of similar societies established in Philadelphia and South Carolina four years later.[29]

Medical societies sprang up in Boston in 1736, New York in 1749, Charleston in 1755, Philadelphia in 1766, and Sharon, Connecticut, in 1767; while a Sodalitas to study law and oratory appeared in Boston in 1765, and a Moot Club in New York in 1770. The list could be extended tenfold with names of more or less ephemeral organizations committed to one form of education or another. The significant point is less that these voluntary societies came and went

29 William Livingston to Noah Welles, February 18, 1749 (Johnson family mss., Yale University).

than that they were widely viewed as instruments for instructing their members and the larger public. And in this respect they set a characteristic American pattern that would be much remarked upon in the nineteenth century and would persist into the twentieth.

V

No single life in provincial America testified more eloquently to the effectiveness of the new education than Franklin's. Indeed, his very success in rising from obscurity to renown, duly celebrated as it was in the *Autobiography,* seemed to justify that new education in uniquely American terms. In the extent to which he came to symbolize the "new man," the educational processes that had shaped him assumed a special significance: in Crèvecoeur's formulation, Franklin had achieved through unfettered and self-interested labor that ample subsistence and proud independence that were characteristically American. Whether Franklin's education was ultimately the source or the outcome of his enterprise must always remain problematical; at the least they were inextricably intertwined. He may well have been, as Max Weber and others have portrayed him, the living embodiment of a secularized Puritanism, demonstrating in his life the explosive power of calling, though one can, of course, find Catholics who were no less vigorous in their enterprise and Congregationalists who seemed called to nothing but lassitude. However one resolves the time-honored controversy—and the interplay of men and traditions in the eighteenth century would seem to make any final resolution improbable—there can be no denying that a spirit of aggressive enterprise was widely manifest in provincial America and that it supported and was in turn strengthened by a variety of educational arrangements, both formal and informal. In the process, men rose from rags to riches.

At least *some* men rose, and, again, that is a fact that must be held in mind despite the cherished American belief that all men could have risen and that many men did. For all its openness, provincial America, like all societies, distributed its opportunities unevenly, and to some groups, particularly those Indians and Afro-Americans who were enslaved and even those who were not, it was for all intents and purposes closed. For the enslaved, slavery itself became a vast system of education—or one might better term it miseducation—deliberately designed to convey values, shape attitudes, and direct behavior. And a few phrases of Christian piety or even, indeed, a modest technical literacy were as nothing compared with the power and decisiveness of that system. It was a system that was never wholly successful in molding men, since isolation from the outside world was impossible to enforce, since there were almost always in the slave community remembered or learned values that conflicted in one way or another with the values of slavery, and since in any case the human species seems less than totally malleable. But it was a system that was immensely effective in setting a large segment of provincial society (perhaps as many as a fifth of the population) apart from the mainstream of affairs and education and depriving it of alternative opportunities.

For the slave, there were few books, few libraries, few schools, and few juntos of the sort Franklin found so instructive; the doors of wisdom were not only not open, they were shut tight and designed to remain that way, cutting the slave off from Franklin's vision and Franklin's world. And by the end of the colonial period there was a well-developed ideology of race inferiority to justify that situation and ensure that it would stand firm against all the heady rhetoric of the Revolution.[30]

[30] For a poignant recognition of slavery as an insidious system of miseducation for masters as well as slaves, see Thomas Jefferson, *Notes on the State of Virginia* (1785), in *The Writings of Thomas Jefferson*, edited by Paul Leicester Ford (10 vols.; New York: G. P. Putnam's Sons, 1892-1899), III, 266-267. In my characterization of slavery as a system of miseducation, I am taking quite the opposite position from Ulrich Bonnell Phillips in *American Negro Slavery* (New York: D. Appleton and Company, 1918), where he argued that the southern plantations were on the whole "the best schools yet invented for the mass training of that sort of inert and backward people which the bulk of American Negroes represented." It is a theme to which I shall return in the next volume.

PART V

REPUBLICANISM

It has been observed that we are all of us lawyers, divines, politicians, and philosophers. And I have good authorities to say, that all candid foreigners who have passed through this country, and conversed freely with all sorts of people here, will allow, that they have never seen so much knowledge and civility among the common people in any part of the world.

JOHN ADAMS

INTRODUCTION

When George Grenville first proposed to Parliament the idea of an American stamp tax in March of 1764, he little knew that in a matter of months not merely the tax but the whole authority of Parliament in America would come under the sharpest challenge. His actual remarks suggesting the tax have not been preserved, but it is known that he indicated the wish of his ministry to consult the interest of the colonists, particularly with respect to any objections they might have to the intended tax and any alternatives they might care to suggest with respect to more satisfactory sources of revenue. What came forth, especially after the colonists discovered that Grenville was not really interested in alternative measures, was an outpouring of colonial rage unprecedented in the annals of the empire. Massachusetts, Rhode Island, Connecticut, Pennsylvania, Virginia, and South Carolina flatly denied the right of Parliament to enact the proposed legislation, while New York and North Carolina declared their right to exemption from any tax not explicitly granted by their own representatives. Pamphlets appeared denouncing the intended levy as an abrogation of the colonists' rights as Englishmen— it was James Otis' *The Rights of the British Colonies Asserted and Proved* (1764) that achieved the greatest notoriety. Newspapers filled their columns with dire predictions concerning the ministry's ultimate intentions, and orators warned of ominous consequences throughout the colonies. Grenville, of course, was unyielding, and Parliament in due course passed the dreaded legislation, chafing over the affront to its authority. But, even before the notable escalation of colonial protest following enactment, it was clear that Westminster was contending with a dramatically new phenomenon in the colonies, namely, the emergence of public opinion. The revenue act of 1764 "set people athinking, in six months more than they had done in their whole lives before," Otis declared in his pamphlet. And their thinking was not merely about sugar, rum, and molasses but about rights, liberties, and government as well.[1]

In the midst of the rising clamor during the early months of 1765, a young Massachusetts lawyer named John Adams, not yet thirty years of age, read three papers before the Sodalitas of Boston, in which he attempted to set the events of the day in the broader perspective of history. Speaking before the most distinguished members of the Massachusetts bar, Adams sketched the ascent of mankind from the enslavement it had suffered under the canon and feudal law during the medieval period. As long as the confederacy of the two heinous tyrannies prevailed, Adams maintained, the people were held in bondage: liberty, knowledge, and virtue seemed absent from the earth and one age of darkness drearily succeeded another. Then God in his benign providence occasioned the Reformation. And from that time until the first settlement of America knowledge gradually spread through Europe (especially England); and, in proportion as knowledge spread, the common people grew restive, until at last, during the reign of the Stuarts, they rid themselves entirely of tyranny. It had been in the course of that greatest of all struggles that England had peopled America.

Those who first came to British North America, Adams continued, were men of intelligence and learning, determined to avoid both the canon and the feudal systems. They brought libraries bearing the wisdom of the ancients; they planted vigorous institutions of learning; and they took every precaution to propagate and perpetuate knowledge, making the education of all ranks of people a central concern of the public. And in one fell swoop they demolished the devices of diocesan and tyrannical authority, substituting a church government consistent with Scripture and a civil government agreeable to the dignity of human nature. The outcome of those decisions was the thriving society of eighteenth-century America. Political authority was widely shared among the people, as was access to knowledge through schools, colleges, churches, and newspapers. "A native of America who cannot read and write is as rare an appear-

---

[1] James Otis, *The Rights of the British Colonies Asserted and Proved* (1764), in Bernard Bailyn, ed., *Pamphlets of the American Revolution, 1750-1776* (4 vols.; Cambridge, Mass.: Harvard University Press, 1965-), I, 461.

ance as a Jacobite or a Roman Catholic, that is, as rare as a comet or an earthquake," Adams declared. "It has been observed that we are all of us lawyers, divines, politicians, and philosophers. And I have good authorities to say, that all candid foreigners who have passed through this country, and conversed freely with all sorts of people here, will allow, that they have never seen so much knowledge and civility among the common people in any part of the world." There could be no denying the design of Providence in making America the model "for the illumination of the ignorant, and the emancipation of the slavish part of mankind all over the earth."[2]

It was this model Adams saw threatened by the schemes of the English hierarchy to introduce episcopacy into America, and of the English ministry to introduce feudalism. And he thought it the high responsibility of the colonists to thwart these schemes via every means of public debate and exposure. "Let us dare to read, think, speak, and write," Adams concluded. "Let every order and degree among the people rouse their attention and animate their resolution. Let them all become attentive to the grounds and principles of government, ecclesiastical and civil. . . . Let the pulpit resound with the doctrines and sentiments of religious liberty. . . . Let the bar proclaim, 'the laws, the rights, the generous plan of power' delivered down from remote antiquity,—inform the world of the mighty struggles and numberless sacrifices made by our ancestors in defense of freedom. . . . Let the colleges join their harmony in the same delightful concern. . . . In a word, let every sluice of knowledge be opened and set aflowing."[3]

One could quarrel with Adams' history but not with his sense of his own generation of Americans and the way in which they themselves perceived their experience. For he had construed the wide diffusion of knowledge and power among them as the result of hard-won victories and as a symbol of God's emerging design for man. And he had articulated their determination to defend their way of life at all costs against the arbitrary designs of distant authority. Thomas Hollis, who was disposed to cheer all forms of provincial republicanism from his house in London, pronounced Adams' analy-

2 John Adams, "A Dissertation on the Canon and Feudal Law," in *The Works of John Adams*, edited by Charles Francis Adams (10 vols.; Boston: Charles C. Little and James Brown, 1851), III, 456, 452.

3 *Ibid.*, III, 462-463. Adams's views changed in time, as is well known; compare the educational views put forth in the "Dissertation" with those asserted in "Discourses on Davila" in *The Gazette of the United States* during 1790 and 1791, and in the Adams-Jefferson correspondence.

sis "one of the very finest productions ever seen from North America," and proceeded to have it reprinted in *The London Chronicle* and in pamphlet form. And Adams' countrymen voted their own assent through the resolution they would display during the ensuing struggles in defense of their liberties.[4]

[4] *Works of John Adams*, III, 447.

Chapter 14

CIVILITY LIBERALIZED

Every government degenerates when trusted to the rulers of the people alone. The people themselves therefore are its only safe depositories. And to render even them safe, their minds must be improved to a certain degree. This indeed is not all that is necessary, though it be essentially necessary. An amendment of our constitution must here come in aid of the public education.

THOMAS JEFFERSON

Much has been made, and rightly so, of the crucial role of rationality in the Lockean theory of government. It is all well and good to argue that no government can have a right to obedience from a people who have not freely consented to it and that in the absence of such consent men are "direct slaves under the force of war." But unless a measure of informed and considered choice is provided for and exercised the words and the concepts are devoid of meaning. Locke came squarely to grips with the problem at several points in his *Two Treatises of Government* (1690), one of the most significant being his discussion of parental responsibility for education. "Adam was created a perfect man," Locke argued, "his body and mind in full possession of their strength and reason, and so was capable from the first instant of his being to provide for his own support and preservation, and govern his actions according to the dictates of the law of reason which God had implanted in him." Yet Adam's descendants, Locke continued, who were born infants without knowledge or understanding, were obviously incapable at birth of so governing their actions and hence not free. It therefore became the responsibility of parents to prepare their offspring for freedom, in the first place by exercising reason on their behalf while they were incapable of doing so, but, more importantly, by educating them to reason. Once children had attained the power to reason independently of their parents, they also attained the right, tacitly or expressly, to consent to government, or, indeed, not to consent to government if they chose to consider themselves in a state of nature with respect to their fellow men. They had, in effect, achieved freedom precisely because they had achieved the power of reason. "The freedom then of man and liberty of acting according to his own will," Locke concluded, "is grounded on his having reason, which is able to instruct him in that law he is to govern himself by, and make him know how far he is left to the freedom of his own will. To turn him loose to an unrestrained liberty, before he has reason to guide him, is not the allowing him the privilege of his nature, to be free; but to thrust him out amongst brutes, and abandon him to a state as wretched, and as much beneath that of a man, as theirs."[1]

Now, there is an educational problem here that goes to the heart of Locke's political theory, on which Locke himself never quite made up his mind, namely, the extent to which men in general are capable of being educated to rationality. On the one hand, there is Locke's persistent tendency to distinguish between the generality of mankind, who can best profit from vocational training in "working schools," along with some elementary instruction in the principles of Christianity, and those few persons of leisure who are able to go beyond the ordinary demands of vocational and religious calling to the true cultivation of the understanding. The distinction is pronounced in the *Essay*, where Locke despairs of the "invincible ignorance" of the elemental principles of rationality manifested by most men; and it is patent too in the Averroist assertions of *The Reasonableness of Christianity* that the greatest part of mankind cannot "know" and must therefore "believe," and in the remark in *Of the Conduct of the Understanding* that knowledge and science in general are the business "only of those who are at ease and leisure."[2]

---

[1] John Locke, *Two Treatises of Government*, edited by Peter Laslett (rev. ed.; New York: New American Library, 1965), pp. 442, 347-352. Notice Locke's insistence upon distinguishing between the power of magistrate over subject, on the one hand, and the power of father over children, master over servant, and lord over slave, on the other (p. 308).

[2] John Locke, *An Essay Concerning Human Understanding*, edited by Alexander Campbell Fraser (2 vols.; Oxford: Clarendon Press, 1894), II, 443; *The Reasonableness of Christianity*, edited by I. T. Ramsey (Stanford: Stanford University Press, 1958), p. 66; *John Locke's "Of the Conduct of the Understanding,"* edited by Francis W. Garforth, Classics in Education, no. 31 (New York: Teachers College Press, 1966), p. 55; and "Memorandum on Working Schools," in H. R. Fox Bourne, *The Life of John Locke* (2 vols.; New York: Harper & Brothers, 1876), II, 377-391.

On the other hand, there is Locke's equally persistent tendency to soften the distinction in light of man's God-given potential. Thus, he also avers in the *Essay* that "God has furnished men with faculties sufficient to direct them in the way they should take, if they will but seriously employ them that way, when their ordinary vocations allow them the leisure." And he points out in the *Conduct* that "there are instances of very mean people who have raised their minds to a great sense and understanding of religion," certainly enough to indicate, he adds, that more might be brought to be "rational creatures and Christians." Men being the common creations of one Omnipotent, he concludes, the original cast of their minds is similar; and, while the differences in their education make for immense differences in the content and character of their understandings, they remain, in the last analysis, born to be rational creatures.[3]

The ambivalence here is not unrelated, of course, to that larger ambivalence in Locke's political theories that made it possible for his writings simultaneously to support a more elite Whiggism in England and a more revolutionary Whiggism in America. Ultimately, the potential for true rationality would determine not only the proportion of a society that could manifest genuine consent to government but also the proportion that could take an active part in the responsible conduct of government. And it would determine, too, the extent to which those participating in the conduct of government could transcend partiality, or the limited view of truth deriving from circumstance, in favor of that true perception of the laws of nature that Locke saw as the essence of just government. Hence, it should be no surprise that the same Locke who became something of a patron saint of the charity-school movement that dominated British attempts to popularize education in the eighteenth century could also inspire the more egalitarian efforts of a Franklin or a Jefferson. Each society, and indeed each author, found a particular Locke in the Lockean corpus; and the Locke the Americans found was likely to be the optimistic utilitarian who seemed to vindicate a growing participation in public affairs by men who worked with their hands, men who also found time to ponder those

---

[3] Locke, *Essay Concerning Human Understanding*, II, 444; *John Locke's "Conduct of the Understanding*," p. 56. See also Locke's assertion in *Some Thoughts Concerning Education* that "of all the men we meet with, nine parts of ten are what they are, good or evil, useful or not, by their education," as contrasted with his advice to Edward Clarke in "The Dedication" that once the education of gentlemen is set right, "they will quickly bring all the rest into order." See *The Educational Writings of John Locke*, edited by James L. Axtell (Cambridge: Cambridge University Press, 1968), pp. 114, 113.

fundamental natural laws that had been declared available to all who would but consult them.[4]

There has long been a tendency to connect Locke's work with the educational traditions of the Commonwealth period and to see his theories as a kind of culmination of certain intellectual movements that patently derived from that era. And in fact if one peruses the principal writings of the 1640's and 1650's, especially those emanating from the circle around Samuel Hartlib, then the connections are apparent. Milton's latitudinarian curricular proposals surely presaged Locke's, though Milton's interest in a complete and generous education that would fit a man "to perform justly, skillfully and magnanimously all the offices both private and public of peace and war" must not be taken as license to confuse his more traditional humanism with Locke's essential utilitarianism. Petty's insistence that children of high social rank be taught "some gentle manufacture in their minority" certainly anticipated Locke's advice that they be taught a manual trade or even two or three. Dury's four aims of education—namely, piety, health, manners, and learning—bear striking resemblance to Locke's virtue, wisdom, breeding, and learning. And Hartlib's 1650 scheme proposing workhouses for the pauper children of London in many ways anticipated Locke's 1697 memorandum on working schools.[5]

But there are elements in the educational thought of the Commonwealth period at least as significant as these, which Locke either ignored or did not know, chief among them those proposals calling for a radically new role on the part of the state in the education of its citizenry. Thus, among Hartlib's friends, Petty recommended the establishment of "literary workhouses" open to all children over seven years of age, "none being to be excluded by reason of the poverty and unability of their parents, for hereby it hath come to

---

[4] It is interesting to note in this respect that the *Essay* and the *Thoughts* seem to have been much better known in America than the *Two Treatises;* see John Dunn, "The Politics of Locke in England and America in the Eighteenth Century," in John W. Yolton, ed., *John Locke: Problems & Perspectives* (Cambridge: Cambridge University Press, 1969), pp. 45-80.

[5] John Milton, "Of Education," *Complete Prose Works of John Milton* (4 vols.; New Haven: Yale University Press, 1953-1966), II, 378-379; *The Advice of W. P. to Mr. Samuel Hartlib for the Advancement of Some Particular Parts of Learning* (London: no publisher, 1647), p. 5; John Dury, *The Reformed School* (London: R. D., c. 1649), p. 24; and S[amuel] H[artlib], *London's Charity Inlarged, Stilling the Orphan's Cry* (London: Matthew Symmons and Robert Ibbitson, 1650). For Milton's fundamental opposition to much of the Comenian program preached by the Hartlib circle, see Ernest Sirluck's remarks in *Complete Prose Works of John Milton,* II, 187 ff.

pass, that many are now holding the plough, which might have been made fit to steer the state." Dury maintained that, in a well-reformed commonwealth, "all the subjects thereof should in their youth be trained up in some schools fit for their capacities, and that over these schools, some overseers should be appointed to look to the course of their education, to see that none should be left destitute of some benefit of virtuous breeding, according to the several kinds of employments, whereunto they may be found most fit and inclinable, whether it be to bear some civil office in the commonwealth, or to be mechanically employed, to be bred to teach others humane sciences, or to be employed in prophetical exercises." And, quite beyond the Hartlib circle, James Harrington reflected views that were widely espoused in pamphlets, petitions, and periodicals when he argued in *The Commonwealth of Oceana* (1656) that the health of a government is intimately bound up with the education of youth, that education is therefore not merely a parental responsibility but a proper concern of the public magistrates, that a uniform system of free schools must be made available to all children between the ages of nine and fifteen, the poor to attend free of charge and all others at their parents' expense, and that it is the responsibility of the magistrates to ensure that the schools are adequate, that parents send their children, and that the children progress.[6]

The extent to which Locke was aware of such arguments must remain problematical. That he chose not to deal with them is significant, not merely because it is additionally indicative of the character of his own liberalism, but also because it documents how selective was his transmission of the liberal tradition, at least as it was handed down to him from the Puritan era.

6 *The Advice of W. P. to Mr. Samuel Hartlib*, pp. 3-4; John Dury, *The Reformed Librarie-Keeper, with a Supplement to the Reformed-School, as Subordinate to Colleges in Universities* (London: William Du-Gard, 1650), pp. 5-6; and James Harrington, *The Oceana and Other Works* (London: A. Millar, 1747), pp. 171-173. See also Charles Hoole's recommendation that all children be sent to a grammar school or writing school as soon as they have learned to read, so that "they may not squander away their time in idleness," a manifestation, incidentally, of Hoole's pedantic fear of mischief rather than any overriding concern for good citizenship (*A New Discovery of the Old Art of Teaching School* [London: J. T., 1660], chap. v). Free primary education for all was also a plank in the Levellers' platform, though it has been fairly well established that Locke was no student of the Leveller tracts; see H. N. Brailsford, *The Levellers and the English Revolution* (Stanford: Stanford University Press, 1961), p. 534. For the possible influence of Harrington on Petty, see H. F. Russell Smith, *Harrington and His Oceana: A Study of a 17th Century Utopia and Its Influence in America* (Cambridge: Cambridge University Press, 1914), pp. 130-132.

II

Not many months after *Some Thoughts Concerning Education* first appeared in the early part of 1693, an Irish admirer of Locke named Robert Molesworth issued a spirited tract entitled *An Account of Denmark, As It Was in the Year 1692* (1694), which was destined to evoke considerable interest on both sides of the Atlantic. Purporting to be an inquiry into the natural history of absolutism—Molesworth believed that the absence of liberty in a body politic is a disease, which, like any disease, requires careful study if a proper remedy is to be determined—the tract was at the same time a historical analysis, a political commentary, and a liberal preachment. But above all, and the fact is impossible to discern from the title alone, *An Account of Denmark* was a treatise on education, in its ancient as well as its modern form and in its English quite as much as its Danish manifestation.[7]

Molesworth had been born in Dublin in 1656, the son of a wealthy merchant and landowner of Cromwellian propensities. Educated first at home and then at Trinity College, Dublin, he had managed successively to incur the wrath of James II and to win the favor of William of Orange, who promptly sent him on a private mission to Denmark in 1689 and then on a formal ambassadorship in 1692. During his second sojourn Molesworth seems to have given offense to the court and was consequently expelled from the country, his *Account* therefore being in some respects the outpouring of an aggrieved Whig smarting under fancied royal capriciousness. But the work from the beginning was much more than that since Molesworth, an ardent admirer of Commonwealth republicanism, was as distressed about the erosion of liberties in England as he was about their disappearance from Denmark; and his tract was patently an effort to reverse what he perceived as a deteriorating situation at home.

The preface to the *Account* is essentially an argument for the inseparability of good education and just government The thoughtful Englishman who wishes to secure the blessing of liberty to himself and his posterity will quickly discover, Molesworth asserts, that it is dependent in substantial measure "upon a good education of

7 [Robert Molesworth], *An Account of Denmark, As It Was in the Year 1692* (3d ed.; London: Timothy Goodwin, 1694).

our youth, and the preservation of our constitution upon its true and natural basis, the original contract." And in discussing the good education of youth Molesworth is severely critical of contemporary English practice, notably the tendency to place the conduct and control of education in the hands of the clergy. It is well enough known, he argues, that "popish countries" depend on the clergy to educate youth to slavery; what is insufficiently recognized is the extent to which Protestant princes have embarked upon much the same course. One need only travel on the Continent, he points out, to realize that since "foreign princes think it their interest that subjects should obey without reserve, and all priests, who depend upon the prince, are for their own sakes obliged to promote what he esteems his interest, 'tis plain, the education of youth, on which is laid the very foundation stones of the public liberty, has been of late years committed to the sole management of such as make it their business to undermine it; and must needs do so, unless they will be false to their fortunes, and make the character of priest give place to that of true patriot."

Good learning, Molesworth insists, is a "great antidote against the plague of tyranny." But good learning involves a constant reference to liberty, law, and patriotism, to those great principles of reason and justice that must be at the heart of all free government. The ancients were well aware of this and placed their academies in the hands of public-spirited philosophers dedicated to teaching the moral virtues associated with duty to country, the preservation of law, and the public liberty. In contrast, the modern priestly class in the schools and universities—and Molesworth sees the Jesuits as the quintessential examples—are content to stress precision of grammar and elegance of style, omitting or passing lightly over the improvement of reason, the love of justice, and the value of liberty in favor of the constant nurture of blind obedience to authority.

As far as Molesworth is concerned, Denmark, Sweden, and Germany teach the lesson of clerical education in the resultant absolutism of their governments, and a people determined to preserve its liberty might well draw the moral and demand a less monkish and more secular education addressed to the political needs of a free society. "And I can't but believe," he concludes, "if in our schools our youth were bred up to understand the meaning of the authors they are made to read, as well as the syntax of the words: If there were as much care taken to inculcate the good maxims, and recom-

mend the noble characters the old historians are so full of, as there
is to hammer into their heads the true grammar of them, and the
fineness of the phrase: If in our universities a proportionable care
were taken to furnish them with noble and generous learning: If
after this they were duly informed in the laws and affairs of their
own country, trained up in good conversation and useful knowledge
at home, and then sent abroad when their heads began to be well
settled, when the heat of youth was worn off, and their judgments
ripe enough to make observation: I say, I cannot but believe that
with this manner of institution a very moderate understanding
might do wonders, and the coming home fully instructed in the
constitutions of other governments, would make a man but the more
resolute to maintain his own."

Molesworth's *Account* was widely consulted in the colonies for
the instruction it appeared to afford on the dangers of surrendering
liberty. And, not surprisingly, it was commonly associated with
Algernon Sidney's *Discourses Concerning Government* (1698), which
Molesworth and the colonists greatly esteemed, as describing the
sort of education that would produce the wise and prudent citizens
who would form the backbone of Sidney's just state. Yet, however
well Molesworth himself was known (and the same might be said
of Harrington and Sidney), the "real Whig" tradition, as Commonwealth ideas were referred to, was even more widely disseminated
in the colonies by two anthologies of essays in which Molesworth
had had a hand but which were largely the work of John Trenchard
and Thomas Gordon.[8]

Trenchard was a contemporary of Molesworth at Trinity College,
though there is no evidence that the two had actually met in Dublin,
or, indeed, that they had met at all before their association in London during the 1690's. A lawyer by training and a man of independent means, Trenchard was an outspoken critic of standing armies

[8] For the particular influence of Sidney's *Discourses* in the colonies, see Caroline Robbins, "Algernon Sidney's *Discourses Concerning Government:* Textbook of
Revolution," *The William and Mary Quarterly*, 3d ser., IV (1947), 267-296. Molesworth's
own definition of a "real Whig" as "one who is exactly for keeping up to the strict-
ness of the true old Gothic constitution, under the estates of king (or queen), lords and
commons; the legislature being seated· in all three together, the executive entrusted
with the first, but accountable to the whole body of the people, in case of maladminis-
tration," a definition that enjoyed wide currency in the colonies, patently assumed the
kind of education that would enable "the whole body of the people" responsibly to
enforce that accountability. See Robert Molesworth, *The Principles of a Real Whig* (London: printed for J. Williams, 1775), p. 6. *Principles* was a reissue of Molesworth's introduction to a translation of François Hotman's *Franco-Gallia* in 1721.

as inherently inconsistent with the principles of free government. In 1719 he entered into a collaboration with Thomas Gordon, a young Scot who may have had some legal training and who was teaching languages in London, first, to produce a number of political tracts on various subjects, then, to edit a weekly paper named *The Independent Whig,* and then, to prepare a series of essays published in the form of *Cato's Letters. The Independent Whig* and *Cato's Letters* subsequently appeared in book form, and were frequently reprinted during the eighteenth century, in whole or in part, on both sides of the Atlantic; at least two full editions of the former were issued in Philadelphia, in 1724 and 1740, and innumerable excerpts, quotations, references, and serializations were published in colonial newspapers from Boston to Savannah. Ultimately, they constituted for the colonists the fullest and most popular expositions of the "real Whig" tradition to appear during the eighteenth century; and they exerted untold influence on the ways in which provincial Americans perceived and responded to the political events of their time.

Nothing shines through the educational discussions of *The Independent Whig* and *Cato's Letters* quite as clearly as their anticlericalism. It is not merely "popishness" the editors fear in schools and colleges but any clergy in any role. "The ancients were instructed by philosophers," Whig laments, "and the moderns are taught by priests. The first thought it their duty to make their pupils as useful as possible to their country, and the latter as subservient as themselves, and the interests of their order." *Vide* Molesworth! But beyond that, beyond all the tyranny and mischief that flow from clerical control, there is the plague of false learning that substitutes endless speculation and scholastic ceremonial for the useful knowledge and agreeable conversation of merchants, mechanics, tradesmen, and young gentlemen. *Vide* Locke! True virtue, wisdom, and breeding are not learned from monkish scholars and stiffened pedants, indeed, they are not learned from schools and colleges at all. They are acquired by living "abroad in the world," by reading and meditation, by conversation with "all sorts of men." They derive from experience reflected upon, from the ability of reason to ascertain truth and the readiness of will to act upon reason. And it is this larger education alone that is worthy of free men and that can vouchsafe their liberties; what is proffered by priests will only erode liberty, or, worse yet, conspire in its suppression. Such strictures doubtless appeared eminently sound to colonists of Whiggish sympathies, who found Trenchard and Gordon so very pertinent and Oxford and Cambridge so very remote.[9]

III

Among the large American audience that regularly perused the writings of Trenchard and Gordon, few read more avidly than William Livingston, William Smith, Jr., and John Morin Scott of New York City. A formidable triumvirate by any criteria of birth or ability, the three shared youth and intelligence, an education at Yale, a commitment to Presbyterianism, a profession of the law, a fondness for scribbling, and a determination to do something about the cultural impoverishment of the colony. Livingston was the eldest, having been born in 1723, the sixth son of Philip Livingston, lord of Livingston Manor. Reared at Albany amid circumstances of ease and affluence, he had been destined for the bar by a father ever mindful of the growing demands of the family's holdings. But he proved a disappointment in this respect, preferring belles-lettres to the law and finding his satisfactions in political rather than business enterprise.

Precisely when Livingston first became acquainted with Smith and Scott is not entirely clear. Smith, who is not to be confused with the William Smith who wrote *A General Idea of the College of Mirania* (1753), had been born in 1728, the oldest son of a distinguished New York lawyer; Scott had been born two years later, the only child of a well-to-do New York merchant. The two younger men had doubtless been acquainted at Yale, and all three may well have met from time to time at one or another of New York's innumerable social events. But it is probable that the triumvirate itself took shape in earnest in the law office of Smith's father, William Smith, Sr., where all three served at least part of their legal apprenticeship. It was surely there, too, that they hatched their plans for a cultural revival in the colony, enlisting a number of older men, such as the senior Smith and the distinguished lawyer James Alexander, in whose office Livingston had labored for a time. One outcome was the informal literary club organized in 1748 as the

---

9 *The Independent Whig* (4 vols. in 1; Hartford, Conn.: William S. Marsh, 1816), no. 29, p. 91; *Cato's Letters* (4 vols.; no place: no publisher, 1754), no. 121, March 23, 1723, IV, 110-112.

Society for the Promotion of Useful Knowledge—but dubbed the "Society of Sage Philosophers" by its critics. Another was the establishment somewhat later of the New York Society Library, a subscription venture open to the public at large. And yet another was the launching of *The Independent Reflector*.

The idea of the *Reflector* seems to have taken form early in 1749, when Livingston wrote to a Yale classmate of "a design of publishing weekly essays as soon as possible upon the plan of *The Spectator*, for correcting the taste and improving the minds of our fellow citizens." At that time Smith and Scott were involved in the plan, along with a Yale contemporary of Livingston named William Peartree Smith, but the latter Smith was destined to be at best a sometime contributor. In any case, three years were to pass before the design came to fruition, and during that time there was a major shift in the model, from *The Spectator* to *The Independent Whig* and *Cato's Letters*. One can only guess at the reasons. They may have been largely temperamental, revolving around the pungent and acerbic style of Trenchard and Gordon, but it is likely that they were substantive as well. For it had become abundantly clear to the triumvirate between 1749 and 1752 that the critical issues in New York affairs had become religious as well as political and that the anticlericalism of *The Independent Whig* was burningly relevant to New York City in general and its projected college in particular.[10]

As early as 1749, Livingston had issued an appeal for legislative action on the projected college entitled *Some Serious Thoughts on the Design of Erecting a College in the Province of New-York*. Nine pages in length, it gave no inkling of the bitter religious controversy that would soon engulf the nascent institution, setting forth its arguments in measured prose that advocated the "numberless advantages" of a "public seminary of learning." When the legislature named trustees for the college in 1751, however, and it turned out that most of those named were members of the Church of England, and when Trinity Church proposed to deed certain lands to the trustees—some of whom were vestrymen of that church—on condition that the president of the institution should be an Anglican, the situation changed drastically. The dissenting sects of the colony, with the Presbyterians in the forefront, viewed the offer as presaging a crass Anglican takeover, not only of the college but of the whole govern-

[10] William Livingston to Noah Welles, February 18, 1749 (Johnson family mss., Yale University).

mental apparatus, under the leadership of Governor De Lancey and his coreligionists on the council. For Livingston, Smith, and Scott, a "monster tyranny" was in the making that could only culminate in the official establishment of the Church of England throughout the colonies—diocese, bishop, and all. The only options open to them were to confront it squarely or suffer the consequences.[11]

Such was the context of politico-religious suspicion and controversy within which *The Independent Reflector* finally emerged, and it is little wonder that *The Independent Whig* struck the editors as an apt model. The first issue appeared on November 30, 1752—it happened to have been Livingston's twenty-ninth birthday—and promised, much in the spirit of Trenchard and Gordon, an uncompromising and nonpartisan crusade in favor of liberty and against public vice and corruption. "In a word," claimed the *Reflector*, "I shall dare to attempt the reforming the abuses of my country, and to point out whatever may tend to its prosperity and emolument." Subsequent issues dealt with the injustice of excise taxes, the advantages of limited monarchy, the unwisdom of unrestricted immigration to the colonies (especially of large numbers of felons), the perils of selling public offices, and the self-serving of those who criticized *The Independent Reflector*.[12]

In March, 1753, the *Reflector* turned to an examination of the projected college. The timing was certainly not fortuitous. Proposals had been solicited by the trustees of the institution concerning its character and curriculum, and at least one, by a friend of the De Lanceys named William Smith, had appeared bearing the recommendation that a member of the established church occupy the presidency. Anticipating a considerable influence for the intended college, the *Reflector* urged that persons of all Protestant denominations be admitted on a basis of complete parity, that the college be founded by an act of the assembly rather than a charter from the Crown, that it be placed under the supervision of civil rather than ecclesiastical authorities, that the president be elected by a majority of the trustees and be responsible to them, that no particular religious

---

[11] [William Livingston,] *Some Serious Thoughts on the Design of Erecting a College in the Province of New-York* (New York: John Zenger, 1749), p. 3; William Livingston to Noah Welles, [March, 1751] (Johnson family mss., Yale University). Livingston himself happened to have been one of the ten trustees named in 1751; but he was far more concerned with the fact that seven of his colleagues were Anglicans than with the opportunities implicit in his own membership.

[12] *The Independent Reflector*, edited by Milton M. Klein (Cambridge, Mass.: Harvard University Press, 1963), no. 1, November 30, 1752, p. 57.

profession be required at the college, the officers and scholars remaining free to attend any Protestant church of their choice, that there be no professor of divinity and that the subject of divinity not be part of the curriculum, and that members of the college have unrestricted access to all books in the library. "Let us, therefore, strive to have the college founded on an ample, a generous, a universal plan," the *Reflector* concluded. "Let not the seat of literature, the abode of the muses, and the nurse of science; be transformed into a cloister of bigots, a habitation of superstition, a nursery of ghostly tyranny, a school of rabbinical jargon. The legislature alone should have the direction of so important an establishment. In their hands it is safer, incomparably safer, than in those of a party, who will instantly discover a thirst for dominion, and lord it over the rest."[13]

The *Reflector* returned to the subject of education soon thereafter, first in an essay on the necessity of county grammar schools as feeders for the college (an essay, incidentally, in which the *Reflector* could not resist the temptation to urge a "generous and catholic" religious foundation for the college) and then in an essay again urging the attractiveness of a college open to students of all denominations on a basis of absolute parity. Moreover, there is evidence of the editors' intention to raise the college issue yet again in subsequent numbers. But the magazine suspended publication with the issue of November 22, 1753, and did not reappear.

It is difficult to determine precisely the influence of *The Independent Reflector* on the development of educational policy. In the short run, the granting of a royal charter for King's College in 1754 and the election of Samuel Johnson as president would seem to have spelled the defeat of the *Reflector's* program. Yet the stigma of sectarianism that appeared to mark the college in its early years may have derived far more from the *Reflector's* columns than from Johnson's curriculum, for the evidence indicates that Johnson's Anglicanism weighed lightly on the day-to-day life of the institution. More importantly, perhaps, the *Reflector* may have prepared the ground for the establishment some years later of the University of the State of New York as an institution to exercise general civic control over the entire educational system. Livingston and his associates had certainly set forth many of the principles that stood at the heart of that institution; whether they were actually instrumental in its coming to be must remain a matter of conjecture.

13 *Ibid.*, no. 22, April 26, 1753, p. 214.

IV

The New York triumvirate had initially taken *The Spectator* as their model for a lively periodical that would correct the tastes and improve the minds of their fellow citizens. Then, in response to changing conditions, they had shifted their loyalty to *The Independent Whig*. A roughly contemporary decision in Boston had gone in quite another direction. There, the booksellers Samuel Eliot and Joshua Blanchard had decided on the need for a journal of affairs that would over time "amount to a treasury of various knowledge and learning, of the serious and pleasant, of the instructive and diverting," furnishing the public "with store of choice well-digested apprehensions of men and things," to be called *The American Magazine and Historical Chronicle*. The model for that journal, however, was not the intensely political variation on *The Spectator* represented by *The Independent Whig* but rather the entertainingly miscellaneous variation represented by *The Gentleman's Magazine* and its competitor, *The London Magazine*. Signifying an important departure from the classic Addison-Steele format, those journals were essentially edited composites of the leading periodicals of their day, presenting not a single original essay in each issue but rather a varied fare of reprinted prose, poetry, and news, along with occasional original contributions. It was such a format that *The American Magazine and Historical Chronicle* adopted for itself, and apparently with some considerable success, given the length of time it lasted and the quality it was able to attain under the versatile editorship of Jeremy Gridley.[14]

In the number for January, 1746, *The American Magazine* carried an announcement that the proprietors, now the Boston printers Rogers and Fowle, hoped would contribute to the instruction of the readership and the financial stability of the enterprise. What was anticipated was the publication "by parcels" of *A Summary, Historical and Political, of the Beginnings, Progressive Improvements, and Present State of the British Settlements in North America*, by "W. D., M.D.," whom the *cognoscenti* quickly identified as the Boston physician William Douglass. As it turned out, the year passed and the magazine expired without the printing of so much as a single parcel; but the parcels did eventually appear, bearing the cover, interestingly enough, of the defunct magazine. By 1749, thirty-six

14 *The American Magazine and Historical Chronicle*, September, 1743, ii.

sections had been presented to the public, and the publishers decided to bind them, with the covers removed, into a single volume. Twenty-six additional sections were issued in the same manner between 1750 and 1752, the project being terminated by Douglass' death in the latter year; and these too were subsequently bound in a single volume. By 1755 a London edition appeared, reprinting both volumes in a uniform format for the first time.

Douglass himself is a fascinating study in catholic interest, encyclopedic knowledge, and confident opinion. Born in 1691 in the town of Gifford in Haddington County, Scotland, he had been educated at Edinburgh, where he had come under the tutelage of a first-rate teacher of medicine, Archibald Pitcairne, and then had gone on to the medical faculties of Leiden and Utrecht to complete the work for the doctorate in medicine. Having attained the degree in 1712, he had worked for a time at hospitals in Paris and Flanders, and had then returned to England in the hope of launching a profitable practice. Through the intervention of his friend Elizeus Burgess he had decided soon thereafter to immigrate to Massachusetts and try his fortunes in the New World. It turned out that Burgess, who was slated for a time to be governor of Massachusetts, eventually changed his mind; but Douglass went ahead with his plan. He crossed the Atlantic in 1716, toured the colonies rather extensively (even visiting the British and French West Indies), and then set down roots in Boston, where he attached himself to the coffeehouse of Richard Hall, surrounded himself with a group of lively friends drawn from high and low places, made a good deal of money and invested it shrewdly in land, and took an active part in the affairs of the colony.

Throughout his life, Douglass was an inveterate author, maintaining a lengthy and voluminous correspondence with his friend Cadwallader Colden of New York (which may have dated from their days at Edinburgh), writing extensively for *The New-England Courant*, and turning out a host of pamphlets on subjects ranging from the wisdom of inoculation to the economics of inflation. Precisely when he first decided to write his *Summary* is not clear. He was a habitual collector of sundry information on a phenomenal variety of topics—legal history, land boundaries, the weather, exports and imports, religious customs, sugar production, fishery, and botany. Much of this was doubtless for his own amusement and edification, in characteristic eighteenth-century fashion. But apparently certain friends urged him to organize and publish his data "for the benefit of the public, and for the use of future historians"; and probably sometime during the 1740's he succumbed to their arguments, concluding that if nothing else a competent effort would provide source material for the future and at the same time correct some of the egregious misimpressions on both sides of the Atlantic concerning the life and character of the colonies. The result was not only the first general history of British North America written from the viewpoint of a resident but also an intriguing potpourri of colonial opinion and Douglassian eccentricity.[15]

In general the *Summary* is prolix, poorly organized, and replete with lengthy digressions and dogmatic dicta. But at the same time it sparkles with keen insights and independent judgments. In an era of much rote piety about the conversion of the heathen, Douglass argued that most missions to the Indians had failed because mission work "requires travel, labor, and hardships: and the British people in general, instead of Christian virtues, teach them European vices; for instance, by introducing the use of intoxicating liquors, for private profit, they dispense more strong liquor than gospel to the Indians; and thus have destroyed, and continue to destroy perhaps more Indians, than formerly the Spaniards did, by their inhumane and execrable cruelties, under the name of conversions; the Spaniards destroyed only their bodies, we destroy body and mind." Douglass observed that John Eliot had spent years translating the Bible into Algonquian but that there were few literate Indians to study it. David Brainerd had at least put forth the time and effort to travel and live among the Indians, but that "true and zealous missionary" had displayed a "weak enthusiastic turn of mind." And, as for the Roman Catholic missionaries, they were ready enough to throw themselves wholly into their work, but one had to grant that they were promoting trade and national interest along with the gospel. Similar acerbity was addressed to religious controversialists ("By the many controversies in revealed religions, the several sects expose the inconsistencies and absurdities of one another's opinions, and occasion the wise and thinking part of mankind to regulate themselves by natural religion only, and to conclude that all religions only are good, which teach men to be good"), to hotheaded enthusiastical preachers ("the vagrant Mr. W——ld, an insignificant person, of no general learning, void of common prudence; his journals are a

[15] William Douglass, *A Summary, Historical and Political, of the First Planting, Progressive Improvements, and Present State of the British Settlements in North-America* (2 vols.; London: R. Baldwin, 1755), I, 1; II, 1.

rhapsody of Scripture texts, and of his own cant expressions"), and to S.P.G. rectors in older, more settled communities ("They are sent to the capitals, richest, and best civilized towns of our provinces; as if the design and institution were only to bring over the tolerated sober, civilized Dissenters, to the formality of saying their prayers liturgy-fashion").[16]

Other observations on education abound throughout the *Summary*, including fairly accurate portrayals of Harvard and Yale (and passing mention of the two other colleges, in Virginia and New Jersey), several strong recommendations that S.P.G. missionaries in New England turn their efforts from the conversion of Dissenters to the establishment of county working schools for both white and Indian children, a sharp criticism of Bishop Berkeley's decision to locate his projected university in Bermuda, and a lengthy commentary on child-rearing, much in the fashion of his fellow physician Locke, which set forth prescriptions regarding health ("I did not allow him to be rocked in a cradle, suspecting that concussions might weaken his brain, and consequently impair his judgment"), advice on the teaching of languages ("Before he was full five years of age, he did distinctly repeat and pronounce the Lord's Prayer in five languages familiar to me, Greek, Latin, English, French and Dutch"), and a fascinating rationalist catechism that conveys as much as any single document Douglass' independence of mind ("Q. When was you born? A. I was born July 25, 1745; but how I was made, and how I came into the world, I have forgotten, and cannot tell").[17]

Most interesting of all, perhaps, is a briefly stated but comprehensive plan for public education obviously modeled on New England practice but clearly extending beyond it:

For the education of youth, there shall be one public school or more in each township or district, for teaching of reading English, writing, and arithmetic: In each shire town a grammar school for the learned dead languages of Greek and Latin, for Hebrew roots recourse may be had to the divinity colleges; the matters of the town and country schools to be approved of by the quarter sessions: In each province, a *schola illustris*, or college, for what are called arts and sciences, to be regulated by the legislatures: And near the center of the North America continent colonies (therefore not in Bermuda, Dr. Berkeley's scheme) a university or academy to be regulated by the board of plantations, to initiate young gentlemen in the learned professions of divinity, law, and medicine; in the modern,

16 *Ibid.*, II, 118; I, 172; II, 117, 118; I, 438; II, 141; I, 232.
17 *Ibid.*, II, 346-347.

commercial and traveling languages of French, Spanish, and Dutch; in other curious sciences of mathematics, belles-lettres, and etc. and gentlemen exercises of riding the great horse, fencing and dancing; from school to college, from college to travel, and from travel to business, are the gradations of a liberal education, but for want of effects the link of travel is frequently wanting.

In every shire-town there shall be a workhouse, to oblige and habituate idlers to some work: it is a better charity to provide work for the idle poor, than to feed them; as also an almshouse for the aged, infirm, and incurable poor of the county: but principally and especially, an orphan house for poor children; where parents are dead or unable to provide for their children, these children become children of the commonwealth, not to be brought up to idle learning (reading and writing excepted) but to trades and labor: generally these poor children may be bound to proper masters, as apprentices or servants, the boys to 21 Æt. the girls to 18 Æt. by the county courts, or by three justices *quorum unus*.[18]

In the last analysis, there is no telling accurately who on either side of the Atlantic imbibed Douglass' zealously gathered data and confidently expressed opinions. There were at least two additional printings after 1755, a Boston edition of 1757 and an English edition of 1760, and one must therefore assume a continuing and widespread interest. But it may in any case be more significant to speculate on how Douglass was actually perceived by those who did in fact read him. Here it is important to recall that he put himself forward and was widely recognized as a colonial commentator seeking to view the colonial scene as a whole and in its entirety. And, for all the faults of his work (which, incidentally, were clearly seen by contemporary critics), the posture he assumed lent an authority to his views that lasted well beyond his lifetime. It must certainly have led more than a few colonials to ponder his educational recommendations with that special consideration one reserves for a landsman, who is familiar with the terrain and therefore knows whereof he speaks.

V

There is evidence that Thomas Jefferson owned a copy of Douglass' *Summary*, though there is no indication as to whether he ever read it or, if he did read it, as to what he made of it. There is a pronounced similarity between the educational proposals of the two men, though that similarity may derive as much from their common reading as from any direct influence of one on the other. Even there,

---

[18] *Ibid.*, I, 256-257.

however, we have too few insights, given Douglass' penchant for using footnotes as obiter dicta rather than acknowledgments of debt. "No person can trace me as a plagiary," Douglass saw fit to remark in the *Summary*; "my own observations, hints from correspondents, and well-approved authors, and from public records are the materials of this essay." Who those well-approved authors were, apart from a few explicit references to Locke on religion, Montaigne on education, Mather on Massachusetts politics, and Pitcairne and Sydenham on materia medica, is impossible to determine.[19]

In the case of Jefferson we know a good deal more. In addition to the interest he manifested in Douglass, he came early to a thorough knowledge of the leading ancient authors, chiefly Plato, Euripides, Cicero, and Virgil; a profound acquaintance with the enduring writers of the Renaissance, notably, Erasmus, More, Machiavelli, Bodin, and Shakespeare; and an easy familiarity with the more modern liberal commentators, from Harrington and Sidney to Locke, Molesworth, Trenchard, and Gordon, and, significantly, their French contemporary Montesquieu. Indeed, given the extraordinary catholicity of his interests and the incredible range of his reading— it is significant that he used Bacon's paradigm of universal knowledge from the *Advancement of Learning* to catalogue his library and found works to list in every category—the problem with Jefferson is not so much to locate the possible sources of his ideas as it is to determine, where possible, the particular sources.

Born in 1743, the son of a rising Virginia planter, Jefferson was fortunate enough to receive the best the colonies could offer by way of formal schooling and instructive experience. His earliest training outside the household of his father was under the tutelage of the Reverend William Douglas, a Scotsman who apparently knew too little Latin and even less Greek. But early in 1758, at the age of fourteen, Jefferson began to attend the log school of the Reverend James Maury, a teacher of considerable ability who nurtured in his student a lifelong interest in the classics. Two years later, Jefferson entered the College of William and Mary, where his chief education seems to have come from another Scotsman named William Small, the professor of natural philosophy, who introduced him not only to mathematics and the sciences but also to some of the leading lights of Williamsburg, especially George Wythe, with whom Jefferson sub- sequently studied law, and Francis Fauquier, the lieutenant governor

[19] *Ibid.*, I, 91.

whose good offices meant so much to Jefferson in coming to know the larger life of Virginia politics. Through these men Jefferson entered the intellectual world of Bacon, Newton, and Locke, whom he considered the "three greatest men that have ever lived, without any exception," and the political world of the Virginia gentry, where the doctrines of universal law and natural right were so well known as to be taken virtually for granted. Both the philosopher and the statesman came alive in Williamsburg during those years of the 1760's, and they interacted for the next half-century in such a way as to make Jefferson the perfect embodiment of the Enlightenment in America.[20]

Jefferson's earliest ideas on education are set forth in correspondence, notably, those few letters dealing with his own schooling at Williamsburg ("By going to the college I shall get a more universal acquaintance, which may hereafter be serviceable to me") and a lengthy advice of August 3, 1771, to his future brother-in-law Robert Skipwith, recommending titles for a basic private library ("A lively and lasting sense of filial duty is more effectually impressed on the mind of a son or daughter by reading *King Lear*, than by all the dry volumes of ethics and divinity that ever were written"). And they are further revealed in his several drafts of the Virginia Constitution of 1776, all of which include provisions for "full and free liberty of religious opinion" and a free press (which provisions, incidentally, were not included in that constitution as adopted). But it was not until Jefferson served as a member of the Virginia assembly's Committee to Revise the Laws of the Commonwealth between 1776 and 1779, along with George Wythe, Edmund Pendleton, George Mason, and Thomas Ludwell Lee, that his views appeared in their larger, more mature form. Indeed, one finds in several of the bills Jefferson drafted on behalf of that committee virtually all the principal ideas on education he would thereafter espouse; and he himself would later remark to George Wythe that the Bill for the More General Diffusion of Knowledge was the single most important measure in the whole proposed code.[21]

The remark itself may have been an exaggeration, though there

[20] Thomas Jefferson to John Trumbull, February 15, 1788, *The Papers of Thomas Jefferson,* edited by Julian P. Boyd (17+ vols.; Princeton: Princeton University Press, 1950–   ), XIV, 561.

[21] Thomas Jefferson to John Harvie, January 14, 1760, *ibid.,* I, 3; Thomas Jefferson to Robert Skipwith, August 3, 1771, *ibid.,* p. 77; "The Virginia Constitution, 1776," *ibid.,* pp. 344-345; and Thomas Jefferson to George Wythe, August 13, 1786, *ibid.,* X, 244. George Mason resigned from the committee of revisers and Thomas Lee died before the work was completed.

is no denying that the bill embodied a crucial element in the Jeffersonian program. Consider it in the perspective of his own political and intellectual development during that critical half-decade following 1774, the year certain resolutions he had drafted to instruct Virginia's delegates to the forthcoming general congress were suddenly published, without his knowledge, as *A Summary View of the Rights of British America.* Based on an implicit doctrine of natural rights, which maintained that the original Anglo-American colonists had been entirely free to depart the country in which chance had placed them (Locke's theory of consent) and to establish new societies "under such laws and regulations as to them shall seem most likely to promote public happiness," the *Summary* had boldly repudiated the right of Parliament to meddle in the internal affairs of the colonies. Then, two years later, the Declaration of Independence had repeated many of these assertions, setting forth as well an explicit statement of the rights doctrine: viz., "that all men are created equal, that they are endowed by their Creator with certain unalienable rights, that among these are life, liberty, and the pursuit of happiness. That to secure these rights, governments are instituted among men, deriving their just powers from the consent of the governed, that whenever any form of government becomes destructive of these ends, it is the right of the people to alter or to abolish it, and to institute new government, laying its foundation on such principles, and organizing its powers in such form, as to them shall seem most likely to effect their safety and happiness." Like Molesworth, however, and like Montesquieu, who taught that in a republican government the whole power of education is required if the virtue that makes men choose public over private interest is to be sustained, Jefferson was well aware that such phrases are empty rhetoric in the absence of widespread public understanding. And it was through the Bill for the More General Diffusion of Knowledge and its companion measures of 1779 that he sought to act on that awareness.[22]

The preamble to the bill is lengthy, but sufficiently significant to bear quotation in its entirety:

[22] "Draft of Instructions to the Virginia Delegates in the Continental Congress," *ibid.,* I, 121; and "The Declaration of Independence," *ibid.,* p. 429. We know that Jefferson had perused Molesworth and Montesquieu by the autumn of 1778, when he drafted the Bill for the More General Diffusion of Knowledge. Whether he had read Harrington's *Oceana* or Douglass' *Summary* by that time cannot be determined. On Jefferson's change of attitude toward Montesquieu during the 1780's, see Gilbert Chinard, ed., *The Commonplace Book of Thomas Jefferson* (Baltimore: Johns Hopkins Press, 1926), pp. 31 ff.

Whereas it appeareth that however certain forms of government are better calculated than others to protect individuals in the free exercise of their natural rights, and are at the same time themselves better guarded against degeneracy, yet experience hath shown, that even under the best forms, those entrusted with power have, in time, and by slow operations, perverted it into tyranny; and it is believed that the most effectual means of preventing this would be, to illuminate, as far as practicable, the minds of the people at large, and more especially to give them knowledge of those facts, which history exhibiteth, that, possessed thereby of the experience of other ages and countries, they may be enabled to know ambition under all its shapes, and prompt to exert their natural powers to defeat its purposes; And whereas it is generally true that that people will be happiest whose laws are best, and are best administered, and that laws will be wisely formed, and honestly administered, in proportion as those who form and administer them are wise and honest; whence it becomes expedient for promoting the public happiness that those persons, whom nature hath endowed with genius and virtue, should be rendered by liberal education worthy to receive, and able to guard the sacred deposit of the rights and liberties of their fellow citizens, and that they should be called to that charge without regard to wealth, birth or other accidental condition or circumstance; but the indigence of the greater number disabling them from so educating, at their own expense, those of their children whom nature hath fitly formed and disposed to become useful instruments for the public, it is better that such should be sought for and educated at the common expense of all, than that the happiness of all should be confided to the weak or wicked.

Based on these assertions, the bill went on to propose the division of the commonwealth into hundreds, each to have a school where reading, writing, common arithmetic, and history (ancient, English, and American) would be taught, which all free children of the hundreds, male and female, might attend gratis for three years and at private expense thereafter, and which would be supported by taxation and overseen by representatives of the public. Further, the bill proposed the establishment under public overseers of twenty grammar schools throughout the commonwealth, where Latin and Greek, English grammar, and more advanced arithmetic would be taught, and which would be open to qualified scholars at appropriate tuition fees as well as to the brightest graduates of the lower schools whose parents were too poor to give them additional education (these to be examined annually for the purpose of weeding out those of "least promising genius and disposition"). Finally, the bill provided for ten of the surviving scholarship students from the grammar schools to be chosen each year to proceed to the College of William and Mary, there to be educated, boarded, and clothed at public expense for three years. "The ultimate result of the whole scheme of education," Jefferson observed in his *Notes on the State of Virginia* (1785), "would be the teaching all the children of the state reading, writing, and common arithmetic; turning out ten annually, of superior genius, well taught in Greek, Latin, geography, and the higher branches of arithmetic; turning out ten others annually, of still superior parts, who, to those branches of learning, shall have added such of the sciences as their genius shall have led them to; the furnishing to the wealthier part of the people convenient schools at which their children may be educated at their own expense.—The general objects of this law are to provide an education adapted to the years, to the capacity, and the condition of everyone, and directed to their freedom and happiness. . . . But of all the views of this law none is more important, none more legitimate, than that of rendering the people the safe, as they are the ultimate, guardians of their own liberty."[23]

Following the Bill for the More General Diffusion of Knowledge in the proposed code, and obviously complementing it, was a Bill for Amending the Constitution of the College of William and Mary, the purpose of which was threefold: first, to provide more certain revenues to the college and at the same time make it more directly responsible to the public by empowering the legislature to choose its visitors, who would not be bound by the royal or ecclesiastical strictures imposed in the original charter; second, to broaden the curriculum to include studies in ethics and the fine arts, history and law, mathematics and medicine, natural philosophy and natural history, and ancient and modern languages; and third, to transform the professorship for the instruction of the Indians—the so-called Brafferton professorship, established under the will of Robert Boyle—into a mission, the prime purpose of which would be to investigate the laws, languages, religions, and customs of the several tribes. And following the college bill was yet another measure, providing for the establishment of a great public library at Richmond, under the supervision of visitors appointed by the assembly.

One other statute completed the educational segment of the

23 "A Bill for the More General Diffusion of Knowledge," *Papers of Thomas Jefferson*, II, 526-527, 533; and *Notes on the State of Virginia* (1785), in *The Writings of Thomas Jefferson*, edited by Paul Leicester Ford (10 vols.; New York: G. P. Putnam's Sons, 1892-1899), III, 252-254.

proposed code, appearing, significantly, directly after the library bill: that was the Bill for Establishing Religious Freedom. According to its provisions, which proclaimed that coercion in matters of conscience is contrary to Christianity, no man "shall be compelled to frequent or support any religious worship, place, or ministry whatsoever, nor shall be enforced, restrained, molested, or burdened in his body or goods, nor shall otherwise suffer, on account of his religious opinions or belief; but that all men shall be free to profess, and by argument to maintain, their opinions in matters of religion, and that the same shall in no wise diminish, enlarge, or affect their civil capacities." To see the religious freedom bill as essentially inseparable from the other education measures is to recognize certain fundamental principles of the Jeffersonian program: first, the assumption that rational men need education to arrive at religious truth quite as much as to achieve political wisdom; second, the insistence that such elemental education as they need for their quest derives more appropriately from state-sponsored schools than from state-sponsored churches; and third, the belief that, given a widespread diffusion of knowledge, the cause of religious truth is best served by permitting all churches to proffer their doctrines in a private capacity.[24]

At no point, it must be said, did Jefferson ever question the fundamental role of the family in the education of youth, though unlike his mentor Locke he seemed relatively unconcerned about the deleterious effects of extramural instruction. What Jefferson did attempt was to shift the prestige and resources of the state from the church to the school as the most appropriate agency for carrying on that extramural education, at least in its public and systematic form. And what should be quickly added is that, withal, Jefferson saw the ultimate education of the citizenry taking place in the world beyond the school, a world in which participation in public affairs, illuminated by the contribution of a free and vigorous press, would play a crucial role. For Jefferson as for Franklin, self-education in the arena of life was of the essence.

Interestingly enough, Jefferson took an exceedingly latitudinarian view of citizenship, providing in one statute of the proposed code that all white persons who might be born in the commonwealth or move to it with the intention of remaining should be deemed citizens.

---

[24] "A Bill for Establishing Religious Freedom," *Papers of Thomas Jefferson*, II, 546.

But the color restriction was stark; and, for all his opposition to the slave trade, for all his recognition of the cruelties of slavery, and for all his support of gradual emancipation, Jefferson seemed at no point ready to accept the blacks into full citizenship, believing them inferior in mental and physical endowment. That being the case, he excluded them from the provisions of the Bill for the More General Diffusion of Knowledge, though later he reported his interest in a plan to educate the blacks "at the public expense, to tillage, arts, or sciences, according to their geniuses," preparatory to their being sent elsewhere as colonists. True, Jefferson's sentiments toward the blacks were more rather than less benign, when measured against those of Virginians—and perhaps white men in general—in the 1770's; but they compare less than favorably with the humane egalitarianism of a John Woolman or an Anthony Benezet.[25]

Finally, it must be said that the Jeffersonian educational program did not fare well in the Virginia legislature during the years following its initial proposal. Only the religious freedom bill passed, and that after seven years of bitter political controversy. The other three measures died in their original form, though Jefferson would spend the rest of his career seeking laws directed to similar ends. Jefferson himself once remarked to Washington that the Bill for the More General Diffusion of Knowledge had been enthusiastically received by the delegates, "and it seemed afterwards that nothing but the extreme distress of our resources prevented its being carried into execution even during the war." But years later William Wirt, a perceptive commentator on commonwealth affairs, put the reason more fundamentally: "What a plan was here to give stability and solid glory to the republic! If you ask me why it has never been adopted, I answer that, as a foreigner, I can perceive no possible reason for it, except that the comprehensive views and generous patriotism which produced the bill, have not prevailed throughout the country, nor presided in the body on whose vote the adoption of that bill depended."[26]

[25] "A Bill Declaring Who Should Be Deemed Citizens of This Commonwealth," *ibid.*, pp. 476-477; "A Bill Concerning Slaves," *ibid.*, pp. 470-472; and *Notes on the State of Virginia*, pp. 243-250, 266-267.

[26] Thomas Jefferson to George Washington, January 4, 1786, *Papers of Thomas Jefferson*, IX, 151; and [William Wirt], *The British Spy* (3d ed.; Newburyport, Mass.: no publisher, 1804), pp. 82-83.

Chapter 15

POLITICS AND EDUCATION

> We are more thoroughly an enlightened people, with respect
> to our political interests, than perhaps any other under heaven.
> Every man among us reads, and is so easy in his circumstances as
> to have leisure for conversations of improvement, and for ac-
> quiring information.
>
> BENJAMIN FRANKLIN

For all its abortiveness, the appearance of *Publick Occurrences*
marked something of an educational milestone for the American
colonies. It is not merely that a monthly was contemplated that
would present for the first time "an account of such considerable
things as have arrived unto our notice" as well as a steady flow of
useful reporting from the "best fountains" of information. It is
rather that there was clearly a concept of the public and its affairs un-
derlying Benjamin Harris' enterprise, which led him to hope that as
a result of *Publick Occurrences* "people everywhere may better
understand the circumstances of public affairs, both abroad and at
home; which may not only direct their thoughts at all times, but at
some times also to assist their business and negotiations." That concept of public affairs was at best nascent in the Anglo-American world
of 1690, but of the utmost import. It was intimately related to the
emerging character of Anglo-American politics and to the peculiar
role of public opinion in that politics. And, though one gathers little
sense of the substance and flavor of Harris' conception from the
single issue of *Publick Occurrences* that appeared, the fact of its
appearance remains remarkable, as, indeed, its prompt suppression
testifies.[1]

---

[1] *Publick Occurrences, Both Forreign and Domestick*, no. 1, September 25, 1690.

Harris' own background is interesting and much to the point. He had associated himself with the earl of Shaftesbury and the Whigs in the Short Parliament of 1679, and had that year launched *Domestick Intelligence: or, News Both from City and Country* (later *The Protestant [Domestick] Intelligence*), which he had continued until its suppression in 1681. He had also published a number of seditious pamphlets, at least one of which had landed him first in the pillory and then in jail. And, characteristically for the time, he had opened a coffeehouse near the Royal Exchange in Cornhill, where he and like-minded Whigs supplemented what they could learn from newspapers and pamphlets with oral intelligence of popish plots and stratagems. With the accession of James II in 1685, Harris' position became increasingly precarious, and he decided to seek refuge in America. Arriving in Boston in the fall of 1686, he set up shop as a printer and bookseller, and in 1690 turned his shop into a coffeehouse as well. What Harris had brought to Boston, then, was not merely a Whiggish newspaper but the whole Whig paraphernalia of opinion-making: newspaper, printing press, bookshop, and coffeehouse. And, though he himself returned to London in 1695 after the English Regulation of Printing Act had expired, the significance of what he had begun could not have been lost upon his fellow Whigs in the colonies, nor, indeed, upon their opponents.

Party politics, of course, was a relatively new phenomenon in the Anglo-American world of 1700, as was any notion of a public opinion that could be influenced in one political direction or another. But, with roughly a third of the adult male population eligible to vote in England and with an even higher percentage of white adult males eligible in the colonies, owing to the virtual omnipresence of freehold property, a dialogue was increasingly necessary between those who wished to exercise power and the electorates who were in a position to bestow it. It was that electorate to whom Whig theorists referred when they spoke of "the people," not the unenfranchised "mobs" that all factions, Whigs included, were wont to use to their own purposes when the occasion arose. And it was to that electorate, already mostly literate and becoming ever more so, that politicians of every persuasion addressed a constant barrage of argument and propaganda. In the process, publics came into being alongside the more traditional ruling elites; and in the interaction between them the ruling elites inevitably changed, initially in their behavior and eventually in their composition. The outcome was the emergence of a political nation whose "business" was public affairs, and one crucial aspect of that business was the continuing formation of public opinion.

In such a context the press became a critically important vehicle of public education, and the traditional restraints on its operation were increasingly viewed as anachronistic by those seeking access to power. In England, opposition to the whole concept of censorship and the licensing of the press dated at least from the Commonwealth, when Leveller and Independent tracts proclaimed the right to freedom of conscience and discourse up to the point where it proved dangerous to the state, and when John Milton in the *Areopagitica* (1644) cried out for "liberty to know, to utter, and to argue freely according to conscience"—at least for Protestants. That opposition had been restated by Locke in the *Essay* and the *Letters on Toleration* (1689, 1690, 1692) as a corollary of his assertions concerning the imperfection and partiality of the human understanding. But it remained for John Trenchard and William Gordon, in *Cato's Letters,* to state the case for freedom of the press in terms that opposed not only prior licensing and censorship but subsequent prosecution for criminal libel, except in extreme cases where the validity of the author's charges could not be demonstrated. Without freedom of speech and of the press, Cato concluded in a "Discourse upon Libels," the world "must soon be overrun with barbarism, superstition, injustice, tyranny, and the most stupid ignorance."[2]

The colonists read Cato on libel along with Cato on everything else, and as newspapers multiplied in the eighteenth century—recall that the number went from one in 1704 to three in 1720 to eight in 1730—conflict between press and government sharpened. The initial battles, as in England, were fought over prior licensing, and it was this question that lay at the heart of James Franklin's conflict with the Massachusetts general court in 1722. Following some acerbic insinuations about the government's lackadaisical attitude toward a pirate vessel that had been reported off the coast, Franklin was arrested and imprisoned for his "high affront" to the authorities. His brother Ben, who was then writing for Franklin's *New-England Courant* under the Silence Dogood pseudonym, promptly penned a communication in which he quoted at length

---

[2] John Milton, *Areopagitica* (1644), in *Complete Prose Works of John Milton* (4 vols.; New Haven: Yale University Press, 1953-1966), II, 560; and *Cato's Letters* (4 vols.; no place: no publisher, 1754), no. 100, III, 256-257.

from Cato on freedom of the press. James Franklin served out his sentence, but the refusal some months later of a grand jury to indict him for printing without a license signaled the demise of an effective licensing system in New England.[3]

Thereafter, the controversy shifted to punishment for seditious libel, and it was this question that was at issue in the celebrated Zenger case of 1735. Printer of a newspaper called *The New-York Weekly Journal*, which had been started in 1733 by James Alexander, William Smith (in whose office William Livingston would serve his apprenticeship), Lewis Morris, and Rip Van Dam as an organ of opposition to the administration of Governor William Cosby, John Peter Zenger was arrested on November 17, 1734, on a warrant charging him with "printing and publishing several seditious libels, dispersed throughout his journals or newspapers entitled *The New-York Weekly Journal, Containing the Freshest Advices, Foreign and Domestic;* as having in them many things tending to raise factions and tumults among the people of this province, inflaming their minds with contempt of His Majesty's government, and greatly disturbing the peace thereof." Alexander and Smith, who volunteered to serve as Zenger's counsel, quickly turned the defense into a political attack on the gubernatorial party and were promptly disbarred by Chief Justice James De Lancey, a gubernatorial appointee to the chief justiceship. Their place was taken by Andrew Hamilton of Philadelphia, an able and eloquent friend of Alexander who had achieved a considerable reputation by opposing the proprietary party in Pennsylvania. When the case came to trial on August 4, 1735, Hamilton's eloquence prevailed; after only a few minutes of deliberation, the jury returned a verdict of not guilty.[4]

And it was indeed Hamilton's eloquence, for the law of the matter was clear, namely, that even if Zenger's printed allegations against the governor and his associates could be established as true, if the jury found that Zenger had printed them—and there was no doubt that he had—the judges could then hold Zenger guilty of sedi-

3 *Journals of the House of Representatives of Massachusetts* (39+ vols.; Boston: The Massachusetts Historical Society, 1919-   ), IV, 23; *The Papers of Benjamin Franklin,* edited by Leonard W. Labaree and Whitfield J. Bell, Jr. (13+ vols.; New Haven: Yale University Press, 1959-   ), I, 27-30.
4 James Alexander, *A Brief Narrative of the Case and Trial of John Peter Zenger, Printer of the New York Weekly Journal,* edited by Stanley Nider Katz (Cambridge, Mass.: Harvard University Press, 1963), p. 48.

tious libel. Hamilton won the case, however, on a political argument, to wit, that citizens have a natural right to protest against abuses of power by their governors, that criticism tends to hold governors responsible by sensitizing them to the costs of abusing power, and that the only restraints on criticism should be in the matter of its truth. And it was doubtless not lost on the jury that Hamilton saw these principles as specially applicable in a colony thousands of miles from the seat of power at Whitehall.

The Zenger case did not end prosecutions for seditious libel in the colonies, particularly in the difficult realm of revelations regarding legislative proceedings. But it did encourage freedom of the press, at least so far as juries might be persuaded to sustain it. And that freedom afforded the press more than enough latitude to serve as a powerful educator of the public during the decade following the Stamp Act crisis of 1765. It was not merely that Parliament in that year enacted the first direct tax ever levied upon the American colonies; it was that the tax was charged upon newspapers, pamphlets, almanacs, and broadsides, along with legal documents, insurance policies, licenses, and the like. Thus, the printer had an economic as well as an ideological grievance, and, with politics wedded to pocketbook, there was no restraining him. "It was fortunate for the liberties of America," David Ramsay wrote in *The History of the American Revolution* (1789), "that newspapers were the subject of a heavy stamp duty. Printers, when uninfluenced by government, have generally arranged themselves on the side of liberty, nor are they less remarkable for attention to the profits of their profession. A stamp duty, which openly invaded the first, and threatened a great diminution of the last, provoked their united zealous opposition."[5]

That zealous opposition, which was clearly in evidence during the year the Stamp Act was under consideration, burst forth with unprecedented vigor between March 22, 1765, when the statute received royal assent, and the following November 1, when it was scheduled to take effect. Indeed, the fury of the printed attack mounted so rapidly that by August it was a potent factor in inciting mob demonstrations against the tax. When November finally arrived, some newspapers appeared unstamped, in open defiance of the legislation, while others, proclaiming they would rather die than be stamped, suspended publication. Still others resorted to one subterfuge after

[5] David Ramsay, *The History of the American Revolution* (2 vols.; Philadelphia: R. Aiken & Son, 1789), I, 61-62.

another to avoid compliance. When word arrived in 1766 that Parliament had rescinded the hated statute, the printers found themselves acutely aware of the power they had wielded—as also did the lawyers, merchants, and popular leaders who had goaded, helped, and applauded them. Thus was laid not only the basis of a crucial political alliance in the movement toward independence but also the foundation of a new relationship between popular education and popular politics in the American colonies.

The role of the press in fomenting the Revolution has been ably discussed in an immense literature that begins with David Ramsay's observation that in the establishment of independence "the pen and the press had a merit equal to that of the sword" and comes down through the magisterial work of Moses Coit Tyler to the more recent analyses of Philip Davidson, Arthur M. Schlesinger, and Bernard Bailyn. Seen from the vantage point of education, several aspects of that role deserve comment. First, once the Tories had learned the techniques of propaganda from their Whig critics, there were the makings of a lively debate over policy that in its very nature instructed the colonial audience at the same time that it propagandized it. Second, with interest running high, the circulation of newspapers, pamphlets, almanacs, and broadsides grew steadily, indicating that ever larger numbers of people were reached by ever larger quantities of material. In the process, technical literacy inevitably enhanced political literacy, and vice versa. Third, these materials were broadcast orally to the illiterate as well as in printed form to the literate, in situations that varied from informal gatherings at taverns, inns, and coffeehouses to more formal assemblies of the Sons of Liberty. And, fourth, with circulation mounting, the products of the press were themselves transformed, as authors and publishers vied with one another to reach the widest possible audiences with the greatest possible impact. Thus the emergence, along with reasoned political argument, of the satirical essay, the inflammatory editorial, the hortatory letter, the atrocity story, the calumnious attack, the pointed cartoon, the blaring headline, the provocative engraving, the inspirational poem, and the patriotic song. And thus, too, the emergence of a characteristically American version of English Whig doctrine, one explicitly rooted in the libertarianism of Sidney, Harrington, Locke, Molesworth, Trenchard, and Gordon but clearly shaped by the experience of colonial politics, and one therefore stressing such concepts as direct rather than virtual representation, the limited jurisdiction of Parliament, the unalienable rights and ultimate sovereignty of the people, and the derivative duty of the people to resist every manner of tyranny and oppression.[6]

Finally, as ever larger publics emerged around particular issues and symbols, the press became crucial in the creation of an intercolonial community, founded on a growing exchange of news, a growing recognition of common problems, and a growing sense of common cause. Between 1767 and 1769 John Dickinson's *Farmer's Letters* appeared in nineteen of the twenty-three English-language newspapers published in the colonies and in seven pamphlet editions as well, on the basis of which Carl F. Kaestle has estimated a readership approaching eighty thousand, spread throughout the colonies. Seven years later, Thomas Paine's *Common Sense* sold a hundred thousand copies in the three months following its appearance on January 10, 1776, and possibly as many as five hundred thousand in all—and this with a total colonial population of two and a half million. "I never saw such a masterly, irresistible performance," Charles Lee wrote of Paine's pamphlet to George Washington. "It will, if I mistake not, in concurrence with the transcendent folly and wickedness of the ministry, give the *coup de grâce* to Great Britain. In short, I own myself convinced, by the arguments, of the necessity of separation." Whether Paine had actually convinced Lee or simply, in the words of Moses Coit Tyler, interpreted to him his own conscience and consciousness, must remain moot. In either case, Paine had educated Lee, and with him a generation of his countrymen.[7]

I I

"Printers," Franklin once observed, "are educated in the belief, that when men differ in opinion, both sides ought equally to have

[6] *Ibid.*, II, 319; Moses Coit Tyler, *The Literary History of the American Revolution, 1763–1783* (2 vols.; New York: G. P. Putnam's Sons, 1897); Philip Davidson, *Propaganda and the American Revolution, 1763–1783* (Chapel Hill: University of North Carolina Press, 1941); Arthur M. Schlesinger, *Prelude to Independence* (New York: Alfred A. Knopf, 1958); and Bernard Bailyn, *The Ideological Origins of the American Revolution* (Cambridge, Mass.: Harvard University Press, 1967).

[7] Carl F. Kaestle, "The Public Reaction to John Dickinson's *Farmer's Letters*," *Proceedings of the American Antiquarian Society*, LXXVIII (1968), 323-359; Moncure Daniel Conway, *The Life of Thomas Paine with a History of His Literary, Political and Religious Career in America, France, and England* (2 vols.; New York: G. P. Putnam's Sons, 1892), I, 69; Charles Lee to George Washington, January 24, 1776, in Peter Force, ed., *American Archives* (4th ser.; 6 vols.; Washington, D.C.: M. St. Clair Clarke and Peter Force, 1837-1846), IV, 839; and Tyler, *Literary History of the Revolution*, II, 42.

the advantage of being heard by the public; and that when truth
and error have fair play, the former is always an overmatch for the
latter: hence they cheerfully serve all contending writers that pay
them well, without regarding on which side they are of the question
in dispute." Like many printers, Franklin himself produced a good
deal of the copy that found its way into his newspaper and almanacs;
and, like many printers, too, he used his press from time to time
to issue a pamphlet or proposal of his own. But, like virtually all
printers, he devoted a substantial portion of his time and energy to
publishing the work of others, and not only the textbooks and legislative proceedings that were inevitably the printer's bread and butter
but also the sermons and discourses that enabled him to fulfill his
traditional didactic responsibilities to the community. In respect to
these latter publications, the printer in the very nature of his work
was required to reach beyond himself to the clergymen, the scholars,
and increasingly the lawyers, who constituted the core of the colonial
intelligentsia. And, while Franklin was quite correct in his assertion
that printers ordinarily served all authors who paid them well, what
he neglected to add was that they also served some who paid them
less well or not at all but whose views they applauded and wished to
disseminate. Not surprisingly, Whiggish printers proved especially
receptive to Whiggish authors, and, particularly after mid-century,
they found such authors in ever greater number in the churches,
colleges, and more popular councils of government that were becoming the nurseries as well as the transmitters of Whig doctrine.[8]

Given their traditional immersion in affairs, it was scarcely possible for the churches to remove themselves from the developing
issues of politics, even in the face of historic precedents and sharpening demands that they do so. The clergy, as the most learned segment
of the colonial community, were inevitably in contact with new ideas
from Great Britain and the Continent, however attractive or repugnant these may have appeared at first sight; and, since most Whig
commentaries were solidly founded on explicit conceptions of human
nature, social justice, and the good life, the clergy were forced to
contend with them, willy-nilly. Then, too, the clergy had traditionally performed many of the functions that newspapers were coming
to assume in the Anglo-American community, especially in the
publicizing of official proclamations, authoritative facts, and useful
intelligence; and they continued to perform these functions in the

8 "Apology for Printers," *Papers of Benjamin Franklin*, I, 195.

local community, both in concert and in competition with the press. In the very nature of their work, therefore, the clergy were caught up in politics, and the pulpit became a vehicle not only for the dissemination of English political opinion but also for the articulation of characteristic colonial positions.

Early in the century in New England, for example, John Wise, the Congregationalist pastor of Chebacco, in Essex County, Massachusetts, took the occasion of the Mathers' proposal to introduce regional ministerial associations into the polity of the Congregational churches to consider the fundamental principles of "man's being and government" and to draw from those principles such inferences as seemed reasonable for the organization of the church. Taking Samuel von Pufendorf as his "chief guide and spokesman," Wise portrayed man as originally in a state of nature, "a free-born subject under the crown of heaven, and owing homage to none but God himself." From that original state civil government emerged, not as the creation of God, but as "the produce of man's reason, of humane and rational combinations." The essential rationale for the emergence of civil government was man's need for protection against his own fellows; the essential basis was a covenant by which sovereignty was conferred and obedience promised. And, since God had decreed no particular form of government in the Scriptures, the covenant could establish a monarchy, an aristocracy, a democracy, or some mixed form (of which the British model, a regular monarchy settled on a noble democracy, was "the fairest in the world"), though there was no mistaking Wise's own preference for democracy, via representative councils in the state and via Congregationalism (as set forth in the Cambridge Platform of 1648) in the church. "For certainly if Christ has settled any form of power in his church he has done it for his church's safety, and for the benefit of every member," Wise concluded. "Then he must needs be presumed to have made choice of that government as should least expose his people to hazard, either from the fraud, or arbitrary measures of particular men. And it is as plain as daylight, there is no species of government like a democracy to attain this end."[9]

However brilliant and forceful his analysis—especially to latterday democrats—Wise was something of a solitary figure in his own time; and even those of his contemporaries disposed to agree with

[9] John Wise, *A Vindication of the Government of New-England Churches* (Boston: J. Allen, 1717), pp. 32, 33, 50-51, 62-63.

him may well have found his analogies to the primitive church more persuasive than his quotations from Pufendorf. A quarter-century later, however, the situation had changed appreciably. New England had become much more familiar with social-contract theory on the one hand and religious revivalism on the other, and, in the interaction of the two, Whig interpretations had become increasingly relevant. For, whatever else revivalism wrought, it crowded the churches with newly enthusiastic communicants, highly conscious of their equal fellowship in Christ; it loosed a spirit of separatism upon the older, more settled regions that in its very nature challenged the standing religious order; and it forced Calvinist and Arminian alike to rethink the nature of the state, the character of the church, and the relation of the one to the other. And all this, incidentally, well in advance of the crisis over the Stamp Act and the public debates it occasioned.

In 1747, for example, the Connecticut New Light minister Nathaniel Hunn, a graduate of Yale and pastor of the parish of Reading, devoted his election sermon before the legislature to *The Welfare of a Government Considered.* The essence of his argument was the right of the people to freedom from civil and religious oppression. "Liberty is New England's property and glory," Hunn perorated. "Let us bless God for it, and prize and improve it." Two years later, interestingly enough, the Old Light pastor of Madison, Connecticut, Jonathan Todd, used his election sermon to castigate his more enthusiastic brethren for their persistent allegations concerning the faithlessness of the established clergy. "I have heard it cast as a reproach upon the clergy," he charged, "that they have been the foremost in propagating the principles of sedition, and disobedience to authority. . . . And I make no doubt but it had an unhappy influence upon the people, and encouraged many to despise government, and to speak evil of dignities."[10]

In Massachusetts, Charles Chauncy warned the magistrates in 1747 that one of their principal responsibilities was "to preserve and perpetuate to every member of the community, so far as may be, the full enjoyment of their liberties and privileges, whether of a civil or religious nature." And these liberties and privileges, Chauncy made clear, derived from rights "naturally" as well as "legally" vested in the

[10] Nathaniel Hunn, *The Welfare of Government Considered* (New London, Conn.: Timothy Green, 1747), p. 18; and Jonathan Todd, *Civil Rulers the Ministers of God, for Good to Men* (New London, Conn.: Timothy Green, 1749), pp. 74-75.

people. The following year, in the series of lectures that eventually appeared as *Seven Sermons* (1749), Jonathan Mayhew asserted the primacy of private judgment in matters of religion, arguing that it was a right given man "by God and nature, and the gospel of Christ: and no man has a right to deprive another of it, under a notion that he will make an ill use of it, and fall into erroneous opinions." And in 1750 Mayhew preached what was to become his most celebrated sermon, *A Discourse, Concerning Unlimited Submission and Non-Resistance to the Higher Powers*, in which he proclaimed the right of the people to rebel against "common tyrants, and public oppressors":

> To say that subjects in general, are not proper judges when their governors oppress them, and play the tyrant; and when they defend their rights, administer justice impartially, and promote the public welfare, is as great treason as ever man uttered;—'tis treason,—not against one single man, but the state—against the whole body politic;—'tis treason against mankind;—'tis treason against common sense;—'tis treason against God. And this impious principle lays the foundation for justifying all the tyranny and oppression that ever any prince was guilty of. The people know for what end they set up, and maintain, their governors; and they are the proper judges when they execute their trust as they ought to do it;—when their prince exercises an equitable and paternal authority over them;—when from a prince and common father, he exalts himself into a tyrant;—when from subjects and children, he degrades them into the class of slaves;—plunders them, makes them his prey, and unnaturally sports himself with their lives and fortunes.

As with the earlier reasoning of John Wise, Mayhew's venture into political theory was ultimately instrumental to a more fundamental effort to clarify the relationship between man and his Maker. But, as also with Wise, the thrust of Mayhew's argument escaped no one, either in his own time or in years to come, when the sermon was repeatedly reprinted as indication of "the principles and feelings which produced the Revolution."[11]

In the middle and southern colonies, as in New England, Whitefield's preaching had emphasized the supremacy of divine over

[11] Charles Chauncy, *Civil Magistrates Must Be Just, Ruling in the Fear of God* (Boston: no publisher, 1747), pp. 33-34; Jonathan Mayhew, *Seven Sermons* (London: printed for John Noon, 1750), pp. 75-76, and *A Discourse Concerning Unlimited Submission and Non-Resistance to the Higher Powers* (Boston: D. Fowle and D. Gookin, 1750), pp. 29, 39; John Adams to William Tudor, April 5, 1818, *The Works of John Adams*, edited by Charles Francis Adams (10 vols.; Boston: Charles C. Little and James Brown, 1851), X, 301.

man-made law, the equality of the truly converted in the eyes of God, and the virtue of toleration as a prime political principle. In New Jersey and Pennsylvania, such ideas fed the fires of New Light Presbyterianism, and ultimately converged with the English libertarianism and Scottish moralism the preachers imbibed from the writings of Locke, Milton, Viscount Bolingbroke, and Francis Hutcheson. In Virginia and the Carolinas, they paved the way not only for the Presbyterianism of men like Samuel Davies, Alexander Craighead, and John Todd but also for the more popular revivalism of Baptist and Methodist itinerants such as Samuel Harris, James Ireland, and Robert Strawbridge, all of whom, incidentally, were perceived as clearly threatening to the dominion of the established church and the landed gentry.

The career of Samuel Davies is instructive in this respect. An alumnus of Samuel Blair's academy at Fagg's Manor, Pennsylvania, Davies had been licensed to preach by the Presbytery of New Castle in 1746 and sent shortly thereafter as a missionary to a number of newly formed Presbyterian congregations in Hanover County, Virginia. From that time until his acceptance of the presidency of the College of New Jersey in 1759, he was for all intents and purposes the mind and heart of the dissenting movement in that colony, the chief issue, of course, being the rights of dissenting ministers and congregations under the 1689 Act of Toleration. Narrowly construed, the problem was simply how the general court would license dissenting clergymen and the meetinghouses they served. More broadly construed, however, the problem was the extent to which the Virginia authorities would countenance the spread of dissent in the colony. In Davies' view, the Dissenters were claiming "no other liberties than those granted by the Act of Toleration—those only upon our compliance with all its requirements—that all our ministers attest their orthodoxy by subscribing [to] the Westminster Confession of Faith and catechism at their licensure and ordination and such of the Articles of the Church of England as that act imposes on us when we settle in this colony; that we attest our loyalty by taking the usual oaths to His Majesty's person and government and by all other public and private methods that belong to our province—and that our very enemies don't pretend to impeach us of any practical immorality." In the view of the established clergy, Virginia was under no obligation to license Presbyterians to preach or to permit them "to send forth their emissaries, or to travel themselves over several counties (to many places without invitation), to gain proselytes to their way, 'to inveigle ignorant and unwary people with their sophistry,' and under pretense of greater degrees of piety among them, than can be found.among the members of the established church, to seduce them from their lawful teachers, and the religion hitherto professed in this dominion."[12]

Davies eventually won, having mustered to his cause not only the diverse dissenting elements in Virginia but also the dissenting community of England (he managed to cement that transatlantic association during a fund-raising trip to Great Britain on behalf of the College of New Jersey between 1753 and 1755). But he won much more than simple toleration, which came, incidentally, as much by default on the part of the Virginia authorities in the face of the need for Presbyterian support during the French and Indian War as it did in response to the legal opinion Davies brought back from the English attorney general, Sir Dudley Ryder. For, during the course of the protracted political conflict, Davies had defined and proclaimed the principle of religious freedom, he had sufficiently united the Dissenters of Hanover County to make their influence felt in Williamsburg and at Fulham Palace, and he had irretrievably shaken the authority of the established clergy in the process. Most importantly, perhaps, he had insisted throughout that he was claiming no more than the "legal as well as natural right" of Englishmen to hear varying versions of the Christian faith, to exercise individual judgment as to which was most true, and to act on that judgment, even in the face of established authority. And, as the established authorities in Virginia quickly recognized, it would require no great leap

[12] "Extract of a Letter from the Reverend Mr. Sam. Davies in Hanover County, Virginia, to Dr. Doddridge, Dated October 2, 1750," in William Stevens Perry, ed., *Historical Collections Relating to the American Colonial Church* (4 vols.; Hartford, Conn.: Church Press Company, 1870-1878), I, 371; and "Address to Burgesses," *ibid.*, I, 382. Davies' acceptance of Doddridge's theology, as embodied in *The Rise and Progress of Religion in the Soul* (1745), is attested in a letter to the bishop of London dated January 10, 1753, in William Foote, *Sketches of Virginia, Historical and Biographical* (1st ser.; Philadelphia: William S. Martien, 1850), pp. 195-196. With respect to the bearing of the Act of Toleration of 1689 on Virginia, one important question concerned whether the act, which had been formally applied to Virginia through a Virginia act of 1699 (William Waller Hening, ed., *The Statutes at Large; Being a Collection of All the Laws of Virginia* [13 vols.; imprint varies, 1819-1823], III, 171) permitted a licensed dissenting minister to preach outside the specific county in which he was licensed; another concerned the possible relevance to Virginia of a parliamentary act of 1711 (10 Anne c. ii), explicitly permitting dissenting ministers to preach from time to time in counties other than the ones in which they had been licensed, an act, incidentally, which had not been formally adopted by the Virginia assembly.

in principle when the situation required it to analogize between religion and politics.[13]

That situation developed, of course, in the early 1760's, when not only the Stamp Act crisis but the rising fear of the appointment of an Anglican bishop for the colonies moved the dissenting clergy to an unprecedented program of political education. For all intents and purposes the pulpit, like the newspaper, became an instrument for the dissemination of radical Whig doctrine and ultimately for the teaching of revolutionary sentiment. Moreover, for all intents and purposes the editor and the preacher worked hand in hand at the instruction; for, as Carl Bridenbaugh has pointed out, there may have been no more threat of an Anglican bishop in 1764 than there had been in earlier years, but there was certainly more concern, occasioned in part by the readiness of the press in London and New England to print and reprint every conceivable rumor emanating from the controversy. That concern had an incalculable effect upon the way in which the colonists perceived the efforts of Parliament in the realm of taxation. The apprehension of episcopacy, John Adams later observed, contributed "as much as any other cause, to arouse the attention, not only of the inquiring mind, but of the common people, and urge them to close thinking on the constitutional authority of Parliament over the colonies." To the colonial, jealous of the rights and prerogatives he exercised in day-by-day affairs, bishops and stamps were inseparable; and even after the stamp issue had died the episcopacy issue remained, driving not only Dissenters but faithful Anglican vestrymen who were used to choosing their ministers into the revolutionary camp.[14]

Be that as it may, the clergy taught politics with a vengeance after 1764, and in a variety of ways. Through sermons, lectures, pamphlets, newspaper articles, and correspondence, they inveighed against particular legislation at the same time that they developed the general principles on which they based their condemnation. Jonathan Mayhew and Charles Chauncy delivered rousing sermons against the Stamp Act, in which they flatly asserted that its enforcement would lead to bloodshed; and it was Mayhew who suggested to James Otis in 1766 the idea of using circular letters to build up a "communion

[13] Samuel Davies to the bishop of London, January 10, 1753, in Foote, *Sketches of Virginia*, I, 190.

[14] Carl Bridenbaugh, *Mitre and Sceptre* (New York: Oxford University Press, 1962), chaps. viii-ix; and John Adams to Jedediah Morse, December 2, 1815, *Works of John Adams*, X, 185.

of colonies" that could maintain and extend the spirit of unity that had forced the repeal of the despised legislation. Not surprisingly, it was James Otis, in turn, who recognized as fully as any revolutionary leader the central role of the "black regiment" in winning the commonality to the revolutionary cause. Samuel Cooke of Massachusetts and Stephen Johnson of Connecticut used their election sermons of 1770 to remind their magistrates that the people have a right to judge the conduct of their rulers, that when rulers break the covenant of the constitution it is the right of the people to take steps to preserve their happiness, and that the failure of the people to do so is a crime. Country ministers like Jonas Clark of Lexington, Massachusetts, and Ebenezer Parkman of Westboro opened up their homes to laymen for the discussion of political theories and strategies. And the grievance committee of the Warren Association of Baptists submitted a report in 1769 suggesting that the position of their sect vis-à-vis the "standing order" was not unlike that of the colonies vis-à-vis England.[15]

As the crisis deepened, so did the intensity of the clergy's effort. Following the Boston massacre, the ministers of Massachusetts raised such an outcry that Governor Hutchinson wrote to John Pownall in June, 1770, "Our pulpits are filled with such dark-covered expressions, and the people are led to think they may as lawfully resist the king's troops as any foreign enemy." Associations of Congregational, Presbyterian, and German Reformed clergymen passed resolutions recommending days of public fasting and prayer, in view of "the dark and threatening aspect of our public affairs, both civil and religious"; and new holidays were created to celebrate the landmarks of the revolutionary movement (March 18, for example, was set aside as the anniversary of the repeal of the Stamp Act), complete with sermons, liberty prayers, and public proclamations. In the end, all the techniques by which the church had traditionally taught, and some

15 Jonathan Mayhew, *The Snare Broken* (Boston: R. & S. Draper, Edes & Gill, and T. & J. Fleet, 1766); Charles Chauncy, *A Discourse on "The Good News from a Far Country"* (Boston: Kneeland and Adams, 1766); Jonathan Mayhew to James Otis, June 8, 1766 (Otis mss., American Antiquarian Society, Worcester, Mass.); *Peter Oliver's Origin & Progress of the American Rebellion,* edited by Douglass Adair and John A. Schutz (San Marino, Calif.: The Huntington Library, 1963), p. 41; Samuel Cooke, *A Sermon Preached at Cambridge* (Boston: Edes and Gill, 1770); Stephen Johnson, *Integrity and Piety the Best Principles of a Good Administration of Government* (New London: Timothy Green, 1770); and Minutes of the Warren (R. I.) Baptist Association, 1769 meeting (unpublished mss., Brown University), p. 4. One should bear in mind that, along with election sermons, there were all manner of artillery sermons, fast-day sermons, and thanksgiving sermons that provided patriot preachers with occasions to teach.

new ones as well, were turned to the service of the revolutionary cause, and with prodigious effect. "When the clergy engage in a political warfare, they become a most powerful engine, either to support or overthrow the state," the loyalist attorney Daniel Leonard wrote in 1774 in *The Massachusetts Gazette*. "What effect must it have had upon the audience, to hear the same sentiments and principles which they had before read in a newspaper, delivered on Sundays from the sacred desk, with a religious awe, and the most solemn appeals to heaven, from lips, which they had been taught, from their cradles, to believe could utter nothing but eternal truths?"[16]

III

Like the churches, the academies and colleges were also caught up in politics, though in ways that may at the same time have been less direct and more enduring. These institutions were in their very nature catholic, gathering in youths from a considerable range of ethnic, religious, and regional backgrounds and exposing them to an extensive common literature and, not unimportantly, to one another. Doubtless different emphases marked different institutions at different times, depending on men, money, and circumstance; and, as in every age, there were characteristic discrepancies between what faculties cared to teach and what students came to learn. But the very number of institutions in evidence by mid-century and the stubborn reality of their need for clientele and funds made them inevitably sensitive to public concern; and, as politics moved to the forefront of public concern, politics, willy-nilly, entered the curriculum.

It did so in various ways. First, and initially foremost, it entered the formal program of instruction, appearing, on the one hand, in the study of certain fundamental classical works considered as quintessential examples of Western learning and, on the other hand, in the study of ethics that formed the core of the culminating course in moral philosophy, frequently given by the president. Eighteenth-century students read the Greek and Latin authors, as had students

---

16 Thomas Hutchinson to John Pownall, June 8, 1770, *The Massachusetts Spy*, no. 233, August 9, 1775; *Records of the Presbyterian Church in the United States of America* (Philadelphia: Presbyterian Board of Publication, 1841), p. 460; and *The Massachusetts Gazette*, no. 904, December 12-19, 1774. See also John Adams' reply to Leonard, in which he contended, "It is the duty of the clergy to accommodate their discourses to the times, to preach against such sins as are most prevalent, and recommend such virtues as are most wanted" (*Works of John Adams*, IV, 56).

for generations, and they no doubt parsed and scanned and construed the texts. But they read the classics in their own ways and could be forgiven, perhaps, if they tended to learn from Aristotle the dangers of violating the immutable laws of God and nature, from Plutarch the glory of opposing tyranny even unto the death, from Cato the power of a virtuous republicanism rooted in the soil, from Cicero the excellence of reasonable laws and the hazards of arbitrary government, and from Tacitus the decadence of the later Roman (read English) empire. Somewhat in the fashion of the Renaissance students who entered school already familiar with the liturgy and only then learned to read it, the provincial student entered his academy or college filled with the political commonplaces of the day and only then learned their sources. In effect, sermon and lecture interacted as fruitfully in the latter era as in the former, and in the process certain elements of education were rendered much more powerful.

Equally significant was the rise to prominence of the course in moral philosophy. An outgrowth of the traditional study of case divinity, in which man was explored first in and of himself and then in relation to God and his fellow men, the course grew up in essentially new forms in the dissenting academies of England under the leadership of Philip Doddridge, Joseph Priestley, and Richard Price, and in the Scottish universities under the leadership of Francis Hutcheson, Adam Ferguson, Adam Smith, and Thomas Reid. In the colonies, it assumed a central place in the academies of Francis Alison (himself a pupil of Hutcheson), Samuel Blair, and Samuel Finley, and later at the College of Philadelphia under William Smith and Francis Alison and at the College of New Jersey under John Witherspoon. Assuming a rational man responsible to a morally perfect God, it considered such fundamental topics as the sources of human action (pneumatology), the purposes of God in creating man for temporal and eternal happiness (divinity and ethics), and the proper balance of rights and obligations in family life (economy) and social affairs (government, jurisprudence, and the law of nations). Politics, of course, entered in, and, however abstruse or arcane the analysis, there was no missing the burning relevance of the central question, What political arrangements are ethically desirable in light of the laws of nature and the teachings of God?[17]

[17] In England, many of the principal moralists, notably Samuel Clarke, William Wollaston, the earl of Shaftesbury, Bernard Mandeville, and Joseph Butler, devised their systems outside the universities, being churchmen or gentlemen of independent means. In Scotland, David Hume and Lord Kames (Henry Home) were the chief examples of moralists who were not professors.

The novelty of the moral philosophy courses envisioned by Smith, Alison, and Witherspoon is best seen, perhaps, in contrast with the roughly contemporary versions of Thomas Clap and Samuel Johnson. Clap acceded to the rectorship of Yale in 1739 (his title was changed to president in the new charter of 1745), having been educated at Harvard under John Leverett, from whom he had doubtless imbibed the vision of a just polity instituted by God and ruled according to the dictates of his word, and having served for more than a decade as the distinguished and much-feared minister of Windham, Connecticut. A powerful and dauntless personality who arrived in New Haven with considerable prestige and reputation, he seized the reins of the college from the trustees and held them firmly in hand until a series of student rebellions forced his resignation in 1766. Under his leadership Yale came into its own, acquiring much-needed funds, books, and buildings, and growing sufficiently rapidly in enrollment to exceed Harvard in number of degrees granted during the later 1750's. A man of firm Calvinist conviction, Clap taught the senior course in ethics from the beginning, and in 1765 published a short textbook to serve as an outline for the work.

Critical of the mistakes of earlier discourses that had treated ethics either as "the laws of nature and nations, or a system of civil laws, generally obtaining among mankind," or as a potpourri called the "religion of nature, whereby every man may obtain the favor of God and eternal happiness, by his own powers, without a mediator or any divine revelation," Clap founded his discussion solidly on God's word, as "the only way and means whereby we can know what the perfections of God are, and what dispositions and conduct in us, are a conformity to these perfections." In effect, the thrust of the volume was almost wholly personal—the problem of ethics is to determine perfection and conform to it in conduct—and such passing comment as occurred toward the end on the duties owed neighbors and mankind in general was essentially incidental. It may have been, of course, that Clap developed this latter sphere in the "public dissertations" he gave from time to time to those students at the college destined for "important stations in civil life." But, given the number of subjects he tried to cover, which ranged from the common law to anatomy, it is doubtful whether the treatment was either extended or profound.[18]

[18] Thomas Clap, *An Essay on the Nature and Foundation of Moral Virtue and Obligation; Being a Short Introduction to the Study of Ethics; for the Use of the Students of Yale-College* (New Haven: B. Mecom, 1765), pp. 1-2, 41; and Thomas Clap, *The Annals or History of Yale-College* (New Haven: John Hotchkiss and B. Mecom, 1766, p. 84.

Clap apparently sent Samuel Johnson a copy of his textbook shortly after it appeared, for Johnson wrote him from Stratford on July 6, 1765, indicating that he agreed wholly with the substance of the work and suggesting that the only difference between them was pedagogical, to wit, that Clap preferred "the synthetical order of thought," while he, Johnson, preferred the analytical, "which to me seems more obvious to young beginners." Johnson's analytical approach had been embodied, of course, in his *Ethices Elementa, or, The First Principles of Moral Philosophy,* initially published in 1746 and then included as the second part of the *Elementa Philosophica,* which Franklin published in 1752. In the traditional mode, Johnson dealt with the duties of man to himself, to God, and to his neighbors, and referred to the limitations of reason and the consequent need to study the holy oracles, "in which we have the sublimest and most advantageous instructions and incentives to practice, with regard to these matters, which are of the utmost importance to our true and everlasting happiness." The burden of Johnson's treatment is speculative, with only a half-dozen paragraphs devoted to social relations, and these of a general nature. Like Clap, Johnson may well have dealt with politics in his oral commentaries, either in the ethics course or in other academic exercises at King's College—certainly the unpublished "Raphael" indicates that he thought seriously about political affairs during the latter years of his presidency. But the *Ethices* itself is essentially a guide to individual conduct and, in the last analysis, virtually devoid of civic concern.[19]

The quite different conception that William Smith held of the moral-philosophy course was first put forth in *A General Idea of the College of Mirania* (1753) which, it will be recalled, he wrote in connection with the founding of King's College. In the fifth and

---

[19] Samuel Johnson to Thomas Clap, July 6, 1765, in Herbert Schneider and Carol Schneider, eds., *Samuel Johnson, President of King's College: His Career and Writings* (4 vols.; New York: Columbia University Press, 1929), II, 343, 444. The minutes of a meeting of the "governors" of King's College on June 3, 1755, set forth the course of studies for the senior year as "metaphysics, logic and moral philosophy with something of criticism and the chief principles of law and government—together with history sacred and profane" (*Early Minutes of the Trustees: Vol. I, 1755-1770* [New York: Columbia University, 1932]). Under this plan, Johnson almost certainly taught the work in philosophy. Later, in 1762, the Reverend Myles Cooper was elected professor of moral philosophy to assist Johnson, and the following year, on Johnson's resignation, Cooper succeeded him in the presidency. The plan of studies adopted by the trustees on March 1, 1763, lists Johnson's *Ethica* as a third-year text and Grotius or Pufendorf as a fourth-year text, with Francis Hutcheson's *A System of Moral Philosophy* (1755) to be read in both years.

highest class of the Latin school of that mighty and flourishing utopia, the principal, Aratus, reviews the salient events of history in the calm light of philosophy, the better to make them lessons in ethics and politics. And, precisely as agriculture is made simpler by a prior knowledge of natural philosophy, so is history rendered more intelligible by a prior knowledge of ethics. "This subject [ethics] Aratus resumes before entering upon history," Smith points out. "He considers man in the solitary state of nature, surrounded with wants and dangers, the whole species at enmity with one another, the stronger lording it over the weaker, and nothing secure to any man, but what he can either acquire or maintain by violence: From thence he takes occasion to show the necessity mankind lay under, of entering into society, and voluntarily resigning some share of their natural freedom and property to secure the rest. Then he explains the different forms of government with the advantages, and inconveniences in the administration of each."[20]

When the time came to define a new three-year curriculum for the College of Philadelphia in 1756, moral philosophy appeared in the second year, rooted in the writings of Francis Hutcheson and Jean Jacques Burlamaqui and developed through supplementary readings from Pufendorf, Sidney, Harrington, and Locke. The choice of Hutcheson was notable, and indeed holds the key to the transformation Smith wrought in the subject. For the eminent Irish academician, who had taught at the University of Glasgow from 1730 until his death in 1746, had done as much as any scholar of the Scottish Enlightenment to change the character of Scottish theology and, with it, the directions of Scottish philosophy. A Presbyterian by birth, a product of Glasgow, the former master of his own dissenting academy at Dublin, and a member of the circle around Lord Molesworth, Hutcheson had first come to be known in the colonies through *An Inquiry into the Original of Our Ideas of Beauty and Virtue* (1725), a treatise in which he vigorously espoused the earl of Shaftesbury's ethical system, especially its concept of an internal human sense capable of perceiving moral excellence in somewhat the same way that the external senses perceive sound and color. It was on that concept of the "moral sense" that Hutcheson erected his moral philosophy, a broad-ranging study not only of human nature, rights, and obligations but also of property, contracts, government, law, and in-

[20] [William Smith], *A General Idea of the College of Mirania* (New York: J. Parker and W. Weyman, 1753), p. 28.

ternational relations, based on Plato, Aristotle, Xenophon, and Cicero among the ancients and Grotius, Pufendorf, Harrington, and Locke among the moderns. To a provincial society in which political issues were coming increasingly to the fore, Hutcheson, the Irish provincial who came to intellectual maturity at a Scottish university, had much to teach, especially in that delicate realm of the right of resistance to metropolitan tyranny. And, when that doctrine was complemented by Burlamaqui's elegant argument that laws are made, not to bring men under a yoke, but rather to oblige them "to act according to their real interests, and to choose the surest and best way to attain the end they are designed for, which is happiness," then its value with respect to the chief controversies of the day became incalculable. In his choice of textbooks alone, quite apart from whatever commentary he introduced, Smith had advanced a generation beyond his contemporaries in New Haven and New York.[21]

Presumably it was Alison rather than Smith himself who actually taught the course in moral philosophy; and, though Alison never produced a textbook of his own, there remain the detailed notes of his student Thomas Mifflin for the years 1758 and 1759, which provide a fairly clear idea of how the field was conceived. The work was about evenly divided between metaphysics and ontology on the one hand and politics on the other, and tended to follow Hutcheson's *System* (1755) both in substance and proportion. Man was portrayed as a rational being, capable of apprehension, memory, reason, and judgment, the last being an "undefinable" power not unlike the "moral sense" of Shaftesbury and Hutcheson. And civil society was portrayed as a necessary institution which enabled wise and virtuous men to rule in the public interest at the same time that it permitted their "more stupid" and wayward brethren to be brought under their beneficent guidance. But it was also an institution born of a voluntary compact and based on "just and wise motives," hence in its very nature contrary to despotism. And indeed when government became destructive of the public liberty and safety,

---

21 Jean Jacques Burlamaqui, *The Principles of Natural Law*, translated by T. Nugent (London: J. Nourse, 1748), p. 99. Students at the College of Philadelphia were introduced to Hutcheson's ideas in three stages, first, via David Fordyce's summary of the *System* in Robert Dodsley's *The Preceptor*, then, through Hutcheson's *A Short Introduction to Moral Philosophy* (Glasgow: Robert Foulis, 1747), and finally through the *System* itself. Fordyce's summary was also published separately as *The Elements of Moral Philosophy* (London: printed for R. and J. Dodsley, 1754).

it was the right of the people to abolish it. "The people have always a right to defend themselves against the abuse of power," Alison concluded. "In a limited monarchy when the rights reserved by the people are invaded the people's right of resistance is unquestionable, and even in absolute governments when the governor neglects the common safety of all and turns everything to the gratification of his own appetites, or when he plainly declares a hatred of his people, so that even their most sacred rights cannot remain secure to them, they have in such cases a right of resistance." The lesson, incidentally, was not lost on young Mifflin, who was an early champion of colonial rights, one of the most radical members of the First Continental Congress, and, at least in the eyes of John Adams, the "animating soul" of the revolutionary movement.[22]

Very much like Alison's course, John Witherspoon's at Princeton after 1768 drew heavily on the Scottish moralists, principally Francis Hutcheson and Lord Kames, whose *Essay on the Principles of Morality and Natural Religion* (1751) stood essentially in the tradition of Hutcheson's *System*. And, like Smith's too, it devoted fully half the lectures to politics, to problems of rights and obligations, government and society, property and contracts, and civil and international law. The theory of the social compact was accepted, the concept of mixed government praised, the necessity of civil liberty detailed, and the right of resistance to tyranny proclaimed. Most important, perhaps, the continuing relevance of moral philosophy for life was explicitly emphasized. "You may plainly perceive both how extensive and how important moral philosophy is," Witherspoon perorated. "As to extent, each of the divisions we have gone through might have been treated at far greater length. Nor would it be unprofitable to enter into a fuller disquisition of many points; but this must be left to every scholar's inclination and opportunities in future life. Its importance is manifest from this circumstance, that it not only points out personal duty, but is related to the whole business of

22 Thomas Mifflin, Notes on (a) Metaphysics and (b) the Elements of the Law of Nature (Mifflin mss., Library of Congress), I, 17-18; II, 11-13, 29-30; and John Adams to Abigail Adams, May 29, 1775, in *Familiar Letters of John Adams and His Wife Abigail Adams, During the Revolution*, edited by Charles Francis Adams (New York: Hurd and Houghton, 1876), p. 59. See also Jasper Yeates, "A Brief Compend of Metaphysics" and "A Compend of Ethics," Samuel Jones, "His Book of Metaphysics," and [John, James, and Andrew Allen], "Ethics" (unpublished mss., University Archives, University of Pennsylvania), all of which bear striking resemblance to Mifflin's notes and to one another, indicating that they may have included translations and précis of common passages in the Scottish philosophers as well as commentaries by Alison.

active life. The languages, and even mathematical and natural knowledge, are but handmaids to this superior science." Handmaids indeed! In effect, what Witherspoon was declaring was that the higher learning was essentially a preparation for public affairs. And, to those who heard his lectures, it would be no surprise when he himself, following his own counsel, became an active member of the Somerset County Committee of Correspondence, a leader in the effort to depose the royal governor of New Jersey, a member of the Continental Congress, and a signer of the Declaration of Independence —the only clergyman, incidentally, to do so.[23]

Beyond the systematic lectures on the ancients and the moderns, politics entered the academies and colleges in the regular oral disputations that constituted a crucial element of the formal curriculum. Thus, Harvard students in the eighteenth century discussed such questions as "Is civil government originally founded on the consent of the people?" (1725) or "Is the voice of the people the voice of God?" (1733) or "Is civil government more favorable to human liberty than entire freedom from legal restriction?" (1737) or "Is an absolute and arbitrary monarchy contrary to right reason?" (1760) or "Are the people the sole judges of their rights and liberties?" (1769). The 1750 commencement of the College of New Jersey included a series of disputations on the following propositions: "In the state of nature with certain exceptions so far as government is concerned men are equal; therefore, the right of kings has its original foundation from a compact of the people; therefore, the rival of George II, our king (by the highest right), vindicates for himself the right to rule in Great Britain not less unjustly than vainly." The 1761 commencement of the College of Philadelphia included disputations on the nature of civil power, the responsibilities of rulers to set virtuous examples by their lives, and the character of reasonable legislation. And the first commencement of the College of Rhode Island in 1769 included a debate on the question "whether British America can under present circumstances consistent with good policy, affect to become an independent state." In the preparation of these debates and disputations, the college library obviously became a basic resource, and it was at this point as much as anywhere in the formal

---

[23] "Lectures on Moral Philosophy," *The Works of the Rev. John Witherspoon* (3 vols.; Philadelphia: William W. Woodward, 1800), III, 372 (the concluding phrase in the edition cited is incorrectly carried as "hard words to this superior science"). For the correction, see John Witherspoon, *Lectures on Moral Philosophy*, edited by Varnum Lansing Collins (Princeton: Princeton University Press, 1912), p. 140.

curriculum that the students were propelled into the larger learning that the library symbolized and encouraged to draw freely upon it.[24]

Withal, it may have been the informal curriculum that had the most profound effect on the younger generation, and in that realm there is abundant evidence of a growing concern with politics, especially after 1765. Literary and debating societies gave increasing attention to rights, freedoms, and obligations, though there was always time for such questions as "whether any sin is unpardonable" or "whether it be fornication to lie with one's sweetheart (after contraction) before marriage." Students at the College of New Jersey attended the commencement of 1765 dressed in American homespun in defiance of English duties, as did students at Harvard in 1768. The following year, a member of the corporation, the Reverend Andrew Eliot, wrote to Thomas Hollis concerning the recent manifestations of student unrest: "The young gentlemen are already taken up with politics. They have caught the spirit of the times. Their declamations and forensic disputes breathe the spirit of liberty. This has always been encouraged; but they have sometimes wrought themselves up to such a pitch of enthusiasm that it has been difficult to keep them within due bounds. But their tutors are fearful of giving too great a check to a disposition which may hereafter fill the country with patriots, and choose to leave it to age and experience to check their ardor."[25]

On July 13, 1770, a public hangman hired especially for the occasion burned a letter from some New York merchants inviting their Philadelphia counterparts to join them in violating the colonial

[24] Edward J. Young, *Subjects for Master's Degree in Harvard College, 1655-1791* (Cambridge, Mass.: John Wilson and Son, 1880). The Latin commencement programs of the College of New Jersey for 1750 and the College of Philadelphia for 1763 are reproduced in facsimile in James J. Walsh, *Education of the Founding Fathers of the Republic* (New York: Fordham University Press, 1935), pp. 166-167, 226-227. And the forensic disputation at the first commencement of the College of Rhode Island is transcribed in its entirety in Reuben A. Guild, "The First Commencement of Rhode Island College, and Especially the Discussion of American Independence, Which Constituted the Prominent Feature of the Commencement Exercises," *Collections of the Rhode Island Historical Society*, VII (1885), 281-298. The "rival" alluded to in the Princeton propositions was the Young Pretender, Charles Edward Stuart, grandson of James II.

[25] William Coolidge Lane, "The Telltale, 1721," *Publications of the Colonial Society of Massachusetts*, XII (1911), 229; and Andrew Eliot to Thomas Hollis, December 25, 1769, Massachusetts Historical Society *Collections*, 4th ser., IV (1858), 447. For another view of the "spirit of liberty" among Harvard students, see Thomas Hutchinson, *The History of the Colony and Province of Massachusetts Bay*, edited by Lawrence Shaw Mayo (3 vols.; Cambridge, Mass.: Harvard University Press, 1936), III, 135-136.

nonimportation agreements, with the students of Nassau Hall suitably in attendance and President Witherspoon conveniently absent in his nearby home. After 1773 students at Harvard, Yale, and the College of New Jersey regularly boycotted, burned, and condemned tea, and by 1774 they were burning British effigies as well. And in 1775 the undergraduates at the College of Rhode Island persuaded the trustees to abandon a public commencement as inappropriate to the political crisis, while their counterparts at Yale publicly exposed one of their number in the press as disloyal to the American cause. By the time of the Revolution, the College of New Jersey under the zealous Witherspoon, Harvard under the ardent Samuel Langdon, and Yale under Acting President Naphtali Daggett were clearly in patriot hands; and the election of Ezra Stiles to the Yale presidency in 1777 threw that institution so decisively to the radicals that a Tory alumnus of 1750, Judge Thomas Jones of the New York supreme court, was moved to portray his alma mater as "a nursery of sedition, of faction and republicanism."[26]

Not all students and not all faculty by any means were caught up in the revolutionary fervor, but there was no mistaking the drift of sentiment. As David Ramsay later observed of the colleges in his characteristically Whiggish rhetoric, "Without the advantages derived from these lights of this New World, the United States would probably have fallen in their unequal contest with Great Britain. Union which was essential to the success of their resistance, could scarcely have taken place in the measures adopted by an ignorant multitude. Much less could wisdom in council, unity in system, or perseverance in the prosecution of a long and self-denying war, be expected from an uninformed people. It is a well-known fact, that persons unfriendly to the Revolution, were always most numerous in those parts of the United States, which had either never been illuminated, or but faintly warmed by the rays of science. The uninformed and the misinformed, constituted a great proportion of those Americans, who preferred the leading strings of the parent state, though encroaching on their liberties, to a government of their own countrymen and fellow citizens."[27]

[26] Thomas Jones, *History of New York During the Revolutionary War*, edited by Edward Floyd De Lancey (2 vols.; New York: printed for the New York Historical Society, 1879), I, 3.
[27] Ramsay, *History of the American Revolution*, II, 321.

IV

For all the talk about churches and colleges as nurseries of republicanism and newspapers as sowers of sedition, the colonists were under no illusions concerning the ultimate source of political wisdom, namely, the direct experience of politics and the systematic reflection on that experience to be derived from individual reading and study. John Adams attended Harvard from 1751 to 1755 and was fortunate enough to partake of John Winthrop's extraordinary tutelage in the fields of mathematics and natural philosophy, along with the usual fare of languages, metaphysics, and disputations. But for all intents and purposes Adams' serious political reading began after he left college, partly in connection with his formal apprenticeship in the law under James Putnam and partly in connection with his personal decision to "assemble an ample and well-chosen assortment of books," which in due course grew into one of the great private libraries of his time, numbering close to five thousand volumes. Thomas Jefferson's experience was essentially the same: it was not until he had left the College of William and Mary for his apprenticeship in the office of George Wythe that he undertook his serious political reading and made the first purchases toward the development of his magnificent library. Moreover, both Adams and Jefferson enjoyed the advantages of a college education. For their less favored contemporaries—Patrick Henry is an excellent case in point—formal instruction came in home, church, and local schoolhouse, and everything else derived from individual effort.[28]

In general, the same indefatigable enterprise that characterized the colonists' activities in the realm of business marked their efforts in the sphere of politics; and, particularly on the part of the lawyers and publicists who stood beside the churchmen and scholars to form the intellectual leadership of the revolutionary cause, the drive toward self-instruction was relentless. "I fly to books, to retirement, to labor, and every moment is an age till I am immersed in study," the youthful John Dickinson wrote his father from London, where he was studying law at the Middle Temple. Some fourteen years later, he observed in the *Farmer's Letters* that he had acquired

[28] *Diary and Autobiography of John Adams,* edited by L. H. Butterfield, Leonard C. Faber, and Wendell D. Garrett (4 vols.; Boston: The Massachusetts Historical Society, 1961), I, 337.

"a greater knowledge in history, and the laws and constitution of my country, than is generally attained by men of my class," a boast, interestingly enough, that he assumed would attract rather than repel the general reader. John Adams admonished himself in 1759: "Labor to get distinct ideas of law, right, wrong, justice, equity. Search for them in your own mind, in Roman, Grecian, French, English treatises of natural, civil, common, statute law. Aim at an exact knowledge of the nature, end, and means of government. Compare the different forms of it with each other and each of them with their effects on public and private happiness. Study Seneca, Cicero, and all other good moral writers. Study Montesquieu, Bolingbroke, . . . and all other good civil writers." For the rest of his life he read and reread his favorite books, making notes for subsequent use, penning lengthy commentaries in the margins, and discussing his insights and opinions with innumerable correspondents. Jefferson complained to a friend about the "malady of bibliomania," learned a half-dozen languages in the process of his reading, and retired time and again from the political fray to mine the treasures of his library.[29]

In the course of this ceaseless self-education, nothing is more striking than the gradual secularizing of the colonists' interests, particularly their drift to history broadly conceived. Carl Becker once observed that history replaced theology at the pinnacle of the eighteenth-century hierarchy of studies, and such was certainly the case in America, at least as far as the informal curriculum was concerned. To be sure, the colonists continued to read the Bible, though more and more of them read it as Jefferson urged his nephew Peter Carr to read it, "as you would read Livy or Tacitus." But in the large their interests shifted to history, politics, and law, to Polybius and Tacitus on ancient history, to Paul Rapin, Henry Care, Catharine Macaulay, and Obadiah Hulme on English history, to Sir Walter Raleigh and Samuel von Pufendorf on European history, to James Harrington, Algernon Sidney, Henry Neville, John Locke, Ben-

29 John Dickinson to Samuel Dickinson, March 8, 1754, in H. Trevor Colbourn, ed., "A Pennsylvania Farmer at the Court of King George: John Dickinson's London Letters, 1754-1756," *The Pennsylvania Magazine of History and Biography*, LXXXVI (1962), 257; John Dickinson, *Letters from a Farmer in Pennsylvania, to the Inhabitants of the British Colonies* (Philadelphia: David Hall and William Seller, 1768), p. 3; *Diary and Autobiography of John Adams*, I, 73; and Thomas Jefferson to Lucy Ludwell Paradise, June 1, 1789, *The Papers of Thomas Jefferson*, edited by Julian P. Boyd (17+ vols.; Princeton: Princeton University Press, 1950-), XV, 163.

jamin Hoadly, James Burgh, Robert Molesworth, Viscount Boling-broke, and Montesquieu on politics (or contemporary history), and to Sir Edward Coke and Sir William Blackstone on the law (or legal history). Moreover, they read their history, not for diversion or even for self-aggrandizement, but for guidance in the affairs of life. And they gleaned from it an unerring devotion to those "rights and liberties of Englishmen" they were claiming in their struggle with the motherland. It was that devotion, illuminating and confirming as it did their own political experience in the New World, that sustained them in their cause and in the last analysis provided them the justification for their revolution.[30]

[30] Carl L. Becker, *The Heavenly City of the Eighteenth-Century Philosophers* (New Haven: Yale University Press, 1932), pp. 17-18, 20, and *passim*; and Thomas Jefferson to Peter Carr, August 10, 1787, *Papers of Thomas Jefferson*, XII, 15.

PART VI

PROVINCIAL EDUCATION

The genius of our people, their way of life, their circumstances in point of fortune, the customs and manners and humors of the country, difference us in so many important respects from Europeans, that a plan of education, however judiciously adapted to these last, would no more fit us, than an almanac, calculated for the latitude of London, would that of Williamsburg.

JAMES MAURY

INTRODUCTION

There is always an ambivalence toward metropolitan education on the part of those who live in the provinces. On the one hand, there is the ever-present sense of metropolitan greatness, as embodied in time-honored institutions conducted by distinguished men moving in assured ways. On the other hand, there is the gnawing sense of metropolitan remove, manifested most poignantly, perhaps, in the common inability of returning youth to readjust to the plainness and crudity of provincial life. The problem is at least as old as the world's cities and the hopes and fears of parents in their surrounding hinterland; and in English America it undoubtedly dates from the 1620's, when the first Virginians began to return to the motherland for their formal schooling.

Obviously, as native institutions became increasingly available in the colonies, the ambivalence of the colonists deepened, until by the end of the seventeenth century the whole question of metropolitan versus provincial education had become one of public as well as parental policy. In 1699, for example, a group of five students at the College of William and Mary addressed the governor, council, and burgesses of Virginia on the general subject of a proper education for the colony's youth. Having been assigned their topics by their "superiors," and having themselves chosen William and Mary for whatever reasons, the speakers revealed little by way of doubt or uncertainty. Yet their arguments were not without insight and sophistication. Assuming that no country "can ever flourish and be in repute and esteem" without learning, the students detailed the difficulties of an English education. In the first place, the trip was long and hazardous and the venture costly, not only to the family involved but to the colony, which was the poorer for the loss of the tuition and living funds. In the second place, the student was removed for extended periods of time from the benevolent surveillance of parents and friends and placed as a "bashful stranger" amidst hostile metropolitan youngsters. Most important, perhaps, the provincial was ruined for subsequent service to his own country by the lavish ways of metropolitan living. "When he is called home he comes fraught more commonly with the luxury than with the learning of England and knows not how to brook our more simple and less costly way of living in Virginia. He has now another gusto that cannot be satisfied with the plainness of his country and so either inclines him to return to the [?] and fleshpots of Egypt, the good eating and drinking, fine plays and jovial company of England or if through the necessity of his affairs he finds himself confined to this country he becomes so uneasy to himself and all that are about him that neither Virginia victuals nor drink or house nor furniture nor wife nor servant nor company nor business nor anything else can suit with his new English humor. And so if he does not mortgage or sell his Virginia estate in England the chief fruit he has reaped by his English education is that he spends all his days in misery cursing his hard fate that has condemned him to a life so unsuitable to his humor and inclination." Not surprisingly, the speakers concluded that "a Virginia education is the most proper and suitable to Virginia children and that, with no such loss of time, health, wealth or reputation and with a great deal more comfort to ourselves and all our relations we may follow our studies at home and improve our naturally good capacities to the service of the church and state in our own country."[1]

Now, for all the provincial bravado in these remarks, there was an essential truth about the metropolitan-provincial relationship that remained at the heart of provincial education. The metropolis was incomparably superior in the intellectual riches it could offer, but with its riches came other educational outcomes that were counterproductive in the provincial environment. Clearly, it was in the colonists' own interest—indeed, clearly, it would eventually be necessary—to develop native institutions that could more effectively blend the requisite degree of knowledge with appropriate qualities of virtue. Many wrestled with this problem of the proper

[1] "Speeches of the Students of the College of William and Mary Delivered May 1, 1699," *William and Mary College Quarterly*, 2d ser., X (1930), 324-329.

blend during the eighteenth century, none more incisively than Jefferson's teacher James Maury. The son of Huguenot immigrants, Maury had attended the College of William and Mary and then served briefly as an usher in its grammar school before going to England for holy orders and returning to Virginia as a minister. A central figure in the bitter battle over the Two-Penny Act, which fixed the price of tobacco used in payment of obligations (including obligations to the clergy) at two pence a pound when the market price was more than twice that amount, Maury was a bitterly disappointed man, ostracized by the laity because of his leadership in the so-called Parsons' Cause and burdened down by the cares of a large family in a poor parish. Yet he was an uncommonly effective teacher, as attested not only by the subsequent career of Jefferson but also by the accomplishments of another student, James Madison, who later became president of William and Mary and the first Episcopal bishop of Virginia.

In Maury's view, it was sheer foolishness for those destined to colonial leadership to undertake the same education as the English gentry. Except for those headed toward the professions, he saw little value in the traditional pursuit of ancient languages and literature, preferring for a Virginian the rudiments of history and geography; some introduction to the laws, interests, and religion of his own country; the more practical parts of mathematics; the grammar of the native tongue and such literature as might be useful "in the approaching active scenes of life"; and an apprenticeship "under some person, eminent in the business he chooses, in order to gain an insight into all its modes, forms and mysteries." Such an education, Maury insisted, would be at the least superior to the half-hearted imitations of English schooling then available in Virginia; for, as Maury concluded, "the genius of our people, their way of life, their circumstances in point of fortune, the customs and manners and humors of the country, difference us in so many important respects from Europeans, that a plan of education, however judiciously adapted to these last, would no more fit us, than an almanac, calculated for the latitude of London, would that of Williamsburg."[2]

The evidence of how closely Maury approached these ideals

2 Helen Duprey Bullock, ed., "A Dissertation on Education in the Form of a Letter from James Maury to Robert Jackson, July 17, 1762," *Papers of the Albemarle County Historical Society*, II (1942), 36-60.

in his own institution is lacking, though neither Jefferson nor Madison ever found himself alienated from the colonial environment. Both went on to the College of William and Mary; both studied under George Wythe; both supported the patriot cause (Madison as a clergyman is reputed to have insisted that heaven was a republic, not a kingdom); both became cultured men of affairs; and both achieved eminence during the early years of the Republic. Indeed, of both it might be said, as Carl Becker once suggested of Franklin, that they tasted in all its fullness the cosmopolitanism of the age but remained to the end quintessentially American.

Chapter 16

INSTITUTIONS

The education of our children is never out of my mind. Train
them to virtue. Habituate them to industry, activity, and spirit.

JOHN TO ABIGAIL ADAMS

By the middle of the eighteenth century, the educational institutions
of provincial America constituted a fascinating kaleidoscope of endless diversity and change. There were newly transplanted German
Lutheran communities in the Lehigh and Schuylkill valleys of
Pennsylvania in which family, church, and school were virtually
perfect replicas of their counterparts in the Palatinate. There were
older communities of French Huguenots in South Carolina in which
cultural institutions were undergoing fundamental change in the
process of gradual assimilation into the dominant English culture
There were frontier communities of second- and third-generation
English Puritans in the recently settled townships of Maine in which
families were performing not only their traditional educational
functions but also those ordinarily carried by church, school, and
even college. And there were deeply rooted coastal communities of
variegated ethnic and religious composition in which autochthonous
educational forms were emerging in response to new social demands.

Furthermore, given the continued novelty and unprecedented
opportunity of the provincial situation, all these institutions, each
in its own way, found themselves wrestling in their day-by-day
operations with insistent problems of stability and change. Parents
were inevitably caught up in heartrending dilemmas as to whether
to hold their offspring to older ways or encourage them along
newer lines—Josiah Franklin must have brooded more than

once about the problem as he watched the dissolution of his plans to make Ben the "tithe of his sons to the service of the church." Orthodox ministers preaching the doctrines of the established faith to empty pews doubtless debated interminably with their consciences and with one another the efficacy and appropriateness of New Light techniques. Schoolmasters who had never for a moment questioned the inherent value of Latin and Greek grammar found themselves teaching youngsters whose most ardent academic ambition was to master commercial arithmetic. And college tutors who had all their lives hearkened to the eternal truths of the ancient poets saw their best students responding to the seemingly ephemeral musings of the Bacons, the Newtons, and the Lockes. For those concerned with the formation of youth, the dilemmas of continuity and novelty were endless and insistent; and, as parents, pastors, and teachers wrestled with these dilemmas and ventured solutions, diversity flourished.[1]

There were common forms, to be sure, for such is the stubborn character of human habit that it persists in the face of the most urgent demands for change—the more so when organized institutionally. And there were inevitably common solutions to common problems, a process that was doubtless facilitated by the continuing expansion of transatlantic and intercolonial communication. Then, too, the edges of diversity were unceasingly blunted as men and institutions sought broader constituencies and support for their teaching. Yet, withal, diversity of form and substance remained regnant: in the coexistence of transplanted European and nascent indigenous patterns lay the key to provincial education.

II

The household remained the single most fundamental unit of social organization in the eighteenth-century colonies and, for the vast majority of Americans, the decisive agency of deliberate cultural transmission. In frontier regions marked by the pattern of dispersed settlement, it continued to educate much as it had in the early years of the middle and southern plantations, taking unto itself functions ordinarily performed by church and school. And, in the older, more

---

[1] *The Autobiography of Benjamin Franklin,* edited by Leonard W. Labaree, Ralph L. Ketchum, Helen C. Boatfield, and Helene H. Fineman (New Haven: Yale University Press, 1964), p. 52.

settled regions, even as churches became more numerous, schools more accessible, and hamlets more common, it continued to discharge its traditional obligations for the systematic nurture of piety, civility, and learning.

Demographically, the rate of population increase for the colonies as a whole remained extraordinarily high, with an average decennial increment of approximately 34 per cent between 1690 and 1780, if immigration is included, and an average decennial increment of somewhere between 25 and 28 per cent, if immigration is factored out. Or, put another way, the best estimates concerning the average birth and death rates for the period, at least among white colonists (the information for blacks and Indians being so fragmentary and ephemeral as to make any conjectures worthless), would be 45 to 50 per thousand per year and 20 to 25 per thousand per year respectively, the resultant rate of natural increase being at least 50 per cent above the contemporary English figure and certainly one of the highest in the contemporary Western world.[2]

Franklin was moved to remark on the phenomenon in his *Observations Concerning the Increase of Mankind,* which he wrote in 1751 and which later enjoyed wide circulation in the colonies and in Great Britain. Land being plentiful and cheap in America, he observed, men were not afraid to marry, since the possibility of subsistence for themselves and their children was ever at hand. "Hence marriages in America are more general, and more generally early, than in Europe. And if it is reckoned there, that there is but one marriage per annum among 100 persons, perhaps we may here reckon two; and if in Europe they have but 4 births to a marriage (many of their marriages being late) we may here reckon 8, of which if one half grow up, and our marriages are made, reckoning one with another at 20 years of age, our people must at least be doubled every 20 years." Moreover, Franklin continued, "the great increase of offspring in particular families, is not always owing to greater fecundity of nature, but sometimes to examples of industry in the heads, and industrious education; by which the children are enabled to provide better for themselves, and their marrying early, is encouraged from the prospect of good subsistence. . . . If there be a sect therefore, in

---

[2] The statistics are from J. Potter, "The Growth of Population in America, 1700-1860," in D. V. Glass and D. E. C. Eversley, *Population in History* (Chicago: Aldine Publishing Company, 1965). chap. xxvii, and D. V. Glass, "Population and Population Movements in England and Wales, 1700 to 1850," *ibid.*, chap. ix.

our nation, that regard frugality and industry as religious duties, and educate their children therein, more than others commonly do; such sect must consequently increase more by natural generation, than any other sect in Britain."[3]

Such evidence as we have indicates the accuracy of Franklin's observation that American marriages were "generally in the morning of life," the average age at the time he wrote having declined to twenty-one or twenty-two, as compared with, perhaps, twenty-five in the Old World. The average family in New England continued to number around six, and the average household between seven and eight, reflecting in part the continued high percentage of households embracing more than one family (more than a third of the families of Massachusetts in 1765, for example, lived with some other family). Household size doubtless ran even higher in New York, Maryland, Virginia, and the Carolinas, where the normal doubling up of white families was compounded by the inclusion of substantial numbers of Negro individuals and families.[4]

Houses themselves tended to become more varied, more spacious, more amply partitioned, and more aesthetically attractive during the provincial era, though the simple cottage of one, two, or four rooms arranged around a central chimney continued to shelter the greater part of the population. Household manufacture also remained the rule, particularly in New England and the middle colonies; indeed, the unbroken productivity of the household economy was a persistent cause of concern to the Board of Trade and to Parliament. And the household farm or plantation persisted as the basic economic unit in all the colonies, as it had been in the seventeenth century. Within such a context, a great deal of formal and informal education, in-

[3] *The Papers of Benjamin Franklin*, edited by Leonard W. Labaree and Whitfield J. Bell, Jr. (13+ vols.; New Haven: Yale University Press, 1959-   ), IV, 228, 232.

[4] Benjamin Franklin to John Alleyne, August 9, 1768, in William Temple Franklin, ed., *Memoirs of the Life and Writings of Benjamin Franklin* (3d ed.; 6 vols.; London: printed for Henry Colburn, 1818-1819), III, 8. For statistical data on the age of marriage, see Potter, "Growth of Population in America, 1700-1860," p. 651, Thomas P. Monahan, *The Pattern of Age at Marriage in the United States* (2 vols.; Philadelphia: Stephenson-Brothers, 1951), I, 100-104, and David Harris Flaherty, "Privacy in Colonial New England, 1630-1776" (unpublished doctoral thesis, Columbia University, 1967), pp. 77-86. For the larger households of New York, Maryland, Virginia, and the Carolinas, see "Census of Slaves, 1755," in E. B. O'Callaghan, ed., *The Documentary History of the State of New-York* (4 vols.; Albany: publisher varies, 1850-1851), III, 505-521 (from which it seems reasonable to surmise that the average slaveholding family had a small family of slaves at its disposal), and "Estimated Population of the American Colonies: 1610-1780, Negro," in *Historical Statistics of the United States, Colonial Times to 1957* (Washington, D.C.: Government Printing Office, 1960), p. 756.

tellectual, technical, and attitudinal, continued to take place in the course of daily life, with the young learning mostly by imitation and partly through explanation. Reading was still taught in the home by parents and siblings, from hornbooks, catechisms, primers, and Bibles, and, as a matter of fact, the common expectation that books would be read aloud in the household (or coffeehouse) is probably the single most important clue to the particular stylistic cast of a good deal of early popular literature—such was certainly the case with the novels of Samuel Richardson, *The Family Instructor* (1715) of Daniel Defoe, and the essays of Addison and Steele. The skills of farming and the trades were also taught within the household, regulated, as earlier, by the institution of apprenticeship. And the values and behaviors associated with piety and civility were systematically nurtured, also as earlier, through an alternating pedagogy of encouragement, emulation, punishment, and casuistry.[5]

A number of subtle changes occurred in the nature and character of household education, however, that are worthy of note. In the first place, as the age of marriage declined and as the death rate fell, particularly in the precarious first few years of life, the place of the child in the household and in the world of his parents became more secure and hence more significant. As a simple pragmatic matter, parents could afford to invest more in their children, emotionally as well as economically, given the enhanced possibilities of their survival. And, as a correlate of that investment, the special sensibility that Philippe Ariès referred to as the concept of childhood was markedly advanced. Childhood in provincial America was a stage during which one attended school (as schools became accessible), participated in special church activities (as children's meetings were organized and children's sermons addressed to them), read a special literature (as children's books came into being as a recognizable genre), wore special clothes (as became the fashion around the time of the

5 In the matter of learning to read at home, the will of Colonel William Ball of Lancaster, Virginia, who died around 1693, is exemplary, requesting as it did that his wife teach each of their youngest children to read until the age of sixteen, at which time their two eldest brothers were to assume their tutelage (Lancaster County, Wills and Codicils [ms. records, Circuit Court, Lancaster, Va.], book VIII, p. 45). Recall also that George Wythe, Thomas Jefferson, James Madison (the United States president), and Patrick Henry were instructed at home, that Samuel Johnson was taught to read by his grandfather, and that Johnson himself later reported that he had written his *Elementa Philosophica* out of the experience of teaching his own children to read in the household. For the relationship of literary style and reading aloud, see Levin L. Schücking, *Die Puritanische Familie in Literar-Soziologischer Sicht* (Bern: Francke Verlag, 1964), pp. 151 ff., 164.

Revolution), and played special games (with hobbyhorses, dollhouses, Noah's arks, battledores, and shuttlecocks). Most fundamentally, perhaps, it was a stage of distinctive needs and capacities, requiring patience, tenderness, and very special forms of nurture. "It will perhaps be wondered that I mention reasoning with children . . . ," the "great Mr. Locke" counseled a new generation of parents. "But when I talk of reasoning, I do not intend any other, but such as is suited to the child's capacity and apprehension. Nobody can think a boy of three, or seven years old, should be argued with, as a grown man. Long discourses, and philosophical reasonings, at best, amaze and confound, but do not instruct children."[6]

Second, as the community life of the tidewater region stabilized in the eighteenth century and as some families became wealthy, peculiarly American versions of the more traditional European extended family developed. A few larger households actually lodged three generations under a single roof, in the fashion of the contemporary English gentry; but more interesting, perhaps, were the families that managed to unite several neighboring nuclear households, representing two or three generations, in a network of relations that inevitably had profound effect on the education of children. Indeed, given the decline of primogeniture and entail in the colonies and the development of a multilineal rather than a patrilineal kinship system, the transmission of certain elements of family style and expertise made possible by such a network may well hold an important key to the distinctive character of the provincial aristocracy.[7]

[6] *The Educational Writings of John Locke*, edited by James L. Axtell (Cambridge: Cambridge University Press, 1968), p. 181. For examples of the special sermon addressed to children, see Cotton Mather *et al.*, *A Course of Sermons on Early Piety* (Boston: S. Kneeland, 1721); and James Janeway, *A Token for Children Being an Exact Account of the Conversion, Holy and Exemplary Lives and Joyful Deaths of Several Young Children* (Boston: printed for Nicholas Boone, 1700). For examples of the new children's literature other than sermons, see not only John Bunyan's *The Pilgrim's Progress* (a work, of course, that was not originally intended especially for the young) but also Daniel Defoe's *Robinson Crusoe* (1719), *The Prodigal Daughter* (Boston: B. Mecom, c. 1760), and Eleazer Moody's *School of Good Manners*, compiled from the English manual of the same name and first published in New London, Connecticut, in 1754.

[7] See, for example, Philip L. White, *The Beekmans of New York in Politics and Commerce 1647-1877* (New York: New-York Historical Society, 1956), James B. Hedges, *The Browns of Providence Plantations* (Cambridge, Mass.: Harvard University Press, 1952), John J. Waters, Jr., *The Otis Family in Provincial and Revolutionary Massachusetts* (Chapel Hill: University of North Carolina Press, 1968), *The Diary of Colonel Landon Carter of Sabine Hall, 1752-1778*, edited by Jack P. Greene (2 vols.; Charlottesville: University Press of Virginia, 1965), and Louis Morton, *Robert Carter*

Third, the stabilization of community life in the older settlements, coupled with the growing prevalence of churches, schools, and colleges, led to a gradual easing of the formal burdens earlier placed on households for the maintenance of social order and stability. One indication of this easing is the relative paucity of eighteenth- as compared with seventeenth-century legislation defining and policing familial responsibility for education. Another is the gradual lapse of legal arrangements subjecting unassociated or immoral individuals to familial authority and the related tendency, at least in New England, to turn instead to houses of correction, workhouses, and almshouses for dealing with the wicked, the idle, and the poor. Interestingly enough, this decline in familial obligation had its principal effect on the households of the English Protestant majority. For families wishing to preserve a measure of ethnic or religious distinctiveness in the face of the dominant culture, whether Dutch Jews in New York or German Catholics in Philadelphia or French Huguenots in Charleston or Yoruban Moslems living as slaves in a Boston household, familial obligation increased rather than declined in proportion to the effectiveness of nearby English Protestant institutions. And in the case of the slaves, to whom the influence of the dominant white household must have seemed ubiquitous and absolute, the conflict must often have been heartrending.[8]

Finally, granting the continued coexistence of virtually every conceivable pattern of family structure in the colonies, from the rigidly stratified choirs of the Pennsylvania Moravians to the matriarchal *ohwachiras* of the New York Iroquois, the related phenomena

---

of *Nomini Hall: A Virginia Tobacco Planter of the Eighteenth Century* (Williamsburg, Va.: Colonial Williamsburg, 1941). Note also Carl Bridenbaugh's assertion in *Cities in Revolt* (New York: Alfred A. Knopf, 1955) concerning the extent of intermarriage and sense of solidarity among the leading families of Boston, Newport, New York, Philadelphia, and Charleston (p. 346).

[8] The poignancy of the situation in which the slave family found itself is indicated in the petition of a group of Boston Negroes to the Massachusetts legislature in 1774: "The endearing ties of husband and wife we are strangers to for we are no longer man and wife than our masters and mistresses thinks proper married or unmarried. Our children are also taken from us by force and sent many miles from us where we seldom or ever see them again there to be made slaves of for life which sometimes is very short by reason of being dragged from their mother's breast. Thus our lives are embittered to us on these accounts. By our deplorable situation we are rendered incapable of showing our obedience to almighty God. How can a slave perform the duties of a husband to a wife or parent to his child? How can a husband leave master and work and cleave to his wife? How can the wife submit themselves to their husbands in all things? How can the child obey their parents in all things?" See Massachusetts Historical Society *Collections*, 5th ser., III (1877), 433.

of cheap land, expanding commerce, geographical and social mobility, and a declining parental authority in the choice of marriage partner interacted to make the nuclear family of husband, wife, and natural children increasingly the rule. And the prevalence of the nuclear family in turn enhanced mobility and freedom of choice, not merely of marriage partners but also of religious affiliation (recall the harvests of revivalism), occupation (consider the enlargement of possibility introduced by the evening school), and, ultimately, of life style. In all of this, the role of the family in nurturing flexibility and institutionalizing novelty remained central.

For obvious reasons, it was the wealthier and better-educated families of provincial America that tended to leave the most abundant records of familial education. In New England, for example, the diaries of Cotton Mather and Samuel Sewall sparkle with comments concerning the nurture of the Mather and Sewall children. Sewall noted as early as 1689 the fright of his seven-year-old daughter Elizabeth on reading a passage from Isaiah during observances; and several years thereafter, under the date February 22, 1696, he observed: "Betty comes to me almost as soon as I was up and tells me the disquiet she had when waked; told me was afraid should go to hell, was like Spira, not elected. Asked her what I should pray for, she said, that God would pardon her sin and give her a new heart. I answered her fears as well as I could, and prayed with many tears on either part; hope God heard us." Some weeks later he noted, "Betty can hardly read her chapter for weeping; tells me she is afraid she is gone back, does not taste that sweetness in reading the word which once she did; fears that what was once upon her is worn off. I said what I could to her, and in the evening prayed with her alone." And shortly before her sixteenth birthday he recorded: "I set Betty to read Ezekiel 37, and she weeps so that can hardly read: I talk with her and she tells me of the various temptations she had; as that [she] was a reprobate, loved not God's people as she should."[9]

Mather took the opportunity in his diary for 1706 to describe in detail the techniques he used in the day-by-day nurture of his children, his remarks there indicating better than any other source a characteristic familial pedagogy of the time:

[9] "Diary of Samuel Sewall, 1674-1729," in Massachusetts Historical Society *Collections*, 5th ser., V (1878), 308, 422-423, 437.

Some Special Points, Relating to the Education of My Children

I. I pour out continual prayers and cries to the God of all grace for them, that he will be a father to my children, and bestow his Christ and his grace upon them, and guide them with his counsels, and bring them to his glory.

And in this action, I mention them distinctly, every one by name unto the Lord.

II. I begin betimes to entertain them with delightful stories, especially Scriptural ones. And still conclude with some lesson of piety; bidding them to learn that lesson from the story.

And thus, every day at the table, I have used myself to tell a story before I rise; and make the story useful to the olive plants about the table.

III. When the children at any time accidently come in my way, it is my custom to let fall some sentence or other, that may be monitory and profitable to them.

This matter proves to me, a matter of some study, and labor, and contrivance. But who can tell, what may be the effect of a continual dropping?

IV. I essay betimes, to engage the children, in exercises of piety; and especially secret prayer, for which I give them very plain and brief directions, and suggest unto them the petitions, which I would have them to make before the Lord, and which I therefore explain to their apprehension and capacity. And I often call upon them; Child, don't you forget every day, to go alone, and pray as I have directed you!

V. Betimes I try to form in the children a temper of benignity. I put them upon doing of services and kindnesses for one another, and for other children. I applaud them, when I see them delight in it. I upbraid all aversion to it. I caution them exquisitely against all revenges of injuries. I instruct them, to return good offices for evil ones. I show them, how they will by this goodness become like to the good God, and his glorious Christ. I let them discern, that I am not satisfied, except when they have a sweetness of temper shining in them.

VI. As soon as 'tis possible, I make the children learn to write. And when they can write, I employ them in writing out the most agreeable and profitable things, that I can invent for them. In this way, I propose to freight their minds with excellent things, and have a deep impression made upon their minds by such things.

VII. I mightily endeavor it, that the children may betimes, be acted by principles of reason and honor.

I first beget in them a high opinion of their father's love to them, and of his being best able to judge, what shall be good for them.

Then I make them sensible, 'tis a folly for them to pretend unto any wit and will of their own; they must resign all to me, who will be sure to do what is best; my word must be their law.

I cause them to understand, that it is a hurtful and a shameful thing to do amiss. I aggravate this, on all occasions; and let them see how amiable they will render themselves by well-doing.

The first chastisement, which I inflict for an ordinary fault, is, to let the child see and hear me in an astonishment, and hardly able to believe that the child could do so base a thing, but believing that they will never do it again.

I would never come, to give a child a blow; except in case of obstinacy: or some gross enormity.

To be chased for a while out of my presence, I would make to be looked upon, as the sorest punishment in the family.

I would by all possible insinuations gain this point upon them, that for them to learn all the brave things in the world, is the bravest thing in the world. I am not fond of proposing play to them, as a reward of any diligent application to learn what is good; lest they should think diversion to be a better and a nobler thing than diligence.

I would have them come to propound and expect, at this rate, *I have done well, and now I will go to my father; he will teach me some curious thing for it.* I must have them count it a privilege, to be taught; and I sometimes manage the matter so, that my refusing to teach them something, is their punishment.

The slavish way of education, carried on with raving and kicking and scourging (in schools as well as families), 'tis abominable; and a dreadful judgment of God upon the world.

VIII. Though I find it a marvelous advantage to have the children strongly biased by principles of reason and honor, (which, I find, children will feel sooner than is commonly thought for): yet I would neglect no endeavors, to have higher principles infused into them.

I therefore betimes awe them with the eye of God upon them.

I show them, how they must love Jesus Christ, and show it, by doing what their parents require of them.

I often tell them of the good angels, who love them, and help them, and guard them; and who take notice of them: and therefore must not be disobliged.

Heaven and hell, I set before them, as the consequences of their behavior here.

IX. When the children are capable of it, I take them alone, one by one; and after my charges unto them, to fear God, and serve Christ, and shun sin, I pray with them in my study and make them the witnesses of the agonies, with which I address the Throne of Grace on their behalf.

X. I find much benefit, by a particular method, as of catechizing the children, so of carrying the repetition of the public sermons unto them.

The answers of the catechism I still explain with abundance of brief questions, which make them to take in the meaning of it, and I see, that they do so.

And when the sermons are to be repeated, I choose to put every truth, into a question, to be answered still, with, yes, or, no. In this way I awaken their attention, as well as enlighten their understanding. And in this way I have an opportunity, to ask, *Do you desire such, or such a grace of God?* and the like. Yea, I have an opportunity to demand, and perhaps, to obtain their consent unto the glorious articles of the new covenant. The spirit of grace may fall upon them in this action; and they may be seized by him, and held as his temples, through eternal ages.

Years later, whether in filiopietistic reverence or simple confirmation, Samuel Mather repeated the "special points" in his biography of his father, by way of discussing his father's methods of child-rearing, following the diary of 1706 virtually word for word.[10]

In New York, a charming picture of the household of Peter and Margarita Schuyler at "The Flatts" near Albany in the 1740's and 1750's is presented in the *Memoirs of an American Lady* (1809) by Mrs. Schuyler's English admirer, Anne Macvicar Grant. Having no children of their own, the well-to-do couple adopted and educated a number of their nieces and nephews; and, even after the death of Colonel Schuyler in 1758, Mrs. Schuyler apparently presided over their "academy" with high competence and aplomb. There was an instructive routine about the household, with the Scriptures read at breakfast, with the daily directives to the domestics conceived as an apprenticeship for the young protégées in "the value and importance of good housewifery," with the conversation during midday dinner and afternoon tea "always rational, generally instructive, and often cheerful," and with madame's incessant knitting ever setting "an example of humble diligence" to all present. For the fortunate children, the experience was doubtless invaluable: "The example of conversation of the family in which they lived, was to them a perpetual school for useful knowledge, and manners easy and dignified, though natural and artless." And, for those adults lucky enough to be included as guests, the household was a veritable "lyceum," where religion and morality "were leisurely and coolly

---

[10] *Diary of Cotton Mather* (2 vols.; New York: Frederick Ungar Publishing Co., 1957), I, 534-537; and Samuel Mather, *The Life of the Very Reverend and Learned Cotton Mather* (Boston: printed for Samuel Gerrish, 1729), pp. 15-19. As a companion document, it is interesting to peruse Christopher Dock's "One Hundred Necessary Rules of Conduct," first published around 1764; it is reprinted in Pennsylvania-German Society, *Proceedings and Addresses at Ephrata*, X (1900), 87-97.

discussed; and plans of policy and various utility arranged." Even with appropriate correction for the rose-colored tint of Mrs. Grant's memory, the extraordinary power of an education in the Schuyler household shines clearly through the pages of her narrative.[11]

Something of the same power is conveyed in accounts of the household education of the Virginia gentry during this period, of whom the Robert Carters of Nomini Hall in Westmoreland County furnish an excellent example. Descended from John Carter, a royalist *émigré* who had fled to Virginia around the time of the execution of Charles I, the family epitomized the traditions of pragmatic intelligence, political acumen, and social cultivation that marked the southern aristocracy during the provincial era. And, given the status of the family and the character of the household, the Carter children must have received an early education not unlike that of Mrs. Schuyler's charges in New York, though with a number of significant differences, relating mostly to the size of the household. The Carter establishment was huge, including the Carters and their children as well as a host of stewards, clerks, artisans, domestics, and overseers, and several hundred Negro slaves; and Carter himself was not only planter, landlord, manufacturer, physician, and judge within this vast household, but a councilor, a colonel in the militia, and a vestryman in the community at large. This alone was an education for the children, both in the diverse sorts of leadership and technical expertise required in such a situation and in the more unfortunate habits of behavior and mind that Jefferson saw as the "unhappy influence" of slavery on the white population. And this quite beyond the careful and apparently well-informed pedagogical efforts of the able and elegant Mrs. Carter.[12]

In addition, the Carters chose to retain a number of tutors, music and dancing masters, and governesses who doubtless played a central role in the formal nurture of the children. One of these tutors, a young Princeton alumnus named Philip Fithian, kept a journal during the year he spent in the household (1773-1774), which

[11] Mrs. [Anne Macvicar] Grant, *Memoirs of an American Lady* (New York: Samuel Campbell, 1809), pp. 140, 151-152, 150. Note also Mrs. Grant's fascinating account of Albany's "companies" of children, "from five or six years of age, till they become marriageable," each one including an equal number of boys and girls of the same age. The companies apparently competed at different useful tasks, for example, berry-picking or knitting, with considerable encouragement from their parents (*ibid.*, pp. 32-35).

[12] It is interesting that Mrs. Grant, who was well aware of the Negroes in the Schuyler household, gave them only passing mention.

presents a revealing picture of life and education at Nomini Hall. Fithian had charge of two of Carter's sons and five of his daughters, as well as a nephew named Harry Willis. He taught a curriculum that ranged in difficulty from the first efforts at letters of Harriot Lucy Carter (a "bold, fearless, noisy and lawless" girl of seven) to the advanced reading in Sallust undertaken by Benjamin Tasker Carter (an eighteen-year-old "youth of genius"); and in addition he catechized the children, drilled them in arithmetic and letter-writing, argued with them over the virtues of fighting, and accompanied them to dances at neighboring plantations.[13]

It is clear from his lengthy letter to his successor, John Peck, that Fithian went about his work with considerable diligence, intelligence, and success. But it is equally clear that the instruction of Fithian's school, so called, was merely one small segment of the larger education of Nomini Hall, an education that proceeded under the able direction of the "judicious" councilor and his "prudent" wife (whom Fithian judged "a remarkable economist, perfectly acquainted [in my opinion] with the good management of children, entirely free from all foolish and unnecessary fondness, and . . . also well acquainted [for she has always been used] with the formality and ceremony we find commonly in high life"), and that extended beyond Nomini to the network of great households within which the children moved easily, as if in a self-enclosed world. It was such an education that formed the gentry of Revolutionary Virginia and nurtured in them the fierce independence and haughty provincialism that were to constitute at the same time their greatest strength and their consummate weakness in the years ahead.[14]

III

The educative influence of the church persisted during the provincial era, though with abated power and in somewhat different form. The actual number of churches rose steadily from 1689 to 1783, as did the number of different sects and denominations those churches represented; but it is questionable whether the increase kept pace with the increase in population, as the following estimates with respect to the larger denominations indicate:

[13] *Journal & Letters of Philip Vickers Fithian, 1773-1774: A Plantation Tutor of the Old Dominion,* edited by Hunter Dickinson Farish (Williamsburg, Va.: Colonial Williamsburg, 1943), pp. 66, 64.
[14] *Ibid.,* p. 64.

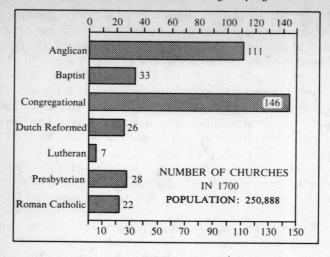

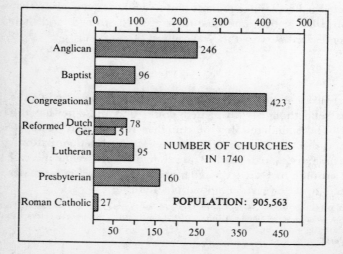

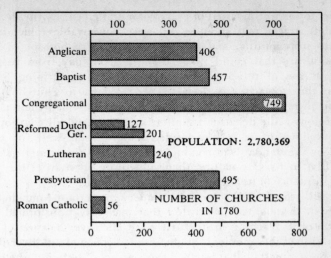

Anglican 406
Baptist 457
Congregational 749
Reformed Dutch 127
Ger. 201
POPULATION: 2,780,369
Lutheran 240
Presbyterian 495
NUMBER OF CHURCHES
IN 1780
Roman Catholic 56

Even these figures, however, tell too little, for the concentration of churches, and hence their accessibility, varied considerably from region to region and according to denomination; and, beyond that, the very nature of their accessibility depended on the different criteria and interpretations that the several denominations held with respect to membership and spiritual communion. On the whole, William Warren Sweet's assertion that by 1760 only 20 to 25 per cent of the population of New England enjoyed church membership and that New England was easily the best-churched section of the country seems a fair estimate of the eighteenth-century situation, though even that estimate may be high.[15]

As has been indicated, the churches continued to serve as centers of instruction, both formal and informal, with ministers preaching, catechizing, and tutoring at every level; visiting the homes of parishioners on matters of doctrine and discipline; itinerating as mis-

[15] The graphs are from Edwin Scott Gaustad, *Historical Atlas of Religion in America* (New York: Harper & Row, 1962), pp. 3-4. Note that French Reformed, German and Moravian sectarian, and Jewish congregations are not included here, nor are Quaker meetings, so that the drift of the ratio of churches to population can be ascertained but not the ratios themselves. Beyond this, there is the ever-present problem of precisely when to call a community of worshipers a church or a congregation, which is not unlike the problem of determining what precisely to call a school. William Warren Sweet, *Religion in Colonial America* (New York: Charles Scribner's Sons, 1949), pp. 334-335.

sionaries to the unconverted of every color and creed; writing books, pamphlets, tracts, and treatises on every conceivable topic, from ethics to iron mining; and in general carrying a host of *ad hoc* responsibilities that could range on any given day from passing on the fitness of prospective schoolteachers to prescribing for a pain in the stomach. Children learned to read in church while learning to repeat the catechism, and adults sharpened their political opinions while debating issues of Scripture. And all who joined in the fellowship of a like-minded congregation were in turn shaped by the standards of conduct and belief in that congregation, willy-nilly. In its very nature, then, and quite apart from the particular substance of its doctrines, the church taught.

Yet, like the family, the church underwent certain fundamental changes in the eighteenth century that markedly transformed the character of its teaching. In the first place, the diversification of the religious life of the colonies brought with it a concomitant diversification of preaching style that touched every aspect of sermonic rhetoric. By mid-century, when revivalism had reached something of a peak, at least four major genres could be distinguished. First, there was the practical sermon of the Old Light New England clergy, which flowered in the eighteenth century as the chief symbol of the triumph of the teaching over the pastoral office of the ministry. Running as long as two hours in length and delivered in plain style from notes or from a full manuscript, particularly after the enthusiasts had given extempore preaching a bad name, the practical sermon was intended as a rational exposition of the work of Christ as revealed in Scripture and an indication of the bearing of that work on the lives of the hearers. The Reverend Samuel Haven of Portsmouth, New Hampshire, characterized the genre magnificently in a portrait of the ideal minister he drew in 1760 under the title *Preaching Christ the Great Business of the Gospel-Ministry:* "And therefore, not entertaining his people with dry speculations, and empty harangues; nor perplexing their minds with vain attempts to pry into those secret things which belong to God only, he will teach and inculcate, with the greatest diligence and care, and press home to men's consciences, in the warmest language, the things which are most plainly taught in the gospel of Christ, oftenest insisted upon by the Saviour, and represented of the highest importance to the souls of men." What is more, Haven continued, the faithful minister would make it an important part of his business to inform himself about the composition of his flock and tailor his instruction accordingly. He would "sound a faithful alarm" to those flirting with sin, comfort the feeble-minded, "not adding affliction to the afflicted," and instruct the ignorant, "adapting himself to their capacities"; in a word, he would "give to everyone his portion in due season."[16]

Second, there was the somewhat more elegant style of the orthodox Anglican clergy, many of whom had received their training in England and then contracted to preach in America as missionaries for the S.P.G. Taking as their most common model the sermons of Archbishop John Tillotson, certainly the greatest and most influential of the Restoration preachers, these ministers conceived the sermon essentially as an essay, simple in structure but informed throughout by allusions to the classical moralists and the most eminent theologians. At their best, Anglican sermons were marked by the same refinement and wit that characterized the best writing of the day, and, indeed, one finds such refinement in the work of Samuel Johnson (though recall that Johnson was initially trained at Yale). At their worst, and they came forth quite often at their worst, they were marked by dullness, pedantry, and irrelevance to the lives of parishioners.

Third, there was the exhortatory style of the New Light preachers, which has already been discussed at some length. A mode of address directed primarily toward the 75 to 90 per cent of the population outside the pale of the churches, or to those within who had not truly experienced Christ, this rhetoric was meant to appeal to the emotions, and, at least in the hands of its more enthusiastic adherents, it tended to eschew organization in favor of immediacy and logic in favor of results, the ultimate criterion of effectiveness being purely and simply the number of declarations for Christ.

Finally, there was what might be called the "morality sermon" of the liberal New England intelligentsia, an outgrowth of the practical sermon but a genre considerably more rationalistic and philosophical in character, tending to rely on certain natural principles of virtue and sobriety rather than a more traditional Scripturalism or Christology. Charles Chauncy and Jonathan Mayhew were the principal architects of the morality sermon in New England, though, like the best of contemporary Anglican preaching, its roots

16 Samuel Haven, *Preaching Christ the Great Business of the Gospel-Ministry* (Portsmouth, N.H.: Daniel Fowle, 1760), pp. 17, 24-25.

lay in the benevolent Platonism of Tillotson. In any case, the genre attracted a good deal of ire from both New Light and Old Light ministers, who tended to view such sermons as "lectures of philosophy" and "harangues on the fitness and decency of things" that seemed "ignorant of God's righteousness."[17]

Another cluster of changes that transformed the teaching of the churches derived from the very fact of religious pluralism. For one thing, even though toleration was only grudgingly granted by the Congregational and Anglican establishments, it had become the rule by the middle of the century—witness the activities of the Anglicans in New England, the Presbyterians in Virginia, and the Quakers practically everywhere. And with toleration came a spirited competition of doctrines and styles that radically altered the teaching situation of the provincial churches. The traditional captive audiences of the older established churches dissolved, and in their place stood a vast audience of the unchurched virtually crying out to be transformed into congregations through which they might receive some dependable instruction with regard to salvation. It was that audience that Whitefield addressed with such power and persuasiveness, and it was the potential of that audience that made America for him "an excellent school to learn Christ in."[18]

Toleration also transformed the economic situation of the churches, as pressures developed from the dissenting sects for a share in ecclesiastical taxes. Traditionally, there had been four principal sources of clerical support: metropolitan governments, metropolitan voluntary agencies and ministerial associations, colonial governments, and the colonists themselves, both as individuals and through their congregations and other voluntary groupings. With the passage of time, however, it became clear that metropolitan sources were at best inadequate and undependable and that the colonists themselves would have to carry the burden of support. In those plantations where no single church had ever attained a monopolistic establishment, namely, Rhode Island, Delaware, and Pennsylvania, this had

[17] Thomas Smith, *The Great Duty of Gospel Ministers to Preach Not Themselves, but Christ Jesus the Lord* (Boston: S. Kneeland, 1751), pp. 3, 35. See also Nathaniel Appleton, *The Great Apostle Paul Exhibited, and Recommended as a Pattern of True Gospel Preaching* (Boston: J. Draper, 1751), p. 13 and *passim*. The phrase "morality sermon" is taken from Alf Edgar Jacobson, "The Congregational Clergy in Eighteenth Century New England" (unpublished doctoral thesis, Harvard University, 1962), p. 359.

[18] *Whitefield's Journals*, edited by William Wale (London: Henry J. Drane, 1905), p. 159.

meant voluntary support from the beginning. In those plantations where there had been an establishment, whether strong and consistent as in Massachusetts, Connecticut, New Hampshire, Virginia, and the Carolinas, or ill-defined and shifting as in New York, New Jersey, Maryland, and Georgia, this commonly involved a struggle on the part of the dissenters, first, for toleration, and then, for a share of ecclesiastical taxes. The New England establishments tended to yield earlier: beginning in 1727, Massachusetts and Connecticut enacted a series of laws granting first to Anglicans and then to Baptists and Quakers the privilege of having their religious assessments given over to teachers of their own faiths. In the South, similar arrangements did not come until the time of the Revolution, when Maryland included provisions for multiple establishment in its Constitution of 1776 and South Carolina in its Constitution of 1778. By then, however, it had become clear that a much more radical effort was developing out of the militant anticlericalism of the "real Whigs," namely, the effort to abolish ecclesiastical taxes entirely and place the support of religion wholly on a voluntary basis. In any case, the implicit shift toward voluntarism was early apparent; and, even in the case of relatively strong establishments, as in Massachusetts and Virginia, the clergy had to go to court from time to time to collect the monies that were owed them—where, incidentally, they were by no means always successful.[19]

---

[19] Ministerial salaries varied considerably from region to region, from denomination to denomination, and from decade to decade during the eighteenth century. S.P.G. missionaries tended to command around fifty pounds sterling per annum. Congregational clergymen ordinarily commanded between fifty and a hundred pounds sterling per annum, with perquisites. The range for the clergy as a whole during the period before the Revolution was probably twenty-five pounds sterling per annum to two hundred. For comparison, one might note that English curacies during the first half of the century commanded an average of thirty to forty pounds per annum, while middling rectorships commanded livings as high as three hundred; that John Leverett was appointed to the Harvard presidency in 1707 at one hundred fifty pounds per annum, Benjamin Wadsworth in 1725 at one hundred fifty pounds per annum plus additional perquisites, and Edward Holyoke in 1737 at two hundred pounds per annum plus additional perquisites; and that the Yale professorship of divinity commanded £113 6s. 8d. per annum in 1767, the Princeton professorship of mathematics and natural philosophy, one hundred fifty pounds in 1768, and the William and Mary professorships between one hundred and two hundred pounds in 1770. The New England and Virginia salaries were presumably paid in New England and Virginia currencies, respectively, and should be reduced by roughly a fourth to convert to pounds sterling. The New Jersey salary was presumably paid in New Jersey currency, and should be reduced by roughly three-fifths to convert to pounds sterling. The problem of equivalence among the various local currencies during the provincial era is a thorny one. See the excellent brief discussion and the table of conversion in Jackson Turner Main, *The Social Structure of Revolutionary America* (Princeton: Princeton University Press, 1965), pp. 289-290.

A final outgrowth of toleration and the concomitant weakening of the provincial establishments was the shift in catechizing from a legally mandated to a customary exercise, as older legislation was permitted to lapse or fall into disuse. In the eighteenth century, ministers simply catechized as part of their teaching office; and, though a steady stream of sermons reaffirmed the importance of catechizing, the threat of ecclesiastical discipline for the laity was not nearly so awesome as the threat of civil penalty, especially for the unchurched. The Westminster Assembly's Shorter Catechism remained the most common text in New England, as did the standard Anglican catechism in New York, Maryland, Virginia, and the Carolinas. But religious diversity brought with it a host of alternative versions in a dozen languages, including a number by native as well as British authors (notably Isaac Watts), setting forth more liberal views of Christianity and assuming more humane views of the child in their efforts to propagate the gospel.[20]

One of the striking characteristics of the provincial clergy was the versatility with which ministers of all denominations performed the multiplicity of educational roles ordinarily associated with the church. Jonathan Edwards, who is properly remembered by subsequent generations for the enduring brilliance of his speculative treatises, was in his own time a practicing clergyman who preached, catechized, lectured, debated, and examined at Northampton, from his arrival there in 1727 until his dismissal in 1750; who then ministered at Stockbridge, Massachusetts, to two congregations, one of them a mission of Christianized Mohawk and Housatunnock Indians bearing no great love for one another; and who at the time of his death in 1758 was preaching and teaching as the newly elected president of the College of New Jersey. His successor, Samuel Davies, came to Princeton in 1759, having spent a decade ministering to the scattered Presbyterian communities of Hanover County, Virginia, where he not only carried on all the standard teaching offices of the ministry, often unaided, but also mounted an extensive program of instruction

---

[20] The evidence on ministerial responsibility for catechizing in New England is contradictory. Jonathan Edwards at Northampton, Massachusetts, apparently concurred in the judgment of the Hampshire Association (October, 1731) that catechizing belongs in the home, with the minister at best encouraging the parents; Thomas Clap at Windham, Connecticut, and Ebenezer Turrell at Medford, Massachusetts, saw catechizing as a prime ministerial obligation. An excellent example of a more liberal native catechism is Samuel Phillips, *The Orthodox Christian* (Boston: S. Kneeland and T. Green, 1738), dedicated "to the children under my pastoral care" (p. i).

for local Negroes by way of preparing them for baptism into the church.

Similar accounts of extraordinary versatility can be endlessly repeated, of S.P.G. missionaries such as John Urmston, who came to North Carolina in 1710 and spent the next twenty years preaching, teaching, baptizing, converting, and haranguing the inhabitants in the attempt, as he put it, to undo the education they had received at "the famous colleges of Bridewell, Newgate or at the mint"; of German Reformed ministers such as Michael Schlatter, who traveled indefatigably through Pennsylvania, Maryland, Virginia, and New Jersey, preaching, catechizing, administering the sacraments, founding schools, organizing missions, and even performing the duties of the military chaplaincy; of Methodist circuit riders such as Francis Asbury, who preached and prayed wherever he could find an audience, proffering the word to the uninstructed in taverns and jails as well as in churches and meetinghouses; or of Quakers such as John Woolman, whose remarkable *Journal* (1774) remains a classic example of spiritual self-education in the course of a ministry wholly dedicated to exposing the evil of slavery, that "dark gloominess hanging over the land." The variegation of pedagogical style was infinite, ranging from the quiet simplicity of the Quaker meeting to the fiery enthusiasm of the Methodist revival. But the commitment to education remained paramount. Indeed, in a society increasingly marked by religious voluntarism, the clergy had no other choice.[21]

IV

It is difficult to generalize with any degree of precision about the extent of schooling in provincial America, largely because of the phenomenal variation in types and modes of instruction and the consequent difficulty of determining exactly what to call a school. We do know, as has already been indicated, that there were individual teachers of reading, writing, ciphering, grammar, bookkeeping, surveying, navigation, fencing, dancing, music, modern languages, embroidery, and every conceivable combination of these and other

[21] John Urmston to secretary (S.P.G.), July 7, 1711, in William L. Saunders, ed., *The Colonial Records of North Carolina* (10 vols.; Raleigh: publisher varies, 1886-1890), I, 767; and *"The Journal of John Woolman" and "A Plea for the Poor,"* edited by Frederick B. Tolles (New York: Corinth Books, 1961), p. 22.

subjects; that these teachers taught part time and full time, by day and by evening, in their homes, in other people's homes, in rented rooms, in churches and meetinghouses, in abandoned buildings, and in buildings erected especially for their use; that they were self-employed and employed by others (acting as individuals or through self-constituted, self-perpetuating, or elected boards); and that they were paid with funds obtained from employers, patrons, subscriptions, lotteries, endowments, tuition rates, and taxes. The combinations and permutations were legion, and the larger and more heterogeneous the community, the greater the latitude and diversity of the arrangements.

Be that as it may, there is every indication that the number of schools and the extent of schooling increased markedly during the eighteenth century and that it increased more rapidly than the increase in population. But the increase was neither linear over time nor uniform from region to region. A particular community, such as New York in the 1730's or Philadelphia in the late 1750's, could suffer a decline in opportunity for schooling, owing to the fortuitous or intentional departure of one or more teachers; while a pair of neighboring communities, such as Norfolk County and Elizabeth City County in Virginia, could experience quite different patterns of institutional growth over a given period of time.

The various types of school were not sharply etched in the provincial era, though if one removes for purposes of analysis elementary household instruction of the sort given by Philip Fithian at Nomini Hall, church-based instruction given by pastors as part of their regular ministerial responsibility, and specialized instruction given by private entrepreneurial teachers of particular subjects, then it is possible to distinguish three general types of institution: the English (or petty, or common) school; the Latin grammar school; and the academy. The English school continued to stress reading, but writing and arithmetic were brought within its purview during the eighteenth century instead of being left, as before, to separate masters, the reasons being simple practicality of purpose and economy of operation. The grammar school was distinguished solely by the inclusion of classical languages and literature within its curriculum. And the academy, being newer and even less well defined than the others, could and did bring any or all of the subjects of the English school, the grammar school, and even the college, within its purview.

Reading was taught from hornbooks and primers that led the

student from the alphabet through a syllabarium and list of syllabified words to an authorized catechism and a varied selection of liturgy, lore, counsel, and rhyming epigrams of a religious character. In schools offering slightly more advanced work, students often used a speller as well, perhaps Henry Dixon's *The Youth's Instructor in the English Tongue*, which was first printed in Boston in 1731 and which included elementary work in arithmetic along with its sections on letters, spelling, and reading, or Thomas Dilworth's popular text *A New Guide to the English Tongue* (1740), which was first reprinted in 1747 by Franklin and went through at least a dozen editions before the Revolution and which included a catechism on spelling, syllabification, punctuation, and grammar in addition to its didactic sentences, poems, Scriptural passages, and fables.

Arithmetic was taught from James Hodder's *Arithmetick* (1661), reprinted in Boston in 1719 as the first purely arithmetic work published in America, Edward Cocker's *Arithmetick* (1670), which was imported in considerable quantities through most of the century, no American edition appearing until 1779, Isaac Greenwood's *Arithmetick Vulgar and Decimal*, first published in Boston in 1729, Greenwood being at the time the Hollis Professor of Mathematics and Natural and Experimental Philosophy at Harvard, and Thomas Dilworth's *The Schoolmaster's Assistant* (1743), the first American edition of which was published in 1773. Cocker's text, which put itself forward as "a plain and familiar method, suitable to the meanest capacity" and which for better or worse decisively shaped the field for a century, began by defining a number system ("A whole or absolute number is a unit, or a composed multitude of units, and it is either a prime or else a compound number") and proceeded through addition, subtraction, multiplication, division, reduction (conversion of shillings into pounds or days into months, and vice versa), the single rule of three, or single proportion ("If 4 yards of cloth cost 12 shillings, what will 6 yards cost?"), the double rule of three, or double proportion ("If £100 in 12 months gain £6 interest, how much will £75 gain in 9 months?"), and vulgar, or common, fractions. Its pedagogy was fairly uncomplicated: a rule was stated, a model problem was worked out with explanation, and then additional problems were supplied without explanation but with answers. A student reaching incorrect answers on the supplementary problems was presumably expected to return to the rule and model for further study:

In the rule of three, the greatest difficulty is (after the question is propounded) to discover the order of the 3 terms, viz. which is the first, which is the second, and which the third, which that you may understand, observe, that (of the three given numbers) two always are of one kind, and the other is of the same kind with the proportional number that is sought; as in this question, viz. If 4 yards of cloth cost 12 shillings, what will 6 yards cost at that rate? Here the two numbers of one kind are 4 and 6, viz. they both signify so many yards, and 12 shillings is the same kind with the number sought, for the price of 6 yards is sought.

Again observe, that of the three given numbers those two that are of the same kind, one of them must be the first, and the other the third, and that which is of the same kind with the number sought, must be the second number in the rule of three, and that you may know which of the said numbers to make your first, and which your third, know this, that to one of their two numbers there is always affixed a demand, and that number upon which the demand lieth must always be reckoned the third number. As in the forementioned question, the demand is affixed to the number 6, for it is demanded, what 6 yards will cost, and therefore 6 must be the third number, and 4 (which is of the same denomination or kind with it) must be the first, and consequently the number 12 must be the second, and then the numbers being placed in the forementioned order will stand as followeth, viz.

yards	s.	yards
4	12	6

In the rule of three direct (having placed the number as is before directed), the next thing to be done will be to find out the fourth number in proportion, which that you may do, multiply the second number by the third, and divide the product thereof by the first, or (which is all one) multiply the third term (or number), by the second, and divide the product thereof by the first, and the quotient thence arising is the 4th number in a direct proportion, and is the number sought, or answer to the question, and is of the same denomination that the second number is of. As thus, let the same question be again repeated, viz. If 4 yards of cloth cost 12 shillings, what will 6 yards cost?

Having placed my numbers according to the sixth rule (of this chapter) foregoing, I multiply (the second number) 12 by (the third number) 6, and the product is 72, which product I divide by (the first number) 4, and the quotient thence arising is 18, which is the 4th proportional or number sought, viz. 18 shillings, (because the second number is shillings) which is the price of 6 yards, as was required by the question. See the work following:[22]

22 *Cocker's Arithmetick* (35th ed.; London: printed for H. Tracy, 1718), title page and pp. 6, 103-104, 130. For the controversy over the authorship of Cocker's text, see

	yds.	s.	yds.	s.
If	4	12	6	18
		6		

$$4)\ \underline{72}\quad(18\text{ shillings}$$

$$\begin{array}{r} \cdot\cdot \\ \underline{4} \\ 32 \\ \underline{32} \\ (0) \end{array}$$

Writing, which remained closely joined to arithmetic as a field of instruction, was probably taught from Hodder's *Arithmetick*, which included several lines of curlicue script, doubtless for purposes of incidental instruction; George Fisher's *The American Instructor*, which included samples of both the older secretary, or gothic cursive, script, and the newer Italian, or italic cursive, script; or possibly one of the older or contemporary metropolitan texts such as William Mather's *The Young Man's Companion* (1681) or Duncan Smith's *The Academical Instructor* (1774). The equipment continued to include quills, along with a knife or razor to sharpen them, paper, ink, and pounce, the fine powder that prevented the ink from spreading; and the pedagogy continued to stress the imitation of fine models, such as the samples on the following page from the Franklin and Hall edition of *The American Instructor*.[23]

The distinguishing mark of the grammar school continued to be the teaching of the Latin and Greek languages and their literatures, though any given grammar school could include an additional offering that ranged from introductory reading and writing in English to arithmetic, geometry, trigonometry, navigation, surveying, bookkeeping, geography, rhetoric, logic, algebra, and astronomy. Latin was taught from newer works such as *A Short Introduction to the Latin Tongue* (1709), attributed to Ezekiel Cheever; Leonhard Culmann's *Sententiae pueriles* (in Charles Hoole's translation of 1658), reprinted at Boston in 1702; and John Clarke's *An Introduction to the Making of Latin* (1740); as well as such older reliables as Comenius' *Orbis sensualium pictus*, Corderius' *Colloquies*, Cato's *Distichs*,

---

Ambrose Heal, *The English Writing-Masters and Their Copy-Books, 1570-1800* (Cambridge: Cambridge University Press, 1931), pp. 30-35.

23 [Mrs. Slack], *The American Instructor: or, Young Man's Best Companion* (Philadelphia: B. Franklin and D. Hall, 1748), pp. 31-33.

The Italian Hand

A B C D E F G H I K L M
N O P 2 R S T U W X Y Z

a b c d e f g h i k l m n o p q
r s s t u v w x y z &c

Art is gain'd by great Labour & Industry

Secretary Hand

A B C D D E F G g H I K L M N
O P P 2 2 R S T H W X Y 3 3

A a b t d e f g h i j k l w
u o p q r s t v u w x y 3 3

Fear God and Honour the King

An easy Copy for Round Hand

A B C D E F G H I K L M N
O P 2 R S T U W W X Y Z

a b c d e f g h i k l m n o p q r s
s t u v w x y z &c 1 2 3 4 5 6 7 8 9 10

Take great Care and you'll Write fair

and *Lily's Grammar*. Aesop, Cicero, Virgil, Hesiod, Caesar, and Ovid remained the staple literature. Greek began with William Camden's *Institutio Graecae grammatices compendiaria* (1595) and then proceeded directly to Isocrates, Homer, and the Greek Testament. The most striking characteristic of the teaching of Latin and Greek was the persistence of traditional methods and materials, though that traditionalism did not necessarily attach to the grammar school as a whole.

As has been indicated, the academy was the least well defined of the three provincial school types, none of which was particularly well defined to begin with. Perhaps the most that can be said of any given academy is that it offered what its master was prepared to teach, or what its students were prepared to learn, or what its sponsors were prepared to support, or some combination or compromise among the three. Francis Alison's academy at New London, Pennsylvania, was for all intents and purposes a dissenting college. The Dummer Academy at Byfield, Massachusetts, under the mastership of Samuel Moody, was essentially a Latin grammar school. The academy Franklin first envisioned for Philadelphia was in effect an English school with advanced offerings in mathematics and the sciences. And the academy Franklin actually established at Philadelphia ultimately combined the English model with the Latin grammar model, on top of which William Smith and the trustees erected the College of Philadelphia. In a sense, then, the academy became the generic—or general—school that brought together under its latitudinarian roof the particular combinations of studies that suited particular American communities at particular times. The English model and the Latin grammar model moved in similar directions, that is, toward latitudinarianism, but no other institutional form so well expressed the fluid, flexible, and loosely defined character of the American educational experience.[24]

The vast majority of schools remained ungraded, and most instruction was therefore individual, with pupils approaching the master's desk or lectern seriatim and reciting orally or displaying their work for praise or correction. The catechetical mode pertained not only in religion but in grammar and arithmetic as well; while the ancient concept of the paradigm—the rule or exemplary model

24 In the sense described here, the academy confirms and symbolizes the widespread movement toward general schools, essentially a movement toward intrainstitutional undifferentiation, remarked upon with respect to the seventeenth century in Geraldine Murphy, "Massachusetts Bay Colony: The Role of Government in Education" (unpublished doctoral thesis, Radcliffe College, 1960).

to be imitated—continued to prevail. Locke's *Thoughts* were widely read and praised, but only indirectly honored in the schoolroom. The more benevolent theology of Isaac Watts made its way into material prepared for younger children, as did a more benignly moralistic emphasis in general; while the *Logick* of Watts and the grammars and textbooks of Locke's disciple John Clarke enjoyed increasing currency in the grammar schools. But it is probably fair to surmise that the same alternating pedagogy of encouragement, emulation, punishment, and casuistry that dominated the household also dominated the schoolroom, though without the leavening effect of familial affection.[25]

As for the masters, they remain ephemeral figures on the provincial scene, the compensation and the character of the work being insufficient to attract and hold many first-class men to permanent careers in the field. A few distinguished exceptions stand apart, however, such as Francis Daniel Pastorius of Germantown, or the Mennonite teacher Christopher Dock, or Nathaneal Williams, who succeeded Cheever at the Boston Latin School, or Thomas Morritt, who taught at the Charleston Free School during the 1720's, or Anthony Benezet, who taught under Quaker sponsorship in Philadelphia, or Nathan Tisdale, who served at Lebanon, Connecticut, for most of the second half of the century, or Samuel Moody of the Dummer Academy.[26]

Benezet, Tisdale, and Moody provide excellent, if quite different, examples. Benezet was born in France in 1713 to a Huguenot family that was forced to flee soon thereafter to Rotterdam and then to London on account of its religious beliefs. He was apparently trained to commerce in England, the elder Benezet having established a successful business there; but, after the family immigrated to Philadelphia in 1731, he determined to follow his own more spiritual bent, associating himself with the Quakers soon after his arrival and eventually choosing teaching as a career. His first post, from 1739 to 1742, was the mastership of the school at Germantown where Pastorius had

[25] For the comment regarding Locke's *Thoughts*, see Jonathan Boucher, "Discourse on American Education," *A View of the Causes and Consequences of the American Revolution; in Thirteen Discourses, Preached in North America Between the Years 1763 and 1775* (London: G. G. and J. Robinson, 1797), pp. 155-156.

[26] Schoolmasters' salaries ranged from the twenty or twenty-five pounds sterling per annum paid to S.P.G. masters to the astronomical three hundred eighty New England pounds apparently paid to Abiah Holbrook in 1749 for conducting Boston's writing school. The average was probably somewhere between twenty-five and fifty pounds sterling per annum during the early part of the century and between fifty and seventy-five pounds sterling per annum on the eve of the Revolution.

taught. He then served for twelve years at the Friends' English School in Philadelphia, resigning in 1754 to accept the mastership of a newly established Quaker girls' school in that same city. Meanwhile, he also undertook around 1750 to conduct an evening class for Negro children in his own home, an activity he continued for some twenty years without charge or compensation. Except for a brief hiatus between 1755 and 1757, he remained at the girls' school until 1766, when he decided to retire to a newly built home in Burlington, New Jersey, for reasons of health. Even then, however, he could not forsake teaching, and the year 1767 found him back in Philadelphia conducting classes for a dozen indigent girls and writing voluminously on the perniciousness of the slave trade. He continued with that until 1782, when, having helped to establish a school for Negroes in Philadelphia, he found its very life threatened by the lack of a master and hence volunteered his services. Appropriately, it was from his post at that school that death took him in 1784.

Whatever else he stood for, Benezet symbolized the Quaker virtue of gentleness: the reports and reminiscences of his teaching, and indeed his own pedagogical writings, portray a man who for more than forty years suffused a half-dozen classrooms with a compassion that knew no limits. He taught all children, rich and poor, boys and girls, deaf and dumb, old and young, black and white, with sensitivity and expertness, preparing his own primer, speller, and grammar for normal children and developing special curricula for handicapped children. And, at a time when some men were debating whether Negroes were men at all, Benezet could insist on the basis of personal experience, "I have found amongst the Negroes as great variety of talents, as among a like number of whites; and I am bold to assert, that the notion entertained by some, that the blacks are inferior in their capacities, is a vulgar prejudice, founded on the pride or ignorance of their lordly masters; who have kept their slaves at such a distance, as to be unable to form a right judgment of them." It is little wonder that the Marquis de Barbé-Marbois, who met him in 1779, could exclaim of him: "For who could have lived a month in Philadelphia without knowing Anthony Benezet! But since he is less known in Paris, I will tell you that he deserves respect as much as any man on the face of the earth."[27]

Tisdale was born at Lebanon in 1732 and returned there after

27 Roberts Vaux, *Memoirs of the Life of Anthony Benezet* (Philadelphia: W. Alexander, 1817), p. 30; and Eugene Parker Chase, ed., *Our Revolutionary Forefathers: The Letters of François, Marquis de Barbé-Marbois* (New York: Duffield & Co., 1929), p. 138.

graduating from Harvard in 1747 to assume charge of a new school that a number of community leaders had organized for the education of their children. Handling some seventy to eighty pupils at a time up to the year of his death in 1787, Tisdale is said to have drawn children from every North American colony and from the West Indies as well. Apparently he was content simultaneously to guide ABCdarians, students working at surveying and navigation for essentially practical purposes, and scholars headed for Harvard and Yale. John Trumbull went to Harvard from Tisdale's school, thoroughly prepared in geography, mathematics, surveying, and navigation as well as in the Latin and Greek classics, having read Virgil, Cicero, Horace, Juvenal, and Homer. Jeremiah Mason recalled having entered Tisdale's school retarded in every major subject of the curriculum. "I read but poorly and spelled worse; my handwriting was bad, and in arithmetic I knew little. . . . In the course of a few months I commenced the study of the Latin, and soon after that of the Greek language. In less than two years I was declared by Master Tisdale to be fitted for college." And, even at the conclusion of his career, Tisdale apparently retained sufficient zest for Dan Huntington to write the following amiable reminiscence:

After a while, however, I found myself pleasantly ensconced with the good old Master Tisdale, in the "brick schoolhouse," where I fitted for college upon very good terms. After prayers, hearing the Bible class, and seating the older scholars, for writing and ciphering, the younger ones came under the more immediate notice of the master. After hearing them read and spell their lesson, he would occasionally indulge himself in a little chat with the children, in their A, B, C. When through reading, he took me, and in "great A, little a, -ron, Aaron," in my turn, betwixt his knees, saying, "Dan what do you intend to be, a minister, or a plough-jogger?" Without hesitating at all, I replied, "A minister, sir." He burst out into a broad laugh. "Well," said he, rubbing my head with his hand, and patting my shoulder, "Sit down, Dan; study your lesson; be a good boy, and we will see about your being a minister."[28]

Samuel Moody presided over the Dummer Academy from 1763 until 1790 with similar, if somewhat more eccentric, benevolence. A native of York, Maine, the son of a Congregational preacher, a member of the Harvard class of 1746, and a sometime minister and justice

[28] *Memoir and Correspondence of Jeremiah Mason* (Cambridge, Mass.: The Riverside Press, 1873), p. 7; [Dan Huntington], *Memories, Counsels, and Reflections* (Cambridge, Mass.: Metcalf and Company, 1857), p. 47; and Clifford K. Shipton, "Nathan Tisdale," in *Sibley's Harvard Graduates*, XII (1962), 490-492.

of the peace, Moody was a superb teacher of Latin and Greek who
managed to inspire affection in his boys at the same time that he
nurtured competence. Indeed, during his tenure as master, Dummer
contributed more than a fourth of Harvard's entering students along
with a significant number to other colleges. He paid small heed to
mathematics and the sciences, but hired a Frenchman to teach dancing at the school and apparently reveled in suspending classes on
hot summer days so he could take the students swimming. And he
claimed that in thirty years he had never had to resort to the rod,
having used praise in place of punishment as his prime pedagogical
device. His was an extraordinary career, during which he helped to
prepare a president of Harvard, a governor of Massachusetts, and
scores of teachers, lawyers, politicians, merchants, and ministers. No
provincial schoolmaster was more respected during the eighteenth
century, and none made a greater impact on the later life of the
Republic.[29]

V

Colleges too sprang up over the provincial countryside with unprecedented alacrity. By the time of the Revolution there were nine
with charters empowering them to grant degrees, by 1783, at least
four more; and, if one were to add the academies that offered
what was clearly collegiate-level instruction, such as Clio's Nursery
in North Carolina and the Newark academy in Delaware, the number might legitimately be put at twenty to twenty-five, which would
represent an incredible increase over the single collegiate institution
available in 1689. "Yesterday by the prints I found that a college was
established in New Hampshire on Connecticut River by the name of
Dartmouth College," the Reverend Ezra Stiles wrote in his diary for
April 5, 1770. "This is Dr. Wheelock's Indian school at Lebanon now
converted into a college by a charter from the Crown. Mr. Whitefield is converting his Georgia orphan house into a college. And by
an advertisement in *South-Carolina Gazette* I find application is made
to that assembly for erecting a college at Charleston. There is now
depending before the general assembly of Rhode Island a petition for
a charter for a college here in Newport, since the first Rhode Island
college is fixed at Providence. College enthusiasm!" Stiles could not

29 Clifford K. Shipton, "Samuel Moody," in *Sibley's Harvard Graduates*, XII (1962),
48-54.

have been more apt: beginning with the founding of the College of New Jersey in 1746, the "college enthusiasm" which he remarked quickly became a permanent feature of the American scene.[30]

Like other educational institutions of the provincial era, the several colleges (and the leading academies) were marked by a striking diversity of character and culture, deriving from their considerable differences in origin, location, leadership, and support. Harvard and Yale had already begun that educational point and counterpoint that would color their relationship for several generations, the more conservative character of Yale stemming as much from its settlement in New Haven as from the particular abilities and weaknesses of the Reverend Thomas Clap. And, interestingly enough, though Harvard was the more venerable and intellectually prestigious of the two, it was Yale that served as the institutional model for the College of New Jersey, King's College, and the College of Rhode Island. The College of William and Mary tended not to grant degrees, though its students seemed to encounter little difficulty in going on to professional study in the colonies and in England and its intimate associations with the Virginia establishment in Williamsburg made it an early nursery of able public servants. The College of Philadelphia displayed a characteristic cosmopolitanism that derived as surely from its urban location as from the Scottish modernism of its rector, William Smith; its New York counterpart, King's College, remained somewhat more provincial, owing to the political ineptitude of the New York Anglican establishment and the self-assured mediocrity of Samuel Johnson's successor, the Reverend Myles Cooper. Yale, Harvard, and the College of New Jersey were quite large, enrolling between one and two hundred students each by 1775; Queens College and the College of Rhode Island remained small, enrolling under fifty. And, while Cambridge and Princeton were early caught up in the revolutionary fervor, there was an undeniable sense of remove at New Brunswick and Hanover.

Granted these differences, the colleges made certain common responses to similar problems and influences that gave them a perceptible American cast by the end of the provincial era. With respect to the curriculum, for example, the influence of Enlightenment thought, particularly as transmitted via the Scottish universities and the Eng-

[30] *The Literary Diary of Ezra Stiles*, edited by Franklin Bowditch Dexter (3 vols.; New York: Charles Scribner's Sons, 1901), I, 45-46.

lish dissenting academies, was such as to broaden the program of studies considerably, especially in the realm of the natural sciences. At Harvard, the program drawn up by Tutor Henry Flynt in 1723 as part of a report to the board of overseers called for juniors to read Charles Morton's "Compendium physicae," which had initially been prepared for Morton's students at Newington Green, one of the earliest and best of the dissenting academies, and Adrian Heereboord's *Meletemata philosophica* (*Philosophical Exercises*, 1654), with its supplement on natural philosophy drawn from the best of the ancient and modern authors; and for seniors to study Pierre Gassendi's *Institutio astronomica* (1653), with its illustrated exposition of the Copernican system. After the establishment of the Hollis professorship of mathematics and natural philosophy in 1727 (which involved an endowment of twelve hundred pounds along with a considerable supply of scientific equipment), upperclassmen were required to study first with Isaac Greenwood, whose publications on arithmetic and meteorology indicate considerable competence but whose alcoholism finally led to his dismissal in 1738, and then under John Winthrop, who in scientific learning was on a par with the best of his contemporaries anywhere. At the College of William and Mary, the statutes of 1727 explicitly spoke of the "progress in philosophy" beyond Aristotle's logic and physics and left it to the "president and masters, by the advice of the chancellor, to teach what systems of logic, physics, ethics, and mathematics, they think fit in their schools"; but it is doubtful whether the prerogative was fully exploited until the appointment of William Small as professor of natural philosophy in 1758. At Yale, Thomas Clap introduced an admirable program in mathematics and natural philosophy that carried the students from arithmetic through geometry and algebra to advanced work on conic sections and fluxions (differential calculus), and put them to work on scientific equipment that included a telescope, a microscope, a homemade orrery, and sundry glasses, globes, weights, and prisms. And at Princeton, almost twenty years before the arrival of Witherspoon, Joseph Shippen wrote to his father of reading Benjamin Martin's *Philosophia Britannica: or A New and Comprehensive System of the Newtonian Philosophy, Astronomy and Geography* (1747) and of undertaking complementary experimental demonstrations. By the 1750's, it was fairly well established that mathematics and the sciences would occupy a significant place in the collegiate curriculum, and in fact in William Smith's plan of 1756 they occupied fully a third or more of the students' time.[31]

Along with the expansion of the mathematical and scientific program came an enlargement of the course in moral philosophy, which has already been traced, and the re-entry of certain traditional professional studies into the formal purview of the colleges. The establishment of medical professorships at the College of Philadelphia in 1765 and at King's College in 1767 not only brought anatomy, physiology, chemistry, and the theory and practice of medicine and surgery into the curriculum, it also brought back into the formal system of higher education a field of training that had devolved from the university in Europe to an apprentice system in the colonies. In similar manner, the appointment of George Wythe as professor of law and police at the College of William and Mary not only introduced lectures on Blackstone and moot courts into the college curriculum, it also brought the formal study of law, which had similarly devolved into an apprenticeship system in the colonies, into the collegiate system—significantly, on the model of the Vinerian professorship of law at Oxford rather than on that of the Inns of Court. And the will of Isaac Royal, endowing a Harvard professorship either in law or in physics and anatomy, militated in much the same direction, even though it took a generation for the corporation and overseers to act on it.[32]

Another major change in the colleges that was intimately related to these shifts in curriculum was the development of the specialized professorship. Recall that Harvard throughout the seventeenth century had adhered to the tutorial system, in which each class was assigned to a tutor, who ideally accompanied the students through their entire four-year program, with the president ranging freely

31 "The Statutes [1727]," *The William and Mary College Quarterly*, XXII (1914), 289; Joseph Shippen, Jr. to Edward Shippen, June 10, 1751, June 24, 1751, September 14, 1751 (Shippen mss., Princeton University Library). (Young Shippen, who used the "Junior" regularly, was named after his paternal grandfather, not his father.) Benjamin Martin's *Philosophia Britannica*, which explicitly provided for complementary "plain, undeniable, and adequate experiments, representing the several parts of the grand machinery and agency of nature" ([2d ed.; 3 vols.; London: printed for M. Cooper, J. Newbery, S. Crowder and Co., B. Collins, J. Leake, and W. Frederick, 1759], I, 2), was also used at Yale during the 1750's.

32 Note also Governor Tryon's land grant to King's College in 1774, on condition that it establish a Tryonian professorship of law (nothing came of the plan), and Ezra Stiles's proposal for a law professorship at Yale in 1777, reprinted in Charles Warren, *A History of the American Bar* (Boston: Little, Brown, and Company, 1911), pp. 563-566.

through all subjects, perhaps concentrating on those of his special interest and competence. The charter of William and Mary, however, clearly contemplated the possibility of professors specializing in different fields, doubtless on the contemporary Scottish pattern, given James Blair's education at Marischal College and the University of Edinburgh; and as early as 1712 a professorship of natural philosophy and mathematics was created, with the Reverend Tanaquil LeFevre as the first—if short-termed—incumbent. Additional professorships were established by the statutes of 1727 in the fields of moral philosophy and divinity. Meanwhile, Harvard created the Hollis professorship of divinity in 1721, installing the energetic young Edward Wigglesworth in the chair, the Hollis professorship of mathematics and natural philosophy in 1727, with Greenwood as incumbent, and the Hancock professorship of Hebrew and other Oriental languages in 1764, with Stephen Sewall as the first occupant. Equally significant was a plan adopted by the governors and the corporation in 1766 reorganizing the work of the tutors so that each might specialize in a particular cluster of subjects, with all students studying under all tutors.

Yale undertook to move in somewhat similar directions in 1745, when the legislative reorganization of that year granted the corporation the explicit right to appoint professors. A chair in divinity was duly created in 1753 (Naphtali Daggett was formally appointed to it in 1756), and one in mathematics and natural philosophy in 1770, with Nehemiah Strong as the initial occupant. But Yale wrestled with the problem of specialization by having the president concentrate on the instruction of the senior class, a pattern that was also followed at the College of New Jersey during its early years. King's College and the College of Philadelphia, on the other hand, moved early to the establishment of professorships and used them freely throughout the eighteenth century to mark the academic and professional areas in which they sought to advertise special competence.

In one sense, the emergence of the professorship was merely the organizational symbol of the larger intellectual and pedagogical transformation involved in the specialization of knowledge. English gradually began to replace Latin as the language of instruction, in textbooks, in the classroom, and in forensic disputations, with Latin in turn slowly assuming the character of a dead but esteemed language. The lecture gradually came into use as a device whereby the professor might present his own ideas or those of others in systematic and critical form, and the experimental lecture developed as a special instance in which the teacher might demonstrate scientific principles, using mechanical equipment, chemicals, or, in the case of the anatomist, the human body itself. And the synthetic approach of Watts's *Logick* gradually won acceptance as a working pedagogy, with its precepts about proceeding from general ideas to particular instances, and from familiar and simple material to less familiar and more complicated material—all carefully, planfully, and without haste.[33]

Of the many scholar-teachers of eighteenth-century America, two more than any others, perhaps, exemplify the new professoriate at its best, John Winthrop and Francis Alison. Winthrop was born in Boston in 1714 to a family that had already enjoyed a measure of eminence in the colonies over four generations. He was educated at the Latin school and at Harvard, and then spent six years in private study in his father's house, emerging in 1738 at the advanced age of twenty-four to accept the Hollis professorship of mathematics and natural philosophy after the dismissal of his former teacher Isaac Greenwood. From that time until his demise in 1779, he proved a versatile scientist, a distinguished teacher, and a scholar of international repute. His investigations, principally in the field of astronomy, ranged from observations of sunspots in 1739 to studies of the transits of Mercury in 1740, 1743, and 1749, and of Venus in 1761 and 1769, to inquiries into the natural history of earthquakes in 1755. His responsibility for the scientific and mathematical instruction at Harvard led him to develop a series of experimental lectures on the laws of mechanics, heat, light, and electricity and to set up an "apparatus chamber" to house the necessary equipment for the demonstrations, to establish the first American laboratory of experimental physics in 1746, to introduce the study of fluxions into the college in 1751, and generally to instruct four decades of Harvard undergrad-

[33] For the relevant sections in Watts's *Logick* (5th ed.; London: printed for Emanuel Matthews, Richard Ford, and Richart Hett, 1733), see pp. 326-365. See also Samuel Johnson's *Noetica* (first part of the *Elementa Philosophica*) in Herbert Schneider and Carol Schneider, eds., *Samuel Johnson, President of King's College: His Career and Writings* (4 vols.; New York: Columbia University Press, 1929), II, 416 and *passim*. Johnson's *Noetica* was used at King's College and at the College of Philadelphia. Watts's *Logick* was used at Harvard in 1746, at the College of New Jersey in 1750, and at Yale in 1778. That with all these changes the provincial colleges left much to be desired is attested by John Trumbull's mordant caricature of Yale in the 1760's in *The Progress of Dulness* (1772-1773), in *The Poetical Works of John Trumbull* (2 vols.; Hartford, Conn.: Samuel C. Goodrich, 1820), II, 7-90.

uates—numbering at least fifteen hundred—in the principles and doctrines of Newtonianism. And his wide-ranging competence and originality earned him election to the Royal Society in 1766, honorary doctorates from Edinburgh in 1771 and from Harvard in 1773 (Harvard's first honorary doctorate of laws), and the friendship of Washington, Franklin, and John Adams. The colonies produced no more distinguished teacher or scholar during the provincial era, and no better symbol of the firm and successful transplantation of Western learning.

Francis Alison was born in County Donegal, Ireland, in 1705, and educated at an academy there and at the University of Edinburgh, after which he immigrated to the colonies, serving first as a tutor in the home of Samuel Dickinson (1735-1737), and then as a Presbyterian pastor at New London in Chester County, Pennsylvania (1737-1752). It was at New London that he opened the academy in 1742 that later became the chief ministerial training school for Old Side ministers under the auspices of the Synod of Philadelphia. His success in teaching the classics and philosophy came to the attention of the trustees of the new academy at Philadelphia, and, when David Martin, the first rector of that institution, died suddenly in 1751, Alison was persuaded to undertake the instruction there in Latin, Greek, logic, and ethics, and, somewhat later on, to accept the rectorship. He apparently worked closely with William Smith in the creation of the College of Philadelphia, and, when the charter of 1755 was granted, he was appointed vice-provost and "professor of the higher classics, logic, metaphysics and geography" and given leave to teach "any of the other arts and sciences that he may judge himself qualified to teach, as the circumstances of the philosophy schools may require." He served in those posts with dedication until the year of his death, when a hostile legislature dissolved the board of trustees and faculty and made new arrangements for the institution.[34]

By all reports, Alison was a superb teacher, occasionally given to mercurial anger but generally deliberate in his instruction and eager to share an unusual fund of learning and knowledge. His list of publications remained brief, including principally sermons dealing with the schisms in contemporary Presbyterianism; but he displayed a keen interest in the religious, political, and philosophical issues

---

[34] Trustees of the College, Academy, and Charitable School of Philadelphia, Minutes (unpublished mss., University of Pennsylvania, Philadelphia), March 7, 1755, April 13, 1756.

of his time and apparently managed to suffuse his teaching with interest and verve. Ezra Stiles remarked of him in 1779 that he was "the greatest classical scholar in America, especially in Greek. Not great in mathematics and philosophy and astronomy—but in ethics, history, and general reading"; while Franklin pronounced him "a person of great ingenuity and learning." And he was awarded honorary degrees by Yale, the College of New Jersey, and the University of Glasgow. Together with Smith, he made the College of Philadelphia a cosmopolitan—if small—institution during the provincial period, and lent a quality of excellence to its instruction that it would not recapture for some decades after his demise.[35]

[35] *Literary Diary of Ezra Stiles,* II, 338; Benjamin Franklin to Joshua Babcock, September 1, 1755, *Papers of Benjamin Franklin,* VI, 174; and Benjamin Franklin to Jared Eliot, September 1, 1755, *ibid.,* p. 175. See also John Ewing, Fragment of a Funeral Sermon on Francis Alison (unpublished ms., Ewing Sermons, University of Pennsylvania Library) and Bird Wilson, *Memoir of the Life of the Rt. Rev. William White, D.D., Bishop of the Protestant Episcopal Church in the State of Pennsylvania* (Philadelphia: Hayes and Zell, 1856), p. 18.

Chapter 17

CONFIGURATIONS

The poorest laborer upon the shore of the Delaware thinks himself entitled to deliver his sentiments in matters of religion or politics with as much freedom as the gentleman or scholar. Indeed, there is less distinction among the citizens of Philadelphia, than among those of any civilized city in the world. Riches give none. For every man expects one day or another to be upon a footing with his wealthiest neighbor;—and in this hope, shows him no cringing servility, but treats him with a plain, though respectful familiarity. Offices or posts of honor give none—but such as every wise and virtuous man would allow to be necessary for the support of government. Literary accomplishments here meet with deserved applause. But such is the prevailing taste for books of every kind, that almost every man is a reader; and by pronouncing sentence, right or wrong, upon the various publications that come in his way, puts himself upon a level, in point of knowledge, with their several authors.

JACOB DUCHÉ

Diversity also flourished among the communities of provincial America, as the interaction of ethnic and religious traditions, settlement patterns, internal and external migration, and economic circumstances produced fundamental differences in modes of life and thought. The result was a considerable variety of contexts in which Americans grew up and were educated to maturity. The New England town was no longer a frontier experiment preoccupied with problems of subsistence and defense but a fully developed institution, firmly rooted in the countryside and solidly established in its ways. The relatively isolated farmsteads of the seventeenth-century Chesapeake region had become by the eighteenth a series of more settled counties, with connecting roads and waterways and occasional hamlets marking diminutive crossroads of trade and communication, though it should be noted that there were persistent efforts throughout the century to develop additional centers of commerce and industry. And the market towns of the seventeenth century, Boston, New York, Philadelphia, and Charleston, had become the thriving cities of the eighteenth, with New York having achieved an unprecedented population of twenty thousand by 1770. Moreover, as settlers pushed out from the initial centers of population, there arose a second and third generation of communities, frontier, back-country settlements that wrestled with many of the same problems that had beset the original pioneers—many, that is, but significantly not all, for what had been learned in the crucible of seventeenth-century experience, from the Indians, from trial and error, and from one another, had been passed along via education to the eighteenth-century frontiersman.

The religious and ethnic composition of these communities varied considerably, according to the fortunes of migration, the receptiveness of the original settlers, and the character and productivity of the regional economy. But at the very least the external immigration and internal migration of the eighteenth century brought increasingly diverse subcommunities into physical and social contiguity, strengthening on the one hand the determination of particular groups to preserve their cultural purity through guarded education (thus, the schools maintained by Quaker meetings throughout the colonies) and on the other hand the need and opportunity to mount common educational ventures toward agreed-upon but limited ends (thus, the neighborhood schools established under multidenominational auspices in the province of Pennsylvania). And, given such diversity, one is not surprised by the significant contrasts between the lives of the young John Adams growing up in Braintree, Massachusetts, in the 1740's and the young Thomas Jefferson coming of age in Albemarle County, Virginia, at roughly the same time; or the equally significant contrasts between the youth of George Plumer, one of the first white children born west of the Alleghenies, near Fort Pitt, Pennsylvania, and the youth of Benjamin Franklin, who had lived in three cities on two continents by the time he was twenty; or the even sharper contrasts between the early lives of those four men and the childhood of Phillis Wheatley, who was brought from Africa as a frail girl of seven or eight and sold as a slave to Mr. and Mrs. John Wheatley of Boston, or the youth of John Antes, who grew up in the Moravian choirs and schools of Bethlehem, Pennsylvania.[1]

Yet, granted the coexistence of communities at different stages of development and granted the contrasts in education deriving from variations in life style from community to community and from group to group within the same community, there remain certain significant changes in the general configuration of provincial educational institutions that are worthy of note. In the first place, there is considerable evidence of a redifferentiation—to employ a neologism —of educational functions that had in the seventeenth-century colonies commonly been carried by the family simply because of the paucity or absence of alternative institutions. Thus, as schools and churches became more readily accessible, certain aspects of the nurture of piety and literacy moved outside the household to the agencies that had borne them in England at the time the colonies were originally settled. And by 1773 the Reverend Jonathan Boucher, who had been a schoolmaster in his youth, was arguing that Americans had generally failed in the execution of parental responsibility for education and that the least they could do was to support decent schools and colleges for their children.[2]

Second, with the proliferation of types of schooling, the concomitant increase in the variety of printed textual materials for instruction and self-instruction, and the development of libraries for the collection and dissemination of such materials, the range of possible life styles open to a given individual beyond the particular version proffered by his family, his church, or even his neighboring school or surrounding community, was vastly enlarged. A particular school might or might not have been liberating for a particular individual; but the institution of schooling in general, when coupled with the flow of didactic material from the press, was indeed liberating, in that it provided genuine life alternatives. And, in an expanding economy with a persistent labor shortage and a consequent dearth of certificatory requirements for entry into careers, the access to alternative life styles provided by education was confirmed by the access

---

[1] For George Plumer, see John S. Van Voorhis, *The Old and New Monongahela* (Pittsburgh: Nicholson, 1893), pp. 476-479. For John Antes, see the unpublished autobiography on deposit in the Archives of the Moravian Church, Bethlehem, Pa. For Phillis Wheatley, see B. B. Thatcher, *Memoir of Phillis Wheatley, A Native African and a Slave* (Boston: Geo. W. Light, 1834).

[2] Jonathan Boucher, *A View of the Causes and Consequences of the American Revolution* (London: printed for G. G. & J. Robinson, 1797), pp. 183-201.

to alternative careers afforded by the economy. The legal career of Patrick Henry, built as it was upon a brief attendance at an English school, the tutelage of his father, John Henry, who had attended King's College at Aberdeen, the preaching of the Reverend Samuel Davies, and some self-instruction in Coke on Littleton and the Virginia code, is a splendid case in point.

Third, there was the emergence of the voluntary association as an instrument of informal education—the young people's societies organized by New England preachers; the neighborhood groups that gathered around the coffeehouses, taverns, and inns of the towns and cities; the salons of Boston and Charleston; the innumerable ministers' organizations, merchant associations, professional societies, Masonic lodges, and Committees of Correspondence through which Americans gathered information, exchanged ideas, debated policy, and in the process formed character and world view. These, too, liberated, in that they afforded opportunity for the creation and development of alternative modes of life and thought.

Finally, though London remained the hub of the empire, growing in size and influence throughout the eighteenth century, and though the colonies remained part of the network of communities that spread out from London to constitute the political, economic, and intellectual empire, it is important to recognize that there was a decided increase in the extent and variety of intercolonial and interprovincial communication, and hence education. London styles of thought, taste, and conduct continued to exert profound influence, especially on the emerging colonial merchant and gentry class that was aware of them and eager and able to imitate them. But equally important were the influence of Scottish styles throughout the colonies, and the influence of particular colonial styles, both imported and indigenous, beyond the bounds of particular colonies. The improvement of the post, the facilitation and increase of travel, the enlargement of trade, the multiplication of newspapers—all enhanced and extended this process of mutual education among the colonists, and in so doing served as a countervailing force to the inherent localism that dominated the culture of provincial America.

II

John Adams once gave a Virginia acquaintance who was lamenting the differences in character between New England and the South his own formula "for making a New England in Virginia," namely, town meetings, militia musters, town schools, and churches. "The virtues and talents of the people are there formed," he observed; "their temperance, patience, fortitude, prudence, and justice, as well as their sagacity, knowledge, judgment, taste, skill, ingenuity, dexterity, and industry." Now, there is no mistaking Adams' patriotism, but his insights into the larger education afforded by provincial New England township life are nonetheless profound. One could add the tavern in some towns or the library in others. But by and large it was the training of the townspeople in free schools—Adams himself had attended Braintree's primary school, kept by Moses Belcher's mother, and then gone on to the local Latin school presided over by Joseph Cleverly—and their subsequent participation as freeholders in the business of politics, religion, and defense that made for the stubborn independence of mind and character traditionally associated with the region. "They seem to be good substantial kind of farmers," an Englishwoman wrote in 1775 after a trip through Connecticut, "but there is no break in their society; their government, religion, and manners all tend to support an equality. . . . They are strangely inquisitive throughout the country, and ask a thousand odd questions about who, and what you are, and etc. and the news of Boston. They are all politicians, and all Scripture learnt."[3]

New England towns varied significantly, of course, in their particular character and traditions, the remote fishing communities of Barnstable and Nantucket bearing at best minimal resemblance to the western agricultural communities of Westfield and Hadley. Yet it is interesting to examine the educational development of a particular township during the eighteenth century, not so much for any generalizations that might be drawn from the data as for the light they shed upon the changing educational configurations of the provincial era. And for this purpose the history of Dedham is instructive.

Dedham was the very model of the seventeenth-century inland agricultural town, even though it was situated only nine miles from the hubbub of commercial Boston. Planted in 1636 by about thirty families "being come together by divine providence from several parts of England: few of them known to one another before," the

3 *The Works of John Adams*, edited by Charles Francis Adams (10 vols.; Boston: Charles C. Little and James Brown, 1851), III, 400; and Anne Hulton, *Letters of a Loyalist Lady* (Cambridge, Mass.: Harvard University Press, 1927), p. 105.

town grew in population to some 650 inhabitants in 1689, to some 1,200 by 1710, and to 1,919 by 1765 (organized into 309 families living in 239 houses). In the classic New England pattern, the first church was gathered late in 1638, growing out of a series of meetings of "all the inhabitants who affected church communion . . . lovingly to discourse and consult together such questions as might further tend to establish a peaceable and comfortable civil society, and prepare for spiritual communion," and with the Reverend John Allin, a graduate of Caius College, Cambridge, as minister. In the early decades most families had at least one member within the church and several had two, though the problems that led eventually to the adoption of the halfway covenant began to afflict Dedham in the later 1650's, with a consequent decline in baptisms and church affiliations. The proportion of freemen was also high, with 75 per cent of the adult males eligible to vote in provincial elections. The first school was authorized by unanimous action of the town meeting on January 2, 1643, and put on a stable financial basis two years later by another unanimous decision to raise twenty pounds annually to maintain a schoolmaster (the first, Ralph Wheelock, was an alumnus of Clare College, Cambridge). Whether in testimony to household or church or school instruction, Dedham's literacy rate, at least among adult males (as measured by the ability to sign their names), remained high: of forty-four settlers in the first generation, signatures have been located for twenty-five, of whom eight made marks; of forty townsmen in the second generation, signatures have been located for at least thirty-six, of whom only two made marks, and at least one of these, John Mac-Kintosh, had come to the town as an adult from Scotland.[4]

Throughout the seventeenth century Dedham was a stable, close-knit community, increasing in wealth and enjoying a substantial measure of internal democracy—at least among admitted townsmen. In the early decades of the eighteenth century, however, population pressures began to exert a perceptible effect. During the 1720's and 1730's, the town found it necessary to take various actions setting new boundaries, annexing surrounding territory, and establishing well-defined precincts. At the same time, the easy prosperity of the first years began to wane: most of the best land had been taken; the num-

[4] Don Gleason Hill, ed., *The Early Records of the Town of Dedham, Massachusetts* (5 vols.; Dedham: Office of the Dedham Transcript, 1886-1899), II, 1; III, 92, 105; and Kenneth Alan Lockridge, "Dedham 1636-1736: The Anatomy of a Puritan Utopia" (unpublished doctoral thesis, Princeton University, 1965), pp. 211, 249, 316.

ber of poor rose; and many sons whose fathers were having difficulty providing for them found themselves forced to leave. An early—and, in retrospect, idyllic—simplicity began to give way to internal conflicts and social complexities.

The increasing diversity of the town and the emergence of divisions along sectional lines are clearly evident in the disputes accompanying the revivals of the 1740's. After initially hedging, the minister of the First Church, the Reverend Samuel Dexter, came gradually to support the Awakening. Two additional parishes had been created in the 1730's, however, and they went in diametrically opposite directions. The South Parish, under the Reverend Thomas Balch, solidly backed the revivals, and on two different occasions invited Eleazar Wheelock and George Whitefield to preach in its pulpit. The West Parish, known as Clapboardtrees, was adamantly opposed to the revivals. Easily the most cosmopolitan of the three congregations, having within it many of the town's *nouveaux riches*, Clapboardtrees pushed its opposition to the point of dismissing its minister, Josiah Dwight, in 1743 and hiring Andrew Tyler from Boston's Brattle Street Church, the citadel of antirevivalist leadership. Family loyalties were obviously involved, since it had been several households of the Gay family who had led the original revolt from the First Church and who continued to maintain the closest contact with the liberal Boston intelligentsia.

Probably the most important outcome of the town's growing size and diversity was the partial breakdown of older communal ties. Before the division into precincts the town meeting had maintained a pervasive influence over all aspects of life, and the selectmen had exercised considerable power. Sharpening internal conflicts, however, slowly disrupted the older functioning of town government. The town meeting was frequently captured by one faction or another for partisan purposes, and appeals were increasingly made over the meeting and selectmen to the provincial authorities and the justices of the peace. Out of the growing impasse came a decentralized system which divided the town's powers between town and precincts. The latter began to hold their own meetings with their own clerks to deal with religious affairs and other local problems; the former continued to handle the administration of town property and finance, the maintenance of roads, and the care of the poor. In one respect, decentralization made possible a new form of political community, one increasingly freed from the assumption that stability depended upon town-wide conformity. In effect, the inability of the town to enforce conformity, coupled with the emergence of alternative agencies for contending with day-by-day problems on the local level, placed the stability of the town on a new basis, leaving greater latitude for individuals to differ and to initiate alternative policies without appearing to threaten the very foundations of social order.

In 1692 the general court enacted a new province law requiring that grammar schools be "constantly kept" by all towns of a hundred families or more. The law was stringently enforced by the courts of session, and in 1701 its terms were strengthened by the requirement that each grammar school be staffed with a full-time certified Latinist. Although Dedham had not been wholly remiss—the town, incidentally, had been indicted in 1690 for failing to maintain a grammar school under the mandate laid down in 1647—it was inevitably affected by the higher standards implicit in the new legislation. In effect, the town could no longer employ a minister or other person to teach part time as an adjunct to his regular occupation; and so, like other towns throughout the province, it was forced to turn to the interim schoolmaster, the college graduate awaiting a call to a church. And, because the laws also demanded that grammar masters be suitably paid, Dedham was forced in addition to pay higher salaries, the figure reaching twenty-eight pounds per annum in 1708, and sixty pounds by 1730.

The difficulties created by rising standards were compounded, too, by the spread of families outward from the center of the town. In 1684 a flexible rate scale was adopted, exempting those living more than two and a half miles from the school from the traditional school assessment upon each householder of five shillings annually for every male child or servant between the ages of four and fourteen. In 1693 the outer limit was extended to three miles, and the following year the assessment was abandoned entirely. Presumably the willingness of the town to release such revenues during a period of economic stringency was testimony to the strength of the assumption that assessments for town services demanded at least their availability to the assessed.

The creation of precincts, which were coterminous with the parishes, only exacerbated the problems of dispersion, for the outlying families now had formal governmental agencies through which to voice their grievances. The town tried to cope initially with the difficulty by having the master teach for a few months in the school-house and then for six- to twelve-week periods in private houses in the several precincts; but the arrangement was inevitably disruptive, since some persons objected to the use of their houses, others disagreed as to which houses ought to be used, and still others refused to be satisfied with anything less than separate money for their own precinct schools. Such disputes, interestingly enough, were indicative of the extent to which the school was looked upon as integral to an ordered community, and the right to maintain one essential to community integrity. Indeed, petitions to the general court for the right to form new towns during this period often based their appeal on the need for better educational services, an appeal, incidentally, which seemed to carry considerable weight with the magistrates.

By 1755, the rotating master arrangement—or the moving school, as it has been called—was abandoned in favor of a new system under which each of Dedham's four precincts (a fourth, the Springfield precinct, had been created contemporaneously with the Springfield Parish in 1748) maintained its own schools, interestingly enough, with those of the first and third (Clapboardtrees) precincts remaining under direct town control and those of the second (South) and fourth (Springfield) precincts coming under local precinct control. The arrangements for 1759-60 are indicative of the new system at work. Three of the schools, at First Parish, South Parish, and Clapboardtrees Parish, had as masters Harvard graduates capable of teaching Latin, and it is probable that the master of the fourth, at Springfield Parish, was at least a certified Latinist. All four of the parishes also had teachers (of whom three were women) offering instruction in reading, writing and ciphering during the summer term. The number of known teachers after 1755 and the regularity with which both the winter and summer sessions were taught in all four parishes strongly suggest that instruction in reading and writing had moved almost wholly into the schools; and, as the statistics below suggest, literacy, which had long been virtually universal among men in Dedham, was coming also to prevail among women. Moreover, the steady flow of Dedhamites through Harvard—there were thirty-six alumni from Dedham during the colonial period, of whom eighteen were graduated between 1760 and 1783—indicates that it was quite possible to obtain a competent Latin education as well, though there is evidence that some boys at least had to supple-

SIGNATURES ON DEDHAM WILLS, DEEDS, AND OTHER DOCUMENTS 1760-1775

	Men		Women	
	Signature	Mark	Signature	Mark
Wills of Adult Males Who Died Between 1760 and 1775	12	1	0	0
Administrations of Wills of Adult Males Who Died Between 1760 and 1775	5	0	5	1
Deeds (Including Divisions or Transfers of Land), 1760-1775	31	1	8	4
Other Documents (Including Official Receipts for Estates, Bonds for Loans, etc.), 1760-1775	23	0	16	4
Total Wills, Administrations, Deeds, and Other Documents	71	2	29	9

CONFIGURATION OF EDUCATIONAL INSTITUTIONS: DEDHAM

	1700	1765	
Population	750	1,919	First Parish —813 Second Parish—441 Third Parish —313 Fourth Parish—352
Households	111	309	
Churches	1	4	
English Schools (summer)		4	
Latin and English Schools (winter)	1	4	

ment the instruction obtained in school with tutoring from the parish minister.[5]

III

However much John Adams stressed the town as the crucible of sagacity, knowledge, judgment, taste, skill, ingenuity, dexterity, and industry, there can be no denying that these same qualities appeared in the Chesapeake region at about the time they appeared in New England, but without towns. As early as 1724, the Reverend Hugh

[5] The number of known teachers who taught in Dedham's parish schools from 1755 to 1776 is 133. Edward M. Cook reports in "The Transformation of Dedham, Massachusetts, 1715-1750" (unpublished honors thesis, Harvard University, 1965) that

Jones, who had taught for a time at the College of William and Mary in the professorship of mathematics and natural philosophy, described the Virginians as bright, of excellent sense, and sharp in trade, apt to learn, fluent of tongue, practical in temper, and independent of mind. "They are more inclinable to read men by business and conversation, than to dive into books," he observed, "and are for the most part only desirous of learning what is absolutely necessary, in the shortest and best method." Moreover, it was neither their interest nor their inclination to cohabit in towns, Jones reported, "so that they are not forward in contributing their assistance towards the making of particular places, every plantation affording the owner the provision of a little market; wherefore they most commonly build upon some convenient spot or neck of land in their own plantation, though towns are laid out and established in each county; the best of which (next Williamsburg) are York, Gloucester, Hampton, Elizabeth Town, and Urbanna." As far as Jones was concerned, the Virginians were England's best hope in the New World, New England having become "an Amsterdam of religion, Pennsylvania, the nursery of Quakers, Maryland the retirement of Roman Catholics, North Carolina the refuge of runaways, and South Carolina the delight of buccaneers and pirates"; and he urged the Crown to give every possible assistance to this most promising of its plantations.[6]

Like Massachusetts townships, Virginia counties varied considerably in their character and traditions, such tidewater communities as James City and King and Queen differing significantly among

---

on a document prepared around 1720, virtually all of the men signed their names, but a majority of the women signed with the mark. The statistics for wills from 1760 to 1775 are based on documents in the Suffolk County Probate Court, Boston; the statistics for deeds and other documents from 1760 to 1775 are based on miscellaneous papers in the Dedham Historical Society. Note in the table "Configuration of Educational Insitutions Dedham" the use of the population figure of 1,919 (from Erastus Worthington, *History of Dedham, from the Beginning of Its Settlement in September, 1635, to May, 1827* [Boston: Dutton and Wentworth, 1827], p. 67)—a figure based on a survey made by Samuel Dexter in 1765—in preference to the figure of 1,929 (in Evarts B. Greene and Virginia D. Harrington, *American Population Before the Federal Census of 1790* [New York: Columbia University Press, 1932], p. 23). There is no way of determining whether the population figure of 1,919 for 1765 includes the 36 Negroes who were listed as residing in the town in the census of Negroes in 1764-65, nor, indeed, what percentage of these Negroes were slaves. An earlier census of 1754-55 had recorded 17 Negro slaves in Dedham (Joseph B. Felt, "Statistics of Population in Massachusetts," *Collections of the American Statistical Association*, I [1847], 208, 211). Presumably, any neighboring Indians lived in Natick, which had originally been part of Dedham.

6 Hugh Jones, *The Present State of Virginia*, edited by Richard L. Morton (Chapel Hill: University of North Carolina Press, 1956), pp. 80-84, 73-74.

themselves and even more sharply from back-country areas like Albemarle and Amherst. Yet, as in the case of Massachusetts, it is useful to examine the educational development of a particular county during the provincial era for the light it sheds upon the changing educational patterns of the eighteenth century. And for this purpose the history of Elizabeth City County is particularly instructive.

Founded by the London company in 1609 as Kecoughtan, after the Indian name for the area, Elizabeth City County was one of the eight original shires of the Virginia plantation. During the early years the settlement existed under the constant threat of Indian attack, but by 1623 a series of military expeditions had driven all hostile Indians from the region. Meanwhile, local government gradually replaced military rule, a church was built, several mills and taverns appeared, and the "savage name," Kecoughtan, was duly changed to Elizabeth City, in honor of the daughter of James I. By 1634, with 859 inhabitants, Elizabeth City was the second most populous county in Virginia, even though it remained the smallest in area.[7]

Originally settled in small scattered plots, the county did not develop a genuine nuclear village until late in the seventeenth century. The rich soil of the "back-river district," comprising about a third of the area, ensured that agriculture would remain, for an initial period at least, the principal element in the county's economy. In 1680, however, in an effort to create trade centers for the colony, the assembly passed an Act for Encouraging Towns, setting aside fifty acres for this purpose in each county; and in Elizabeth City the Jarvis plantation on the west side of the Hampton River, with its fine harbor and easy access to the hinterland via waterway, was chosen as the natural site for such a community. Despite initial resistance from the local farmers, the town of Hampton slowly took root and soon became, with nearby Norfolk, one of the foremost commercial centers of the region.[8]

During the first half of the eighteenth century, relentless tobacco-

[7] "Proceedings of the Virginia Assembly, 1619," in Lyon Gardiner Tyler, ed., *Narratives of Early Virginia, 1606-1625*, Original Narratives of Early American History, edited by J. Franklin Jameson (New York: Charles Scribner's Sons, 1907), p. 259.

[8] William Waller Hening, ed., *The Statutes at Large; Being a Collection of All the Laws of Virginia, from the First Session of the Legislature in the Year 1619* (13 vols.; imprint varies, 1819-1823), II, 471-478. For the subsequent suspension of the act of 1680 and for the efforts to encourage towns thereafter, see *ibid.*, p. 508 and III, 53-69, 108-109, 404-419.

farming soon depleted the rich soil of the back-river district, and agriculture began to decline. But commerce flourished, and by mid-century the total tonnage of ships arriving in Hampton harbor was nearly equal to that of New York's. Not surprisingly, the town began to take on urban characteristics: streets multiplied; hogs were ordered penned (by act of the general assembly); ferries were built; and the number and variety of craftsmen increased steadily. White and black servants were present in roughly equal numbers during the early eighteenth century, but as indentures decreased Negro slavery became basic to the local economy.

Not surprisingly, too, population rose markedly. During most of the seventeenth century the number of inhabitants had grown slowly, from 859 in 1634 to about 1,000 in 1693. During the nineties, however, coincident with the rise of the town, the population appears to have jumped almost 10 per cent, to approximately 1,100 in 1698. Thereafter, the rate of growth remained fairly high, with the number of inhabitants doubling to 2,250 by 1747 and standing at 3,100 in 1782.

Church records for Elizabeth City are virtually nonexistent for the initial decades, the earliest extant vestry book covering the years from 1751 through 1784. Various other sources reveal the names of at least fourteen different clergymen who served the parish during the seventeenth century; and, although the backgrounds of many remain obscure, it is known that the minister who settled in 1687, the Reverend Cope D'Oyley, was a graduate of Merton College, and that his successor, the Reverend James Wallace, served the county simultaneously as physician and pastor during his incumbency between 1691 and 1712.

According to the Reverend James Falconer in his 1724 report to the bishop of London, the parish was "about fifty miles in circumference"; and, although it was smaller than many in Virginia, a family living at the perimeter would have found the trip to church long, uncomfortable, and occasionally dangerous. For obvious reasons, church attendance throughout the century was scant and sporadic, with one estimate for the 1720's placing the figure as low as one out of seven families. Yet, given the overlap of civil and ecclesiastical government in provincial Virginia, church attendance is at best only one index of ecclesiastical effectiveness; and the vestry book for 1751-1784 reveals a number of other things about the Elizabeth City church and its place in the community. First, the vestry was exceedingly active in caring for the large number of charity cases within the parish. During a sample twelve-year period, 1751-1763, the vestry administered and paid for the boarding of at least seventy individuals (roughly thirty of whom were children), assuming the costs of food, clothing, and medicine and occasionally meeting funeral and burial expenses as well. The vestry also protected itself from assuming unnecessary burdens by paying representatives from time to time to escort unwanted vagabonds to the parish edge. Second, the vestry appears to have given Elizabeth City's ministers considerable security in office during the eighteenth century, engaging only nine during the entire period between 1691 and 1783, and at least three of these for more than a decade each. And, third, it is clear that this particular vestry was fairly tightly controlled by a small group of well-to-do parishioners. Of the thirty-four vestrymen from 1751 through 1784, at least half served for ten years or more, nearly a third for fifteen years or more, and almost a fourth for twenty years or more. Nine of these men were also members of the House of Burgesses at some time during their careers, and almost all held one or more county offices at some time or other. Indeed, the control of public offices by a relatively small number of leading families appears to have been generally more pronounced in Elizabeth City than it was, for example, in contemporary Dedham, or even, for that matter, in some of the inland counties of contemporary Virginia.[9]

The establishment of the Syms and Eaton schools in the seventeenth century has already been discussed, and there are references to the affairs of the two institutions from time to time in the county records, though not in sufficient number or detail to establish whether they were in continuous operation. In 1753 the Syms free school and in 1759 the Eaton charity school were incorporated by formal acts of the assembly, the Syms school remaining free to all its students, the Eaton school remaining free only to poor children. The legal trustees were identical for both institutions and included the county justice, the two churchwardens, and the minister; but actually the vestry seems to have been the most consistently active agency in administering the two schools. Rogers D. Whichard, the

[9] William Stevens Perry, ed., *Historical Collections Relating to the American Colonial Church* (4 vols.; Hartford, Conn.: Church Press Company, 1870-1878), I, 293. Note also Falconer's assertion that he catechized the youth of the parish only at Lent (*ibid.*, p. 294).

historian of lower tidewater Virginia, has remarked that this was natural, if extralegal, owing to the traditional connection between church and school. It was especially natural in Elizabeth City, given the overlap of civil and ecclesiastical functions and the control of both by a fairly small number of families.[10]

The county also had a continuing tradition of official concern for the maintenance of minimal educational standards, and from the beginning the authorities consistently held parents and masters responsible for the education of their children and servants. Thus, the court in 1688 ordered a family to put its apprentice to school "and learn him to read a chapter in the Bible," and in 1725 upheld the claim of a boy's mother that his master "has not learned her son, Armistead House, to read, write, and cipher" as agreed in the boy's indenture. And in the years between 1756 and 1762 the court called at least four Elizabeth City fathers before it "to show cause why they have neglected the education of their children." There is no way of ascertaining whether these last cases represented special attempts to enforce laws that were being widely flouted or routine actions against occasional instances of parental neglect. What is clear, however, is that instruction in basic literacy by parents and masters was as acceptable, and possibly as ordinary, as formal schooling in Elizabeth City, even given the presence of Syms and Eaton.[11]

Some light is thrown upon education in eighteenth-century Elizabeth City by the existence in the county records of a guardians' account book covering the twelve-year period between 1737 and 1749. Bearing in mind that the children listed were orphans with estates, that is, the children of well-to-do families, and that their education was for that reason scarcely representative, one can draw a number of inferences. First, over half of the orphans listed are recorded as having received some kind of formal education. From a total of twenty-four accounts, fourteen included schooling costs, as compared with ten which failed to mention schooling at all. Such payments may have gone either to private teachers or to one of the local free schools. And those children whose accounts did not include

[10] Hening, ed., *Statutes at Large; Being a Collection of All the Laws of Virginia,* VI, 389-392; VII, 317-320; Whichard, *History of Lower Tidewater Virginia,* I, 149.

[11] *The William and Mary College Quarterly,* XXIV (1915-16), 35-36; and Lyon G. Tyler, *History of Hampton and Elizabeth City County, Virginia* (Hampton, Va.: The Board of Supervisors of Elizabeth City County, 1922), p. 33; and Marion L. Starkey, *The First Plantation: A History of Hampton and Elizabeth City County, Virginia, 1607-1887* (Hampton, Va.: Houston Printing and Publishing House, 1936), p. 35.

payments for schooling might nevertheless have received instruction from the families of their guardians, or they might have attended one of the free schools without cost—a practice sufficiently prevalent to have elicited complaints from the Eaton school's trustees in the 1750's. It would also seem a valid surmise that other families with means were probably providing for their children in much the same way as the guardians of the orphans.

Second, the records indicate a substantial number of persons in the community apparently capable of teaching. Ten persons (possibly eleven) appear in the account book as teachers during the twelve-year period, and three additional names are cited in a separate account for John Tabb covering the years 1762-1764. These teachers may have included persons recruited from within the county as private tutors, persons brought in from outside specifically for the purpose, or local schoolmasters paid to take the orphans into their classes or instruct them privately.

Third, the records include payments for Latin books in at least two of the accounts, indicating that some of these teachers, if not all, were instructing in grammar-school subjects. Whether these same teachers taught English as well as Latin is not known; but, given the character of the local economy, which would place no special premium on a classical education, most teachers who taught Latin probably also taught English, the extent of instruction received by a particular pupil doubtless being a function of family taste and aspiration. In any case, some twenty Elizabeth City youths are known to have attended the College of William and Mary during the eighteenth century, a number that is certainly significant in its own right, though not particularly high in light of the special attributes of Elizabeth City County.[12]

Using the guardians' account book along with other sources, one can identify the names of twenty-two different persons—and possibly as many as twenty-four—who taught in the county at one time or another from 1690 through 1770. This list includes teachers in the Syms and Eaton schools, teachers named in the guardians' accounts and in deeds and wills, and at least one private schoolmaster. Taking the year 1745 as a base, it is possible to construct a rough estimate

---

[12] John Bell Henneman, "Historic Elements in Virginia Education and Literary Effort," Virginia Historical Society *Collections*, new series, XI (1892), 41-46. In addition to those who attended the College of William and Mary, Wilson Cary attended Trinity College, Cambridge, in 1721, and James McClurg, who later became professor of surgery at the College of William and Mary, attended the University of Edinburgh, in 1770.

of the minimum number of teachers in the community around mid-century. In that year three names appear in the guardians' accounts as teachers, a Mrs. Parker, a Mr. Booth, and a Captain Wallace, and one person, Mr. Hunter, is known to have been a schoolmaster at either Syms or Eaton. To these the rector of the church, the Reverend William Fyfe, can be added as in all probability the instructor of some youngsters. This would indicate a minimum of five teachers in the community during 1745, probably covering the full range of English and grammar-school subjects. And, by way of gross result, a sampling of signature counts from records in the county reveals a substantial measure of literacy among women as well as men:[13]

SIGNATURES ON ELIZABETH CITY DEEDS AND DEPOSITIONS 1693-1699

Men		Women	
Signature	Mark	Signature	Mark
142	48	16	29

SIGNATURES ON WILLS, DEEDS AND MORTGAGES, AND OTHER DEPOSITIONS 1763-1771

	Men		Women	
	Signature	Mark	Signature	Mark
Wills	15	5	7	1
Deeds and Mortgages	111	11	35	18
Other Depositions	35	0	0	0
Total	161	16	42	19

There is scant evidence concerning the education of Elizabeth City's blacks. The Reverend James Falconer remarked in his 1724 report that slaveowners "are generally careful to instruct those capable of instruction, and to bring them to baptism, but it is impossible to instruct these that are grown up before they are carried from their own country they never being able either to speak or understand our language perfectly." Of course, there remains the central question of what such instruction comprised even when it

[13] The statistics regarding signatures on deeds and wills for 1693-1699 are from Philip Alexander Bruce, *Institutional History of Virginia in the Seventeenth Century* (2 vols.; New York: G. P. Putnam's Sons, 1910), I, 453, 457. The statistics regarding signatures on deeds and wills for 1763-1771 are from "Wills and Deeds, 1763-1771" (ms. records, Elizabeth City County, Va.).

was given, and, in any case, one may doubt whether too much energy was expended, since there were more expedient ways of keeping slaves docile. A few blacks must have learned to read, however, for in 1739 a slave named Ned, convicted of stealing, managed to escape execution by successfully pleading benefit of clergy. And, given the attitude toward slaves who stole, Ned at the very least must have read fluently and well.[14]

CONFIGURATION OF EDUCATIONAL INSTITUTIONS: ELIZABETH CITY

	1700	1782
Population	1,200	3,100
Households	170	248
Churches	1	1
Schools	2	5

IV

Industry, ingenuity, and independency apparently flourished in the cities of eighteenth-century America, as well as in its northern towns and southern counties, that is, if the Reverend Andrew Burnaby's much-read account of 1775 can be believed. An amiable and cultivated English clergyman who traveled through the colonies in 1759 and 1760, Burnaby was so much taken with the character and resourcefulness of the inhabitants that he saw fit to publish a narrative of his trip during the most trying days of the developing crisis over independence, maintaining that while his first attachment was naturally to his native England his second was most assuredly to America, and urging that conciliation was by far the wisest and most prudent course for the two countries in resolving their "present unhappy differences."[15]

Burnaby was not without his criticisms of the colonies, predicting that internal antagonisms and inherent weaknesses would ultimately combine to prevent them from coalescing into a great nation. But he was unstinting in his admiration of the unparalleled natural beauties of the new continent—the colorful grandeur of Virginia

[14] Perry, ed., *Historical Collections Relating to the American Colonial Church*, I, 293.

[15] Andrew Burnaby, *Travels Through the Middle Settlements in North-America* (2d ed.; Ithaca: Cornell University Press, 1960), p. x.

(where he sojourned with Colonel Washington), the extraordinary falls at Passaic, New Jersey, the elegant terrain of Long Island, and the prodigious flights of pigeons southward across New England— and he was lavish in his praise of its thriving young cities. "Philadelphia," he observed, "if we consider that not eighty years ago the place where it now stands was a wild and uncultivated desert, inhabited by nothing but ravenous beasts, and a savage people, must certainly be the object of everyone's wonder and admiration." The climate was delightful. The streets were crowded with people, and the port with vessels. The arts and sciences, though nascent, were daily gaining ground. And the inhabitants were frugal and industrious, sprightly and enterprising, and on the whole great republicans full of erroneous ideas about independence. New York was much the same, well situated, enjoying a fine climate and "a very wholesome air," possessed of extensive trade, and peopled by habitually frugal, industrious, and parsimonious men and women who much resembled the Philadelphians. So far as Burnaby was concerned, America was a land formed for happiness, if not for empire. In the course of twelve hundred miles, he had not seen "a single object that solicited charity."[16]

The two cities that captured Burnaby's attention were indeed flourishing in the eighteenth century, and in many ways served as foundries for the richest variety of character types produced in provincial America. Situated in the greatest natural harbor on the eastern coast of North America, New York grew from a respectable-sized market town of 4,300 in 1690 to a bustling city of 21,863 by 1771; while Philadelphia, serving as the chief port of entry for immigrants from the Palatinate and Ulster, expanded from a nascent trading center of 1,444 in 1693 to a thriving city of 13,708 by 1779 —or, if one prefers to include the population for Philadelphia County as a whole, an astronomical 41,144. Both cities continued to display the phenomenal range of ethnic, religious, and racial types that marked seventeenth-century New York: a dozen languages and dialects might be heard at any given time, particularly in the market and wharf sections of the two cities; whites, Indians, and blacks, and every conceivable combination of the three, mingled in the houses and streets; and one could worship in any of a dozen

---

16 *Ibid.*, pp. 53-54, 77, 110. In view of Adams' disparaging comments about Virginia, and Jones's about New England, it is interesting to note Burnaby's lack of enthusiasm for either region.

liturgies. An English visitor to New York in 1768 enumerated eighteen principal churches in the city, including three Anglican congregations, three Dutch Reformed, three Presbyterian, two Lutheran, and single congregations of German Reformed, French Reformed, Baptists, Moravians, Quakers, Methodists, and Jews. And
this obviously did not include the smaller congregations and splinter
groups that worshiped in households or in temporary quarters.
Similarly, Philadelphia could boast twenty churches at the time of
the Revolution, spanning the same range of denominations with the
exception of the Dutch and French Reformed, but including two
of Roman Catholic profession.[17]

This same striking diversity that marked the households and
churches of the two cities also appeared in their schools. Recall that
most formal schooling during the seventeenth century had been
carried out under the joint auspices of the ecclesiastical and civil
authorities. The initial town school in New Amsterdam, begun in
1638, became after the accession of the English essentially a parochial
school of the Dutch Reformed church, which continued to teach in
the Dutch language until 1773, when English became an optional
vehicle of instruction. On the English side, official provision for
schooling was desultory at best. In 1702 the assembly voted to provide a free school for the city and two years later George Muirson
was employed as master; but Muirson served only a few months and
was succeeded by Andrew Clarke in 1705. A few years thereafter the
school seems to have expired. Another effort by the assembly in
1732 appears to have lasted about as long. Meanwhile in 1702 William Huddleston, a private schoolmaster, began to conduct a charity
school at Trinity Church, and in 1709 the S.P.G. made him its
official schoolmaster in New York. Aside from the catechetical
schools maintained for Negroes by the Society and the Bray Associates and the preparatory school begun by King's College in 1763,
these exhaust New York's official efforts at schooling. The dissenting
congregations doubtless carried on some formal instruction for their
children, in the fashion of the day, but, aside from the efforts of
Congregation Shearith Israel to teach Hebrew, the indications of

[17] G. Taylor, *A Voyage to North America, Perform'd by G. Taylor, of Sheffield, in
the Years 1768 and 1769* (Nottingham: S. Cresswell, 1771), pp. 69, 171; and Nelson Waite
Rightmyer, "Churches Under Enemy Occupation, Philadelphia, 1777-8," *Church History*,
XIV (1945), 33-60. For the social composition of Philadelphia's population in 1774, see
Sam Bass Warner, Jr., "If All the World Were Philadelphia: A Scaffolding for Urban
History, 1774-1930," *The American Historical Review*, LXXIV (1968-69), 26-43.

such ventures are at best ephemeral. Little wonder that in 1757 William Smith leveled a blistering indictment of the educational efforts of his countrymen: "Our schools are in the lowest order—the instructors want instruction; and, through a long shameful neglect of all arts and sciences, our common speech is extremely corrupt, and the evidences of a bad taste, both as to thought and language, are visible in all our proceedings, public and private."[18]

In Philadelphia, the Friends, of course, were active from the start. Recall that in 1683 the provincial council appointed Enoch Flower to instruct children in reading, writing, and ciphering, and six years later the monthly meeting employed George Keith to conduct public Latin classes for rich and poor alike, the latter work subsequently evolving into the William Penn Charter School. The 1760's and 1770's also saw the establishment of schools for Negroes under the auspices of the Friends and the Bray Associates, while there is direct evidence that the Anglican, Lutheran, German Reformed, Moravian, and Baptist churches conducted schools for greater or lesser periods of time, depending on the needs of their congregations and the availability of alternative institutions. And, as in New York, there were doubtless other such ventures that simply failed to appear in the records.

Even in the seventeenth century, however, it was the private entrepreneurial schoolmaster who carried an increasing share of the formal education in New York City; and during the eighteenth it was entrepreneurial schooling that expanded most impressively in the two cities. Several factors may have contributed, including the general restrictiveness of the congregational schools and their tendency to favor Latin or Hebrew instruction over English; but easily the most important was the concentration of artisans, tradesmen, and shopkeepers in the two cities (Bridenbaugh has estimated that between a third and two-thirds of the population of the two cities was made up of such men and their families) and the considerable mobility into and within their ranks—a mobility, incidentally, to which many a private schoolmaster made subtle and indirect appeal in his advertising. In any case, for the period to 1783 it is possible

18 William Smith, *The History of the Late Province of New-York, from Its Discovery, to the Appointment of Governor Colden, in 1762* (2 vols.; New York: New-York Historical Society, 1829), I, 278. For an earlier indictment, see Memorandum of the Reverend John Sharpe, March 11, 1713, "Bibliotheca Lambethana" (unpublished mss., Lambeth Palace Library, London), vol. DCCCXLI, no. 18.

to identify by name at least 260 teachers in New York and 283 teachers in Philadelphia; and upon grouping them the following patterns emerge:

NEW YORK CITY SCHOOLMASTERS 1638-1783

	1638-1688	1689-1783
Parochial and town schoolmasters	11	27
Private schoolmasters	16	206
Total	27	233

PHILADELPHIA SCHOOLMASTERS 1689-1783

Parochial and town schoolmasters	76	(includes Philadelphia academy)
Private schoolmasters	207	
Total	283	

In addition, if one averages the population figures of the two cities for five-year periods, derives the number of households and school-aged children, and averages the number of teachers for five-year periods to soften the impact of fortuitous shifts, the striking change in the availability of formal schooling after mid-century becomes readily apparent.[19]

In assessing these data, several cautions must be borne in mind. First, the listing of teachers gleaned from advertisements and other records probably provides fairly reliable information with respect to minimum numbers, though there were almost certainly teachers who advertised but never actually taught and teachers who taught but never appeared in any records. Second, there is no way of estimating the number of children from surrounding areas, or even from distant colonies, who came to New York and Philadelphia for their schooling, but it is almost certain that there were such children, especially from the populous suburbs of Philadelphia. And third, since there is evidence that some private teachers offered basic instruction in reading, writing, and ciphering even when their advertised specialties lay elsewhere, all teachers of all subjects have been included—there being only the most ephemeral evidence in most instances as to which students actually studied which subjects under

[19] For the procedures employed in the development of these statistics, see Appendix A.

NEW YORK CITY HOUSEHOLDS AND TEACHERS
(Five-Year Averages)

Years	Population	House-holds	Children	Teachers	Children per Teacher	
1700-1704	4,587	829	1,241	5	248.2	
1705-1709	5,060	888	1,378	5.6	246.1	
1710-1714	5,862	1,028	1,586	2.8	566.4	
1715-1719	6,805	1,194	1,789	4.2	426.0	
1720-1724	9,670	1,696	1,991	6.4	311.1	Average
1725-1729	8,635	1,515	2,197	7.2	305.1	357.6
1730-1734	9,600	1,684	2,388	7.2	331.7	
1735-1739	10,619	1,862	2,592	6.2	418.1	
1740-1744	11,249	1,974	2,704	7.4	365.4	
1745-1749	11,852	2,079	2,799	9.8	285.6	
1750-1754	12,511	2,195	2,960	15.8	187.3	
1755-1759	13,719	2,407	3,246	15.6	208.1	Average
1760-1764	16,569	2,907	3,882	16.6	233.9	254.7
1765-1769	19,510	3,423	4,528	13.6	332.9	
1770-1774	21,885	3,822	5,184	18.5	280.2	

PHILADELPHIA HOUSEHOLDS AND TEACHERS
(Five-Year Averages)

Years	Population	House-holds	Children	Teachers	Children per Teacher	
1700-1704	2,132	374	581	3.0	193.7	
1705-1709	2,514	441	684	2.8	244.3	
1710-1714	2,896	508	775	2.0	387.5	
1715-1719	3,278	576	861	2.2	391.4	
1720-1724	3,877	680	1,001	2.4	417.1	Average
1725-1729	4,803	843	1,218	5.0	243.6	308.4
1730-1734	5,728	1,005	1,425	6.2	229.8	
1735-1739	6,948	1,219	1,696	5.8	292.4	
1740-1744	8,529	1,496	2,029	5.4	375.7	
1745-1749	9,991	1,753	2,359	8.4	280.8	
1750-1754	11,298	1,982	2,675	15.2	176.0	
1755-1759	12,140	2,130	2,868	20.0	143.4	Average
1760-1764	12,710	2,230	2,979	16.8	177.3	175.4
1765-1769	12,913	2,262	2,997	23.4	128.1	
1770-1774	13,115	2,301	3,106	21.2	146.5	

which teachers. Yet, even if one were to remove the specialized teachers of sewing, dancing, fencing, art, and music from the tables, it would not significantly affect the trend, since the number of such teachers totaled only 27 for New York (out of 260 for the period) and 14 for

Philadelphia (out of 283). The conclusion seems valid, then, that the availability of schooling of various sorts increased markedly in New York and Philadelphia during the eighteenth century, and not merely as a function of population growth. One outcome, as elsewhere, was a continuing high rate of literacy among men, and a perceptibly rising rate among women. Another, in effect, was the same institutionalized extension of alternative possibilities that had appeared in the households and churches of the two cities.[20]

SIGNATURES ON NEW YORK CITY WILLS 1692-1775

	Men		Women	
	Signature	Mark	Signature	Mark
1692-1703	40	4	10	3
1760-1775 (City proper)	91	12	13	5
1760-1775 (Harlem and Bloomingdale)	5	2	1	2
1760-1775 (Combined)	96	14	14	7

SIGNATURES ON PHILADELPHIA WILLS 1699-1775

	Men		Women	
	Signature	Mark	Signature	Mark
1699-1706	32	8	6	4
1773-1775 (City proper)	66	12	26	7
1773-1775 (Northern liberties)	14	6	4	1
1773-1775 (Combined)	80	18	30	8

That extension of possibilities appeared elsewhere as well, in the colleges and subscription libraries that grew up in both cities during the 1740's and 1750's, in the enlarged range of apprenticeships made possible by the greater variety of craftsmen, in the increased opportunity for informal association afforded by coffeehouses, taverns, clubs, and scientific societies, and in the mounting flow of printed materials that issued from a steadily rising number of printers. One need not live in the city of publication, of course, to enjoy the benefits of literature, a fact that was amply demonstrated by the spirited

[20] The statistics for New York City are based on New York City Wills (ms. records, Surrogate's Court, New York), Libers V-VII (1692-1703) and XXVIII-XXXI (1760-1775). The statistics for Philadelphia are based on Philadelphia Register of Wills (ms. records, City Hall Annex, Philadelphia), Book B (1699-1706) and Philadelphia Wills (microfilm records, City Hall, Philadelphia), 1773-1775.

circulation of English and French books in both communities. But to live in the city of publication is to have easier, more immediate, and more assured access to those benefits. And that is what the residents of New York and Philadelphia had in increasing measure during the provincial era, to the inevitable enhancement of their knowledge, taste, and most important, perhaps, imagination.

NEW YORK CITY AND PHILADELPHIA PRINTERS AND NEWSPAPERS

	1700	1710	1720	1730	1740	1750	1760	1770	1780
New York City Printers	1	2	1	2	2	3	4	7	9
New York City Newspapers				1	2	2	3	3	5
Philadelphia Printers	1	1	1	5	4	8	8	16	14
Philadelphia Newspapers			1	2	3	3	4	6	7

V

There is less to be said about the back country, not because it was less significant during the provincial era, but only because there are fewer reliable data from which to draw generalizations. Certainly no simple evolutionism will suffice, for the communities of the frontier were not merely nascent replicas of tidewater communities a century earlier. For one thing, they were founded by men and women from quite different circumstances—on the one hand, emigrants from the Palatinate or Ulster rather than from England or Holland; on the other hand, emigrants from the older settled communities of New England, New York, and the Chesapeake region. For another, they were founded by men and women bearing the fruits of a hundred years of colonial experience. The elements and the Indians were still there and often still hostile. But the farm family bearing the Bible, a primer, Franklin's almanacs, Jared Eliot's *Essays upon Field-Husbandry in New-England* (1760), and *The American Instructor*, and an oral tradition based on a century of New England or Chesapeake lore, was simply in a better position to survive and multiply than its progenitors who arrived with the Bible, Tusser, Bayly, and dreams of earthly or heavenly glory. The frontier may have been the crucible of the American experience, but it was education that filtered, synthesized, and transmitted what was learned, and enabled men to profit from the testing.

The early history of Kent, Connecticut, a town founded in 1738 in the westernmost part of that colony, lends impressive documentation to this thesis. Of the forty original families who settled Kent, sixteen had moved west from such river towns as Colchester, Tolland, Mansfield, and Windham, and twenty-four, north from such Long Island Sound towns as Danbury, Fairfield, and Norwalk. A majority were fourth-generation descendants of "first-comers" to the earlier communities; and a majority came to Kent in groups of three or more families. The first cabin was erected early in 1738; the first school is mentioned in the minutes of the proprietors' meeting in May, 1739; the town was formally settled by act of the general assembly on October 13, 1739; and the covenant formally gathering the Congregational church was made on April 29, 1741. Within three years all the formal institutions of education had been initially constituted. Most of the town's inhabitants appear to have joined the new church, and all the town's children appear to have received an English education at school—and, indeed, as the settlers dispersed in the 1740's, additional schools were built to serve the several localities. So far as can be determined, no member of a Kent family ever had to sign with a mark during the eighteenth century, and at least two young men, Samuel Mills and Edmund Mills, the sons of John Mills, one of the original proprietors, were prepared for Yale by the Reverend Joel Bordwell, who acceded to the pulpit of the town church in 1758.[21]

The settlement of the South Carolina back country, which began in earnest about the same time Kent was founded, proceeded quite differently. There the story is one of rapid population by emigrants from Europe, the British Isles, Africa, the tidewater communities of South Carolina, and the older frontier communities of Pennsylvania and Virginia. Arriving in groups, in families, and as individuals, these men and women settled in townships, hamlets, and dispersed farmsteads. The established religion being Anglican, parishes were laid out in Charleston, but the back country was so poorly served that as late as 1767 the Reverend Charles Woodmason, the itinerant rector of St. Mark's Parish, traveled some four thousand miles in caring for some twenty congregations numbering over three

[21] These data are taken from Charles S. Grant, *Democracy in the Connecticut Frontier Town of Kent* (New York: Columbia University Press, 1961). For a contemporary example of a school and church being founded before a town was settled, in this instance by the German Lutherans who established Upper Milford Township in Bucks County, Pennsylvania, see Andrew S. Berky, *The Schoolhouse Near the Old Spring* (Norristown, Pa.: Pennsylvania German Society, 1955).

thousand individuals. Equally important, perhaps, the various communities of Dissenters started their own churches, and within Woodmason's parish alone there were knots and clusters of Regular Baptists, Seventh Day Baptists, New Light Baptists, Presbyterians, Huguenots, Quakers, Lutherans, and German Reformed. "It is very few families whom I can bring to join in prayer," Woodmason lamented in his journal, "because most of them are of various opinions the husband a Churchman, wife, a Dissenter, children nothing at all."[22]

It was essentially within these churches, as well as within the households of the settlers, that most formal education took place. True, Woodmason himself conducted a school for some twenty poor children in the hope that through them he could "make impression on their relations," and there is also occasional indication of a schoolhouse on maps of the parish and surveyors' records. But in the main the settlers were forced to depend on their pastors and themselves. Yet, surprisingly perhaps, literacy rates remained relatively high, as indicated by signatures on deeds, wills, and mortgages, not falling much below 80 per cent for any substantial group of white male settlers and running around 90 per cent among the Germans. Given the isolation of particular families and the persistent difficulties of obtaining and retaining pastors, these rates are extraordinary, and stand as eloquent testimony to the power the tradition of learning had acquired in the minds of provincial Americans.[23]

[22] Richard J. Hooker, ed., *The Carolina Backcountry on the Eve of the Revolution: The Journal and Other Writings of Charles Woodmason, Anglican Itinerant* (Chapel Hill: University of North Carolina Press, 1953), p. 52.

[23] *Ibid.*, p. 85; Robert L. Meriwether, *The Expansion of South Carolina, 1729-1765* (Kingsport, Tenn.: Southern Publishers, Inc., 1940), pp. 177-183; and David Duncan Wallace, *The History of South Carolina* (4 vols.; New York: The American Historical Society, 1934), I, 403. William Willis Boddie notes in his *History of Williamsburg*, a back-country community just beyond the eastern border of St. Mark's Parish that was originally settled by Scotch-Irish Presbyterians: "Not more than one man out of the first one hundred wills and transfers of property made and recorded between 1765 and 1775 had to make his mark, nor did a greater percentum of women releasing rights fail to write legibly their names. Out of more than three hundred of Marion's Men from Williamsburg who filed their statements for pay, only six made their marks where they should have signed their names. Almost every one of these men was born in Williamsburg later than 1740" (Columbia, S.C.: The State Company, 1923), p. 91.

Chapter 18

CHARACTERISTICS

It is a common argument that the power and strength of a nation consists in its riches and money. No doubt money can do great things but I think the power of a nation consists in the knowledge and virtue of its inhabitants and in proof of this history everywhere almost shows us that the richest nations abounding most in silver and gold have been generally conquered by poor but in some sense virtuous nations. If riches be not accompanied with virtue they on that very account expose a nation to ruin by their being a temptation for others to invade them while luxury the usual consequence of riches makes them an easy prey.

CADWALLADER COLDEN

However variegated the patterns of provincial education, there were certain larger tendencies that already gave it a characteristic cast by the time of the Revolution. Chief among these was the prevalence of schooling and its accessibility to most segments of the population —the Negroes and Indians, of course, being the leading exceptions. "The education of children among the English in this country was well established in many ways," observed the Swedish naturalist Peter Kalm, who had traveled through America between 1748 and 1751 in search of a mulberry tree that could endure the rigors of the Swedish climate. "They had separate schools for small boys and girls. When a child was a little over three it was sent to school both morning and afternoon. They probably realized that such little children would not be able to read much, but they would be rid of them at home and thought it would protect them from any misbehavior. Also they would acquire a liking for being with other children."[1]

[1] *Peter Kalm's Travels in North America*, edited by Adolph B. Benson (2 vols.; New York: Dover Publications, 1934), I, 204.

Several explanations may be ventured for the general expansion of schooling in the eighteenth-century colonies. For one thing, it is well to bear in mind that schools had been firmly transplanted to America during the initial decades of settlement, as part of the "transit of civilization" from a metropolis that had valued schooling quite highly—indeed, that had markedly increased the number of its schools at precisely the time of initial colonization. Moreover, one key segment of the colonizing population had been led by Puritans of the very same sort as had been in the vanguard of the educational revolution in England. At the least, then, there was from the beginning a solid foundation for the further development of schooling in the colonies.

That development came during the provincial era, in connection with a number of significant social changes. First, schooling expanded because a rapid rate of economic growth in the colonies combined with a considerable degree of social mobility to create a situation in which schooling was widely perceived and used as a vehicle for personal advancement—the pattern was the same as had prevailed in Elizabethan and early Stuart England, when schooling had so effectively aided the movement of new men from the yeoman and artisan classes into the professions and the gentry (recall Sir Thomas Smith's observation in 1583 that "whosoever studieth the laws of the realm, who studieth in the universities, who professeth liberal sciences, and to be short, who can live idly and without manual labor, and will bear the port, charge and countenance of a gentleman, he shall be called master . . . and shall be taken for a gentleman"). Second, schooling expanded because, as denomination-alism became the characteristic form of American Protestantism, the competing sects increasingly used schools as agencies of missionary endeavor, though the schools, as institutions are wont to do, frequently developed along lines that had little to do with their original purposes. And third, schooling expanded because of a growing participation in public affairs during the latter half of the eighteenth century. As almanacs, newspapers, pamphlets, and books dealt with matters of topical interest, especially after the Stamp Act crisis of the 1760's, a premium was placed on literacy in segments of the population where illiteracy had long been no stigma. In the process, the pressure for schooling mounted. And, as schools became more generally available, families and churches that had earlier been forced to undertake the teaching of reading and writing in the absence of schools (or because available schools were too narrowly sectarian) found themselves increasingly prepared to turn that teaching back to the institutions where it seemed to belong.[2]

One outcome, of course, was the rapid spread of literacy among the population. At a time when the estimates of adult male literacy in England ran from 48 per cent in the rural western midlands to 74 per cent in the towns, on the basis of signatures on marriage registers, adult male literacy in the American colonies seems to have run from 70 per cent to virtually 100 per cent, on the basis of signatures on deeds and wills, militia rolls, and voting rosters. Now, there are several obvious problems here that merit attention. For one thing, the assumption that the ability to write one's name implies the ability to read, or, conversely, that the inability to write one's name implies the inability to read, is open to all sorts of questions that are not downed by simple-minded assertions that all data are useful so long as one is aware of their limitations. In this particular instance, the limitations remain distressingly unclear. In addition, there is a patent discrepancy between the English and the American statistics, since marriage registers are obviously more inclusive than deeds and wills, which are ordinarily relevant only where substantial property is involved, and even, perhaps, than militia rolls and voting rosters, so that the two sets of figures may not be at all comparable. Beyond that, if one were to include white nonproperty holders, nonvoters, and nonparticipants in the militia in the American statistics, which would probably affect them more significantly than the inclusion of bachelors in the English statistics, those American statistics would presumably fall to a point much closer to the English. And, additionally, if one were to include Negro and Indian nonproperty holders, nonvoters, and nonparticipants in the militia, the American statistics would drop even farther, almost certainly ending up below the English. Indeed, though comparable statistics for eighteenth-century Ireland are not presently available, it is probable that literacy rates among the American Negroes and Indians would be considerably lower than those among the rural Irish Catholic peasantry, but that literacy rates among the Irish generally would be lower than those in England or among American whites. In any case, this is certainly what one would be led to expect from the descrip-

---

[2] Thomas Smith, *De Republica Anglorum*, edited by L. Alston (Cambridge: Cambridge University Press, 1906), pp. 39-40.

tions of contemporaries, as gross and partial as such descriptions might have been.[3]

Another quite different measure of literacy, one especially useful for comparative purposes, is the number and circulation of newspapers; and, though precise figures are difficult to obtain, the gross estimates for the three societies around 1775 are revealing:

NUMBER OF NEWSPAPERS AND SUBSCRIBERS IN ENGLAND AND WALES, IRELAND, AND THE AMERICAN COLONIES 1775

| | England and Wales | | | | |
	Total	London	Provincial	Ireland	American Colonies
Population	7,244,000	788,000	6,456,000	3,678,000	2,464,000
Number of Newspapers	67	23	44	16	37
Estimated Number of Subscribers	112,500	57,500	55,000	16,000	35,000

The discrepancies are significant in and of themselves, but it is important to recognize in addition that a very large portion of the Irish circulation was concentrated in Dublin, while in both England and the American colonies there was a substantial production and circulation of newspapers in the hinterland.[4]

To leave the dubious realm of signature counts and turn to the

---

[3] Lawrence Stone, "Literacy and Education in England, 1640-1900," *Past & Present*, no. 42 (February, 1969), p. 104. With respect to the literacy of American Indians, note the assertion in Oliver N. Bacon, *History of Natick, from Its First Settlement in 1651 to the Present Time* (Boston: Damrell & Moore, 1856), p. 27, that in 1698 only one child in seventy in that Indian town could read. The problem of literacy among the native Irish was complicated by the prevalence of oral Gaelic as the language of the Roman Catholic indigenes, as contrasted with written English as the language used in much that appeared in print. Such data as I have been able to obtain, using manuscript depositions, deeds, agreements, marriage certificates, and declarations of civil principles, suggest that literacy rates were consistently high in Dublin during the seventeenth and eighteenth centuries—roughly comparable to those in Philadelphia, perhaps, in the latter period, that they were considerably lower in the outlying regions, and that they ran between 40 and 60 per cent among Roman Catholic men at the time of the declaration of civil principles in 1792. Some of the better data are reported in Appendix B.

[4] The statistics for England and Wales are derived from Phyllis Deane and W. A. Cole, *British Economic Growth, 1688-1959* (2d ed.; Cambridge: Cambridge University Press, 1969), p. 16; E. A. Wrigley, "A Simple Model of London's Changing Importance in Changing English Society and Economy 1650-1750," *Past & Present*, no. 37 (July, 1967), pp. 44-45; R. S. Crane and F. B. Kaye, *A Census of British Newspapers and Periodicals, 1620-1800* (Chapel Hill: University of North Carolina Press, 1927); G. A. Cranfield, *The Development of the Provincial Newspaper, 1700- 760* (Oxford: Clarendon Press, 1962); Lucyle Werkmeister, *The London Daily Press, 1772-1792* (Lincoln: University of Nebraska Press, 1963); and Robert R. Rea, *The English Press*

grosser but perhaps more significant realm of newspaper circulation is to raise the fundamental question of what one means by literacy in the first place. At the minimum, literacy implies the technical ability to read and comprehend writing and printing. But there are inevitably the ancillary questions, What sort of writing and printing, and to what purpose? Certainly the English yeoman of the sixteenth century who could read certain passages from Scripture and the liturgy and little else, and who indeed had little need or opportunity to read anything else, was literate in a fundamentally different sense from his counterpart in the eighteenth century who could read a newspaper and who in fact looked forward to reading that newspaper as a source of information on public affairs. In effect, one must distinguish between what might be termed inert literacy, in which a minimal technical competence is combined with limited motivation, need, and opportunity, and a more liberating literacy, in which a growing technical competence is combined with expanding motivation, expanding need, and expanding opportunity. Used in this

in Politics, 1760-1774 (Lincoln: University of Nebraska Press, 1963). The statistics for Ireland are derived from K. H. Connell, The Population of Ireland, 1750-1845 (Oxford: Clarendon Press, 1950), p. 25; Robert Munter, The History of the Irish Newspaper, 1685-1760 (Cambridge: Cambridge University Press, 1967), pp. 87-88 and passim; and Richard Robert Madden, The History of Irish Periodical Literature, from the End of the 17th to the Middle of the 19th Century (2 vols.; London: T. C. Newby, 1867). The statistics for the American colonies are derived from Historical Statistics of the United States, Colonial Times to 1957 (Washington, D.C.: Government Printing Office, 1960), p. 756; Clarence S. Brigham, History and Bibliography of American Newspapers, 1690-1820 (2 vols.; Worcester, Mass.: American Antiquarian Society, 1947); and Arthur M. Schlesinger, Prelude to Independence: The Newspaper War on Britain 1764-1776 (New York: Alfred A. Knopf, 1958), "Appendix A: Newspaper Circulations." The English subscription statistics are based on Cranfield's estimate of 1,000, on the average, for each provincial newspaper in 1760 (I used the figure 1,250 for 1775) and Werkmeister's estimate of under 3,000, on the average, for London newspapers (I used the figure 2,500). The Irish subscription statistics are based on Munter's estimate of 1,000, on the average, for each newspaper, the Dublin newspapers tending to run higher. The American subscription statistics assume 3,600 for Rivington's New-York Gazetteer, 3,500 for The Massachusetts Spy, 3,500 for The Connecticut Courant, and Hartford Weekly Intelligencer, 2,000 for The Boston-Gazette, and Country Journal, 1,500 for The Massachusetts Gazette; and the Boston Weekly News-Letter, 800 for The Providence Gazette; and Country Journal, 1,000 for all other English-language newspapers issuing from Boston, New York, and Philadelphia, and 500 for all other newspapers. Obviously, subscription statistics do not distinguish among weeklies, triweeklies, and dailies; obviously, too, London newspapers enjoyed a healthy circulation in the provinces. And finally, while subscription figures are roughly related to literacy rates, they are also affected by the location of printing facilities and the efficiency of distribution techniques, for example, the post. So far as can be determined, newspaper prices in the three countries were roughly comparable in 1775. There are only the grossest estimates of how many people actually read each copy of each newspaper, though the number seems to have been significantly larger than in the twentieth century.

sense, literacy becomes, not merely the technical ability of an individual, but that technical ability in interaction with a literary environment. And it is with this meaning in mind that one can assert with some confidence, for example, that eighteenth-century literacy rates were generally higher in the American colonies than in Ireland, and roughly equivalent as between English and American white males, with the Americans possibly having a slight edge.

Given these definitions, a special relationship emerges between literacy and schooling that is worthy of note. One can acquire the technical competence of literacy anywhere, in the household, in church, in school, and even in relative isolation. And, in a society with a free press, any individual can turn that technical competence to liberal ends almost entirely on his own, limited only by financial wherewithal, the availability of materials, and his particular horizons. But whether one is encouraged to become literate in the liberating sense can depend in large measure on the context in which one is initially educated. The households of back-country South Carolina, the sectarian churches of western Pennsylvania, and the town schools of Massachusetts and Connecticut all imparted literacy during the 1740's and 1750's, but they imparted different kinds of literacy. And the chances were greater that one would develop a liberating literacy—that is, that one would reach out to intellectual worlds beyond one's own—via the schools. This is not to say that schools were without limitations of philosophy or vision, that schoolmasters did not vary widely in the extent of their training and cosmopolitanism, that there were not households and churches deeply committed to learning, or that the means were not at hand for individuals to transcend the particular limitations of given households or churches. It is merely to suggest a difference in probability, deriving from the historic relationship of schools to learning and to the traditional academic mechanisms for refining, extending, correcting, and communicating knowledge.

Now, it is the historical interaction of a relatively expansive literacy with a relatively inclusive politics that explains much of the character of American society during the latter decades of the eighteenth century. As popular interest in public affairs mounted, a greater number of readers fed the press, which in turn only heightened the motivation to read among ever larger segments of the population. The culmination came during the period from 1774 and 1775, when the great propaganda battles over independence were fought, through the debates over the Constitution in 1787 and 1788. Indeed, it may well be that Revolutionary America achieved the highest intensity of popular interest and participation in politics that any Western society had achieved to that time. American historians have made much in the past of that brilliant galaxy of leaders that came to the fore during the crisis of 1774 to 1789: Franklin, Washington, Jefferson, Madison, Hamilton, Jay, Rush, the Adamses, and a score of others; but they have paid insufficient attention to the extraordinary followership that emerged during the same era, the sort of followership that permitted Jefferson to talk about the wisdom of the people without ultimately sounding like a fool. One can speak of deference politics in describing the social mechanisms of the period, but one must grant that it was deference with taste.[5]

Then, there is the quality of the leadership itself, certainly as extraordinary a generation of statesmen as any in history. If one considers the eighty-nine men who signed either the Declaration of Independence or the Constitution or both, it is clear that the group is a collective outcome of provincial education in all its richness and diversity. Of the fifty-six signers of the Declaration, twenty-two were products of the provincial colleges, two had attended the academy conducted by Francis Alison at New London, Pennsylvania, and the others represented every conceivable combination of parental, church, apprenticeship, school, tutorial, and self- education, including some who had studied abroad. Of the thirty-three signers of the Constitution who had not also signed the Declaration, fourteen were products of the provincial colleges, one was a product of the Newark academy, and the remainder spanned the same wide range of alternative patterns.[6]

Education, then, both formal and informal, played a significant role in the creation of the Republic, though it was education broadly conceived and in constant interaction with politics. But there was even a larger sense in which education and politics converged in the

[5] It was also deference with a sense of psychic identity between leader and follower, as documented in Lloyd I. Rudolph's discussion of leader-follower relationships in European and American eighteenth-century mobs in *American Quarterly*, XI (1959), 447-469. For a more general analysis of American political culture during the Revolutionary period, see Gordon S. Wood, *The Creation of the American Republic, 1776-1787* (Chapel Hill: University of North Carolina Press, 1969).

[6] Conversely, an equally high rate of political leadership, as indicated by office-holding, is evidenced by college graduates. See Donald O. Schneider, "Education in Colonial American Colleges, 1750-1770, and the Occupations and Political Offices of Their Alumni" (unpublished doctoral thesis, George Peabody College for Teachers, 1965), pp. 181 ff.

creation of the Republic and the drafting of the various state constitutions of the 1770's and 1780's, and that is the sense in which education and politics inevitably come together in any act of creative statesmanship. Immersed as they were in the heritage of classical learning, whether popularly conveyed via newspapers, pamphlets, and almanacs, or systematically studied in colleges, academies, or programs of preparation for the law, the founders knew full well that the law educates, inasmuch as it guides, shapes, and ideally governs conduct, and that therefore as they made the laws they were inevitably forming the education of generations of unborn children. Indeed, they had an explicit sense of this as they went about the writing, revising, and ratifying of the various instruments of government. "You and I, my dear friend," John Adams wrote to George Wythe in 1776, "have been sent into life at a time when the greatest lawgivers of antiquity would have wished to live. How few of the human race have ever enjoyed an opportunity of making an election of government, more than of air, soil, or climate, for themselves or their children! When, before the present epoch, had three millions of people full power and a fair opportunity to form and establish the wisest and happiest government that human wisdom can contrive? I hope you will avail yourself and your country of that extensive learning and indefatigable industry which you possess, to assist her in the formation of the happiest governments and the best character of a great people." That same year, Adams put it even more succinctly in a letter to his friend Mercy Warren: "It is the form of government which gives the decisive color to the manners of the people, more than any other thing."[7]

II

The accessibility of education in its many forms was doubtless enhanced by its diversification during the provincial era, for at the very least, as genuine options emerged, larger segments of the populace found themselves attracted to education in the particular terms of

[7] *The Works of John Adams,* edited by Charles Francis Adams (10 vols.; Boston: Charles C. Little and James Brown, 1851), IV, 200. The letter to Wythe was written in response to a query Wythe had put to Adams during an evening's conversation in January, 1776, as to what plan Adams would advise a colony to pursue "in order to get out of the old government and into a new one." Adams' reply, which he drafted the following day, was subsequently published as *Thoughts on Government.* The letter to Mercy Otis Warren was written on January 8, 1776 ("Warren-Adams Letters," Massachusetts Historical Society *Collections,* LXXII [1917], 202).

their own goals and aspirations. This was certainly true in the case of the churches, which reached out to the unaffiliated with novel styles and substance during the course of the awakenings. It was equally true of apprenticeship, as the range of possibilities increased with the proliferation of trades and crafts in the towns and cities. And it was also true of the schools and colleges, as curricula broadened in response to new social demands and intellectual opportunities.

Given the openness of the provincial situation, virtually every major character type of a socially acceptable sort came to be institutionalized, in a manner of speaking, in some major form of education. Thus, Benjamin Franklin, who found the curriculum at the Boston Latin School suffocating, was forced in his own youth to utilize such options as the classes of George Brownell, the apprenticeship to his brother James, and the road he finally chose above all others, self-instruction. Fifty years later, the Philadelphia academy offered in institutionalized form much that Franklin had been forced to obtain on his own. In a sense, the academy had dedicated itself to nurturing the character type subsequently celebrated in Franklin's *Autobiography.* Or, to take another example, David Brainerd was expelled from Yale in 1742 for his revivalist propensities and was forced to complete his education under the Reverend Jedediah Mills of Ripton, Connecticut, before embarking upon his extraordinary career as a missionary to the Indians. Yet, only a few years later, the College of New Jersey was nurturing the very character type Yale had found objectionable, a character type celebrated, incidentally, in the edition of Brainerd's journal that appeared posthumously in 1749 with a panegyrical biography by Jonathan Edwards. Or, to take still another example, Thomas Jefferson, like many Virginians of his time, left the College of William and Mary in 1762 after two years to obtain his real education in the office of George Wythe and the larger society of Williamsburg. Less than a decade later, his younger countryman James Madison was able to obtain under John Witherspoon at the College of New Jersey an education explicitly directed to the goal of public service; twenty-one years later, Madison joined with Patrick Henry and a group of fellow Virginians in obtaining a charter for Hampden-Sydney College, hoping to nurture there precisely the same commitment Witherspoon had taught so well; and meanwhile, of course, George Wythe had been appointed professor of law and police at the College of William and Mary, owing largely to Jefferson's efforts. To cite such instances is not in the least to suggest naïvely that formal institutions pre-empted all of informal education; it is merely to point to the ease and rapidity with which formal institutions, even at the collegiate level, were able to diversify in response to the outgrowths and needs of the American environment.

On the utilitarian side, the diversification of apprenticeships and schooling bore intimate relation to the economy, in that a high birth rate combined with relatively easy access to training, a chronic labor shortage, and an ample supply of raw materials to encourage the rapid development of human capital, that is, the productive potential inherent in human skills. The same encouragement to population increase that Franklin saw in the existence of cheap land was also present in the ready availability of training and employment, with the result that education was a factor not only in the burgeoning of the population but also in the rising productivity of that population. In respect to schooling, this was enhanced by the relative absence of sharp social distinctions between various sorts of institutions. Unlike contemporary England and Ireland, the colonies never maintained any substantial system of charity schooling as a rescue or disciplinary enterprise for the "poor" as a clearly defined social class. The largest American attempt toward such a system was the one developed by the S.P.G., which the colonists seem to have used for their own purposes; the closest American counterpart was the effort of the Society for the Propagation of Christian Knowledge Among the Germans in Pennsylvania, and that simply did not last. At the collegiate level, productivity was enhanced by the preparation of substantial numbers of graduates who chose secular occupations in preference to the ministry. Thus, whereas slightly over half of Harvard's alumni had embarked upon ministerial careers at the beginning of the eighteenth century, that proportion had declined to around a quarter by the late 1760's; and, while the trend was somewhat different at Yale and the College of New Jersey, the two largest institutions after Harvard, both contributed substantial numbers of physicians, lawyers, teachers, and businessmen to the economy.[8]

The colonists themselves were well aware of the close relationship between education and productivity and commented upon it from time to time in their correspondence. For example, when Cadwallader Colden, who for a half-century stood at the center of political and intellectual affairs in New York, first read Franklin's *Proposals*

---

[8] The statistics, presented in detail on page 554, are adapted from Schneider, "Education in Colonial Colleges, 1750-1770."

OCCUPATIONS OF GRADUATES OF HARVARD, YALE,
AND THE COLLEGE OF NEW JERSEY 1700-1770

	Harvard					Yale				College of New Jersey		
	1700	'25	'50	'60	'70	'25	'50	'60	'70	'50	'60	'70
Number of graduates	15	47	19	27	34	9	16	33	19	6	11	22
Ministers	7	17	7	6	9	4	3	13	8	2	4	10
Physicians	1	6	1	3	4	0	4	5	1	2	1	1
Lawyers	0	1	1	4	7	0	2	4	2	0	0	3
Teachers	2	3	1	0	1	0	0	0	0	0	0	2
Merchants	1	5	1	2	2	2	2	1	3	0	2	0
Farmers	0	4	1	2	1	0	0	3	0	0	0	0
Public servants	1	3	1	1	1	1	0	0	0	0	0	1
Minister-teachers	0	1	0	0	0	0	0	1	0	0	1	0
Physician-merchants	0	0	0	0	0	0	1	0	0	0	0	0
Minister-lawyers	0	0	0	1	0	1	0	0	0	0	0	0
Teacher-merchants	0	1	0	0	0	0	0	0	0	0	0	0
Minister-farmers	0	0	0	0	1	0	0	0	0	0	1	0
Minister-public servants	0	1	0	0	1	0	0	0	0	0	1	1
Teacher-farmers	0	0	0	1	1	0	0	0	0	0	0	0
Minister-physicians	0	1	0	0	0	0	0	0	0	0	0	0
Other	3	4	6	7	6	1	4	6	5	2	1	4

Relating to the Education of Youth in Pennsylvania, he wrote to Franklin expressing his pleasure at the inclusion of agriculture in the curriculum—"it is truly the foundation of the wealth and welfare of the country"—and then went on to state his own abiding faith in the union of virtue and useful learning: "It is a common agreement that the power and strength of a nation consists in its riches and money. No doubt money can do great things but I think the power of a nation consists in the knowledge and virtue of its inhabitants and in proof of this history everywhere almost shows us that the richest nations abounding most in silver and gold have been generally conquered by poor but in some sense virtuous nations." Franklin responded several weeks later, conveying the trustees' appreciation for "the useful hints you have favored us with."[9]

[9] Cadwallader Colden to Benjamin Franklin, November, 1749, in *The Papers of Benjamin Franklin,* edited by Leonard W. Labaree and Whitfield J. Bell, Jr. (13+ vols.; New Haven: Yale University Press, 1959-), III, 431-432; Franklin to Colden, February 13, 1750, *ibid.,* p. 462. Note Franklin's return to the theme in much the same language as Colden had used in a letter to Samuel Johnson (August 23, 1750, *ibid.,* IV, 41).

Colden, of course, was never wholly sympathetic with the colonial drift toward utilitarianism, exhibiting throughout his life what Ezra Stiles once referred to as "a superlative contempt for American learning." But Franklin was at the same time its most distinguished embodiment and its most perceptive student. Some years later, when Franklin visited Scotland to accept a doctorate from the University of St. Andrews, he may well have discussed such questions with Professor Adam Smith of Glasgow, and may even have sent along data after his return to America—at the least it is known that Smith had copies of Franklin's *Observations Concerning the Increase of Mankind* in his library. However that may be, when *An Inquiry into the Nature and Causes of the Wealth of Nations* was published in 1776, it devoted a substantial section to the American colonies, flatly stating that the discovery of America and of the passage to the East Indies via the Cape of Good Hope had been the two most important events in the recorded history of mankind.[10]

Smith's views on the bases of prosperity in North America were one with Franklin's, whether or not there had been a shred of influence: he listed the plenitude of land, which kept it cheap; the scarcity of labor, which forced wages up; the rapid increase in population, which he considered the single most decisive index of prosperity; and the availability of metropolitan knowledge and technique, which were in their very nature superior to those of the indigenes. Smith starkly contrasted the situation of Ireland, which had been viciously exploited by a Protestant aristocracy, with that of the colonies, which had enjoyed the benefits of remove from the heavy-handed authority of the metropolis. And he ably detailed the "mean and malignant expedients of the mercantile system," which he saw as deleterious to metropolis and colony alike. Yet, more clearly than anyone else, perhaps, he recognized that the very productivity of the American colonies had made a mockery of mercantilism, for, given the free flow of technical information and the presence of institutions for disseminating it, there was no preventing the colonials from developing their own manufacturing in the attempt to supply their own markets—and any other markets they could reach for that mat-

[10] *The Literary Diary of Ezra Stiles,* edited by Franklin Bowditch Dexter (3 vols.; New York: Charles Scribner's Sons, 1901), II, 78. It is difficult to determine the events surrounding and succeeding Franklin's meeting with Smith at the home of William Robertson, since much of Franklin's correspondence for 1759 has been lost.

ter. In the last analysis, it was distance and education that rendered mercantilism untenable.[11]

Smith concluded his treatise with a plea for the union of Ireland and America with Great Britain, warning that any other policy would leave Ireland to languish under oppression and America to splinter under "democratical" factionalism. Like his contemporary Burke, however, he was too late with his plea for reconciliation: the same educational institutions that had stimulated productivity had sparked independency, and the Atlantic remained as wide as it had ever been.[12]

III

Distance from Whitehall, of course, was only one factor in the general dispersal of authority that raised the continuing specter of independency in eighteenth-century America. Given the multiplicity of original settlements, there was no central capital in the New World itself from which to exercise political, social, and cultural authority, and indeed the several capitals that were attempting to do so found themselves contending daily with a stubborn and insistent localism. Distance had joined with need to create the opportunity for experiment, and the result was a profusion of social innovations on the part of people who, in the very business of living, were forced to modify or abandon traditions simply to survive. It was this interplay of distance, need, and opportunity with human character that elicited the resourcefulness, the industry, and the ingenuity that John Adams associated with the New England town, Hugh Jones with the Virginia county, and Andrew Burnaby with the provincial city. And it led in education to a popularizing of conduct and control as well as of access and substance. In the churches, that popularization manifested itself in the congregationalism that marked most American denominations and in the widespread willingness, at least during the awakenings, to accept the leadership of inspired but unlearned pastors. Among printers, it appeared in the growing effort to meet

[11] Adam Smith, *An Inquiry into the Nature and Causes of the Wealth of Nations,* edited by Edwin Cannan (New York: Random House, 1937), p. 577. The slender evidence for the belief that Franklin may have read *The Wealth of Nations* chapter by chapter as Smith wrote it is summarized in J. Bennett Nolan, *Benjamin Franklin in Scotland and Ireland, 1759 and 1771* (Philadelphia: University of Pennsylvania Press, 1956), p. 200.

[12] Smith, *Wealth of Nations,* p. 897.

the needs and desires of audiences in preference to the wishes and instruction of the authorities. And, in the schools and colleges, it colored the entire developing pattern of management and administration.[13]

In New England, for example, owing to the uncertainties of support by endowment and tuition rates, schooling had early become a function of the towns, with funds generally deriving from taxation supplemented by tuition and control increasingly exercised by the town meeting and the selectmen. But the development had been far from uniform, with constables, justices, elders, deacons, ministers, and overseers of the poor assuming various roles at different times in the several localities. Meanwhile, the selectmen of a number of towns began to appoint special committees or subcommittees to give continuing attention to the care and oversight of schools and especially to the employment of teachers, the erection of schoolhouses, and the management of school funds—the town of Dorchester provided for a committee to oversee such matters as early as 1645. And as towns dispersed precincts were created, which were either assigned or arrogated unto themselves the responsibility for managing education—this development in Dedham has already been sketched. The result, by the time of the Revolution, was the popular control of schooling as a civil responsibility by elected laymen at the provincial, town, and precinct (later, district) levels. Elsewhere, the pattern was less pronounced but entirely discernible. Legislatures and governors in all the colonies regarded education as a legitimate—and, indeed, traditional—domain of public policy. Vestries considered parish schooling as much within their purview as any other aspect of ecclesiastical affairs—recall the intimate involvement of the Elizabeth City vestry with the management of the Syms and Eaton schools. County justices expended a good deal of effort on the proper placement and education of orphans and paupers. And the standard practice with endowed or chartered schools was to have a lay board of trustees, on the early Stuart pattern.

Obversely, the regulation of the teaching profession proved even more difficult than the regulation of the clergy, with the result that movement into teaching was restricted only by halfhearted efforts

[13] We have here, of course, the character traits that Turner attributed to the frontier. But while Turner saw clearly the conservative—in fact, repressive—function of formal education in respect to these traits, he missed the consolidating and transmissive function that education also performed. See Frederick Jackson Turner, *The Frontier in American History* (New York: Henry Holt and Company, 1920), pp. 35-37.

to secure religious uniformity. Licensing requirements failed to prevent Dissenters from teaching in Virginia and South Carolina—recall the incessant complaints of the Reverend Charles Woodmason against Dissenter competition; and the single most conspicuous instance of clerical control and sponsorship, the S.P.G. program, came under widespread suspicion in the 1760's and 1770's, and was eventually suspended. In more populous communities such as Boston, New York, and Philadelphia, virtually anyone who could command a clientele could conduct classes, and indeed the same labor shortage that afflicted every other occupation in the colonies affected teaching, with the result that as salaries approached seventy-five to a hundred pounds per annum for competent individuals, greater numbers of contributors were needed, which in provincial America meant a greater constituency of overseers. As in other realms, the politics and the economics of participation were mutually reinforcing.

These same tendencies affected the provincial colleges, which, like the newborn of any species, seemed perpetually on the brink of starvation. In the first place, the very existence of nine chartered institutions with degree-granting powers was unprecedented, given the size of the population; but the phenomenon itself was indicative, for when the Crown refused to grant a charter, there was always a provincial legislature. And, as has been documented, the search for political and financial support, to say nothing of an adequate clientele, led the various colleges to look well beyond their own constituencies for funds—first, to the colonies at large, and then, increasingly, to Great Britain. This is not to say that the colleges fell into what contemporaries would have called "democratical" hands: their boards of trustees, like provincial assemblies and local vestries, tended to comprise the "better sort" among the merchant and landed gentry and the professional classes. But they did tend increasingly to laicism, in that with the notable exception of Yale they were not composed exclusively or even primarily of clergymen or of the professors who actually offered the instruction.

The boards of the newer dissenting colleges also tended to be interdenominational, another characteristic mark of provincial educational control. Those institutions founded by the establishments, Harvard, William and Mary, Yale, and King's, were ordinarily granted liberal endowments or reasonably assured revenues in their formative years, and remained under the watchful eyes of the dominant ecclesiastical authorities. Yet even they were subject to continuing oversight and interference by their respective legislatures, most directly in Massachusetts and Connecticut. The dissenting institutions, on the other hand, were forced from the beginning to stress their interdenominational character in the composition of both their boards and their student bodies, advertising themselves as "catholic, comprehensive, and liberal." No one, of course, could deny the Presbyterian proclivities of the College of New Jersey or the Baptist proclivities of the College of Rhode Island; but the fact is that non-Presbyterians helped to shape the former, non-Baptists the latter. And the very presence of these dissenters from dissent affected the character of both institutions. Many of the same factors were operative in the case of academies, schools, and libraries that reached across denominational lines for funds and clientele. Indeed, it was such institutions, rather than the churches themselves, that furnished the principal evidence of eighteenth-century denominationalism, once the revivalists had left, and such institutions that in turn were the earliest to be decisively shaped by the new denominationalist sentiments.

Inevitably, the openness of the environment and the competition for clients made the institutions themselves responsive, in that they displayed a characteristic readiness to introduce what the populace seemed to demand. Thus, the printers printed almanacs; the churches sponsored revivals; the grammar schools taught navigation; the academies offered agriculture; the colleges introduced politics; and innumerable private teachers specialized in everything from embroidery to fiddling. In the last analysis, it seemed less important to maintain traditional definitions of education than it did to accommodate those who desired it. Virtually anyone could teach and virtually anyone could learn, at least among whites, and the market rather than the church or the legislature governed through multifarious contractual relationships.

Whether anything was lost in the process is difficult to determine, though there is no denying contemporary concern with the question. Thus, when the Abbé Guillaume Raynal, in the face of mounting provincial self-congratulation about the widespread dissemination of education, charged that America had yet to produce "a good poet, an able mathematician, a man of genius in a single art, or a single science," Jefferson replied:

In war we have produced a Washington, whose memory will be adored while liberty shall have votaries, whose name will triumph over time, and will in future ages assume its just station among the most celebrated worthies of the world, when that wretched philosophy shall be forgotten which would have arranged him among the degeneracies of nature. In physics we have produced a Franklin, than whom no one of the present age has made more important discoveries, nor has enriched philosophy with more, or more ingenious solutions of the phenomena of nature. We have supposed Mr. Rittenhouse second to no astronomer living; that in genius he must be the first, because he is self-taught. As an artist he has exhibited as great a proof of mechanical genius as the world has ever produced. He has not indeed made a world; but he has by imitation approached nearer its Maker than any man who has lived from the creation to this day. As in philosophy and war, so in government, in oratory, in painting, in the plastic art, we might show that America, though but a child of yesterday, has already given hopeful proofs of genius, as well as of the nobler kinds, which arouse the best feelings of men, which call him into action, which substantiate his freedom, and conduct him to happiness, as of the subordinate, which serve to amuse him only.[14]

Jefferson, characteristically, was attempting to answer the good abbé on his own terms. Others might have sounded the common provincial theme that, in the rise of commonwealths, ages of war and agriculture invariably precede ages of art and education, and that when America had endured as long as Greece and Rome it would doubtless have produced its share of genius. And still others, perhaps, might even have suggested that the abbé's terms themselves needed reformulation for republics, where the enlightenment of the people at large was the initial goal of education, and where the invention of institutions to attain that goal was therefore meritorious in its own right.[15]

[14] Thomas Jefferson, *Notes on the State of Virginia* (1785), in *The Writings of Thomas Jefferson*, edited by Paul Leicester Ford (10 vols.; New York: G. P. Putnam's Sons, 1892-1899), III, 166-169.

[15] Jefferson himself discussed the question of the youth of America in *Notes on the State of Virginia*, p. 168. See also Benjamin Franklin to Mary [Polly] Stevenson, March 25, 1763, in *Papers of Benjamin Franklin*, X, 232-233, with its envy of England's concentration of "virtuous and elegant minds" and its allusion to Bishop Berkeley's oft-quoted line, "Westward the course of empire takes its way," from "Verses, on the Prospect of Planting Arts and Learning in America," in *The Works of George Berkeley*, edited by Alexander Campbell Fraser (4 vols.; Oxford: Clarendon Press, 1871), III, 232; Franklin to Charles Willson Peale, July 4, 1771, in *The Crayon*, I (1855), 82; and Franklin to David Hartley, September 6, 1783, in *The Writings of Benjamin Franklin*, edited by Albert Henry Smyth (10 vols.; New York: The Macmillan Company, 1904-1907), IX, 87-88.

IV

Popularization, then, with respect to access, substance, and control, became early and decisively the single most characteristic commitment of American education. It was an optimistic and in many ways messianic commitment, which envisioned America as the new Israel living under a special covenant with God and dedicated to carrying the benefits of the arts and sciences in their highest form to all mankind. It was also a highly utilitarian commitment, which saw no end to the improvement knowledge could effect in the day-by-day lives of ordinary people. And it was ultimately a peaceful commitment, which conceived of education as a means for reconciling hitherto insurmountable differences both within and among the nations of the world. Ezra Stiles articulated it eloquently in his election sermon before the governor and assembly of Connecticut in 1783: "We shall have a communication with all nations in commerce, manners, and science, beyond anything heretofore known in the world. Manufacturers and artisans, and men of every description, may, perhaps, come and settle among us. They will be few indeed in comparison with the annual thousands of our natural increase, and will be incorporated with the prevailing hereditary complexion of the first settlers:—we shall not be assimilated to them, but they to us, especially in the second and third generations. This fermentation and communion of nations will doubtless produce something very new, singular, and glorious. . . . That prophecy of Daniel is now literally fulfilling—there shall be a universal traveling to and fro, and knowledge shall be increased. This knowledge will be brought home and treasured up in America: and being here digested and carried to the highest perfection, may reblaze back from America to Europe, Asia and Africa, and illumine the world with truth and liberty." It was a pompous millennialism, made the more so by a prideful sense that the colonies would soon themselves be a metropolis with all the world as its province; but it was at least humane, preaching nothing more dangerous, so to speak, than the doctrine of universal education, the dominion of the useful arts and sciences, and the ultimate triumph of truth and liberty.[16]

---

[16] Ezra Stiles, *The United States Elevated to Glory and Honor* (New-Haven, Conn.: Thomas & Samuel Green, 1783), pp. 50-52.

Yet, with all its exuberance, Stiles's vision of "God's American Israel" was not without its problems, many of which were incisively analyzed by the Reverend Samuel Miller in *A Brief Retrospect of the Eighteenth Century* (1803). Looking back on the era just completed, Miller had high praise for the educational revolution that was obviously under way. The means of learning had been brought to almost every door, the curriculum had been rendered "more conducive to the useful purposes of life," servility and "monkish habits" had been abandoned, opportunity had been opened to women, and the advantages of education had been "more extensively diffused through the different grades of society than in any former age." And to all this America, given its youth, had made a remarkable contribution.[17]

But along with these admirable advances had come a new doctrine that Miller thought "too pregnant with mischief to be suffered to pass without more particular consideration." It was the doctrine that education "has a kind of intellectual and moral omnipotence; that to its different forms are to be ascribed the chief, if not all the differences observable in the genius, talents, and dispositions of men; and that by improving its principles and plan, human nature may, and finally will, reach a state of absolute perfection in this world, or at least go on to a state of unlimited improvement. In short, in the estimation of those who adopt this doctrine, man is the child of circumstances; and by meliorating these, without the aid of religion, his true and highest elevation is to be obtained; and they even go so far as to believe that, by means of the advancement of light and knowledge, all vice, misery and death may finally be banished from the earth." In good Presbyterian fashion, Miller criticized the doctrine as contrary to the nature of man, inconsistent with the experience of history, and ultimately incompatible with the Scriptural account of the creation and destiny of man. And he warned that both the world and the men who inhabited it would have to change drastically—by which he really meant miraculously—before any such doctrine could prove efficacious. "The millennium of Scripture is represented as a period of knowledge, benevolence, peace, purity, and universal holiness," he concluded; "but the millennium depicted in philosophic dreams, is an absurd portrait of knowledge without

[17] Samuel Miller, *A Brief Retrospect of the Eighteenth Century* (2 vols.; New York: T. and J. Swords, 1803), II, 272-277.

real wisdom, of benevolence without piety, and of purity and happiness without genuine virtue."[18]

Now, however one may judge Miller's strictures, or even his caricature of Enlightenment aspirations, he had surely captured that peculiar mixture of religious enthusiasm and secular yearning that was both the boon and the bane of the American commitment to popular education. At its best, it moved men to dream impossible dreams and then set out to realize them; but, at its worst, it filled them with unfulfillable hopes that could only be answered in some other, more perfect world. In short, for all its nobility, it led men inexorably to the brink of hubris, and then tempted them beyond with visions of the true, the good, and the beautiful.

[18] *Ibid.*, pp. 295, 300.

EPILOGUE

The American war is over; but this is far from being the case
with the American revolution. On the contrary, nothing but the
first act of the great drama is closed. It remains yet to establish
and perfect our new forms of government; and to prepare the
principles, morals, and manners of our citizens for these forms
of government, after they are established and brought to perfection.

BENJAMIN RUSH

Wars interrupt and destroy, and the American Revolution was no
exception. In the clash of arms, custom stands suspended, and, in
education as elsewhere, the cause reigns supreme. Churches and colleges are commandeered for troops; the clergy march off as "fighting
parsons"; schoolmasters and their students don uniforms; and shortages and inflation become the order of the day. And in communities
across the land there are burning and bloodshed and destruction.

"A state of war," Benjamin Trumbull once remarked, "is peculiarly unfriendly to religion. It dissipates the mind, diminishes the
degree of instruction, removes great numbers almost wholly from it,
connects them with the most dangerous company, and presents them
with the worst examples. It hardens and emboldens men in sin; is
productive of profaneness, intemperance, disregard to property, violence and all licentious living." Trumbull had every reason to know,
having served as chaplain to General Jeremiah Wadsworth's brigade
during the latter months of 1776 and having captained a company of
sixty volunteers during the remainder of the war. And, though as
pastor of North Haven's Congregational church he was wont to
confuse deism with profanity and churchlessness with infidelity, his
sense that the Revolution had loosened the bonds of Christian piety
was undeniably accurate. Churches had been burned; loyalist min-

isters had fled their pulpits; schism had rent several of the leading denominations; clergymen had been ordained under the most dubious circumstances; and congregations had fallen to new lows in size and fervency. Everywhere, it seemed to Trumbull and his contemporaries, the war had unhinged the principles, the morality, and the religion of the country.[1]

In the schools and colleges there was similar turmoil. Local institutions undoubtedly continued in their traditional ways, subject to the incessant depredations of inflation and the occasional depredations of the contending armies. The colleges, however, were more severely affected. Harvard's buildings were appropriated by the provincial congress in the spring of 1775—tradition has it that Professor Winthrop spent two days packing his apparatus and books, assisted by the future Count Rumford—and the following fall the faculty and students reassembled at Concord for instruction, using the meetinghouse, the courthouse, and the schoolhouse for recitations. Yale suffered persistent food shortages during 1776 and 1777, and was actually dispersed in March of the latter year to three inland towns, the freshmen to Farmington, the sophomores and juniors to Glastonbury, and the seniors to Wethersfield. Having reconvened in New Haven in the summer of 1778, the faculty and students were present to assist in the defense of the town against the British invasion of July 5, 1779, when Professor Daggett distinguished himself by taking on a detachment of regulars singlehandedly, assisted only by a large and unwieldy fowling piece.[2]

The College of New Jersey was caught squarely in the midst of the hostilities during 1776 and 1777, serving alternately as barracks and hospital for a succession of British and Continental troops, with neither side treating the facilities gently. By the end of it all, Nassau was a heap of ruin. Nearby Queen's College, located precisely at the center of the British stronghold at New Brunswick, was forced to move, first to a small hamlet on the Raritan known as North Branch, and then to Millstone, some eight miles west of New Brunswick. The College of William and Mary was more fortunate, having to suspend instruction for only a few months directly preceding and

---

[1] Benjamin Trumbull, *A Complete History of Connecticut* (2 vols.; New-Haven: Maltby, Goldsmith and Co. and Samuel Wadsworth, 1818), II, 18. See also Timothy Dwight, *Travels in New-England and New-York* (4 vols.; London: printed for William Baynes and Son, and Ogle, Duncan, & Co., 1823), IV, 353-359.
[2] See Peter Colt's description of the encounter in the Massachusetts Historical Society *Collections*, 7th ser., II (1902), 401-404.

following the siege of Yorktown. But the president's house was badly damaged by French troops who occupied it after the surrender of General Cornwallis in October, 1781.[3]

King's College witnessed mob violence in 1775, and it was only through the prompt intervention of the youthful Alexander Hamilton that President Myles Cooper was able to escape to an English sloop of war lying at anchor in New York harbor. Several months later, the college's buildings were commandeered as a hospital by a local Committee of Safety, only to be taken over a few weeks after that by occupying British troops. Meanwhile, instruction went forward for the remainder of the war on a vastly reduced basis in a private house under the leadership of Acting President Benjamin Moore. The College of Philadelphia experienced similar difficulty with the Committee of Safety there and finally suspended operation entirely in the spring of 1777, being used first as a Continental billet and then as a British hospital. And the College of Rhode Island served successively as a barracks for Continental and French troops and did not actually return to its proper work until June of 1782. Only Dartmouth escaped the immediacies of the Revolution, and it was later to lose heavily through withdrawals of English pledges of support.

The press also suffered the ravages of war, being hurt as much by shortages of paper and rags as by mob or military violence. Of thirty-seven newspapers circulating in April, 1775, only twenty survived the hostilities, and some of these were forced to suspend publication from time to time. In addition, of another thirty-three launched during the course of the conflict, only fifteen lasted until the surrender at Yorktown. Of course, the survival rate of newspapers had never been high during the eighteenth century, but these statistics clearly indicate the toll taken by the war. Interestingly enough, such censorship as was actually enforced during the period of hostilities was mostly by the mob action of patriot groups against the Tory press, the royal governors having long abandoned the effort to curb printers because of the unwillingness of juries to sustain their charges. The number of issues as a whole fell sharply as the war progressed, reaching a nadir in 1782 and then turning rapidly upward with the signing of the peace treaty.

[3] For a description of Princeton as "a deserted village" and Nassau in ruin, see Benjamin Rush to Richard Henry Lee, January 7, 1777, in Richard H. Lee, *Memoir of the Life of Richard Henry Lee* (2 vols.; Philadelphia: H. C. Carey and I. Lea, 1825), II, 164.

The Revolution interrupted and destroyed, then, though the destruction was limited and in some considerable measure temporary. Yet in the clash of arms men are also thrown together for new purposes and under new circumstances, and hence wars frequently teach and originate at the same time as they interrupt and destroy. Here, too, the Revolution was no exception. The sense of cohesion and nationality that had been developing in Americans since the 1740's and 1750's—nurtured, incidentally, by all the major institutions of education—was deepened and enlarged as common goals were defined, common efforts mounted, and common adversities endured. And, almost as if to symbolize this quickening patriotism, primers began to appear in Philadelphia as early as 1779 bearing engraved portraits of General Washington. Beyond this, there was a vast process of mutual instruction and accommodation as English, French, and German troops mixed with Americans, and as the Continentals rubbed shoulders with one another. Particularly in medicine, there were associations of inestimable value in lifting the general state of the art. The youthful James Thacher of Massachusetts marveled at the incredible "skill and dexterity" of the English army surgeons and reported his own sustained excitement over a conversation with the "learned Doctor Shippen" of Philadelphia; while John Warren, who had first studied medicine as an apprentice to his brother, was moved after serving with French physicians in Boston and with the eminent Dr. Morgan at Cambridge and in New York to assume leadership in the subsequent establishment of the Harvard Medical School. For hundreds of other physicians, military service afforded literally their first opportunity to see the inside of a hospital, however primitive and however filthy. Many of the same fruitful exchanges occurred in engineering, the sciences, and the arts, and especially in politics, where the members of the Continental Congress seem to have been ever conscious of their role in mutual education. In fact, John Adams went so far as to liken that body to a "school of political prophets," in which successive groups of Americans might be prepared for the arduous responsibilities of statesmanship.[4]

In these and countless other ways, the Revolution proved a piv-

---

[4] *A Primer. Adorned with a Beautiful Head of General Washington and Other Copper Plate Cuts* (Philadelphia: printed for Walters and Norman, 1779); James Thacher, *Military Journal During the Revolutionary War, from 1775-1783* (Hartford: Silas Andrus & Son, 1854), pp. 112, 195; and *The Works of John Adams,* edited by Charles Francis Adams (10 vols.; Boston: Charles C. Little and James Brown, 1851), IX, 339.

otal occasion in the history of American education. But it was an occasion rather than a social movement, a cataclysmic event that confirmed a century of provincial educational experience at the same time that it created new circumstances and set in motion new developments. On the very eve of hostilities, Edmund Burke, in his moving speech on conciliation with the colonies, masterfully portrayed that experience in seeking the sources of the "disobedient spirit" Parliament stood determined to crush. "Then, sir," he observed, summing up a lengthy discourse on the American temper, "from these six capital sources, of descent, of form of government, of religion in the northern provinces, of manners in the southern, of education, of the remoteness of situation from the first mover of government,—from all these causes a fierce spirit of liberty has grown up. It has grown with the growth of the people in your colonies, and increased with the increase of their wealth: a spirit, that, unhappily meeting with an exercise of power in England, which, however lawful, is not reconcilable to any ideas of liberty, much less with theirs, has kindled this flame that is ready to consume us." In short, rooted as it was in the English heritage and removed as it was from the sources of metropolitan authority, provincial life had served the Americans as a schooling in freedom. Many years later, John Adams reiterated the assertion in his oft-quoted remark that the real revolution was effected before the war ever began, "in the minds and hearts of the people." Conciliation failing, the war itself simply confirmed the experience from which it had derived.[5]

But the war also transformed the meaning of the provincial experience; for in severing the political ties to England it hastened the need for that rethinking and recasting of American education that was already under way but not yet completed. However jubilant the young republicans were at their triumph over tyranny, their dominant sense was one of beginning rather than culmination, in the words of Adams to Wythe, of instituting "the wisest and happiest government that human wisdom can contrive." That government would be free but also virtuous, and, to ensure both freedom and virtue, the citizenry would require education. "America must be as independent in literature as she is in politics—as famous for arts as

[5] "Speech on Moving His Resolutions for Conciliation with the Colonies, March 22, 1775," in The Works of the Right Honorable Edmund Burke (rev. ed.; 12 vols.; Boston: Little, Brown, and Company, 1865-1867), II, 125, 126-127; and John Adams to Hezekiah Niles, February 13, 1818, Works of John Adams, X, 282.

for arms—and it is not impossible, but a person of my youth may have some influence in exciting a spirit of literary industry," a fervent but unknown young schoolmaster named Noah Webster wrote in 1783 to his friend John Canfield. And, later that same year, he boldly issued a new spelling book, the first part of *A Grammatical Institute, of the English Language, Comprising, an Easy, Concise, and Systematic Method of Education, Designed for the Use of English Schools in America,* the purpose of which was nothing less than the instruction of American youth in the love of virtue, liberty, and learning:

The author wishes to promote the honor and prosperity of the confederated republics of America; and cheerfully throws his might into the common treasure of patriotic exertions. This country must in some future time, be as distinguished by the superiority of her literary improvements, as she is already by the liberality of her civil and ecclesiastical constitutions. Europe is grown old in folly, corruption and tyranny—in that country laws are perverted, manners are licentious, literature is declining and human nature debased. For America in her infancy to adopt the present maxims of the Old World, would be to stamp the wrinkles of decrepit age upon the bloom of youth and to plant the seeds of decay in a vigorous constitution. American glory begins to dawn at a favorable period, and under flattering circumstances. We have the experience of the whole world before our eyes; but to receive indiscriminately the maxims of government, the manners and the literary taste of Europe and make them the ground on which to build our systems in America, must soon convince us that a durable and stately edifice can never be erected upon the moldering pillars of antiquity. It is the business of Americans to select the wisdom of all nations, as the basis of her constitutions,—to avoid their errors,—to prevent the introduction of foreign vices and corruptions and check the career of her own,—to promote virtue and patriotism,—to embellish and improve the sciences,—to diffuse a uniformity and purity of language,—to add superior dignity to this infant empire and to human nature.[6]

The sense of young Webster and his contemporaries, then, was that the Revolution had ushered in a new era during which for the first time in history men could live in true freedom and dignity under forms of their own devising. "The American war is over," Benjamin Rush wrote in 1787. "But this is far from being the

6 Noah Webster to John Canfield, January 6, 1783 (Webster mss., New York Public Library); and Noah Webster, *A Grammatical Institute, of the English Language, Comprising, an Easy, Concise, and Systematic Method of Education, Designed for the Use of English Schools in America. In Three Parts. Part I* (Hartford: Hudson & Goodwin, [1783]), pp. 14-15.

case with the American revolution. On the contrary, nothing but the first act of the great drama is closed. It remains yet to establish and perfect our new forms of government, and to prepare the principles, morals, and manners of our citizens for these forms of government after they are established and brought to perfection." And no one was more eager than Philadelphia's indefatigable young physician to get on with the play.[7]

[7] Benjamin Rush, "Address to the People of the United States (1787)," in Hezekiah Niles, *Republication of the Principles and Acts of the Revolution in America* (New York: A. S. Barnes & Co., 1876), p. 234.

APPENDICES

The method I take to do this, is not yet very usual; for instead of using only comparative and superlative words, and intellectual arguments, I have taken the course (as a specimen of the political arithmetic I have long aimed at) to express myself in terms of number, weight, or measure.

WILLIAM PETTY

APPENDIX A. *Derivation of New York City and Philadelphia Population Statistics in Chapter 17*

NEW YORK CITY

1. *Source of population statistics*

   All statistics are based on data in Evarts B. Greene and Virginia D. Harrington, *American Population Before the Federal Census of 1790* (New York: Columbia University Press, 1932).

2. *Area*

   All statistics are for the county (which was co-existent with the city). Thus, teachers in Harlem or the Bowery are included.

3. *Interpolation*

   A. Ten available statistics were used as a skeleton for population growth. The first two, for 1656 and 1664, represent contemporary estimates. The other eight are based on actual city censuses.

1656	1,000	1737	10,664
1664	1,500	1746	11,717
1698	4,937	1756	13,040
1703	4,436	1771	21,863
1712	5,840	1786	23,614

   B. For all the "ghost" years between these ten statistics, population was assumed to increase (and in one instance to decrease) in constant numbers per year. Statistics for the "ghost" years were therefore determined by calculating simple arithmetic progressions, not by calculating constant percentage increases or decreases.

C. For example:

$$\text{Total population, New York City, } 1698 = 4,937$$
$$\text{Total population, New York City, } 1664 = 1,500$$
$$\text{Population increase, } 1664\text{–}1698 = 3,437$$

Dividing 3,437 by 34 years, the assumed increase in population per year is 101

Therefore, estimated population, 1665 = 1,500 + 101 = 1,601
Therefore, estimated population, 1666 = 1,601 + 101 = 1,702

D. This method obviously results in such awkward assertions as:

New York City's population increased by 101 persons from 1697 to 1698; *but* New York City's population decreased by 100 persons from 1698 to 1699.

E. To soften such awkward and unverified shifts, five-year averages were computed and used in the tables.

4. *Numbers of children*

A. For five of the ten skeleton years, the percentage of white children under sixteen years of age is known. For those years, the ratio of white children under sixteen to the total population was computed:

1703	41.2%
1746	35.2
1756	35.4
1771	34.3
1786	47.0

B. For the years between 1703 and 1786, the same method of arithmetic increase or decrease was used as with the total population (see 3B above), but percentages were computed rather than actual numbers of children. This was indicated since both the total population and the ratio of children to adults can change independently.

C. For the years between 1656 and 1703, no ratios of children to adults are available. For lack of a better statistic, an average of the five known ratios from the later period—or 38%—was used for 1656 and the same arithmetic increases were computed to reach a ratio of 41.2% in 1703.

D. Numbers of children were calculated by multiplying the estimated total population for a given year by the estimated percentage of children.

5. *Numbers of children of school age*

It was assumed that children between the ages of five and sixteen were of school age. It was also assumed that, owing to high infant mortality, there were more children between the ages of birth and four than between the ages of five and nine or ten and fourteen. Therefore, an arbitrary ratio of .67 was used to estimate the number of children of school age within the total child population. This estimate is probably somewhat high.

PHILADELPHIA

1. *Source of population statistics*

Much less is known about the population of Philadelphia than of New York City, there having been no actual census until 1790. The statistics here are based on data in Greene and Harrington, *American Population Growth Before the Federal Census of 1790*, p. 117, and on tax rolls reprinted in the *Pennsylvania Archives*, 3d ser., XIV (1897), and in *The Pennsylvania Magazine of History and Biography*, VIII (1884), 82–105. Population estimates derived from the number of taxable individuals were computed using a multiplier of 4, as discussed in the introduction to Greene and Harrington, *American Population Growth*.

2. *Area*

Unlike New York City, a large part of Philadelphia County's population resided outside the town (city), in relatively isolated communities. Most commonly cited population estimates are for the county. The actual relationship of the town (city) population to the county population is known at only a few points:

	Town (City)	County	Percentage
1693	1,444	3,016	47.9%
1769	11,336	34,412	32.9
1774	13,196	33,440	39.4
1779	13,708	41,144	33.3

The average of the percentages of 1769, 1774, and 1779 is 35.2. Therefore the assumption is made that the town (city) population decreased steadily in relation to the total county population between 1693 and 1779, from 48% to approximately 35%. Arithmetic interpolation was used, as before, to estimate the ratio of town (city) to county population in years for which only the latter datum is available. Since only two basic statistics are involved, the interpolation formula may be written as follows:

$$\frac{\text{Town (City) Population}}{\text{County Population}} = .48 - [(Y - 1693) \times .0015]$$

where Y is the year in question and .0015 is the annual decrease in the ratio of town (city) population to county population.

3. *Skeleton*

Year	Town (City) Population	Derivation
1693	1,444	Town taxables (from list in the *Pennsylvania Magazine of History and Biography*, VIII [1884], 82-105) multiplied by 4.

1720	3,507	County taxables (from Greene and Harrington, *American Population Growth*, p. 117) multiplied by 4; and interpolation formula.
1735	6,284	Town taxables (from Greene and Harrington, *American Population Grow.h*, p. 117) multiplied by 4.
1740	7,944	County taxables (from Greene and Harrington, *American Population Growth*, p. 117) multiplied by 4; and interpolation formula.
1751	11,161	*Ibid.*
1760	12,629	*Ibid.*
1774	13,196	Town taxables (from list in the *Pennsylvania* Archives, 3d ser., XIV [1897]) multiplied by 4.
1779	13,708	*Ibid.*

A population statistic for the town (city) of 11,336 for 1769, derived from the list for that year in the *Pennsylvania Archives*, 3d ser., XIV (1897), has been omitted from the skeleton, since it would seem to imply a population decrease during the 1760's, which is improbable. More likely the decrease reflects a change in tax qualifications or some other factor than an actual population decline.

4. *Interpolation*

Once the skeleton had been constructed, statistics for "ghost" years were derived following the procedures used for New York City.

5. *Numbers of children*

Since no statistics are available for colonial Philadelphia, the percentages computed for New York City were used for Philadelphia. The procedure assumes that Philadelphia was more like New York City in this respect than it was like the rest of Pennsylvania, an assumption concurred in by W. S. Rossiter in *A Century of Population Growth from the First Census of the United States to the Twelfth, 1790-1900* (Washington, D.C.: Government Printing Office, 1909), chap. i. In calculating numbers of children of school age, the procedures used for New York City were followed.

APPENDIX B. *Signatures and Marks on Seventeenth- and Eighteenth-Century Irish Documents*

CITY OF DUBLIN

1. In a collection of depositions and petitions regarding the rebellion of 1641, made principally by upper-class Protestants in 1642 and 1643, 90 signed their names, 3 made marks. Interestingly, of 24 "gentlewomen" in the sample, 23 signed their names (Supplementary Volume to Collection of Depositions Regarding the Rebellion of 1641, Manuscripts Room, Trinity College, Dublin).

2. In the records of the Guild of St. Luke, indicating the admission of apprentices and the signing of the bylaws, between 1670 and 1695, 297 signed their names, 11 made marks (Records of the Guild of St. Luke, National Library of Ireland, Dublin).

3. In the same records, for the years 1701 to 1723, 147 signed their names, 3 made marks.

4. In the records of the Corporation of Barber Surgeons, indicating bonds and witnesses to bonds, between 1705 and 1719, 89 signed their names, 8 made marks (Records of the Corporation of Barber Surgeons, No. 9 Book of Bonds, Manuscripts Room, Trinity College, Dublin).

5. In collections of Quaker marriage settlements and certificates, dating from 1710 to 1755 and involving 117 men and 65 women (including brides, bridegrooms, and guests), 181 signed their names, 1 made his mark. It would appear that a significant number of women failed to sign these documents for one reason or another, some, perhaps, because of potential embarrassment over their inability to write their names (Quaker Marriage Certificates [D 8959, D 10,085-10,094], National Library of Ireland, Dublin).

6. In articles of agreement of the Broadcloth Manufacturers, drawn in 1730, 62 men signed their names, 19 made marks (Articles of Agreement of the Broadcloth Manufacturers [M 739], Public Records Office, Dublin).

COUNTY CORK

1. On various deeds, marriage agreements, and inventories dating from c. 1607 to 1698, 179 signed their names, 55 made marks. Of the 89 known men in the group, 69 signed their names, 20 made marks; of the 9 known women in the group, 1 signed her name, 8 made marks (Caulfield mss., Manuscripts Room, Trinity College, Dublin).

2. On various deeds, marriage agreements, and inventories, dating from 1709 to 1780, 48 signed their names, 2 made marks. Of the 20 known men in the group, 20 signed their names; of the 6 known women in the group, 4 signed their names, 2 made marks (Caulfield mss., Manuscripts Room, Trinity College, Dublin).

COUNTIES TYRONE AND ARMAGH

1. In 1792 the General Committee of the Catholics in Ireland sponsored a movement to persuade the authorities that Roman Catholics could be good citizens despite the fact that they did not belong to the established church. The committee circulated a declaration of civil principles throughout the country, to which a large number of subscriptions was obtained. Of 3,820 subscribers in County Tyrone, 1,904 signed their names (904 of these seem to have had their names written by others owing to the striking similarity of their signatures), 553 appear as explicitly having asked that their names be written by others since "they are persons who write not themselves," 1,346 appear on lists that may well fall into the preceding category but may also have been drawn up by parish priests without reference to the subscribers'

ability to sign their names, and 17 made marks (Sirr mss., Manuscripts Room, Trinity College, Dublin).

2. Of 3,230 subscribers in County Armagh, 2,665 signed their names (986 of these seem to have had their names written by others owing to the striking similarity of their signatures), 111 appear as explicitly having asked that their names be written by others since they "could not write themselves," and 454 made their marks (Sirr mss., Manuscripts Room, Trinity College, Dublin).

3. Of 949 subscribers in one parish of County Armagh (included in the 3,230 mentioned above), 591 signed their names (the document is difficult to read, but there are at least a few signatures clearly done by a single hand), 358 made marks. The priest, Father James Crowley, noted the following on the declaration: "The enclosed subscription amounts to about 1,200 and this parish contains many more women and 3,000 children at the lowest computation who with the voice of their parents do make the same declaration and do expect from the goodness of their sovereign a participation in the franchise election and the benefit of trial by jury" (Sirr mss., Manuscripts Room, Trinity College, Dublin).

BIBLIOGRAPHICAL ESSAY

Of making many books there is no end; and much study is a weariness of the flesh.

ECCLESIASTES

Anyone who would undertake a fresh study of American education during the colonial era must perforce begin with Bernard Bailyn's remarkable little book *Education in the Forming of American Society* (Chapel Hill: University of North Carolina Press, 1960). Bailyn called it an essay in hypothetical history, because it was based on scattered and incompletely assembled evidence. Yet, there is no escaping its extraordinarily provocative analysis. Seeking to depart from the traditional account of colonial education, which had been marred throughout by the search for the origins of the public school, Bailyn approached his problem with a new definition of education—namely, "the entire process by which a culture transmits itself across the generations." His attention was thereby directed not merely to the schools and colleges but also to other time-honored educators: family, church, and community. And on the basis of this broader exploration he suggested five major theses: first, that formal schooling assumed new cultural burdens in the colonies because of drastic changes in the character and composition of the family (he referred here to a shift from an extended family structure in England to a nuclear family structure in the colonies); second, that with land abundant and labor at a premium, apprenticeship rapidly surrendered certain of its traditional educative functions; third, that the initial effort to convert the Indians to Christianity introduced a new social role for schools as agencies of acculturation; fourth, that public support for education derived not from ideological principles but from a chronic lack of surplus private wealth; and, finally, that by the end of the eighteenth century American education had undergone a radical transformation, which can be understood only as part of a larger transformation in the social, economic, and religious life of the colonies and that it is this transformation, rather than the early Puritan educational legislation, that marked the genesis of the later public-school movement. Taken together, of course, these theses reflect what has now become a fairly familiar account of the colonial era: a story of transplantation followed by transformation, resulting in the emergence of a distinctively American culture in the eighteenth century. The approach is apparent in Bailyn's studies of eighteenth-century politics, in which the Revolution confirms and ratifies changes that have long been in the making; and it is inherent in more general form in Daniel Boorstin's engaging work *The Americans: The Colonial Experience* (New York: Random House, 1958), though Boorstin's analysis tends in my opinion to overemphasize the autochthonous at the expense of the transplanted in the development of American culture and to undervalue ideas as moving forces in the lives of men.

Since it was initially prepared as a volume in the consistently excellent *Needs and Opportunities for Study* series of the Institute of Early American History and Culture at Williamsburg, Virginia, Bailyn's book is replete with bibliographical suggestions and commentary; and, apart from his tendency to distinguish too sharply and neatly between the interpretations of academic historians and those of educational historians, I find myself generally in agreement with his appraisals. My own essay *The Wonderful World of Ellwood Patterson Cubberley* (New York: Teachers College, Columbia University, 1965) represented an effort to carry forward the historiographical discussion Bailyn had initiated, giving particular attention to his definition of education, which I found so latitudinarian as to afford the would-be chronicler of education too few canons for the selection of his material, and sketching somewhat more fully than Bailyn had been able to do the history of the historiography of American education. Other discussions in somewhat the same vein are Paul H. Buck *et al.*, *The Role of Education in American History* (New York: Fund for the Advancement of Education, 1957), Wilson Smith, "The New Historian of American Education," *Harvard Educational Review*, XXXI (1961), 136-143, William W. Brickman, "Revision and the Study of the History of Education," *History of Education Quarterly*, IV (1964), 209-223, and the several articles on "new directions" in the *History of Education Quarterly*, IX (1969), 329-375. The generic problems of the relation of history and the social sciences are incisively raised by John Herman Randall in Salo W. Baron, Ernest Nagel, and Koppel S. Pinson, eds., *Freedom and Reason* (Glencoe, Ill.: The Free Press, 1951), pp. 287-308, and by George W. Stocking in "On the Limits of 'Presentism' and 'Historicism' in the Historiography of the Behavioral Sciences," *Journal of the History of the Behavioral Sciences*, I (1965), 211-217; while the more general context of American historiography within which all such problems must be discussed is ably sketched by Robert Allen Skotheim in *American Intellectual Histories and Historians* (Princeton: Princeton University Press, 1966). A useful anthropological analysis evoked by Bailyn's definition of education is John D. Herzog, "Deliberate Instruction and Household Structure: A Cross-Cultural Study," *Harvard Educational Review*, XXXII (1962), 301-342.

Given my own approach to education, certain standard works in social and intellectual history proved consistently valuable during the course of my research, notably, Perry Miller, *The New England Mind* (2 vols.; Cambridge, Mass.: Harvard University Press, 1939-1953), Max Savelle, *Seeds of Liberty: The Genesis of the American Mind* (New York: Alfred A. Knopf, 1948), Clinton Rossiter,

Seedtime of the Republic: The Origin of the American Tradition of Political Liberty (New York: Harcourt, Brace & World, 1953), the first four volumes of A History of American Life, edited by Arthur M. Schlesinger and Dixon Ryan Fox—namely, Herbert I. Priestley, *The Coming of the White Man, 1492-1848* (New York: The Macmillan Company, 1929), Thomas Jefferson Wertenbaker, *The First Americans, 1607-1690* (New York: The Macmillan Company, 1927), James Truslow Adams, *Provincial Society, 1690-1763* (New York: The Macmillan Company, 1927), and Evarts Boutell Greene, *The Revolutionary Generation, 1763-1790* (New York: The Macmillan Company, 1943), Louis B. Wright, *The Cultural Life of the American Colonies* (New York: Harper & Brothers, 1957), Edward Eggleston, *The Transit of Civilization from England to America in the Seventeenth Century* (New York: D. Appleton and Company, 1900), Moses Coit Tyler, *A History of American Literature, 1607-1765* (2 vols.; G. P. Putnam's Sons, 1878), Vernon Louis Parrington, *Main Currents in American Thought: The Colonial Mind, 1620-1800* (New York: Harcourt, Brace, and Company, 1927), Constance Rourke, *The Roots of American Culture and Other Essays,* edited by Van Wyck Brooks (New York: Harcourt, Brace and Company, 1942), Louis Hartz, *The Founding of New Societies* (New York: Harcourt, Brace & World, 1964), I. Woodbridge Riley, *American Philosophy: The Early Schools* (New York: Dodd, Mead & Company, 1907), Howard Mumford Jones, *O Strange New World: American Culture, The Formative Years* (New York: The Viking Press, 1964), and Daniel J. Boorstin, *The Americans: The Colonial Experience,* already alluded to.

Also valuable were such standard demographic materials as Charles O. Paullin, *Atlas of the Historical Geography of the United States,* edited by John K. Wright (Washington, D.C.: Carnegie Institution of Washington, 1932), Herman R. Friis, *A Series of Population Maps of the Colonies and the United States, 1625-1790* (New York: The American Geographical Society, 1940), *A Century of Population Growth from the First Census of the United States to the Twelfth, 1790-1900* (Washington, D.C.: Government Printing Office, 1909), Evarts B. Greene and Virginia D. Harrington, *American Population Before the Federal Census of 1790* (New York: Columbia University Press, 1932), and Stella H. Sutherland, *Population Distribution in Colonial America* (New York: Columbia University Press, 1936). My practice in general was to cite the Sutherland statistics on colonial population from *Historical Statistics of the United States: Colonial Times to 1957* (Washington, D.C.: Government Printing Office, 1960), p. 756, in the absence of overwhelming evidence to the contrary.

Like every American historian, I derived invaluable assistance throughout from such bibliographical aids as Justin Winsor, ed., *Narrative and Critical History of America* (8 vols.; Boston: Houghton, Mifflin and Company, 1884-1889), an older work whose continuing worth is too infrequently acknowledged, Oscar Handlin *et al.,* eds., *Harvard Guide to American History* (Cambridge, Mass.: Harvard University Press, 1954), Roy P. Basler, Donald H. Mugridge, and Blanche P. McCrum, *A Guide to the Study of the United States of America* (Washington, D.C.: Government Printing Office, 1960), George Howe *et al.,* eds., *Guide to Historical Literature* (New York: The Macmillan Company, 1961), and Nelson R. Burr *et al., A Critical Bibliography of Religion in America* (2 vols.; Princeton: Princeton University Press, 1961). And, like everyone who has studied the colonial era, I found Charles Evans, ed., *American Bibliography* (12 vols. with a 13th edited by Clifford K. Shipton; imprint varies, 1903-1955) and Joseph Sabin and Wilberforce Eames, eds., *Bibliotheca Americana* (29 vols.; New York: publisher varies, 1868-1936), along with the *Early American Imprints* series based on them, issued by the American Antiquarian Society under the editorship of Clifford K. Shipton, absolutely indispensable.

For comparable assistance in the field of British history, I turned to Conyers Read, ed., *Bibliography of British History: Tudor Period, 1485-1603* (2d ed.; Oxford: Clarendon Press, 1959), Godfrey Davies, *Bibliography of British History: Stuart Period, 1603-1714* (Oxford: Clarendon Press, 1928), Perez Zagorin, "English History, 1558-1640: A Bibliographical Survey," *The American Historical Review*, LXVIII (1962-63), 364-384, Robert Walcott, "The Later Stuarts (1660-1714): Significant Work of the Last Twenty Years (1939-1959)," *ibid.*, LXVII (1961-62), 352-370, William A. Bultmann, "Early Hanoverian England (1714-1760): Some Recent Writings," *The Journal of Modern History*, XXXV (1963), 46-61, Lawrence Henry Gipson, *A Bibliographical Guide to the History of the British Empire, 1748-1776* (New York: Alfred A. Knopf, 1969), the last volume of his magisterial work *The British Empire Before the American Revolution* (rev. ed.; 14 vols.; New York: Alfred A. Knopf, 1958-1969), and, of course, the short-title catalogues, A. W. Pollard and G. R. Redgrave, *A Short-Title Catalogue of Books Printed in England, Scotland & Ireland and of English Books Printed Abroad, 1475-1640* (London: The Bibliographical Society, 1926) and Donald Wing, *Short-Title Catalogue of Books Printed in England, Scotland, Ireland, Wales, and British America and of English Books Printed in Other Countries, 1641-1700* (3 vols.; New York: Columbia University Press, 1945-1951).

INTRODUCTION TO BOOK I

The most valuable source for material relating to the colonization movements of Renaissance Europe is the series published by the Hakluyt Society, which now numbers well over two hundred volumes. Of particular relevance to the *Discourse of Western Planting* and the historical context within which it was written are *The Original Writings & Correspondence of the Two Richard Hakluyts*, edited by E. G. R. Taylor, Works Issued by the Hakluyt Society, 2d ser., vols. LXXVI-LXXVII (2 vols.; London: The Hakluyt Society, 1935), David Beers Quinn, ed., *The Voyages and Colonising Enterprises of Sir Humphrey Gilbert*, Works Issued by the Hakluyt Society, 2d ser., vols. LXXXIII-LXXXIV (2 vols.; London: The Hakluyt Society, 1940), and David Beers Quinn, ed., *The Roanoke Voyages, 1584-1590*, Works Issued by the Hakluyt Society, 2d ser., vols. CIV-CV (2 vols.; London: The Hakluyt Society, 1955). English theories of colonization during the Renaissance are ably discussed by Howard Mumford Jones in "Origins of the Colonial Idea in England," *Proceedings of the American Philosophical Society*, LXXXV (1942), 448-465, and in *O Strange New World: American Culture, The Formative Years* (New York: The Viking Press, 1964), chap. v, by R. Dunlop in "Sixteenth Century Schemes for the Plantation of Ulster," *The Scottish Historical Review*, XXII (1925), 51-60, 115-126, 199-212, by David Beers Quinn in "Sir Thomas Smith (1513-1577) and the Beginnings of

English Colonial Theory," *Proceedings of the American Philosophical Society,* LXXXIX (1945), 543-560, by Louis B. Wright in *Religion and Empire: The Alliance Between Piety and Commerce in English Expansion, 1558-1625* (Chapel Hill: University of North Carolina Press, 1943), and by Klaus E. Knorr in *British Colonial Theories, 1570-1850* (Toronto: University of Toronto Press, 1944). Dutch theories of colonization, particularly as they affected New Netherland, are discussed in Van Cleaf Bachman, *Peltries or Plantations: The Economic Policies of the Dutch West India Company in New Netherland, 1623-1639* (Baltimore: Johns Hopkins Press, 1969). The colonizing movement itself is vividly portrayed by J. H. Parry in *The Age of Reconnaissance* (Cleveland, O.: The World Publishing Company, 1963). And the first English accounts of the New World are presented in Louis B. Wright, ed., *The Elizabethans' America* (Cambridge, Mass.: Harvard University Press, 1965). The definitive biography of Hakluyt is George Bruner Parks, *Richard Hakluyt and the English Voyages,* edited by James A. Williamson (2d ed.; New York: Frederick Ungar Publishing Co., 1961).

The settlement of New England, New York, and the Chesapeake colonies is the subject of a vast literature, much of it contentiously filiopietistic in character. Charles Andrews' monumental *The Colonial Period of American History* (4 vols.; New Haven: Yale University Press, 1934-1938) remains the most balanced and comprehensive account; while the Original Narratives of Early American History, edited by J. Franklin Jameson (19 vols.; Charles Scribner's Sons, 1906-1917) and Peter Force, ed., *Tracts and Other Papers, Relating Principally to the Origin, Settlement, and Progress of the Colonies in North America, from the Discovery of the Country to the Year 1776* (4 vols.; Washington, D.C.: Peter Force, 1836-1846) remain the most useful collections of source material. Among older works, Herbert L. Osgood, *The American Colonies in the Seventeenth Century* (3 vols.; New York: The Macmillan Company, 1904-1907) proved exceedingly helpful, as did Thomas Jefferson Wertenbaker's more recent trilogy, *The Founding of American Civilization* (3 vols.; New York: Charles Scribner's Sons, 1938-1947). The best anthology of recent perspectives and interpretations is James Morton Smith, ed., *Seventeenth-Century America: Essays in Colonial History* (Chapel Hill: University of North Carolina Press, 1959).

For Virginia, beyond the traditional compilations of Alexander Brown, Susan Myra Kingsbury, and others conveniently listed in Oscar Handlin *et al., Harvard Guide to American History* (Cambridge, Mass.: Harvard University Press, 1954), I found Wesley Frank Craven's *Dissolution of the Virginia Company* (New York: Oxford University Press, 1932), and *The Southern Colonies in the Seventeenth Century, 1607-1689,* A History of the South, edited by Wendell Holmes Stephenson and E. Merton Coulter (Baton Rouge: Louisiana State University Press, 1949), Sigmund Diamond's *The Creation of Society in the New World* (Chicago: Rand McNally & Company, 1963), and Richard L. Morton, *Colonial Virginia* (2 vols.; Chapel Hill: University of North Carolina Press, 1960) especially germane to my concerns; while Philip Alexander Bruce's *Institutional History of Virginia in the Seventeenth Century* (New York: G. P. Putnam's Sons, 1910) afforded a comprehensive overview of educational developments, outdated, perhaps, in some of its interpretations, but not in the accuracy of its data.

For Massachusetts, in addition to the wealth of primary source material available through the *Collections* and *Proceedings* of the Massachusetts Historical Society, the *Publications* of the Colonial Society of Massachusetts, the *Proceedings* of the American Antiquarian Society, and the *Publications* of the Prince Society, and beyond the standard accounts listed in the *Harvard Guide to American History,* I found Bernard Bailyn's *The New England Merchants in the Seventeenth Century* (Cambridge, Mass.: Harvard University Press, 1955), Perry Miller's *Errand into the Wilderness* (Cambridge, Mass.: Harvard University Press, 1956), Edmund S. Morgan's *The Puritan Dilemma* (Boston: Little, Brown and Company, 1958) and *Visible Saints* (New York: New York University Press, 1963), David D. Hall's "The Faithful Shepherd: The Puritan Ministry in Old and New England, 1570-1660" (unpublished doctoral thesis, Yale University, 1963), and Darrett B. Rutman's *Winthrop's Boston* (Chapel Hill: University of North Carolina Press, 1965) especially valuable. Samuel Eliot Morison's engaging polemic *The Puritan Pronaos: Studies in the Intellectual Life of New England in the Seventeenth Century* (New York: New York University Press, 1936), reprinted in 1956 as *The Intellectual Life of Colonial New England,* remains the most comprehensive overview of early New England education, though it does not deal with the family.

The so-called middle colonies present a special historiographical problem, which is ably discussed by Richard H. Shryock in "Historical Traditions in Philadelphia and in the Middle Atlantic Area: An Editorial," *The Pennsylvania Magazine of History and Biography,* LXVII (1943), 115-141. For New Netherland and New York, the best collections of source materials remain E. B. O'Callaghan, ed., *Documents Relative to the Colonial History of the State of New York* (10 vols. and General Index; Albany: Weed, Parsons and Company, 1856-1861), and *The Documentary History of the State of New York* (4 vols.; Albany: publisher varies, 1850-1851), Berthold Fernow, ed., *The Records of New Amsterdam, from 1653 to 1674 Anno Domini* (7 vols.; New York: The Knickerbocker Press, 1897), and Edward T. Corwin, ed., *Ecclesiastical Records, State of New York* (7 vols.; Albany: J. B. Lyon and Company, 1901-1916). Of the works listed in the *Harvard Guide to American History,* Albert E. McKinley, "The Transition from Dutch to English Rule in New York," *The American Historical Review,* VI (1900-01), 693-724, I. N. Phelps Stokes, *The Iconography of Manhattan Island, 1498-1909* (6 vols.; New York: Robert H. Dodd, 1915-1928), Mrs. Schuyler Van Rensselaer, *History of the City of New York in the Seventeenth Century* (2 vols.; The Macmillan Company, 1909), and Ellis Lawrence Raesly, *Portrait of New Netherland* (New York: Columbia University Press, 1945) proved the more valuable, though, as Shryock suggests, the historiography of colonial New York is neither as advanced nor as sophisticated as that of colonial Virginia and New England. A recent effort to review the commercial origins of New Netherland is Thomas J. Condon, *New York Beginnings* (New York: New York University Press, 1968). No single volume affords a comprehensive introduction to education in seventeenth-century New York, in the fashion of Bruce's *Institutional History of Virginia in the Seventeenth Century* or Morison's *The Puritan Pronaos.* The closest approach, though a limited one, is William Heard Kilpatrick, *The Dutch Schools of New Netherland and Colonial New York* (Washington, D.C.: Government Printing Office, 1912).

Obviously, the theory of cultural diffusion asserted in the final pages of the introduction is a refinement of the position first put forth by Edward Eggleston in *The Transit of Civilization from England to America in the Seventeenth Century* (New York: D. Appleton and Company, 1900) and more recently argued by Louis B. Wright in *Culture on the Moving Frontier* (Bloomington: Indiana University Press, 1955) and by Bernard Bailyn in *Education in the Forming of American Society* (Chapel Hill: University of North Carolina Press, 1960). Brief overviews of England during the era of settlement may be gleaned from Wallace Notestein, *The English People on the Eve of Colonization, 1603-1630* (New York: Harper & Brothers, 1954), Christopher Hill, *The Century of Revolution, 1603-1714*, A History of England, edited by Christopher Brooke and Denis Mack Smith (Edinburgh: Thomas Nelson and Sons, 1961), and Carl Bridenbaugh, *Vexed and Troubled Englishmen, 1590-1642* (New York: Oxford University Press, 1968); of the Netherlands during the same era, from Pieter Geyl, *The Netherlands in the 17th Century* (2 vols.; New York: Barnes and Noble, 1961), Charles R. Boxer, *The Dutch Seaborne Empire, 1600-1800*, The History of Human Society, edited by J. H. Plumb (New York: Alfred A. Knopf, 1965), and J. A. van Houtte *et al.*, eds., *Algemene Geschiedenis der Nederlanden* (12 vols.; Utrecht: W. De Hann, 1949-1958), V-VI; and of Europe during the same era, from G. N. Clarke, *The Seventeenth Century* (2d ed.; Oxford: Clarendon Press, 1947), Carl J. Friedrich, *The Age of the Baroque, 1610-1660* (New York: Harper & Brothers, 1952), and E. E. Rich and C. H. Wilson, eds., *The Economy of Expanding Europe in the Sixteenth and Seventeenth Centuries*, The Cambridge Economic History of Europe (Cambridge: Cambridge University Press, 1967). A sense of the multifarious relationships between English and Continental culture may be obtained from Albert Hyma, "The Continental Origins of English Humanism," *The Huntington Library Quarterly*, IV (1940-1941), 1-25, D. W. Davies, *Dutch Influences on English Culture, 1558-1625* (Ithaca: Cornell University Press, 1964), Lewis Einstein, *The Italian Renaissance in England* (New York: Columbia University Press, 1902), and Sidney Lee, *The French Renaissance in England* (Oxford: Clarendon Press, 1910). Vera Brown Holmes, *A History of the Americas: From Discovery to Nationhood* (New York: The Ronald Press Company, 1950) affords a perspective on the larger New World context of North American settlement, as does Silvio Zavala, "A General View of the Colonial History of the New World," *The American Historical Review*, LXVI (1960-61), 913-929. And James E. Gillespie discusses the impact of the New World on England in *The Influence of Oversea Expansion on England to 1700* (New York: Longmans, Green & Co., 1920).

INTRODUCTION TO PART I

My conception of the English Renaissance, which I use as a convenient phrase for referring to the period roughly from 1480 to 1660, derives from a line of argument that received early statement in Douglas Bush's Alexander Lectures at the University of Toronto, published under the title *The Renaissance and English Humanism* (Toronto: University of Toronto Press, 1939), that underwent further development in the Renaissance Conferences held at the Huntington Library in 1940 and 1941 and reported in volumes IV and V of *The Huntington Library Quarterly* (1940-1942), and that was thereafter accepted, both implicitly and explicitly, by a vastly significant school of educational scholarship that included J. H. Hexter's now-classic essay "The Education of the Aristocracy in the Renaissance," *The Journal of Modern History*, XXII (1950), 1-20, Conyers Read's *Social and Political Forces in the English Reformation* (Houston: The Elsevier Press, 1953), R. R. Bolgar's *The Classical Heritage and Its Beneficiaries* (Cambridge: Cambridge University Press, 1954), Fritz Caspari's *Humanism and the Social Order in Tudor England* (Chicago: University of Chicago Press, 1954), Mark H. Curtis' *Oxford and Cambridge in Transition, 1558-1642* (Oxford: Clarendon Press, 1959), W. K. Jordan, *Philanthropy in England, 1480-1660* (London: George Allen & Unwin, 1959), Lawrence Stone's "The Educational Revolution in England, 1560-1640," *Past & Present*, no. 23 (July, 1964), 41-80, and Kenneth Charlton's *Education in Renaissance England* (London: Routledge and Kegan Paul, 1965). Within this view, the Renaissance describes a period of English history to which, in the words of F. Smith Fussner, the Reformation gave "peculiar and distinctive character." For a discussion of this and alternative modes of viewing the Renaissance, see Fussner's *The Historical Revolution: English Historical Writing and Thought, 1580-1640* (London: Routledge and Kegan Paul, 1962) and Wallace K. Ferguson, *The Renaissance in Historical Thought* (Boston: Houghton Mifflin Company, 1948).

That the colonies were settled during the time when the West was moving from an oral to a typographic culture is of incalculable significance for the present work. The movement itself and its bearing on culture and education are explicated in Walter J. Ong, *The Presence of the Word* (New Haven: Yale University Press, 1967), which includes an excellent bibliography, Albert B. Lord, *The Singer of Tales* (Cambridge, Mass.: Harvard University Press, 1960), Marshall McLuhan, *The Gutenberg Galaxy* (Toronto: University of Toronto Press, 1962), Joan Marie Lechner, *Renaissance Concepts of the Commonplaces* (New York: Pageant Press, 1962), Frances Yates, *The Art of Memory* (Chicago: University of Chicago Press, 1966), and Elizabeth L. Eisenstein, "Some Conjectures About the Impact of Printing on Western Society and Thought: A Preliminary Report," *The Journal of Modern History*, XL (1968), 1-56, and "The Advent of Printing and the Problem of the Renaissance," *Past & Present*, no. 45 (November, 1969), 19-89. It is only against an understanding of this movement and the inevitable limitations it imposes on writings as source materials that one can consider using writings as vehicles for an understanding of Renaissance educational ideas. Frederick Bailey, "The Historical Ballad: Its Tradition in Britain and America" (unpublished doctoral thesis, University of Tennessee, 1963) and Tristram P. Coffin, *The British Traditional Ballad in North America* (rev. ed.; Philadelphia: The American Folklore Society, 1963) are useful introductions to the substance of the oral tradition.

Given my argument that we cannot, on the one hand, confine our attention to the writings of the colonists themselves, as, for example, Moses Coit Tyler did in *A History of American Literature, 1607-1765* (2 vols.; New York: G. P. Putnam's Sons, 1878), nor, on the other hand, assume that writings available in England were necessarily or even widely known in the colonies, as, for example,

Perry Miller did in *The New England Mind* (2 vols.; Cambridge, Mass.: Harvard University Press, 1939-1953), I have devoted particular attention to the books the colonists owned or had access to, as evidenced by letters, wills, diaries, inventories, printed catalogues, and records of colonial imprints. Apart from the notations in individual volumes in the Harvard College Library, the Massachusetts Historical Society Library, the American Antiquarian Society Library, the Yale University Library, the Columbia University Library, the New York Public Library, the Folger Shakespeare Library, and the Newberry Library, and the particular letters, wills, and diaries I was able to examine, I relied in substantial measure on studies of American book ownership, such as Louis B. Wright, *The Cultural Life of the American Colonies* (New York: Harper & Brothers, 1957), and *The First Gentlemen of Virginia: Intellectual Qualities of the Early Colonial Ruling Class* (San Marino, Calif.: The Huntington Library, 1940), Thomas Goddard Wright, *Literary Culture in Early New England* (New Haven: Yale University Press, 1920), Philip Alexander Bruce, *Institutional History of Virginia in the Seventeenth Century* (2 vols.; New York: G. P. Putnam's Sons, 1910), Samuel Eliot Morison, *The Puritan Pronaos: Studies in the Intellectual Life of New England in the Seventeenth Century* (New York: New York University Press, 1936), George K. Smart, "Private Libraries in Colonial Virginia," *American Literature*, X (1938), 24-52, George Emery Littlefield, *Early Boston Booksellers, 1642-1711* (Boston: The Club of Odd Volumes, 1900), Worthington Chauncey Ford, *The Boston Book Market, 1679-1700* (Boston: The Club of Odd Volumes, 1917), Franklin B. Dexter, "Early Private Libraries in New England," *Proceedings of the American Antiquarian Society*, new ser., XVIII (1907), 135-147, Charles F. Robinson and Robin Robinson, "Three Early Massachusetts Libraries," *Publications of the Colonial Society of Massachusetts*, XXVIII (1935), 107-175, William S. Powell, "Books in the Virginia Colony Before 1624," *The William and Mary Quarterly*, 3d ser., V (1948), 177-184, Ellis Lawrence Raesly, *Portrait of New Netherland* (New York: Columbia University Press, 1945), James D. Hart, *The Popular Book: A History of America's Literary Taste* (Berkeley: University of California Press, 1961), Louis Shores, *Origins of the American College Library, 1638-1800* (New York: Barnes & Noble, 1934), and Joe Walker Kraus, "Book Collections of Five Colonial College Libraries; A Subject Analysis" (unpublished doctoral thesis, University of Illinois, 1960). Wright's chapter on "Books, Libraries, and Learning" in *The Cultural Life of the American Colonies* conveys an excellent sense of the purposefulness with which the colonists read the books they brought with them to the New World; the Kraus thesis contains a comprehensive bibliography of articles detailing the holdings of seventeenth-century Harvard. In addition, I derived considerable benefit from Carl F. Kaestle's "Index to Seventeen Colonial New England Libraries, 1629-1776," an unpublished paper in the library of the Institute of Philosophy and Politics of Education at Teachers College.

CHAPTER 1: THE PRACTICE OF PIETY

The most balanced recent treatment of the Reformation in England is A. G. Dickens, *The English Reformation* (New York: Schocken Books, 1964), while the most interesting recent discussion of the intellectual history of the English

Reformation is Charles H. George and Katherine George, *The Protestant Mind of the English Reformation, 1570-1640* (Princeton: Princeton University Press, 1961). The Georges' tendency to see common strains in Anglican and Puritan thought is ably challenged by John F. H. New in *Anglican and Puritan: The Basis of Their Opposition, 1558-1640* (Stanford: Stanford University Press, 1964), though I continue to find the Georges' treatment persuasive. The broader movement of the Continental Reformation is vividly sketched in Roland H. Bainton, *The Reformation of the Sixteenth Century* (Boston: The Beacon Press, 1952), Harold J. Grimm, *The Reformation Era* (New York: The Macmillan Company, 1954), and Preserved Smith's older but immensely readable *The Age of the Reformation* (New York: Henry Holt and Company, 1920). E. Harris Harbison's *The Christian Scholar in the Age of the Reformation* (New York: Charles Scribner's Sons, 1955) is a sensitive portrayal of the various intellectual roles that came to the fore during the Reformation. The particular nature of English Puritanism is imaginatively characterized in William Haller, *The Rise of Puritanism* (New York: Columbia University Press, 1938), and *Liberty and Reformation in the Puritan Revolution* (New York: Columbia University Press, 1955), Marshall M. Knappen, *Tudor Puritanism* (Chicago: University of Chicago Press, 1939), Patrick Collinson, *The Elizabethan Puritan Movement* (Berkeley: University of California Press, 1967), Christopher Hill, *Puritanism and Revolution* (London: Secker & Warburg, 1958), and *Society and Puritanism in Pre-Revolutionary England* (New York: Schocken Books, 1964), Michael Walzer, *The Revolution of the Saints* (Cambridge, Mass.: Harvard University Press, 1965), and G. R. Cragg, *From Puritanism to the Age of Reason* (Cambridge: Cambridge University Press, 1950), and *Puritanism in the Period of the Great Persecution, 1660-1688* (Cambridge: Cambridge University Press, 1957). Richard B. Schlatter, *The Social Ideas of Religious Leaders, 1660-1688* (London: Oxford University Press, 1940) is a valuable general discussion. Brian Magee, *The English Recusants* (London: Burns, Oates & Washbourne, 1938), Patrick McGrath, *Papists and Puritans Under Elizabeth I* (London: Blandford Press, 1967), William R. Trimble, *The Catholic Laity in Elizabethan England* (Cambridge, Mass.: Harvard University Press, 1964), and A. C. F. Beales, *Education Under Penalty: English Catholic Education from the Reformation to the Fall of James II, 1547-1689* (London: The Athlone Press, 1963) are useful guides to Recusancy.

The most recent scholarly biography of Desiderius Erasmus is Roland H. Bainton, *Erasmus of Christendom* (New York: Charles Scribner's Sons, 1969); given the nature of its subject, it complements rather than supersedes earlier works such as Preserved Smith, *Erasmus: A Study of His Life, Ideals and Place in History* (New York: Harper & Brothers, 1923), Margaret Mann Phillips, *Erasmus and the Northern Renaissance* (London: Hodder & Stoughton, 1949), and Johan Huizinga, *Erasmus of Rotterdam* (London: Phaidon Press, 1952). *Erasmi opera omnia,* edited by Johannes Clericus (10 vols.; Leiden: J. Leclercq, 1703-1706) and *Opus epistolarum Des. Erasmi Roterodamo, denuo recognitum et auctum,* edited by P. S. Allen, H. M. Allen, and H. W. Garrod (12 vols.; Oxford: Clarendon Press, 1906-1958), remain invaluable, though there are good English editions of most of the major works and there is the splendid edition of *The Epistles of Erasmus*, translated and edited by Francis Morgan Nichols (3 vols.; London: Longmans, Green, and Co., 1901-1918). Frederic Seebohm's classic, *The Oxford Reformers: John Colet, Erasmus, and Thomas More* (2d ed.; London: Longmans, Green, and Co., 1869) still serves as an excellent guide to English Erasmianism, though it should be supplemented by later works such as Fritz Caspari, *Humanism and the Social Order in Tudor England* (Chicago: University of Chicago Press, 1954) and James Kelsey McConica, *English Humanists and Reformation Politics Under Henry VIII and Edward VI* (Oxford: Clarendon Press, 1965).

J. F. Mozley, *William Tyndale* (New York: The Macmillan Company, 1937) is the best biography of the Protestant Erasmian, while R. W. Chambers, *Thomas More* (London: Jonathan Cape, 1935) is the standard work on the Catholic statesman. W. E. Campbell, *Erasmus, Tyndale and More* (London: Eyre & Spottiswoode, 1949) discusses the intellectual relations among the three contemporaries. The development of the English Bible and its rise to pre-eminence as a popular book are traced in Margaret Deansley, *The Lollard Bible* (Cambridge: Cambridge University Press, 1920), C. C. Butterworth, *The Literary Lineage of the King James Bible, 1340-1611* (Philadelphia: University of Pennsylvania Press, 1941), S. L. Greenslade, ed., *The Cambridge History of the Bible* (Cambridge: Cambridge University Press, 1963), and Alfred W. Pollard, ed., *Records of the English Bible: The Documents Relating to the Translation and Publication of the Bible in English, 1525-1611* (London: Oxford University Press, 1911). And Tyndale's vernacular style is discussed in educational terms by George Philip Krapp in *The Rise of English Literary Prose* (New York: Oxford University Press, 1915) and by Richard Foster Jones in *The Triumph of the English Language* (Stanford: Stanford University Press, 1953).

The Bible itself, particularly the Geneva edition of 1560 and the Authorized Version of 1611, is the single most important primary source for the intellectual history of colonial America. A good deal of work remains to be done on the character and scope of that influence; meanwhile, P. Marion Simms, *The Bible in America* (New York: Wilson-Erickson, 1936) serves as a useful guide to the editions that have circulated at different periods in American history.

The English devotional literature is brilliantly discussed by Helen C. White in *English Devotional Literature [Prose], 1600-1640* (Madison: University of Wisconsin, 1931), *The Tudor Books of Private Devotion* (Madison: University of Wisconsin Press, 1951), and *Tudor Books of Saints and Martyrs* (Madison: University of Wisconsin Press, 1963). Louis B. Wright also deals with the genre in *Middle-Class Culture in Elizabethan England* (Chapel Hill: University of North Carolina Press, 1935), as does H. S. Bennett in *English Books & Readers, 1558 to 1603: Being a Study in the History of the Book Trade in the Reign of Elizabeth I* (Cambridge: Cambridge University Press, 1965).

William Haller's *Foxe's Book of Martyrs and the Elect Nation* (London: Jonathan Cape, 1963) is a splendid account of the development of the *Actes and Monuments,* and nicely complements J. F. Mozley's older work *John Foxe and His Book* (London: Society for Promoting Christian Knowledge, 1940). There is a sketch of Lewis Bayly in *The Dictionary of National Biography,* while *The Practise of Pietie* is dealt with in J. E. Bailey, "Bishop Lewis Bayly and His 'Practice of Piety,' " *The Manchester Quarterly*, II (1883), 201-219. Bayly's manual was read in New Netherland, incidentally, under the title *De Practycke ofte Oeffeninghe der Godsaligheyt*. Richard Allestree has been dealt with more systematically than Bayly. In addition to the sketch in *The Dictionary of National Biography*, there are Paul H. Elman, "The Works of Richard Allestree: A Critical Study" (unpublished doctoral thesis, Harvard University, 1947), which makes an irrefutable case for Allestree's authorship of *The Whole Duty of Man*, and John Alfred Thomas, "The Sermons and Attributed Works of Richard Allestree" (unpublished doctoral thesis, University of Maryland, 1963).

The best introduction to Richard Baxter is Irvonwy Morgan, *The Nonconformity of Richard Baxter* (London: The Epworth Press, 1946). Critical insights may also be gleaned from Charles F. Kemp, *A Pastoral Triumph: The Story of Richard Baxter & His Ministry at Kidderminster* (New York: The Macmillan Company, 1948), Hugh Martin, *Puritanism and Richard Baxter* (London: SCM Press, 1954), Richard Schlatter, ed., *Richard Baxter and Puritan Politics* (New Brunswick: Rutgers University Press, 1957), and N. H. Mair, "Christian Sanctification and Individual Pastoral Care in Richard Baxter" (unpublished doctoral thesis, Union Theological Seminary, 1967). Baxter wrote an autobiography, which became widely available in the Everyman's Library edition issued by J. M. Dent & Sons in 1931; in addition, the biography by William Orme in *The Practical Works of the Rev. Richard Baxter* (23 vols.; London: James Duncan, 1830), I, 1-412, is still useful. There is an excellent collection of Baxter correspondence (with an index by Geoffrey F. Nuttall) and Baxter manuscripts (with a catalogue by Roger Thomas) at Dr. Williams's Library in London.

Roger Sharrock, *John Bunyan* (London: Hutchinson House, 1954), Henri Talon, *John Bunyan: The Man and His Works* (London: Rockliff Publishing Corporation, 1951), Robert Morris O'Neil, "The Role of Christian in *The Pilgrim's Progress*" (unpublished doctoral thesis, University of Washington, 1964), and William York Tindall, *John Bunyan: Mechanick Preacher* (New York: Columbia University Press, 1934) are the best introductions to Bunyan and his work. David Edwin Smith's "John Bunyan in America: A Critical Inquiry" (unpublished doctoral thesis, University of Minnesota, 1962) deals principally with the influence of *The Pilgrim's Progress* in the nineteenth century, but the first three chapters bear on the colonial era.

The domestic conduct books are discussed in Wright, *Middle-Class Culture in Elizabethan England*, Chilton Latham Powell, *English Domestic Relations, 1487-1653* (New York: Columbia University Press, 1917), Charles H. George and Katherine George, *The Protestant Mind of the English Reformation* (Princeton: Princeton University Press, 1961), and Michael Walzer, *The Revolution of the Saints* (Cambridge, Mass.: Harvard University Press, 1965). The role of the domestic conduct books in the life of the American colonies is treated in Sandford Fleming, *Children & Puritanism: The Place of Children in the Life and Thought of the New England Churches, 1620-1847* (New Haven: Yale University Press, 1933) and Edmund S. Morgan, *The Puritan Family: Religion and Domestic Relations in Seventeenth-Century New England* (rev. ed.; New York: Harper & Row, 1966).

Renaissance preachments on preaching are discussed in Edward Charles

Dargan, *A History of Preaching* (2 vols.; New York: publisher varies, 1905-1912), W. Fraser Mitchell, *English Pulpit Oratory from Andrewes to Tillotson* (London: Society for Promoting Christian Knowledge, 1932), William Haller, *The Rise of Puritanism* (New York: Columbia University Press, 1938), Alan Fager Herr, *The Elizabethan Sermon: A Survey and Bibliography* (Philadelphia: no publisher, 1940), Christopher Hill, *Society and Puritanism in Pre-Revolutionary England* (New York: Schocken Books, 1964), Irvonwy Morgan, *The Godly Preachers of the Elizabethan Church* (London: The Epworth Press, 1965), and George and George, *The Protestant Mind of the English Reformation;* while the particular contributions of William Perkins are ably set forth by Louis B. Wright in "William Perkins: Elizabethan Apostle of 'Practical Divinity,' " *The Huntington Library Quarterly,* II (1939-40), 171-196, and by I. Breward in "The Life and Theology of William Perkins, 1558-1602" (unpublished doctoral thesis, University of Manchester, 1963). Preaching in the seventeenth-century colonies is explicated in Babette May Levy, *Preaching in the First Half Century of New England History* (Hartford, Conn.: The American Society of Church History, 1945), Roy Fred Hudson, "The Theory of Communication of Colonial New England Preachers, 1620-1670" (unpublished doctoral thesis, Cornell University, 1953), David D. Hall, "The Faithful Shepherd: The Puritan Ministry in Old and New England, 1570-1660" (unpublished doctoral thesis, Yale University, 1963), and Norman Pettit, *The Heart Prepared: Grace and Conversion in Puritan Spiritual Life* (New Haven: Yale University Press, 1966). The substance and context of this preaching are dealt with in Perry Miller, *The New England Mind* (2 vols.; Cambridge, Mass.: Harvard University Press, 1939-1953), Herbert W. Schneider, *The Puritan Mind* (New York: Henry Holt and Company, 1930). Alan Simpson, *Puritanism in Old and New England* (Chicago: University of Chicago Press, 1955), and George Maclaren Brydon, *Virginia's Mother Church and the Political Conditions Under Which It Grew* (2 vols.; imprint varies, 1947-1952).

There is a brief sketch of John Brinsley in *The Dictionary of National Biography;* the context of his life and work may be gleaned from Foster Watson, *The English Grammar Schools to 1660: Their Curriculum and Practice* (Cambridge: Cambridge University Press, 1908), T. W. Baldwin, *William Shakspere's Small Latine & Lesse Greeke* (2 vols.; Urbana: University of Illinois Press, 1944), and Kenneth Charlton, *Education in Renaissance England* (London: Routledge and Kegan Paul, 1965).

CHAPTER 2: THE NURTURE OF CIVILITY

The Renaissance civility book, as both a literary and an educational genre, is discussed in Ruth Kelso, *The Doctrine of the English Gentleman in the Sixteenth Century* (Urbana: University of Illinois, 1929), and *Doctrine for the Lady of the Renaissance* (Urbana: University of Illinois Press, 1956), W. Lee Ustick, "The English Gentleman in the Sixteenth and the Early Seventeenth Century: Studies in the Literature of Courtesy and Conduct" (unpublished doctoral thesis, Harvard University, 1931), John E. Mason, *Gentlefolk in the Making* (Philadelphia: University of Pennsylvania Press, 1935), Fritz Caspari, *Humanism and the Social Order in Tudor England* (Chicago: University of Chicago Press, 1954), Arthur B. Ferguson, *The Indian Summer of English Chivalry* (Durham: Duke University Press, 1960), and *The Articulate Citizen and the English Renaissance* (Durham: Duke University Press, 1965), and Patricia Ann Lee, "The Ideal of the English Gentleman in the Early Seventeenth Century" (unpublished doctoral thesis, Columbia University, 1966). In addition, the introduction to Desiderius Erasmus, *The Education of a Christian Prince,* edited by Lester K. Born (New York: Columbia University Press, 1936) includes a lengthy analysis of the prince's mirror as a medieval genre, while George C. Brauer, Jr., *Theories of Gentlemanly Education in England, 1660-1775* (New York: Bookman Associates, 1959) carries the analysis forward into Restoration and eighteenth-century England.

The comparison of Erasmus's *Christian Prince,* Thomas More's *Utopia,* and Niccolò Machiavelli's *The Prince* is a common theme in writings on Renaissance political thought, though the bearing on education of the similarities and differences among the three treatises has not been adequately explored. The works on Erasmus cited in connection with Chapter 1 are relevant here. More's political philosophy is ably explicated in Russell Ames, *Citizen Thomas More and His Utopia* (Princeton: Princeton University Press, 1949), J. H. Hexter, *More's Utopia: The Biography of an Idea* (Princeton: Princeton University Press, 1952), Edward Surtz, *The Praise of Pleasure: Philosophy, Education, and Communism in More's Utopia* (Cambridge, Mass.: Harvard University Press, 1957), and the introduction to the *Utopia* in *The Complete Works of St. Thomas More,* edited by Edward Surtz and J. H. Hexter (14 vols.; New Haven: Yale University Press, 1963-   ), vol. IV. Machiavelli's political philosophy is brilliantly analyzed in Giuseppe Prezzolini, *Machiavelli* (New York: Farrar, Straus & Giroux, 1967), which is a translation and condensation of Prezzolini's *Machiavelli Anticristo* (Rome: Gherardo Casini Editore, 1954). Felix Gilbert, "The Humanist Concept of the Prince and *The Prince* of Machiavelli," *The Journal of Modern History,* XI (1939), 449-483, Robert P. Adams, "Designs by More and Erasmus for a New Social Order," *Studies in Philology,* XLII (1945), 131-145, and C. R. Thompson, "Erasmus as Internationalist and Cosmopolitan," *Archiv für Reformationsgeschichte,* XLVI (1955), 167-195, were particularly relevant to my concern with civility as an educational concept; while J. W. Allen, *A History of Political Thought in the Sixteenth Century* (London: Methuen & Co., 1928), Pierre Mesnard, *L'Essor de la Philosophie Politique au XVIe Siècle* (Paris: Boivin, 1936), and Christopher Morris, *Political Thought in England: Tyndale to Hooker* (London: Oxford University Press, 1953) provided useful general background.

Sir Thomas Elyot has been the subject of a good deal of recent work, including Stanford E. Lehmberg, *Sir Thomas Elyot: Tudor Humanist* (Austin: University of Texas Press, 1960), John M. Major, *Sir Thomas Elyot and Renaissance Humanism* (Lincoln: University of Nebraska Press, 1964), and Pearl Hogrefe, *The Life and Times of Sir Thomas Elyot, Englishman* (Ames: Iowa State University Press, 1967). Thomas Elyot, *The Boke Named the Governour,* edited by Henry Herbert Stephen Croft (2 vols.; London: Kegan Paul, Trench, & Co., 1883) remains the best edition of the classic. William Harrison Woodward, *Studies in Education During the Age of the Renaissance, 1400-1600* (Cambridge:

Cambridge University Press, 1906) and Kenneth Charlton, *Education in Renaissance England* (London: Routledge and Kegan Paul, 1965) are excellent guides to the debates over education that marked the Renaissance in Italy and England and to the influence of the Italian debates on the English. Caspari's *Humanism and the Social Order in Tudor England* is the best account of the triumph of the humanist ideal in education, though Caspari's optimism about the triumph needs the qualification that derives from a perusal of Anthony Esler's *The Aspiring Mind of the Elizabethan Younger Generation* (Durham: Duke University Press, 1966), which views the alienation of the later Elizabethans as partly a result of the failure of humanism triumphant. Eugene Rice's *The Renaissance Idea of Wisdom* (Cambridge, Mass.: Harvard University Press, 1958) is indispensable for its contextual material on the relation of learning to the art of living, as is Herschel Baker's *The Dignity of Man: Studies in the Persistence of an Idea* (Cambridge, Mass.: Harvard University Press, 1947).

Henry Peacham's life and work are discussed in a sketch in *The Dictionary of National Biography*, as well as in the introduction to *Peacham's Compleat Gentleman* (1634), with an introduction by G. S. Gordon (Oxford: Clarendon Press, 1906) and Henry Peacham, *The Complete Gentleman,* edited by Virgil B. Heltzel (Ithaca: Cornell University Press, 1962). Richard Brathwaite's life and work are also sketched in *The Dictionary of National Biography*. For a splendid comparison of the Peacham and Brathwaite treatises, see W. Lee Ustick, "Changing Ideals of Aristocratic Character and Content in Seventeenth-Century England," *Modern Philology*, XXX (1932-33), 147-166.

There is no adequate treatment of education in the political thought of the sixteenth and seventeenth centuries. The more particular theme of patriarchalism is dealt with at length in Peter Laslett's introduction to Sir Robert Filmer, *Patriarcha and Other Political Works of Sir Robert Filmer,* edited by Peter Laslett (Oxford: Basil Blackwell, 1949), W. H. Greenleaf, *Order, Empiricism and Politics: Two Traditions of English Political Thought, 1500-1700* (London: Oxford University Press, 1964), and Michael Walzer, *The Revolution of the Saints* (Cambridge, Mass.: Harvard University Press, 1965). Julian H. Franklin, *Jean Bodin and the Sixteenth-Century Revolution in Law and History* (New York: Columbia University Press, 1963) is a useful introduction to the thought of Bodin; Leo Strauss, *The Political Philosophy of Hobbes: Its Basis and Its Genesis,* translated by Elsa M. Sinclair (Chicago: University of Chicago Press, 1952), Howard Warrender, *The Political Philosophy of Hobbes: His Theory of Obligation* (Oxford: Clarendon Press, 1957), and M. N. Goldsmith, *Hobbes's Science of Politics* (New York: Columbia University Press, 1966) are illuminating introductions to the thought of Hobbes.

W. Lee Ustick, "Advice to a Son: A Type of Seventeenth-Century Conduct Book," *Studies in Philology*, XXIX (1932), 409-441, is an incisive introduction to the genre. *The Political Works of James I,* edited by Charles Howard McIlwain (Cambridge, Mass.: Harvard University Press, 1918), includes a fine edition of the *Basilikon Doron,* as well as a useful analysis of James's political ideas. An excellent edition of Francis Osborne's *Advice to a Son,* along with a suitable introduction, is included in Louis B. Wright, ed., *Advice to a Son: Precepts of Lord Burghley, Sir Walter Raleigh, and Francis Osborne* (Ithaca:

Cornell University Press, 1962). The role of travel as an element in the education of upper-class children is dealt with in George B. Parks, "Travel as Education," in Richard Foster Jones *et al., The Seventeenth Century: Studies in the History of English Thought and Literature from Bacon to Pope* (Stanford: Stanford University Press, 1951), pp. 264-290.

Lawrence V. Ryan's *Roger Ascham* (Stanford: Stanford University Press, 1963), is definitive; while *The Babees' Book: Medieval Manners for the Young: Done into Modern English from Dr. Furnivall's Texts by Edith Rickert* (London: Chatto & Windus, 1923) remains the standard anthology of early Renaissance civility manuals for young children.

Howard Mumford Jones, *O Strange New World: American Culture, The Formative Years* (New York: The Viking Press, 1964) is the best discussion of Renaissance traditions of civility in early America; Edwin Harrison Cady, *The Gentleman in America: A Literary Study in American Culture* (Syracuse: Syracuse University Press, 1949) deals more specifically with the transplantation and development of gentlemanly ideals. Richard M. Gummere, *The American Colonial Mind and the Classical Tradition* (Cambridge, Mass.: Harvard University Press, 1963) provides an excellent introduction to the colonists' awareness of classical political theory.

CHAPTER 3: THE ADVANCEMENT OF LEARNING

The humanist program for the reconstitution of learning is the subject of a considerable literature, including such classics as William Harrison Woodward, *Studies in Education During the Age of the Renaissance, 1400-1600* (Cambridge: Cambridge University Press, 1906), Frederic Seebohm, *The Oxford Reformers: John Colet, Erasmus, and Thomas More* (2d ed.; London: Longmans, Green and Co., 1869), and John Edwin Sandys, *A History of Classical Scholarship* (3 vols.; Cambridge: Cambridge University Press, 1903-1908), and such modern works as T. W. Baldwin, *William Shakspere's Small Latine & Lesse Greeke* (2 vols.; Urbana: University of Illinois Press, 1944), R. R. Bolgar, *The Classical Heritage and Its Beneficiaries* (Cambridge: Cambridge University Press, 1954), James Kelsey McConica, *English Humanists and Reformation Politics Under Henry VIII and Edward VI* (Oxford: Clarendon Press, 1965), Kenneth Charlton, *Education in Renaissance England* (London: Routledge and Kegan Paul, 1965), and Joan Simon, *Education and Society in Tudor England* (Cambridge: Cambridge University Press, 1966).

The friendship of Erasmus and More is a time-honored theme in the history of letters. Among the better works that deal with it are E. M. G. Routh, *Sir Thomas More and His Friends, 1477-1535* (London: Oxford University Press, 1934), Jesse Kelley Sowards, "Thomas More and the Friendship of Erasmus, 1499-1517: A Study in Northern Humanism" (unpublished doctoral thesis, University of Michigan, 1951), and E. E. Reynolds, *Thomas More and Erasmus* (New York: Fordham University Press, 1965). More's household and its educational activities are discussed at length in Thomas Stapleton's classic *The Life and Illustrious Martyrdom of Sir Thomas More,* first published in Latin in 1588 and recently reissued in an English translation by Philip E. Hallett, edited and annotated by E. E. Reynolds (New York: Fordham University Press, 1966); a more modern treatment is given in R. W. Chambers, *Thomas More* (London: Jonathan Cape, 1935). J. H. Lupton, *A Life of John Colet* (2d ed.; London: George Bell and Sons, 1909) is the standard biography; Roger K. Warlick, "John Colet and Renaissance Humanism" (unpublished doctoral thesis, Boston University, 1965) is an able analysis of Colet's thought; while the educational activities of Colet and his associates at St. Paul's School are detailed in Baldwin, *William Shakspere's Small Latine & Lesse Greeke,* William Harrison Woodward, *Desiderius Erasmus Concerning the Aim and Method of Education* (Cambridge University Press, 1904), and Bolgar, *The Classical Tradition and Its Beneficiaries.* Vives is ably discussed in Edward J. Baxter, "The Educational Thought of Juan Luis Vives" (unpublished doctoral dissertation, Harvard University, 1943), Ruth Kuschmierz, "The Instruction of the Christian Woman: A Critical Edition of the Tudor Translations" (unpublished doctoral dissertation, University of Pittsburgh, 1961), and Marian Leona Tobriner, "Juan Luis Vives' Introduction to Wisdom: A Renaissance Textbook—Its Author, Its Era, and Its Use" (unpublished doctoral dissertation, Stanford University, 1966), as well as in Foster Watson's older works, *Vives and the Renascence Education of Women* (New York: Longmans, Green & Co., 1912) and *Vives: On Education; A Translation of the "De tradendis disciplinis" of Juan Luis Vives* (Cambridge: Cambridge University Press, 1913). And the humanist effort in the English universities is detailed in McConica, *English Humanists and Reformation Politics Under Henry VIII and Edward VI* and in H. C. Porter, *Reformation and Reaction in Tudor Cambridge* (Cambridge: Cambridge University Press, 1958).

William Warthin Taylor details the Western ambivalence toward learning in "The History of the Attacks on Profane Learning in the Christian Tradition to about 1675" (unpublished doctoral thesis, University of Michigan, 1945); while Richard Foster Jones, *Ancients and Moderns: A Study of the Rise of the Scientific Movement in Seventeenth-Century England* (2d ed.; St. Louis: Washington University Press, 1961), Judah Bierman, "Of Learning and Knowledge: An Analysis of the Discussion of Learning in Seventeenth-Century English Essays" (unpublished doctoral thesis, University of California, Los Angeles, 1951), Leo Solt, *Saints in Arms* (Stanford: Stanford University Press, 1959), and David Johnston Maitland, "Three Puritan Attitudes Toward Learning: An Examination of the Puritan Controversy over a Learned Ministry" (unpublished doctoral thesis, Columbia University, 1959), Richard Schlatter, "The Higher Learning in Puritan England," *Historical Magazine of the Protestant Episcopal Church,* XXIII (1954), 167-187, and J. J. O'Brien, "Commonwealth Schemes for the Advancement of Learning," *British Journal of Educational Studies,* XVI (1968), 30-42, illumine the controversy over the nature and function of learning that marked the seventeenth century. Walter E. Houghton, Jr., explicates a leading ideal of the learned man in "The English Virtuoso in the Seventeenth Century," *Journal of the History of Ideas,* III (1942), 51-73, 190-219.

The view of the history of Renaissance science set forth here is based on Marie Boas, *The Scientific Renaissance, 1450-1630* (New York: Harper & Brothers, 1962) and A. Rupert Hall, *From Galileo to Newton, 1630-1720* (New

York: Harper & Row, 1963). Lynn Thorndike, *A History of Magic and Experimental Science* (8 vols.; New York: Columbia University Press, 1923-1941) is obviously an indispensable reference work, as is Charles Singer *et al.*, *A History of Technology* (5 vols.; New York: Oxford University Press, 1954-1958). George Sarton, *The Appreciation of Ancient and Medieval Science During the Renaissance (1450-1600)* (Philadelphia: University of Pennsylvania Press, 1955), and *Six Wings: Men of Science in the Renaissance* (Bloomington: Indiana University Press, 1957), Francis R. Johnson, *Astronomical Thought in Renaissance England: A Study of the English Scientific Writings from 1500 to 1645* (Baltimore: The Johns Hopkins Press, 1937), E. G. R. Taylor, *Tudor Geography: 1485-1583* (London: Methuen & Co., 1930), and *Late Tudor and Early Stuart Geography, 1583-1650* (London: Methuen & Co., 1934), C. D. O'Malley, *English Medical Humanists: Thomas Linacre and John Caius* (Lawrence: University of Kansas Press, 1965), A. Wolf, *A History of Science, Technology and Philosophy in the 16th & 17th Centuries* (New York: The Macmillan Company, 1950), and A. C. Crombie, *Medieval and Early Modern Science* (rev. ed.; 2 vols.; Garden City, N.Y.: Doubleday & Company, 1959) are also patently relevant.

The most interesting of the recent works on Bacon is Paolo Rossi, *Francesco Bacone: Dalla Magia alla Scienza* (Bari: Editori Laterza, 1957), published in an excellent English translation by Sacha Rabinovitch as *Francis Bacon: From Magic to Science* (Chicago: University of Chicago Press, 1968). Benjamin Farrington's *Francis Bacon: Philosopher of Industrial Science* (London: Lawrence and Wishart, 1951) is useful, though it overstates Bacon's practicalism and fails to place Bacon's philosophy sufficiently within its Renaissance context. The standard collections of Bacon's writings are *The Letters and Life of Francis Bacon*, edited by James Spedding (7 vols.; London: Longman, Green, Longman, and Roberts, 1861-1874) and *The Works of Francis Bacon*, edited by James Spedding, Robert Leslie Ellis, and Douglas Denon Heath (new ed.; 7 vols.; London: Longmans & Co., 1876-1890); the standard bibliography is R. W. Gibson, *Francis Bacon: A Bibliography of His Works and Baconiana to the Year 1750* (Oxford: Scrivener Press, 1950). Geoffrey Bullough, "Bacon and the Defence of Learning," in J. Dover Wilson, ed., *Seventeenth Century Studies Presented to Sir Herbert Grierson* (Oxford: Clarendon Press, 1938), F. H. Anderson, *The Philosophy of Francis Bacon* (Chicago: University of Chicago Press, 1948), George Vernon Tovey, "Francis Bacon, The Reformer of Learning" (unpublished doctoral thesis, Columbia University, 1950), Raymond Canning Cochrane, "Francis Bacon and the Advancement of Learning" (unpublished doctoral thesis, Columbia University, 1953), and Moody E. Prior, "Bacon's Man of Science," *Journal of the History of Ideas*, XV (1954), 348-370, are unusually incisive with respect to Bacon's ideas on education.

The Colloquies of Erasmus, translated by Craig R. Thompson (Chicago: University of Chicago Press, 1965) is a splendid new edition of the old classic, and Thompson's introduction there is an important contribution to the Erasmus literature, along with his introduction to the reissue of William Harrison Woodward, *Desiderius Erasmus Concerning the Aim and Method of Education*, Classics in Education No. 19 (New York: Bureau of Publications,

Teachers College, Columbia University, 1964). Bolgar discusses the special relation of the *Colloquies,* the *De copia,* and the *Adages* in *The Classical Tradition and Its Beneficiaries.*

Donald M. Frame, *Montaigne's Discovery of Man: The Humanization of a Humanist* (New York: Columbia University Press, 1955), and *Montaigne: A Biography* (New York: Harcourt, Brace & World, 1965) are excellent companions to *The Complete Essays of Montaigne,* translated by Donald M. Frame (Stanford: Stanford University Press, 1958), as is Philip P. Hallie's imaginative essay *The Scar of Montaigne* (Middletown: Wesleyan University Press, 1966). Gabriel Compayré, *Montaigne and Education of the Judgment,* translated by J. E. Mansion (New York: Thomas Y. Crowell & Co., 1908) and Paul Porteau, *Montaigne et la Vie Pédagogique de Son Temps* (Paris: Libraire E. Droz, 1935) are older works still worthy of study. Jacob Zeitlin, "The Development of Bacon's Essays—with Special Reference to the Question of Montaigne's Influence upon Them," *The Journal of English and Germanic Philology,* XXVII (1928), 496-519, proved especially useful, as did Rebecca Patterson Hein, "Montaigne in America" (unpublished doctoral thesis, University of Michigan, 1966).

Walter J. Ong, *Ramus, Method, and the Decay of Dialogue* (Cambridge, Mass.: Harvard University Press, 1958), and *Ramus and Talon Inventory* (Cambridge, Mass.: Harvard University Press, 1958) are the definitive works on Ramism. Wilbur Samuel Howell, *Logic and Rhetoric in England, 1500-1700* (Princeton: Princeton University Press, 1956) discusses Ramism in the English context; while Neal W. Gilbert, *Renaissance Concepts of Method* (New York: Columbia University Press, 1960) discusses Ramism in the Western context. Perry Miller, *The New England Mind: The Seventeenth Century* (Cambridge, Mass.: Harvard University Press, 1939), Samuel Eliot Morison, *Harvard College in the Seventeenth Century* (2 vols.; Cambridge, Mass.: Harvard University Press, 1936), and Herbert W. Schneider, *A History of American Philosophy* (New York: Columbia University Press, 1946) establish the significance of Ramism in the American colonies. It is Louis B. Wright who first suggested the substantial influence of *The French Academie* in the New World; Madalene Shindler's "The Vogue and Impact of Pierre de la Primaudaye's *The French Academie* on Elizabethan and Jacobean Literature" (unpublished doctoral thesis, University of Texas, 1960) proved valuable in my consideration of that work.

INTRODUCTION TO PART II

Some years ago, in a fascinating aside in *State Intervention in English Education: A Short History from the Earliest Times down to 1833* (Cambridge: Cambridge University Press, 1902), J. E. G. de Montmorency remarked that the earliest use of the word "education" in its modern meaning appeared in the preamble to the act incorporating the Universities of Oxford and Cambridge in 1571 (13 Eliz. I, c. xxix). One can actually trace it back earlier, to the 1530's, when it appeared in Thomas Starkey's "Dialogue Between Reginald Pole and Thomas Lupset" (c. 1534), later published in S. J. Herrtage, ed., *England in*

the Reign of King Henry VIII: Starkey's Life and Letters, Part I, Early English
Text Society, Extra Series, Vol. XXXII (London: N. Trübner & Co., 1878),
pp. 18, 129, 132, 165. But the several decades of difference in these estimates
do not alter Montmorency's fundamental point—namely, that the term was
relatively new to the English language during the Tudor era. It was rather the
term "institution" (or the Latin "institutio") that appeared again and again in
Tudor discussions of the deliberate attempt to form human beings in accordance with certain cultural ideals, and it is in this essentially educational sense
that the term "institution" is used in this introduction to Part II.

   The social ferment that marked the Tudor and early Stuart periods and
hence that inevitably conditioned both English and American education in the
seventeenth century is ably discussed in Barry E. Supple, Commercial Crisis
and Change in England, 1600-1642: A Study in the Instability of a Mercantile
Economy (Cambridge: Cambridge University Press, 1959), Christopher Hill,
The Century of Revolution, 1603-1714, A History of England, edited by Christopher Brooke and Denis Mack Smith (Edinburgh: Thomas Nelson and Sons,
1961), and Intellectual Origins of the English Revolution (Oxford: Clarendon
Press, 1965), Trevor Aston, ed., Crisis in Europe, 1560-1660 (London: Routledge
& Kegan Paul, 1965), E. E. Rich and C. H. Wilson, eds., The Economy of Ex-
panding Europe in the Sixteenth and Seventeenth Centuries, The Cambridge
Economic History of Europe (Cambridge: Cambridge University Press, 1967),
Michael Walzer, The Revolution of the Saints (Cambridge, Mass.: Harvard
University Press, 1965), Lawrence Stone, "Social Mobility in England, 1500-
1700," Past & Present, no. 33 (April, 1966), 16-55, Alan Everitt, "Social Mobility
in Early Modern England," ibid., 56-73, and Carl Bridenbaugh, Vexed and
Troubled Englishmen, 1590-1642 (New York: Oxford University Press, 1968),
all of which have valuable bibliographical leads. In the same realm, Wallace
Notestein's older work, The English People on the Eve of Colonization, 1603-
1630 (New York: Harper & Brothers, 1954) is also useful. It is from E. E.
Rich's excellent article "The Population of Elizabethan England," The
Economic History Review, 2d ser., II (1949-50), 247-265, that I first derived
the sense that the transatlantic migration might have been something less than
the uniquely extreme social and cultural shock assumed by Oscar Handlin in
"The Significance of the Seventeenth Century," in James Morton Smith, ed.,
Seventeenth-Century America: Essays in Colonial History (Chapel Hill: Uni-
versity of North Carolina Press, 1959), pp. 3-12, and by Bernard Bailyn in
Education in the Forming of American Society (Chapel Hill: University of
North Carolina Press, 1960); while it was from Zevedei Barbu's Problems of
Historical Psychology (New York: Grove Press, 1960) that I derived several
of my hypotheses concerning the psychological impact of Renaissance upheavals.

   As already suggested, the most interesting considerations of the social
ferment that marked the institutions of English-speaking America in the
seventeenth century are the several essays in James Morton Smith, ed., Seventeenth-Century America, Bernard Bailyn's Education in the Forming of
American Society, and Daniel J. Boorstin's The Americans: The Colonial Experience (New York: Random House, 1958).

CHAPTER 4: HOUSEHOLD

Two lines of work have dominated the recent study of the early modern house-hold in the West, one represented by Philippe Ariès' remarkable book *Centuries of Childhood: A Social History of Family Life*, translated by Robert Baldick (New York: Alfred A. Knopf, 1962), the other represented by Peter Laslett's popular work *The World We Have Lost* (London: Methuen and Company, 1965). For all its seminal quality, the Ariès book rests principally on Continental sources, and its theses need a good deal of additional testing before they can be established as wholly or even generally applicable to Renaissance England or colonial America. (At those points in the present work where I have used Ariès' theses, I have taken pains to establish their validity, not only from written sources, but also from an examination of relevant paintings and artifacts.) David Hunt's intriguing examination of Ariès' theses against a background of Eriksonian personality theory, published under the title *Parents and Children in History: The Psychology of Family Life in Early Modern France* (New York: Basic Books, 1970), came to my attention after the present volume had gone to press, but would seem in any case to refine rather than to contradict the broader histori-cal arguments advanced by Ariès. Laslett's book is located squarely within the burgeoning literature of historical demography and should be read along with D. V. Glass and D. E. C. Eversley, eds., *Population in History: Essays in Historical Demography* (Chicago: Aldine Publishing Company, 1965) and E. A. Wrigley, ed., *An Introduction to English Historical Demography* (London: Weidenfeld and Nicolson, 1966).

The general literature on the English Renaissance household, while useful and interesting in its own right, tends to rest on source material that is at best fragmentary and frequently prescriptive rather than descriptive: certainly this is true of Chilton Latham Powell, *English Domestic Relations, 1487-1653: A Study of Matrimony and Family Life in Theory and Practice as Revealed by the Literature, Law, and History of the Period* (New York: Columbia Uni-versity Press, 1917), the relevant sections of Willystine Goodsell, *A History of the Family as a Social and Educational Institution* (New York: The Macmillan Company, 1915), the several works of Elizabeth Burton, notably, *The Jacobeans at Home* (London: Secker & Warburg, 1962) and *The Elizabethans at Home* (London: Secker & Warburg, 1963), and, the most detailed of the genre, Lu Emily Pearson, *Elizabethans at Home* (Stanford: Stanford University Press, 1957). The result is that the student of family life is forced back to collections of papers or monographs relating to particular families, or to fugitive chapters in works dealing with special segments of society, for example, the studies pursued at Yale during the 1930's and 1940's under the direction of Wallace Notestein, notably, Francis Squire, "The English Country Gentleman in the Early Seven-teenth Century" (unpublished doctoral thesis, Yale University, 1935), Alice Kimball Smith, "The English Country Clergy in the Early Seventeenth Cen-tury" (unpublished doctoral thesis, Yale University, 1938), John Roach, "The English Country Doctor in the Province of Canterbury, 1603-1643" (unpublished doctoral thesis, Yale University, 1941), and Mildred Campbell, *The English Yeoman Under Elizabeth and the Early Stuarts* (New Haven: Yale University Press, 1942), or such recent works as Lawrence Stone, *The Crisis of the Aristocracy, 1558-1641* (Oxford: Clarendon Press, 1965), W. G. Hoskins, *Provincial England* (London: The Macmillan Company, 1964), and *The Midland Peasant* (London: The Macmillan Company, 1957), Jerome Frank Brown, "Five Somerset Families, 1590-1640" (unpublished doctoral thesis, University of California, Berkeley, 1966), Christopher Hill, *Economic Problems of the Church, from Archbishop Whitgift to the Long Parliament* (Oxford: Clarendon Press, 1956), and G. E. Aylmer, *The King's Servants: The Civil Service of Charles I, 1625-42* (New York: Columbia University Press, 1961).

For an understanding of the oral culture of households and localities, Albert B. Lord, *The Singer of Tales* (Cambridge, Mass.: Harvard University Press, 1960) and Walter J. Ong, *The Presence of the Word* (New Haven: Yale University Press, 1967) are incisive. For the content of the emerging print culture in England, Louis B. Wright, *Middle-Class Culture in Elizabethan England* (Chapel Hill: University of North Carolina Press, 1935) and H. S. Bennett, *English Books and Readers, 1475 to 1603* (2 vols.; Cambridge: Cambridge University Press, 1952-1965) provide excellent introductions. The particular content of treatises on child rearing is dealt with in Kathleen Kessler Shepherd, "Better Unborn than Untaught: Sixteenth-Century Popular Advice on Child Rearing in England" (unpublished master's thesis, Columbia University, 1965).

With respect to the Tudor effort to utilize households in the pursuit of religious, economic, and political ends, I. Pinchbeck's article "The State and the Child in Sixteenth Century England," *The British Journal of Sociology*, VII (1956), 273-285, and VIII (1957), 59-74, is invaluable. Norman Wood, *The Reformation and English Education* (London: George Routledge & Sons, 1931) deals with the various efforts at church regulation of household education; while Walter Howard Frere and William McClure Kennedy, eds., *Visitation Articles and Injunctions of the Period of the Reformation*, Alcuin Club Collections, vols. XIV-XVI (3 vols.; London: Longmans, Green & Co., 1910), W. P. M. Kennedy, ed., *Elizabethan Episcopal Administration*, Alcuin Club Collections, vols. XXV-XXVII (3 vols.; London: A. R. Mowbray & Co., 1924), and Henry Gee and William John Hardy, eds., *Documents Illustrative of English Church History* (London: Macmillan and Co., 1896) present much of the relevant source material on which an analysis such as Wood's must rest. The crucial role of the household as an instrument of mercantilist policy is discussed in O. Jocelyn Dunlop, *English Apprenticeship & Child Labor* (New York: The Macmillan Company, 1912), Eli F. Hechscher, *Mercantilism*, edited by E. F. Söderlund (2 vols.; London: George Allen & Unwin, 1955), John U. Nef, *Industry and Government in France and England, 1540-1640* (Philadelphia: American Philosophical Society, 1940), Margaret Gay Davies, *The Enforcement of English Apprenticeship: A Study in Applied Mercantilism, 1563-1642* (Cambridge, Mass.: Harvard University Press, 1956), and E. A. J. Johnson, "The Place of Learning, Science, Vocational Training, and 'Art' in Pre-Smithian Economic Thought," *The Journal of Economic History*, XXIV (1964), 129-144; many of the relevant documents are included in R. H. Tawney and Eileen Power, eds.,

Tudor Economic Documents (3 vols.; London: Longmans, Green and Co., 1924). David J. Rothman, "A Note on the Study of the Colonial Family," *The William and Mary Quarterly*, 3d ser., XXIII (1966), 627-634, Philip J. Greven, Jr., "Historical Demography and Colonial America," *ibid.*, XXIV (1967), 438-454, and Edward N. Saveth, "The Problem of American Family History," *American Quarterly*, XXI (1969), 311-329, are the best reviews of recently published work on the family in colonial America. Other useful writings include Herbert Moller, "Sex Composition and Correlated Culture Patterns of Colonial America," *The William and Mary Quarterly*, 3d ser., II (1945), 113-153, John Demos, "Notes on Life in Plymouth Colony," *ibid.*, XXII (1965), 264-286, and *A Little Commonwealth: Family Life in Plymouth Colony* (New York: Oxford University Press, 1970), Philip J. Greven, Jr., "Family Structure in Seventeenth-Century Andover, Massachusetts," *The William and Mary Quarterly*, 3d ser., XXIII (1966), 234-256, and *Four Generations: Population, Land, and Family in Colonial Andover, Massachusetts* (Ithaca: Cornell University Press, 1970), Kenneth A. Lockridge, "The Population of Dedham, Massachusetts, 1636-1736," *The Economic History Review*, 2d ser., XIX (1966), 318-344, and *A New England Town: The First Hundred Years* (New York: W. W. Norton & Company, 1970), and John J. Waters, "Hingham, Massachusetts, 1631-1661: An East Anglian Oligarchy in the New World," *Journal of Social History*, I (1967-68), 351-370. Richard S. Dunn undertakes a useful comparative analysis of family size in "The Barbados Census of 1680: Profile of the Richest Colony in English America," *The William and Mary Quarterly*, 3d ser., XXVI (1969), 3-30.

David Harris Flaherty, "Privacy in Colonial New England, 1630-1776" (unpublished doctoral thesis, Columbia University, 1967) reveals much, both directly and indirectly, about the character of seventeenth-century family life, as do various studies in the history of domestic architecture, for example, Fiske Kimball, *Domestic Architecture of the American Colonies and of the Early Republic* (New York: Charles Scribner's Sons, 1922), of community structure, for example, Edward Spaulding Perzel, "The First Generation of Settlement in Colonial Ipswich, Massachusetts: 1633-1660" (unpublished doctoral thesis, Rutgers University, 1967), of children's toys, for example, Antonia Fraser, *A History of Toys* (New York: Delacorte Press, 1966), and of painting, for example, Mary Black and Jean Lipman, *American Folk Painting* (New York: Clarkson N. Potter, 1966). Several of the papers at the Smithsonian Institution's Conference on the History of the Family, held on October 26-27, 1967, proved relevant, chiefly, Philip J. Greven, Jr., "An Historical Perspective on Family Structure." The collections of the Museum of the City of New York and of the Metropolitan Museum of Art, particularly the American Wing, were patently invaluable, as were any number of diaries and autobiographies listed in William Matthews, *American Diaries: An Annotated Bibliography of American Diaries Written Prior to the Year 1861* (Boston: J. S. Canner & Company, 1959), and Louis Kaplan *et al.*, *A Bibliography of American Autobiographies* (Madison: University of Wisconsin Press, 1961).

Edmund S. Morgan's *The Puritan Family: Religion & Domestic Relations in Seventeenth-Century New England* (new ed.; New York: Harper & Row, 1966) is interesting and suggestive, though it rests more heavily on normative than on descriptive sources; of the older literature, the several works of Alice Morse Earle, especially *Child Life in Colonial Days* (New York: The Macmillan Company, 1899), *Home Life in Colonial Days* (New York: The Macmillan Company, 1898), and *Colonial Days in Old New York* (New York: Charles Scribner's Sons, 1896), are generally accurate and richly detailed, as are Arthur W. Calhoun, *A Social History of the American Family from Colonial Times to the Present* (3 vols.; Cleveland: The Arthur H. Clark Co., 1917-1919), Mary Newton Stanard, *Colonial Virginia: Its People and Customs* (Philadelphia: J. B. Lippincott Company, 1917), and Sandford Fleming, *Children & Puritanism: The Place of Children in the Life and Thought of the New England Churches, 1620-1847* (New Haven: Yale University Press, 1933).

Colonial legislation relating to households and children is excerpted and discussed in Elsie W. Clews, *Educational Legislation and Administration of the Colonial Governments* (New York: no publisher, 1899) and Marcus Wilson Jernegan, *Laboring and Dependent Classes in Colonial America, 1607-1783* (Chicago: University of Chicago Press, 1931). Richard B. Morris, *Government and Labor in Early America* (New York: Columbia University Press, 1946) and Geraldine Joanne Murphy, "Massachusetts Bay Colony: The Role of Government in Education" (unpublished doctoral thesis, Radcliffe College, 1960) are prime examples of detailed modern studies and illustrate the need to go beyond formal legislative documents to court orders, indentures, probate records, and other local source materials in assessing the real impact of governmental policy. Many of these records have been published, for example, Berthold Fernow, ed., *The Minutes of the Orphanmasters of New Amsterdam, 1655-1663*, Publications of the Committee on History and Tradition of the Colonial Dames of the State of New York, no. 1 (New York: Francis P. Harper, 1902); others are available in the original and in manuscript transcriptions in historical societies and local government archives.

The household as an economic unit and the inevitable consequences for education are dealt with in Rolla Milton Tryon, *Household Manufactures in the United States, 1640-1860: A Study in Industrial History* (Chicago: University of Chicago Press, 1917), Philip Alexander Bruce, *Economic History of Virginia in the Seventeenth Century* (2 vols.; New York: The Macmillan Company, 1895), William B. Weeden, *Economic and Social History of New England, 1620-1789* (2 vols.; Boston: Houghton, Mifflin, and Company, 1890), Abbot Emerson Smith, *Colonists in Bondage: White Servitude and Convict Labor in America, 1607-1776* (Chapel Hill: University of North Carolina Press, 1947), Lawrence William Towner, "A Good Master Well Served: A Social History of Servitude in Massachusetts, 1620-1750" (unpublished doctoral thesis, Northwestern University, 1955), and Darrett B. Rutman, *Husbandmen of Plymouth: Farms and Villages in the Old Colony, 1620-1692* (Boston: Beacon Press, 1967).

The American literature on the history of reading instruction is scandalously thin when it comes to the colonial period; the best recent treatise, Mitford M. Mathews' *Teaching to Read: Historically Considered* (Chicago: University of Chicago Press, 1966), literally ignores the first two centuries of the American experience, while the standard older treatise, Rudolph Reeder's *The Historical Development of School Readers and of Method in Teaching Reading* (New

York: The Macmillan Company, 1900), begins with *The New-England Primer*. This being so, the best available literature on methods of colonial instruction is the literature on contemporary English instruction, notably, T. W. Baldwin, *William Shakspere's Petty School* (Urbana: University of Illinois Press, 1943), Harris Francis Fletcher, *The Intellectual Development of John Milton* (2 vols.; Urbana: University of Illinois Press, 1956-1961), and William Robert Hart, "*The English Schoole-Maister* (1596) by Edmund Coote: An Edition of the Text with Critical Notes and Introductions" (unpublished doctoral thesis, University of Michigan, 1963). Andrew W. Tuer, *History of the Horn-Book* (London: The Leadenhall Press, 1897) is definitive, while Wilberforce Eames, "Early New England Catechisms," *Proceedings of the American Antiquarian Society*, new ser., XII (1899), 76-182, is the most comprehensive discussion available.

The problems of acculturation occasioned by the spread of Western culture are explored in the various articles constituting Paul Bohannan and Fred Plog, eds., *Beyond the Frontier: Social Process and Cultural Change* (Garden City, N.Y.: The Natural History Press, 1967). Obviously, such problems marked the multifarious contacts of various European ethnic and religious groups in the New World, but they were most severe in the contacts of white Europeans with American Indians and African blacks. William N. Fenton, *American Indian and White Relations to 1830: Needs and Opportunities for Study*, with a bibliography compiled by L. H. Butterfield, Wilcomb E. Washburn, and William N. Fenton (Chapel Hill: University of North Carolina Press, 1957) is the most recent discussion of the relevant literature. Harold E. Driver, *Indians of North America* (Chicago: University of Chicago Press, 1961) depicts Indian institutions as they prevailed at the time of initial contact with the whites, though its ethnological approach tends to telescope time scale in favor of geographical and cultural differentiation. Maurice Marc Wasserman, "The American Indian as Seen by Seventeenth Century Chroniclers" (unpublished doctoral thesis, University of Pennsylvania, 1954), Roy Harvey Pearce, *The Savages of America* (Baltimore: The Johns Hopkins Press, 1953), and Alden T. Vaughan, *New England Frontier: Puritans and Indians, 1620-1675* (Boston: Little, Brown and Company, 1965) are the best recent histories; Almon Wheeler Lauber, *Indian Slavery Within the Present Limits of the United States* (New York: privately printed, 1913) is an older work replete with valuable information. Winthrop D. Jordan's *White over Black: American Attitudes Toward the Negro, 1550-1812* (Chapel Hill: University of North Carolina Press, 1968) is a tour de force that goes far beyond the subject of its subtitle and includes an excellent bibliography. On the relation of race prejudice and slavery, Oscar and Mary F. Handlin argue in "Origins of the Southern Labor System," *The William and Mary Quarterly*, 3d ser., VII (1950), 199-222, that it was the actuality of the slave system that engendered feelings of prejudice toward blacks; while Carl N. Degler argues the contrary in "Slavery and the Genesis of American Race Prejudice," *Comparative Studies in Society and History*, II (1959-60), 49-66. The actuality doubtless strengthened the prejudice; but I was moved to accept the Degler argument in large measure by Jordan's analysis, along with David Brion Davis' in *The Problem of Slavery in Western Culture* (Ithaca: Cornell University Press, 1966) and Charles Lyons' in "'To Wash an Aethiop White':

British Ideas About Black African Educability, 1530-1865" (unpublished doctoral thesis, Columbia University, 1970). The best brief discussions of West African civilization at the time of the great "involuntary migrations" of the seventeenth and eighteenth centuries are Jan Vansina, *Kingdoms of the Savanna* (Madison: University of Wisconsin Press, 1968), Basil Davidson, *A History of West Africa to the Nineteenth Century* (Garden City, N.Y.: Doubleday & Company, 1966), J. D. Fage, *An Introduction to the History of West Africa* (Cambridge: Cambridge University Press, 1955), and Melville J. Herskovits' revisionist classic, *The Myth of the Negro Past* (New York: Harper & Brothers, 1941). The best introduction to the slave trade itself is Elizabeth Donnan, ed., *Documents Illustrative of the History of the Slave Trade to America* (4 vols.; Washington, D.C.: The Carnegie Institution of Washington, 1930-1935).

CHAPTER 5: CHURCH

The problem of dealing with the church as an educational institution is not any lack of source material—indeed, the sheer quantity of primary and secondary sources is overwhelming; it is rather one of establishing appropriate categories and perspectives for discussion. The more one works in the literature of ecclesiastical and theological history, the more one realizes that, while the concerns of the church historian and the educational historian are related and overlapping, they are not identical. And it is the establishment of that which is characteristically and consistently the concern of the educator in church history that has proved one of the more interesting aspects of the study.

The long view of the minister as teacher, from the time of the primitive church to the early modern period, is provided in three works that were especially useful, H. Richard Niebuhr and Daniel D. Williams, eds., *The Ministry in Historical Perspectives* (New York: Harper & Row, 1956), James L. Ainslie, *The Doctrine of Ministerial Order in the Reformed Churches of the Sixteenth and Seventeenth Centuries* (Edinburgh: T. & T. Clark, 1940), and Robert W. Henderson, *The Teaching Office in the Reformed Tradition: A History of the Doctoral Ministry* (Philadelphia: The Westminster Press, 1962). The particular characteristics of the church's teaching in late medieval and early Renaissance England are discussed in H. Maynard Smith, *Pre-Reformation England* (London: Macmillan and Co., 1938), Bernard Lord Manning, *The People's Faith in the Time of Wyclif* (Cambridge: Cambridge University Press, 1919), and Ted Hayden McDonald, "The Piety of Englishmen Under Henry VII, 1484-1509" (unpublished doctoral thesis, University of Washington, 1957); while the stubborn continuities in popular piety in the face of the ecclesiastical and doctrinal upheavals of the Reformation are documented in James Francis Hitchcock, "Popular Religion in Elizabethan England" (unpublished doctoral thesis, Princeton University, 1965).

A. G. Dickens, *The English Reformation* (New York: Schocken Books, 1964) provides the best overview of early Tudor policy with respect to the churches; the Elizabethan settlement as it evolved in theory and practice is dealt with in Walter H. Frere, *The English Church in the Reigns of Elizabeth and James I* (London: Macmillan and Co., 1904), Henry Gee, *The Elizabethan Clergy and the Settlement of Religion, 1558-64* (Oxford: Clarendon Press, 1898), and the first volume of W. K. Jordan, *The Development of Religious Toleration in England* (4 vols.; London: G. Allen & Unwin, 1932-1940). Norman Wood deals generally with the educational responsibilities of the church in *The Reformation and English Education* (London: George Routledge & Sons, 1931), though his treatment tends to be overly legal and institutional; more useful, perhaps, are the specialized discussions of preaching in William Haller, *The Rise of Puritanism* (New York: Columbia University Press, 1938), Irvonwy Morgan, *The Godly Preachers of the Elizabethan Church* (London: The Epworth Press, 1965), Caroline Francis Richardson, *English Preachers and Preaching, 1640-1670* (New York: The Macmillan Company, 1928), W. Fraser Mitchell, *English Pulpit Oratory from Andrewes to Tillotson* (London: Society for Promoting Christian Knowledge, 1932), and Ruth B. Bozell, "English Preachers of the Seventeenth Century on the Art of Preaching" (unpublished doctoral thesis, Cornell University, 1938), or the specialized discussions of the clergy in Alice Kimball Smith, "The English Country Clergy in the Early Seventeenth Century" (unpublished doctoral thesis, Yale University, 1936), A. Tindal Hart, *The Country Clergy in Elizabethan and Stuart Times* (London: Phoenix House, 1958), D. M. Barratt, "The Condition of the Parish Clergy Between the Reformation and 1660, with Special Reference to the Dioceses of Oxford, Worcester and Gloucester" (unpublished doctoral thesis, Somerville College, University of Oxford, 1949), and Christopher Hill, *Economic Problems of the Church, from Archbishop Whitgift to the Long Parliament* (Oxford: Clarendon Press, 1956), and *Society and Puritanism in Pre-Revolutionary England* (New York: Schocken Books, 1964). Carl Russell Fish's older article "The English Parish and Education at the Beginning of American Colonization," *The School Review*, XXIII (1915), 433-449, provides an interesting set of categories, but Fish's discussion needs considerable amplification.

The standard work on the colonial church is William Warren Sweet, *Religion in Colonial America* (New York: Charles Scribner's Sons, 1949); more recent perspectives are given in the relevant sections of H. Shelton Smith, Robert T. Handy, and Lefferts A. Loetscher, eds., *American Christianity: An Historical Interpretation with Representative Documents* (2 vols.; New York: Charles Scribner's Sons, 1960), Winthrop S. Hudson, *Religion in America* (New York: Charles Scribner's Sons, 1965), and Edwin Scott Gaustad, *A Religious History of America* (New York: Harper & Row, 1966). The Smith, Handy, and Loetscher volumes and Nelson R. Burr, *A Critical Bibliography of Religion in America* (2 vols.; Princeton: Princeton University Press, 1961) are the best sources of bibliographical commentary. David D. Hall, "The Faithful Shepherd: The Puritan Ministry in Old and New England, 1570-1660" (unpublished doctoral thesis, Yale University, 1963) goes farther than any other analysis in attempting to specify the "Americanization" of the Puritan ministry in the seventeenth century, though Hall points out, quite rightly, that the New England clergy performed what was in the main a traditional role. Edwin Scott Gaustad's *Historical Atlas of Religion in America* (New York: Harper & Row, 1962) is uniquely useful, though Gaustad tends to avoid the question of what actually constitutes a church, particularly among more marginal religious groups.

George Maclaren Brydon, *Virginia's Mother Church and the Political Con-*

ditions Under Which It Grew (2 vols.; imprint varies, 1947-1952) is the best general account of the development of Anglicanism in that colony, while the *Historical Magazine of the Protestant Episcopal Church* is replete with special accounts of Anglicans and Anglicanism throughout colonial America—the issue of March, 1957, marking the 350th anniversary of the founding of Virginia, is an excellent example. Philip Alexander Bruce, *Institutional History of Virginia in the Seventeenth Century* (2 vols.; New York: G. P. Putnam's Sons, 1910), Guy Fred Wells, *Parish Education in Colonial Virginia* (New York: Teachers College, Columbia University, 1923), and Sadie Bell, *The Church, the State, and Education in Virginia* (Philadelphia: The Science Press, 1930) provide the best general accounts of Virginia churches as centers of education.

Of the vast literature on colonial Puritanism, I found Williston Walker, *The Creeds and Platforms of Congregationalism* (New York: Charles Scribner's Sons, 1893), Perry Miller, *Orthodoxy in Massachusetts, 1630-1650: A Genetic Study* (Cambridge, Mass.: Harvard University Press, 1933), and *The New England Mind* (2 vols.; Cambridge, Mass.: Harvard University Press, 1939-1953), and Edmund Sears Morgan, *Visible Saints: The History of the Puritan Idea* (New York: New York University Press, 1963) especially valuable, along with Williston Walker's older *A History of the Congregational Churches in the United States* (New York: The Christian Literature Company, 1894) in The American Church History Series. On the educational side, Vergil V. Phelps, "The Pastor and Teacher in New England," *The Harvard Theological Review*, IV (1911), 388-399, George Stewart, Jr., *A History of Religious Education in Connecticut to the Middle of the Nineteenth Century* (New Haven: Yale University Press, 1924), and Sandford Fleming, *Children & Puritanism: The Place of Children in the Life and Thought of the New England Churches, 1620-1847* (New Haven: Yale University Press, 1933) are centrally relevant.

The works of Frederick Lewis Weis are essential to any effort to generalize about the colonial clergy, including *The Colonial Clergy and the Colonial Churches of New England, 1620-1776* (Lancaster, Mass.: Society of the Descendants of the Colonial Clergy, 1936), *The Colonial Churches and the Colonial Clergy of the Middle and Southern Colonies, 1607-1776* (Lancaster, Mass.: Society of the Descendants of the Colonial Clergy, 1938), *The Colonial Clergy of Maryland, Delaware and Georgia* (Lancaster, Mass.: Society of the Descendants of the Colonial Clergy, 1950), and *The Colonial Clergy of Virginia, North Carolina, and South Carolina* (Boston: Society of the Descendants of the Colonial Clergy, 1955). Beyond these minimal listings are the biographical sketches in William Buell Sprague, *Annals of the American Pulpit* (9 vols.; New York: Robert Carter and Brothers, 1857-1869) and Allen Johnson and Dumas Malone, eds., *Dictionary of American Biography* (20 vols.; New York: Charles Scribner's Sons, 1928-1936), such lengthier studies as Kenneth Murdock, *Increase Mather* (Cambridge, Mass.: Harvard University Press, 1925), Raymond Phineas Stearns, *The Strenuous Puritan: Hugh Peter, 1598-1660* (Urbana: University of Illinois Press, 1954), Ola Elizabeth Winslow, *Master Roger Williams: A Biography* (New York: The Macmillan Company, 1957), Larzer Ziff, *The Career of John Cotton: Puritanism and the American Experience* (Princeton: Princeton University Press, 1962), Gerald Francis de Jong, "Dominie Johannes Megapolensis: Minister to New Netherland," *The New-York His-*

torical Society Quarterly, LII (1968), 7-47, and Harry Culverwell Porter, "Alexander Whitaker: Cambridge Apostle to Virginia," *The William and Mary Quarterly,* 3d ser., XIV (1957), 317-343, and such primary materials as Thomas Shepard's autobiography (*Publications of the Colonial Society of Massachusetts,* XXVII [1932], 345-400), Increase Mather's diary (Massachusetts Historical Society *Proceedings,* 2d ser., XIII [1899-1900], 340-374), and Jonas Michaëlius' correspondence (Dingman Versteeg, *Manhattan in 1628* [New York: Dodd, Mead and Company, 1904]).

The colonial church as a center of social and educational activities is vividly portrayed by Ola Elizabeth Winslow in *Meetinghouse Hill, 1630-1783* (New York: The Macmillan Company, 1952), and, from a quite different perspective, by Emil Oberholzer, Jr., in "The Church in New England Society," in James Morton Smith, ed., *Seventeenth-Century America: Essays in Colonial History* (Chapel Hill: University of North Carolina Press, 1959), chap. vii, and *Delinquent Saints: Disciplinary Action in the Early Congregations of Massachusetts* (New York: Columbia University Press, 1956), and Kai T. Erikson, *Wayward Puritans: A Study in the Sociology of Deviance* (New York: John Wiley & Sons, 1966). Theodore C. Gambrall's *Church Life in Colonial Maryland* (Baltimore: George Lycett, 1885) deals with the same sort of materials, but more superficially. William H. Seiler, "The Anglican Parish in Virginia," in Smith, ed., *Seventeenth-Century America,* chap. vi, Borden W. Painter, Jr., "The Anglican Vestry in Colonial America" (unpublished doctoral thesis, Yale University, 1965), and Gerald Eugene Hartdagen, "The Anglican Vestry in Colonial Maryland" (unpublished doctoral thesis, Northwestern University, 1965) deal with the control of the churches and, therefore, of church education. Babette May Levy, *Preaching in the First Half Century of New England History* (Hartford, Conn.: The American Society of Church History, 1945) discusses the education and rhetoric of New England's preachers and the reception accorded their sermons; Roy Fred Hudson deals with their pedagogy in "The Theory of Communication of Colonial New England Preachers, 1620-1670" (unpublished doctoral thesis, Cornell University, 1953).

The missionary efforts of the seventeenth-century churches among the Indians are discussed in Alden T. Vaughan, *New England Frontier: Puritans and Indians, 1620-1675* (Boston: Little, Brown and Company, 1965), R. Pierce Beaver, "Methods in American Missions to the Indians in the Seventeenth and Eighteenth Centuries: Calvinist Models for Protestant Foreign Missions," *Journal of Presbyterian History,* XLVII (1969), 124-148, and William Kellaway, *The New England Company, 1649-1776: Missionary Society to the American Indians* (New York: Barnes & Noble, 1961), as well as in such older studies as Edward Payson Johnson, "Early Missionary Work Among the North American Indians," *Papers of the American Society of Church History,* 2d ser., III (1912), 13-39, and Charles E. Corwin, "Efforts of the Dutch-American Colonial Pastors for the Conversion of the Indians," *Journal of the Presbyterian Historical Society,* XII (1924-27), 225-246. What can be gleaned concerning the missionary efforts among the blacks, from the most fragmentary sources, is reported in Winthrop D. Jordan, *White over Black: American Attitudes Toward the Negro, 1550-1812* (Chapel Hill: University of North Carolina Press, 1968).

The best biography of John Eliot is Frederick Farnham Harling, "A

Biography of John Eliot" (unpublished doctoral thesis, Boston University, 1965); Ola Elizabeth Winslow's *John Eliot: "Apostle to the Indians"* (Boston: Houghton Mifflin Company, 1968) is a useful complement, with an excellent bibliography listing the published letters, the translations into Algonquian, and the so-called Eliot tracts separately and with their places and dates of publication. There are a few unpublished Eliot letters in the Massachusetts Historical Society, and there are the unpublished records of the First Church in Roxbury, written by Eliot during his tenure there.

Charles E. Corwin, "The First Dutch Minister in America," *Journal of the Presbyterian Historical Society*, XII (1924-1927), 144-151, and "The First Ministers in the Middle Colonies," *ibid.*, 346-384, are useful for the educational activities of the Dutch Reformed church during the seventeenth century, as is de Jong, "Dominie Johannes Megapolensis: Minister to New Netherland," *The New-York Historical Society Quarterly*, LII (1968), 7-47. Edward T. Corwin, ed., *Ecclesiastical Records, State of New York* (7 vols.; Albany: J. B. Lyon Company, 1901-1916) is invaluable as a documentary collection. E. T. Corwin, J. H. Dubbs, and J. T. Hamilton, *A History of the Reformed Church, Dutch, the Reformed Church, German, and the Moravian Church in the United States* (New York: The Christian Literature Company, 1895) and Edward Tanjore Corwin, *A Manual of the Reformed Church in America* (2d ed.; New York: Board of Publication of the Reformed Church in America, 1869) are also valuable. William H. Kilpatrick, *The Dutch Schools of New Netherland and Colonial New York* (Washington, D.C.: Government Printing Office, 1912) also deals with the church, though with reference to the work of the schools. John Tracy Ellis documents the educational activities of the Roman Catholic church in *Catholics in Colonial America* (Baltimore, Md.: Helicon Press, 1965). The educational activities of the Quakers in the seventeenth-century colonies are the subject of a large literature, including Rufus M. Jones, *The Quakers in the American Colonies* (London: Macmillan and Co., 1911).

CHAPTER 6: SCHOOL

There has recently been a revival of interest in English Renaissance schooling, sparked largely by the work of Joan Simon, Kenneth Charlton, and A. C. F. Beales. The traditional view, which maintained that the Reformation did fundamental damage to English schooling, derived from the classic works of A. F. Leach, notably, *The Schools of Medieval England* (2d ed.; London: Methuen & Co., 1915), which includes, incidentally, a bibliography of Leach's writings on education, *English Schools at the Reformation* (London: Archibald Constable & Co., 1894), and *Educational Charters and Documents* (Cambridge: Cambridge University Press, 1911). This view prevailed until the mid-1950's, when it was sharply challenged by Joan Simon in "A. F. Leach on the Reformation," *British Journal of Educational Studies*, III (1954-55), 128-143, and IV (1955-56), 32-48, and "The Reformation and English Education," *Past & Present*, no. 11 (April, 1957), 48-65. W. N. Chaplin responded in "A. F. Leach: A Reappraisal," *British Journal of Educational Studies*, XI (1962-63), 99-124, and Mrs. Simon replied in *ibid.*, XII (1963-64), 41-50. Mrs. Simon's *Education and Society in Tudor England* (Cambridge: Cambridge University Press, 1966) sets forth the developed statement of her views; Kenneth Charlton's *Education in Renaissance England* (London: Routledge and Kegan Paul, 1965) presents a comprehensive view of the period; while A. C. F. Beales, *Education Under Penalty: English Catholic Education from the Reformation to the Fall of James II, 1547-1689* (London: The Athlone Press, 1963) deals with the special problems of the Recusants. Clara P. McMahon presents a convenient review of late medieval and early Renaissance traditions in *Education in Fifteenth-Century England* (Baltimore: The Johns Hopkins Press, 1947), as do John Nelson Miner in "Schools and Literacy in Later Medieval England," *British Journal of Educational Studies*, XI (1962-63), 16-27, and W. E. Tate in "Some Sources for the History of English Grammar Schools," *ibid.*, I (1952-53), 164-175. W. A. L. Vincent reviews developments in the Commonwealth period in *The State and School Education 1640-1660 in England and Wales* (London: S.P.C.K., 1950).

The laicizing of school control during the Tudor era is documented in Simon, *Education and Society in Tudor England* and W. K. Jordan, *Philanthropy in England, 1480-1660* (London: George Allen & Unwin, 1959), as well as in A. Monroe Stowe's older but still useful *English Grammar Schools in the Reign of Queen Elizabeth* (New York: Teachers College, Columbia University, 1908). The drive toward curricular uniformity during the same period is discussed in Norman Wood, *The Reformation and English Education* (London: George Routledge & Sons, 1931), T. W. Baldwin, *William Shakspere's Small Latine & Lesse Greeke* (2 vols.; Urbana: University of Illinois Press, 1941), and *William Shakspere's Petty School* (Urbana: University of Illinois Press, 1943), and J. E. G. de Montmorency, *State Intervention in English Education* (Cambridge: Cambridge University Press, 1902), which remains illuminating though vastly in need of updating.

The curriculum of English schools at the time of the founding of the North American colonies is portrayed in Foster Watson, "The Curriculum and Text-Books of English Schools in the First Half of the Seventeenth Century," *Transactions of the Bibliographical Society*, VI (1900-01), part I, 166-267, *The English Grammar Schools in 1660: Their Curriculum and Practice* (Cambridge: Cambridge University Press, 1908), and *The Beginnings of the Teaching of Modern Subjects in England* (London: Sir Isaac Pitman & Sons, 1909), and in Harris Francis Fletcher's distinguished work *The Intellectual Development of John Milton* (2 vols.; Urbana: University of Illinois Press, 1956-1961). The social role of schooling is admirably dealt with in Lawrence Stone, "The Educational Revolution in England, 1560-1640," *Past & Present*, no. 28 (July, 1964), 41-80, and in the relevant chapters of Wallace Notestein, *The English People on the Eve of Colonization, 1603-1630* (New York: Harper & Row, 1954) and Carl Bridenbaugh, *Vexed and Troubled Englishmen, 1590-1642* (New York: Oxford University Press, 1968).

Brian Simon's excellent examination of "Leicestershire Schools, 1625-1640," *British Journal of Educational Studies*, III (1954-55), 42-58, is complemented by Brian Simon, ed., *Education in Leicestershire, 1540-1940* (Leicester: Leicester University Press, 1968), and the relevant chapters of such works as *A History of the County of Leicester,* The Victoria History of the Counties of England (5 vols.; London: publisher varies, 1907-1964), and W. G. Hoskins, *Essays in Leicestershire History* (Liverpool: Liverpool University Press, 1950), *The Midland Peasant: The Economic and Social History of a Leicestershire Village* (London: Macmillan and Company, 1957), and *Provincial England: Essays in Social and Economic History* (London: Macmillan and Company, 1963).

My own essay *The Wonderful World of Ellwood Patterson Cubberley* (New York: Bureau of Publications, Teachers College, Columbia University, 1965) includes a discussion of the historiography of American schooling. The best general view of schooling in the seventeenth-century colonies is provided in Rena Lee Vassar's "Elementary and Latin Grammar School Education in the American Colonies, 1607-1700" (unpublished doctoral thesis, University of California, Berkeley, 1958). Richard Boyd Ballou's "The Grammar Schools in 17th Century Colonial America" (unpublished doctoral thesis, Harvard University, 1940), though older, is an excellent complementary study. Geraldine Joanne Murphy's "Massachusetts Bay Colony: The Role of Government in Education" (unpublished doctoral thesis, Radcliffe College, 1960) is exemplary in the richness of its detail and the firm rooting of its educational considerations in the political life of the colony, and, indeed, furnishes a model for the kind of intensive analysis that is needed for the other colonies. All three studies have extensive bibliographies.

There is a substantial older literature dealing with the development of schooling in particular colonies or regions, though much of it is marred by the search for the origins of the public school. Henry Suzzallo, *The Rise of Local School Supervision in Massachusetts* (New York: Teachers College, Columbia University, 1906), George L. Jackson, *The Development of School Support in Colonial Massachusetts* (New York: Teachers College, Columbia University, 1909), Walter Herbert Small, *Early New England Schools* (Boston: Ginn and Company, 1914), Bernard C. Steiner, *The History of Education in Connecticut* (Washington, D.C.: Government Printing Office, 1893) and Marcus Wilson Jernegan, *Laboring and Dependent Classes in Colonial America, 1607-1783* (Chicago: University of Chicago Press, 1931) are useful for New England. Herbert H. Vreeland, "Public Secondary Schooling in Connecticut, 1636-1800" (unpublished doctoral thesis, Yale University, 1941) and Norwood Marion Cole, "The Origin and Development of Town-School Education in Colonial Massachusetts, 1635-1775" (unpublished doctoral thesis, University of Washington, 1957) are replete with valuable detail but cast in a traditional mold; Clifford K. Shipton, "Secondary Education in the Puritan Colonies," *The New England Quarterly,* VII (1934), 646-661, and Samuel Eliot Morison, *The Puritan Pronaos: Studies in the Intellectual Life of New England in the Seventeenth Century* (New York: New York University Press, 1936) are sharply revisionist but not overly detailed. William Heard Kilpatrick, *The Dutch Schools of New Netherland and Colonial New York* (Washington, D.C.: Government Printing Office, 1912) remains definitive; Daniel J. Pratt, *Annals of Public Education in the State of New York from 1626 to 1746* (Albany, N.Y.: The Argus Company, 1872) and the earlier sections of James Pyle Wickersham, *A History of Education in Pennsylvania* (Lancaster, Pa.: Inquirer Publishing Company, 1886) and of Nelson

R. Burr, *Education in New Jersey, 1630-1871* (Princeton: Princeton University Press, 1942) are also useful for the middle colonies. Philip Alexander Bruce, *Institutional History of Virginia in the Seventeenth Century* (2 vols.; New York: G. P. Putnam's Sons, 1910), Allen George Umbreit, "Education in the Southern Colonies" (unpublished doctoral thesis, State University of Iowa, 1932), Jernegan, *Laboring and Dependent Classes in Colonial America, 1607-1783*, Sadie Bell, *The Church, the State, and Education in Virginia* (Philadelphia: The Science Press, 1930), and the first chapter of Leo Joseph McCormick, *Church-State Relationships in Education in Maryland* (Washington: Catholic University of America Press, 1942) are of value for the Chesapeake colonies, as are the documents in the first two volumes of Edgar W. Knight, ed., *A Documentary History of Education in the South Before 1860* (5 vols.; Chapel Hill: University of North Carolina Press, 1949-1953). Richard Walden Hale, Jr., *Tercentenary History of the Roxbury Latin School, 1645-1945* (Cambridge, Mass.: The Riverside Press, 1946), Charles D. Yetman, "The Hartford Public High School, 1639-1865" (unpublished doctoral thesis, Yale University, 1956), and Jean Parker Waterbury, *A History of Collegiate School, 1638-1963* (New York: Clarkson N. Potter, 1965) are characteristic histories of particular schools dating from the seventeenth century; Carlos Slafter, *A Record of Education: The Schools and Teachers of Dedham, Massachusetts, 1644-1904* (Dedham, Mass.: Dedham Transcript Press, 1905) and Mary Hall James, *The Educational History of Old Lyme, Connecticut, 1635-1935* (New Haven: Yale University Press, 1939) are characteristic histories of schooling in particular communities. Thomas Woody, *A History of Women's Education in the United States* (2 vols.; New York: Science Press, 1929) considers a subject that is too often ignored amid airy generalizations from what was happening to males.

The titles of textbooks used in the colonies may be gleaned from the sources listed in the bibliography for the introduction to Part I (pp. 584-585 *supra*), supplemented, perhaps, by a work such as George Emery Littlefield, *Early Schools and School-Books of New England* (Boston: The Club of Odd Volumes, 1904). George A. Plimpton discusses "The Hornbook and Its Use in America" in the *Proceedings of the American Antiquarian Society,* new ser., XXVI (1916), 264-272, providing an interesting addendum to Andrew Tuer's classic *History of the Horn-Book* (London: The Leadenhall Press, 1897). Ray Nash's "American Writing Masters and Copybooks," *Publications of the Colonial Society of Massachusetts,* XLII (1964), 343-412, serves similarly to complement Ambrose Heal, *The English Writing-Masters and Their Copy-Books, 1570-1800* (Cambridge: Cambridge University Press, 1931). Robert F. Roden speculates in *The Cambridge Press, 1638-1692: A History of the First Printing Press Established in English America, Together with a Bibliographical List of the Issues of the Press* (New York: Dodd Mead & Company, 1905) as to whether the so-called speller that issued from the Cambridge Press in the 1640's was actually Edmund Coote's *The English Schoole-Maister* (1596).

A good deal of work is needed on the seventeenth-century colonial schoolmaster. The one serious book in the field, Willard Elsbree's *The American Teacher* (New York: American Book Company, 1939), takes as its leitmotif the rise of professionalism and hence passes quickly and lightly over the colonial period. Wilson Smith ably examines Puritan attitudes toward teaching in "The Teacher in Puritan Culture," *Harvard Educational Review,* XXXVI (1966), 394-411; but his discussion there includes Harvard tutors as well as schoolmasters and his primary concern is to distinguish between the teaching and the ministerial careers—a distinction that was probably more social than educational in its essence. Bruce mentions a number of schoolmasters in his *Institutional History of Virginia in the Seventeenth Century,* though not much is known about any of them. Emma Van Vechten does likewise in "Early Schools and Schoolmasters of New Amsterdam," in Maud Wilder Goodwin *et al.,* eds., *Historic New York* (New York: G. P. Putnam's Sons, 1899), pp. 321-343, as do William Heard Kilpatrick in *The Dutch Schools of New Netherland and Colonial New York* and Ellis Lawrence Raesly in *Portrait of New Netherland* (New York: Columbia University Press, 1945). There are several brief portraits in the *Dictionary of American Biography* and in John Langdon Sibley's *Biographical Sketches of Graduates of Harvard University, in Cambridge, Massachusetts* (3 vols.; Cambridge, Mass.: Charles William Sever, 1873-1885). George E. Littlefield's "Elijah Corlet and the 'Faire Grammar Schoole' at Cambridge," *Publications of the Colonial Society of Massachusetts,* XVII (1915), 131-142, exemplifies what is needed.

Much of what we know about Ezekiel Cheever derives from Cotton Mather, *Corderius Americanus: An Essay upon the Good Education of Children* (Boston: John Allen, 1708). There is also a book-length biography by Elizabeth Porter Gould, entitled *Ezekiel Cheever: Schoolmaster* (Boston: The Palmer Company, 1904), and an excellent article by Thomas Woody in the *Dictionary of American Biography.* John T. Hassam's book, *Ezekiel Cheever and Some of His Descendants* (Boston: David Clapp & Son, 1879) is useful with respect to matters bibliographical and genealogical; there are a few unpublished documents in the Massachusetts Historical Society.

The development of a "public concernment" with schooling in Massachusetts is ably discussed by Geraldine Murphy in "Massachusetts Bay Colony: The Role of Government in Education." Obviously, any such consideration raises the age-old question of what was meant by a "free school" in the colonies and in contemporary England, a question on which A. F. Leach, *English Schools at the Reformation, 1546-8,* Elmer Ellsworth Brown, *The Making of Our Middle Schools* (New York: Longmans, Green, and Co., 1903), and Clara McMahon, "A Note on the Free School Idea in Colonial Maryland," *Maryland Historical Magazine,* LIV (1959), 149-152, are illuminating. The licensing of colonial schoolmasters is touched upon briefly in Kilpatrick, *The Dutch Schools of New Netherland and Colonial New York,* Bell, *The Church, the State, and Education in Virginia,* Small, *Early New England Schools,* and Norwood M. Cole, "The Licensing of Schoolmasters in Colonial Massachusetts," *History of Education Journal,* VIII (1957), 68-74; but the sketchiness of the material and its emphasis on legal codes rather than their application in specific instances is indicative of the work that is needed. The accessibility of schooling to Negroes and Indians is discussed in C. G. Woodson, *The Education of the Negro Prior to 1861: A History of the Education of the Colored People of the United States from the Beginning of Slavery to the Civil War* (2d ed.; Washington, D.C.:

The Associated Publishers, 1919) and in Alden T. Vaughan, *New England Frontier: Puritans and Indians, 1620-1675* (Boston: Little, Brown and Company, 1965).

CHAPTER 7: COLLEGE

The standard history of the medieval European universities is Hastings Rashdall, *The Universities of Europe in the Middle Ages,* edited by F. M. Powicke and A. B. Emden (3 vols.; Oxford: Clarendon Press, 1936). The standard histories of Oxford and Cambridge are Charles Edward Mallet, *A History of the University of Oxford* (3 vols.; London: Methuen & Co., 1924-1927) and James Bass Mullinger, *The University of Cambridge* (3 vols.; Cambridge: Cambridge University Press, 1873-1911). The development of the Inns of Court is sketched by W. S. Holdsworth in *A History of English Law* (12 vols.; London: Methuen & Co., 1903-1938). Gordon Leff deals incisively with medieval Oxford in *Paris and Oxford Universities in the Thirteenth and Fourteenth Centuries* (New York: John Wiley & Sons, 1968), which includes a discriminating bibliography; while John M. Fletcher deals with curricular matters in "The Teaching of Arts at Oxford, 1400-1520," *Paedagogica Historica,* VII (1967), 417-454, an article based on his unpublished doctoral thesis at the University of Oxford. The standard bibliography of printed Oxfordiana is E. H. Cordeaux and D. H. Merry, *A Bibliography of Printed Works Relating to the University of Oxford* (Oxford: Clarendon Press, 1968). The recent literature on medieval Cambridge is sparse by comparison, the burden of attention having gone to later periods. Developments at both universities are touched upon by Clara P. McMahon in *Education in Fifteenth-Century England* (Baltimore: The Johns Hopkins Press, 1947). The many histories of the individual Inns and colleges are also of obvious value.

The best book on the transformation of Oxford and Cambridge during the Tudor and early Stuart eras is Mark H. Curtis, *Oxford and Cambridge in Transition, 1558-1642* (Oxford: Clarendon Press, 1959). Joan Simon, *Education and Society in Tudor England* (Cambridge: Cambridge University Press, 1966) and James Kelsey McConica, *English Humanists and Reformation Politics Under Henry VIII and Edward VI* (Oxford: Clarendon Press, 1965) deal with both universities during the earlier decades of the Renaissance; H. C. Porter vividly portrays sixteenth-century Cambridge in *Reformation and Reaction in Tudor Cambridge* (Cambridge: Cambridge University Press, 1958); while Kenneth Charlton presents an overview of developments at both the universities and the Inns of Court in *Education in Renaissance England* (London: Routledge and Kegan Paul, 1965), challenging Curtis' assertion that the period between 1558 and 1642 marked a transformation in the character of Oxford and Cambridge.

Lawrence Stone brings together the recent studies on the changing size and social composition of the student bodies at the universities and Inns of Court in "The Educational Revolution in England, 1560-1640," *Past & Present,* no. 28 (July, 1964), 41-80 (including Joan Simon's analysis of "The Social Origins of Cambridge Students, 1603-1640," *Past & Present,* no. 26 [November,

1968], which is critical of Curtis). Data on the curriculum of the universities and Inns at the time of North American colonization can be gleaned from the works of Curtis, Charlton, and Porter, cited above, as well as from Wilbur Samuel Howell, *Logic and Rhetoric in England, 1500-1700* (Princeton: Princeton University Press, 1956), Phyllis Allen, "Medical Education in 17th Century England," *Journal of the History of Medicine and Allied Sciences,* I (1946), 115-163, and "Scientific Studies in the English Universities of the Seventeenth Century," *Journal of the History of Ideas,* X (1949), 219-253, Nan Cooke Carpenter, "The Study of Music at the University of Oxford in the Renaissance (1450-1600)," *The Musical Quarterly,* XLI (1955), 191-214, W. R. Prest, "The Learning Exercises at the Inns of Court 1590-1640," *The Journal of the Society of Public Teachers of Law,* new ser., IX (1966-67), 301-313, and "Legal Education of the Gentry at the Inns of Court, 1560-1640," *Past & Present,* no. 38 (December, 1967), 20-39, Richard S. Westfall, *Science and Religion in Seventeenth-Century England* (New Haven: Yale University Press, 1958), William T. Costello, *The Scholastic Curriculum at Early Seventeenth-Century Cambridge* (Cambridge, Mass.: Harvard University Press, 1958), Francis R. Johnson, *Astronomical Thought in Renaissance England* (Baltimore: The Johns Hopkins Press, 1937), E. G. R. Taylor, *Late Tudor and Early Stuart Geography, 1583-1650* (London: Methuen & Co., 1934), and *The Mathematical Practitioners of Tudor and Stuart England* (Cambridge: Cambridge University Press, 1954), and Christopher Hill, *Intellectual Origins of the English Revolution* (Oxford: Clarendon Press, 1965).

Richard Holdsworth's "Directions for a Student" are printed in their entirety and brilliantly explicated in Harris Francis Fletcher, *The Intellectual Development of John Milton* (2 vols.; Urbana: University of Illinois Press, 1956-1961), though the significance which Fletcher assigns them (a position concurred in by Curtis in *Oxford and Cambridge in Transition* and by Samuel Eliot Morison in *The Founding of Harvard College* [Cambridge, Mass.: Harvard University Press, 1935]) is challenged by Hill in *Intellectual Origins of the English Revolution.*

Dixon Ryan Fox's elaboration of Edward Eggleston's thesis is stated in "Civilization in Transit," the first essay of *Ideas in Motion* (New York: D. Appleton-Century Company, 1935). It is, of course, a latter-day version of "the arts move westward" thesis commonly held in the colonial period (see pp. 559-562 *supra*) and has been sharply challenged by those like Constance Rourke in *The Roots of American Culture and Other Essays,* edited by Van Wyck Brooks (New York: Harcourt, Brace and Company, 1942), who would stress the search for autochthonous traditions rather than cultural importations. A recent refinement of Fox's argument with special reference to the field of science is George Basalla, "The Spread of Western Science," *Science,* CLVI (1967), 611-621. The remarkable early influence of the English universities and Inns of Court on the colonies is treated in Franklin Bowditch Dexter, "The Influence of the English Universities in the Development of New England," in Dexter, *A Selection from the Miscellaneous Historical Papers of Fifty Years* (New Haven: The Tuttle, Morehouse & Taylor Company, 1918), Samuel Eliot Morison, *The Founding of Harvard College,* and John B. Prizer, *Some Aspects of the*

Influence of Cambridge Men and Their University in the American Colonies (Philadelphia: Society of Colonial Wars in the Commonwealth of Pennsylvania, 1956), the Prizer discussion being one of the few that looks beyond New England. Obversely, the attendance of Americans at Oxford, Cambridge, and the Inns of Court is dealt with in C. E. A. Bedwell, "American Middle Templars," *The American Historical Review*, XXV (1919-20), 680-689, E. Alfred Jones, *American Members of the Inns of Court* (London: The Saint Catherine Press, 1924), J. G. de Roulhac Hamilton, "Southern Members of the Inns of Court," *The North Carolina Historical Review*, X (1933), 278-279, Willard Connely, "Colonial Americans in Oxford and Cambridge," *The American Oxonian*, XXIX (1942), 6-17, 75-77, and William L. Sachse, "Harvard Men in England, 1642-1714," *Publications of the Colonial Society of Massachusetts*, XXXV (1951), 119-144, and *The Colonial American in Britain* (Madison: University of Wisconsin Press, 1956).

The development of indigenous medical, legal, and theological education under an apprenticeship system is dealt with, often indirectly, in Richard Harrison Shryock, *Medicine and Society in America, 1660-1860* (New York: New York University Press, 1960), Otho T. Beall, Jr. and Richard H. Shryock, *Cotton Mather: First Significant Figure in American Medicine* (Baltimore: Johns Hopkins Press, 1954), William Frederick Norwood, *Medical Education in the United States Before the Civil War* (Philadelphia: University of Pennsylvania Press, 1944), Paul Mahlon Hamlin, *Legal Education in Colonial New York* (New York: New York University Law Quarterly Review, 1939), Anton-Hermann Chroust, *The Rise of the Legal Profession in America* (2 vols.; Norman: University of Oklahoma Press, 1965), and William Orpheus Shewmaker, "The Training of the Protestant Ministry in the United States of America Before the Establishment of Theological Seminaries," *Papers of the American Society of Church History*, VI (1921), 71-202.

The ill-fated effort to establish Henrico College in Virginia is reviewed in Robert Hunt Land, "Henrico and Its College," *William and Mary College Quarterly*, 2d ser., XVIII (1938), 453-498. John Stoughton's proposal for a college is discussed in Morison, *The Founding of Harvard College*. The literature on seventeenth-century Harvard is dominated, of course, by Morison's magisterial histories, *The Founding of Harvard College* and *Harvard College in the Seventeenth Century* (2 vols.; Cambridge, Mass.: Harvard University Press, 1936). The volumes set a model for the historiography of individual institutions of higher learning, though Morison has tended to exaggerate the humanistic and rationalistic character of Puritan higher education in contrast to its theological and doctrinal character (see Winthrop S. Hudson, "The Morison Myth Concerning the Founding of Harvard College," *Church History*, VIII [1939], 148-159). The three volumes of "Harvard College Records" published as volumes XV, XVI, and XXXI of the *Publications of the Colonial Society of Massachusetts*, with excellent introductions by Albert Matthews and Samuel Eliot Morison, provide an invaluable complement to Morison's histories, as do the individual biographies in John Langdon Sibley, *Biographical Sketches of Graduates of Harvard University, in Cambridge, Massachusetts* (3 vols.; Cambridge, Mass.: Charles William Sever, 1873-1885) and, most significant of all, the collections in the Harvard College Archives, which, under the distinguished supervision of Clifford K. Shipton, have become a model for other institutions to imitate. Albert Matthews' listing of temporary students at Harvard College between 1639 and 1800 in the *Publications of the Colonial Society of Massachusetts*, XVII (1915), 271-285, is a useful addendum to Sibley.

With respect to the traditional, well-established links between Harvard and early seventeenth-century Cambridge, it is well to bear in mind Father Costello's observation in *The Scholastic Curriculum at Early Seventeenth-Century Cambridge* (p. 110): "The Whig historians have made of Cambridge a Puritan university, coloring a place like Trinity with Emmanuel; the Tories, on the other hand, will urge the loyalty of Cambridge divinity, arguing that Emmanuel was a separatist little seedbed, which can be ignored as far as the whole University is concerned. The truth lies somewhere between. Cambridge was as loyal, on the whole, as Oxford (we yield the confusion of orthodoxy with loyalty) and, if Cambridge be theologically suspect in the earlier decades of the 1600's, it is because two of her colleges, Emmanuel and Sidney Sussex, smelled of Puritanism."

Colyer Meriwether presents much useful information about the higher learning in the colonies in *Our Colonial Curriculum, 1607-1776* (Washington, D.C.: Capital Publishing Company, 1907), though the work is essentially a compilation and difficult to read. Beyond the ample information in the Morison histories, there is valuable material on the Harvard curriculum in Edward Kenneth Rand, "Liberal Education in Seventeenth-Century Harvard," *The New England Quarterly*, VI (1933), 525-551, Arthur O. Norton, "Harvard Textbooks and Reference Books of the Seventeenth Century," *Publications of the Colonial Society of Massachusetts*, XXVIII (1935), 361-438, Alfred C. Potter, "Catalogue of John Harvard's Library," *ibid.*, XXI (1919), 190-230, Henry J. Cadbury, "John Harvard's Library," *ibid.*, XXXIV (1943), 353-377, Porter C. Perrin, "Possible Sources of *Technologia* at Early Harvard," *The New England Quarterly*, VII (1934), 718-724, and Keith L. Sprunger, "Technometria: A Prologue to Puritan Theology," *Journal of the History of Ideas*, XXIX (1968), 115-122. And, given the special role of Ramist logic at early Harvard, Walter J. Ong's *Ramus, Method, and the Decay of Dialogue* (Cambridge, Mass.: Harvard University Press, 1958) is indispensable.

The most authoritative essay on Henry Dunster is in Samuel Eliot Morison, *Builders of the Bay Colony* (Boston: Houghton Mifflin Company, 1930); it patently supersedes Jeremiah Chaplin, *Life of Henry Dunster, First President of Harvard College* (Boston: J. R. Osgood and Company, 1872).

The evolution of lay control at Harvard is discussed in Morison, *Harvard College in the Seventeenth Century* and in Richard Hofstadter and Walter P. Metzger, *The Development of Academic Freedom in the United States* (New York: Columbia University Press, 1955). The evolving aims of the college are dealt with at length by Jerome Fink in "The Purposes of the American Colonial Colleges" (unpublished doctoral thesis, Stanford University, 1958), while the changing bases of support are explicated by Margery Somers Foster, *"Out of Smalle Beginnings . . ."* (Cambridge, Mass.: Harvard University Press, 1962). Finally, the events surrounding the founding and failure of the Indian College are discussed by Alden T. Vaughan, *New England Frontier: Puritans and Indians, 1620-1675* (Boston: Little, Brown and Company, 1965) and William Kellaway, *The New England Company, 1649-1776* (New York: Barnes & Noble, 1962), as well as by Morison in *Harvard College in the Seventeenth Century*.

CHAPTER 8: COMMUNITY

The character of English communities in the earlier seventeenth century is discussed in Wallace Notestein, *The English People on the Eve of Colonization, 1603-1630* (New York: Harper & Row, 1954), Carl Bridenbaugh, *Vexed and Troubled Englishmen, 1590-1642* (New York: Oxford University Press, 1968), Peter Laslett, *The World We Have Lost* (London: Methuen and Company, 1965), D. V. Glass and D. E. C. Eversley, eds., *Population in History* (Chicago: Aldine Publishing Company, 1965), Joan Thirsk, ed., *The Agrarian History of England and Wales, 1500-1640*, The Agrarian History of England and Wales, edited by H. P. R. Finberg (Cambridge: Cambridge University Press, 1967), W. G. Hoskins, *Essays in Leicestershire History* (Liverpool: University Press of Liverpool, 1950), *The Midland Peasant: The Economic and Social History of a Leicestershire Village* (London: Macmillan and Company, 1957), and *Provincial England: Essays in Social and Economic History* (London: Macmillan and Company, 1963), Wallace T. MacCaffrey, *Exeter, 1540-1640* (Cambridge, Mass.: Harvard University Press, 1958), Norman G. Brett-James, *The Growth of Stuart London* (London: G. Allen & Unwin, [1935]), Harold Priestley, *London: The Years of Change* (New York: Barnes & Noble, 1965), and, more generally, G. M. Trevelyan, *English Social History: A Survey of Six Centuries, Chaucer to Queen Victoria* (London: Longmans and Company, 1942). Contemporary sources such as William Harrison, *The Description of England* (1587), edited by Georges Edelen (Ithaca: Cornell University Press, 1968), John Stow, *A Survey of London* (1598), edited by Charles L. Kingsford (3 vols.; Oxford: Clarendon Press, 1908), and Thomas Wilson, *The State of England Anno. Dom. 1600*, edited by F. J. Fisher, *Camden Miscellany*, XVI, 3d ser., lii (1936), 1-47, are of course invaluable.

My conception of the relation between London and the realm is based on Lewis Mumford's brilliant portrayal of the role of the baroque capital in *The City in History: Its Origins, Its Transformations, and Its Prospects* (New York: Harcourt, Brace & World, 1961), and *The Culture of Cities* (New York: Harcourt, Brace and Company, 1938), as complemented by the data on demography in E. A. Wrigley, "A Simple Model of London's Importance in Changing English Society and Economy 1650-1750," *Past & Present*, no. 37 (July, 1967), 44-70, on travel in Joan Parkes, *Travel in England in the Seventeenth Century* (London: Oxford University Press, 1925) and R. W. Franz, *The English Traveller and the Movement of Ideas, 1660-1732* (Lincoln: University of Nebraska Press, 1934), on trade in Dorothy Davis, *Fairs, Shops, and Supermarkets: A History of English Shopping* (Toronto: University of Toronto Press, 1966), and on printing and the distribution of English printed matter in H. S. Bennett, *English Books & Readers, 1558-1603* (Cambridge: Cambridge University Press, 1965), P. M. Handover, *Printing in London from 1476 to Modern Times* (Cambridge, Mass.: Harvard University Press, 1960), W. W. Greg, *Some Aspects and Problems of*

London Publishing Between 1550 and 1650 (Oxford: Clarendon Press, 1956), Cyprian Blagden, *The Stationers' Company: A History, 1403-1959* (Cambridge, Mass.: Harvard University Press, 1960), William M. Clyde, *The Struggle for the Freedom of the Press from Caxton to Cromwell* (London: Oxford University Press, 1934), Leona Rostenberg, *Literary, Political, Scientific, Religious & Legal Publishing, Printing & Bookselling in England, 1551-1700: Twelve Studies* (2 vols.; New York: Burt Franklin, 1965), Oliver M. Willard, "The Circulation of Books in Elizabethan England: Observations upon the Available Evidence, and Suggestions for Its Interpretation" (unpublished doctoral thesis, Harvard University, 1936), and Pearl Beattie Mitchell, "The England of the First General Reading Public, 1643-1645" (unpublished doctoral thesis, Stanford University, 1935).

The Puritan lectureships are dealt with in Christopher Hill, *Society and Puritanism in Pre-Revolutionary England* (New York: Schocken Books, 1964) and Paul Siddall Seaver, "The Puritan Lectureships in London: A Study in Institutional Development and Ecclesiastical Politics, 1560-1662" (unpublished doctoral thesis, Harvard University, 1964). The early English newspapers are discussed in M. A. Shaaber, *Some Forerunners of the Newspaper in England, 1476-1622* (Philadelphia: University of Pennsylvania Press, 1929) and Joseph Frank, *The Beginnings of the English Newspaper, 1620-1660* (Cambridge, Mass.: Harvard University Press, 1961). The rise of the coffeehouses is portrayed in Aytoun Ellis, *The Penny Universities: A History of the Coffee-Houses* (London: Secker & Warburg, 1956). And the founding of the Royal Society is recounted, from quite different perspectives, by Dorothy Stimson, *Scientists and Amateurs: A History of the Royal Society* (New York: Henry Schuman, 1948), and Margery Purver, *The Royal Society: Concept and Creation* (London: Routledge and Kegan Paul, 1967).

The conception of a transatlantic community in the seventeenth century is derived from E. E. Rich, "The Population of Elizabethan England," *The Economic History Review*, 2d ser., II (1949-50), 247-265, Bernard Bailyn, "Communications and Trade: The Atlantic in the Seventeenth Century," *The Journal of Economic History*, XIII (1953), 378-387, and *The New England Merchants in the Seventeenth Century* (Cambridge, Mass.: Harvard University Press, 1955), Frederick B. Tolles, *Quakers and the Atlantic Culture* (New York: The Macmillan Company, 1960), Frederick E. Brasch, "The Royal Society of London and Its Influence upon Scientific Thought in the American Colonies," *The Scientific Monthly*, XXXIII (1931), 336-355, 448-469, Raymond P. Stearns, "Colonial Fellows of the Royal Society of London, 1661-1778," *The William and Mary Quarterly*, 3d ser., III (1946), 206-268, and, more generally, William L. Sachse, *The Colonial American in Britain* (Madison: University of Wisconsin Press, 1956).

Glenn T. Trewartha develops a morphology of early American communities in "Types of Rural Settlement in Colonial America," *The Geographical Review*, XXXVI (1946), 568-596; his essay should be read in conjunction with Herman R. Friis, *A Series of Population Maps of the Colonies and the United States, 1625-1790* (New York: The American Geographical Society, 1940), H. Roy Merrens, "Historical Geography and Early American History," *The William and*

Mary Quarterly, 3d ser., XXII (1965), 529-548, Lewis Cecil Gray, *History of Agriculture in the Southern United States to 1860* (2 vols.; Washington, D.C.: The Carnegie Institution of Washington, 1933), Percy Wells Bidwell and John I. Falconer, *History of Agriculture in the Northern United States, 1620-1860* (Washington, D.C.: The Carnegie Institution of Washington, 1925), and Carlos Richard Allen, "Travel and Communication in the Early Colonial Period, 1607-1720" (unpublished doctoral thesis, University of California, Berkeley, 1956).

Anne Bush Maclear, *Early New England Towns: A Comparative Study of Their Development* (New York: Longmans, Green & Co., 1908), Edna Scofield, "The Origin of Settlement Patterns in New England," *The Geographical Review*, XXVIII (1938), 652-663, F. Grave Morris, "Some Aspects of the Rural Settlement of New England in Colonial Times," in L. Dudley Stamp and S. W. Wooldridge, eds., *London Essays in Geography: Rodwell Jones Memorial Volume* (Cambridge, Mass.: Harvard University Press, 1951), pp. 219-227, William Haller, *The Puritan Frontier: Town-Planting in New England Colonial Development 1630-1660* (New York: Columbia University Press, 1951), Anthony N. B. Garvan, *Architecture and Town Planning in Colonial Connecticut* (New Haven: Yale University Press, 1951), Kenneth A. Lockridge, *A New England Town: The First Hundred Years* (New York: W. W. Norton & Company, 1970), and Edward Spaulding Perzel, "The First Generation of Settlement in Colonial Ipswich, Massachusetts, 1633-1660" (unpublished doctoral thesis, Rutgers University, 1967) convey a sense of the nature and character of the early New England town. The explicit values of the New England *paideia* are detailed in Perry Miller, *The New England Mind* (2 vols.; Cambridge, Mass.: Harvard University Press, 1939-1953). The clash between the "Puritan" and the "Yankee" is depicted in Vernon L. Parrington, *Main Currents in American Thought* (3 vols.; New York: Harcourt, Brace and Company, 1927-1930), I, 88, as well as in "The Apologia of Robert Keayne," edited by Bernard Bailyn, *Publications of the Colonial Society of Massachusetts*, XLII (1964), 243-341, and Darrett B. Rutman, *Winthrop's Boston: A Portrait of a Puritan Town, 1630-1649* (Chapel Hill: University of North Carolina Press, 1960.

Richard L. Morton, *Colonial Virginia* (2 vols.; Chapel Hill: University of North Carolina Press, 1960) discusses land policy in the seventeenth century, complementing the earlier analyses of Philip Alexander Bruce in the *Economic History of Virginia in the Seventeenth Century* (2 vols.; New York: Macmillan and Company, 1895), Wesley Frank Craven in *Dissolution of the Virginia Company* (New York: Oxford University Press, 1932), and Thomas J. Wertenbaker in *The Shaping of Colonial Virginia* (New York: Russell and Russell, 1958)— an anthology of *Patrician and Plebeian in Virginia* (1910), *The Planters of Colonial Virginia* (1922), and *Virginia Under the Stuarts* (1914). Seventeenth-century spokesmen such as Richard Green in *Virginia's Cure: or, An Advisive Narrative Concerning Virginia* (London: W. Goodbid, 1662), in Peter Force, ed., *Tracts and Other Papers, Relating Principally to the Origin, Settlement, and Progress of the Colonies in North America, from the Discovery of the Country to the Year 1776* (4 vols.; Washington, D.C.: Peter Force, 1836-1846), vol. III, no. 15, were eloquent concerning the bearing of the dispersed farmstead pattern of settlement on Virginia's education and culture; John C. Rainbolt undertakes a historical assessment of the pattern in "The Absence of Towns in Seventeenth-Century Virginia," *The Journal of Southern History*, XXXV (1969), 343-360.

Irving Elting sketches the Dutch patterns of settlement in the middle colonies in *Dutch Village Communities on the Hudson River* (Baltimore: N. Murray, 1886). Amandus Johnson does likewise for Swedish patterns in *The Swedish Settlements on the Delaware, 1638-1664* (2 vols.; New York: D. Appleton and Company, 1911), while John H. Wuorinen portrays Finnish patterns in *The Finns on the Delaware, 1638-1655* (New York: Columbia University Press, 1938). Adrian C. Leiby's *The Early Dutch and Swedish Settlers of New Jersey* (Princeton, N.J.: D. Van Nostrand Company, Inc., 1964) is a more recent work, with a useful critical bibliography. The Johnson, Wuorinen, and Leiby volumes convey something of the communal character of Swedish, Finnish, and Dutch colonial education, as does William Heard Kilpatrick's *The Dutch Schools of New Netherland and Colonial New York* (Washington, D.C.: Government Printing Office, 1912).

The character of life in the colonial market towns of the seventeenth century is vividly portrayed by Carl Bridenbaugh in *Cities in the Wilderness: The First Century of Urban Life in America 1625-1742* (2d ed.; New York: Alfred A. Knopf, 1955). Darrett B. Rutman's detailed study of *Winthrop's Boston* is also valuable, as is Mrs. Schuyler Van Rensselaer's older but still useful *History of the City of New York in the Seventeenth Century* (2 vols.; New York: The Macmillan Company, 1902).

The value of comparing the Irish with the North American colonial ventures, given their contemporaneity, was first suggested to me by my colleague Harold J. Noah, who should not be held responsible for the outcome. The comparison is not meant to draw invidious distinctions, nor to cast aspersion on the native Irish or their English conquerors, nor to establish the superiority of the American Indians and their English conquerors. Rather, it is meant, first, to dramatize the similarities in the educational development of the several English-speaking North American colonies, as something of a corrective to a century of polemical historiography attempting to establish the differences with a view to indicating the superiority of one over the others, and, second, to raise questions concerning the relation of education to economic and political development, granting that education is far from the only or even the most significant factor in economic and political development and allowing that the data for both economics and education in both societies during the seventeenth century are primordial. Those interested in pursuing the comparison will find David Beers Quinn, *The Elizabethans and the Irish* (Ithaca: Cornell University Press, 1966) a good place to begin; J. C. Beckett, *The Making of Modern Ireland, 1603-1923* (New York: Alfred A. Knopf, 1966) is an excellent general history, with a valuable critical bibliography; Aidan Clarke, *The Old English in Ireland, 1625-42* (London: Macgibbon & Kee, 1966), Edward MacLysaght, *Irish Life in the Seventeenth Century: After Cromwell* (London: Longmans, Green & Co., 1939), Richard Bagwell, *Ireland Under the Stuarts and During the Interregnum* (3 vols.; London: Longmans, Green, and Co., 1909-16), K. Theodore Hoppen, "The Dublin Philosophical Society and the New Learning in Ireland," *Irish Historical Studies*, XIV (1964-65), 99-118, James Johnston Auchmuty,

Irish Education: A Historical Survey (Dublin: Hodges Figgis & Co., 1937), and Sister Anthony Marie Gallagher, *Education in Ireland* (Washington: Catholic University of America Press, 1948) are replete with pertinent information.

INTRODUCTION TO BOOK II

George Macaulay Trevelyan's little classic *The English Revolution, 1688-1689* (London: Thornton Butterworth, 1938) presents the traditional Whig view of the events of 1688-1689 as a triumph of constitutional monarchy and individual liberty; Maurice Ashley's *The Glorious Revolution of 1688* (New York: Charles Scribner's Sons, 1966) is more skeptical, placing greater emphasis on the particular personalities of James II and William III. David Ogg deals more generally with the closing years of the seventeenth century in *England in the Reigns of James II and William III* (Oxford: Clarendon Press, 1955), while the impact of the Glorious Revolution in America is treated in Michael G. Hall, Lawrence H. Leder, and Michael G. Kammen, eds., *The Glorious Revolution in America* (Chapel Hill: University of North Carolina Press, 1964), which presents documents, commentary, and an excellent brief bibliography.

The direct and immediate connections between the political upheavals of 1688-1689 and the intellectual revolution associated with Newton and Locke can easily be pressed too far, particularly in light of such recent works on Newton as Thomas S. Kuhn's *The Copernican Revolution: Planetary Astronomy in the Development of Western Thought* (Cambridge, Mass.: Harvard University Press, 1957) and Alexandre Koyré's *From the Closed World to the Infinite Universe* (Baltimore: Johns Hopkins Press, 1957), and such recent works on Locke as Maurice Cranston's *John Locke: A Biography* (London: Longman's Green and Co., 1957), Philip Abrams' "The Locke Myth," *Past & Present*, no. 15 (April, 1959), 87-90, and *John Locke: Two Tracts on Government* (Cambridge: Cambridge University Press, 1967), Peter Laslett's *Locke's Two Treatises of Government* (Cambridge: Cambridge University Press, 1960), and John Dunn's *The Political Thought of John Locke: An Historical Account of the Argument of the "Two Treatises of Government"* (Cambridge: Cambridge University Press, 1969). Yet a broad and general connection between the two revolutions is inescapable and is brilliantly explicated by John Herman Randall, Jr., in *The Career of Philosophy: From the Middle Ages to the Enlightenment* (New York: Columbia University Press, 1962).

The literature on Newton and Locke was already immense by the middle of the twentieth century, when a spirited concern with the history of science, on the one hand, and the opening of the Lovelace collection of Locke papers, on the other, sparked a revival of scholarly interest in both men. Maurice Cranston's *John Locke: A Biography* and Richard I. Aaron's *John Locke* (2d ed.; Oxford: Clarendon Press, 1955) are the best general works, while John W. Yolton, ed., *John Locke: Problems and Perspectives* (Cambridge: Cambridge University Press, 1969) is indicative of the directions of recent scholarship. Frank E. Manuel's *A Portrait of Isaac Newton* (Cambridge, Mass.: Harvard University Press, 1968) throws new light on Newton's personality from a psychoanalytical perspective, though it remains to be seen whether Manuel's explanation suffices for Newton's philosophical insights; Louis Trenchard More's *Isaac Newton: A Biography* (New York: Charles Scribner's Sons, 1934) remains the fullest portrait, though it has been superseded at points by subsequent research. E. A. Burtt, *The Metaphysical Foundations of Modern Physical Science* (New York: Harcourt, Brace & Company, 1925) and Alexandre Koyré, *Newtonian Studies* (Cambridge, Mass.: Harvard University Press, 1965) are incisive expositions of Newtonian philosophy; the principal lines of recent Newton scholarship are indicated in I. Bernard Cohen, "Newton in the Light of Recent Scholarship," *Isis*, LI (1960), 489-514, and D. T. Whiteside, "The Expanding World of Newtonian Research," *History of Science: An Annual Review of Literature, Research and Teaching*, I (1962), 16-29. And, for the general western context, there is no better discussion than Peter Gay's brilliant study *The Enlightenment: An Interpretation* (2 vols.; New York: Alfred A. Knopf, 1966-1969).

The general impact of Newtonian and Lockean ideas on American thought is a subject in need of considerable work. P. Emory Aldrich's discussion of Locke's influence in the *Proceedings of the American Antiquarian Society*, LXXIII (1879), 22-39, is primitive, while Merle Curti's "The Great Mr. Locke, America's Philosopher, 1783-1861," in *Probing Our Past* (New York: Harper & Brothers, 1955), pp. 69-118, gives only passing mention to the pre-Revolutionary period. Frederick E. Brasch, "The Newtonian Epoch in the American Colonies (1680-1783)," *Proceedings of the American Antiquarian Society*, new ser., XLIX (1940), 314-332, is valuable, but sketchy. Carl Becker included an urbane discussion on Newton and Locke in *The Declaration of Independence: A Study in the History of Political Ideas* (New York: Harcourt, Brace and Company, 1922); Max Savelle and Clinton Rossiter include similarly instructive discussions, respectively, in *Seeds of Liberty: The Genesis of the American Mind* (New York: Alfred A. Knopf, 1948) and *Seedtime of the Republic: The Origin of the American Tradition of Political Liberty* (New York: Harcourt, Brace & World, 1953). John Dunn's detailed essay "The Politics of Locke in England and America in the Eighteenth Century," in John W. Yolton, ed., *John Locke: Problems and Perspectives* is indicative of the kind of analysis that is needed to supplement these earlier works.

The provincial America that took unto itself the ideas of Newton and Locke is the subject of a considerable general literature, including Herbert L. Osgood, *The American Colonies in the Eighteenth Century* (4 vols.; New York: Columbia University Press, 1924-25), Lawrence Henry Gipson, *The British Empire Before the American Revolution* (rev. ed.; 14 vols.; New York: Alfred A. Knopf, 1958-1969), James Truslow Adams, *Provincial Society, 1690-1763*, A History of American Life, edited by Arthur M. Schlesinger and Dixon Ryan Fox (New York: The Macmillan Company, 1927), Evarts Boutell Greene, *The Revolutionary Generation, 1763-1790*, A History of American Life, edited by Arthur M. Schlesinger and Dixon Ryan Fox (New York: The Macmillan Company, 1950), Charles M. Andrews, *Colonial Folkways: A Chronicle of American Life in the Reign of the Georges* (New Haven: Yale University Press, 1919), Michael Kraus, *Intercolonial Aspects of American Culture on the Eve of the Revolution, with Special Reference to the Northern Towns* (New York: Columbia University

Press, 1928), and *The Atlantic Civilization: Eighteenth-Century Origins* (Ithaca: Cornell University Press, 1949), Leonard Woods Labaree, *Royal Government in America: A Study of the British Colonial System before 1783* (New Haven: Yale University Press, 1930), and *Conservatism in Early American History* (New York: New York University Press, 1948), Carl Bridenbaugh, *Cities in Revolt: Urban Life in America, 1743-1776* (New York: Alfred A. Knopf, 1955), and *Mitre and Sceptre: Transatlantic Faiths, Ideas, Personalities, and Politics, 1689-1775* (New York: Oxford University Press, 1962), Thomas J. Wertenbaker, *The Golden Age of Colonial Culture* (New York: New York University Press, 1949), Brooke Hindle, *The Pursuit of Science in Revolutionary America, 1735-1789* (Chapel Hill: University of North Carolina Press, 1956), William S. Sachs and Ari Hoogenboom, *The Enterprising Colonials: Society on the Eve of the Revolution* (Chicago: Argonaut, 1965), Alan Heimert, *Religion and the American Mind from the Great Awakening to the Revolution* (Cambridge, Mass.: Harvard University Press, 1966), Arthur M. Schlesinger, *The Birth of the Nation: A Portrait of the American People on the Eve of Independence* (New York: Alfred A. Knopf, 1968), Bernard Bailyn, *The Ideological Origins of the American Revolution* (Cambridge, Mass.: Harvard University Press, 1967), and *The Origins of American Politics* (New York: Alfred A. Knopf, 1968), and Max Savelle, *Seeds of Liberty* and Clinton Rossiter, *Seedtime of the Republic,* already cited. There are superb notes in *Seedtime of the Republic,* and there is a splendid bibliography in Daniel J. Boorstin's *The Americans: The Colonial Experience* (New York: Random House, 1958), already cited at the beginning of this essay.

The changing social composition of the American population in the eighteenth century is discussed in Maldwyn Allen Jones, *American Immigration* (Chicago: University of Chicago Press, 1960) and Marcus Lee Hansen, *The Atlantic Migration, 1607-1860,* edited by Arthur M. Schlesinger (Cambridge, Mass.: Harvard University Press, 1940). Albert Bernhardt Faust, *The German Element in the United States, with Special Reference to Its Political, Moral, Social, and Educational Influence* (2 vols.; Boston: Houghton Mifflin Company, 1909), Henry Jones Ford, *The Scotch-Irish in America* (Princeton: Princeton University Press, 1915), James G. Leyburn, *The Scotch-Irish: A Social History* (Chapel Hill: University of North Carolina Press, 1962), R. J. Dickson, *Ulster Emigration to Colonial America, 1718-1775* (London: Routledge and Kegan Paul, 1966), Lucian J. Fosdick, *The French Blood in America* (New York: F. H. Revell Company, 1906), and Philip D. Curtin, *The Atlantic Slave Trade: A Census* (Madison: University of Wisconsin Press, 1969) discuss the immigration of particular social groups; while J. Potter, "The Growth of Population in America, 1700-1860," in D. V. Glass and D. E. C. Eversley, eds., *Population in History* (Chicago: Aldine Publishing Company, 1965), pp. 631-688, discusses the natural increase of the native white population in the eighteenth century. The national origins of the white population in 1790 are discussed in the report of the American Council of Learned Societies' Committee on Linguistic and National Stocks in the Population of the United States, *Annual Report of the American Historical Association for the Year 1931* (Washington, D.C.: Government Printing Office, 1932), pp. 103-441.

For the social history of early Pennsylvania, the older work of Sidney George Fisher, notably, *The Making of Pennsylvania* (Philadelphia: J. B. Lippincott Company, 1896), and Wayland F. Dunaway's general textbook *A History of Pennsylvania* (2d ed.; New York: Prentice-Hall, 1948) remain useful, along with such specialized works as Frederick B. Tolles, *Meeting House and Counting House: The Quaker Merchants of Colonial Philadelphia: 1682-1763* (Chapel Hill: University of North Carolina Press, 1948), and *James Logan and the Culture of Provincial America* (Boston: Little, Brown and Company, 1957), Carl and Jessica Bridenbaugh, *Rebels and Gentlemen: Philadelphia in the Age of Franklin* (New York: Reynal & Hitchcock, 1942), Edwin B. Bronner, *William Penn's "Holy Experiment": The Founding of Pennsylvania, 1681-1701* (New York: Columbia University Press, 1962), Joseph E. Illick, *William Penn the Politician: His Relations with the English Government* (Ithaca: Cornell University Press, 1965), Mary Maples Dunn, *William Penn: Politics and Conscience* (Princeton: Princeton University Press, 1967), Gary B. Nash, *Quakers and Politics: Pennsylvania, 1681-1726* (Princeton: Princeton University Press, 1968), Wayland F. Dunaway, *The Scotch-Irish of Colonial Pennsylvania* (Chapel Hill: University of North Carolina Press, 1944), Ralph Wood, ed., *The Pennsylvania Germans* (Princeton: Princeton University Press, 1942), Charles H. Browning, *Welsh Settlement of Pennsylvania* (Philadelphia: W. J. Campbell, 1912), and Gillian Lindt Gollin, *Moravians in Two Worlds: A Study of Changing Communities* (New York: Columbia University Press, 1967).

The effort to "Americanize" the Pennsylvania Germans is discussed in Samuel Edwin Weber, *The Charity School Movement in Colonial Pennsylvania* (Philadelphia: George F. Lasher, 1905), Horace Wemyss Smith, *Life and Correspondence of the Rev. William Smith* (2 vols.; Philadelphia: S. A. George & Co., 1879-80), Glenn Weaver, "The Lutheran Church During the French and Indian War," *The Lutheran Quarterly*, VI (1954), 248-256, Whitfield J. Bell, "Benjamin Franklin and the German Charity Schools," *Proceedings of the American Philosophical Society*, XCIX (1955), 381-387, Glenn Weaver, "Benjamin Franklin and the Pennsylvania Germans," *The William and Mary Quarterly*, 3d ser., XIV (1957), 536-559, and Jonathan Messerli, "Benjamin Franklin: Colonial and Cosmopolitan Educator," *British Journal of Educational Studies*, XVI (1968), 43-59.

For the larger process of social integration that "Americanized" the Germans at the same time as it created a self-conscious American community, see Michael Kraus, *Intercolonial Aspects of American Culture on the Eve of the Revolution*, Max Savelle, *Seeds of Liberty*, Hans Kohn, *American Nationalism: An Interpretive Essay* (New York: The Macmillan Company, 1957), Lawrence Henry Gipson, *The Triumphant Empire: Thunder-Clouds Gather in the West, 1763-1766* (New York: Alfred A. Knopf, 1961), Edmund S. Morgan, *The Birth of the Republic, 1763-1789* (Chicago: University of Chicago Press, 1956), and Richard L. Merritt, "Nation-Building in America: The Colonial Years," in Karl W. Deutsch and William J. Foltz, eds., *Nation-Building* (New York: Atherton Press, 1963), and *Symbols of American Community, 1735-1775* (New Haven: Yale University Press, 1966). And for the shifting perceptions of Europeans with respect to the emergent American community, see Durand Echeverria,

Mirage in the West: A History of the French Image of American Society, to 1815 (Princeton: Princeton University Press, 1957) and R. R. Palmer, *The Age of the Democratic Revolution: A Political History of Europe and America, 1760-1800* (2 vols.; Princeton: Princeton University Press, 1959-1964).

The relationship between the North American colonies and the English metropolis in the eighteenth century is incisively explicated by John Clive and Bernard Bailyn in "England's Cultural Provinces: Scotland and America," *The William and Mary Quarterly*, 3d ser., XI (1954), 200-213. Contemporary England is portrayed in Dorothy Marshall, *English People in the Eighteenth Century* (London: Longmans, Green and Co., 1956), and *Eighteenth Century England*, A History of England, edited by W. N. Medlicott (New York: David McKay Company, 1962), J. H. Plumb, *England in the Eighteenth Century (1714-1815)* (Baltimore, Md.: Penguin Books, 1950), and T. S. Ashton, *An Economic History of England: The 18th Century* (London: Methuen & Co., 1955). Contemporary Scotland is discussed in William Law Mathieson, *Scotland and the Union: A History of Scotland from 1695 to 1747* (Glasgow: James Maclehose & Sons, 1905), and *The Awakening of Scotland: A History from 1747 to 1797* (Glasgow: James Maclehose & Sons, 1910), George S. Pryde, *Scotland from 1603 to the Present Day* (London: Thomas Nelson and Sons, 1962), Henry Hamilton, *An Economic History of Scotland in the Eighteenth Century* (Oxford: Clarendon Press, 1963), and Henry Grey Graham's older work, *The Social Life of Scotland in the Eighteenth Century* (2 vols.; London: A. & C. Black, 1899). The best recent bibliography is Stanley Pargellis and D. J. Medley, *Bibliography of British History: The Eighteenth Century, 1714-89* (Oxford: Clarendon Press, 1951).

INTRODUCTION TO PART III

My general view of denominationalism as the shape of American Protestantism, with roots in the provincial era, is based on Winthrop S. Hudson, "Denominationalism as a Basis for Ecumenicity," *Church History*, XXIV (1955), 37-47, *American Protestantism* (Chicago: University of Chicago Press, 1961), and *Religion in America* (New York: Charles Scribner's Sons, 1965), on Sidney Mead, *The Lively Experiment: The Shaping of Christianity in America* (New York: Harper & Row, 1963), on H. Richard Niebuhr, *The Social Sources of Denominationalism* (New York: Henry Holt and Company, 1929), and on Timothy L. Smith, "Congregation, State, and Denomination: The Forming of the American Religious Structure," *The William and Mary Quarterly*, 3d ser., XXV (1968), 155-176. For George Whitefield as the quintessential denominationalist, one can profitably peruse Albert David Belden, *George Whitefield: The Awakener* (New York: The Macmillan Company, 1953), Stuart C. Henry, *George Whitefield: Wayfaring Witness* (New York: Abingdon Press, 1957), Roderic Hall Pierce, "George Whitefield and His Critics" (unpublished doctoral thesis, Princeton University, 1962), and William Howland Kenney III, "George Whitefield and Colonial Revivalism: The Social Sources of Charismatic Authority, 1737-1770" (unpublished doctoral thesis, University of Pennsylvania, 1966).

CHAPTER 9: PIETY RATIONALIZED

The development of English religious thought from the Restoration through the eighteenth century is brilliantly explicated in the works of G. R. Cragg, notably, *From Puritanism to the Age of Reason: A Study of Changes in Religious Thought Within the Church of England, 1600 to 1700* (Cambridge: Cambridge University Press, 1950), *Puritanism in the Period of the Great Persecution, 1660-1688* (Cambridge: Cambridge University Press, 1957), *Reason and Authority in the Eighteenth Century* (Cambridge: Cambridge University Press, 1964), and an admirable collection of documents entitled *The Cambridge Platonists* (New York: Oxford University Press, 1968), in Roland N. Stromberg's *Religious Liberalism in Eighteenth-Century England* (London: Oxford University Press, 1954), and in L. P. Curtis' *Anglican Moods of the Eighteenth Century* (Hamden, Conn.: Archon Books, 1966). Norman Sykes discusses the ecclesiastical context in *Church and State in England in the XVIIIth Century* (Cambridge: Cambridge University Press, 1934). Richard Burgess Barlow traces the development of toleration in *Citizenship and Conscience: A Study in the Theory and Practice of Religious Toleration in England During the Eighteenth Century* (Philadelphia: University of Pennsylvania Press, 1962). Sir Leslie Stephen's classic *History of English Thought in the Eighteenth Century* (3d ed.; 2 vols.; New York: G. P. Putnam's Sons, 1902) remains invaluable, as does Anthony Lincoln's lesser-known work, *Some Political and Social Ideas of English Dissent, 1763-1800* (Cambridge: Cambridge University Press, 1938).

John W. Yolton's *John Locke and the Way of Ideas* (Oxford: Clarendon Press, 1956) examines the substance and impact of Locke's *Essay Concerning Human Understanding* against a background of the religious and moral controversies of the late seventeenth and early eighteenth centuries; H. McLachlan's *The Religious Opinions of Milton, Locke and Newton* (Manchester: Manchester University Press, 1931) deals more directly with the theological and ecclesiastical ideas of the three men. *Some Thoughts Concerning Education* is available in a splendid critical edition edited by James L. Axtell under the title *The Educational Writings of John Locke* (Cambridge: Cambridge University Press, 1968). M. G. Mason, "How John Locke Wrote 'Some Thoughts Concerning Education,' 1693," *Paedagogica Historica,* I (1961), 244-290, and "The Literary Sources of John Locke's Educational Thoughts," *ibid.,* V (1965), 65-108, are useful with respect to the genesis of *Thoughts*; while Daniel Calhoun treats its pedagogy in an interesting unpublished paper entitled "Repression: The Lockean Tradition in American Child-Rearing." Maurice Cranston's *John Locke: A Biography* (London: Longmans, Green and Co., 1957) and Richard I. Aaron's *John Locke* (2d ed.; Oxford: Clarendon Press, 1955) provide valuable background information, though, particularly for matters of religion and education, H. R. Fox Bourne's older biography, *The Life of John Locke* (2 vols.; London: Henry S. King, 1876) remains pertinent.

The standard biography of Watts is Arthur Paul Davis, *Isaac Watts: His Life and Works* ([New York]: privately printed, 1943), which includes a detailed guide to Watts's published and unpublished papers; a convenient edition of his writings is *The Works of the Rev. Isaac Watts* (9 vols.; Leeds: Edward Baines, 1812-1813). Wilbur Macey Stone's *The Divine and Moral Songs of Isaac Watts* (New York: privately printed for the Triptych, 1918) and Phyllis Jane Wetherell's "Education and the Children's Hymn in Eighteenth Century England," in Samuel Clyde McCulloch, ed., *British Humanitarianism: Essays Honoring Frank J. Klingberg* (Philadelphia: Church Historical Society, 1950) are instructive with respect to the phenomenal influence of the *Divine and Moral Songs* in England and America; Paul J. Fay's "Isaac Watts—An Unsung Singer of Education," *School and Society*, XXVIII (1928), 217-224, is a useful essay. Of the several volumes that deal with dissenting education, H. McLachlan, *English Education Under the Test Acts, Being the History of the Nonconformist Academies, 1662-1820* (Manchester: Manchester University Press, 1931) and J. W. Ashley Smith, *The Birth of Modern Education: The Contribution of the Dissenting Academies, 1660-1800* (London: Independent Press, 1954) are most valuable in explicating Watts's critical influence.

The best recent writings on Philip Doddridge came on the two hundredth anniversary of his death, notably the several critical articles in Geoffrey F. Nuttall, ed., *Philip Doddridge, 1702-1751: His Contribution to English Religion* (London: Independent Press, 1951) and Nuttall's lecture *Richard Baxter and Philip Doddridge: A Study in a Tradition* (London: Oxford University Press, 1951). The standard edition of Doddridge's writings, *The Works of the Rev. P. Doddridge* (10 vols.; Leeds: Edward Baines, 1802-1805), includes a memoir of Doddridge by the Reverend Job Orton. Other useful biographies include D. A. Harsha, *Life of Philip Doddridge* (Albany, N.Y.: J. Munsell, 1865) and Charles Stanford, *Philip Doddridge* (London: Hodder & Stoughton, 1880). *The Correspondence and Diary of Philip Doddridge*, edited by John Doddridge Humphreys (5 vols.; London: Henry Colburn and Richard Bentley, 1829-31) is also useful, though marred by inaccurate transcription from the originals. Irene Parker, *Dissenting Academies in England: Their Rise and Progress and Their Place Among the Educational Systems of the Country* (Cambridge: Cambridge University Press, 1914), H. McLachlan, *English Education Under the Test Acts*, J. W. Ashley Smith, *The Birth of Modern Education*, and Bobbie G. Henderson, "Philip Doddridge and the Northampton Academy: Dissenting Education in England in the Eighteenth Century" (unpublished doctoral thesis, George Peabody College for Teachers, 1967) deal with Doddridge's crucial role in the development of the dissenting academies. There are significant collections of Doddridge manuscripts and correspondence at New College, London, the residuary legatee of the academy at Northampton, and at Dr. Williams's Library. Geoffrey F. Nuttall has compiled an immensely useful "Doddridge Intercalation: Interim Intercalated List of Correspondence of Rev. Philip Doddridge, D.D. (D.N.B.), the Greater Part of Which Is Held by New College, London" (London: Historical Manuscripts Commission, 1969).

Given his influence in England and especially in America, too little is known of the work of James Burgh. Significantly, his *Thoughts on Education* was one of the first pamphlets bearing the term "education" in its title to be reprinted in the colonies, though obviously many earlier colonial imprints had dealt with matters educational. There is a brief biography of Burgh in the

1795 edition of *The Dignity of Human Nature* (London: C. Dilly, 1795) and there is a sketch in *The Dictionary of National Biography*.

That the works of Watts, Doddridge, and Burgh were well known in the colonies is attested by the correspondence and writings of American contemporaries, as well as by Clinton Rossiter, *Seedtime of the Republic: The Origin of the American Tradition of Political Liberty* (New York: Harcourt, Brace & World, 1953), Conrad Wright, *The Beginnings of Unitarianism in America* (Boston: Starr King Press, 1955), and Bernard Bailyn, *The Ideological Origins of the American Revolution* (Cambridge, Mass.: Harvard University Press, 1967), among others. But I have been particularly attentive in assessing the scope of their influence, to colonial reprintings of their works, as indicated by Charles Evans, ed., *American Bibliography* (12 vols. with a 13th edited by Clifford K. Shipton; imprint varies, 1903-1955).

There is a considerable literature dealing with Cotton Mather, though no study addressed primarily to his educational views. The standard biography is Barrett Wendell, *Cotton Mather: The Puritan Priest*, first published in 1891 and republished in 1963 with a favorable introduction by Alan Heimert (New York: Harcourt, Brace & World, Inc., 1963). Ralph and Louise Boas, *Cotton Mather: Keeper of the Puritan Conscience* (New York: Harper and Brothers, 1928) is also instructive, as are Philip Storer Campbell, "Cotton Mather" (unpublished doctoral thesis, Brown University, 1954) and John Portz, "Cotton Mather and Rationalism" (unpublished doctoral thesis, Harvard University, 1947). David Levin is critical of Mather's biographers in "The Hazing of Cotton Mather," *The New England Quarterly*, XXXVI (1963), 147-171. Kenneth Ballard Murdock's *Increase Mather: The Foremost American Puritan* (Cambridge, Mass.: Harvard University Press, 1925) is obviously pertinent.

Perry Miller deals with Mather as a major figure in New England intellectual history in *The New England Mind: From Colony to Province* (Cambridge, Mass.: Harvard University Press, 1953). George L. Kittredge deals with Mather as scientist in "Cotton Mather's Election into the Royal Society," *Publications of the Colonial Society of Massachusetts*, XIV (1913), 81-114, and "Cotton Mather's Scientific Communications to the Royal Society," *Proceedings of the American Antiquarian Society*, XXVI (1916), 18-57; while Otho T. Beall, Jr. and Richard H. Shryock focus on his particular contributions to medicine in *Cotton Mather: First Significant Figure in American Medicine* (Baltimore: The Johns Hopkins Press, 1954). Peter Gay deals with Mather as historian in *A Loss of Mastery: Puritan Historians in Colonial America* (Berkeley: University of California Press, 1966). Robert Middlekauff deals with Mather as pedagogue in an unpublished paper entitled "Cotton Mather's Educational Ideas," as well as more generally in "Piety and Intellect in Puritanism," *The William and Mary Quarterly*, 3d ser., XXII (1965), 457-470.

The standard bibliography of Mather's works is Thomas J. Holmes, *Cotton Mather: A Bibliography of His Works* (3 vols.; Cambridge, Mass.: Harvard University Press, 1940). Mather's diaries, as originally published by the Massachusetts Historical Society in 1911 and 1912, are available in a reprint edition (New York: Frederick Ungar Publishing Co., 1957); the long-missing diary of 1712 is also available with an introduction and notes by William R. Manuerre

II (Charlottesville: University Press of Virginia, 1964). Until Kenneth Murdock's long-awaited edition of the *Magnalia Christi Americana* appears, scholars will be forced to rely on older versions: I used the edition published at Hartford, Conn., by S. Andrus & Son in 1853. There is an excellent new edition of *Bonifacius: An Essay upon the Good,* edited by David Levin (Cambridge, Mass.: Harvard University Press, 1966), while many formerly unobtainable items are now readily available through the *Early American Imprints* series under the editorship of Clifford K. Shipton. There are significant collections of unpublished Mather materials in the American Antiquarian Society and the Massachusetts Historical Society.

For the views of Jonathan Mayhew and Charles Chauncy, see Charles W. Akers, *Called unto Liberty: A Life of Jonathan Mayhew, 1720-1766* (Cambridge, Mass.: Harvard University Press, 1964) and Edward Michael Griffin, "A Biography of Charles Chauncy (1705-1787)" (unpublished doctoral thesis, Stanford University, 1966), and, more generally, Conrad Wright, *The Beginnings of Unitarianism in America* and Joseph Haroutunian, *Piety Versus Moralism: The Passing of New England Theology* (New York: Henry Holt and Company, 1932). In addition to *Seven Sermons* (London: John Noon, 1750) and other published preachings, there is a significant collection of unpublished Mayhew sermons at the Henry E. Huntington Library. For the views of Edwards, see Ola Elizabeth Winslow, *Jonathan Edwards, 1703-1758* (New York: The Macmillan Company, 1940), Perry Miller, *Jonathan Edwards* (New York: William Sloan Associates, 1949), William Hartshorne Becker, "The Distinguishing Marks of the Christian Man in the Thought of Jonathan Edwards" (unpublished doctoral thesis, Harvard University, 1964), *A Treatise Concerning Religious Affections* (1746), edited by John E. Smith (New Haven: Yale University Press, 1959), and the sources discussed on pp. 632-633 *infra.*

The principal collection of Samuel Johnson's works is Herbert and Carol Schneider, eds., *Samuel Johnson, President of King's College: His Career and Writings* (4 vols.; New York: Columbia University Press, 1929), which includes an autobiographical memoir and a splendid selection of correspondence. Two traditional biographical works are Thomas Bradbury Chandler, *The Life of Samuel Johnson* (New York: T. & J. Swords, 1805), based almost entirely on the then unpublished memoir, and E. Edwards Beardsley, *Life and Correspondence of Samuel Johnson* (Boston: Houghton, Mifflin and Company, 1887); more recent considerations include Larry Lee Bothell, "Cloak and Gown: A Study of Religion and Learning in the Early Career of Samuel Johnson of Connecticut" (unpublished doctoral thesis, Princeton University, 1967) and a work in progress at Columbia University by my student Donald Gerardi, which views Johnson as a case study of the transformation of the colonial intellectual class suggested by Edmund Morgan in "The American Revolution Considered as an Intellectual Movement," in Arthur M. Schlesinger, Jr. and Morton White, eds., *Paths of American Thought* (Boston: Houghton Mifflin Company, 1963). Johnson's role as a central figure in eighteenth-century Anglicanism is dealt with in Gerald Joseph Goodwin, "The Anglican Middle Way in Early Eighteenth-Century America: Anglican Religious Thought in the American Colonies, 1702-1750" (unpublished doctoral thesis, University of

Wisconsin, 1965) and Carl Bridenbaugh, *Mitre and Sceptre;* his role as an eighteenth-century philosopher is discussed in I. Woodbridge Riley, *American Philosophy: The Early Schools* (New York: Dodd, Mead & Company, 1907), and Graham P. Conroy, "Berkeley and Education in America," *Journal of the History of Ideas,* XXI (1960), 211-221. There are significant collections of Johnson papers at Columbia University, the New York Historical Society, and Yale University; much of the correspondence in the Fulham Papers at Lambeth Palace and in the archives of the Society for the Propagation of the Gospel in Foreign Parts is available on microfilm at the Library of Congress and the University of Virginia. An invaluable guide to the Fulham Papers is William Wilson Manross, *The Fulham Papers in the Lambeth Palace Library: American Colonial Section, Calendar and Indexes* (Oxford: Clarendon Press, 1965).

The standard biography of John Witherspoon is Varnum Lansing Collins, *President Witherspoon: A Biography* (2 vols.; Princeton: Princeton University Press, 1925), which is now well complemented by George Eugene Rich, "John Witherspoon: His Scottish Intellectual Background" (unpublished doctoral thesis, Syracuse University, 1964) with respect to the Scottish years, by Wayne William Witte, "John Witherspoon: An Exposition and Interpretation of His Theological Views as the Motivation of His Ecclesiastical, Educational, and Political Career in Scotland and America" (unpublished doctoral thesis, Princeton Theological Seminary, 1953) with respect to Witherspoon's theology, by L. H. Butterfield, *John Witherspoon Comes to America* (Princeton: Princeton University Press, 1953) with respect to the negotiations concerning the Princeton presidency, and by Douglas Milton Sloan, "The Scottish Enlightenment and the American College Ideal: Early Princeton Traditions" (unpublished doctoral thesis, Columbia University, 1969) with respect to Witherspoon's educational ideas. John Maclean, *History of the College of New Jersey, from Its Origin in 1746 to the Commencement of 1854* (2 vols.; Philadelphia: J. B. Lippincott & Co., 1877), Varnum Lansing Collins, *Princeton* (2 vols.; New York: Oxford University Press, 1914), and Thomas Jefferson Wertenbaker, *Princeton, 1746-1896* (Princeton: Princeton University Press, 1946) are valuable on the Princeton context before and during Witherspoon's presidency; Gladys Bryson, *Man and Society: The Scottish Inquiry of the Eighteenth Century* (Princeton: Princeton University Press, 1945), George S. Pryde, *The Scottish Universities and the Colleges of Colonial America* (Glasgow: Jackson, Son & Company, 1957), Andrew Dunnett Hook, "Literary and Cultural Relations Between Scotland and America, 1763-1830" (unpublished doctoral thesis, Princeton University, 1960), and Douglas Milton Sloan, "The Scottish Enlightenment and the American College Ideal: Early Princeton Traditions" are useful with respect to more general Scottish influences on American education; while Leonard J. Trinterud, *The Forming of an American Tradition: A Re-examination of Colonial Presbyterianism* (Philadelphia: The Westminster Press, 1949) and Elwyn A. Smith, *The Presbyterian Ministry in American Culture: A Study in Changing Concepts, 1700-1900* (Philadelphia: The Westminster Press, 1962) deal with Witherspoon's fundamental contribution to American Presbyterianism. James L. McAllister, "John Witherspoon: Academic Advocate for American Freedom," in Stuart C. Henry, ed., *A Miscellany of American Christianity: Essays in Honor of H.*

Shelton Smith (Durham: Duke University Press, 1963) provides another case study in the transformation of the clerical role in eighteenth-century America, using Witherspoon as an example; I. Woodbridge Riley deals at length in *American Philosophy: The Early Schools* with Witherspoon's philosophical realism. There are various collections of Witherspoon's writings, the most useful being *The Works of the Rev. John Witherspoon* (3 vols.; Philadelphia: William W. Woodward, 1800) and *The Works of the Rev. John Witherspoon* (2d ed., rev.; 4 vols.; Philadelphia: William W. Woodward, 1802), the former including a number of works not included in the latter. The principal collection of Witherspoon papers is at Princeton University.

A good deal of work is needed on eighteenth-century didactic literature as self-conscious education. For the eighteenth-century conduct books in their various popular forms, see Michael Shinagel, *Daniel Defoe and Middle-Class Gentility* (Cambridge, Mass.: Harvard University Press, 1968), Katherine Gee Hornbeak, *The Complete Letter Writer in English, 1568-1800*, Smith College Studies in Modern Languages, vol. XV, nos. 3-4 (Northampton, Mass.: The Collegiate Press, 1934), and *Richardson's "Familiar Letters" and the Domestic Conduct Books: Richardson's Aesop*, Smith College Studies in Modern Languages, vol. XIX, no. 2 (Northampton: Smith College, 1938), Ralph Straus, *Robert Dodsley* (London: John Lane, 1910), Herbert Schöffler, *Protestantismus und Literatur: Neue Wege zur Englischen Literatur des Achtzehnten Jahrhunderts* (Leipzig: Bernhard Tauchnitz, 1922), and Levin L. Schücking, "Die Grundlagen des Richardson'schen Romans," *Germanisch-romanische Monatsschrift*, XII (1924), 21-42, 88-110.

There is no study of the interrelations of American deism and education, though there are many studies of the educational activities of particular deists, especially Benjamin Franklin and Thomas Jefferson. For the development of Deism in England and America, see Roger Lee Emerson, "English Deism, 1670-1755: An Enlightenment Challenge to Orthodoxy" (unpublished doctoral thesis, Brandeis University, 1962), Roland N. Stromberg, *Religious Liberalism in Eighteenth-Century England*, Herbert M. Morais, *Deism in Eighteenth Century America* (New York: Columbia University Press, 1934), G. Adolf Koch, *Republican Religion: The American Revolution and the Cult of Reason* (New York: Henry Holt and Company, 1933), and Conrad Wright, *The Beginnings of Unitarianism in America*.

CHAPTER 10: MODES OF ENTHUSIASM

The classic work on enthusiastic religion is Ronald A. Knox's *Enthusiasm: A Chapter in the History of Religion with Special Reference to the Seventeenth and Eighteenth Centuries* (Oxford: Clarendon Press, 1950). I found Knox's distinction between mysticism and evangelicism as different but related versions of enthusiasm exceedingly useful in the present analysis. The idea of a "left wing" of the Reformation is obviously taken from Roland H. Bainton's well-known essay under that title in *The Journal of Religion*, XXI (1941), 124-134; the relation of certain of the left-wing sects to the general movement of Puritanism in England is explicated in a highly original way in Geoffrey F.

Nuttall, *The Holy Spirit in Puritan Faith and Experience* (Oxford: Basil Blackwell, 1946). Of the considerable literature on enthusiasm in eighteenth-century America, I found several works particularly valuable, notably, William Warren Sweet, *Revivalism in America: Its Origin, Growth and Decline* (New York: Charles Scribner's Sons, 1944), Felix James Schrag, "Pietism in Colonial America" (unpublished doctoral thesis, University of Chicago, 1945), Lawrence Gene Lavengood, "The Great Awakening and New England Society" (unpublished doctoral thesis, University of Chicago, 1953), Edwin Scott Gaustad, *The Great Awakening in New England* (New York: Harper & Brothers, 1957), John Opie, Jr., "Conversion and Revivalism: An Internal History from Jonathan Edwards through Charles Grandison Finney" (unpublished doctoral thesis, University of Chicago, 1963), Martin Ellsworth Lodge, "The Great Awakening in the Middle Colonies" (unpublished doctoral thesis, University of California, Berkeley, 1964), C. C. Goen, *Revivalism and Separatism in New England, 1740-1800* (New Haven: Yale University Press, 1962), Alan Heimert, *Religion and the American Mind from the Great Awakening to the Revolution* (Cambridge, Mass.: Harvard University Press, 1966), Alan Heimert and Perry Miller, eds., *The Great Awakening: Documents Illustrating the Crisis and Its Consequences* (Indianapolis: The Bobbs-Merrill Company, 1967), and David Taft Morgan, Jr., "The Great Awakening in the Carolinas and Georgia, 1740-1775" (unpublished doctoral thesis, University of North Carolina, 1967). Two older works, Charles Hartshorn Maxson, *The Great Awakening in the Middle Colonies* (Chicago: University of Chicago Press, 1920) and Wesley M. Gewehr, *The Great Awakening in Virginia, 1740-1790* (Durham: Duke University Press, 1930), remain useful.

On the antinomian controversy in Massachusetts, two recent books supersede most of the prior work in the wealth of their detail and the incisiveness of their analysis, Emery Battis, *Saints and Sectaries: Anne Hutchinson and the Antinomian Controversy in the Massachusetts Bay Colony* (Chapel Hill: University of North Carolina Press, 1962) and David D. Hall, ed., *The Antinomian Controversy, 1636-1638* (Middletown: Wesleyan University Press, 1968). Hugh Stewart Barbour, "The Early Quaker Outlook upon 'the World' and Society, 1647-1662" (unpublished doctoral thesis, Yale University, 1952) and Joseph Walford Martin, "The English Revolution and the Rise of Quakerism (1650-1660)" (unpublished doctoral thesis, Columbia University, 1965) are excellent with respect to the beginnings of Quakerism, while Rufus M. Jones, *The Quakers in the American Colonies* (London: Macmillan and Co., 1911) is authoritative with respect to the seventeenth-century Quaker missionaries.

There is a rich literature on the educational ideas and activities of the English and American Quakers. Luella M. Wright, *Literature and Education in Early Quakerism* (Iowa City: University of Iowa, 1933), Walter Joseph Homan, *Children & Quakerism* (Berkeley, Calif.: Gillick Press, 1939), Howard Brinton, *Quaker Education in Theory and Practice* (Wallingford, Pa.: Pendle Hill, 1940), and Richard L. Greaves, "The Early Quakers as Advocates of Educational Reform," *Quaker History*, LVIII (1969), 22-30, sketch the historical development of Quaker educational principles and policies. W. A. Campbell Stewart, *Quakers and Education as Seen in Their Schools in England* (London: The Epworth Press, 1953) is the best general history of the English experience. Thomas Woody, *Early Quaker Education in Pennsylvania* (New York: Teachers College, Columbia University, 1920), and *Quaker Education in the Colony and State of New Jersey* (Philadelphia: published by the author, 1923), Zora Klain, *Quaker Contributions to Education in North Carolina* (Philadelphia: Westbrook Publishing Company, 1925), and *Educational Activities of New England Quakers: A Source Book* (Philadelphia: Westbrook Publishing Company, 1928), Frederick B. Tolles, *Meeting House and Counting House: The Quaker Merchants of Colonial Philadelphia, 1682-1783* (Chapel Hill: University of North Carolina Press, 1948), and *James Logan and the Culture of Provincial America* (Boston: Little, Brown and Company, 1957), Carl and Jessica Bridenbaugh, *Rebels and Gentlemen: Philadelphia in the Age of Franklin* (New York: Reynal & Hitchcock, 1942), and Sydney V. James, *A People Among Peoples: Quaker Benevolence in Eighteenth-Century America* (Cambridge, Mass.: Harvard University Press, 1963) explicate the American experience, as do studies such as Janet Whitney, *John Woolman: American Quaker* (Boston: Little, Brown and Company, 1942), George S. Brookes, *Friend Anthony Benezet* (Philadelphia: University of Pennsylvania Press, 1937), and Edward C. O. Beatty, *William Penn as Social Philosopher* (New York: Columbia University Press, 1939). Professor James's volume also presents a splendid critical bibliography. Thomas E. Drake, *Quakers and Slavery in America* (New Haven: Yale University Press, 1950) and Rayner Wickersham Kelsey, *Friends and the Indians, 1655-1917* (Philadelphia: The Associated Executive Committee of Friends on Indian Affairs, 1917) are sympathetic accounts of race relations; Carter G. Woodson deals with Quaker educational efforts on behalf of black children in *The Education of the Negro Prior to 1861* (Washington, D. C.: The Associated Publishers, Inc., 1919). Needless to say, the writings of George Fox—the most comprehensive edition is *The Works of George Fox* (8 vols.; Philadelphia: Marcus T. C. Gould, 1831)—and *The Select Works of William Penn* (3d ed.; 5 vols.; London: James Phillips, 1782) are invaluable, as are the *Epistles from the Yearly Meeting of Friends, Held in London, to the Quarterly and Monthly Meetings in Great Britain, Ireland, and Elsewhere, from 1681 to 1817 Inclusive* (London: W. & S. Graves, 1818), the various minutes and pronouncements of the Philadelphia Meeting, most of which are in the Department of Records of the Society of Friends in Philadelphia, and the chief didactic writings of the Quaker leaders, such as [George Fox and Ellis Hookes,] *A Primmer and Catechism for Children: Or a Plain and Easie Way for Children to Learn to Spell and Read Perfectly in a Little Time* (no place: no publisher, 1670), which Sydney James has characterized as the Quaker antidote to *The New-England Primer*.

Marion Dexter Learned, *The Life of Francis Daniel Pastorius* (Philadelphia: William J. Campbell, 1908) is a scholarly biography; there is a significant collection of Pastorius papers in the Historical Society of Pennsylvania, including his commonplace book, "Alvearialia: Or Such Phrases and Sentences Which in Haste Were Booked Down Here, Before I Had Time to Carry Them to Their Respective Proper Places in My English-Folio-Bee-hive." Martin F. Brumbaugh, *The Life and Works of Christopher Dock* (Philadelphia: J. B. Lippincott Company, 1908) is invaluable, presenting as it does the *Schulordnung* in German and in English; Frank Henry Klassen, "Christopher Dock: Eighteenth Century American Educator" (unpublished doctoral thesis, University of Illinois, 1962) is a useful complementary study. Mabel Haller, *Early Moravian Education in Pennsylvania* (Nazareth, Pa.: Moravian Historical Society, 1953), Gillian Lindt Gollin, *Moravians in Two Worlds* (New York: Columbia University Press, 1967), Menno Simon Harder, "The Origin, Philosophy and Development of Education Among the Mennonites" (unpublished doctoral thesis, University of Southern California, 1949), Frederick George Livingood, *Eighteenth Century Reformed Church Schools* (Norristown, Pa.: Pennsylvania German Society, 1930), and Andrew S. Berky, *The Schoolhouse Near the Old Spring: A History of the Union School and Church Association, Dillingersville, Pennsylvania, 1735-1955* (Norristown, Pa.: Pennsylvania German Society, 1955) are also instructive. Janice Leonora Gorn presents a wealth of information on education in eighteenth-century Pennsylvania in "John Locke's Educational Theory and Some Evidences Thereof in Pennsylvania, 1682-1755" (unpublished doctoral thesis, New York University, 1963), along with an excellent bibliography.

Felix James Schrag's "Pietism in Colonial America" is the best brief history of the impact of Continental Pietism on the American colonies, though Schrag's assertions concerning the origins of Frelinghuysen's evangelicism must be modified on the basis of F. Ernest Stoeffler's *The Rise of Evangelical Pietism* (Leiden: E. J. Brill, 1965) and James Tanis' *Dutch Calvinistic Pietism in the Middle Colonies: A Study in the Life and Theology of Theodorus Jacobus Frelinghuysen* (The Hague: Martinus Nijhoff, 1967). Tanis has also criticized the "imprecise, mid-Victorian English translation" of the Reverend William Demarest's edition of Frelinghuysen's *Sermons* (New York: Board of Publication of the Reformed Protestant Dutch Church, 1856). Miles Douglas Harper, Jr., "Gilbert Tennent: Theologian of the 'New Light'" (unpublished doctoral thesis, Duke University, 1958) is a modern scholarly biography, with a sophisticated theological analysis and an excellent bibliographical guide to the Tennent manuscripts at the Presbyterian Historical Society in Philadelphia, and at the Princeton Theological Seminary, the Historical Society of Pennsylvania, and Princeton University. William J. Mann, *Life and Times of Henry Melchior Mühlenberg* (Philadelphia: G. W. Frederick, 1887) has rightly been characterized as "a masterpiece of scholarship and understanding"; Henry Harbaugh, *The Life of Rev. Michael Schlatter* (Philadelphia: Lindsay & Blakiston, 1857) is less satisfactory.

Roderic Hall Pierce, "George Whitefield and His Critics" (unpublished doctoral thesis, Princeton University, 1962) and William Howland Kenney III, "George Whitefield and Colonial Revivalism: The Social Sources of Charismatic Authority, 1737-1770" (unpublished doctoral thesis, University of Pennsylvania, 1966) are excellent on Whitefield's career in America.

Edwin Scott Gaustad, *The Great Awakening in New England*, Lawrence Gene Lavengood, "The Great Awakening and New England Society," and C. C. Goen, *Revivalism and Separatism in New England, 1740-1800*, are modern scholarly studies with excellent bibliographies; Joseph Tracy, *The Great Awakening: A History of the Revival of Religion in the Time of Edwards and Whitefield* (Boston: Tappan and Dennet, 1842) remains of value. The literature on Jonathan Edwards is already substantial and growing rapidly as the stature of the man and the influence of his work are more fully perceived by present-day scholars. In addition to the general works mentioned on pp. 624-627 *supra*, Thomas Herbert Johnson, "Jonathan Edwards as a Man of Letters" (unpublished doctoral thesis, Harvard University, 1932), William Sparkes Morris, "The Young Jonathan Edwards: A Reconstruction" (unpublished doctoral thesis, University of Chicago, 1955), Douglas J. Elwood, *The Philosophical Theology of Jonathan Edwards* (New York: Columbia University Press, 1960), Wallace Earl Anderson, "Mind and Nature in the Early Philosophical Writings of Jonathan Edwards" (unpublished doctoral thesis, University of Minnesota, 1961), Emily Stipes Watts, "Jonathan Edwards and the Cambridge Platonists" (unpublished doctoral thesis, University of Illinois, 1963), Edward H. Davidson. *Jonathan Edwards: The Narrative of a Puritan Mind* (Cambridge, Mass.: Harvard University Press, 1968), and Paul Ramsey's introduction to Jonathan Edwards, *Freedom of the Will* (1754) (New Haven: Yale University Press, 1957) are instructive. There is a superb collection of Edwards manuscripts at Yale University.

Wayland J. Chase, " 'The Great Awakening' and its Educational Consequences," *School and Society*, XXXV (1932), 443-449, deals principally with the colleges that grew out of the awakenings after 1746 but not with the transformation of the church as an educational institution. Otherwise, what serious scholarly consideration there is of the subject lies in works focusing on other matters, notably, the books by Gaustad, Lavengood, and Goen, mentioned above, as well as in Leonard J. Trinterud, *The Forming of an American Tradition: A Re-examination of Colonial Presbyterianism* (Philadelphia: The Westminster Press, 1949), Martin Ellsworth Lodge, "The Great Awakening in the Middle Colonies," Alf Edgar Jacobson, "The Congregational Clergy in Eighteenth Century New England" (unpublished doctoral thesis, Harvard University, 1962), and Alan Heimert, *Religion and the American Mind from the Great Awakening to the Revolution,* which includes an exemplary chapter on "The Danger of an Unconverted Ministry." Miles Douglas Harper's biography of Tennent is excellent on the ambivalence of the New Lights toward nurture and conversion.

Douglas Milton Sloan explicates the Scottish influence on eighteenth-century higher education in the colonies in "The Scottish Enlightenment and the American College Ideal: Early Princeton Traditions" (unpublished doctoral thesis, Columbia University, 1969); the tradition of the English dissenting academies is analyzed in Irene Parker, *Dissenting Academies in England: Their Rise and Progress and Their Place Among the Educational Systems of the Country* (Cambridge: Cambridge University Press, 1914), H. McLachlan, *English Education under the Test Acts, Being the History of the Nonconformist Academies, 1662-1820* (Manchester: Manchester University Press, 1931), Olive M. Griffiths, *Religion and Learning: A Study in English Presbyterian Thought from the Bartholomew Ejections (1662) to the Foundation of the Unitarian Movement* (Cambridge: Cambridge University Press, 1935), Nicholas Hans, *New Trends in Education in the Eighteenth Century* (London: Routledge & Kegan Paul, 1951), and J. W. Ashley Smith, *The Birth of Modern Education: The Contribution of the Dissenting Academies, 1660-1800* (London: Independent Press, 1954). And the character of ministerial training in provincial

America is discussed in William O. Shewmaker, "The Training of the Protestant Ministry in the United States of America Before the Establishment of Theological Seminaries," *Papers of the American Society of Church History*, 2d ser., VI (1921), 73-202, Mary Latimer Gambrell, *Ministerial Training in Eighteenth Century New England* (New York: Columbia University Press, 1937), Samuel Simpson, "Early Ministerial Training in America," *Papers of the American Society of Church History*, 2d ser., II (1910), 117-129, B. Sadtler, "The Education of Ministers by Private Tutors, Before the Establishment of Theological Seminaries," *The Lutheran Church Review, XIII* (1894), 167-183, and Roland H. Bainton, *Yale and the Ministry: A History of Education for the Christian Ministry at Yale from the Founding in 1701* (New York: Harper & Brothers, 1957).

The Presbyterian academies are dealt with generally by Douglas Milton Sloan, "The Scottish Enlightenment and the American College Ideal" and by Henry D. Funk, "The Influence of the Presbyterian Church in Early American History," *Journal of the Presbyterian Historical Society*, XII (1924-25), 152-224. The specific role of the Log College is discussed in George H. Ingram, "The Story of the Log College," *ibid.*, 487-511, and Thomas C. Pears, Jr., and Guy S. Klett, "Documentary History of William Tennent, and the Log College," *Journal of the Department of History (The Presbyterian Historical Society)*, XXVIII (1950), 37-64, 105-128, 167-204, and in Archibald Alexander's classic, *Biographical Sketches of the Founder, and Principal Alumni of the Log College* (Princeton, N.J.: T. Robinson, 1845). The best modern history of Princeton is Thomas Jefferson Wertenbaker, *Princeton, 1746-1896* (Princeton: Princeton University Press, 1946), though John Maclean, *History of the College of New Jersey from Its Origin in 1746 to the Commencement of 1854* (2 vols.; Philadelphia: J. B. Lippincott & Co., 1877) has not been superseded for the early years. The best modern history of Brown is Walter C. Bronson, *The History of Brown University, 1764-1914* (Providence: published by the University, 1914). The best modern history of Dartmouth is Leon Burr Richardson, *History of Dartmouth College* (2 vols.; Hanover: Dartmouth College Publications, 1932). And the best modern history of Rutgers is Richard P. McCormick, *Rutgers: A Bicentennial History* (New Brunswick: Rutgers University Press, 1966), though the volume contains little on the colonial period. All four universities maintain archives of unpublished materials relating to their origins and early years. The story of Whitefield and Bethesda is best told in Robert L. McCaul, Jr., "A Documentary History of Education in Colonial Georgia" (unpublished doctoral thesis, University of Chicago, 1953).

Eighteenth-century Harvard and Yale are in need of good scholarly histories; in the meantime, Samuel Eliot Morison's charming *Three Centuries of Harvard, 1636-1936* (Cambridge, Mass.: Harvard University Press, 1946) and Edwin Oviatt's *The Beginnings of Yale (1701-1726)* (New Haven: Yale University Press, 1916) must suffice, along with Josiah Quincy's *The History of Harvard University* (2 vols.; Cambridge, Mass.: John Owen, 1840) and Benjamin Peirce's *A History of Harvard University, from Its Foundation, in the Year 1636, to the Period of the American Revolution* (Cambridge, Mass.: Brown, Shattuck, and Company, 1833). Franklin Bowditch Dexter, ed., *Documentary History of Yale University Under the Original Charter of the Collegiate School of Connecti-

cut, 1701-1745 (New Haven: Yale University Press, 1916) is an invaluable collection of documents. Arthur Daniel Kaledin, "The Mind of John Leverett" (unpublished doctoral thesis, Harvard University, 1965) is instructive on early eighteenth-century Harvard and corrects the common misimpression of Leverett as a theological liberal; Kaledin's work in progress under the title "Harvard in Transition, 1707-1737: The Transformation of a Puritan Institution" promises to be immensely useful. Richard Warch, "Yale College: 1701-1740" (unpublished doctoral thesis, Yale University, 1967) is also a valuable monograph. Both Harvard and Yale possess excellent collections of papers relating to their affairs during the provincial era.

Richard Hofstadter raises fundamental questions concerning the ambivalence of enthusiasm toward intellect—very much in a Lockean mode—in *Anti-intellectualism in American Life* (New York: Alfred A. Knopf, 1963), as do Leonard W. Labaree in "The Conservative Attitude Toward the Great Awakening," *The William and Mary Quarterly*, 3d ser., I (1944), 331-352, and William G. McLoughlin in *Isaac Backus and the American Pietistic Tradition* (Boston: Little, Brown and Company, 1967).

CHAPTER 11: MISSIONS AND ENCOUNTERS

Colonial Anglicanism during the provincial era is admirably dealt with in Carl Bridenbaugh, *Mitre and Sceptre: Transatlantic Faiths, Ideas, Personalities, and Politics, 1689-1775* (New York: Oxford University Press, 1962) and Gerald Joseph Goodwin, "The Anglican Middle Way in Early Eighteenth-Century America: Anglican Religious Thought in the American Colonies, 1702-1750" (unpublished doctoral thesis, University of Wisconsin, 1965), as well as in such older works as Arthur Lyon Cross, *The Anglican Episcopate and the American Colonies* (Cambridge, Mass.: Harvard University Press, 1902), Evarts B. Greene, "The Anglican Outlook on the American Colonies in the Early Eighteenth Century," *The American Historical Review*, XX (1914-15), 64-85, and William Stevens Perry's invaluable collection of documents, *Historical Collections Relating to the American Colonial Church* (4 vols.; Hartford, Conn.: Church Press Company, 1870-1878).

The standard biography of Henry Compton is Edward Carpenter, *The Protestant Bishop, Being the Life of Henry Compton, 1632-1713, Bishop of London* (London: Longmans, Green and Co., 1956). The best discussion of the ecclesiastical commissary, which Compton used to such effect in the colonies, is Howard E. Kimball, "The Ecclesiastical Commissary: A Study of the Migration of an English Institution to British North America" (unpublished doctoral thesis, University of California, Los Angeles, 1956). And the best work on James Blair, Compton's first major emissary to continental North America, is Samuel Roop Mohler, "Commissary James Blair, Churchman, Educator, and Politician of Colonial Virginia" (unpublished doctoral thesis, University of Chicago, 1940), a study that is usefully complemented by George Maclaren Brydon, *Virginia's Mother Church and the Political Conditions Under Which It Grew* (2 vols.; imprint varies, 1947-52) and Jerome Walker Jones, "The Anglican Church in Colonial Virginia, 1690-1760" (unpublished doctoral thesis, Harvard University, 1959). There is no first-class study of the College of William and Mary during the colonial period; among the more useful works are *The History of the College of William and Mary from Its Foundation, 1660, to 1874* (Richmond, Va.: J. W. Randolph & English, 1874), Herbert B. Adams, *The College of William and Mary: A Contribution to the History of Higher Education, with Suggestions for Its National Promotion* (Washington, D.C.: Government Printing Office, 1887), Lyon G. Tyler, "Education in Colonial Virginia: The Higher Education," *William and Mary College Quarterly,* VI (1897-98), 171-187, "Education in Colonial Virginia: Influence of William and Mary College," *ibid.,* VII (1898-99), 1-9, and *Williamsburg: The Old Colonial Capital* (Richmond, Va.: Whittet & Shepperson, 1907), chap. iii, and John E. Kirkpatrick, "The Constitutional Development of the College of William and Mary," *William and Mary College Quarterly,* 2d ser., VI (1926), 95-108. Many of the records of the college during the eighteenth century have been printed in *The William and Mary Quarterly;* there is an abundance of unpublished material in the college's archive.

The best recent work on Thomas Bray is Samuel C. McCulloch, "The Life and Times of Dr. Thomas Bray, 1656-1730: A Study in Humanitarianism" (unpublished doctoral thesis, University of California, Los Angeles, 1943), parts of which have appeared as "Dr. Thomas Bray's Commissary Work in London," *The William and Mary Quarterly,* 3d ser., II (1945), 333-348, "Dr. Thomas Bray's Trip to Maryland: A Study in Militant Anglican Humanitarianism," *ibid.,* 15-32, "Dr. Thomas Bray's Final Years at Aldgate, 1706-1730," *Historical Magazine of the Protestant Episcopal Church,* XIV (1945), 322-336, "The Importance of Dr. Thomas Bray's Bibliotheca Parochialis," *ibid.,* XV (1946), 50-59, "The Foundation and Early Work of the Society for Promoting Christian Knowledge," *ibid.,* XVIII (1949), 3-22, and "A Plea for Further Missionary Activity in Colonial America: Dr. Thomas Bray's Missionalia," *ibid.,* XV (1946), 232-245. Edgar L. Pennington, *The Reverend Thomas Bray* (Philadelphia: Church Historical Society, 1934), Joseph Towne Wheeler, "Thomas Bray and the Maryland Parochial Libraries," *Maryland Historical Magazine,* XXXIV (1939), 246-265, and John Wolfe Lydekker, "Thomas Bray (1658-1730): Founder of Missionary Enterprise," *Historical Magazine of the Protestant Episcopal Church,* XII (1943), 186-224, are also useful, as are Bernard C. Steiner's older works, "Rev. Thomas Bray and His American Libraries," *The American Historical Review,* II (1896-97), 59-75, and *Rev. Thomas Bray: His Life and Selected Works Relating to Maryland* (Baltimore: Maryland Historical Society, 1901). Herbert Lyman Searcy, "Parochial Libraries in the American Colonies" (unpublished doctoral thesis, University of Illinois, 1963) is an excellent study with a comprehensive bibliography. Photostatic reproductions of the Thomas Bray manuscripts in the Sion College Library, London, and in the archives of the United Society for the Propagation of the Gospel, successor to the Society for the Propagation of the Gospel in Foreign Parts, are available in the Library of Congress.

Norman Sykes, "The Theology of Divine Benevolence," *Historical Magazine of the Protestant Episcopal Church,* XVI (1947), 278-291, Frank J. Klingberg, "The Expansion of the Anglican Church in the Eighteenth Century," *ibid.,* 292-301, Dudley W. R. Bahlman, *The Moral Revolution of 1688* (New Haven: Yale University Press, 1957), and Hans Cnattingius, *Bishops and Societies: A Study of Anglican Colonial and Missionary Expansion, 1698-1850* (London: Society for Promoting Christian Knowledge, 1952) provide valuable perspective on the origins and context of the Society for Promoting Christian Knowledge and the Society for the Propagation of the Gospel in Foreign Parts, as do the standard histories of the two organizations, William O. B. Allen and Edmund McClure, *Two Hundred Years: The History of the Society for Promoting Christian Knowledge, 1698-1898* (London: Society for Promoting Christian Knowledge, 1898) and Henry P. Thompson, *Into All Lands: The History of the Society for the Propagation of the Gospel in Foreign Parts, 1701-1950* (London: Society for Promoting Christian Knowledge, 1951).

John Calam's "Parsons and Pedagogues: The S.P.G. Adventure in American Education" (unpublished doctoral thesis, Columbia University, 1969) presents a fresh appraisal of the Society's educational activities in the American colonies, conceiving of education broadly and adopting a critical posture toward the traditional historiography. The result is an incisive history complemented by a splendid bibliography, both of which have proved immensely valuable. Among other recent writings, I found John Kendall Nelson, "Anglican Missions in America, 1701-1725: A Study of the Society for the Propagation of the Gospel in Foreign Parts" (unpublished doctoral thesis, Northwestern University, 1962) and Charles Bronislaw Hirsch, "The Experiences of the S.P.G. in Eighteenth Century North Carolina" (unpublished doctoral thesis, Indiana University, 1953) especially useful. Among older writings, I found Frank J. Klingberg, *Anglican Humanitarianism in Colonial New York* (Philadelphia: The Church Historical Society, 1940), and *An Appraisal of the Negro in Colonial South Carolina: A Study in Americanization* (Washington, D.C.: The Associated Publishers, 1941), Alfred W. Newcombe, "The Organization and Procedure of the S.P.G., with Special Reference to New England" (unpublished doctoral thesis, University of Michigan, 1943), William Webb Kemp, *The Support of Schools in Colonial New York by the Society for the Propagation of the Gospel in Foreign Parts* (New York: Teachers College, Columbia University, 1913), and C. F. Pascoe, *Two Hundred Years of the S.P.G.: An Historical Account of the Society for the Propagation of the Gospel in Foreign Parts, 1701-1900* (London: published by the Society, 1901) of continuing value. Beyond these general works, Edgar Legare Pennington, "The Reverend Francis Le Jau's Work Among Indians and Negro Slaves," *The Journal of Southern History*, I (1935), 442-458, deals with the particular problems of the Society's efforts with Indians and blacks, while William A. Bultmann, "The S.P.G. and the Foreign Settler in the American Colonies," in Samuel Clyde McCulloch, ed., *British Humanitarianism: Essays Honoring Frank J. Klingberg* (Philadelphia: The Church Publishing Company, 1950), and Bultmann, "The S.P.G. and the French Huguenots in Colonial America," *Historical Magazine of the Protestant Episcopal Church*, XX (1951), 156-172, deal with the Society vis-à-vis other ethnic groups in the colonies. The closely related philanthropic work of Thomas Bray's Associates in the colonies is discussed in Edgar Legare Pennington, "Thomas Bray's Associates and Their Work Among the Negroes," *Proceedings of the American Antiquarian Society*, new ser., XLVIII (1939), 311-403, and "The Work of the Bray Associates in Pennsylvania," *The Pennsylvania Magazine of History and Biography*, LVIII (1934), 1-25.

The published sermons, annual reports, statements of policy, teaching materials, and other documents of the Society, most of which are available at the Missionary Research Library of Union Theological Seminary and at the New York Public Library, are invaluable. And the manuscript collections in the archives of the Society, which include its journals as well as thousands of letters and reports from American missionaries, schoolmasters, and catechists to the secretary of the Society in London (and, needless to say, a great many communications in return), are a remarkably rich resource with respect to the culture of provincial America, and, more generally, of the eighteenth-century Anglo-American community. Reproductions of the minute books and other papers of Thomas Bray's Associates are available in the Library of Congress.

Edward Payson Johnson, "Christian Work Among the North American Indians During the Eighteenth Century," *Papers of the American Society of Church History,* 2d ser., VI (1921), 3-41, Herbert E. Bolton, "The Mission as a Frontier Institution in the Spanish-American Colonies," *The American Historical Review,* XXII (1917-18), 42-61, and the theoretical papers collected by Paul Bohannan and Fred Plog in *Beyond the Frontier: Social Process and Cultural Change* (Garden City, N.Y.: The Natural History Press, 1967) provide a useful general introduction to the problem of missionary education as cultural and political imperialism. John Tracy Ellis, *Catholics in Colonial America* (Baltimore: Helicon Press, 1965) includes a good deal of material on Catholic missions, superseding John Gilmary Shea's useful but outdated *History of the Catholic Missions Among the Indian Tribes of the United States, 1529-1854* (New York: Edward Dunigan & Brother, 1855). Charles Edwards O'Neill, *Church and State in French Colonial Louisiana: Policy and Politics to 1732* (New Haven: Yale University Press, 1966) is a sensitive introduction to mission work in that French territory, and is usefully complemented by Claude L. Vogel, *The Capuchins in French Louisiana (1722-1766)* (Washington: Catholic University of America, 1928), Jean Delanglez, *The French Jesuits in Lower Louisiana (1700-1763)* (Washington: Catholic University of America, 1935), and Norman Ward Caldwell, *The French in the Mississippi Valley, 1740-1750* (Urbana: University of Illinois Press, 1941). Edward Spicer, *Cycles of Conquest: The Impact of Spain and the United States on the Indians of the Southwest, 1533-1960* (Tucson: University of Arizona Press, 1962) and John Augustine Donohue, "Jesuit Missions in Northwestern New Spain, 1711-1767" (unpublished doctoral thesis, University of California, 1957) are mines of information, supplementing Herbert E. Bolton's older but still valuable *Rim of Christendom: A Biography of Eusebio Francisco Kino, Pacific Coast Pioneer* (New York: The Macmillan Company, 1936), and Bolton and Thomas Maitland Marshall, *The Colonization of North America, 1492-1783* (New York: The Macmillan Company, 1920).

Introduction to Part IV

In the absence of a comprehensive scholarly history of the colonial economy, one must piece together the economic picture of provincial America from a variety of sources. William S. Sachs and Ari Hoogenboom, *The Enterprising Colonials: Society on the Eve of the Revolution* (Chicago: Argonaut, 1965) is a useful, though popular, introduction; Jackson Turner Main, *The Social Structure of Revolutionary America* (Princeton: Princeton University Press, 1965) provides the complementary social analysis. Robert E. Brown, *Middle-Class Democracy and the Revolution in Massachusetts, 1691-1780* (Ithaca: Cornell University Press, 1955) and Robert E. and B. Katherine Brown, *Virginia, 1702-1786: Aristocracy or Democracy?* (East Lansing: Michigan State University Press, 1964) are exemplary studies of particular colonies. Stuart Bruchey, *The Roots of American Economic Growth, 1607-1861: An Essay in Social Causation* (New York: Harper & Row, 1965), Carl Bridenbaugh, *The Colonial Craftsman* (New York: New York University Press, 1950), Curtis P. Nettels, "British Mercantilism and the Development of the Thirteen Colonies," *The Journal of Economic History,* XII (1952), 105-114, John H. Andrews, "Anglo-American Trade in the Early Eighteenth Century," *The Geographical Review,* XLV (1955), 99-110, Arthur Meier Schlesinger, *The Colonial Merchants and the American Revolution, 1763-1776* (New York: Columbia University, 1918), Percy Wells Bidwell and John I. Falconer, *History of Agriculture in the Northern United States, 1620-1860* (Washington, D.C.: The Carnegie Institution of Washington, 1925), Lewis Cecil Gray, *History of Agriculture in the Southern United States to 1860* (2 vols.; Washington, D.C.: The Carnegie Institution of Washington, 1933), and Victor S. Clark, *History of Manufactures in the United States* (2 vols.; Washington, D.C.: The Carnegie Institution of Washington, 1916-1928), vol. I, are replete with pertinent material. Stuart Bruchey, ed., *The Colonial Merchant: Sources and Readings* (New York: Harcourt, Brace & World, 1966) is broader in scope than its title indicates and includes a number of excellent statistical tables.

The best biography of J. Hector St. John de Crèvecoeur is Howard C. Rice, *Le Cultivateur Américain: Étude sur l'Oeuvre de Saint John de Crèvecoeur* (Paris: H. Champion, 1933). *Letters from an American Farmer,* with an introduction and notes by Warren Barton Blake (London: J. M. Dent & Sons, 1912) should be read in conjunction with *Crèvecoeur's Eighteenth-Century Travels in Pennsylvania & New York,* translated and edited by Percy G. Adams (Lexington: University of Kentucky Press, 1961).

CHAPTER 12: THE USES OF LEARNING

All of the bibliographical citations referring to Locke on pp. 619-624 are relevant here. In addition, the first sections of Janice Leonora Gorn, "John Locke's Educational Theory and Some Evidences Thereof in Pennsylvania, 1682-1755" (unpublished doctoral thesis, New York University, 1963) are useful with respect to Locke's epistemological and pedagogical theories, as are John Herman Randall, *The Career of Philosophy: From the Middle Ages to the Enlightenment* (New York: Columbia University Press, 1962), D. J. O'Connor, *John Locke* (London: Penguin Books, 1952), and Nina Reicyn, *La Pédagogie de John Locke* (Paris: Hermann & Cie., 1941).

James Benjamin League, Jr., "Addison and Steele as Educational Realists in the *Tatler,* the *Spectator,* and the *Guardian*" (unpublished doctoral thesis, Johns Hopkins University, 1965) is a useful general study, though League's rigid categories of "social realism," "empirical realism," and "humanistic realism" seem to me to obfuscate rather than clarify his presentation. Rae Blanchard, "Richard Steele as Moralist and Social Reformer" (unpublished doctoral thesis,

University of Chicago, 1928), Willard Connely, *Sir Richard Steele* (New York: Charles Scribner's Sons, 1934), Ernest Claude Coleman, "The Influence of the Addisonian Essay in America Before 1910" (unpublished doctoral thesis, University of Illinois, 1936), Edward A. Bloom and Lillian D. Bloom, "Joseph Addison and Eighteenth-Century 'Liberalism,' " *Journal of the History of Ideas,* XII (1951), 560-583, Peter Smithers, *The Life of Joseph Addison* (Oxford Clarendon Press, 1954), Lee A. Elioseff, *The Cultural Milieu of Addison's Literary Criticism* (Austin: University of Texas Press, 1963), and Arthur R. Humphreys, *The Augustan World: Society, Thought, Letters in Eighteenth-Century England* (London: Methuen & Co., 1954) are useful contextual studies. The bibliographical citations referring to James Burgh and Isaac Watts on pp. 624-626 *supra* are also relevant here. The edition of Watts's work I used was *The Improvement of the Mind: or a Supplement to the Art of Logic. In Two Parts. To Which Is Added, a Discourse on the Education of Children and Youth* (Exeter, N.H.: J. Lamson and T. Odiorne, 1793); the coupling of the two works in this edition is indicative of how Watts in general and *The Improvement of the Mind* in particular were perceived in America.

The best and fullest biography of Franklin is Carl Van Doren, *Benjamin Franklin* (New York: The Viking Press, 1938); while *The Autobiography of Benjamin Franklin,* edited by Leonard W. Labaree, Ralph L. Ketcham, Helen C. Boatfield, and Helene H. Fineman (New Haven: Yale University Press, 1964) is the most informative version of that classic. *The Papers of Benjamin Franklin,* edited by Leonard W. Labaree and Whitfield J. Bell, Jr. (13+ vols.; New Haven: Yale University Press, 1959-) is the most recent and authoritative edition of Franklin's writings; *The Writings of Benjamin Franklin,* edited by Albert Henry Smyth (10 vols.; New York: The Macmillan Company, 1904-1907) also remains a highly useful collection. I have always found Carl L. Becker's sketch, written initially for the *Dictionary of American Biography* and published subsequently as *Benjamin Franklin* (Ithaca: Cornell University Press, 1946), an unsurpassed model of its kind.

David Levin, "The Autobiography of Benjamin Franklin: The Puritan Experimenter in Life and Art," *The Yale Review,* LIII (1963-64), 258-275, John William Ward, " 'Who Was Benjamin Franklin?' " *The American Scholar,* XXXII (1963), 541-553, and Robert F. Sayre, *The Examined Self: Benjamin Franklin, Henry Adams, Henry James* (Princeton: Princeton University Press, 1964) are incisive explorations of Franklin's character, as are some of the older essays collected in Charles L. Sanford, ed., *Benjamin Franklin and the American Character* (Boston: D. C. Heath and Company, 1955). For the fortunes of Franklin's junto, see Milton Rubincam, "History of Benjamin Franklin's Junto Club," *Junto Selections: Essays on the History of Pennsylvania* (Washington, D.C.: Pennsylvania Historical Junto, 1946) and Brooke Hindle, "The Rise of the American Philosophical Society, 1766-1787" (unpublished doctoral thesis, University of Pennsylvania, 1949). For Franklin's role in the development of the subscription library, see Dorothy Fear Grimm, "A History of the Library Company of Philadelphia, 1731-1835" (unpublished doctoral thesis, University of Pennsylvania, 1955) and Margaret Barton Korty, *Benjamin Franklin and Eighteenth-Century American Libraries,* Transactions of the American Philosophical

Society, new ser., vol. LV, part 9 (Philadelphia: The American Philosophical Society, 1965). For Franklin's role in the development of American science, see I. Bernard Cohen, *Franklin and Newton: An Inquiry into Speculative Newtonian Experimental Science and Franklin's Work in Electricity as an Example Thereof* (Philadelphia: The American Philosophical Society, 1956) and Brooke Hindle, *The Pursuit of Science in Revolutionary America, 1735-1789* (Chapel Hill: University of North Carolina Press, 1956). For Franklin as printer, see John Clyde Oswald, *Benjamin Franklin, Printer* (Garden City, N.Y.: Doubleday, Page & Company, 1917), Lawrence C. Wroth, *The Colonial Printer* (2d ed.; Portland, Me.: The Southworth-Anthoensen Press, 1938), and Alfred Owen Aldridge, "Benjamin Franklin and the *Pennsylvania Gazette*," *Proceedings of the American Philosophical Society*, CVI (1962), 77-81.

The sources of the proverbial sayings of Poor Richard are traced in Robert Newcomb, "The Sources of Benjamin Franklin's Sayings of Poor Richard" (unpublished doctoral thesis, University of Maryland, 1957). The sources of Franklin's *Proposals Relating to the Education of Youth in Pennsylvania* are discussed in Eugene D. Owen, "Where Did Benjamin Franklin Get the Idea for His Academy?" *The Pennsylvania Magazine of History and Biography*, LVIII (1934), 86-94, and John J. O'Neill, "An Analysis of Franklin's *Proposals Relating to the Education of Youth in Pennsylvania* as a Selection of Eighteenth Century Cultural Values" (unpublished doctoral thesis, Harvard University, 1960). Franklin's role in the founding of the Academy of Philadelphia is treated in detail in James Mulhern, *A History of Secondary Education in Pennsylvania* (Philadelphia: published by the author, 1933); while his role in the development of the College of Philadelphia is sketched in Francis N. Thorpe, *Benjamin Franklin and the University of Pennsylvania* (Washington, D.C.: Government Printing Office, 1893) and Thomas Harrison Montgomery, *A History of the University of Pennsylvania from Its Foundation to A.D. 1770* (Philadelphia: George W. Jacobs & Co., 1900). The best recent estimates of Franklin's general contribution to American education are M. Roberta Warf Keiter, "Benjamin Franklin as an Educator" (unpublished doctoral thesis, University of Maryland, 1957) and Jonathan Messerli, "Benjamin Franklin: Colonial and Cosmopolitan Educator," *British Journal of Educational Studies*, XVI (1968), 43-59. The most significant collections of Franklin papers are in the American Philosophical Society, the Historical Society of Pennsylvania, and the Library of Congress.

The merit of Carl and Jessica Bridenbaugh's *Rebels and Gentlemen: Philadelphia in the Age of Franklin* has already been alluded to at several points in this essay; that merit also marks the discussion of the debates over educational theory and philosophy during the provincial era. With respect to William Smith, whose work and influence have been insufficiently noted by historians of American education, the traditional source is Horace Wemyss Smith, *Life and Correspondence of the Rev. William Smith* (2 vols.; Philadelphia: S. A. George & Co., 1879-80), which is somewhat marred by filiopietism, while the standard recent biography is Albert Frank Gegenheimer, *William Smith: Educator and Churchman, 1727-1803* (Philadelphia: University of Pennsylvania Press, 1943). Smith's chief educational essays from the New York period are *Some Thoughts on Education: With Reasons for Erecting a College in*

This Province, and Fixing the Same at the City of New York (New York: J. Parker, 1752), and *A General Idea of the College of Mirania* (New York: J. Parker and W. Weyman, 1753), both published anonymously, while his curriculum of 1756 for the College of Philadelphia is reprinted in Thomas Harrison Montgomery, *A History of the University of Pennsylvania from Its Foundation to A.D. 1770* (Philadelphia: George W. Jacobs & Co., 1900). Theodore Hornberger, "A Note on the Probable Source of Provost Smith's Famous Curriculum for the College of Philadelphia," *The Pennsylvania Magazine of History and Biography*, LVIII (1934), 370-377, and *Scientific Thought in the American Colonies, 1638-1800* (Austin: University of Texas Press, 1945) are excellent with respect to both the sources and the far-reaching significance of Smith's conception of the higher learning. Bruce Richard Lively, "William Smith, the College and Academy of Philadelphia and Pennsylvania Politics, 1753 1758," *Historical Magazine of the Protestant Episcopal Church*, XXXVIII (1969), 237-258, is a useful contextual analysis. The best collections of Smith papers are in the New York Historical Society and the Historical Society of Pennsylvania.

The best discussion of John Morgan's contributions to American education is in Whitfield J. Bell, Jr., *John Morgan: Continental Doctor* (Philadelphia: University of Pennsylvania Press, 1965); while the best collection of papers—one recently augmented by microfilm, photostatic, and typewritten copies of the material Bell gathered in connection with his research—is in the library of the College of Physicians of Philadelphia. Betsy Copping Corner, *William Shippen, Jr.: Pioneer in American Medical Education* (Philadelphia: American Philosophical Society, 1951) is a useful complementary discussion, as are Francis R. Packard, *History of Medicine in the United States* (2 vols.; New York: P. B. Hoeber, 1931), and "How London and Edinburgh Influenced Medicine in Philadelphia in the Eighteenth Century," *Annals of Medical History*, new ser., IV (1932), 219-244, and William Frederick Norwood, *Medical Education in the United States Before the Civil War* (Philadelphia: University of Pennsylvania Press, 1944). Isabel Kenrick's "The University of Edinburgh 1660-1715: A Study in the Transformation of Teaching Methods and Curriculum" (unpublished doctoral thesis, Bryn Mawr College, 1956) provides excellent background.

CHAPTER 13: THE BUSINESS OF LIVING

Lawrence C. Wroth's *The Colonial Printer* (2d ed.; Portland, Me.: The Southworth-Anthoensen Press, 1938) is the leading work on the subject, and includes an excellent bibliography; Isaiah Thomas' *The History of Printing in America, With a Bibliography of Printers* (2d ed.; 2 vols.; Albany, N.Y.: J. Munsell, 1874) remains a mine of information. The best studies of individual printers are Lawrence C. Wroth, *William Parks: Printer and Journalist of England and Colonial America* (Richmond, Va.: The William Parks Club, 1926), Clifford K. Shipton, *Isaiah Thomas: Printer, Patriot and Philanthropist, 1749-1831* (Rochester, N.Y.: Leo Hart, 1948), Anna Janney DeArmond, *Andrew Bradford: Colonial Journalist* (Newark: University of Delaware Press, 1949), William Reed Steckel, "Pietist in Colonial Pennsylvania: Christopher Sauer, Printer, 1738-1758" (unpublished doctoral thesis, Stanford University, 1949), Alexander A. Lawrence, *James Johnson: Georgia's First Printer* (Savannah, Ga.: Pigeonhole Press, 1956), Robert Wilson Kidder, "The Contribution of Daniel Fowle to New Hampshire Printing, 1756-1787" (unpublished doctoral thesis, University of Illinois, 1960), Anna Kathryn Oller, "Christopher Saur, Colonial Printer: A Study of the Publication of the Press, 1738-1758" (unpublished doctoral thesis, University of Michigan, 1963), Robert Hurd Kany, "David Hall: Printing Partner of Benjamin Franklin" (unpublished doctoral thesis, Pennsylvania State University, 1963), Mary Louise Dunham Meder, "Timothy Green III, Connecticut Printer, 1737-1796: His Life and Times" (unpublished doctoral thesis, University of Michigan, 1964), and, of course, Carl Van Doren, *Benjamin Franklin* (New York: The Viking Press, 1938). A number of shorter biographies appear in the early volumes of *The Americana Collector*.

The almanac has intrigued American literary historians at least since Moses Coit Tyler's oft-quoted remark of 1878, "No one who would penetrate to the core of early American literature, and would read in it the secret history of the people in whose minds it took root and from whose minds it grew, may by any means turn away, in lofty literary scorn, from the almanac,—most despised, most prolific, most indispensable of books, which every man uses, and no man praises; the very quack, clown, pack-horse, and pariah of modern literature, yet the one universal book of modern literature; the supreme and only literary necessity even in households where the Bible and the newspaper are still undesired or unattainable luxuries." (*A History of American Literature, 1607-1765* [2 vols.; G. P. Putnam's Sons, 1878], II, 120). The most comprehensive study of the almanacs as didactic literature is Robert T. Sidwell, "The Colonial American Almanacs: A Study in Non-Institutional Education" (unpublished doctoral thesis, Rutgers University, 1965); Joseph Philip Goldberg, "The Eighteenth-Century Philadelphia Almanac and Its English Counterpart" (unpublished doctoral thesis, University of Maryland, 1962) is a useful complementary study, particularly with respect to contemporary English backgrounds. Milton Drake, ed., *Almanacs of the United States* (New York: Scarecrow Press, 1962) is the best general checklist. Richard M. Gummere, "The Classical Element in Early New England Almanacs," *The Harvard Library Bulletin*, IX (1955), 181-196, and Francisco Guerra, "Medical Almanacs of the American Colonial Period," *Journal of the History of Medicine and Allied Sciences*, XVI (1961), 234-255, are illustrative of a large literature dealing with the content of the almanacs on special subjects.

The standard history of American newspapers is Frank Luther Mott, *American Journalism: A History of Newspapers in the United States Through 260 Years: 1690 to 1950* (rev. ed.; New York: The Macmillan Company, 1950). Sidney Kobre, *The Development of the Colonial Newspaper* (Pittsburgh: Colonial Press, 1944) is a useful specialized study, though the circulation figures therein, based largely on the analyses of William A. Dill of the University of Kansas (*The First Century of American Newspapers* [Lawrence: Department of Journalism, University of Kansas, 1925] and *Growth of Newspapers in the United States* [Lawrence: Department of Journalism, University of Kansas, 1928]), are not wholly accurate. Elizabeth Christine Cook, *Literary Influences in*

Colonial Newspapers, 1704-1750 (New York: Columbia University Press, 1912), Brooks Edward Kleber, "The Colonial Newspaper and the Emergence of an American Community" (unpublished doctoral thesis, University of Pennsylvania, 1957), Robert H. Riefe, "The Newspaper and the Development of American Culture, 1704-1754" (unpublished doctoral thesis, Boston University, 1952), Arthur M. Schlesinger, *Prelude to Independence: The Newspaper War on Britain, 1764-1776* (New York: Alfred A. Knopf, 1957), and Robert Mangum Barrow, "Newspaper Advertising in Colonial America, 1704-1775" (unpublished doctoral thesis, University of Virginia, 1967) are also pertinent, as are G. A. Cranfield, *The Development of the Provincial Newspaper, 1700-1760* (Oxford: Clarendon Press, 1962), Laurence Hanson, *Government and the Press, 1695-1763* (London: Oxford University Press, 1936), and Robert R. Rea, *The English Press in Politics, 1760-1774* (Lincoln: University of Nebraska Press, 1963) for contemporary English newspapers. Hennig Cohen's *The South Carolina Gazette, 1732-1775* (Columbia: University of South Carolina Press, 1953) is an exemplary study of an individual newspaper. Clarence S. Brigham, *History and Bibliography of American Newspapers, 1690-1820* (2 vols.; Worcester, Mass.: American Antiquarian Society, 1947) is the authoritative checklist.

Frank Luther Mott, *A History of American Magazines* (5 vols.; Cambridge, Mass.: Harvard University Press, 1930-1968) is the standard work; Lyon N. Richardson, *A History of Early American Magazines, 1741-1789* (New York: Thomas Nelson and Sons, 1931) is a valuable specialized study. Both works include checklists for the colonial period.

Paul Leicester Ford, *The New-England Primer: A History of Its Origin and Development with a Reprint of the Unique Copy of the Earliest Known Edition and Many Fac-Simile Illustrations and Reproductions* (New York: Dodd, Mead and Company, 1897) is the best introduction to the *Primer*, though it must be supplemented by the later checklists and commentaries of Charles F. Heartman, *The New-England Primer Issued Prior to 1830* (New York: R. R. Bowker Company, 1934), and *American Primers, Indian Primers, Royal Primers, and Thirty-Seven Other Types of Non-New-England Primers Issued Prior to 1830* (Highland Park, N. J.: Harry B. Weiss, 1935). The best works on the self-instructors are Robert Francis Seybolt, *Source Studies in American Colonial Education: The Private School* (Urbana: University of Illinois, 1925), and *The Evening School in Colonial America* (Urbana: University of Illinois, 1925).

Thomas Goddard Wright, *Literary Culture in Early New England, 1620-1730* (New Haven: Yale University Press, 1920), Louis B. Wright, *The First Gentlemen of Virginia: Intellectual Qualities of the Early Colonial Ruling Class* (San Marino, Calif.: Henry E. Huntington Library & Art Gallery, 1940), Lawrence C. Wroth, *An American Bookshelf, 1755* (Philadelphia: University of Pennsylvania Press, 1934), and Joseph T. Wheeler, "Literary Culture in Eighteenth Century Maryland" (unpublished doctoral thesis, University of Maryland, 1938) afford insight into individual libraries during the provincial era, as do the particular studies of the Mather and Logan libraries in Julius Herbert Tuttle, "The Libraries of the Mathers," *Proceedings of the American Antiquarian Society*, new ser., XX (1911), 269-356, and Frederick B. Tolles, *James Logan and the Culture of Provincial America* (Boston: Little, Brown and Company, 1957).

College libraries are dealt with in Louis Shores, *Origins of the American College Library, 1638-1800* (Nashville: George Peabody College for Teachers, 1934), John M. Jennings, *The Library of the College of William and Mary in Virginia, 1693-1793* (Charlottesville: University Press of Virginia, 1968), and Joe Walker Kraus, "Book Collections of Five Colonial College Libraries; A Subject Analysis" (unpublished doctoral thesis, University of Illinois, 1960), which includes an excellent bibliography. Parish and town libraries are dealt with in Herbert Lyman Searcy, "Parochial Libraries in the American Colonies" (unpublished doctoral thesis, University of Illinois, 1963), Jesse H. Shera, *Foundations of the Public Library: The Origins of the Public Library Movement in New England, 1629-1855* (Chicago: University of Chicago Press, 1949), and Carl Bridenbaugh, *Cities in Revolt: Urban Life in America, 1743-1776* (New York: Alfred A. Knopf, 1955). Dorothy Fear Grimm, "A History of the Library Company of Philadelphia, 1731-1835" (unpublished doctoral thesis, University of Pennsylvania, 1955), Margaret Barton Korty, *Benjamin Franklin and Eighteenth-Century Libraries,* Transactions of the American Philosophical Society, new ser., vol. LV, part 9 (Philadelphia: The American Philosophical Society, 1965), and Austin Baxter Keep, *History of the New York Society Library, with an Introductory Chapter on Libraries in Colonial New York, 1698-1776* (New York: De Vinne Press, 1908) are instructive on the development of subscription libraries.

The best early works on the private entrepreneurial teacher during the provincial era are Robert Francis Seybolt, *The Evening School in Colonial America* (Urbana: University of Illinois, 1925), *Source Studies in American Colonial Education* (Urbana: University of Illinois, 1925), "The Evening Schools of Colonial New York City," in *Fifteenth Annual Report of the [New York State] Education Department* (1919), I, 630-652, and "New York Colonial Schoolmasters," *ibid.,* 653-669, "The S.P.G. Myth: A Note on Education in Colonial New York," *Journal of Educational Research,* XIII (1926), 129-137, "Schoolmasters of Colonial Philadelphia," *The Pennsylvania Magazine of History and Biography,* LII (1928), 361-371, and *The Private Schools of Colonial Boston* (Cambridge, Mass.: Harvard University Press, 1935), which are admirably complemented by the pertinent material in Carl and Jessica Bridenbaugh, *Rebels and Gentlemen: Philadelphia in the Age of Franklin* (New York: Reynal & Hitchcock, 1942), and Carl Bridenbaugh, *Cities in the Wilderness: The First Century of Urban Life in America, 1625-1742* (2d ed.; New York: Alfred A. Knopf, 1955), and *Cities in Revolt.*

The early development of the Academy of Philadelphia is detailed in James Mulhern, *A History of Secondary Education in Pennsylvania* (Philadelphia: published by the author, 1933), while the subsequent development of the College of Philadelphia is detailed in Thomas Harrison Montgomery, *A History of the University of Pennsylvania from Its Foundation to A.D. 1770* (Philadelphia: George W. Jacobs & Co., 1900) and Edward Potts Cheyney, *History of the University of Pennsylvania, 1740-1940* (Philadelphia: University of Pennsylvania Press, 1940). The connection with the earlier charitable school is explicated in Charles W. Dulles, "The Charity School of 1740—The Foundation of the University of Pennsylvania," *University of Pennsylvania Medical Bulletin,* XVII

(1904-1905), 302-311. The early history of King's College is admirably dealt with in David Churchill Humphrey, "King's College in the City of New York, 1754-1776" (unpublished doctoral thesis, Northwestern University, 1968), a study that sets forth somewhat different interpretations from my own; Herbert and Carol Schneider, eds., *Samuel Johnson, President of King's College: His Career and Writings* (4 vols.; New York: Columbia University Press, 1929) is obviously of direct relevance. There are excellent archives at both the University of Pennsylvania and Columbia University.

The delineation of the history of the American academy as a reform movement proceeding from the dissenting academies through Franklin's academy through the Phillips academies and eventually to the Boston English classical school derives from a long line of studies that begins at least as early as 1902, with the publication of Elmer Ellsworth Brown's *The Making of Our Middle Schools: An Account of the Development of Secondary Education in the United States* (New York: Longmans, Green, and Co., 1902). It was Douglas Sloan's analysis in "The Scottish Enlightenment and the American College Ideal: Early Princeton Traditions" that alerted me to the crucial role of the Scottish universities on the one hand and the Presbyterian academies on the other. And it is Sloan's analysis that renders so stark the gap between the richness and modernity of the curriculum of those academies and the more narrowly traditional classical curriculum reported in Harriet Webster Marr, *Old New England Academies Founded Before 1826* (New York: Comet Press Books, 1959) or John W. Ragle, *Governor Dummer Academy History, 1763-1963* (South Byfield, Mass.: Governor Dummer Academy, 1963), or, indeed, Claude M. Fuess's *An Old New England School: A History of the Phillips Academy, Andover* (Boston: Houghton Mifflin Company, 1917).

The best work on the organization of early American science in general and the American Philosophical Society in particular has been done by Brooke Hindle in *The Pursuit of Science in Revolutionary America, 1735-1789* (Chapel Hill: University of North Carolina Press, 1956) and in "The Rise of the American Philosophical Society, 1766-1787" (unpublished doctoral thesis, University of Pennsylvania, 1949). Francis R. Packard, "Medicine and the American Philosophical Society," *Proceedings of the American Philosophical Society*, LXXXVI (1942-43), 91-102, Gilbert Chinard, "The American Philosophical Society and the World of Science (1768-1800)," *ibid.*, LXXXVII (1943-44), 1-11, Carl Van Doren, "The Beginnings of the American Philosophical Society," *ibid.*, 277-289, Ralph S. Bates, *Scientific Societies in the United States* (New York: John Wiley & Sons, 1945), and G. Brown Goode's older essay, *The Origin of the National Scientific and Educational Institutions of the United States*, Papers of the American Historical Association, vol. IV, part 2 (New York: G. P. Putnam's Sons, 1890) are also useful. A number of recent biographies are directly relevant, notably, Josephine Herbst, *New Green World: John Bartram and the Early Naturalists* (New York: Hastings House, 1954), Brooke Hindle, *David Rittenhouse* (Princeton: Princeton University Press, 1964), Whitfield J. Bell, Jr., *John Morgan: Continental Doctor* (Philadelphia: University of Pennsylvania Press, 1965), Carl Binger, *Revolutionary Doctor: Benjamin Rush, 1746-1813* (New York: W. W. Norton & Company, 1966), and Edmund Berkeley and

Dorothy Smith Berkeley, *John Clayton: Pioneer of American Botany* (Chapel Hill: University of North Carolina Press, 1963), and *Dr. Alexander Garden of Charles Town* (Chapel Hill: University of North Carolina Press, 1969). Whitfield J. Bell, Jr. critically assesses the earlier literature in *Early American Science: Needs and Opportunities for Study* (Williamsburg, Va.: Institute of Early American History and Culture, 1955).

The historiography of the thesis set forth in Max Weber, *The Protestant Ethic and the Spirit of Capitalism* (1904-1905), translated by Talcott Parsons (New York: Charles Scribner's Sons, 1930) is tersely summarized in Robert W. Green, *Protestantism and Capitalism: The Weber Thesis and Its Critics* (Boston: D. C. Heath and Company, 1959). The data are appraised in Gabriel Kolko, "Max Weber on America: Theory and Evidence," *History and Theory,* I (1961), 243-260. Robert S. Michaelson's "The American Gospel of Work and the Protestant Doctrine of Vocation" (unpublished doctoral thesis, Yale University, 1951) marshals what evidence there is for relating Franklin to Puritanism in the Weber tradition.

The lives of the excluded blacks and Indians are dealt with in the sources discussed on pp. 601-602, as well as in Lorenzo Johnston Greene, *The Negro in Colonial New England* (New York: Columbia University Press, 1942) and the relevant sections of John Hope Franklin, *From Slavery to Freedom: A History of Negro Americans* (3d ed.; New York: Alfred A. Knopf, 1967), which also includes an excellent bibliography. Given the economic and social interrelationships between the West Indies and the mainland, the development of black institutions in the West Indies during the eighteenth century is highly relevant, rendering such discussions as J. Harry Bennett, *Bondsmen and Bishops: Slavery and Apprenticeship on the Codrington Plantations of Barbados, 1710-1838* (Berkeley: University of California Press, 1958), M. G. Smith, "Some Aspects of Social Structure in the British Caribbean about 1820," in *The Plural Society in the British West Indies* (Berkeley: University of California Press, 1965), chap. v, and Elsa V. Goveia, *Slave Society in the British Leeward Islands at the End of the Eighteenth Century* (New Haven: Yale University Press, 1965) also pertinent. Elsa V. Goveia, *A Study on the Historiography of the British West Indies to the End of the Nineteenth Century* (Mexico: Instituto Panamericano de Geografía e Historia, 1956) is the leading analysis of its kind.

INTRODUCTION TO PART V

Edmund S. and Helen M. Morgan, *The Stamp Act Crisis: Prologue to Revolution* (rev. ed.; New York: Collier Books, 1963) is the best general introduction to the portentous events of 1764-1766; it is admirably complemented by the pertinent sections of Bernard Bailyn, ed., *Pamphlets of the American Revolution, 1750-1776* (4 vols.; Cambridge, Mass.: Harvard University Press, 1965-   ).

John Adams, "Dissertation on the Canon and Feudal Law," *The Works of John Adams,* edited by Charles Francis Adams (10 vols.; Boston: Charles C. Little and James Brown, 1851), III, 448-464, has been vastly overshadowed by Jefferson's contemporary pronouncements on education, partly because of Adams' later conservatism in matters educational, partly because of Jefferson's willingness to put forward specific organizational proposals, and partly because of the title of Adams' treatise. Yet Adams' dissertation doubtless had more in common with Jefferson's proposals of 1779 than either had with the latter-day ideological commitments of an American educational profession that honored Jefferson and forgot Adams. Page Smith, *John Adams* (2 vols.; Garden City, N. Y.: Doubleday & Company, 1962) is the fullest modern biography; John R. Howe, Jr., *The Changing Political Thought of John Adams* (Princeton: Princeton University Press, 1966) and Zoltán Haraszti, *John Adams and the Prophets of Progress* (Cambridge, Mass.: Harvard University Press, 1952) are the best recent analyses of Adams' social ideas. The Adams Papers, now issuing from the Harvard University Press under the distinguished general editorship of L. H. Butterfield, promise to be definitive.

CHAPTER 14: CIVILITY LIBERALIZED

All of the bibliographical citations referring to Locke on pp. 619-624 are relevant here. In addition, Peter Laslett's notes and commentaries in his edition of John Locke, *Two Treatises of Government* (rev. ed.; Cambridge: Cambridge University Press, 1963), John Dunn, "Consent in the Political Theory of John Locke," *The Historical Journal*, X, 2 (1967), 153-182, and *The Political Thought of John Locke: An Historical Account of the Argument of the Two Treatises of Government* (Cambridge: Cambridge University Press, 1969), and Philip Abrams, *John Locke: Two Tracts on Government* (Cambridge: Cambridge University Press, 1967) are invaluable for an understanding of Locke's political philosophy, while Sterling Power Lamprecht, *The Moral and Political Philosophy of John Locke* (New York: Columbia University Press, 1918) remains useful. The connection of Lockean thought and the charity school movement is explicated in M. G. Jones's excellent work, *The Charity School Movement: A Study of Eighteenth Century Puritanism in Action* (Cambridge: Cambridge University Press, 1938), which also presents a discriminating bibliography.

The educational thought of the Commonwealth period is discussed in J. W. Adamson, *Pioneers of Modern Education, 1600-1700* (Cambridge: Cambridge University Press, 1905), G. H. Turnbull, *Samuel Hartlib: A Sketch of His Life and His Relation to J. A. Comenius* (London: Oxford University Press, 1920), and *Hartlib, Dury and Comenius: Gleanings from Hartlib's Papers* (London: Hodder & Stoughton, 1947), Matthew Spinka, *John Amos Comenius: That Incomparable Moravian* (Chicago: University of Chicago Press, 1943), W. A. L. Vincent, *The State and School Education 1640-1660 in England and Wales* (London: Society for Promoting Christian Knowledge, 1950), Judah Bierman, "Of Learning and Knowledge: An Analysis of the Discussion of Learning in Seventeenth-Century English Essays" (unpublished doctoral thesis, University of California, Los Angeles, 1951), David Johnston Maitland, "Three Puritan Attitudes Toward Learning: An Examination of the Puritan Controversies over a Learned Ministry, 1640-1660, and the Consequences of This Struggle for Puritan Concern About the Reformation of Learning" (unpublished doctoral thesis, Columbia University, 1959), Richard Foster Jones, *Ancients and Moderns: A Study of the Rise of the Scientific Movement in Seventeenth-Century England*

(2d ed.; St. Louis: Washington University Press, 1961), Malcolm Gordon Parks, "Milton and Seventeenth-Century Attitudes to Education" (unpublished doctoral thesis, University of Toronto, 1963), John Edward Sadler, *J. A. Comenius and the Concept of Universal Education* (New York: Barnes & Noble, 1966), J. J. O'Brien, "Commonwealth Schemes for the Advancement of Learning," *British Journal of Educational Studies,* XVI (1968), 30-42, Richard L. Greaves, *The Puritan Revolution and Educational Thought: Background for Reform* (New Brunswick: Rutgers University Press, 1969), and Charles Webster, ed., *Samuel Hartlib and the Advancement of Learning* (Cambridge: Cambridge University Press, 1970), as well as in H. R. Trevor-Roper's sharply revisionist essay, "Three Foreigners: The Philosophers of the Puritan Revolution," in *Religion, the Reformation, and Social Change* (London: Macmillan and Company, 1967), which is more interesting, perhaps, than persuasive.

The transmission of Commonwealth political and educational thought to England and America in the eighteenth century is explicated in Caroline Robbins, *The Eighteenth-Century Commonwealthman: Studies in the Transmission, Development and Circumstances of English Liberal Thought from the Restoration of Charles II Until the War with the Thirteen Colonies* (Cambridge, Mass.: Harvard University Press, 1961), Zera S. Fink, *The Classical Republicans: An Essay in the Recovery of a Pattern of Thought in Seventeenth Century England* (Evanston: Northwestern University, 1945), J. R. Pole, *Political Representation in England and the Origins of the American Republic* (London: Macmillan and Company, 1966), and "Machiavelli, Harrington, and English Political Ideologies in the Eighteenth Century," *The William and Mary Quarterly,* 3d ser., XXII (1965), 549-583, Bernard Bailyn, *The Ideological Origins of the American Revolution* (Cambridge, Mass.: Harvard University Press, 1967), Clinton Rossiter, *Seedtime of the Republic: The Origin of the American Tradition of Political Liberty* (New York: Harcourt, Brace & World, 1953), and H. F. Russell Smith's older work, *Harrington and His Oceana: A Study of a 17th Century Utopia and Its Influence in America* (Cambridge: Cambridge University Press, 1914). Staughton Lynd's *Intellectual Origins of American Radicalism* (New York: Pantheon Books, 1968) was also valuable in forcing me to query my conclusions, and the fact of my disagreement with its theses does not negate that value. Caroline Robbins, "Algernon Sidney's *Discourses Concerning Government:* Textbook of Revolution," *The William and Mary Quarterly,* 3d ser., IV (1947), 267-296, and John Dunn, "The Politics of Locke in England and America in the Eighteenth Century," in John W. Yolton, ed., *John Locke: Problems and Perspectives* (Cambridge: Cambridge University Press, 1969) were also exceedingly useful.

The Independent Reflector is available in a splendid critical edition prepared for the John Harvard Library under the editorship of Milton M. Klein (Cambridge, Mass.: Harvard University Press, 1963). Klein's introduction there is the best starting place for an assessment of Livingston's career. It is usefully complemented by Klein's monograph, "The American Whig: William Livingston of New York" (unpublished doctoral thesis, Columbia University, 1954), by Klein's two essays, "The Rise of the New York Bar: The Legal Career of William Livingston," *The William and Mary Quarterly,* 3d ser., XV (1958),

334-358, and "The Cultural Tyros of Colonial New York," *The South Atlantic Quarterly*, LXVI (1967), 218-232, and by Harold Wesley Thatcher, "The Social Philosophy of William Livingston" (unpublished doctoral thesis, University of Chicago, 1935), Dorothy Rita Dillon, *The New York Triumvirate: A Study of the Legal and Political Careers of William Livingston, John Morin Scott, and William Smith, Jr.* (New York: Columbia University Press, 1949), and L. S. F. Upton, *The Loyal Whig: William Smith of New York & Quebec* (Toronto: University of Toronto Press, 1969). There are significant collections of Livingston papers at the Massachusetts Historical Society, the New York Historical Society, and the New York Public Library.

Raymond Muse's "William Douglass, Man of the Enlightenment, 1691-1752" (unpublished doctoral thesis, Stanford University, 1948) is a competent biographical study, which includes, *inter alia*, a full bibliography and a useful listing of the printed sources mentioned in the *Summary*. The "Letters from Dr. William Douglass to Cadwallader Colden," published in the Massachusetts Historical Society *Collections*, 4th ser., II (1854), 164-189, are the most valuable sources after the *Summary* itself. Lawrence C. Wroth includes an excellent review of the several editions of the *Summary* in *An American Bookshelf, 1755* (Philadelphia: University of Pennsylvania Press, 1934).

In contrast to Douglass, the sources and literature on Jefferson are voluminous. The best recent biography is Dumas Malone, *Jefferson and His Time* (4+ vols.; Boston: Little, Brown and Company, 1948-   ); Marie Kimball, *Jefferson: The Road to Glory, 1743 to 1776* (New York: Coward-McCann, 1943), and *Jefferson: War and Peace, 1776 to 1784* (New York: Coward-McCann, 1947) are also valuable. *The Papers of Thomas Jefferson*, edited by Julian P. Boyd *et al.* (17+ vols.; Princeton: Princeton University Press, 1950-   ) promises to be the definitive edition of Jefferson's writings; meanwhile, *The Writings of Thomas Jefferson*, edited by Paul Leicester Ford (10 vols.; New York: G. P. Putnam's Sons, 1892-1899) and *The Writings of Thomas Jefferson*, edited by Andrew A. Lipscomb and A. E. Bergh (20 vols.; Washington, D.C.: Thomas Jefferson Memorial Association, 1903) remain useful. *The Autobiography of Thomas Jefferson*, edited by Paul Leicester Ford (New York: G. P. Putnam's Sons, 1914) is a convenient edition; while Gilbert Chinard, ed., *The Commonplace Book of Thomas Jefferson: A Repertory of His Ideas on Government*, The Johns Hopkins Studies in Romance Literatures and Languages, extra vol. II (Baltimore: The Johns Hopkins Press, 1926), and *The Literary Bible of Thomas Jefferson: His Commonplace Book of Philosophers and Poets* (Baltimore: The Johns Hopkins Press, 1928) are invaluable with respect to Jefferson's early intellectual development. E. Millicent Sowerby's *Catalogue of the Library of Thomas Jefferson* (5 vols.; Washington: The Library of Congress, 1952-1959) contains, as Dumas Malone once remarked, all that anyone could ask about Jefferson's books and a great deal more of value.

Roy J. Honeywell, *The Educational Work of Thomas Jefferson* (Cambridge, Mass.: Harvard University Press, 1931) is the standard discussion, though it is somewhat dated and narrow in its view of education. Gilbert Chinard, *Jefferson et les Idéologues d'après Sa Correspondance Inédite avec Destutt de Tracy, Cabanis, J.-B. Say, et Auguste Comte*, The Johns Hopkins Studies in Romance Literatures and Languages, extra vol. I (Baltimore: The Johns Hopkins Press,

1925) is excellent on the French motif in Jefferson's thought; Adrienne Koch, *The Philosophy of Thomas Jefferson* (New York: Columbia University Press, 1943) deals incisively with Jefferson's philosophy, devoting appropriate attention to Chinard's theme. Chinard's own *Thomas Jefferson: The Apostle of Americanism* (Boston: Little, Brown and Company, 1943) and Douglass Greybill Adair, "The Intellectual Origins of Jeffersonian Democracy: Republicanism, the Class Struggle, and the Virtuous Farmer" (unpublished doctoral thesis, Yale University, 1943) are also valuable. Frank Luther Mott, *Jefferson and the Press* (Baton Rouge: Louisiana State University Press, 1943) and Edwin T. Martin, *Thomas Jefferson: Scientist* (New York: Henry Schuman, 1952) are useful specialized studies.

Winthrop D. Jordan, *White over Black: American Attitudes Toward the Negro, 1550-1812* (Chapel Hill: University of North Carolina Press, 1968), Frederick M. Binder, *The Color Problem in Early National America as Viewed by John Adams, Jefferson and Jackson* (The Hague: Mouton, 1968), and William Cohen, "Thomas Jefferson and the Problem of Slavery," *The Journal of American History*, LVI (1969-70), 503-526, present intelligent analyses of the complexities of Jefferson's position, the last offering also an incisive historiographical commentary.

Richard Beale Davis, *Intellectual Life in Jefferson's Virginia, 1790-1830* (Chapel Hill: University of North Carolina Press, 1964) and Daniel J. Boorstin, *The Lost World of Thomas Jefferson* (New York: Henry Holt and Company, 1948) are excellent contextual studies, though they stress the period after 1783. Merrill D. Peterson, *The Jeffersonian Image in the American Mind* (New York: Oxford University Press, 1960) and Charles Maurice Wiltse, *The Jeffersonian Tradition in American Democracy* (Chapel Hill: University of North Carolina Press, 1935) trace the continuing relevance of Jeffersonian ideas and American perceptions of that relevance. The chief collections of Jefferson papers are at the Library of Congress, the University of Virginia, and the Massachusetts Historical Society.

CHAPTER 15: POLITICS AND EDUCATION

The recent works of J. H. Plumb and Bernard Bailyn, notably, Plumb's *England in the Eighteenth Century* (Baltimore, Md.: Penguin Books, 1950), and *The Origins of Political Stability: England, 1675-1725* (Boston: Houghton Mifflin Company, 1967), and Bailyn's "Political Experience and Enlightenment Ideas in Eighteenth-Century America," *The American Historical Review*, LXVII (1961-62), 339-351, and *The Origins of American Politics* (New York: Alfred A. Knopf, 1968), provide a splendid introduction to the new politics of the eighteenth-century Anglo-American world and the role of public opinion in that new politics. In addition, Laurence Hanson, *Government and the Press, 1695-1763* (London: Oxford University Press, 1936) and Robert R. Rea, *The English Press in Politics, 1760-1774* (Lincoln: University of Nebraska Press, 1963) are valuable for the English side, while Arthur M. Schlesinger, *Prelude to Independence: The Newspaper War on Britain, 1764-1776* (New York: Alfred A. Knopf, 1958), Edmund S. and Helen M. Morgan, *The Stamp Act Crisis: Pro-*

logue to Revolution (rev. ed; New York: Collier Books, 1963), Bernard Bailyn, *The Ideological Origins of the American Revolution* (Cambridge, Mass.: Harvard University Press, 1967), and Philip Davidson, *Propaganda and the American Revolution* (Chapel Hill: University of North Carolina Press, 1941) are valuable for the American side. Lawrence Henry Gipson's *The British Empire Before the American Revolution* (14 vols.; New York: Alfred A. Knopf, 1958-1969) is a mine of information, including, of course, the comprehensive bibliography that constitutes the fourteenth volume.

Frederick S. Siebert, *Freedom of the Press in England, 1476-1776* (Urbana: University of Illinois, 1952) is the best and most comprehensive survey of the English tradition; Leonard W. Levy, *Legacy of Suppression: Freedom of Speech and Press in Early American History* (Cambridge, Mass.: Harvard University Press, 1960) and Levy, ed., *Freedom of the Press from Zenger to Jefferson* (Indianapolis: The Bobbs-Merrill Company, Inc., 1966) serve similarly for colonial America. Clyde Augustus Duniway, *The Development of Freedom of the Press in Massachusetts* (New York: Longmans, Green, and Co., 1906) is a splendid older study. Stanley Nider Katz's recent critical edition of James Alexander's *A Brief Narrative of the Case and Trial of John Peter Zenger, Printer of The New York Weekly Journal* (Cambridge, Mass.: Harvard University Press, 1963) is excellent, though usefully complemented by Livingston Rutherford's older work, *John Peter Zenger: His Press, His Trial, and a Bibliography of Zenger Imprints* (New York: Dodd, Mead & Company, 1904). Ralph E. McCoy, *Freedom of the Press: An Annotated Bibliography* (Carbondale: Southern Illinois University Press, 1968) will probably be definitive for some time to come, though its alphabetical organization, without topical breakdown, makes it difficult to use for particular subjects.

The role of the press in the coming of the Revolution has been debated at least since David Ramsay's assertions about that role in *The History of the American Revolution* (2 vols.; Philadelphia: R. Aiken & Son, 1789). Ramsay's assertions are documented in Moses Coit Tyler, *The Literary History of the American Revolution, 1763-1783* (2 vols.; New York: G. P. Putnam's Sons, 1897) and in the works by Philip Davidson, Arthur M. Schlesinger, and Bernard Bailyn mentioned above. And they are reviewed against a background of subsequent historiography in Page Smith, "David Ramsay and the Causes of the American Revolution," *The William and Mary Quarterly*, 3d ser., XVII (1960), 51-77. Solomon Lutnick's *The American Revolution and the British Press, 1775-1783* (Columbia: University of Missouri Press, 1967) is a useful complementary study. Carl F. Kaestle's essay "The Public Reaction to John Dickinson's Farmer's Letters," *Proceedings of the American Antiquarian Society*, LXXVIII (1968), 323-359, is a model of the sort of detailed analysis that must eventually document the traditional case.

John Wingate Thornton, *The Pulpit of the American Revolution: Or, the Political Sermons of the Period of 1776* (2d ed.; Boston: D. Lathrop & Co., 1876), Edward Frank Humphrey, *Nationalism and Religion in America, 1774-1789* (Boston: Chipman Law Publishing Company, 1924), Alice M. Baldwin, *The New England Clergy and the American Revolution* (Durham: Duke University Press, 1928), *The Clergy of Connecticut in Revolutionary Days* (New Haven:

Yale University Press, 1936), and "Sowers of Sedition: The Political Theories of Some of the New Light Presbyterian Clergy of Virginia and North Carolina," *The William and Mary Quarterly*, 3d ser., V (1948), 52-76, Martha Louise Counts, "The Political Views of the Eighteenth Century New England Clergy as Expressed in Their Election Sermons" (unpublished doctoral thesis, Columbia University, 1956), Carl Bridenbaugh, *Mitre and Sceptre: Transatlantic Faiths, Ideas, Personalities, and Politics, 1689-1775* (New York: Oxford University Press, 1962), Bernard Bailyn, ed., *Pamphlets of the American Revolution, 1750-1776* (4 vols.; Cambridge, Mass.: Harvard University Press, 1965-), and Alan Heimert, *Religion and the American Mind from the Great Awakening to the Revolution* (Cambridge, Mass.: Harvard University Press, 1966) discuss the role of the clergy in propagating Whiggish ideas.

George Allan Cook, *John Wise: Early American Democrat* (New York: King's Crown Press, 1952), John Meyer Ericson, "John Wise: Colonial Conservative" (unpublished doctoral thesis, Stanford University, 1961), Edward Michael Griffin, "A Biography of Charles Chauncy (1705-1787)" (unpublished doctoral thesis, Stanford University, 1966), Charles W. Akers, *Called unto Liberty: A Life of Jonathan Mayhew, 1720-1766* (Cambridge, Mass.: Harvard University Press, 1964), and Earl Edward Lewis, "The Theology and Politics of Jonathan Mayhew" (unpublished doctoral thesis, University of Minnesota, 1966) deal with the religious teachings of Wise, Chauncy, and Mayhew and the inescapable bearing of those teachings on political questions. George S. Sensabaugh's discussion of Milton's influence on Mayhew in *Milton in Early America* (Princeton: Princeton University Press, 1964) is an excellent study in the transmission of Commonwealth thought to America. George William Pilcher, "Preacher of the New Light: Samuel Davies, 1724-1761" (unpublished doctoral thesis, University of Illinois, 1963) is an excellent biography, while Robert Sutherland Alley, "The Reverend Mr. Samuel Davies: A Study in Religion and Politics, 1747-1759" (unpublished doctoral thesis, Princeton University, 1962) deals perceptively with Davies' career in Virginia. Pilcher's essay, "Samuel Davies and the Instruction of Negroes in Virginia," *The Virginia Magazine of History and Biography*, LXXIV (1960), 293-300, details Davies' efforts with the blacks; while his edition of *The Reverend Samuel Davies Abroad: The Diary of a Journey to England and Scotland, 1753-55* (Urbana: University of Illinois Press, 1967) made available Davies' account of his activities on behalf of the College of New Jersey and his former constituents in Virginia. There are miscellaneous Davies letters at the Library of Congress (in the William and Thomas Dawson manuscripts), at Princeton University, and in the Fulham Palace Papers, London; many of the more important are available in the first volume of William Stevens Perry, ed., *Historical Collections Relating to the American Colonial Church* (4 vols.; Hartford, Conn.: Church Press Company, 1870-1878) and in William Foote, *Sketches of Virginia Historical and Biographical* (1st ser.; Philadelphia: William S. Martien, 1850).

Charles F. Mullett, "Classical Influences on the American Revolution," *The Classical Journal*, XXXV (1939-40), 92-104, and Richard M. Gummere, *The American Colonial Mind and the Classical Tradition: Essays in Comparative Culture* (Cambridge, Mass.: Harvard University Press, 1963) are excellent analyses of the ways in which eighteenth-century Americans knew and used the ancients. The development of the moral philosophy course is discussed in Anna Haddow, *Political Science in American Colleges and Universities, 1636-1900* (New York: D. Appleton Century, 1939) and James Doyle Casteel, "Professors and Applied Ethics: Higher Education in a Revolutionary Era, 1750-1800" (unpublished doctoral thesis, George Peabody College for Teachers, 1964), as well as more generally in Gladys Bryson, "The Emergence of the Social Sciences from Moral Philosophy," *The International Journal of Ethics,* XLII (1931-32), 304-323, and "The Comparable Interests of the Old Moral Philosophy and the Modern Social Sciences," *Social Forces,* XI (1932-33), 19-27.

Gladys Bryson, *Man and Society: The Scottish Inquiry of the Eighteenth Century* (Princeton: Princeton University Press, 1945) is easily the best book on the social thought of the Scottish moralists. Henry Grey Graham, *The Social Life of Scotland in the Eighteenth Century* (2 vols.; London: A. & C. Black, 1899) and George S. Pryde's more recent *Scotland, from 1603 to the Present Day* (London: Thomas Nelson and Sons, 1962) are excellent contextual works, while Louis Schneider, ed., *The Scottish Moralists on Human Nature and Society* (Chicago: University of Chicago Press, 1967) is a useful collection of documents, commentary, and bibliography.

William Robert Scott, *Francis Hutcheson: His Life, Teaching and Position in the History of Philosophy* (Cambridge: Cambridge University Press, 1900) is the standard biography; William Frankena, "Hutcheson's Moral Sense Theory," *Journal of the History of Ideas,* XVI (1955), 356-375, is a valuable explication of the leitmotif in Hutcheson's philosophy. Douglas Milton Sloan, "The Scottish Enlightenment and the American College Ideal: Early Princeton Traditions" (unpublished doctoral thesis, Columbia University, 1969), Sydney E. Ahlstrom, "The Scottish Philosophy and American Theology," *Church History,* XXIV (1955), 257-272, and Caroline Robbins, " 'When It Is That Colonies May Turn Independent': An Analysis of the Environment and Politics of Francis Hutcheson (1694-1746)," *The William and Mary Quarterly,* 3d ser., XI (1954), 214-251, are useful expositions of Hutcheson's influence in America.

Louis Leonard Tucker, *Puritan Protagonist: President Thomas Clap of Yale College* (Chapel Hill: University of North Carolina Press, 1962) is a thorough biography; Clap's efforts in the field of moral philosophy are exemplified by his textbook, *An Essay on the Nature and Foundation of Moral Virtue and Obligation; Being a Short Introduction to the Study of Ethics; for the Use of the Students of Yale-College* (New Haven: B. Mecom, 1765), and his teaching, as described in *The Annals or History of Yale-College* (New Haven: John Hotchkiss and B. Mecom, 1766). The chief work on Samuel Johnson is Herbert and Carol Schneider, eds., *Samuel Johnson, President of King's College: His Career and Writings* (4 vols.; New York: Columbia University Press, 1929), which includes the full text of Johnson's *Ethices Elementa, or the First Principles of Moral Philosophy* (1746).

William Smith's ideas concerning the moral philosophy course are set forth in *A General Idea of the College of Mirania* (New York: J. Parker and W. Weyman, 1753). Witherspoon's ideas are set forth in his "Lectures on Moral Philosophy," in *The Works of the Rev. John Witherspoon* (3 vols.; Philadelphia: William W. Woodward, 1800), and commented upon in James L. McAllister, "John Witherspoon: Academic Advocate for American Freedom," in Stuart C. Henry, ed., *A Miscellany of American Christianity: Essays in Honor of H. Shelton Smith* (Durham: Duke University Press, 1963), pp. 183-224.

Student debates and disputations are dealt with in David Potter, *Debating in the Colonial Chartered Colleges: An Historical Survey, 1642 to 1900* (New York: Bureau of Publications, Teachers College, Columbia University, 1944) and " 'Exercises' Presented During the Commencements of the College of Philadelphia and Other Colonial Colleges" (unpublished doctoral thesis, University of Pennsylvania, 1962), as well as in the several individual college histories already alluded to. Student exercises in some of the eighteenth-century academies are portrayed in Douglas Milton Sloan, "The Scottish Enlightenment and the American College Ideal: Early Princeton Traditions." A history of student life in America is desperately needed; Henry D. Sheldon, *Student Life and Customs* (New York: D. Appleton and Company, 1901) is primordial.

For the colonists' self-education in the classics, the law, and history, Richard M. Gummere, *The American Colonial Mind and the Classical Tradition: Essays in Comparative Culture,* H. Trevor Colbourn, *The Lamp of Experience: Whig History and the Intellectual Origins of the American Revolution* (Chapel Hill: University of North Carolina Press, 1965), George L. Haskins, *Law and Authority in Early Massachusetts: A Study in Tradition and Design* (New York: Macmillan Company, 1960), George Athan Billias, ed., *Law and Authority in Colonial America: Selected Essays* (Barre, Mass.: Barre Publishers, 1965), and Daniel J. Boorstin, *The Mysterious Science of the Law* (Cambridge, Mass.: Harvard University Press, 1941) are valuable, though Boorstin's analysis of the influence of Blackstone's *Commentaries* needs to be complemented by additional analyses of the influence of Coke's *Institutes* and, indeed, of available volumes of colonial legislation.

Introduction to Part VI

The peculiar character of provincial education and the extent of its similarities to and differences from seventeenth-century colonial education, on the one hand, and eighteenth-century metropolitan education, on the other, are the leading theme of most discussions of eighteenth-century American education. Traditional views, defining education almost wholly as schooling, tended to make the case for fundamental differences on the basis of the social and political aspirations of the American people; thus, for example, Ellwood P. Cubberley's assertions in *Public Education in the United States: A Study and Interpretation of American Educational History* (rev. ed.; Boston: Houghton Mifflin Company, 1934) to the effect that by 1760 it was evident that European traditions and types of schools were no longer satisfactory and that the new confidence born of Braddock's defeat was creating among the colonists a widespread sense of the need for uniquely American institutions. The more recent works of Bernard Bailyn *(Education in the Forming of American Society* [Chapel Hill: University of North Carolina Press, 1960]) and Daniel J. Boorstin *(The Americans: The Colonial Experience* [New York: Random House, 1958]), defining education far more broadly than Cubberley and his contemporaries, tend to make the case for fundamental differences largely in response to the more general colonial environment, though this case is disputed in part by Robert Middlekauff in his review of Bailyn's volume, *Harvard Educational Review*, XXXI (1961), 213-215.

The best published account of the Reverend James Maury is Helen D. Bullock's discussion in the *Papers of the Albemarle County Historical Society*, II (1942), 36-39, based on the Maury papers at the University of Virginia. *Memoirs of a Huguenot Family: Translated and Compiled from the Original Autobiography of the Rev. James Fontaine, and Other Family Manuscripts*, edited by Ann Maury (New York: G. P. Putnam & Co., 1853) is also pertinent.

CHAPTER 16: INSTITUTIONS

Most of the traditional literature on colonial households, for example, Alice Morse Earle, *Home Life in Colonial Days* (New York: The Macmillan Company, 1898), and *Child Life in Colonial Days* (New York: The Macmillan Company, 1899), Arthur W. Calhoun, *A Social History of the American Family from Colonial Times to the Present* (3 vols.; Cleveland: The Arthur H. Clark Company, 1917-1919), vol. I, and Mary Newton Stanard, *Colonial Virginia: Its People and Customs* (Philadelphia: J. B. Lippincott Company, 1917), is especially useful for the provincial era since there is a dramatic increase in the number and variety of available sources. Nevertheless, since seventeenth-century records have always been scarcer, there is little of a developmental character in the accounts set forth in that literature: time is telescoped and the story homogenized, with the colonial period taken as a unit and the evidence drawn haphazardly from one decade or another. Something of the same criticism can be addressed to Percy B. Caley, "Child Life in Colonial Western Pennsylvania," *Western Pennsylvania Historical Magazine*, IX (1926), 33-275, Lorenzo Johnston Greene, *The Negro in Colonial New England* (New York: Columbia University Press, 1942), Elizabeth Andrews Wilson, "Hygienic Care and Management of the Child in the American Family Prior to 1860" (unpublished master's thesis, Duke University, 1940), Monica Kiefer, "Early American Childhood in the Middle Atlantic Area," *The Pennsylvania Magazine of History and Biography*, LXVIII (1944), 3-37, and Charles Edward Ironside, *The Family in Colonial New York: A Sociological Study* (New York: no publisher, 1942).

Most of the studies mentioned on pp. 599-602 of the bibliography are relevant here. In addition, Edmund S. Morgan, *Virginians at Home: Family Life in the Eighteenth Century* (Williamsburg, Va.: Colonial Williamsburg, 1952) and Jerry William Frost, "The Quaker Family in Colonial America: A Social History of the Society of Friends" (unpublished doctoral thesis, University of Wisconsin, 1968) colorfully portray provincial households, with emphasis on those of the upper social strata; Monica Kiefer, *American Children Through Their Books, 1700-1835* (Philadelphia: University of Pennsylvania Press, 1948) traces the development of child life through books addressed primarily to children; John Demos, "Families in Colonial Bristol, Rhode Island: An Exercise in Historical Demography," *The William and Mary Quarterly*, 3d ser., XXV (1968), 40-57, deals with the size, structure and composition of households;

while William R. Taylor, "Domesticity in England and America, 1770-1840," a paper prepared for the Symposium on the Role of Education in Nineteenth-Century America at Chatham, Massachusetts, in June, 1964, discusses the character of late eighteenth-century domesticity books. Several of the papers at the Smithsonian Institution's Conference on the History of the Family, held on October 26-27, 1967, proved relevant, especially Anthony N. B. Garvan, "Architectural Space and Family Customs, 1700-1850" and Stephen Brobeck, "Family Group Portrait Paintings as Indices of Family Culture, 1730 to 1855."

A number of recent works make possible a more serious and systematic study of characteristic family style, including Lawrence Shaw Mayo, *The Winthrop Family in America* (Boston: The Massachusetts Historical Society, 1948), James B. Hedges, *The Browns of Providence Plantations* (Cambridge, Mass.: Harvard University Press, 1952), Philip L. White, *The Beekmans of New York in Politics and Commerce, 1647-1877* (New York: New-York Historical Society, 1956), Maurice Alfred Crouse, "The Manigault Family of South Carolina, 1685-1783" (unpublished doctoral thesis, Northwestern University, 1964), John J. Waters, Jr., *The Otis Family in Provincial and Revolutionary Massachusetts* (Chapel Hill: University of North Carolina Press, 1968), Alice P. Kenney, *The Gansevoorts of Albany: Dutch Patricians in the Upper Hudson Valley* (Syracuse: Syracuse University Press, 1969), and Alden Hatch, *The Byrds of Virginia* (New York: Holt, Rinehart and Winston, 1969). Such older volumes as *Memoirs of a Huguenot Family: Translated and Compiled from the Original Autobiography of the Rev. James Fontaine, and Other Family Manuscripts,* edited by Ann Maury (New York: G. P. Putnam & Co., 1853), George Francis Dow, ed., *The Holyoke Diaries, 1709-1856* (Salem, Mass.: The Essex Institute, 1911), and Mrs. Robert W. de Forest, *A Walloon Family in America: Lockwood de Forest and His Forbears, 1500-1848* (Boston: Houghton Mifflin Company, 1914) remain useful, of course. Bernard Bailyn's review of the White book on the Beekmans in *The William and Mary Quarterly,* 3d ser., XIV (1957), 598-608, is especially evocative with respect to the development of a multilineal kinship system in America. Lawrence H. Leder, "Robert Livingston's Sons: Preparation for Futurity," *New York History,* L (1969), 235-249, is an exemplary analysis.

The shifts in modes of dealing with indigent children and families are explicated in Marcus Wilson Jernegan, *Laboring and Dependent Classes in Colonial America, 1607-1783* (Chicago: University of Chicago Press, 1931), Richard B. Morris, *Government and Labor in Early America* (New York: Columbia University Press, 1946), Ian M. G. Quimby, "Apprenticeship in Colonial Pennsylvania" (unpublished master's thesis, University of Delaware, 1963), and Lawrence William Towner, "A Good Master Well Served: A Social History of Servitude in Massachusetts, 1620-1750" (unpublished doctoral thesis, Northwestern University, 1955), and "The Indentures of Boston's Poor Apprentices, 1734-1805," *Publications of the Colonial Society of Massachusetts,* XLIII (1966), 416-468. Slave families are discussed in Lorenzo Johnston Greene, *The Negro in Colonial New England,* Edmund S. Morgan, *Virginians at Home: Family Life in the Eighteenth Century,* Thad W. Tate, Jr., *The Negro in Eighteenth-Century Williamsburg* (Charlottesville: University Press of Virginia, 1965), and, more generally, Winthrop D. Jordan, *White over Black: American Attitudes*

Toward the Negro, 1550-1812 (Chapel Hill: University of North Carolina Press, 1968).

The biographies and diaries of Cotton Mather are discussed on pp. 626-627. Samuel Mather, *The Life of the Very Reverend and Learned Cotton Mather* (Boston: Samuel Gerrish, 1729) is useful for a son's view of family nurture, however filiopietistic; Elizabeth Bancroft Schlesinger, "Cotton Mather and His Children," *The William and Mary Quarterly*, 3d ser., X (1953), 181-189, is a more detached commentary. Theodore B. Strandness, "Samuel Sewall: The Man and His Work" (unpublished doctoral thesis, Michigan State College, 1951) is a competent recent biography; the Sewall diary is at the Massachusetts Historical Society, and is printed in the Massachusetts Historical Society *Collections*, 5th ser., V-VII (1878-82). The account of the Schuyler household is given in Mrs. [Anne Macvicar] Grant, *Memoirs of an American Lady* (New York: Samuel Campbell, 1809). The best accounts of the Carter household can be gleaned from the *Journal & Letters of Philip Vickers Fithian, 1773-1774*, edited by Hunter Dickinson Farish (Williamsburg, Va.: Colonial Williamsburg, 1943), Louis B. Wright, *The First Gentlemen of Virginia: Intellectual Qualities of the Early Ruling Class* (San Marino, Calif.: Henry E. Huntington Library and Art Gallery, 1940), and Louis Morton, *Robert Carter of Nomini Hall* (Williamsburg, Va.: Colonial Williamsburg, 1941).

With respect to the educational work of the eighteenth-century churches, many of the sources referred to on pp. 603-606 and 629-635 are pertinent, along with William Warren Sweet, *Religion in the Development of American Culture, 1765-1840* (New York: Charles Scribner's Sons, 1952), Howard Charles Emrick, "The Role of the Church in the Development of Education in Pennsylvania" (unpublished doctoral thesis, University of Pittsburgh, 1959), and James Reed Young's informative but poorly organized "Relation of the Church and Clergy to Education in the American Colonies" (unpublished doctoral thesis, University of Chicago, 1916). Jerome Walker Jones, "The Anglican Church in Colonial Virginia, 1690-1760" (unpublished doctoral thesis, Harvard University, 1959) and Alf Edgar Jacobson, "The Congregational Clergy in Eighteenth Century New England" (unpublished doctoral thesis, Harvard University, 1962) are exemplary with respect to the educational role of the clergy, broadly conceived, as is John Calam, "Parsons and Pedagogues, The S.P.G. Adventure in American Education" (unpublished doctoral thesis, Columbia University, 1969) with respect to the educational role of the S.P.G. missionaries. In addition, the Jacobson thesis includes an excellent bibliography of eighteenth-century ministerial diaries, both published and unpublished. Arthur Pierce Middleton, "The Colonial Virginia Parson," *The William and Mary Quarterly*, 3d ser., XXVI (1969), 425-440, is a vivid portrayal of dissenting as well as establishment ministers. Donald George Smith, "Eighteenth Century American Preaching— An Historical Survey" (unpublished doctoral thesis, Northern Baptist Theological Seminary, 1956) is a mine of information.

The movement toward pluralism, toleration, and disestablishmentarianism is the subject of a considerable polemical literature, owing to fundamental differences concerning what the First Amendment to the United States Constitution meant in its own time and what it has meant since. The most judicious work is Anson Phelps Stokes, ed., *Church and State in the United States* (3 vols.; New York: Harper & Brothers, 1950). R. Freeman Butts, *The American Tradition in Religion and Education* (Boston: The Beacon Press, 1950) and Leo Pfeffer, *Church, State, and Freedom* (Boston: The Beacon Press, 1953) are also useful. The concept of pluralism inherent in denominationalism, as explicated by Winthrop S. Hudson in "Denominationalism as a Basis for Ecumenicity," *Church History*, XXIV (1955), 37-47, and by Sidney E. Mead in *The Lively Experiment: The Shaping of Christianity in America* (New York: Harper & Row, 1963), has already been alluded to.

Some of the best efforts of traditional historians of education have been concerned with the delineation of eighteenth-century schooling in the colonies. I have commented in detail upon that literature in *The Wonderful World of Ellwood Patterson Cubberley: An Essay in the Historiography of American Education* (New York: Bureau of Publications, Teachers College, Columbia University, 1965). Among the better general sources are Ellwood P. Cubberley, *Public Education in the United States: A Study and Interpretation of American Educational History*, Paul Monroe, *Founding of the American Public School System* (New York: The Macmillan Company, 1940), part of which is a microfilm of documents in typescript numbering close to two thousand pages, and Allen George Umbreit, "Education in the Southern Colonies" (unpublished doctoral thesis, University of Iowa, 1932). Many of the monographs cited on pp. 608-611 *supra* are pertinent, as are James Mulhern, *A History of Secondary Education in Pennsylvania* (Philadelphia: published by the author, 1933), Thomas Woody, *Early Quaker Education in Pennsylvania* (New York: Teachers College, Columbia University, 1920), Elmer Ellsworth Brown, *The Making of Our Middle Schools: An Account of the Development of Secondary Education in the United States* (New York: Longmans, Green, and Co., 1902), Frederick George Livingood, *Eighteenth Century Reformed Church Schools* (Norristown, Pa.: The Pennsylvania German Society, 1930), Charles Lewis Maurer, *Early Lutheran Education in Pennsylvania* (Philadelphia: Dorrance & Company, 1932), and Robert Francis Seybolt, *The Evening School in Colonial America* (Urbana: University of Illinois, 1925), *Source Studies in American Colonial Education: The Private School* (Urbana: University of Illinois, 1925), *The Private Schools of Colonial Boston* (Cambridge, Mass.: Harvard University Press, 1935), and *The Public Schools of Colonial Boston* (Cambridge, Mass.: Harvard University Press, 1935).

Among the better histories of individual schools are Claude M. Fuess, *An Old New England School: A History of Phillips Academy, Andover* (Boston: Houghton Mifflin Company, 1917), Pauline Holmes, *A Tercentenary History of the Boston Public Latin School, 1635-1935* (Cambridge, Mass.: Harvard University Press, 1935), Thomas W. Davis, Jr., *Chronicles of the Hopkins Grammar School, 1660-1935* (New Haven: Quinnepiack Press, 1938), John W. Ragle, *Governor Dummer Academy History, 1763-1963* (South Byfield, Mass.: Governor Dummer Academy, 1963), Edward Stewart Moffat, "Trinity School, New York, 1709-1959" (unpublished doctoral thesis, Columbia University, 1963), and Andrew S. Berky, *The Schoolhouse Near the Old Spring: A History of the Union School and Church Association, Dillingersville, Pennsylvania, 1735-1955* (Norristown, Pa.: Pennsylvania German Society, 1955).

Among more recent writings, Mabel Haller, *Early Moravian Education in Pennsylvania* (Nazareth, Pa.: The Moravian Historical Society, 1953), Thomas Kirby Bullock, "Schools and Schooling in Eighteenth Century Virginia" (unpublished doctoral thesis, Duke University, 1961), Robert Middlekauff, *Ancients and Axioms: Secondary Education in Eighteenth-Century New England* (New Haven: Yale University Press, 1963), Robert L. McCaul, Jr., "A Documentary History of Education in Colonial Georgia" (unpublished doctoral thesis, University of Chicago, 1953), John Calam, "Parsons and Pedagogues: The S.P.G. Adventure in American Education" (unpublished doctoral thesis, Columbia University, 1969), and Douglas Milton Sloan, "The Scottish Enlightenment and the American College Ideal: Early Princeton Traditions" (unpublished doctoral thesis, Columbia University, 1969), and Alice Elaine Mathews, "Pre-College Education in the Southern Colonies" (unpublished doctoral thesis, University of California, 1968) are noteworthy.

As mentioned earlier, there is a paucity of works dealing with the teaching of reading, writing, spelling, and arithmetic in colonial America. The references cited on pp. 608-609 are relevant, as are Monica Kiefer, *American Children Through Their Books,* John Nietz, *Old Textbooks* (Pittsburgh: University of Pittsburgh Press, 1961), Charles Carpenter, *History of American Schoolbooks* (Philadelphia: University of Pennsylvania Press, 1963), Lydia A. H. Smith, "Three Spelling Books of American Schools, 1740-1800," *Harvard Library Bulletin,* XII (1968), 72-93, David Eugene Smith and Jekuthiel Ginsburg, *A History of Mathematics in America Before 1900* (Chicago: The Open Court Publishing Company, 1934), and Florence A. Yeldham, *The Teaching of Arithmetic Through Four Hundred Years (1535-1935)* (London: George G. Harrap & Co., 1936). The best discussions of grammar-school and academy curricula are in the works by Brown, Mulhern, Seybolt, Middlekauff, Calam, and Sloan cited above.

Marion Dexter Learned, *The Life of Francis Daniel Pastorius,* (Philadelphia: William J. Campbell, 1908), Joseph Jackson, "A Philadelphia Schoolmaster of the Eighteenth Century [David James Dove]," *The Pennsylvania Magazine of History and Biography,* XXXV (1911), 315-332, Frank Henry Klassen, "Christopher Dock: Eighteenth Century American Educator" (unpublished doctoral thesis, University of Illinois, 1962), George S. Brookes, *Friend Anthony Benezet* (Philadelphia: University of Pennsylvania Press, 1937), and Helen E. Livingston, "Thomas Morritt, Schoolmaster at the Charleston Free School, 1723-1728," *Historical Magazine of the Protestant Episcopal Church,* XIV (1945), 151-167, are exemplary biographies of eighteenth-century teachers. James Edwin Hendricks, Jr., "Charles Thomson and the American Enlightenment" (unpublished doctoral thesis, University of Virginia, 1961) deals in some detail with Thomson's activities at the Academy of Philadelphia and the Friends' Public School during the 1750's. The *Dictionary of American Biography* includes a number of useful sketches of provincial pedagogues, while Clifford K. Shipton's profiles in *Sibley's Harvard Graduates: Biographical Sketches of Those Who Attended Harvard College,* vols. IV-XIII (imprint varies, 1933-1965) and Franklin Bowditch Dexter's in *Biographical Sketches of the Graduates of Yale College, with Annals of the College History, October, 1701 to June, 1792* (4 vols.; New York: Henry Holt and Company, 1885-1907) include some superb characterizations of eighteenth-century schoolmasters.

Among the better schoolmaster diaries are *Journal & Letters of Philip Vickers Fithian, 1773-1774: A Plantation Tutor of the Old Dominion*, edited by Hunter Dickinson Farish (Williamsburg, Va.: Colonial Williamsburg, 1943) and *The Journal of John Harrower: An Indentured Servant in the Colony of Virginia, 1773-1776*, edited by Edward Miles Riley (Williamsburg, Va.: Colonial Williamsburg, 1963). "The Autobiography of the Reverend Devereux Jarratt, 1732-1763," edited by Douglass Adair, *The William and Mary Quarterly*, 3d ser., IX (1952), 346-393, is similarly revealing. Schoolchildren's diaries are few and far between, the best-known being *Diary of Anna Green Winslow: A Boston School Girl of 1771*, edited by Alice Morse Earle (Boston: Houghton Mifflin and Company, 1894). Children's copybooks turn up from time to time, most often in family papers; children's graffiti on textbooks are ubiquitous.

Donald G. Tewksbury, *The Founding of American Colleges and Universities Before the Civil War, with Particular Reference to the Religious Influences Bearing upon the College Movement* (New York: Bureau of Publications, Teachers College, Columbia University, 1932) has long been the standard source, though its content is limited by Tewksbury's decision to consider only permanent chartered colleges. More recently, the work of Beverly McAnear has been notable with respect to the eighteenth century, especially "College Founding in the American Colonies, 1745-1774," *The Mississippi Valley Historical Review*, XLII (1955-56), 24-44, "The Raising of Funds by the Colonial Colleges," *ibid.*, XXXVIII (1951-52), 591-612, "The Charter of the Academy of Newark," *Delaware History*, IV (1950-51), 149-156, and "The Selection of an Alma Mater by Pre-Revolutionary Students," *The Pennsylvania Magazine of History and Biography*, LXXIII (1949), 429-440. Albert Frank Gegenheimer, *William Smith: Educator and Churchman, 1727-1803* (Philadelphia: University of Pennsylvania Press, 1943), Donald Robert Come, "The Influence of Princeton on Higher Education in the South Before 1825," *The William and Mary Quarterly*, 3d ser., II (1945), 359-396, Francis L. Broderick, "Pulpit, Physics, and Politics: The Curriculum of the College of New Jersey, 1746-1794," *ibid.*, VI (1949), 42-68, and Douglas Milton Sloan, "The Scottish Enlightenment and the American College Ideal: Early Princeton Traditions" are useful on the College of New Jersey. Louis Leonard Tucker, *Puritan Protagonist: President Thomas Clap of Yale College* (Chapel Hill: University of North Carolina Press, 1962), Edmund S. Morgan, *The Gentle Puritan: A Life of Ezra Stiles, 1727-1795* (New Haven: Yale University Press, 1962), and Richard Warch, "Yale College: 1701-1740" (unpublished doctoral thesis, Yale University, 1967) are valuable with respect to Yale. And Arthur Daniel Kaledin, "The Mind of John Leverett" (unpublished doctoral thesis, Harvard University, 1965) is illuminating with respect to Harvard. The standard histories of the colleges chartered prior to the Revolution are cited on pp. 613-614, 633-635, and 645-646; Willard Wallace Smith, "The Relations of College and State on Colonial America" (unpublished doctoral thesis, Columbia University, 1950) considers their multifarious political relationships.

Jerome Sanford Fink, "The Purposes of the American Colonial Colleges" (unpublished doctoral thesis, Stanford University, 1958) is a convenient survey of changing published statements. Carl Albert Hangartner, "Movements to Change American College Teaching, 1700-1830" (unpublished doctoral thesis, Yale University, 1955) is the best general consideration of curriculum and pedagogy. The movement of science into the curriculum of the provincial colleges is dealt with in Broderick, Sloan, and Morgan references cited above, as well as in Winthrop Tilley, "The Literature of Natural and Physical Science in the American Colonies from the Beginning to 1765" (unpublished doctoral thesis, Brown University, 1933), Theodore Hornberger, *Scientific Thought in the American Colleges, 1638-1800* (Austin: University of Texas Press, 1945), Galen W. Ewing, *Early Teaching of Science at the College of William and Mary in Virginia* (Williamsburg: College of William and Mary, 1938), I. Bernard Cohen, *Some Early Tools of American Science: An Account of the Early Scientific Instruments and Mineralogical and Biological Collections in Harvard University* (Cambridge, Mass.: Harvard University Press, 1950), and Ronald Sterne Wilkinson, "John Winthrop, Jr., and the Origins of American Chemistry" (unpublished doctoral thesis, Michigan State University, 1969).

There are no major biographies of John Winthrop and Francis Alison, and few decent biographies of other eighteenth-century academics, the works of Tucker on Clap, Morgan on Stiles, Kaledin on Leverett, Bell on Morgan, the Schneiders on Johnson, Collins on Witherspoon, and Gegenheimer on Smith being notable exceptions. A convenient listing of provincial professors and a social analysis of the provincial professoriate are presented in William D. Carrell, "American College Professors: 1750-1800," *History of Education Quarterly*, VIII (1968), 289-305, and "Biographical List of American College Professors to 1800," *ibid.*, 358-374. There is a significant collection of Winthrop papers in the Harvard College Archives and at the Massachusetts Historical Society, and of Alison papers at the Presbyterian Historical Society in Philadelphia. Malcolm Freiberg of the Massachusetts Historical Society has compiled what is probably the most comprehensive available guide to Winthrop's papers in connection with his more general work on the Winthrop family. The University of Pennsylvania library has the notes taken by Jasper Yeates and Samuel Jones in Alison's moral philosophy course.

CHAPTER 17: CONFIGURATIONS

Carl Bridenbaugh's "The New England Town: A Way of Life," *Proceedings of the American Antiquarian Society*, new ser., LVI (1946), 19-48, is a classic; it is usefully complemented by Robert E. Brown, *Middle-Class Democracy and the Revolution in Massachusetts, 1691-1780* (Ithaca: Cornell University Press, 1955) and Michael Zuckerman, *Peaceable Kingdoms: New England Towns in the Eighteenth Century* (New York: Alfred A. Knopf, 1970). The commentary on Dedham is based on Edward M. Cook, "The Transformation of Dedham, Massachusetts, 1715-1750" (unpublished honors thesis, Harvard College, 1965), Kenneth A. Lockridge, *A New England Town: The First Hundred Years* (New York: W. W. Norton & Company, 1970), Carlos Slafter, *A Record of Education: The Schools and Teachers of Dedham, Massachusetts, 1644-1904* (Dedham: Dedham Transcript Press, 1905), Frank Smith, *A History of Dedham,*

Massachusetts (Dedham: The Transcript Press, 1936), Erastus Worthington, *The History of Dedham, from the Beginning of Its Settlement in September, 1635, to May, 1827* (Boston: Dutton and Wentworth, 1827), Herman Mann, *Historical Annals of Dedham, from Its Settlement in 1635, to 1847* (Dedham: Herman Mann, 1847), Alvan Lamson, *A History of the First Church and Parish in Dedham* (Dedham: H. Mann, 1839), and George Willis Cooke, *A History of the Clapboard Trees or Third Parish* (Boston: G. H. Ellis, 1887), as well as on Don Gleason Hill, ed., *The Early Records of the Town of Dedham* (5 vols.; Dedham: Dedham Transcript Press, 1886-1899) and on various wills, depositions, minutes, maps, and other papers in the Dedham Historical Society.

Carl Bridenbaugh's *Myths and Realities: Societies of the Colonial South* (Baton Rouge: Louisiana State University Press, 1952) includes an incisive analysis of the structure and values of the Chesapeake society; it is admirably complemented by Hugh Jones, *The Present State of Virginia,* edited by Richard L. Morton (Chapel Hill: University of North Carolina Press, 1956), by Richard L. Morton, *Colonial Virginia* (2 vols.; Chapel Hill: University of North Carolina Press, 1960), and by Robert E. and B. Katherine Brown, *Virginia, 1705-1786: Aristocracy or Democracy* (East Lansing: Michigan State University Press, 1964). The commentary on Elizabeth City County is based on Marion L. Starkey, *The First Plantation: A History of Hampton and Elizabeth City County, Virginia, 1607-1887* (Hampton: Houston Printing and Publishing House, 1936), Lyon G. Tyler, *History of Hampton and Elizabeth City County, Virginia* (Hampton: The Board of Supervisors of Elizabeth City County, 1922), Rogers D. Whichard, *The History of Lower Tidewater Virginia* (3 vols.; New York: Lewis Historical Publishing Company, Inc., 1959), Jacob Heffelfinger, *Kecoughton Old and New; or, Three Hundred Years of Elizabeth City Parish* (Hampton: Houston Printing & Publishing House, 1910). W. H. Brown, *The Education and Economic Development of the Negro in Virginia* (Charlottesville: University of Virginia Phelps-Stokes Fellowship Papers, 1923), Blanche Adams Chapman, ed., "Wills and Administrations of Elizabeth City County" (Hampton: mimeographed copy in New York Public Library, 1941), and Marion Ruth Van Doenhoff, "The Vestry Book of Elizabeth City Parish, 1751-1784" (unpublished master's thesis, College of William and Mary, 1957), as well as on various wills, depositions, deeds, minutes, maps, guardians' accounts, and other papers in the City of Hampton Court House and in St. John's Church, Hampton.

Carl and Jessica Bridenbaugh, *Rebels and Gentlemen: Philadelphia in the Age of Franklin* (New York: Reynal & Hitchcock, 1942) and Carl Bridenbaugh, *Cities in the Wilderness: The First Century of Urban Life in America, 1625-1742* (2d ed.; New York: Alfred A. Knopf, Inc., 1955), and *Cities in Revolt: Urban Life in America, 1743-1776* (New York: Alfred A. Knopf, 1955) are indispensable with respect to provincial cities. In addition, Herman LeRoy Collins and Wilfred Jordan, *Philadelphia: A Story of Progress* (4 vols.; Lewis Historical Publishing Company, 1941) is useful for Philadelphia, and I. N. Phelps Stokes, *The Iconography of Manhattan Island, 1408-1909* (6 vols.; New York: Robert H. Dodd, 1915-28), Arthur Everett Peterson, *New York as an Eighteenth Century Municipality Prior to 1731* (New York: Columbia University, 1917), George William Edwards, *New York as an Eighteenth Century Municipality, 1731-1776* (New York: Columbia University, 1917) are helpful for New York.

The discussion of education in New York is based on the contemporary reports of G. Taylor in *A Voyage to North America, Perform'd by G. Taylor, of Sheffield, in the Years 1768 and 1769* (Nottingham: S. Cresswell, 1771); on William Heard Kilpatrick, *The Dutch Schools of New Netherland and Colonial New York* (Washington, D.C.: Government Printing Office, 1912), William Webb Kemp, *The Support of Schools in Colonial New York by the Society for the Propagation of the Gospel in Foreign Parts* (New York: Teachers College, Columbia University, 1913), Michael J. O'Brien, "Irish Schoolmasters in the American Colonies," *The Journal of the American Irish Historical Society,* XXV (1926), 35-61, Daniel G. Pratt, *Annals of Public Education in the State of New York, from 1626 to 1746* (Albany, N.Y.: The Argus Company, 1872), and Robert Francis Seybolt, "The Evening Schools of Colonial New York City," in *Fifteenth Annual Report of the [New York State] Education Department* (1919), I, 630-652, "New York Colonial Schoolmasters," *ibid.,* pp. 653-669, and "The S.P.G. Myth: A Note on Education in Colonial New York," *Journal of Educational Research,* XIII (1926), 129-137; and on miscellaneous wills, deeds, petitions, receipt books, and bills and accounts in the New York Historical Society, the New York City Archives, and the New York City Surrogate's Court. Also, Carl F. Kaestle graciously shared with me the early drafts of his doctoral dissertation at Harvard University on education in New York City during the century following 1750.

The discussion of education in Philadelphia is based on Nelson Waite Rightmyer, "Churches Under Enemy Occupation, Philadelphia, 1777-8," *Church History,* XIV (1945), 33-60, James Mulhern, *History of Secondary Education in Pennsylvania,* Richard J. Purcell, "Irish Educational Contribution to Colonial Pennsylvania," *Catholic Educational Review,* XXXVII (1939), 425-439, Robert Francis Seybolt, "Schoolmasters of Colonial Philadelphia," *The Pennsylvania Magazine of History and Biography,* LII (1928), 361-364, and Thomas Woody, *Early Quaker Education in Pennsylvania,* as well as on unpublished wills in the Philadelphia City Hall.

For education in the back-country regions, I found Charles S. Grant, *Democracy in the Connecticut Frontier Town of Kent* (New York: Columbia University Press, 1961), Carl Bridenbaugh, *Myths and Realities: Societies of the Colonial South,* Robert L. Meriwether, *The Expansion of South Carolina, 1729-1765* (Kingsport, Tenn.: Southern Publishers, 1940), Verner W. Crane, *The Southern Frontier, 1670-1732* (Ann Arbor: University of Michigan Press, 1929), and Richard J. Hooker, *The Carolina Backcountry on the Eve of the Revolution: The Journal and Other Writings of Charles Woodmason, Anglican Itinerant* (Chapel Hill: University of North Carolina Press, 1953) invaluable.

CHAPTER 18: CHARACTERISTICS

The problem of literacy and its relationship to economic and political development has received increasing scholarly attention in recent years, resulting in several summaries of the leading investigations to date. Among the more useful writings are Lawrence Stone, "The Educational Revolution in England, 1560-1640," *Past & Present,* no. 28 (July, 1964), 41-80, and "Literacy and Education in England, 1640-1900," *ibid.,* no. 42 (February, 1969), 68-139, C. Arnold Anderson, "Literacy and Schooling on the Developmental Threshold: Some Historical Cases," in C. Arnold Anderson and Mary Jean Bowman, eds., *Education and Economic Development* (Chicago: Aldine Publishing Company, 1965), chap. xviii, Jack Goody, ed., *Literacy in Traditional Societies* (Cambridge: Cambridge University Press, 1968), Carlo M. Cipolla, *Literacy and Development in the West* (Baltimore, Md.: Penguin Books, 1969), and two unpublished papers, one by C. Arnold Anderson entitled "Equity, Efficiency, and Educational Opportunity in Relation to Economic Development" and one by C. Arnold Anderson and Mary Jean Bowman entitled "Human Capital and Economic Modernization in Historical Perspective." But there have been too few analyses, first, of what the statistics themselves mean about actual rates of popular literacy (given the selected samples surveyed and the technique of counting signatures versus marks), and, second, of what literacy means at different stages of social development. Estimates of literacy in colonial America are scattered through the observations of contemporary commentators and differ vastly, depending on the social vantage point of the commentator and the segment of the population about which he is generalizing. They are also scattered through the secondary literature, including, *inter alia,* Philip Alexander Bruce, *Institutional History of Virginia in the Seventeenth Century* (2 vols.; New York: G. P. Putnam's Sons, 1910), William Heard Kilpatrick, *The Dutch Schools of New Netherland and Colonial New York* (Washington, D.C.: Government Printing Office, 1912), Samuel Eliot Morison, *The Puritan Pronaos* (New York: New York University Press, 1936), Clifford K. Shipton, "Secondary Education in the Puritan Colonies," *The New England Quarterly,* VII (1934), 646-661, I. Daniel Rupp, *A Collection of Upwards of Thirty Thousand Names of German, Swiss, Dutch and Other Immigrants in Pennsylvania, from 1727 to 1776* (2d ed.; Philadelphia: I. Kohler, 1876), Robert L. Meriwether, *The Expansion of South Carolina, 1729-1765* (Kingsport, Tenn.: Southern Publishers, 1940), David Duncan Wallace, *The History of South Carolina* (4 vols.; New York: The American Historical Society, 1934), and Charles S. Grant, *Democracy in the Connecticut Frontier Town of Kent* (New York: Columbia University Press, 1961). I undertook my own studies of Dedham, Elizabeth City County, Philadelphia, and New York, using the traditional method of signature counts (about which, as noted in the text, I am highly dubious). The fascinating question of the role of the school in varying ecologies of education is incisively raised in Anthony F. C. Wallace, "Schools in Revolutionary and Conservative Societies," in Frederick C. Gruber, ed., *Anthropology and Education* (Philadelphia: University of Pennsylvania Press, 1961), pp. 25-54.

Comparative studies of the number and circulation of eighteenth-century newspapers are lacking, though Dewey Eugene Carroll, "Newspaper and Periodical Production in Countries of Europe, 1600-1950: A Quantitative Historical Analysis of Patterns of Growth" (unpublished doctoral thesis, University of Illinois, 1965) represents an interesting exploration. To be effective as studies in education, such investigations would have to take into account comparative costs, comparative distribution systems, and comparative numbers of readers per publication circulated. The relevant literature on English and American newspapers during the eighteenth century is referred to on pp. 643-644. For Irish newspapers during the same period, Richard Robert Madden, *The History of Irish Periodical Literature, from the End of the 17th to the Middle of the 19th Century* (2 vols.; London: T. C. Newby, 1867), Constantia Maxwell, *Dublin Under the Georges, 1714-1830* (London: G. G. Harrap and Company, 1936), and *Country and Town in Ireland Under the Georges* (London: George G. Harrap & Company, 1940), Robert Munter, *The History of the Irish Newspaper, 1685-1760* (Cambridge: Cambridge University Press, 1967), and William Raymond Hunt, "The Traveler in Ireland 1732 to 1850" (unpublished doctoral thesis, University of Washington, 1967) are useful—the last two for their bibliographies as well as their excellent texts.

The problem of provincial leadership has been much discussed in a substantial literature. Among the more recent writings I found useful were Henry Steele Commager, "Leadership in Eighteenth-Century America and Today," *Daedalus*, XC (1961), 652-673, Robert E. Brown, *Middle-Class Democracy and the Revolution in Massachusetts, 1691-1780* (Ithaca: Cornell University Press, 1955), Robert E. and B. Katherine Brown, *Virginia, 1705-1786: Democracy or Aristocracy* (East Lansing: Michigan State University Press, 1964), Charles S. Sydnor, *Gentlemen Freeholders: Political Practices in Washington's Virginia* (Chapel Hill: University of North Carolina Press, 1952), Oscar Zeichner, *Connecticut's Years of Controversy, 1750-1776* (Chapel Hill: University of North Carolina Press, 1949), Jack P. Greene, "Foundations of Political Power in the Virginia House of Burgesses, 1720-1776," *The William and Mary Quarterly*, 3d ser., XVI (1959), 485-506, and *The Quest for Power: The Lower Houses of Assembly in the Southern Royal Colonies, 1689-1776* (Chapel Hill: University of North Carolina Press, 1963), J. R. Pole, "Historians and the Problem of Early American Democracy," *The American Historical Review*, LXVII (1961-62), 626-646, and Bernard Bailyn, *The Origins of American Politics* (New York: Alfred A. Knopf, 1968). Donald O. Schneider, "Education in Colonial American Colleges 1750-1770 and the Occupations and Political Offices of Their Alumni" (unpublished doctoral thesis, George Peabody College for Teachers, 1965) is the most comprehensive study of the particular role of the colleges in the education of political leaders; P. M. G. Harris, "The Social Origins of American Leaders: The Democratic Foundations," *Perspectives in American History*, III (1969), 157-344, is easily the most imaginative.

The relation of education to provincial economic development and the colonists' perceptions of that relation have not been much studied. Bailey B. Burritt, *Professional Distribution of College and University Graduates* (Washington, D.C.: Government Printing Office, 1912) is a classic analysis; it is usefully complemented by Walter Crosby Eells, *Baccalaureate Degrees Conferred by American Colleges in the 17th and 18th Centuries* (Washington, D.C.: U.S. Office of Education, 1958) and Donald O. Schneider, "Education in Colonial American Colleges 1750-1770 and the Occupations and Political Offices of Their Alumni." Criticisms of the quality of apprenticeships in medicine and law were vociferous during the provincial era and, indeed, led to the establishment of professional instruction in these fields during the latter decades of the eighteenth century; and, from the evidence in Carl Bridenbaugh's engrossing study, *The Colonial Craftsman* (New York: New York University Press, 1950), criticisms of the quality of apprenticeships in the trades and crafts were ubiquitous, especially in light of the persistent labor shortage in the colonies.

The economic views of provincial Americans, and of Benjamin Franklin and Cadwallader Colden, are dealt with in Joseph Dorfman, *The Economic Mind in American Civilization, 1606-1865* (2 vols.; New York: The Viking Press, 1946). Lewis J. Carey, *Franklin's Economic Views* (New York: Doubleday, Doran and Company, 1928) and Paul W. Conner, *Poor Richard's Politics: Benjamin Franklin and His New American Order* (New York: Oxford University Press, 1965) are also useful for Franklin's views, while Alice Mapelsden Keys, *Cadwallader Colden: A Representative Eighteenth Century Official* (New York: The Macmillan Company, 1906) is helpful on Colden. With respect to Adam Smith, Gladys Bryson, *Man and Society: The Scottish Inquiry of the Eighteenth Century* (Princeton: Princeton University Press, 1945), Charles R. Fay, *Adam Smith and the Scotland of His Day* (Cambridge: Cambridge University Press, 1956), and Eli Ginzberg, *The House of Adam Smith* (New York: Columbia University Press, 1934) are valuable commentaries, as is John Rae's older *Life of Adam Smith,* recently reissued with a new introduction by Jacob Viner (New York: Augustus M. Kelley, 1965).

The popularism implicit, on the one hand, in lay control of educational institutions and, on the other hand, in the accessibility and openness of these institutions, is a major theme in Daniel J. Boorstin, *The Americans: The Colonial Experience* (New York: Random House, 1958). It is also dealt with in Sidney E. Mead, *The Lively Experiment: The Shaping of Christianity in America* (New York: Harper & Row, 1963), Borden W. Painter, Jr., "The Anglican Vestry in Colonial America" (unpublished doctoral thesis, Yale University, 1965), Henry Suzzallo, *The Rise of Local School Supervision in Massachusetts* (New York: Teachers College, Columbia University, 1906), Richard Hofstadter and Walter P. Metzger, *The Development of Academic Freedom in the United States* (New York: Columbia University Press, 1955), Lawrence C. Wroth, "Book Production and Distribution from the Beginning to the American Revolution," in Hellmut Lehmann-Haupt *et al., The Book in America: A History of the Making and Selling of Books in the United States* (2d ed.; New York: R. R. Bowker Company, 1951), and Frank Luther Mott, *American Journalism* (rev. ed.; New York: The Macmillan Company, 1950). The substantial differences between English and American schools in the eighteenth century are revealed in considering M. G. Jones, *The Charity School Movement: A Study of Eighteenth-Century Puritanism in Action* (Cambridge: Cambridge University Press, 1938), Joe J. Keen, "William Shenstone and the English Dame School" (unpublished doctoral thesis, University of Colorado, 1966), Richard Stevens Thompson, "Classics and Charity: The English Grammar School in the Eighteenth Century" (unpublished doctoral thesis, University of Michigan, 1967), W. A. L. Vincent, *The Grammar Schools: Their Continuing Tradition, 1660-1714* (London: John Murray, 1969), W. R. Ward, *Georgian Oxford: University Politics in the Eighteenth Century* (Oxford: Clarendon Press, 1958), and Nicholas Hans, *New Trends in Education in the Eighteenth Century* (London: Routledge & Kegan Paul, 1951).

The eighteenth-century debate over the capacity of America to nurture greatness is ably dealt with in Brooke Hindle, *The Pursuit of Science in Revolutionary America, 1735-1789* (Chapel Hill: University of North Carolina Press, 1956), Constance Rourke, *The Roots of American Culture and Other Essays*, edited by Van Wyck Brooks (New York: Harcourt, Brace & Company, 1942), Durand Echeverria, *Mirage in the West: A History of the French Image of American Society to 1815* (Princeton: Princeton University Press, 1957), and Joseph Jay Jones, "British Literary Men's Opinions About America, 1750-1832" (unpublished doctoral thesis, Yale University, 1934).

Epilogue

The best general history of the Revolution as a military encounter is Christopher Ward, *War of the Revolution*, edited by John R. Alden (2 vols.; New York: Macmillan, 1952); Howard H. Peckham, *The War for Independence: A Military History* (Chicago: University of Chicago Press, 1958) is also useful. The classic consideration of the social significance of the Revolution is J. Franklin Jameson, *The American Revolution Considered as a Social Movement* (Princeton: Princeton University Press, 1926). Frederick B. Tolles, "The American Revolution Considered as a Social Movement: A Re-Evaluation," *The American Historical Review*, LX (1954-55), 1-12, is a thoughtful assessment of Jameson's thesis; Clarence L. Ver Steeg, "The American Revolution Considered as an Economic Movement," *The Huntington Library Quarterly*, XX (1956-57), 361-372, is an admirable extension. R. R. Palmer, *The Age of the Democratic Revolution: A Political History of Europe and America, 1760-1800* (2 vols.; Princeton: Princeton University Press, 1959-1964) and Richard B. Morris, *The American Revolution Reconsidered* (New York: Harper & Row, 1967) provide valuable context.

Dixon Ryan Fox, "Culture in Knapsacks," in Fox, *Ideas in Motion* (D. Appleton-Century Company, 1935), pp. 37-76, and Evarts B. Greene, "Some Educational Values of the American Revolution," *Proceedings of the American Philosophical Society*, LXVIII (1929), 185-194, deal generally with the impact of the Revolution on the schools and colleges, and with the larger educational effect of the conflict. Evelyn Marie Walsh, "Effects of the Revolution upon the Town of Boston: Social, Economic, and Cultural" (unpublished doctoral thesis, Brown University, 1964) is a model study with respect to the work that needs to be done on education in specific localities.

Benjamin Rush and Noah Webster will be considered more extensively in the next volume of this study. Harry R. Warfel, *Noah Webster: Schoolmaster to America* (New York: The Macmillan Company, 1936) is the standard biography; I used the Webster papers at the New York Public Library in connection with the present work. Nathan Goodman, *Benjamin Rush: Physician and Citizen, 1746-1813* (Philadelphia: University of Pennsylvania Press, 1934) is the standard biography; Donald John D'Elia, "Benjamin Rush: An Intellectual Biography" (unpublished doctoral thesis, Pennsylvania State University, 1965) is the best brief consideration of Rush's ideas; L. H. Butterfield, "A Survey of the Benjamin Rush Papers," *The Pennsylvania Magazine of History and Biography*, LXX (1946), 78-111, is a useful guide to the extant manuscripts.

INDEX

ABC, 129, 171n, 185

Aaron, Richard I., 624

Abney, Sir Thomas, 279

Abrams, Philip, 619, 648

Academia Virginiensis et Oxoniensis, 177

academy: British dissenting, 323-324, 460; eighteenth-century American, 322-326, 402-404; proposals of Benjamin Franklin, 375-378; proposals of William Douglass, 435; as characteristic provincial school, 500, 505; writings on, 633-634, 645-646

Academy of Complements, The, 131

Academy of Philadelphia, 265, 266, 505, 552, 645-646

Act of Supremacy (1559), 144

Act of Toleration (1689), 251-252, 455-456

Act of Uniformity (1559), 144

Act of Uniformity (1662), 324

Actes and Monuments. See Foxe, John

Adair, Douglass Greybill, 651, 661

Adams, Charles Francis, 647

Adams, John: on Americans, 413; "A Dissertation on the Canon and Feudal Law," 416-418; reply to Daniel Leonard, 459n; on Thomas Mifflin, 465; reading, 470; on familial education, 479; on New England towns, 520-521, 526, 556; on the polity as educator, 551; on the Continental Congress as educator, 567; cited, 410, 457n, 469, 515, 518, 535n, 568; writings on, 647-648

Adams, Sir John, 197, 212

Adams, Percy G., 639

Adams, Robert P., 590

Adams, Samuel, 550

Adamson, John William, 28, 231n, 648

Addison, Joseph, 366-367, 368, 376, 393n, 483, 639-640

Aesop's Fables, 63, 175, 185, 204, 505

Afro-Americans: seventeenth-century families in America, 136; efforts to Christianize, 161-162; baptism and emancipation, 161-162; schooling, 194-195; Quaker attitudes toward, 307-308; S.P.G. missions to, 350-353; economic restrictions, 360; miseducation under slavery, 411-412; slave family life, 485n; attitudes of Anthony Benezet, 507; in Elizabeth City County (Va.), 533-534; in New York City and Philadelphia, 536-537; cited, 19, 257, 264; writings on, 601-602, 605-606, 610-611, 631, 637, 647, 651

Agricola, Rodolphus, 63, 103

agriculture, 84, 376, 380, 408-409, 554

Ahlstrom, Sydney E., 654

Ainslie, James L., 602

Akers, Charles W., 627, 653

Albany Plan of Union, 263

Albert (of York), 168

Alcuin, 167-168

Alden, John R., 668

Aldrich, P. Emory, 620

Aldridge, Alfred Owen, 641

Alexander, Archibald, 323n, 634

Alexander, James, 428, 447, 652

algebra, 380, 503

Alison, Francis: life and education, 325, 515; academy at New London (Pa.), 325, 326, 505; role at Academy and College of Philadelphia, 380, 403, 404, 515; moral philosophy course, 460, 461, 464-465; characterized, 515-516; papers, 662

Allen, Andrew, 465n

Allen, Carlos Richard, 617

Allen, H. M., 586

Allen, J. W., 590

Allen, James, 465n

Allen, John, 465n

Allen, P. S., 586

Allen, Phyllis, 612

Allen, William, 262

Allen, William O. B., 637

Allestree, Richard: characterized, 44; *The Whole Duty of Man,* 46-47; conception of piety, 47; ideas on education, 49-50; *The Gentleman's Calling,* 71; cited, 301, 346; writings on, 588

Alley, Robert Sutherland, 653

Allin, John, 522

almanac, 389-391, 540

Alsted, Johann Heinrich, 103-104, 215, 216

Ambrose, 34

Ambrose, Joshua, 208

American Academy of Arts and Sciences, 410

American Council of Learned Societies, Committee on Linguistic and National Stocks in the Population of the United States, 621

American Instructor, The, 395, 503-504

American Philosophical Society, 374, 408-410, 646

American Revolution, 564-570, 652-655, 668

American Society Held at Philadelphia for Promoting and Propagating Useful Knowledge, 408, 409

Ames, Nathaniel, 390, 393

Ames, Russell, 590

Ames, William, 212, 215

Amicable [Library] Company, 399
Amish, 258, 308
anatomy, 362, 380
ancient languages, 441. *See also* Greek language instruction; Hebrew language instruction; Latin language instruction
Anderson, C. Arnold, 664-665
Anderson, F. H., 594
Anderson, James S. M., 12n
Anderson, Wallace Earl, 633
Andrew, 351-352
Andrews, Charles M., 14, 581, 620
Andrews, Jedediah, 316-317
Andrews, John H., 639
Andrews, Samuel, 345
Andrews, William, 350
Andros, Sir Edmund, 20, 187, 288
Angelus, Jacobus, 90
Anglican church: *See* Church of England
Anglicans, 148, 165, 259, 332
Annapolis (Md.), 340, 398
Anne (of England), 258
Antes, John, 519
apprenticeship education: in Renaissance England, 120-122; in seventeenth-century America, 133-134; in eighteenth-century America, 483; writings on, 598-599, 600, 657-658
Aquinas, Thomas, 255
Arcaeus, Franciscus, 340
Archer, Gabriel, 207
Ariès, Philippe, 118, 483, 597
Aristophanes, 85, 97
Aristotle, 60, 63, 68, 85, 89, 91, 103, 106, 197, 205, 244, 365, 380, 382, 464, 511
arithmetic, 86, 173, 185, 197, 214, 362, 376, 382, 403, 406, 435, 440, 441, 499, 501-503, 538, 609, 660
Arminianism, 276, 311
Asbury, Francis, 499
Ascham, Roger: early life and career, 76; *The Scholemaster*, 76-78; conception of civility, 77-78; cited, 66, 86, 88, 100; writings on, 591
Ashley, Maurice, 619
Ashton, T. S., 623
Association Library, 399
Aston, Trevor, 596
astronomy, 214, 296, 362, 376, 380, 383, 503
Atkins, Samuel, 389
Auchmuty, James Johnston, 618
Auchmuty, Samuel, 351
Augustine (354-430), 23, 34, 89, 291n
Augustine (d. 604), 167
Axtell, James L., 624
Aylmer, G. E., 598
Aylmer, John, 173

Bachman, Van Cleaf, 581

Backus, Issac, 328n
Bacon, Sir Francis: on plantations, 14n; on scientific inquiry, 80; early life and career, 91-92; projects *The Great Instauration*, 92-93; *Advancement of Learning*, 93-94; *New Atlantis*, 94-96; conception of learning, 92-96; reputation in the American colonies, 96, 100-102; *Essays*, 100-102; cited, 104, 203, 255, 282, 362, 363, 365, 381, 383, 437, 438; writings on, 594
Bacon, Nathaniel (1593-1660), 383
Bacon, Nathaniel (1647-1676), 192
Bacon, Oliver N., 547n
Bagwell, Richard, 618
Bahlman, Dudley W. R., 636
Bailey, Frederick, 584
Bailey, J. E., 587
Bailyn, Bernard, 233, 372, 449, 450n, 577, 578, 582, 583, 596, 616, 617, 621, 623, 626, 647, 649, 651, 652, 653, 655-656, 657, 666
Bainton, Roland H., 39n, 586, 629, 634
Baker, Herschel, 591
Balch, Thomas, 523
Baldwin, Alice M., 652-653
Baldwin, T. W., 589, 592, 593, 601, 607
Ball, William, 483n
Ballou, Richard Boyd, 608
Bancroft, George, 259n
Banneker, Benjamin, 354
Baptist church: transplanted to America, 153, 163; establishment of the College of Rhode Island, 327-328; itinerant preachers, 455
Baptists, 304, 536, 543
Barbé-Marbois, François de, 507
Barbour, Hugh Stewart, 630
Barbu, Zevedei, 596
Bard, Samuel, 407
Barker, Sir Ernest, 66
Barlow, Richard Burgess, 624
Barnard, John, 129n
Barratt, D. M., 146-147, 175, 603
Barrow, Isaac, 253, 294, 382
Barrow, Robert Mangum, 644
Bartlet, Phoebe, 319
Bartram, John, 408
Basalla, George, 612
Basler, Roy P., 579
Bates, Ralph S., 646
Battis, Emery, 630
Bauman, John, 281
Baxter, Edward J., 593
Baxter, Richard: characterized, 45; *The Poor Man's Family Book*, 47; conception of piety, 47; ideas on education, 50; *Gildas Salvianus; The Reformed Pastor*, 55; *A Call to the Unconverted* translated into Algonquian, 159-160; cited, 48, 301; writings on, 588
Bay Psalm Book, 163
Bayly, Lewis: characterized, 44, 45; *The Practise of Pietie*, 46; conception of piety, 46; ideas on education, 49; *The Practise of Pietie* translated into Algonquian, 159-160; cited, 185, 277, 301, 340, 541; writings on, 587-588
Beales, A. C. F., 586, 606, 607
Beall, Otho T., Jr., 613, 626
Beardsley, E. Edwards, 627
Beatty, Edward C. O., 631
Beauvois, Carel de, 242
Beaver, R. Pierce, 605
Becker, Carl L., 471n, 478, 620, 640
Becker, William Hartshorne, 627
Becket, Thomas à, 196
Beckett, J. C., 618
Bedwell, C. E. A., 613
Belden, Albert David, 623
Bell, Sadie, 604, 609, 610
Bell, Whitfield J., Jr., 260n, 622, 640, 642, 646, 647, 662
Bellamy, Joseph, 326
Benezet, Anthony, 308, 373, 443, 506-507
Bennett, H. S., 28, 587, 598, 615
Bennett, J. Harry, 647
Bergh, A. E., 650
Berkeley, Dorothy Smith, 647
Berkeley, Edmund, 646-647
Berkeley, George, 295, 296, 297, 298, 398, 560
Berkeley, Sir William, 178n, 192
Berky, Andrew S., 542n, 632, 659
Bernard, Richard, 54-55
Bertrand, John, 189
Bethesda Orphan Asylum, 329-330
Bethlehem (Pa.), 265
Bible: translation into English, 35-38; Renaissance versions, 38; source of educational wisdom, 40-41, 587; translated into Algonquian, 159-160; as textbook, 34, 40, 60, 63, 73, 86, 129-130, 142-144, 159-160, 175, 185, 191, 204, 214, 277, 340, 346, 362, 383, 483, 505, 540; writings on, 587
Bidwell, Percy Wells, 617, 639
Bierman, Judah, 593, 648
Billias, George Athan, 655
Bilney, Thomas, 35, 43
Binder, Frederick M., 651
Binger, Carl, 646
Birch, Thomas, 232n
Bisset, Charles, 382
Black, Mary, 128n, 599
blacks. *See* Afro-Americans
Blackstone, Sir William, 471, 512

Blagden, Cyprian, 616
Blair, James, 322n, 334-338, 513
Blair, Samuel, 323, 325, 460
Blake, Warren Barton, 639
Blanchard, Joshua, 432
Blanchard, Rae, 639
Blanton, Wyndham B., 207n
Bloom, Edward A., 640
Bloom, Lillian D., 640
Blount, Charles, 88
Blount, William, 31-32
Boas, Louise, 626
Boas, Marie, 593
Boas, Ralph, 626
Boatfield, Helen C., 640
Boddie, William Willis, 543n
Bodin, Jean, 72, 437
Boerhaave, Hermann, 383, 385
Boethius, Anicius Manlius Severinus, 197
Boétie, Etienne de la, 99
Bohannan, Paul, 601, 638
Bohun, Laurence, 207
Bolgar, R. R., 97, 584, 592, 594
Bolingbroke, Henry St. John, 295, 455, 470, 471
Bolton, Herbert F., 638
Bond, Thomas, 409
Bonner, Edmund, 172
Book of Common Prayer, 144-145, 155-156, 340, 346
Book of Martyrs. See Foxe, John
bookkeeping, 401, 499, 503
Boorstin, Daniel J., 578, 579, 596, 621, 651, 655, 667
Booth, Mr., 533
Bordwell, Joel, 542
Borgia, Cesare, 61
Born, Lester K., 590
Boston (Mass.): as early center of culture production, 152; use of pastor and teacher, 155; first formal schooling, 180, 181, 182, 184; school of Ezekiel Cheever, 189-191; printing, 389, 390, 391-392, 444-445; libraries, 398; private schooling, 400-401; American Academy of Arts and Sciences, 410; Sodalitas, 416; James Franklin's imprisonment, 446-447; cited, 130, 134, 151, 189, 243, 272, 518. See also Chauncy, Charles (1705-1787); Douglass, William; Mather, Cotton; Mayhew, Jonathan
Boston Latin School, 180, 184, 189-191, 266, 552
Boswell, James, 75-76
Bothell, Larry Lee, 627
Boucher, Jonathan, 506n, 519
Bouhours, Dominique, 382
Bourne, H. R. Fox, 281n, 624
Bowdoin, James, 410
Bowen, Richard Le Baron, 238n
Bowman, Mary Jean, 665
Boxer, Charles R., 583
Boyd, Julian P., 650
Boyle, Robert, 159, 234, 235n, 294, 337, 365

Bozell, Ruth B., 603
Bradford, Andrew, 388, 391
Bradford, William (1590-1657), 15
Bradford, William (1663-1752), 389
Bradley, Richard, 399
Bradstreet, Anne, 68n
Bradstreet, Samuel, 208
Brahe, Tycho, 255
Brailsford, H. N., 423n
Brainerd, David, 283, 319, 353, 434, 552
Brant, Sebastian, 82
Brasch, Frederick E., 256n, 616, 620
Brathwaite, Richard: quoted, 58; early life and education, 70; The English Gentleman, 70-72; conception of civility, 70-72; writings on, 591
Brattle, Thomas, 234-235, 256
Brauer, George C., Jr., 590
Bray, Thomas: early life, 338, 341; plans for parochial libraries, 339; establishment of S.P.C.K., 339; ecclesiastical work in Maryland, 339-340; parochial libraries, 340-341, 398; writings on, 636
Bray's Associates. See Thomas Bray's Associates
Brereton, William, 234
Brethren of the Common Life, 31, 33
Brett-James, Norman G., 615
Breward, I., 589
Brewster, Nathaniel, 208
Brewster, William, Jr., 15, 134, 150
Brickman, William W., 578
Bridenbaugh, Carl, 378, 401n, 457, 485, 537, 583, 596, 607, 615, 618, 621, 622, 628, 631, 635, 639, 641, 645, 653, 662, 663, 664, 666-667
Bridenbaugh, Jessica, 378, 401n, 622, 631, 641, 645, 663
Brigham, Clarence S., 391n, 548n, 644
Brinsley, John: writings consulted by Virginia Company, 13; A Consolation for Our Grammar Schooles, 55-56; Ludus Literarius, 56; influenced by Roger Ascham, 78; ideals of piety and civility, 78; recommends The French Academie, 106; cited, 174, 185; writings on, 589
Brinton, Howard, 630
Broderick, Francis L., 661, 662
Bronner, Edwin B., 622
Bronson, Walter C., 328n, 634
Brooke, Christopher, 583, 596
Brookes, George S., 631, 660
Brooks, Van Wyck, 579, 612, 668
Brown, B. Katherine, 639, 663, 666

Brown, Elmer Ellsworth, 610, 659, 660
Brown, Jerome Frank, 117n, 598
Brown, Robert E., 639, 662, 663, 666
Brown, W. H., 663
Browne, Daniel, 294-295, 345
Browne, Robert, 211
Brownell, George, 266, 401, 552
Browning, Charles H., 622
Bruce, Philip Alexander, 533n, 581, 582, 585, 600, 604, 609, 617, 665
Bruchey, Stuart, 639
Brueghel, Pieter, 98
Brumbaugh, Martin G., 309n, 631-632
Bruner, Jerome, 227n
Brydon, George Maclaren, 589, 603-604, 635
Bryson, Gladys, 299n, 628, 654, 667
Buck, Sir George, 229
Buck, Paul L., 578
Buck, Richard, 149, 154
Budd, Thomas, 306-307
Budé, Guillaume, 88
Budgell, Eustace, 366
Bulkley, John, 218
Bullock, Helen D., 656
Bullock, Thomas Kirby, 660
Bullough, Geoffrey, 594
Bultmann, William A., 580, 637
Bunyan, John: characterized, 48; The Pilgrim's Progress, 48-49; conception of piety, 48-49; ideas on education, 50; A Book for Boys and Girls, 279; cited, 301, 372, 484n; writings on, 588
Burgess, Elizeus, 433
Burgh, James: life and education, 285; conception of piety, 285-286; Thoughts on Education, 285; The Dignity of Human Nature, 286, 367-368; conception of learning, 367-368; cited, 471; writings on, 625-626
Burke, Edmund, 568
Burkitt, William, 394
Burlamaqui, Jean Jacques, 383, 463, 464
Burnaby, Andrew, 534-535, 556
Burnet, Gilbert, 336n
Burr, Aaron (1716-1757), 299, 327
Burr, Aaron (1756-1836), 301
Burr, Nelson R., 579, 603, 608-609
Burritt, Bailey B., 322n, 666
Burton, Elizabeth, 597
Burtt, E. A., 620
Bush, Douglas, 583
Butler, Joseph, 460n
Butterfield, Lyman H., 299, 601, 628, 648, 668
Butterworth, C. C., 587
Butts, R. Freeman, 659

Buxtorf, John, 186
Byrd, William II, 396

Cadbury, Henry J., 614
Cady, Edwin Harrison, 592
Caesar, Julius, 63, 77, 175, 505
Calam, John, 342, 637, 658, 660
Caley, Percy B., 656
Calhoun, Arthur W., 600, 656
Calhoun, Daniel, 624
California, 355-356
Calvert, George, 241n
Calvin, John, 41
Calvinism, 41, 142, 143. *See also* Dutch Reformed church; French Reformed church; German Reformed church
Cambridge (Mass.), 130, 131, 181, 189
Cambridge Group for the Study of Population and Social Structure, 116
Cambridge Platform of 1648, 138, 152, 163, 452
Cambridge University: *See* University of Cambridge
Camden, William, 175, 185, 505
Campanius, John, 162
Campbell, Helen Jones, 178n
Campbell, John, 391
Campbell, Mildred, 231n, 598
Campbell, Philip Storer, 626
Campbell, W. E., 587
Canada, 355-356
Canfield, John, 569
Care, Henry, 470
Carey, Lewis J., 667
Carleill, Christopher, 4, 5
Carpenter, Charles, 660
Carpenter, Edward, 635
Carpenter, Nan Cooke, 612
Carr, Peter, 470
Carrel, William D., 662
Carroll, Dewey Eugene, 665
Carter, Benjamin Tasker, 491
Carter, Frances Tasker, 490
Carter, Harriot Lucy, 491
Carter, John, 134, 490
Carter, Robert, 490-491
Cartwright, Richard, 143
Caspari, Fritz, 39n, 66, 584, 587, 589, 591
Casteel, James Doyle, 654
Castiglione, Baldassare, 23, 65-66, 68
casuistry, 45-46
catechism: of John Colet, 87; of Desiderius Erasmus, 87; of William Perkins, 130; in New England, 130, 156, 498; in Virginia, 149; catechizing, 156-157, 176, 498n; Indian, 160, 350; in Renaissance England, 171, 174n; of Isaac Watts, 280; of William Douglass, 435; of Westminster Assembly, 498; cited, 50, 129, 144, 147, 164n, 185, 483; writings on, 601
Catherine of Aragon, 88
Cato, Dionysius, 175, 185, 191, 503

Cato, Marcus Porcius, 460
Cato's Letters, 427-428, 429, 446
Caussin, Nicolas, 205
Caxton, William, 114
Cecil, Sir Robert, 6, 92
Cecil, William (Lord Burghley), 67, 92, 201
Chaderton, Laurence, 211
Chambers, R. W., 587, 593
Chandler, Thomas Bradbury, 627
Chaplin, Jeremiah, 614
Chaplin, W. N., 606
Chapman, Blanche Adams, 663
Charles I, 221, 231
Charles II, 17, 94, 145, 188, 251
Charleston (S.C.), 399, 485, 518
Charlestown (Mass.), 151, 180, 181, 184, 189, 190
Charlton, Kenneth, 584, 589, 591, 592, 606, 607, 612
Charlton, Richard, 351
Charteris, Laurence, 335
Chase, Wayland J., 633
Chaucer, Geoffrey, 169n
Chauncy, Charles (1592-1672), 57, 186, 216, 217, 220, 222-223
Chauncy, Charles (1705-1787), 293, 316, 453-454, 457, 495-496, 653
Cheeshahteaumuck, Caleb, 223
Cheever, Ezekiel: early life and education, 189-190; career at Ipswich, Charlestown, and Boston, 190-191; eulogized by Cotton Mather, 190-191; cited, 287, 503, 506; writings on, 610
Cheke, Sir John, 78
chemistry, 380, 383
Cheyney, Edward Potts, 645
child. *See* household
Chillingworth, William, 40
Chilton, Edward, 322n, 336n
Chinard, Gilbert, 646, 650, 651
chivalric education, 114
Christina (of Sweden), 182
Chroust, Anton-Hermann, 613
church: conception of William Perkins, 53-54; conception of Richard Bernard, 54-55; conception of Richard Baxter, 55; conception of Paul, 138-139; in Renaissance England, 139-148; in seventeenth-century America, 148-166; political education, 451-459; in eighteenth-century America, 491-499; cited, 8; writings on, 602-606, 623-638, 653, 658-659
Church of England: established in England, 141-145; transplanted to Virginia, 148-150, 152; development in eighteenth-century Connecticut, 294-295; eighteenth-century missions, 333-356; in New York City, 536; in Phila-

delphia, 536; writings on, 602-604, 624, 635-638
Churchill, Awnsham, 256
Churchill, John, 256
Cicero, Marcus Tullius, 23, 60, 63, 64, 68, 78, 85, 86, 97, 106, 175, 185, 191, 197, 204, 205, 365, 380, 382, 383, 406, 437, 460, 464, 470, 505, 508
ciphering. *See* mathematics
Cipolla, Carlo M., 665
city. *See* community
Clap, Thomas, 330, 331n, 461-462, 498n, 510, 511
Clark, John, 209
Clark, Jonas, 458
Clark, Victor S., 639
Clarke, Aidan, 618
Clarke, Andrew, 536
Clarke, Edward, 276, 421n
Clarke, G. N., 583
Clarke, John, 503, 506
Clarke, Richard Samuel, 345
Clarke, Samuel, 285, 460n
Classis of Amsterdam, 178-179, 183, 187
Claudian, 205
Clayton, John, 235n, 245, 410
Cleaver, Robert, 50-51, 284
Cleland, James, 66
clergy. *See* church
Clerk, David, 385
Cleverly, Joseph, 521
Clews, Elsie, 600
Clio's Nursery, 509
Clive, John, 623
Clossy, Samuel, 406
Cluver, Hans, 205
Clyde, William M., 616
Cnattingius, Hans, 636
Cobbett, Thomas, 52-53, 113
Cochrane, Raymond Canning, 594
Cocker, Edward, 185, 501
coffeehouse, 367, 445, 520
Coffin, Tristram, 584
Cogenhoe (Northamptonshire), 116-117
Cohen, Hennig, 644
Cohen, I. Bernard, 620, 641
Cohen, William, 651
Coke, Sir Edward, 255, 471, 520
Colbourn, H. Trevor, 470n, 655
Colden, Cadwallader, 408, 409, 433, 544, 553-554
Cole, Norwood Marion, 608, 610
Cole, W. A., 547n
Coleman, Ernest Claude, 640
Colet, John: lectures on Paul, 32; friendship with Erasmus, 32-33, 86; refounding of St. Paul's School, 86-87; deplores quality of clergy, 141; cited, 88, 171; writings on, 593
college. *See* higher education
College of New Jersey: Witherspoon's presidency, 299-301, 465-466; origins, 326-327; library, 398; fundraising by Samuel Davies,

College of New Jersey (*cont.*)
456; moral philosophy course,
465-466; disputations, 466;
student politics, 467, 468;
professorial salaries, 497n;
curriculum, 511, 512; occupations of alumni, 553-554;
impact of the Revolution,
565; cited, 510, 513, 514n,
516, 552, 559; writings on,
634, 661, 662
College of Philadelphia: curriculum of 1756, 380-383;
medical education, 385-386,
512; library, 398; origins,
404; moral philosophy course,
463-465; disputations, 466;
cosmopolitanism, 510; professorships, 513; career of
Francis Alison, 515-516; impact of the Revolution, 566;
cited, 505, 514n; writings on,
645-646, 662
College of Rhode Island, 327-
328, 466-467, 468, 509, 510,
559, 634, 662
College of William and Mary:
origins and early years, 321,
335-338; library, 398; student
addresses of 1699, 475-476;
professorial salaries in 1770,
497n; tendency not to grant
degrees, 510; curriculum,
511, 512; professorships, 513;
endowment, 558-559; impact
of the Revolution, 565-566;
cited, 532, 552; writings on,
635-636, 662
college teacher. *See* higher
education
collegium (dormitory), 198
Collins, Herman LeRoy, 663
Collins, John, 218
Collins, Varnum Lansing, 628,
662
Collinson, Patrick, 586
Collinson, Peter, 261
Colman, Benjamin, 279
Colombo, Matteo Realdo, 91
Colt, Peter, 565n
Come, Donald Robert, 661
Comenius, John Amos, 104,
185, 213, 503
Commager, Henry Steele, 666
commissary, 334-341
Committees of Correspondence,
520
community: as educator, 225-
226, 550-551; dispersed farmsteads of the Chesapeake colonies, 135-136, 238-241; New
England townships, 135-136,
236-238; Renaissance English
villages and towns, 226-228;
Renaissance London, 228-232;
seventeenth-century American market towns, 242-243;
eighteenth-century New England towns, 520-526; eighteenth-century Chesapeake
counties, 526-534; eighteenth-
century cities, 534-541; eighteenth-century back country,

541-543; cited, 338, 552;
writings on, 615-619, 662-664
Company for Propagacion of
the Gospell in New England,
159-160
Compayré, Gabriel, 595
Compton, Henry, 233, 334, 336,
338, 341
Comrie, J. D., 385n
Condon, Thomas J., 582
Congregational church: established in New England,
151-152; use of pastors and
teachers, 154-155; halfway
covenant, 314; "harvests,"
314; eighteenth-century revivals, 314-316; political preaching, 452-454, 457; eighteenth-
century sermons, 494-495; dis-
establishment, 497; writings
on, 604-607, 632, 653, 658-
659
Congregational Fund Board, 279,
324
Connecticut: education law of
1650, 125, 182; beginnings of
Congregational church, 152;
education law of 1672, 182;
Hopkins Grammar School,
186; S.P.G. activities, 345;
political preaching, 453; cited,
153, 415. *See also* New Haven Colony; Tisdale, Nathan;
Yale College
Connell, K. H., 247n, 548n
Connely, Willard, 208n, 613,
640
Conner, Paul W., 667
Conroy, Graham P., 628
Constitution of the United
States, 550
control of education: in medieval England, 168-169; in
Renaissance England, 119-121,
144, 170-173, 174-175, 200-
201, 230-231; in seventeenth-
century America, 125, 155-
156, 183-184, 193-194, 221-
222; in eighteenth-century
England, 323-324, 423, 424-
426, 445, 446; in eighteenth-
century America, 322, 325-
326, 391, 405, 429-431, 439-
442, 445, 446-448, 485, 496-
497, 500, 556-559. *See also*
licensing of teachers
Conway, Moncure Daniel, 450n
Cook, Edward M., 662
Cook, Elizabeth Christine, 643-
644
Cook, George Allan, 653
Cooke, George Willis, 663
Cooke, Samuel, 458
Cooper, Anthony Ashley (earl
of Shaftesbury), 445, 460n,
463, 464
Cooper, Myles, 462n, 510, 566
Coote, Edmund, 129, 174, 185
Copernicus, Nicolaus, 90
Copland, Patrick, 12, 26, 177,
210
Cordeaux, E. H., 611
Corderius, Mathurin, 185, 503

Corlet, Elijah, 189, 191, 194
Cornelissen, Jan, 179
Corner, Betsy Copping, 642
Cornwallis, Charles, 566
Corwin, Charles E., 605, 606
Corwin, Edward T., 164n, 582,
606
Cosby, William, 447
cosmography. *See* geography
Costello, William T., 612
Cotes, Roger, 383
Cotton, John, 128, 130, 281
Cotton, Josiah, 128
Coulter, E. Merton, 581
Counts, Martha Louise, 653
county. *See* community
Coverdale, Miles, 38
Coward Trust, 278
Cowing, Cedrick B., 319n
Cragg, G. R., 586, 624
Craighead, Alexander, 455
Cranach, Lucas, 98
Crane, R. S., 547n
Crane, Verner W., 664
Cranfield, G. A., 547n, 644
Cranmer, Thomas, 35, 38, 43
Cranston, Maurice, 619, 624
Craven, Wesley Frank, 581,
617
Cremin, Lawrence A., 578, 608,
659
Crèvecoeur, J. Hector St. John
de, 251, 359-360, 411, 639
Croft, Henry Herbert Stephen,
590
Crombie, A. C., 594
Cromwell, Thomas, 38, 65, 141,
200
Cross, Arthur Lyon, 635
Cross, Wilford Oakland, 157n
Crouch, Ralph, 182
Crousaz, Jean Pierre de, 382
Crouse, Maurice Alfred, 657
Cubberley, Ellwood P. 655, 659
Cullen, William, 378, 385
Culmann, Leonhard, 175, 185,
191, 503
Cumberland, Richard, 383
Curti, Merle, 620
Curtin, Philip D., 621
Curtis, L. P., 624
Curtis, Mark H., 203, 584, 611,
612
Cutler, Timothy, 295, 345
Cutting, Leonard, 406

Daggett, Naphtali, 468, 513,
565
Dale, Thomas, 10
dame school, 129. *See also*
household; petty school
dancing, 63, 199, 362, 499, 509,
539
Danckaerts, Jasper, 246
Danforth, Samuel, 218
Dargan, Edward Charles, 589
Dartmouth College, 328, 509,
510, 566, 634, 662
Davenant, Charles, 383
Davenport, John, 152, 180, 189
Davidson, Basil, 602
Davidson, Edward H., 633
Davidson, Philip, 449, 450n,
652

Davies, D. W., 583
Davies, Godfrey, 231n, 580
Davies, Margaret Gay, 598
Davies, Samuel: as president of the College of New Jersey, 299; work with Negroes in ership of Virginia Dissenters, Virginia, 354, 498-499; lead-455-457; cited, 520; writings on 653
Davis, Arthur Paul, 369n, 624
Davis, David Brion, 601
Davis, Dorothy, 615
Davis, Richard Beale, 651
Davis, Thomas W., Jr., 659
Davy, Sir Humphry, 377-378
Deane, Phyllis, 547n
Deansley, Margaret, 587
DeArmond, Anna Janney, 642
declamations, 214-215, 382, 383
Declaration of Independence, 439, 550
Dedham (Mass.), 181, 193, 521-526, 662-663
Dee, John, 90, 91
Defoe, Daniel, 302, 360, 372, 483, 484n, 629
De Forest, Emily Johnston (Mrs. Robert W.), 657
Degler, Carl N., 136n, 601
deism, 302, 629
De Jong, Gerald Francis, 604, 606
De Lancey, James, 379, 430, 447
Delanglez, Jean, 638
Delaware, 22, 258, 496, 509, 618
D'Elia, Donald John, 668
Dell, William, 57n, 220
Demarest, William, 632
Demetrius Phalereus, 383
Demos, John, 599, 656
Demosthenes, 63, 205, 380
Dent, Arthur, 48
Depellians, 258
Derham, William, 383
Desaguliers, J. T., 383
Descartes, René, 103, 244, 253, 278, 294
Deutsch, Karl W., 622
Dexter, Franklin Bowditch, 207, 585, 612, 634-635, 660, 661
Dexter, Samuel, 523
Diamond, Sigmund, 581
Dickens, A. G., 36, 585, 602
Dickinson, John, 450, 469-470
Dickinson, Jonathan, 299, 326, 327
Dickinson, Samuel, 515
Dickson, R. J., 621
didactic literature: in medieval England, 197-198; in Renaissance England, 40-41, 111, 171, 203-205; in seventeenth-century America, 29-30, 129-131, 184-186; in eighteenth-century England, 365-367, 446; in eighteenth-century America, 301-302, 346, 382-383, 388-395, 446-450, 460, 469-471, 483, 484n, 500-505, 511-512, 541. See also almanac; Bible; catechism; hornbook; library; primer; Psalter

Digges, Edward, 207
Digges, Thomas, 90, 91
Dike, Mr., 177
Dill, William A., 643
Dillon, Dorothy Rita, 650
Dilworth, Thomas, 501
Dionysius of Halicarnassus, 382
Dionysius Periegetes, 382, 383
Dioscorides, 85
disputations, 197, 214, 215-216, 382, 466-467
Distichs. See Cato, Dionysius
divinity. See theology
Dixon, Henry, 501
Dixon, Richard Watson, 36n
Dock, Christopher, 308-309, 489n, 506, 631-632
Dod, John, 50-51, 143, 284
Doddridge, Philip: life and education, 281-282; conception of piety, 282-284; relationship with Isaac Watts, 282; The Principles of the Christian Religion, 284; cited, 265, 278, 301, 456n, 460; writings on, 625
Dodsley, Robert, 302, 381, 382, 383, 464n
Dominicans, 355
Dominion of New England, 187
Donatus, Aelius, 169, 172, 197
Dongan, Thomas, 20
Donnan, Elizabeth, 602
Donohue, John Augustine, 638
Dorchester (Mass.), 151, 180, 181
Dorfman, Joseph, 667
Dorp, Martin, 34n, 83
Douglas, William, 437
Douglass, William: suggests scientific academy, 408; life and education, 433; Summary, 432-433, 434-436, 437; proposals on education, 435-436; cited, 347n; writings on, 650
Dove, David James, 403
Dow, George Francis, 657
Downing, George, 218
D'Oyley, Cope, 529
Drake, Sir Francis, 6
Drake, Milton, 643
Drake, Thomas E., 631
drawing, 69, 376
Driver, Harold E., 601
Drummond, Colin, 385
Dryden, John, 382
Dubbs, J. J., 606
Dublin Philosophical Society, 409
Duché, Jacob, 517
Dulles, Charles W., 645
Dummer, Jeremiah, 294
Dummer Academy, 505, 509
Dunaway, Wayland F., 622
Duncan, William, 382
Duniway, Clyde Augustus, 652
Dunkers, 258, 304, 308
Dunlop, O. Jocelyn, 122n, 598
Dunlop, R., 580
Dunn, John, 422n, 619, 648, 649
Dunn, Mary Maples, 622
Dunn, Richard, 599

Dunster, Henry, 186, 213-219
Dunton, John, 396
Dürer, Albrecht, 98
Dury, John, 305, 422, 423
Dutch-Americans, 18, 19, 22, 123, 333, 485
Dutch language instruction, 436
Dutch Reformed church: transplanted to America, 153, 164; missionary efforts of Johannes Megapolensis, 162; "comforters of the sick" and precentors, 164; sponsorship of schooling in New Netherland, 178-180; eighteenth-century revivalism, 311; establishment of Queen's College, 328; in eighteenth-century New York City, 536; cited, 333; writings on, 606
Dutch West India Company, 18-19, 178-180, 183, 187
Dwight, Josiah, 523
Dwight, Timothy, 565n

Eames, Wilberforce, 580, 601
Earle, Alice Morse, 600, 656, 661
East India School, 12-13, 177
Eaton, Isaac, 327
Eaton, Nathaniel, 212-213, 219
Eaton, Samuel, 218
Eaton, Theophilus, 152, 189
Eaton, Thomas, 178, 183
Eaton School, 178, 183, 530-531, 533
Echeverria, Durand, 622-623, 668
economics, 340
Edelen, Georges, 615
Edinburgh University. See University of Edinburgh
education, control of. See control of education
education, definition of, xi-xii, xiii
education, earliest use of term, 595-596
education, support of. See support of education
Edward VI, 38, 43, 119-120, 144, 170, 171-172
Edwards, George William, 663
Edwards, Jonathan: early life and education, 314-315; ministry at Northampton, 315-316; A Treatise Concerning Religious Affections, 315-316; on catechizing, 498n; cited, 266, 293, 299, 303, 317, 318, 353, 552; writings on, 627, 632-633
Edwards, Sarah Pierrepont, 319n
Eells, Walter Crosby, 666
Eggleston, Edward, 23, 112, 264, 579, 583, 612
Einstein, Lewis, 583
Eisenstein, Elizabeth L., 584
elementary education. See petty school; school
Elioseff, Lee A., 640
Eliot, Andrew, 467
Eliot, Jared, 360, 541

Eliot, John: missionary work among the Indians, 158-160, 194-195; early life and education, 162; ministry at Roxbury, 162-163; participation in New England cultural life, 163; encouragement of schooling, 163, 167; characterized by William Douglass, 434; writings on, 605-606
Eliot, Samuel, 432
Elizabeth I, 3, 5, 38, 43, 119, 145, 171-172, 230
Elizabeth City County (Va.), 11, 528-534, 663
Ellis, Aytoun, 616
Ellis, John Tracy, 606, 638
Ellis, Robert Leslie, 594
Elman, Paul L., 588
Elsbree, Willard, 609
Elting, Irving, 618
Elwood, Douglas J., 633
Elyot, Sir Thomas: life and education, 62; *The Boke Named the Governour*, 62-67; conception of civility, 62-64, 67; absence of *The Governour* in the colonies, 68n; influence on Roger Ascham, 78; cited, 277; writings on, 590-591
Emden, A. B., 196n, 611
Emerson, Roger Lee, 629
Emerson, William, 382
Emrick, Howard Charles, 658
English-Americans, 9-24, 257
English language instruction. *See* reading; writing
English school. *See* petty school
Epictetus, 383
Erasmus, Desiderius: quoted, 31; early life and education, 31-32; relationship with the Oxford reformers, 32-33; *Enchiridion militis Christiani*, 33-34; *Paraclesis*, 34-35; conception of piety, 33-34, 39; reputation in America, 39-40, 96-98; *The Education of a Christian Prince*, 58-61; conception of civility, 60-61; influence on Roger Ascham, 78; friendship with Thomas More, 80-86; *The Praise of Folly*, 80-83; prepares metrical catechism, 87; collaborates on *Lily's Grammar*, 87; compiles *De copia*, 87; writes *De ratione studii*, 87; mockery of the sciences, 89; *Colloquies*, 96-98; relationship of *Colloquies*, *Adages*, and *De copia*, 97; conception of learning, 82-83, 97-98; cited, 23, 63, 88, 171, 175, 204, 275-276, 367, 437; writings on, 587-588, 590, 592, 594
Erikson, Erik, 597
Erikson, Kai T. 605
Esler, Anthony, 591
Estienne, Charles, 91
Ethelbert, 167
ethics. *See* moral philosophy
Euclid, 197, 382
Euripides, 85, 175, 382, 437

Eusebius of Caesarea, 43
Evans, Charles, 388, 580, 626
Everitt, Alan, 596
Eversley, D. E. C., 597, 615, 621
Ewing, Galen W., 662
Ewing, John, 516
Eyton, Sampson, 208

Fabricius, Heironymus, 91
Fage, J. D., 602
Falconer, James, 529, 533, 534n
Falconer, John I., 617, 639
Fallopius, Gabriel, 91
Familists, 304
family. *See* household
Farish, Hunter Dickinson, 658, 661
Farrington, Benjamin, 594
Fauquier, Francis, 437-438
Faust, Albert Bernhardt, 621
Fay, Paul J., 625
Felt, Joseph B., 238n
Fénelon, François, 378
Fenton, William N., 601
Ferguson, Adam, 460
Ferguson, Arthur B., 590
Ferguson, Wallace K., 39n, 584
Fernow, Berthold, 582, 600
Ferrar, William, 207
Fifth Monarchists, 304
Finberg, H. P. R., 117n, 615
fine arts, 441
Fineman, Helene H., 640
Fink, Jerome, 614, 662
Fink, Zera S., 649
Finley, Samuel, 299, 323, 325, 384, 460
Finnish-Americans, 19, 123, 241
Firmin, Giles, 209n
Fish, Carl Russell, 603
Fisher, F. J., 615
Fisher, George, 503. *See* Slack, Mrs.
Fisher, John, 87
Fisher, Sidney George, 622
Fiston, William, 79n, 131
Fithian, Philip, 490-491, 500
Fitzhugh, William, 189
Five Mile Act (1665), 324
Flaherty, David Harris, 238n, 482n, 599
Fleet, Thomas, 389, 394
Fleetwood, William, 349-350
Fleming, Sandford, 588, 600, 604
Fletcher, Harris Francis, 205n, 601, 607, 612
Fletcher, John M., 611
Florus, 204
Flower, Enoch, 307, 537
Flynt, Henry, 511
Foltz, William J., 622
Foote, William, 653
Force, Peter, 581, 617
Ford, Henry Jones, 621
Ford, Paul Leicester, 644, 650
Ford, Worthington Chauncey, 585
Fordyce, David, 265, 464n
Fortescue, Sir John, 114, 199-200, 383
Fosdick, Lucian J., 621
Foster, John, 389

Foster, Margery Somers, 614
Fowle, Daniel, 391
Fox, Dixon Ryan, 206, 208, 210, 579, 612, 620, 668
Fox, Edward, 36
Fox, George, 164n, 233, 307, 309, 310
Fox, Richard, 88
Foxe, John: *Actes and Monuments*, 42-43; conception of piety, 43-44; certifies authority of Church of England doctrine, 49; advocacy of Hugh Latimer, 143; cited, 53, 185; writings on, 587
Frame, Donald M., 594
Francis, Tench, 402
Francis, W. Nelson, 6n
Franciscans, 355
Francke, August Hermann, 304, 314, 329
Francke, Gotthilf, 312
Frank, Joseph, 616
Frankland, Richard, 324
Franklin, Benjamin: on Pennsylvania Germans, 260-262; early life, 371-372; Silence Dogood letters, 371, 446-447; education, 371-373; junto, 373, 407-408; idea of self-education, 374-375; *Poor Richard's Almanack*, 374-375; conception of schooling, 375-378; *Proposals Relating to the Education of Youth in Pennsylvania*, 375-376; *Idea of the English School*, 376; relationship with William Smith, 378-379, 380; as printer, 388; organizes Library Company of Philadelphia, 398-400; establishes Academy and College of Philadelphia, 402-405; as personification of provincial education, 411-412; on freedom of the press, 446-447; on printers, 450-451; *Observations Concerning the Increase of Mankind*, 481-482; on the relation of economics and education, 553-555; cited, 259n, 266, 302, 310, 316, 336n, 354, 360, 361, 381, 390, 391, 405, 442, 444, 478, 501, 505, 515, 516, 518, 550, 552, 560; writings on, 629, 640-641
Franklin, James, 267, 371, 389, 390, 446-447, 552
Franklin, John Hope, 647
Franklin, Josiah, 266
Franklin, Julian H., 591
Franklin, Samuel, 267
Franklin College, 263
Franz, R. W., 615
Fraser, Antonia, 599
Freiberg, Malcolm, 662
Frelinghuysen, Theodore, 328-329
Frelinghuysen, Theodorus Jacobus, 311, 314, 317, 319
French Academie, The. See La Primaudaye, Pierre de

French-Americans, 19, 22, 241, 257, 259, 264, 333, 479, 485
French language instruction, 362, 383, 436
French Reformed church, 163, 493n, 536
Frere, Walter Howard, 598, 602
Friedrich, Carl J., 583
Friis, Herman R., 579, 616
Froben, Johann, 34, 97
Frost, Jerry William, 656
Froude, J. A., 6, 33n
Fuess, Claude M., 646, 659
Fuller, Thomas (1608-1661), 66
Fuller, Thomas (1654-1734), 374
Funk, Henry D., 634
Fussner, F. Smith, 584
Fyfe, William, 533

Gale, Benjamin, 330n
Galen, 85, 90, 91, 106, 197, 198, 206n
Galiani, Ferdinando, 267
Gallagher, Sister Anthony Marie, 619
Gambrall, Theodore C., 605
Gambrell, Mary Latimer, 634
Garden, Alexander, 344, 351-352
Gardiner, Stephen, 35
Garland, Madge, 128n
Garrod, H. W., 586
Garvan, Anthony N. B., 617, 657
Gates, Sir Thomas, 7, 149
Gaustad, Edwin Scott, 164n, 492-493, 603, 630, 632, 633
Gay, Peter, 620, 626
Gee, Henry, 598, 602
Gee, Joshua, 383
Gegenheimer, Albert Frank, 641, 661, 662
Gellius, Aulus, 205
general school, 173-174, 187, 505
geography, 69, 362, 376, 441, 503, 508
geology, 296
geometry, 69, 86, 197, 214, 362, 376, 380, 382, 503
George, Charles H., 586, 589
George, Katherine, 586, 589
Georgia, 271-272, 329-330, 352, 497
Gerardi, Donald, 627
German-Americans, 22, 257, 259-264, 333, 485
German Reformed, 258, 264, 543
German Reformed church, 258, 312-313, 499
Gewehr, Wesley M., 630
Geyl, Pieter, 583
Gibson, R. W., 594
Gichtelians, 258
Gilbert, Felix, 590
Gilbert, Sir Humphrey, 3, 8, 66
Gilbert, Neal W., 595
Gilbert, William, 90-91
Gillespie, James E., 583
Ginsburg, Jekuthiel, 660
Ginzberg, Eli, 667
Gipson, Lawrence Henry, 580, 620

Glasgow University. See University of Glasgow
Glass, D. V., 228n, 597, 615, 621
Glorious Revolution, 251-252, 257
Glover, Jose, 213
Godfrey, Thomas, 399
Godwin, Thomas, 204
Godwyn, Morgan, 161, 195
Goen, C. C., 630, 632, 633
Goldberg, Joseph Philip, 643
Goldsmith, M. N., 591
Gollin, Gillian Lindt, 622, 632
Goode, G. Brown, 646
Goodman, Nathan, 668
Goodnestone-next-Wingham (Kent), 116-117
Goodsell, Willystine, 597
Goodwin, Gerald Joseph, 627-628, 635
Goodwin, Gordon, 464n
Goodwin, Maud Wilder, 610
Gordon, G. S., 591
Gordon, Thomas, 376, 426-428, 430, 437, 446, 449
Gorges, Sir Ferdinando, 7
Gorn, Janice Leonora, 632, 639
Gouge, William, 50, 51-52, 111, 284
Gould, Elizabeth Porter, 610
Goveia, Elsa V. 647
Grace, Robert, 398
Graham, Henry Grey, 623, 654
grammar, 168-169, 172, 197, 214, 215, 296, 340, 376, 403, 499
grammar school: in manses and churches, 147; in medieval England, 167-169; in Renaissance England, 169-176; in seventeenth-century America, 181-187; Thomas Jefferson's proposals, 440; in eighteenth-century America, 503, 505, 524, 532-533. See also school
Grant, Anne Macvicar, 489-490, 658
Grant, Charles S., 542n, 664, 665
Gratian, 198
Gravesande, Willem Jakob, 383
Gray, Lewis Cecil, 617, 639
Great Awakening, 310-332, 494-496
Greaves, Richard L., 630, 649
Greek language instruction, 63-64, 69, 86, 173, 174-175, 185, 214, 215, 380, 406, 435, 441, 503, 505, 516
Green, Bartholomew, 389, 391, 394
Green, John Richard, 38
Green, Joseph, 129n
Green, Richard, 154n, 240, 617
Green, Robert W., 647
Greene, Evarts B., 238n, 259n, 571, 573, 574, 597, 635, 668
Greene, Jack P., 666
Greene, Lorenzo Johnston, 647, 656, 657
Greenham, Richard, 211
Greenleaf, W. H., 591
Greenslade, S. L., 587

Greenwood, Isaac, 501, 511, 514
Greg, W. W., 615-616
Gregory IX, 198
Gregory, David, 323, 382, 383
Grenville, George, 415-416
Gresham College, 229, 232
Greven, Philip J., Jr., 599
Grew, Nehemiah, 235n
Grew, Theophilus, 390, 403
Gridley, Jeremy, 432
Griffin, Edward Michael, 627, 653
Griffiths, Olive M., 633
Grimm, Dorothy Fear, 640, 645
Grimm, Harold J., 586
Grocyn, William, 32, 87
Grotius, Hugo, 282, 285, 300, 383, 464
Gruber, Frederick C., 665
Guardian, The, 325, 365-368, 399
Guerra, Francisco, 643
Guild, Reuben A., 467n
Gummere, Richard M., 592, 643, 653-654, 655

Haak, Theodore, 235
Haddow, Anna, 654
Hakluyt, Richard, 3-8, 148, 581
Hakluyt, Richard (the lawyer), 4
Hakluyt Society, 580
Hale, Richard Walden, 609
halfway covenant, 314
Hall, A. Rupert, 593
Hall, David, 388
Hall, David D., 582, 589, 603, 630
Hall, Michael G., 619
Hall, Richard, 433
Halle, Edward, 36n
Haller, Mabel, 632, 660
Haller, William (1885-   ), 46, 586, 587, 589, 603
Haller, William (1914-   ), 617
Hallett, Philip E., 593
Hallie, Philip P., 595
Hamilton, Andrew, 447-448
Hamilton, Henry, 623
Hamilton, J. G. De Roulhac, 207n, 613
Hamilton, J. T., 606
Hamilton, James, 262
Hamlin, Paul Mahlon, 613
Hampden-Sydney College, 552
Handlin, Mary F., 601
Handlin, Oscar, 579, 596, 601
Handover, P. M., 615
Handy, Robert T., 603
Hangartner, Carl Albert, 662
Hanover County (Va.), 354, 455-457
Hans, Nicholas, 633, 667
Hansen, Marcus Lee, 621
Hanson, Laurence, 644, 651
Haraszti, Zoltán, 648
Harbaugh, H., 262n, 632
Harbison, E. Harris, 586
Harder, Menno Simon, 632
Hardy, William John, 598
Harling, Frederick Farnham, 605-606
Haroutunian, Joseph, 627

Harper, Miles Douglas, Jr., 632, 633
Harper, Robert, 406
Harpsfield, Nicholas, 86n
Harrington, James, 255, 300, 377, 383, 423, 426, 437, 449, 463, 464, 470, 649
Harrington, Virginia D., 238n, 259n, 571, 573, 574
Harris, Benjamin, 185n, 391, 394, 444-445
Harris, P. M. G., 666
Harris, Samuel, 455
Harrison, John, 116n
Harrison, William, 67n, 615
Harry, 352-353
Harsha, D. A., 625
Hart, A. Tindal, 603
Hart, James D., 585
Hart, William Robert, 601
Hartdagen, Gerald Eugene, 605
Hartford (Conn.), 152, 181, 184
Hartlib, Samuel, 305, 422
Hartopp, Sir John, 278, 336n
Hartwell, Henry, 322n
Harvard, John, 103, 196, 212, 397
Harvard College: founding, 210-212; seventeenth-century program, 212-219; early purposes, 219-220; occupations of early alumni, 220-221; early control, 221; early financing, 222; the Indian College, 159, 222-223; eighteenth-century theological liberalism, 330-331; library, 397; eighteenth-century disputations, 466; student politics, 467, 468; presidential salaries, 497n; eighteenth-century curriculum, 509, 510, 513-515; Dedham alumni, 525; occupations of eighteenth-century alumni, 553-554; impact of the Revolution, 565; cited, 246, 469, 508, 512, 558-559; writings on, 613-615, 634, 661, 662
Harvey, William, 91
Haskins, George L., 655
Hassam, John T., 610
Hassel, Thomas, 344
Hatch, Alden, 657
Haven, Samuel, 494
Haynes, John, 208
Heal, Ambrose, 185n, 609
Heartman, Charles F., 393n, 644
Heath, Douglas Denon, 594
Hebrew language instruction, 173, 174-175, 185, 214, 435, 513, 536
Hechscher, Eli F., 598
Hedges, James B., 484n, 657
Heereboord, Adrian, 511
Heffelfinger, Jacob, 663
Heimert, Alan, 621, 626, 630, 633, 653
Hein, Rebecca Patterson, 595
Helsham, Richard, 382
Heltzel, Virgil B., 591

Henderson, Bobbie G., 625
Henderson, Robert W., 602
Hendricks, James Edwin, Jr., 660
Henrico College, 13, 158, 210, 613
Henry II, 196
Henry VI, 199
Henry VII, 231
Henry VIII, 32, 43, 83, 119-120, 141-142, 144, 170, 171
Henry, John, 520
Henry, Patrick, 469, 483n, 520, 552
Henry, Stuart C., 623, 628, 655
heraldry, 70
Herbert, George, 55, 147-148
Herbst, Josephine, 646
Hermogenes, 63
Herodian, 85
Herodotus, 85
Herr, Alan Fager, 589
Herrtage, S. J., 595
Herskovits, Melville J., 602
Herzog, John D., 578
Hesiod, 63, 175, 185, 205, 505
Hesychius, 85
Hexter, J. H., 584, 590
Hiacoomes, 158
Hibbins, William, 222
Higginson, Francis, 151
higher education: in medieval England, 197-200; in Renaissance England, 200-206; in seventeenth-century America, 206-224; in eighteenth-century America, 321-330, 335-338, 379-386, 404-406, 429-431, 441, 460-468, 509-516; writings on, 611-615, 633-635, 645-646, 654-656, 661-662
Hildreth, Joseph, 345
Hill, Christopher, 205n, 583, 586, 589, 596, 603, 612, 616
Hill, Don Gleason, 663
Hill, John, 394
Hill, Nathaniel, 210
Hindle, Brooke, 621, 640, 641, 646, 668
Hippocrates, 85, 91, 197, 198, 206n
Hirsch, Charles Bronislaw, 637
history, 63, 69, 100, 296, 340, 362, 376, 380, 383, 441
Hitchcock, James Francis, 603
Hoadly, Benjamin, 470
Hoar, Leonard, 208, 209, 217
Hobbes, Thomas, 72, 203, 255, 300
Hobsbawm, E. J., 109
Hodder, James, 501, 503
Hofstadter, Richard, 614, 635, 667
Hogrefe, Pearl, 62n, 590
Holbein, Hans, 98
Holbrook, Abiah, 506n
Holdsworth, Richard, 203-206, 611
Holdsworth, W. S., 200
Holinshed, Raphael, 67n, 88n
Hollis, Thomas, 397, 417, 467
Holmes, Pauline, 659

Holmes, Thomas J., 626
Holmes, Vera Brown, 583
Holt, John, 393
Holyoke, Edward, 331, 497n
Homan, Walter Joseph, 630
Home, Henry (Lord Kames), 378, 460n, 465
Homer, 63, 68, 85, 97, 175, 185, 205, 365, 382, 399, 505, 508
Honeywell, Roy J., 650
Hoogenboom, Ari, 621, 638
Hook, Andrew Dunnett, 628
Hooke, Robert, 234
Hooker, Richard, 383
Hooker, Richard J., 664
Hooker, Thomas, 151-152, 162
Hoole, Charles, 129n, 172, 185, 423n, 503
Hopewell Academy, 327
Hopkins, Edward, 184
Hopkins Grammar School, 186
Hoppen, K. Theodore, 618
Horace, 63, 175, 185, 205, 382, 508
Hornbeak, Katherine Gee, 629
Hornberger, Theodore, 381, 642, 662
hornbook: character, 129; role in teaching of reading, 129, 185, 483; recommended by John Locke, 277, 362; cited, 350; writings on, 592-593, 601, 609
Horton, Azariah, 353
Hoskins, W. G., 115, 117n, 598, 608, 615
hospitium (dormitory), 198
Hotman, François, 426n
Houghton, Walter E., Jr., 593
House, Armistead, 531
household: ideas of John Dod and Robert Cleaver, 50-51; ideas of William Gouge, 51-52; ideas of Thomas Cobbett, 52-53; ideas of Thomas More, Jean Bodin, and Thomas Hobbes, 92; in Renaissance England, 113-122; in seventeenth-century America, 123-137; ideas of Cotton Mather, 292; in eighteenth-century America, 480-491; writings on, 597-602, 656-658
Houtte, J. A. van, 583
Howard, Francis (Lord Effingham), 188, 252
Howe, George P., 579
Howe, John R., Jr., 648
Howell, David, 328n
Howell, James, 374
Howell, Wilbur Samuel, 104, 595, 612
Howes, Edmond, 229n
Hubbard, William, 213n
Huddleston, William, 21, 345, 351, 536
Hudson, Roy Fred, 589, 605
Hudson, Winthrop S., 603, 613, 623, 659
Hughes, John, 366
Hughes, Lewis, 185
Huguenots, 22, 148, 164, 241, 257, 333, 479, 485, 543

Huizinga, Johan, 32n, 586
Hulme, Obadiah, 470
Hume, David, 373, 460n
Humphrey, David Churchill, 646
Humphrey, Edward Frank, 652
Humphrey, Laurence, 66
Humphreys, Arthur R., 640
Humphreys, John Doddridge, 625
Hunn, Nathaniel, 453
Hunt, David, 597
Hunt, Robert, 148-149, 154
Hunt, William Raymond, 666
Hunter, William, 384-385, 406
Huntington, Dan, 508
Hutcheson, Francis, 265, 299, 300, 324, 325, 377, 380, 381, 382, 383, 460, 463-464, 465
Hutchins, John, 401
Hutchinson, Anne, 153, 163, 304
Hutchinson, Thomas, 458
Huygen, Jan, 18
Huygens, Christian, 254, 255
Hyma, Albert, 583
hymnody, 279

Illick, Joseph E., 622
Imborch, Gysberg van, 134
Independent Reflector, The, 429-431, 649-650
Independent Whig, The, 427-428, 429, 432
Indians (American): seventeenth-century family life, 136; seventeenth-century missions to, 158-163; availability of schooling, 194-195; opportunities at Harvard College, 222-223; Quaker attitudes toward, 307-308; mission of Eleazar Wheelock, 328; S.P.G. missions to, 348-356; economic restrictions, 360; miseducation under slavery, 411-412; Brafferton professorship at College of William and Mary, 441; Iroquois ohwachiras, 485; Jonathan Edwards' mission, 498; writings on, 601, 605-606, 610-611, 631, 637, 638, 647
Inglis, Mungo, 337
Ingram, George H., 634
Inns of Chancery, 199
Inns of Court: origins, 198-200; Renaissance developments, 201-202; alumni in seventeenth-century America, 207; seventeenth-century Americans at, 208; cited, 512; writings on, 611-612
Inspired, 258, 304
Institucion of a Gentleman, The, 66
Institution of a Christian Man, The, 171
Ipswich (Mass.), 130, 155, 180, 181, 190, 193
Ireland: colonization by England, 246-247; English colonial policy, 247; comparison

with American colonies in the seventeenth century, 247-248; eighteenth-century literacy, 547-548, 574-576; Adam Smith on, 555-556; writings on, 618-619, 665-666
Ireland, James, 455
Irish-Americans, 259, 266
Ironside, Charles Edward, 656
Isaac, 198
Isocrates, 63, 64, 175, 185, 505

Jackson, George L., 608
Jackson, Joseph, 660
Jacobson, Alf Edgar, 496n, 633, 658
James I: letter soliciting contributions for Virginia, 12; idea of colonization, 21; Basilikon Doron, 73-75; conception of civility, 74; relationship with Sir Francis Bacon, 92; policy of religious uniformity, 145; instructions on religion in Virginia, 148, 150; cited, 201
James II, 17-18, 187, 251, 252, 334, 445
James, Mary Hall, 609
James, Sydney V., 631
Jameson, J. Franklin, 581, 668
Jamestown (Va.), 9-11, 148-149, 335
Janeway, James, 484n
Jardine, David, 324
Jay, John, 550
Jefferson, Thomas: on slavery as miseducation, 412n; life and education, 437-438; reading, 437; conception of civility, 438-439; ideas on education, 438-443; Bill for the More General Diffusion of Knowledge, 438-441; Notes on the State of Virginia, 441; Bill for Amending the Constitution of the College of William and Mary, 441; library bill, 441; Bill for Establishing Religious Freedom, 441-442; ideas on educating Negroes, 442-443; "malady of bibliomania," 470; replies to Abbé Raynal, 560; cited, 266, 302, 419, 469, 483n, 518, 550, 552; writings on, 650-651
Jennings, David, 324
Jennings, John, 281-282
Jennings, John M., 645
Jernegan, Marcus Wilson, 600, 608, 609, 657
Jerome, 34, 89
Jesuits, 56, 182, 183, 211n, 342, 355, 425
Jesus, 34, 59, 60, 138-139, 191, 275-276, 280
Jews, 24, 148, 164, 485, 493n, 536
Jogues, Isaac, 19n
Johnson, Allen, 604
Johnson, Amandus, 618
Johnson, E. A. J., 598

Johnson, Edward, 196, 238
Johnson, Edward Payson, 605, 638
Johnson, Francis R., 594, 612
Johnson, Samuel (1696-1772): life and education, 294-296; conception of piety, 294-297; Elementa Philosophica, 296-297; "Raphael," 297; as president of King's College, 405-406, 431; conception of moral philosophy, 461, 462; Ethices Elementa, 462; use of Noetica in the colleges, 514n; cited, 345, 356, 376, 380, 483n, 495; writings on, 627-628
Johnson, Samuel (1709-1784), 75, 381
Johnson, Stephen, 458
Johnson, Thomas Herbert, 633
Johnson, William Samuel, 406
Johnston, Gideon, 344
Jones, E. Alfred, 208n, 612
Jones, Howard Mumford, 579, 580, 592
Jones, Hugh, 337, 526-527, 535n, 556, 663
Jones, Jerome Walker, 635, 658
Jones, John, 406
Jones, Joseph Jay, 668
Jones, M. G., 648, 667
Jones, Maldwyn Allen, 621
Jones, Richard Foster, 232n, 587, 592, 593, 648
Jones, Rufus M., 309-310, 606, 630
Jones, Samuel, 465n
Jones, Thomas, 468
Jordan, W. K., 111, 170, 584, 603, 607
Jordan, Wilfred, 663
Jordan, Winthrop D., 601, 605, 651
Judaism, 138. See also Jews
Justinian, 197, 198
Justinus, Marcus Junianus, 204
Juvenal, 175, 185, 205, 382, 508

Kaestle, Carl F., 450, 585, 652, 664
Kaledin, Arthur Daniel, 635, 661, 662
Kalm, Peter, 544
Kammen, Michael G., 619
Kany, Robert Hurd, 643
Kaplan, Louis, 599
Katz, Stanley Nider, 652
Kaye, F. B., 547n
Keayne, Robert, 237
Keckermann, Bartholomaüs, 103-104, 215
Keen, Joe J., 667
Keep, Austin Baxter, 645
Keill, John, 382, 383
Keimer, Samuel, 372, 391, 392, 408
Keiter, M. Roberta Warf, 641
Keith, George, 537
Kellaway, William, 605, 615
Kelsey, Rayner Wickersham, 631

Kelso, Ruth, 589
Kemp, Charles F., 588
Kemp, Richard, 207
Kemp, William Webb, 637, 664
Kempe, William, 174n
Kennedy, W. P. M., 598
Kennedy, William McClure, 598
Kenney, Alice P., 657
Kenney, William Howland III, 312, 319, 623, 632
Kenrick, Isabel, 642
Kent (Conn.), 541-542
Kepler, Johannes, 255
Ketcham, Ralph L., 640
Keys, Alice Mapelsden, 667
Kidder, Robert Wilson, 643
Kiefer, Monica, 656
Kilpatrick, William Heard, 19n, 582, 606, 608, 610, 618, 665
Kimball, Fiske, 599
Kimball, Howard E., 635
Kimball, Marie, 650
King, William, 382
King Philip's War, 159, 160
King's College: contribution of S.P.G., 345; library, 398; origins, 405-406; observations of The Independent Reflector, 429-431; Samuel Johnson's course in moral philosophy, 462; professorships, 512-513; medical education, 512; prepatory school, 536; endowment, 558-559; impact of the Revolution, 566; cited, 295, 328, 510, 514n; writings on, 627-628, 646, 662
King's College (Aberdeen), 381
Kingsbury, Susan Myra, 581
Kingsford, Charles L., 615
Kinnersley, Ebenezer, 403
Kirkpatrick, John E., 636
Kittredge, George L., 626
Klain, Zora, 631
Klassen, Frank Henry, 632, 660
Kleber, Brooks Edward, 644
Klein, Milton M., 649
Klett, Guy S., 634
Klingberg, Frank J., 636, 637
Klotz, Edith L., 41n
Knappen, Marshall M., 586
Knight, Edgar W., 609
Knight, William, 208
Knolles, Richard, 72
Knorr, Klaus E., 581
Knox, John, 41
Knox, Ronald, 310, 629
Kobre, Sidney, 643
Koch, Adrienne, 651
Koch, G. Adolf, 629
Kohn, Hans, 622
Kolko, Gabriel, 647
Korty, Margaret Barton, 640, 645
Koyré, Alexandre, 619, 620
Krapp, George Philip, 587
Kraus, Joe Walker, 397n, 585, 645
Kraus, Michael, 620-621, 622
Krol, Bastiaen, 18
Kuhn, Thomas S., 619
Kuschmierz, Ruth, 593

Labadists, 258
Labaree, Leonard Woods, 621, 640
Lake, Stephen, 208
Lamb, Andrew, 401
Lamprecht, Sterling Power, 648
Lamson, Alvan, 663
Land, Robert Hunt, 12n, 613
Langdon, Samuel, 468
language instruction. See Dutch, French, Greek, Hebrew, Latin, and Spanish language instruction; grammar; reading; rhetoric; writing
La Primaudaye, Pierre de, 105-106, 594
La Rochefoucauld, François de, 374
La Rochefoucauld d'Enville, Louis Alexandre, Duc de, 373
Lascaris, Constantine, 85
Laslett, Peter, 116-117, 228n, 229, 591, 597, 615, 619, 648
Latimer, Hugh, 35, 43, 143
Latin grammar school. See grammar school
Latin language instruction, 62-63, 69, 77, 86, 97, 168-169, 173, 174-175, 185, 215, 362, 380, 382, 435, 441, 503, 505
Lauber, Almon Wheeler, 601
Laud, William, 201
Lavengood, Lawrence Gene, 321, 630, 632, 633
law, study of, 198, 199-200, 208-209, 340, 362, 435, 441, 512, 613
Lawrence, Alexander A., 643
Leach, A. F., 193n, 606, 610
League, James Benjamin, Jr., 639
Learned, Marion Dexter, 631, 660
Le Bossu, René, 382
Lechford, Thomas, 155n
Lechner, Joan Marie, 584
Le Clerc, Jean, 368, 382, 383
lectures, 198, 215-216, 513-514
Leder, Lawrence H., 619, 657
Lee, Charles, 450
Lee, John, 208
Lee, Patricia Ann, 590
Lee, Sidney, 583
Lee, Thomas Ludwell, 438
Leeds, Daniel, 102n
LeFevre, Tanaquil, 513
Leff, Gordon, 611
Lehmann-Haupt, Hellmut, 667
Lehmberg, Stanford E., 590
Leicestershire, 115, 175-176
Leiden University. See University of Leiden
Le Jau, Francis, 344, 352-353
Lenthal, Robert, 181
Leonard, Daniel, 459
Levellers, 423n
Leverett, John, 288, 461, 497n
Levin, David, 626, 627, 640
Levy, Babette May, 589, 605
Levy, Leonard W., 652
Lewis, Earl Edward, 653
Lewis, Ezekiel, 190
Leyburn, James G., 621
library: of the first colonists,

28-30; established by Thomas Bray, 338-341; in the eighteenth century, 396-400; writings on, 644-645
Library Company of Philadelphia, 373-374, 398-400
licensing of teachers: English clergymen, 144, 147; English schoolmasters, 172, 175-176, 324; American schoolmasters, 187-188, 557-558; English printers, 230-231, 445, 446; American clergymen, 455-456
Lily, William, 87, 88, 171, 175, 185, 191, 505
Linacre, Thomas, 32, 87, 90
Lincoln, Anthony, 624
Lipman, Jean, 128n, 599
Lipscomb, Andrew A., 650
literacy: in Tudor and Stuart England, 176, 231n; in Dedham (Mass.), 522, 526; in Elizabeth City County (Va.), 533; in New York City and Philadelphia, 540; in Kent (Conn.), 542; in back-country South Carolina, 543; in eighteenth-century America, 546-549; and schooling, 549; and politics, 549-550; comparison of American, English, and Irish in the eighteenth century, 546-549; writings on, 664-665
Littlefield, George Emery, 585, 609, 610
Littleton, Sir Thomas, 520
Lively, Bruce Richard, 642
Livingood, Frederick George, 632, 659
Livingston, Helen E., 660
Livingston, Philip, 428
Livingston, William, 410, 428-431, 649-650
Livy, 63, 382
Locke, John: life and career, 253-255; An Essay Concerning Human Understanding, 273-275, 303; conception of piety, 273-278; The Reasonableness of Christianity, 275-278, 285, 420; Some Thoughts Concerning Education, 276-278, 284, 360-363; distaste for enthusiasm, 303-304; Of the Conduct of the Understanding, 361, 363-364, 420, 421; conception of learning, 361-364; conception of civility, 363-364, 419-421; reputation in America, 365, 421-422, 506; Two Treatises of Government, 419-420; "Memorandum on Working Schools," 420n; use of Commonwealth traditions, 422-423, 427; cited, 102, 265, 282, 284, 287, 294, 295, 298, 300, 301, 368, 376, 377, 378, 380, 381, 382, 383, 437, 438, 439, 446, 455, 463, 464, 470; writings on, 619-620, 624, 639, 648

Lockridge, Kenneth Alan, 236n, 238n, 599, 617, 662
Lodge, Martin Ellsworth, 630, 633
Loetscher, Lefferts A., 603
Log College, 311, 322-323, 326
Logan, James, 256, 260
logic, 63, 86, 103-104, 197, 204-205, 214, 215, 340, 362, 380, 382, 503
London, 228-235, 267, 520
Longinus, Dionysius Cassius, 382
Lord, Albert B., 584, 598
Lovelace, Francis, 20
Lucan, 63, 205
Lucian, 65, 85, 97
Lucretius, 205
Lull, Ramón, 114
Lupset, Thomas, 88
Lupton, J. H., 593
Luther, Martin, 36, 41
Lutheran church: transplanted to America, 162-163; missionary efforts of John Campanius, 162; eighteenth-century revivalism, 312-313; shortage of clergy, 321-322
Lutheranism, 36, 37, 41, 142, 143. See also Lutheran church
Lutherans, 241, 258, 264, 333, 542n, 543
Lutnick, Solomon, 652
Lydekker, John Wolfe, 636
Lydgate, John, 140
Lyly, John, 66
Lynd, Staughton, 649
Lyons, Charles, 601

McAllister, James L., 628, 655
McAnear, Beverly. 661
MacCaffrey, Wallace T., 615
McCaul, Robert L., Jr., 634, 660
McClure, Edmund, 637
McColloch, Samuel Clyde, 625, 636, 637
McConica, James Kelsey, 82, 587, 592, 593, 611
McCormick, Leo Joseph, 609
McCormick, Richard P., 634
McCoy, Ralph E., 652
McCrum, Blanche P., 579
McDonald, Ted Hayden, 602
McGrath, Patrick, 586
McIlwain, Charles Howard, 591
McKinley, Albert E., 20n, 582
MacKintosh, John, 522
McLachlan, H., 624, 625, 633
McLelland, Colin, 350
McLoughlin, William G., 635
McLuhan, Marshall, 584
MacLysaght, Edward, 618
McMahon, Clara P., 193n, 607, 610, 611
Macaulay, Catharine, 470
Macaulay, Thomas Babington, 248
Machiavelli, Niccolò, 60-61, 65, 68, 101, 255, 437, 590
Maclaurin, Colin, 382, 383

Maclean, John, 301n, 634
Maclear, Anne Bush, 617
Macrobius Saturnus, 205
Madden, Richard Robert, 548n, 666
Madison, James (1749-1812), 478
Madison, James (1751-1836), 301, 483n, 550, 552
magazine, 391-392, 644
Magee, Brian, 586
Main, Jackson Turner, 497n, 638
Mair, N. H., 588
Maitland, David Johnston, 57n, 593, 648
Major, John M., 65, 590
Mallet, Charles Edward, 611
Malone, Dumas, 604, 650
Mandeville, Bernard, 460n
Mann, Herman, 663
Mann, Horace, 384
Mann, William J., 632
Manning, Bernard Lord, 602
Manning, James, 327
Manross, William Wilson, 628
Mansfield, Richard, 345
manual arts, 362
Manuel, Frank E., 255n, 619-620
Manuerre, William R. II, 626-627
Marischal College (Aberdeen), 334, 381, 513
Markham, Gervase, 340
Marshall, Dorothy, 623
Marshall, Thomas Maitland, 638
Martha's Vineyard (Mass.), 160
Martial, 205
Martin, Benjamin, 383, 511
Martin, David, 402, 403, 515
Martin, Edward T., 651
Martin, Hugh, 588
Martin, Joseph Walford, 630
Martin, Josiah, 378
Mary I, 88
Mary II, 251, 254
Maryland: early religious policies, 153, 165; school conducted by Ralph Crouch, 182; number of schools in 1689, 183; abortive effort of 1671 to establish a school, 194; church act of 1702, 339-340; libraries, 340, 398; Constitution of 1776, 497; cited, 187, 192, 211n, 482, 499. See also Bray, Thomas
Mason, George, 438
Mason, Jeremiah, 508
Mason, John E., 589
Mason, M. G., 277n, 624
Masons, 520
Massachusetts: plantation, 14-16; initial educational efforts, 16-17; education law of 1642, 124-125; education law of 1668, 126; ecclesiastical laws of 1635 and 1638, 152; seventeenth-century schooling, 180-182, 184, 187, 189-191, 193, 194; education law of 1647,

181-182; number of schools in 1689, 183; requirements for teaching, 187; configuration of educational institutions in 1650 and 1689, 238; eighteenth-century printing, 389, 391; eighteenth-century church life, 452, 453-454, 495, 496, 497; eighteenth-century life and education, 521-526; cited, 415, 482; writings on, 581-582, 617, 662-663. See also Adams, John; Boston; Douglass, William; Edwards, Jonathan; Harvard College; Mather, Cotton; Moody, Samuel; Plymouth Colony
Massys, Quentin, 98
mathematics, 86, 173, 185, 197, 296, 340, 380, 382, 404, 406, 436, 508, 509, 511, 513
Mather, Cotton: notes influence of Richard Baxter on Jonathan Mitchell, 55; on his brother Nathaniel's education, 131-132; eulogizes Ezekiel Cheever, 190-191; on the "collegiate way of living," 203; life and education, 287-288; conception of piety, 288-293; Manuductio ad Ministerium, 289-290; Corderius Americanus, 290-291; Bonifacius, 291-292; library, 396; familial pedagogy, 486-489; cited, 238, 245, 256, 279, 372, 437; writings on, 626-627, 658
Mather, Increase, 130, 132, 134, 208, 217, 235, 252, 605
Mather, Richard, 163
Mather, Samuel, 208, 218, 489, 658
Mather, William, 503
Mathews, Alice Elaine, 660
Mathews, Mitford M., 600
Mathews, Samuel, 127-128
Mathieson, William Law, 623
Matthew, Thomas, 38
Matthews, Albert, 218n, 613, 614
Matthews, William, 599
Maud, Daniel, 184
Maurer, Charles Lewis, 659
Maury, Ann, 657
Maury, James, 437, 473, 477-478, 656
Maxson, Charles Hartshorn, 630
Maxwell, Constantia, 666
Mayhew, Jonathan, 272, 293, 347, 454, 457, 495-496, 627
Mayhew, Thomas, Jr., 158-159
Mayo, Lawrence Shaw, 657
Mead, Sidney, 331, 623, 659, 667
Mease, William, 149
mechanics, 296
Mecom, Benjamin, 392
Mecom, Jane, 373
Meder, Mary Louise Dunham, 643
medical societies, 410
medicine, study of, 198, 209-210, 340, 384-386, 410, 435, 512, 513, 642
Medley, D. J., 623
Medlicott, W. N., 623

Megapolensis, Johannes, 162
Mein, John, 398
Mennonites, 163, 258, 304, 308
mental philosophy, 197, 204, 214, 215, 296, 380, 382
mercantilism, 5, 120-122, 126, 415-416, 482, 553-556, 580-581, 598-599, 600, 638-639, 667
Mercator, Gerhardus, 4, 90, 91
Mercers' Company of London, 86
Meredith, Hugh, 372
Meriwether, Colyer, 614
Meriwether, Robert L., 543n, 664, 665
Merrens, H. Roy, 616-617
Merritt, Richard L., 622
Merry, D. H., 611
Mesnard, Pierre, 590
Messerli, Jonathan, 622, 641
metaphysics. See mental philosophy
Methodist church, 499
Methodists, 271, 312, 455, 536
Metzger, Walter P., 614, 667
Michaëlius, Jonas J., 18, 164n, 605
Michaelson, Robert S., 647
Middlekauff, Robert, 291n, 626, 656, 660
Middleton, Arthur Pierce, 658
Middleton, Peter, 406
Mifflin, Thomas, 464-465
Mildmay, Sir Walter, 111, 211
Miller, Perry, 29n, 578, 582, 585, 589, 595, 604, 617, 626, 630
Miller, Samuel, 562
Mills, Edmund, 542
Mills, Jedediah, 552
Mills, John, 542
Mills, Samuel, 542
Milton, John: influenced by Renaissance civility, 67; as source of Benjamin Franklin's Proposals, 265, 376-377; conception of education, 422; on freedom of thought, 446; cited, 203, 294, 368, 378, 455; writings on, 648-649
Miner, John Nelson, 607
minister. See church
missionary education: in seventeenth-century America, 157-162; in eighteenth-century America, 338-356; writings on, 605-606, 636-638
Mitchell, Jonathan, 55, 177, 211n, 218, 220
Mitchell, Pearl Beattie, 616
Mitchell, W. Fraser, 589, 603
modern languages, 441, 499. See also Dutch, French, and Spanish language instruction
Moffat, Edward Stewart, 659
Mohler, Samuel Roop, 336n, 635
Molesworth, Robert: early life and education, 424; An Account of Denmark, 424-426; anticlericalism, 425; conception of civility, 425-426; reputation in America, 426, 427; influence on Thomas Jefferson, 437; cited, 439,

449, 463, 471; writings on, 649
Moller, Herbert, 599
Molyneux, William, 361
Monahan, Thomas P., 482n
Monmouth, Humphrey, 36
Monroe, Paul, 659
Montagne, Jan de la, 19
Montaigne, Michel Eyquem de: early life and career, 98-99; Essays, 99-100; conception of learning, 100; cited, 23, 362, 437; writings on, 594
Montesquieu, 300, 383, 437, 439, 470, 471
Montegomery, Thomas Harrison, 641, 642, 645
Montmorency, J. E. G. de, 595, 596
Moody, Eleazer, 484n
Moody, Samuel, 505, 506, 508-509
Moore, Benjamin, 566
Moore, Thoroughgood, 349
Moot Club (New York), 410
Morais, Herbert M., 292, 629
moral philosophy, 63, 197, 204, 214, 215, 296-297, 340, 362, 376, 380, 382-383, 441, 460-466
Moravians, 259, 265, 485, 493n, 536
Moray, Sir Robert, 234
More, Louis Trenchard, 620
More, Thomas: early relationship with Desiderius Erasmus, 32-33; conception of civility in Utopia, 61; influence on Sir Thomas Elyot, 65; knowledge of Utopia in America, 68; centrality of the family in Utopia, 72; friendship with Desiderius Erasmus, 80-85; conception of learning in Utopia, 83-86; More's "school," 86; praise of the sciences, 89; reputation in America, 96; cited, 88, 255, 384, 437; writings on, 590, 592-593
Morgan, David Taft, Jr., 630
Morgan, Edmund S., 17n, 582, 588, 599-600, 604, 622, 627, 647, 651-652, 656, 657, 661, 662
Morgan, Helen M., 647, 651-652
Morgan, Irvonwy, 143n, 588, 589, 603
Morgan, John, 378, 384-386, 407, 567, 642
Morison, Samuel Eliot, 16n, 207, 210, 211n, 220n, 221, 582, 585, 595, 608, 613, 614, 615, 634, 665
Morris, F. Grave, 617
Morris, Lewis, 404, 447
Morris, Richard B., 600, 668
Morris, William Sparkes, 633
Morritt, Thomas, 506
Morton, Charles, 244, 511
Morton, Louis, 484n, 658
Morton, Richard L., 581, 617, 663
Moslems, 485
Mott, Frank Luther, 393n, 643, 644, 651, 667

Mountain Men, 258
moving school, 525
Mozley, J. F., 587
Mugridge, Donald H., 579
Mühlenberg, Henry Melchior, 263n, 312, 313
Muirson, George, 536
Mulhern, James, 641, 645, 659, 660
Müller, Johann. See Regiomontanus
Mullett, Charles F., 653-654
Mullinger, James Bass, 87, 611
Mumford, Lewis, 228, 232, 615
Munro, Alexander, 385
Munter, Robert, 548n, 666
Murdock, Kenneth, 604, 626, 627
Murphy, Geraldine Joanne, 182, 193, 505n, 600, 608, 610
Muse, Raymond, 650
museum, 399n
music, 69, 84, 197, 199, 309, 539
Musschenbroek, Pieter van, 383

Nantucket (Mass.), 160
Nash, Gary B., 622
Nash, Ray, 609
Nashe, Thomas, 28
Nassau Hall. See College of New Jersey
natural history, 214, 296, 376, 380, 383, 441
natural philosophy, 197, 204, 214, 215, 340, 362, 380, 383, 441, 511, 513
navigation, 380, 499, 503, 508
Neau, Elias, 351
Ned, 534
Nef, John U., 598
Negroes. See Afro-Americans
Nelson, John Kendall, 343n, 637
Neshaminy (Pa.), 322-323, 324
Nettels, Curtis P., 63
Neville, Henry, 470
New, John F. H., 586
New Amsterdam: plantation, 18-19; Dutch Reformed church, 164; schooling, 178-180; town school, 182; cited, 134, 189, writings on, 582, 606
New Born, 258
New England. See Connecticut; Massachusetts; New Hampshire; Rhode Island
New England Confederation, 152
New-England Primer, The, 394, 644
New France, 22, 355-356
New Hampshire, 164, 222, 497, 509. See also Dartmouth College
New Haven Colony, 125, 152, 180, 184
New Jersey, 241, 258, 399, 454, 497, 499, 535, 618. See also College of New Jersey; Queen's College; Witherspoon, John
New Light-Old Light controversy, 310-332, 494-496
New Mooners, 258
New Mexico, 355-356

New Netherland: plantation, 18-19; Dutch Reformed church, 164; schooling, 178-180; town school at New Amsterdam, 182; regulation of schoolmasters, 187; configuration of educational institutions in 1650, 243; writings on, 582, 606

New Spain, 21-22, 355-356

New Sweden, 22, 182

New York: Duke's Laws of 1665, 125; seventeenth-century religious situation, 164; number of schools in 1689, 183; licensing of teachers, 187-188; configuration of educational institutions in 1689, 243; S.P.G. activities, 345, 349-351, 356; eighteenth-century printing, 389; writings on, 582, 618. See also King's College; New Amsterdam; New Netherland; New York City

New York City: beginnings, 17-21; Elias Neau's school for Negroes, 351; Bray's Associates school for Negroes, 354; printing, 389, 392; library, 399; provincial life and education, 537-541; population statistics, 571-572; cited, 518; writings on, 663-664. See also Johnson, Samuel (1696-1772); King's College; Livingston, William; New Amsterdam

Newark (Del.) academy, 509

Newbury (Mass.), 180

Newcomb, Robert, 641

Newcombe, Alfred W., 637

Newport (R.I.), 181, 243, 389

newspaper, 391, 393, 643-644, 651-652

Newton, Sir Isaac: life and career, 253-254; Principia mathematica, 254-255; cited, 102, 234, 294, 295, 363, 365, 368, 383, 438, 515; writings on, 619-620

Newton (Mass.), 155

Newtown (Md.), 182, 183, 211n

Newtown (Mass.), 152. See also Cambridge (Mass.)

Nicholas, 198

Nichols, Francis Morgan, 587

Nicholson, Sir Francis, 338, 339

Nicolls, Richard, 17, 18, 19-21

Niebuhr, H. Richard, 602, 623

Nietz, John, 660

Nieuwentijt, Bernard, 383

Noah, Harold J., 618

Noel, Garrat, 398

Nolan, J. Bennett, 556n

Nomini Hall, 490-491, 500

Norris, Edward, 130

Norris, John, 294

North Carolina, 258, 415, 482, 497, 498, 509

Norton, Arthur O., 614

Norton, John, 130

Norwood, William Frederick, 613, 642

Notestein, Wallace, 583, 596, 597, 607, 615

Noxon, Thomas, 345

Noyes, James, 130

Nuttall, Geoffrey F., 588, 625, 629-630

Oakes, Thomas, 208

Oakes, Urian, 107, 217, 218

Oberholzer, Emil, Jr., 605

O'Brien, J. J., 593, 649

O'Brien, Michael J., 664

O'Callaghan, E. B., 582

Occom, Samson, 328, 354

O'Connor, D. J., 639

Ogg, David, 619

Old Light–New Light controversy, 310-332, 494-496

Oldenburg, Henry, 234

Oldham, Hugh, 88

Oller, Anna Kathryn, 643

O'Malley, C. D., 594

O'Neil, Robert Morris, 588

O'Neill, Charles Edwards, 638

O'Neill, John J., 641

Ong, Walter J., 104, 584, 595, 598, 614

Opie, John, Jr., 630

oral tradition, 29, 119, 133, 584

Origen, 34

Orme, William, 588

Orton, Job, 625

Osborne, Francis, 74-76

Osgood, Herbert L., 581, 620

Oswald, John Clyde, 641

Otis, James, 415-416, 458

Ottolenghe, Joseph, 352

Oviatt, Edwin, 634

Ovid, 63, 68, 175, 185, 191, 203, 204, 205, 505

Owen, Eugene D., 641

Oxford Diocese (England), 146

Oxford University. See University of Oxford

Packard, Francis R., 642, 646

Packington, Augustine, 36

Paine, Thomas, 450

Painter, Borden W., Jr., 605, 667

Palladio, Andrea, 382

Palmer, Edward, 13, 177

Palmer, R. R., 623, 668

Pardies, Ignace Gaston, 382

parent. See household

Pargellis, Stanley, 623

Paris University. See University of Paris

Parker, Mrs., 533

Parker, Irene, 625, 633

Parker, James, 260

Parkes, Joan, 615

Parkman, Ebenezer, 458

Parks, George Bruner, 3n, 149n, 581, 592

Parks, Malcolm Gordon, 649

Parks, William, 389

Parrington, Vernon L., 237, 579, 617

Parry, J. H., 90, 581

Parsons' Cause, 477

Pascoe, C. F., 341n, 637

Pastorius, Francis Daniel, 308, 506, 631

Patoun, Archibald, 382

Patrick, Simon, 294

Paul, 138

Paul's Cross, 229

Paulett, Robert, 210

Paullin, Charles O., 579

Peacham, Henry: early life and education, 69; The Compleat Gentleman, 69-70; conception of civility, 69-70; writings on, 591

Pearce, Roy Harvey, 601

Pears, Thomas C., Jr., 634

Pearson, Eliphalet, 404

Pearson, Lu Emily, 597

Peck, John, 491

Peckham, Howard H., 668

pedagogy: in Renaissance devotional writers, 49-52; in Renaissance manuals of homiletics, 54-55; ideas of Sir Thomas Elyot, 62-63; ideas of Roger Ascham, 77-78; in Thomas More's household, 86; in Ramist writings, 103-104; in Renaissance English households, 115; in seventeenth-century American households, 129-130, 131-133; in medieval English churches, 139-140; in seventeenth-century English churches, 147-148; in seventeenth-century American churches, 155-157; in medieval English schools, 168; recommendations of Richard Holdsworth, 203-204; at seventeenth-century Harvard, 216-217; ideas of John Locke, 277-278, 362-363, 484; ideas of Samuel Johnson (1696-1772), 296; ideas of William Penn, 305; teaching of Christopher Dock, 309; of New Light preaching, 317-319; teaching of Francis Le Jau, 352-353; teaching of Cotton Mather, 486-489, 291n; teaching of Margarita Schuyler, 489-490; in eighteenth-century American churches, 494-496; in eighteenth-century American schools, 501-503, 505-506; in eighteenth-century American colleges, 513-514

Peirce, Benjamin, 634

Pemberton, Henry, 256

Pendleton, Edmund, 438

Penn, John, 260

Penn, William: idea of colonization, 21; conception of community, 225; theory of education, 305-306; attitudes on race, 307-308; cited, 241; writings on, 630-631

Penn Charter School. See William Penn Charter School

Pennington, Edgar Legare, 636, 637

Pennsylvania: education law of 1683, 125; early religious policies, 153; early settlement, 258-260; conflicts between English and German colonists, 260-262; effort to Anglicize the Germans, 262-264; schooling, 305-310, 401-403; printers, 388-389; libraries, 398-399; cited, 415; writings on, 622, 630-631. See also College of Philadelphia; Franklin, Benjamin; Morgan, John;

Pennsylvania (*cont.*)
  Philadelphia; Smith, William (1727-1803)
Pennsylvania Hospital, 407
Perkins, William: concept of calling, 52n; *The Arte of Prophecying*, 53-54; *The Foundation of Christian Religion*, 130; conception of "godly preaching," 143; cited, 46n, 47, 71, 111; writings on, 589
Perrin, Porter C., 614
Perrott, Henry, 208
Perry, William Stevens, 635, 653
Persius, 205
Perzel, Edward Spaulding, 236n, 599, 617
Petau, Denys, 383
Peter, Hugh, 130, 213, 222
Peter the Lombard, 198
Peters, Richard, 262
Peterson, Arthur Everett, 663
Petit, Jean Louis, 406
Pettit, Norman, 589
Petty, Sir William, 246-248, 305, 422, 571
petty school: in colonial households, 129; in manses and churches, 147; in medieval England, 169; in Renaissance England, 173-175; in seventeenth-century America, 181-183, 184-185; proposals of Thomas Jefferson, 440; in eighteenth-century America, 500-503, 505-506; cited, 423, 435. *See also* school
Pfeffer, Leo, 659
Phelps, Vergil V., 155n, 604
Philadelphia: educational ferment of the 1750's and 1760's, 378; printing, 388-389, 391-392; libraries, 398-399; schooling, 401-403; character of the citizenry, 517; eighteenth-century life and education, 535-541; population statistics, 572-574; writings on, 663-664. *See also* College of Philadelphia; Franklin, Benjamin; Morgan, John; Smith, William (1727-1803)
Philip II, 5
Phillips, Margaret Mann, 586
Phillips, Samuel, 498
Phillips, Ulrich Bonnell, 412n
Phillips academies, 403-404
Philogrammatical Library, 399-400
philosophy. *See* logic; mental philosophy; moral philosophy; natural philosophy
physical education, 63, 66, 70, 199, 362, 376, 436, 499
physics. *See* natural philosophy
physiology, 340
Pierce, Roderic Hall, 623, 632
Pierce, William, 389
Pierrepont, Sarah. See Edwards, Sarah Pierrepont
Pietersen, Evert, 189
pietism, 259, 266, 304-332, 495, 632
Pigot, George, 345

Pilcher, George William, 653
Pilgrim's Progress, The. See Bunyan, John
Pinchbeck, I., 122n, 598
Pindar, 382
Pitcairne, Archibald, 433, 437
Plato, 59, 60, 63, 65, 68, 78, 84, 85, 86, 97, 106, 365, 380, 383, 437, 464
Plautus, 205
Plimpton, George A., 609
Plog, Fred, 601, 638
Plomer, Henry R., 231n
Pluche, N. A., 383
Plumb, J. H., 583, 623, 651
Plumer, George, 518
Plutarch, 60, 64, 68, 78, 85, 97, 399, 460
Plymouth Colony: plantation, 14-15; initial educational efforts, 15; education law of 1671, 125; ecclesiastical law of 1655, 152; absence of schools during initial years, 180; education laws of 1658 and 1677, 182; cited, 134, 150-151, 219; writings on, 581, 599
pneumatology, 460
Pocahontas, 158
Pole, J. R., 649, 666
Pole, Reginald, 172
Pollard, A. W., 580, 587
Poor Law of 1601, 120-122, 126
Poor Man's Family Book, The. See Baxter, Richard
Pope, Alexander, 366, 376
Pormont, Philemon, 180, 184
Porteau, Paul, 595
Porter, H. C., 593, 605, 611, 612
Portuguese-Americans, 19, 22
Portz, John, 626
Potter, Alfred C., 614
Potter, David, 655
Potter, J., 481n, 621
Potts, John, 207
Powell, Chilton Latham, 588, 597
Powell, William, 585
Power, Eileen, 598
Powicke, Sir Maurice, 38, 611
Pownall, John, 458
Practise of Pietie, The. See Bayly, Lewis
Pratt, Daniel J., 608, 664
preaching: casuistry, 45-46; ideas of William Perkins, 53-54; ideas of Richard Bernard, 54-55; ideas of Richard Baxter, 55; in Renaissance England, 143, 147-148; in seventeenth-century America, 154-155, 165-166; in eighteenth-century America, 317-320, 494-496; writings on, 589, 602-603, 629-630, 632-633, 658
Presbyterian church: in seventeenth-century America, 163; Old Light–New Light controversy, 299-300, 311-312, 317-319; eighteenth-century academies, 323-327; missions, 353; in Virginia, 455-457; in New York City, 536; in Philadelphia, 536; writings

Presbyterian church (*cont.*)
  on, 632-634. *See also* College of New Jersey; Davies, Samuel; Witherspoon, John
Presbyterians, 543
Prest, W. R., 612
Prezzolini, Giuseppe, 590
Price, Richard, 460
Priestley, Harold, 615
Priestley, Herbert I., 579
Priestley, Joseph, 324, 460
Primaudaye, Pierre de la. *See* La Primaudaye, Pierre de
primer: character, 129; role in teaching of reading, 129, 185, 483; recommended by John Locke, 277, 362; *The New-England Primer*, 394; cited, 350; writings on, 592-593, 601, 644
Prince, Thomas, Jr., 317n
Pring, Martin, 6
printer: Cambridge (Mass.) press, 185; Stationers' Company, 230-231; early colonial presses, 234; eighteenth-century didactic publishing, 388-395; as political educator, 444, 450, 457; in New York City and Philadelphia, 540-541; cited, 42; writings on, 642-644, 651-653
Prior, Moody E., 594
Priscian, 169, 172, 197
Prizer, John B., 612-613
Prodigal Daughter, The, 484n
professor. *See* higher education
professorship, 512-514
Protestantism, 5, 31-76, 141-166, 271-356, 585-589, 602-606, 623-639, 653
Pryde, George S., 623, 628, 654
Psalter, 185, 277, 362
Ptolemy, 63, 90, 91, 106, 197
Pufendorf, Samuel von, 300, 381, 383, 452, 453, 463, 464, 470
Purcell, Richard J., 664
Puritanism: in the establishment of Massachusetts, 15-17; in Renaissance England, 31-56; Puritan preaching, 143; Puritan objections to Elizabethan settlement, 145; New England Congregationalism and early Virginia Anglicanism, 151-163; New England schooling, 180-182, 183-184; Puritan intellectuals in New England, 207; Harvard College, 211-220; New England *paideia*, 236-238; eighteenth-century forms, 271-293, 303-332; writings on, 581-582, 585-589, 599-600, 602-603, 613-614, 617, 624-627, 629-631, 632-635, 653
Purver, Margery, 616
Putnam, James, 469

Quakers, 163, 258, 259, 333, 344, 443, 499, 506-507, 536, 537, 543. *See also* Society of Friends
Queen's College, 328, 510, 565, 634, 662

Quimby, Ian M. G., 657
Quincy, Josiah, 634
Quinn, David Beers, 580, 618
Quintilian, 63, 68, 78, 106, 205, 380, 382
Quintus Curtius, 63, 205

Rae, John, 667
Raesly, Ellis Lawrence, 582, 585, 610
Ragle, John W., 646, 659
Rainbolt, John C., 617-618
Raleigh, Sir Walter, 3, 8, 67, 470
Rambler, The, 382
Ramsay, David, 448, 449, 468, 652
Ramsey, Paul, 633
Ramus, Petrus, 103-104, 215, 244, 595
Rand, Edward Kenneth, 614
Randall, John Herman, 578, 619, 639
Ranters, 304
Rapin, Paul, 470
Rashdall, Hastings, 196n, 611
Ray, John, 383
Raynal, Guillaume, 559-560
Rea, Robert R., 547n, 651
Read, Conyers, 580, 584
reading, 130, 173-175, 184-185, 277, 435, 440, 441, 483, 499, 503, 538, 600-601, 660. *See also* Dutch, French, Greek, Hebrew, Latin, and Spanish language instruction
Récollets, 355
Recorde, Robert, 90
Recusancy, 38, 145, 586
Redgrave, G. R., 580
Redman, John, 323, 384
Redwood, Abraham, 400
Redwood Library, 400
Reed, Solomon, 321
Reeder, Rudolph, 600
Reformation, 38-39, 109-112, 141-145, 585-586
Regiomontanus, 90
Reicyn, Nina, 639
Reid, Thomas, 298, 299, 300, 460
Reif, Sister Mary Richard, 104n
Renaissance, 28-29, 38-39, 109-112, 583-584
Revolutionary War, 564-570
Reynolds, E. E., 592
rhetoric, 63, 103-104, 106, 197, 214, 215, 296, 340, 362, 376, 380, 382, 404, 503
Rhode Island, 153, 165, 181, 187, 415, 496, 509. *See also* College of Rhode Island
Rhodes, Hugh, 131, 174, 185
Rice, Eugene, 591
Rice, Howard C., 639
Rich, E. E., 110, 232, 583, 596, 616
Rich, George Eugene, 298n, 628
Richardson, Caroline Francis, 603
Richardson, Leon Burr, 634
Richardson, Lyon N., 392n, 644
Richardson, Samuel, 302, 374, 483

Richelieu, Louis François Armand, Duc de, 22
Richmond (Va.), 441
Ridley, Nicholas, 43
Riefe, Robert H., 644
Rightmyer, Nelson Waite, 536n
Riley, Edward Miles, 661
Riley, I. Woodbridge, 579, 628, 629
Rind, William, 398
Rittenhouse, David, 264, 560
Roach, John, 597
Robbins, Caroline, 426n, 649, 654
Robertson, William, 378, 555n
Robinson, Charles F., 585
Robinson, John, 132, 150
Robinson, Robin, 585
Robinson, William, 323
Roden, Robert F., 185n, 609
Roelantsen, Adam, 18-19
Rogers, Ezekiel, 130
Rogers, Gamaliel, 391, 432
Rogers, John (c.1500-1555), 38
Rogers, John (1630-1684), 209, 217
Rogers, Richard, 143
Rohault, Jacques, 383
Rolfe, John, 239
Rollin, Charles, 265, 377
Roman Catholic church: transplanted to America, 163; missionary efforts of Andrew White, 162; eighteenth-century missionary efforts, 355-356; in eighteenth-century Philadelphia, 536
Roman Catholicism, 138-141. *See also* Roman Catholic church
Roman Catholics, 148, 165, 333, 342, 485
Rondelet, Guillaume, 383
Ronsdorfer, 258
Roper, Margaret, 86
Ross, Alexander, 204
Rossi, Paolo, 104, 594
Rossiter, Clinton, 579, 620, 621, 626
Rossiter, W. S., 574
Rostenberg, Leona, 616
Rothman, David J., 599
Rourke, Constance, 265, 579, 612, 668
Rousseau, Jean Jacques, 378
Routh, E. M. G., 592
Rowe, Thomas, 278, 281
Rowley (Mass.), 155
Rowning, John, 382, 383
Roxbury (Mass.), 155, 158, 162-163, 181, 184, 193
Royal, Isaac, 512
Royal College of Physicians (Edinburgh), 385
Royal College of Physicians (London), 224, 385
Royal Society, 94, 232, 234-235, 254-255, 288, 305, 367, 385, 409, 515
Rubincam, Milton, 640
Rudolph, Lloyd I., 550n
Rupp, I. Daniel, 665
Rush, Benjamin, 264, 299, 564, 566n, 569-570

Russell, Walter, 207
Rutherford, Livingston, 652
Rutman, Darrett B., 582, 600, 617, 618
Ryan, Lawrence V., 78, 592
Ryder, Sir Dudley, 456
Ryece, Robert, 27

S.P.C.K. *See* Society for Promoting Christian Knowledge
S.P.G. *See* Society for the Propagation of the Gospel in Foreign Parts
Sabin, Joseph, 580
Sachs, William S., 621, 638
Sachse, William L., 208n, 613, 616
Sackville, Sir Richard, 76-77
Sadler, John Edward, 649
Sadtler, B., 634
St. Paul's School, 86, 170
salaries of teachers, 188, 497
Salem (Mass.), 130, 151, 155, 180, 193
Sallust, 63, 77, 86, 175, 204, 491
Saltonstall, Henry, 208
Sandys, Sir Edwin, 10, 11, 12
Sandys, George, 207
Sandys, John Edwin, 592
Sanford, Charles L., 640
Sansovino, Francisco, 28n
Sarton, George, 594
Sassamon, John, 223
Saur, Christopher, 262-263, 389, 392
Savelle, Max, 620, 621, 622
Saveth, Edward N., 599
Saybrook Platform of 1708, 152
Sayre, Robert F., 640
Scaliger, Joseph Justus, 383
Scaliger, Julius Caesar, 205
Schickard, William, 185
Schirmer, Walter F., 141n
Schlatter, Michael, 261, 262, 312, 313, 499
Schlatter, Richard B., 586, 588, 593
Schlesinger, Arthur M., 449, 450n, 548n, 579, 620, 621, 627, 639, 644, 651, 652
Schlesinger, Elizabeth Bancroft, 658
Schneider, Carol, 627, 646, 654, 662
Schneider, Donald O., 550n, 553n, 666
Schneider, Herbert W., 589, 595, 627, 646, 654, 662
Schneider, Louis, 654
Schöffler, Herbert, 302n
school: advocacy of John Brinsley, 55-56; advocacy of Charles Chauncy, 57; in medieval England, 167-170; in Renaissance England, 170-176; in seventeenth-century America, 176-195; in eighteenth-century America, 400-404, 499-509, 544-546; and literacy, 546-549; writings on, 606-611, 634, 645-646, 655-656, 659-661. *See also* academy; general school; gram-

school (cont.)
mar school; higher education;
petty school
schoolmaster. See school
schoolmistress. See school
Schrag, Felix James, 630, 632
Schücking, Levin L., 483n, 629
Schuyler, Margarita, 489-490
Schwenkfelders, 258, 304, 308
science, 89-96, 106, 197-198,
203, 204-205, 214, 232, 234-
235, 244, 254-256, 382-383,
384-386, 404, 406, 407-411,
511-515, 593-594, 619-620,
642, 646-647, 661-662
Scotch-Irish Americans, 257,
259, 264
Scottish-Americans, 22, 257,
259, 266
Scott, John, 294
Scott, John Morin, 410, 428-
431
Scott, William Robert, 654
Seager, Francis, 79n, 131, 174,
185
Searcy, Herbert Lyman, 636,
645
Seaver, Paul Siddall, 616
Secker, Thomas, 329-330
secondary education. See acad-
emy; grammar school; school
Seebohm, Frederic, 587, 592
Seekers, 304
Seiler, William H., 605
Selden, John, 383
self-education, 33-34, 104-107,
363, 367-368, 372-374, 387-
395, 442, 469-471
Sellers, William, 388
Seneca, 60, 64, 68, 205, 383,
470
Sensabaugh, George S., 653
Sententiae pueriles. See Cul-
mann, Leonhard
Separatists, 14-15, 150-151, 153
sermon. See preaching
Servetus, Michael, 91
Settle, Elkanah, 333
Seven Years' War, 356
Sewall, Elizabeth, 486
Sewall, Samuel, 237, 486
Sewall, Stephen, 513
Seybolt, Robert Francis, 401n,
644, 645, 659, 664
Seymour, Sir Edward, 336n
Shaaber, M. A., 616
Shaftesbury, earl of. See
Cooper, Anthony Ashley
Shakespeare, William, 229n,
294, 437, 438
Sharp, John, 294
Sharpe, John, 351n, 537n
Sharrock, Roger, 588
Shea, John Gilmary, 638
Shearith Israel congregation,
536
Sheldon, Henry D., 655
Shepard, Thomas, 102n, 130,
605
Shepherd, Kathleen Kessler, 598
Shera, Jesse H., 645
Sherlock, William, 294
Sherwin, Henry, 382
Sherman, Roger, 390

Shewmaker, William Orpheus,
613, 634
Shinagel, Michael, 629
Shindler, Madalene, 595
Shippen, Joseph, Jr., 511
Shippen, William, Jr., 385, 567
Shipton, Clifford K., 508n, 509n,
580, 608, 614, 626, 627, 642,
660-661, 665
Shores, Louis, 585, 645
Shryock, Richard H., 582, 613,
626
Sibbald, Robert, 323
Sibley, John Langdon, 610, 613,
614
Sidney, Algernon, 255, 300,
376, 377, 381, 383, 399, 426,
437, 449, 463, 470, 649
Sidney, Sir Philip, 4, 5, 66, 67,
68
Sidwell, Robert T., 643
Siebert, Frederick S., 652
Sieur d'Allone (Abel Tassin),
353
Silius Italicus, 63
Simms, P. Marion, 587
Simon, Brian, 175-176, 607
Simon, Joan, 202n, 592, 606,
607, 611
Simpson, Alan, 589
Simpson, Samuel, 634
Simpson, Thomas, 382
Singer, Charles, 594
Sirluck, Ernest, 422n
Skelton, Samuel, 151
Skotheim, Robert Allen, 578
Slack, Mrs., 394, 503-504, 540
Slafter, Carlos, 609, 662
slavery, 348-349, 350-353, 354,
360, 411-412
Sloan, Douglas Milton, 378,
628, 633, 634, 654, 655, 660,
661, 662
Small, Walter Herbert, 608, 610
Small, William, 337, 386, 511
Smart, George K., 585
Smith, Abbot Emerson, 600
Smith, Adam, 378, 460, 555-556
Smith, Alice Kimball, 597, 603
Smith, David Edwin, 588
Smith, David Eugene, 660
Smith, Denis Mack, 583, 596
Smith, Donald George, 658
Smith, Duncan, 503
Smith, Elwyn A., 628
Smith, Frank, 662
Smith, H. F. Russell, 649
Smith, H. Maynard, 602
Smith, H. Shelton, 603
Smith, Henry, 211
Smith, Horace Wemyss, 622
Smith, J. W. Ashley, 625, 633
Smith, James, 407
Smith, James Morton, 581, 596,
605
Smith, Captain John, 9, 12n,
148-149
Smith, John E., 627
Smith, Lydia A. H., 660
Smith, M. G., 647
Smith, Page, 648, 652
Smith, Preserved, 38-39, 586
Smith, Sir Thomas (1513-1577),
67, 255, 545

Smith, Sir Thomas (c.1558-
1625), 7
Smith, Timothy L., 623
Smith, Willard Wallace, 661
Smith, William (1697-1769),
447
Smith, William (1727-1803):
efforts to Anglicize Pennsylvania Germans, 261-262; early
life and education, 378; A
General Idea of the College of
Mirania, 378-380, 462-463;
proposed curriculum for the
College of Philadelphia, 380-
383; conception of learning,
380-384; as provost of the
College of Philadelphia, 402,
404; conception of moral phi-
losophy, 461, 462-464; cited,
261, 357, 405, 460, 505, 515;
writings on, 641-642
Smith, William, Jr. (1728-
1793), 410, 428-431, 537, 650
Smith, William Peartree, 429
Smith, Wilson, 578, 610
Smithers, Peter, 640
Society for Promoting Christian
Knowledge, 339
Society for Propagacion of the
Gospell in New England, 159-
160, 194
Society for the Promotion of
Agriculture, Commerce, and
Art, 410
Society for the Promotion of
Useful Knowledge (New
York), 410, 428-429
Society for the Promotion of
Useful Knowledge (Virginia),
410
Society for the Propagation of
Christian Knowledge Among
the Germans in Pennsylvania,
261-262, 553, 636-637
Society for the Propagation of
the Gospel in Foreign Parts:
organization and purposes,
341-342; educational program
in the colonies, 342-347; criticisms, 346-347, 435; missions
to the Indians, 347-350; missions to the Negroes, 347, 350-
353; competition with Roman
Catholicism, 354-355, 356;
support of libraries, 397, 398;
cited, 499, 536, 553, 558;
writing on, 636-638
Society in London for Promoting Knowledge Among the
Poor, 354
Society in Scotland for Propagating Christian Knowl-
edge, 353
Society of Friends: transplanted
to America, 163-164; international character, 233; settlement of Pennsylvania, 258;
ideas on education, 304-308;
educational policies and practices, 307-310; writings on,
630-631
Society of the Hospital in the
City of New-York in Amer-
ica, 407

Socrates, 97, 106
Sodalitas, 410, 416
Söderlund, E. F., 598
Solt, Leo, 593
Somerby, Anthony, 180, 181
Sons of Liberty, 449
Sophocles, 85
South, Robert, 294
South Carolina: S.P.G. activities, 344-345, 349, 351-353; Constitution of 1778, 497; back-country life and education, 542-543; cited, 399, 415, 482; writings on, 664
Sowards, Jesse Kelley, 592
Sowerby, E. Millicent, 650
Spanish-Americans, 21-22, 333
Spanish language instruction, 436
Spectator, The, 282, 325, 365-368, 399, 429, 432
Spedding, James, 594
Spence, Joseph, 382
Spencer, William, 208
Spener, Philipp Jakob, 304, 314
Spenser, Edmund, 66
Spicer, Edward, 638
Spinka, Matthew, 648
Sprague, William Buell, 604
Sprat, Thomas, 206, 232n
Sprunger, Keith L., 614
Squire, Francis, 117n, 597
Stafford, Sir Edward, 3-4
Stamp, L. Dudley, 617
Stamp Act (1765), 415-416, 448-450, 453, 457, 458, 545, 647, 656
Stanard, Mary Newton, 600, 656
Stanford, Charles, 625
Stanhope, Philip Dormer (earl of Chesterfield), 302n
Stanley, William, 346
Stapleton, Thomas, 592
Starkey, Marion L., 531n, 663
Starkey, Thomas, 595
Starr, Comfort, 218
Stationers' Company, 230-231
Statute of Artificers (1563), 120-122, 126
Stearns, Raymond Phineas, 604, 616
Steckel, William Reed, 642-643
Steele, Richard, 365-367, 368, 393n, 483, 639-640
Steiner, Bernard C., 608, 636
Stephen, Sir Leslie, 624
Stephenson, Wendell Holmes, 581
Stevenson, John, 298, 325
Stewart, George, Jr., 604
Stewart, W. A. Campbell, 630-631
Stiles, Ezra, 397, 468, 509, 512n, 516, 561-562
Stillingfleet, Edward, 275
Stimson, Dorothy, 616
Stocking, George W., 578
Stoddard, Solomon, 315, 319
Stoeffler, F. Ernest, 632
Stokes, Anson Phelps, 659
Stokes, I. N. Phelps, 20n, 582, 663
Stone, Edmund, 382
Stone, John, 208

Stone, Lawrence, 117n, 118n, 147n, 171n, 176, 202, 231n, 547n, 584, 596, 598, 607, 611, 664
Stone, Samuel, 152
Stone, Wilbur Macey, 625
Stoughton, John, 210-211
Stoughton, William, 208
Stow, John, 229n, 615
Stowe, A. Monroe, 607
Strachey, William, 10n
Strada, Famianus, 205, 382
Strahan, William, 373, 388
Strandness, Theodore, 658
Straus, Ralph, 302n, 629
Strauss, Leo, 591
Strawbridge, Robert, 455
Stromberg, Roland N., 624, 629
Strong, Nehemiah, 513
Stuart, Charles Edward, 467n
student. See church; community, as educator; didactic literature; higher education; household; library; oral tradition; printer; school; self-education; voluntary association
student life (college), 466-469.
See also higher education
Sturm, Johannes, 78, 103
Stuyvesant, Peter, 20, 179
Suetonius, 205
Sulpicians, 356
Supple, Barry E., 596
support of education: in medieval England, 168-169; in Renaissance England, 121-122, 170, 200-201; in seventeenth-century America, 126, 152, 159, 160, 183-184, 193-194, 222; in eighteenth-century England, 339, 423; in eighteenth-century America, 393, 395, 439-442, 496-497, 500, 556-559
Surtz, Edward, 590
surveying, 380, 382, 499, 503, 508
Sutherland, Stella H., 19n, 238n, 259n
Suzzallo, Henry, 608, 667
Swedish-Americans, 19, 123, 241
Swedish Reformed, 241
Sweet, William Warren, 493, 603, 630, 658
Swift, Jonathan, 366
Sydenham, Thomas, 437
Sydnor, Charles S., 666
Sykes, Norman, 624, 636
Sylvius, Jacques Dubois, 91
Syms, Benjamin, 177-178, 182, 183
Syms School, 177-178, 182, 183, 530-531, 533

Tacitus, 63, 460
Tanis, James, 632
Tate, Thad W., Jr., 657
Tate, W. E., 607
Tatler, The, 282, 365-368, 399
Tawney, R. H., 598
Taylor, E. G. R., 580, 594, 612
Taylor, G., 536n, 664
Taylor, William Warthin, 593

teacher. See church; community, as educator; didactic literature; higher education; household; library; licensing of teachers; oral tradition; printer; school; voluntary association
technologia, 104
Tedder, Henry, 302n
Temple, J. H., 321n
Temple, Sir William, 255
Tenison, Thomas, 341
Tennent, Gilbert: preaching style, 317; The Danger of an Unconverted Ministry, 318, 322; reading list for penitents, 319; sermons for the newly converted, 320; cited, 311-312; 314, 332n; writings on, 632, 634
Tennent, John, 317
Tennent, John V. B., 407
Tennent, William, 311-312, 314, 317, 322-323, 325, 326, 384, 634
Tennent, William, Jr., 317
Terence, 87, 175, 204
Tewksbury, Donald G., 661
textbook. See didactic literature
Thacher, James, 567
Thacher, Thomas, 209
Theocritus, 205
Theognis, 204
theology, study of, 198, 435, 513, 613
Theophrastus, 85, 91
Thirsk, Joan, 615
Thirty Years' War, 257
Thomas, Isaiah, 390, 642
Thomas, John Alfred, 588
Thomas, Roger, 588
Thomas, Samuel, 349
Thomas a Kempis, 33
Thomas Bray's Associates, 308, 353-354, 536, 537, 636, 638
Thompson, Benjamin (Count Rumford), 565
Thompson, Craig R., 98, 590, 594
Thompson, Henry P., 637
Thompson, Richard Stevens, 667
Thomson, David, 261
Thorndike, Lynn, 594
Thornton, John W., 652
Thorpe, Francis N., 641
Thrupp, Sylvia L., 231n
Thucydides, 85, 382
Tienhoven, Cornelis van, 179
Tilley, Winthrop, 662
Tillotson, John, 282, 294, 336, 376, 495
Tindal, Matthew, 295
Tindall, William York, 588
Tisdale, Nathan, 506, 507-508
Tobriner, Marian Leona, 593
Todd, John, 455
Todd, Jonathan, 453
Tolles, Frederick B., 616, 622, 631, 644, 668
Tompson, Benjamin, 189, 190
Toner, Joseph M., 209n
Tovey, George Vernon, 594
town. See community

Towner, Lawrence William, 600, 657
Tracy, Joseph, 632
Trapp, Joseph, 382
travel as education, 75, 77, 102, 362, 436
Treadwell, Daniel, 406
Trenchard, John, 376, 426-428, 430, 437, 446, 449
Trevelyan, George Macaulay, 251, 615, 619
Trevor-Roper, H. R., 109, 649
Trewartha, Glenn T., 236n, 616
trigonometry, 503
Trimble, William R., 586
Trinity College (Dublin), 208, 212, 217, 248
Trinterud, Leonard J., 628, 633
Trumbull, Benjamin, 565n
Trumbull, John, 508, 514n
Tryon, Rolla Milton, 600
Tryon, Thomas, 373
Tryon, William, 512n
Tucker, Louis Leonard, 654, 661, 662
Tuer, Andrew W., 601, 609
Tunstall, Cuthbert, 35, 36
Turnbull, G. H., 648
Turnbull, George, 265, 377
Turner, Robert, 205
Turrell, Ebenezer, 498n
Tusser, Thomas, 133, 541
Tuttle, Julius Herbert, 644
Two-Penny Act (1755, 1758), 477
Twombly, Robert C., 162n
Tycho. See Brahe, Tycho
Tyler, Andrew, 523
Tyler, Lyon G., 531n, 636, 663
Tyler, Moses Coit, 29n, 300, 449, 450, 579, 584, 643, 652
Tyndale, William: early life and education, 35; translation of Desiderius Erasmus' *Enchiridion*, 35; translation of the Bible into English, 35-36; controversy with Thomas More, 36-38; conception of piety, 35, 39; reputation in America, 40; cited, 43; writings on, 587
Tyrrell, James, 274

Umbreit, Allen George, 609, 659
Union Library Company, 399
university. *See* higher education
University of Cambridge: origins, 197-199; Renaissance developments, 200-206; Emmanuel College, 201, 211; Sidney Sussex College, 201, 211; alumni in seventeenth-century America, 206; seventeenth-century Americans at, 208; cited, 159, 211, 216, 217, 219, 253, 315, 324; writings on, 611-612
University of Edinburgh, 219, 323, 325, 334, 337, 384, 385, 407, 513
University of Glasgow, 325, 463, 516
University of Leiden, 323, 384, 385n

University of Oxford: Corpus Christi College, 87-88; origins, 196-199; Renaissance developments, 200-206; alumni in seventeenth-century America, 207; seventeenth-century Americans at, 208; cited, 159, 211, 216, 219, 253, 271, 324; writings on, 611-612, 667
University of Paris, 196
University of the State of New York, 431
Upton, L. S. F., 650
Urmston, John, 499
Ursulines, 266
Ustick, W. Lee, 72n, 589, 591

Valla, Lorenzo, 32, 204
Van Dam, Rip, 447
Van Doren, Carl, 640, 643, 646
Van Doenhoff, Marion Ruth, 663
Van Rensselaer, Mariana Griswold (Mrs. Schuyler), 20n, 582, 618
Vansina, Jan, 602
Van Vechten, Emma, 610
Varenius, Bernardus, 382
Varro, Marcus Terentius, 77
Vassar, Rena Lee, 608
Vaughan, Alden T., 136n, 601, 605, 611, 615
Vaux, Roberts, 507n
Ver Steeg, Clarence L., 668
Versteeg, Dingman, 19n
Vesalius, Andreas, 90, 91
Vigerius, Franciscus, 204
Vincent, W. A. L., 607, 648, 667
Viner, Jacob, 667
Virgil, 23, 63, 68, 86, 175, 185, 205, 406, 437, 505, 508
Virginia: plantation, 9-11; initial educational efforts, 12-14; education law of 1631, 125; ecclesiastical code of 1619, 149-150; revival of office of lay reader in 1661, 154; number of schools in 1689, 183; licensing of schoolmasters, 188, abortive effort of 1661 to establish a college, 193; configuration of educational institutions in 1650 and 1689, 241; eighteenth-century dissenting education, 455-457; eighteenth-century citizenry, 527; eighteenth-century life and education, 527-534; Act for Encouraging Towns (1680), 528; cited, 415, 482; writings on, 581, 617-618, 663. *See also* College of William and Mary; Davies, Samuel; Jefferson, Thomas
Virginia Company of London, 7, 9-14, 148-150, 194, 233, 581
Vives, Juan Luis, 23, 88, 593
Voetius, Gysbertus, 304, 314
Vogel, Claude L., 638
voluntary association, 291, 373, 407-411, 520
Volz, Paul, 34
voorlezer (reader), 18, 164, 189

voorsanger (precentor), 164, 189
Vossius, Gerhard Johannes, 382
Vreeland, Herbert H., 608

Wadsworth, Benjamin, 288, 497n
Wake, William, 346
Walcott, Robert, 580
Walker, Obadiah, 265, 377
Walker, Williston, 604
Wallace, Captain, 533
Wallace, Anthony F. C., 665
Wallace, David Duncan, 543n, 665
Wallace, James, 529
Wallis, John, 253
Walloon-Americans, 18, 19, 123
Walsh, Evelyn Marie, 668
Walsh, James J., 467n
Walsh, Sir John, 35
Walsingham, Sir Francis, 4, 5
Walzer, Michael, 111, 586, 588, 591, 596
Warch, Richard, 635, 661
Ward, Christopher, 668
Ward, James, 208
Ward, John, 382
Ward, John William, 640
Ward, Seth, 253
Ward, W. R., 667
Warfel, Harry R., 668
Warlick, Roger K., 593
Warren, John, 567
Warren, Mercy, 551
Warrender, Howard, 591
Washburn, Wilcomb E., 601
Washington, George, 450, 515, 535, 550, 567n
Wassenaer, Nicolaes van, 18n
Wasserman, Maurice Marc, 601
Waterbury, Jean Parker, 609
Waters, John J., 484n, 599, 657
Watertown (Mass.), 151
Watson, Foster, 174n, 593, 607
Watts, Emily Stipes, 633
Watts, Isaac: life and education, 278-279; conception of piety, 279-281; *Divine Songs*, 279-280, 284; relationship with Philip Doddridge, 282; *The Improvement of the Mind*, 369-370; *Discourse on the Education of Children and Youth*, 370; conception of learning, 369-371; *Logick* used in America, 506, 514; cited, 256, 287, 301, 378, 381, 382, 498; writings on, 624-625
Weaver, Glenn, 622
Weber, Max, 411, 647
Weber, Samuel Edwin, 263n, 622
Webster, Charles, 649
Webster, John, 203
Webster, Noah, 373, 568-569
Weeden, William B., 600
Weis, Frederick Lewis, 164n, 207n, 604
Weiser, Conrad, 262
Weld, Daniel, 194
Weld, Thomas, 163, 213, 222
Wells, Guy Fred, 604
Welsh-Americans, 258

Wendelin, Marcus Frederik, 205
Wendell, Barrett, 626
Werkmeister, Lucyle, 547n
Wertenbaker, Thomas Jefferson, 579, 581, 617, 621, 628, 634
Wesley, Charles, 270-271, 329, 354
Wesley, John, 270-271, 354
West, Richard, 131
West, Thomas (Lord Delaware), 149, 207
Westfall, Richard S., 612
Wetherell, Phyllis Jane, 625
Wetmore, James, 295n, 345, 351
Wharton, William, 208
Wheatley, Phillis, 518-519
Wheeler, Joseph Towne, 636, 644
Wheelock, Eleazar, 328, 353, 509, 523
Wheelock, Ralph, 522
Whichard, Rogers D., 530, 663
Whiston, William, 287
Whitaker, Alexander, 149, 154, 155, 156, 157-158, 162
Whitaker, Nathaniel, 328
Whitby, Daniel, 294
White, Andrew, 162
White, Helen C., 41, 587
White, John, 14n
White, Philip L., 484n, 657
Whitefield, George: enthusiasm for America as "school" of Christ, 269, 496; early preaching in England, 270; first visit to America, 271-272; subsequent visits to America, 312-313; as quintessentially undenominational, 312, 354; description of the Log College, 322-323; unsuccessful effort to convert Bethesda Orphan Asylum into a college, 329-330, 509; denounced by Harvard faculty, 331; acquaintance with Benjamin Franklin, 377; criticized by William Douglass, 434-435; cited, 283, 316, 317, 402, 523; writings on, 622, 632
Whiteman, Anne, 116n
Whiteside, D. T., 620
Whitford, Richard, 80
Whitgift, John, 201
Whitney, Janet, 631
Whittemore, Nathaniel, 390
Whole Duty of Man, The. See Allestree, Richard
Whytt, Robert, 385
Wickersham, James Pyle, 608
Wigglesworth, Edward, 331
Wigglesworth, Michael, 130, 218
Wilkinson, Ronald Sterne, 662
Willard, Oliver M., 616
William III, 251, 254, 334, 353

William Penn Charter School, 307, 537
Williams, David D., 602
Williams, Elisha, 279
Williams, John, 349n
Williams, Nathaneal, 506
Williams, Roger, 153, 165-166, 234
Williams, Solomon, 399-400
Williamsburg (S.C.), 543n
Williamsburg (Va.), 338, 354, 477, 552. See also College of William and Mary
Williamson, James A., 581
Willis, Harry, 491
Willis, Richard, 347
Wilson, Bird, 516
Wilson, C. H., 583, 596
Wilson, Elizabeth Andrews, 656
Wilson, Henry, 382
Wilson, J. Dover, 594
Wilson, John, 209
Wilson, Thomas, 615
Wiltse, Charles Maurice, 651
Wing, Donald, 580
Wingate, Roger, 207
Winship, George Parker, 16n
Winslow, Ola Elizabeth, 604, 605, 606, 627
Winsor, Justin, 579
Winthrop, John (1588-1649), 3, 14-16, 27
Winthrop, John, Jr., (1606-1676), 234-235
Winthrop, John (1714-1779), 386, 469, 511, 514-515, 565, 662
Wise, John, 451, 454
Witherell, William, 180
Witherspoon, John: life and education, 298-299; conception of piety, 299-301; moral philosophy course, 461, 465-466; cited, 378, 460, 552; writings on, 628-629
Witte, Wayne William, 628
Wolf, A., 594
Wolf, Edwin, 2nd, 256n
Wollaston, William, 460n
Wolsey, Thomas, 88
women's education, 71n, 86, 88, 186-187, 440, 507, 609
Wood, George, 398
Wood, Gordon S., 550n
Wood, Norman, 598, 603, 607
Wood, Ralph, 622
Woodbridge, William, 404
Woodmason, Charles, 542-543
Woods, Leonard, 3n
Woodson, Carter G., 610, 631
Woodward, William Harrison, 591, 592, 594
Woody, Thomas, 307n, 609, 610, 631, 659, 664
Wooldridge, S. W., 617

Woolman, John, 308, 443, 499
Worcester Diocese (England), 146
Wormeley, Ralph, 208
Worthington, Erastus, 527n, 662-663
Wren, Sir Christopher, 337
Wright, Conrad, 293, 626, 627, 629
Wright, John K., 579
Wright, Louis B., 28, 118n, 579, 581, 582, 585, 587, 588, 589, 591, 644, 658
Wright, Luella M., 630
Wright, Thomas Goddard, 585, 644
Wrigley, E. A., 116, 547n, 597, 615
writing, 173, 185, 376, 403, 406, 435, 440, 441, 499, 503, 538, 609, 660, 661
Wroth, Lawrence C., 396n, 641, 642, 644, 650, 667
Wuorinen, John H., 618
Wyatt, Sir Francis, 207
Wycliffe, John, 43, 142-143
Wythe, George, 437, 438, 468, 478, 483n, 512, 551, 552, 568

Xenophon, 63, 78, 383, 464

Yale College, Dummer library, 294, 398; founding, 321; occupations of alumni, 330, 553-554; teaching of Thomas Clap, 461; student politics, 468; professorial salaries, 497n; professorships, 513; John Trumbull's caricature, 514n; ecclesiastical control, 558-559; impact of the Revolution, 565; cited, 508, 516, 542, 553; writings on, 634, 635, 661, 662
Yarranton, Andrew, 307n
Yates, Frances, 584
Yeardley, Sir George, 11, 12
Yeates, Jasper, 465n
Yeldham, Florence A., 660
Yetman, Charles D., 609
Yolton, John W., 619, 620, 624, 649
Young, Edward J., 467n
Young, James Reed, 658

Zagorin, Perez, 580
Zavala, Silvio, 583
Zeichner, Oscar, 466
Zeitlin, Jacob, 595
Zenger, John Peter, 389, 447-449
Ziff, Larzer, 604
Zinzendorf, Nikolaus Ludwig von, 283, 304
Zion's Brueder, 258
Zuckerman, Michael, 662

ABOUT THE AUTHOR

LAWRENCE A. CREMIN is Frederick A. P. Barnard Professor of Education and Director of the Institute of Philosophy and Politics of Education at Columbia University. He has been a member of the Teachers College faculty since 1949 and chairman of the college's Department of Philosophy and the Social Sciences since 1958. Since 1961 he has also been a member of the university's Department of History.

Professor Cremin was born in New York City on October 31, 1925, and attended the Townsend Harris High School and the College of the City of New York, where he was elected to Phi Beta Kappa. He received the Master of Arts and Doctor of Philosophy degrees from Columbia University.

He won a Guggenheim Fellowship in 1957-1958 for research in the history of American education, and was a Fellow at the Center for Advanced Study in the Behavioral Sciences in 1964-1965. He was also recipient of the 1969 Award of the American Educational Research Association for his contributions to educational research.

Professor Cremin was president of the History of Education Society in 1959, and of the National Society of College Teachers of Education in 1961. He is currently President of the National Academy of Education. Professor Cremin serves on the Board of Trustees of both the Dalton Schools and the Children's Television Workshop.

A historian and interpreter of education, his most notable book is *The Transformation of the School,* a history of the progressive education movement in the United States. The book was awarded the Bancroft Prize in American History for 1962. He has been the author or co-author of eight other books, and has contributed numerous articles to various journals and magazines. He also edits the Classics in Education series published at Teachers College.

Professor Cremin lives in New York City with his wife and two children.